ORGANIZATION AND GOVERNANCE IN HIGHER EDUCATION

AN ASHE READER

FOURTH EDITION

Edited by

MARVIN W. PETERSON
Center for the Study of Higher and Postsecondary Education
School of Education, University of Michigan

Associate Editors

ELLEN E. CHAFFEE
North Dakota State Board of Higher Education

and

THEODORE H. WHITE
Center for the Study of Higher and Postsecondary Education
School of Education, University of Michigan

ASHE READER SERIES
Bruce Anthony Jones, Series Editor

 SIMON & SCHUSTER CUSTOM PUBLISHING

Printed in the United States of America

10 9 8 7 6

ISBN 0-536-57981-4
BA 97152

SIMON & SCHUSTER CUSTOM PUBLISHING
160 Gould Street/Needham Heights, MA 02194
Simon & Schuster Education Group

Copyright Acknowledgments

Contents

Part III. Leadership Perspectives

Acknowledgements

The Association for the Study of Higher Education wishes to express its appreciation to the following publishers and organizations for their permission to reprint copyrighted material: *Academe, Academy of Management Review, Administrative Science Quarterly,* American Council on Education, Carnegie Foundation for the Advancement of Teaching, Education Commission of the States, *Educational Record, Educational Researcher, Human Resource Management,* Jossey-Bass Publishers, Inc., *The Journal of Higher Education,* McCutchan Publishing Corporation, Prentice Hall, Inc., Princeton University Press, *Research in Higher Education, The Review of Higher Education,* and the Western Interstate Commission for Higher Education. The Association for the Study of Higher Education also wishes to thank James March for his permission to reprint chapters from *Leadership and Ambiguity.*

More than sixty members of ASHE who teach courses in the organization and administration of higher education and have used the third edition of this *Reader* were asked to critique the prior volume and assist in the identification and selection of new items for this fourth edition. Especially helpful was the thoughtful critique and commentary from an Advisory Group for this edition. Those members included: Robert Birnbaum, Patricia Gumport, Yvonna Lincoln, Anna Neumann, Michael Olivas, William Tierney, and Frank Schmidtlein.

Introduction

Perhaps no area more reflects the growing complexity and sophistication in the study of higher education than that dealing with organization and governance. We now have almost four decades of serious scholarly publication research and graduate seminars in higher education programs dealing with this focus or perspective on higher education.

In the 1950's, 60's, and 70's higher education drew heavily on the study of formal organization and from models developed outside higher education. Psychology, sociology, political science, anthropology, public administration, business administration, management science, and law are among the disciplines and professional fields that have provided concepts and models and shaped our thinking about the organization and governance of higher education. In the 1980's we began to look more seriously at the nature of colleges and universities as educational organizations with their own special cultures and patterns. That trend has not abated and is currently providing a rich new array of concepts, perspectives, and insights.

In selecting items for this volume, a special attempt was made to reflect these new conceptual perspectives and models. Older selections were continued only if they were "classics." Preference was given to articles which emphasized conceptual topics rather than practical issues or applications. To do the latter would have created an extensive volume. Similarly, articles not dealing explicitly with higher education were not included although most faculty indicated they regularly use non-higher education materials (they also reflected an impossibly eclectic set of preferences!). Thus over half the articles in this fourth edition are new even though the third edition was published a scant four years ago. The selections not only reflect the changing views of colleges and universities as organizations, but they also highlight the areas of literature applied to higher education that need to be addressed.

This edition of the *Reader* is divided into three sections: Organization Theory and Models; Governance and Management Processes; and Leadership Perspectives. The first section focuses on our concept of colleges and universities as organizations; the second on how we govern ourselves and the nature of the primary management processes; the final takes a broad perspective on the leadership domain.

There is no satisfactory definition of "organization" that captures the essence of colleges and universities. Rather we view them from several perspectives. The first section presents the different primary models and concepts of organization that are currently employed to describe and analyze colleges and universities. They are not mutually exclusive nor are they completely sufficient. They do suggest ways to think about the organized patterns of colleges and universities, how they function or differ from one another, and how they are similar to or different from non-collegiate organizations because of higher education's unusual goals, structures, technologies, and environments.

"Governance" refers to the processes and structures through which individuals and groups participate in and influence decisions. Governance focuses on broad institutional decision processes and issues. "Management" refers to the major functions we assume the governance process serves: How strategy is conceived, how planning and resource allocation occur, how change is stimulated or managed, how one knows whether the institution is effective. Limitations of space do not allow the inclusion of articles on more specific management processes or the myriad of decision issues or topics which attract the attention of management processes.

"Leadership" refers to the process or attempts to give an institution a sense of purpose or direction. Clearly this *Reader* cannot completely survey this comprehensive topic. However, it is difficult to discuss organization and governance without recognizing the importance of this topic. Leadership is crucial because we live in a world of increased complexity, constraint, and demand for change. This section only deals with the topic conceptually and with the key participants as groups.

Organization Models and Theory

In the first chapter Duryea provides a brief historical and developmental view of the "Evolution of University Organization" and governance. He traces the influence of past practices and suggests the need for continual change to meet evolving circumstances. Peterson's article, "Emerging Developments In the Study of Organizations" captures the recent shifts in our paradigms and conflicts about how to view colleges and universities as organizations. In "Higher Education and Organizational Theory", Bensimon et al. provide a more comprehensive perspective for our conceptual thinking to date. These three articles provide a historical overview and a current conceptual context for the concepts and models in the following chapters.

In "Alternative Models of Governance in Higher Education", Baldridge et al. describe some of the unique organizational characteristics of colleges and universities, and provide a concise summary of the bureaucratic, collegial, and political models identified over a decade ago that remain useful models from which to study and analyze colleges and universities today. They reflect our early rational, behavioral, and open systems perspectives and provide a basis for many other models that address some unique characteristics of colleges and universities as organizations. Mintzberg's "Professional Bureaucracy" elaborates on the collegial model in a manner befitting higher education. Within this conceptual context, Alpert's "Performance and Paralysis: The Organizational Context of the American Research University" provides a matrix model to show how the externally oriented research function and the disciplinary-oriented internal structure can be understood and contrasted as universities strive to cope with a changing social environment. The movement away from a formal, rational, or political model toward a cultural perspective was one explored two decades ago in Clark's "The Organizational Saga in Higher Education," which focuses on an analysis of institutions in which participants develop deep emotional commitments and express a unified sense of belonging to a unique community of exceptional accomplishment.

Many administrative and managerial systems in higher education implicitly assume (but rarely articulate) a view of organizations as structured, goal-directed, and rational. When actions do not have the intended effects, organizational pathology or personal incompetence is suspected and doses of new and improved management are prescribed. There are, however, newer and more provocative concepts in the study of organizations that go beyond the view of colleges and universities as either hierarchical, community, or political systems. In "Educational Organizations as Loosely Coupled Systems", Weick proposes a paradigm in which organizational elements are often tied together loosely rather than tightly. Although there is a tendency for managers to focus their attention on the problems caused by such relationships, Weick suggests that they have many organizational advantages as well.

Loose coupling is one of the major conceptual bases of the "organized anarchy," the name given by Cohen and March to organizations characterized by problematic goals, unclear technology, and fluid participation. How can organizations of this kind, of which the university is perhaps the archetype, make decisions when they are not quite certain what their goals are, nor how they could accomplish these goals even if they could agree on them? The answer presented in Cohen and March's *Leadership and Ambiguity*, is the concept of "garbage can decision-making," in which choices are partially decoupled from problems (see Reference Text).

The shift away from rational paradigms begun by the works of Clark, Weick, and Cohen and March is most obvious in our recently expanded interest in college and university cultures. Masland's article on "Organizational Culture in the Study of Higher Education" provides a bridge between our models of higher education and the recent theoretical and practical views of organizations as cultural entities in popularized versions such as Peters and Waterman's *In Pursuit of Excellence*. This piece, however, builds on some of our earlier higher education views of colleges as communities or sagas and provides a different way of examining the more fluid conceptualization of colleges and universities as loosely coupled or organized anarchies. Tierney's more in depth anthropological treatment in "Organizational Culture in Higher Education: Defining the Essentials" expands the concept. In "Understanding Organizational Culture and Climate", Peterson and Spencer distinguish between these constructs by focusing on some conceptual dimensions.

Governance and Management Processes

The practical uniqueness of higher education's governance context is captured in the AAUP/ACE/AGB's "Statement on Government of Colleges and Universities." It is reflected conceptually in Mortimer and McConnell's "Process of Academic Governance" in which they suggest ways of moving toward systems of joint participation that permit both full consultation and appropriate levels of administrative discretion. However, Cohen and March's "The Processes of Choice" suggests that the differences in professional groups and how they approach choice may make such an integrative approach (rationally or politically) more difficult or perhaps, at times, undesirable. Dill draws a further distinction by focusing on "The Management of Academic Culture," which is neither as malleable nor as easily influenced as the political, professional, or paradoxical organizations assumed by the first three authors.

Switching from conceptual views of governance, Birnbaum's "The Latent Organizational Functions of the Academic Senate" and Rice and Austin's "High Faculty Morale: What Exemplary Colleges Do Right" deal with issues of the faculty constituency in governance and management. Berdahl further highlights the conceptual difficulty imposed by "Shared Governance and External Constraints."

No current discussion of governance can avoid the concept of strategy and planning, the concern for linking where the organization is going with its environment. Chaffee's "Three Models of Strategy" provides some way of thinking about this very vague concept. Kotler and Murphy consider managerial behavior to be the most critical factor, and argue that only organizational leaders can respond to environmental changes. In "Strategic Planning for Higher Education" they present a framework for a market-oriented and systematic long-range planning process through which institutions can develop goals and strategies after careful assessment of their resources and their environment.

Another critical management function for governance is the allocation of resources. Two articles in this section reflect our preponderant concern with resource allocation in the early 1990's. Chaffee's article discusses the limits of "The Role of Rationality in University Budgeting," but suggests it still plays a major role. "Power and Centrality in the Allocation of Resources in Colleges and Universities" by Hackman emphasizes political dynamics as well as consideration for institutional mission.

Two articles by Cameron provide conceptual perspective into two other major management functions of governance: institutional adaptation and judging effectiveness. As the environment changes, institutions must also change if they are to survive. In "Organizational Adaptation and Higher Education," Cameron develops a continuum of approaches to the way colleges respond to their environment, based upon the degree to which either managerial behavior or environmental influences are presumed to be the most important force in influencing organizational adaptation. In "Measuring Organizational Effectiveness in Institutions of Higher Education," Cameron suggests that in loosely coupled organizations there are a number of dimensions of effectiveness and that no institution can operate effectively at once on all dimensions. This means that no college or university can simultaneously maximize each of the various outcomes expected by its multiple constituencies — an uncomfortable truth for those responsible for managing their economic and political accountability. Terenzini amplifies this in his concern for facing "Assessment With Open Eyes."

Leadership Perspectives

It is almost redundant to have to remind ourselves of Pfeffer's discussion of "The Ambiguity of Leadership," but it is useful to be reminded that this requires careful attention, thought and cultivation if higher education's complex organizational needs and governance demands are to be addressed. Trow amplifies and provides perspective on that idea in his "Comparative Reflections of Leadership in Higher Education". Further, Dill helps us conceptualize it in his "Nature of Administrational Behavior In Higher Education." Cohen and March then return us to the complexity of "Leadership in an Organized Anarchy."

Against this conceptual background, the readings shift to the role of key players. Bensimon draws on her research to discuss "The Meaning of Good Presidential Leadership" while Tierney introduces his cultural perspective to a discussion of "Symbolism and Presidential Perceptions of Leadership." While we view presidents as the expected repository of leadership, it is a truism that faculty may provide a major element of that resource (if it exists). Two older, classic articles Etzioni's "Administrative and Professional Authority" and Clark's "Faculty Organization and Authority" are still instructive reminders of the critical power/authority that faculty can wield to lead or resist.

A key ingredient is knowing when leadership is doing the right thing or when it is having a desirable influence. The question is not answerable but a final article provides some help, as Whetton and Cameron suggest ways to view "Administrative Effectiveness in Higher Education."

A Comment

No reader is ever complete. Topics are left uncovered, user's have differing interests, and readings become dated. However, the process of assembling a reader also identifies gaps and invites new initiatives. As readers use this set of selections (including the additional resources at the end of each Part) please consider significant conceptual topics that are absent. These are fruitful areas for research and writing.

This *Reader* has not attempted to deal with the many critical organizational and governance issues of the 1990's: Improving academic quality, serving minority and underprepared students, contributing to economic productivity, using educational telecommunications, global or international education, and commercial competition. The list goes on. For those of us interested in this *Reader*, I would suggest we should incorporate and address these topics but attempt to go beyond them. We should be learning about the new organizational and governance models and concepts that emerge as we attempt to address these issues. If we understand what these concepts and models are and what works, we will have important contributions to make to the next edition of the *ASHE Reader on Organization and Governance*.

A Note to the Reader

The ASHE Reader on Organization and Governance in Higher Education was the first volume in a series of publications sponsored by the Association for the Study of Higher Education (ASHE). Other volumes currently available focus on academic programs, faculty, finance, and history. The purpose of the Reader Series is to provide supplementary text material for use in graduate courses in the field of higher education.

More than fifty faculty members from programs around the country participated in the process which led to the selection of the articles, chapters, and other documents included in this volume. Many of these faculty had adopted the earlier editions of the *ASHE Reader on Organization and Governance*; this edition reflects their classroom experiences.

This *ASHE Reader* is intended for use in introductory graduate courses on organization and governance. College and university organization and governance are complex subjects with a large, growing, and increasingly sophisticated literature. The *ASHE Reader* contains only a sample of the best of that literature. Because of limitations of size, many scholarly and professional works of equal quality and importance could not be included. For example, many faculty identified excellent selections that do not deal explicitly with higher education, but because of the extensive array of quality articles dealing only with colleges and universities, these other selections could not be included.

Since this is the fourth edition of the *ASHE Reader on Organization and Governance in Higher Education*, a fifth is planned in three to four years; your assistance in determining the contents of the next edition would be greatly appreciated. We would like to know which articles you would recommend be retained, which should be replaced, and what you have read or discussed in class that should be included in future versions of this *ASHE Reader*. Please send your comments to: Marvin W. Peterson, 2117 School of Education Building, The University of Michigan, Ann Arbor, MI 48109.

PART I
ORGANIZATION THEORY AND MODELS

Evolution of University Organization

E. D. DURYEA

It has become customary in histories of American higher education to begin with a description of medieval origins. In general, there is good basis for looking back to those distant and turbulent days. The idea of a university itself as a formal, organized institution is a medieval innovation, which contrasts to the Greek schools and to the rudimentary organizational precedents in ancient Alexandria and in the Byzantine and Arabian cultures. The medieval universities instituted the use of many contemporary titles such as *dean, provost, rector,* and *proctor.* They initiated the idea of formal courses and of the curriculum leading to the baccalaureate and the master's and doctor's degrees. Our commencements are graced annually by the color and distinction of medieval garb. Fascinating anecdotes confirm that student violence has early precedents.

The point is, of course, that complex institutions such as universities do not appear full-blown at a particular point in time. They evolve through that complicated process by which men and cultures mingle over a history fraught with traditions and happenstance. Contemporary Western culture itself originated in the centuries that followed the "dark ages," and the university has served as one of the major institutions by which this culture he been transmitted over the years.

Within this context, certain aspects of the university's organization do have some important medieval precedents. Other aspects of its organization reflect the more direct influence of the English colleges of the sixteenth and seventeenth centuries. A history of American colleges and universities must be written also with due recognition of that educational revolution which took place in this country during the four decades following the Civil War. As Laurence R. Veysey (1965, p. 2) comments in his detailed interpretation of that era, "The American university of 1900 was all but unrecognizable in comparison to the colleges of 1860." The contemporary system of higher education dominated by the large, multifunctional university stands as a heritage of those years. Organizationally as well as educationally, its form and function were set by the time of the First World War. Its history during this century is primarily a chronicle of expansion and consolidation.

Reflecting these major historical influences, the following analysis examines the evolution of university organization from three major perspectives. The first deals with (1) the origins and use of the corporate form by which authority was granted to lay governing boards and (2) how their legal control has been modified by alumni and faculty influences that go back well into the nineteenth century. The second views the origins and expansion of the organizational structure of universities, an evolution epitomized by the comment that the old-time college president has all but disappeared behind a bureaucracy of academic and administrative offices and councils. In this sense the transition from the small, struggling colleges of the past to the large multiversity with its complex administration is first of all the history of the presidency. The third views the twentieth-century period of organizational expansion and consolidation. A concluding section identifies very briefly the evidences of dysfunction that have emerged in recent years.

Corporate Origins

By the twelfth century in Europe the church not only reigned supreme as a ruler of man's conscience but also exercised great temporal power over his mundane affairs. Rare were the individuals who would, when threatened with excommunication, choose to face an uncertain future in the hereafter. As the arbitrator of an ultimate destiny which included the possibility so vividly described in Dante's *Inferno* and as the only effective organization for all Europe, the church entered into the total life of the culture. But early in the thirteenth century, the more astute popes began to feel the rumblings of a shift of temporal power to political states and kings. The remote threat of hell began to give way to the more tangible thrust of the sword. As a result, the church hierarchy moved to bring its scattered organizations — religious orders, cathedral chapters, and universities — under more effective papal control. To this end, canon lawyers looked back to Roman law and its concept of corporations as fictitious legal entities. Their learned investigations led to a number of papal statements in the first decades of the thirteenth century and in 1243 to the famous bull or proclamation of Pope Innocent IV. The central idea in the Innocentean doctrine was that each cathedral chapter, collegiate church, religious fraternity, and university constituted a *Universitas*, i.e., a free corporation. Its corporate personality, however, was not something natural in the sense of a social reality but rather "an artificial notion invented by the sovereign for convenience of legal reasoning," existent only in the contemplation of law. This was a theoretical conception but nonetheless a very real one, since the corporation thereby derived its right to exist from an external authority and not from the intrinsic fact of its being (Brody, 1935, pp. 3-4).

The efforts of the papacy, the need of universities for protection against the immediate threats to their freedom from local bishops and townspeople, and the fact that the kings also intruded on their sovereignty — all these supported the corporate idea. The theory of corporate existence meant ultimately the end of the guild system and, for universities, of the idea of an independent association of scholars. The history of this development is complex and detailed, certainly beyond the scope of this particular analysis. It is sufficient to note that Emperor Frederick II rivaled Pope Gregory IX during the later years of the thirteenth century in the issuance of grants of authorization to universities, which in turn did not hesitate to strengthen their own hand by playing off pope against king (Rashdall, 1936, vol. 1, pp. 8-9). As national states gained dominance, however, universities ultimately had to look solely to kings for their charters, and what the king gave the king could take away.

The concept of corporations which served as precedent for the early colleges in this country matured in England during the fifteenth and sixteenth centuries. It provided an effective legal by which the king and later parliament would delegate in an orderly way authority for designated activities, not only to universities but to municipalities, trading companies, charitable establishments, and various other institutions. Charters provided for perpetual succession and the freedom for corporate bodies to set up and maintain the rules and regulations which in effect constituted internal or private governments. They also carried the right of supervision and visitation by representatives of the state. They established, in addition, legal protections associated with the rights of individuals in the sense that the corporation existed as an artificial or juristic individual. This conception of governmental grant of authority served also as the basis for the charters and statutes of the colleges of the English universities, which in general included provisions for external visitors or overseers, a head elected by the teaching staff or fellows, and a formal body constituted of these fellows which "exercised the legislative powers" (Davis, 1961, pp. 303-305).

The influence of this English college model was evident in the founding of the first two colonial colleges, Harvard (1636) and William and Mary (1693). For example, the language of the 1650 charter for Harvard is very similar to that of the royal charters for the colleges of Oxford and Cambridge (Morison, 1935, p. 10). Both these institutions were formed with governing councils composed of internal members (the presidents and teaching fellows) in tandem with external supervising boards that held final approval powers and the right of visitation.[1]

Another medieval precedent, however, came to the colonies with the early settlers and caused a significant modification of the English practice. In place of immediate control of the colleges by the teachers or professors, the practice evolved of granting complete corporate power to governing boards composed of external members. The origins of the use of external control lie in the medieval universities of northern Italy. Initially guilds of students who hired their professors, universities proved good for local business. The Italian towns competed for their presence in part by subsidizing salaries of outstanding teachers. The inexorable result was a blunting of student economic power and the establishment of municipal committees, in effect the first lay governing boards, to guard their financial interests (Rashdall, 1936, vol. 2, p. 59). Again, the detailing of the history of this tradition goes beyond the scope of this chapter. The lay board of control proved an appropriate mechanism for the direction of advanced education under the Calvinists at Geneva in the early sixteenth century, at the Dutch University of Leyden a few years later, at the Scottish universities of that same era, and finally at the Protestant Trinity College in Dublin. It was in part from these Dutch, Scottish, and Irish sources that the concept of lay boards came to the colonies (Cowley, 1964; 1971).

The English pattern of internal control by academics which was followed by Harvard and William and Mary did not set the precedent for university government in this country. That distinction fell to Yale College, established in 1701. Whether because of direct influences from the European Calvinistic practices noted above or simply because of parallel sectarian desires to maintain religious orthodoxy, the founders of Yale petitioned for a single nonacademic board of control. As a consequence, the colonial legislature of Connecticut granted authority to a board of "Trustees, Partners, or Undertakers" to "erect a collegiate school." Renamed in the revised 1745 charters as the "President and Fellows of Yale College," it continued as an external board with the right of self-perpetuation and with final control of the affairs of the institution (*The Yale Corporation*, 1952; see also Brody, 1935, Ch. 1).

Meanwhile, yet another deviation from English precedents also had begun to emerge. The right of the king and parliament to grant a charter carried with it an equal right to withdraw this charter. In fact, during the times of religious conflict in England this did occur, as first a Protestant and then a Catholic sovereign reconstituted the organization of the English universities in terms of religious biases. In the eighteenth century a new philosophy, that formalized by John Locke, gained acceptance, especially in the American colonies so strongly committed to a separation of church and state. This view stressed the nature of government as a compact among individuals, with sovereignty held by the people. In these terms of reference, having legal status as a person in law, although a fictitious or juridical person, corporations gained protection from legislative intrusions associated with the rights of individuals. Early in the nineteenth century court decisions began to interpret charters as contracts equally as binding upon the state as upon their recipients. The first intimation of this position regarding corporate auton3omy appeared in the 1763 statement of President Clap of Yale to the colonial legislature. He was protesting a threatened legislative visitation of the college on the grounds that such action would be contrary to the nature of the charter and the private legal nature of the institution.[2] Clap's position was novel in his day, but after the turn of the eighteenth century support of a judicial theory which interpreted charters to private corporations as contracts or compacts between the state and the founders began to appear. This point of view received its legal judicial confirmation in the famous Dartmouth College case decision of the Supreme Court under Chief Justice Marshall. In that decision, the Court viewed the college as a private institution and interpreted its charter as a contract binding upon the state of New Hampshire as well as the trustees, "a contract, the obligation of which cannot be impaired without violating the constitution of the United States" (Wright, 1938, p. 45).

The Dartmouth College decision led to a reexamination of the state-college relationship. Faced with a loss of control, legislators understandably questioned the award of public funds to private corporations. As a result there emerged in subsequent decades a number of public or state colleges, but not as agencies of state government under ministers of education in the continental tradition. Rather, the early public colleges took the form of public corporations parallel in their general organization to the private colleges. In the nineteenth century, it became common practice for legislatures to delegate governing power over state institutions to boards of control established as public corporations.[3] These boards received authority to control property, contracts, finances, forms of internal governance, and relationships with internal personnel — students, faculty members, and administrative employees (Brody, 1935, Ch. 6).[4]

Modification of Board Control: Faculty and Alumni Participation

Whatever the legal authority inherent in lay governing boards, continuing modification of their actual power is documented by a history of university organization. Early in the nineteenth century, accounts of the administration of Jeremiah Day at Yale College attest to the influence of faculty members with whom Day conferred regularly on policy decisions. Students, while rarely a direct component of government until recent years, have traditionally participated as alumni.

Earlier precedents than Yale exist. Professor W. H. Cowley (1964, Ch. 7) has uncovered a number of such instances. Overall, it is clear from his analysis and from histories of the leading universities that faculties greatly expanded their influence over academic affairs during the nineteenth century. The period from 1869 to 1900 illustrates the gradual but decisive involvement of professors in academic policies (Morison, 1930, p. xxxiv). The trustees at Cornell in 1889, for example, established a University Senate of the president and full professors (Kingsbury, 1962, pp. 263-264). Similar arrangements existed at Michigan, Illinois, Wisconsin, and other Midwestern institutions. At Johns Hopkins and Chicago, professors were accepted as the guiding force for all matters concerned with education and research. Faculty influence reached the point that, by the 1890s, President Jacob G. Schurman of Cornell saw his influence in educational affairs limited to final approval of appointments and his role as "the only man in the University who is a member of all boards, councils and organizations" (Kingsbury, 1962, p. 323).

By the turn of the century the trend to faculty participation was definite in the larger universities and major colleges. The decades that followed have chronicled the extension of faculty control over academic affairs, a development influenced by the policies and pressures of the American Association of University Professors subsequent to its founding in 1915.[5]

During the nineteenth century, alumni also entered actively into the government of colleges and universities. In doing this, they had well-established precedents in both England and Scotland, though little evidence exists to support a causal relationship. It is probably more accurate to explain alumni participation as the result of a unique commitment epitomized by the spirit of alma mater and reinforced by recollections of campus camaraderie. The college class has constituted a primary social as well as academic unit which, early in the history of the colleges, led to campus reunions and thus served regularly to reinforce the loyalty of graduates. In turn, it was natural for the members of governing boards and leaders of state governments to look to graduates of colleges for service on these boards when openings occurred. "From the very beginnings," Professor Cowley (1964, Ch. 10, p. 10) has written, "alumni have contributed to the support of private colleges and universities; and as legislators, lobbyists, and moulders of public opinion they have strategically influenced the subsidizing of civil institutions." Formal representation by means of elected members to governing boards first appeared at Harvard in 1865, a pattern that was followed by many other institutions in the subsequent decades.[6]

In summary, university government had coalesced into the pattern we know today by shortly after the turn of the century. It reflected a continuation of medieval and English precedents whereby institutional autonomy received a high degree of protection, modified perhaps in American higher education by a more overt sense of commitment to societal needs. Private colleges and universities had the protection afforded them by their status as corporations under law.[7] In practice, public institutions obtained much of this same autonomy through their status as public corporations under the control of boards established by state constitution or legislative law. But even before the end of the nineteenth century, evidences of growing restrictions upon the actual power of governing boards had begun to emerge.

Over and above any incipient faculty militance, the practical result of growing size and complexity necessitated the delegation of some policy-making and managerial responsibilities to presidents and faculties. Finally, the unique role and influence of presidents during this era require recognition. In contrast to earlier periods when presidents served more as principals responsible for campus conduct and morality — of professor and student alike — and trustees sat importantly at commencements to examine graduating seniors, by 1900 presidents had become a positive force. Every university to rise to major status did so under the almost dominating influence of such presidential leaders as Charles W. Eliot at Harvard, Andrew D. White at Cornell, Daniel Coit Gilman at Johns Hopkins, Charles R. Van Hise at Wisconsin, William Rainey Harper at Chicago, David S. Jordan at Stanford, and Benjamin Ide Wheeler at California. The office of president emerged as the central force that has given United States higher education a distinctive character among systems of higher education in the world. Whether one viewed the president as the alter ego of boards or as a discrete unit in institutional government had little bearing on practice. Whatever faculty voices may have been raised to the contrary, university government by the twentieth century centered upon the office of the president.

Administrative Structure

In his history of Williams College, *Mark Hopkins and the Log* (1956), Frederick Rudolph vividly portrays a typical college from 1836 to 1872. President Hopkins presides as the paternal head of a small and personal college family, responsible for the character of its children, the students. The curriculum was fixed and limited. In any event, what the students studied was secondary to the quality of personal moral life. In contrast, the "new education" of the last half of the nineteenth century reflected the new morality of the times, a turning away from Christian theology as the basis for life's judgments and toward values oriented far more to the marketplace and material success. In the words of Veysey (1965, Ch. 2), "discipline and piety" gave way to "utility" as the hallmark of a college education. Specialized knowledge replaced the "disciplining of the mind and character" as the raison d'être for higher education. Adherents of reform rallied to elective ideas which supported, to a degree at least, the rights of students to choose their subjects and thus to open the universities to the new studies of science and technology and of specialization in the humanities, all of which stressed the advancement of knowledge and a utilitarian commitment. By 1900 graduate studies, professional schools, and professors whose careers rested upon their published research rather than upon their role as teachers were moving to positions of the highest status in the academic hierarchy. Harvard University offered good evidence of the impact of this influence upon the curriculum. The 1850 catalog described the entire four years of undergraduate study on four pages; in 1920, 30 times that number of pages were required to list the courses offered at the university.

Two shifts in organizational structure inevitably followed. On the one hand, by the turn of the century departments and professional schools had become the basic units for academic affairs. The academic structure of the university coincided with the structure of knowledge. On the other hand, the impact of this "new education" fitted the times. In contrast to the declining enrollment of the 1840s and 1850s, the latter half of the nineteenth century marked the beginning of what has become a constantly increasing rate of college attendance. More students meant more professors, more buildings, more facilities and equipment, and, above all, more money from private and public sources. As chief executive, the president inherited the responsibility both for securing this support and for coordinating and managing the inevitable internal complexities that resulted. Initially, a vice-president and a few professors who served as part-time registrars, bursars, and librarians assisted him. By 1900, however, such staffs proved insufficient; the managerial burden of the president had begun to necessitate what has become a burgeoning administrative bureaucracy.

Academic Organization

Some imitations of the specialized departments and professional schools which have become the basic organizational units of universities do appear in the early colleges. The University of Virginia, for example, opened in 1825 with eight schools, each headed by a professor and each offering a program of studies. In that same year, the statutes reorganizing Harvard College established nine "departments" for instruction, each of which (in the pattern already set for medicine, law, and divinity) would be "governed by a board of its full professors" (Cowley, 1964, Ch. 7, p. 4). The use of departments appeared also in 1826 at the University of Vermont, a decade later at Wisconsin, and at Michigan in 1841. But these departments served only as progenitors of the disciplinary and professional units that fashioned the academic organization of universities later in the century.

The appearance of departments as organizational entities accompanied the expansion of knowledge — particularly scientific and technological — and the elective system, by means of which the adherents of specialized study forced their point of view into institutions with traditions of a fixed, classical curriculum. But the reason for the association of departments of scholars in this country (in contrast to the chair held by one professor in foreign universities) has not been documented historically. That they had become the established structural units by 1900 is evident nonetheless in the histories of all major universities.[8]

A similar development occurred in the various professional studies, which appeared with few exceptions first as departments and later as schools, which in turn procreated their own departments. Certainly by 1900 professional specializations in more than a dozen areas were well established, ranging from the traditional trinity of medicine, law, and theology to such new areas as business administration, veterinary medicine, journalism, librarianship, and architecture.

The departmental structure that followed in the wake of specialized knowledge was accompanied by other evidence of disciplinary and professional segmentation, such as journals and national societies. Professors, as the authorities for their respective specializations, assumed more and more control over academic affairs. This revolutionary change from the earlier colleges had evolved by 1910 to the extent that a study of physics departments complains about their having "too much autonomy." The report describes the department as "usually practically self-governing" in control of its own affairs — that is, its students, staff, and curriculum (Cooke, 1910).

Administrative Organization

Responding to the pressures of office work, travel, supervising new construction, employing new faculty, and initiating educational programs, in 1878 President Andrew Dickson White of the new Cornell University appointed a professor of modern languages and history, William C. Russel, as vice-president. Russel functioned as a kind of executive associate — hiring and dismissing junior faculty members, answering correspondence, and carrying out routine responsibilities as well as acting as institutional head in White's absence. The same year, a presidential colleague at Harvard, Charles W. Eliot, appointed Professor Ephriam W. Gurney as dean of the college faculty. In contrast to Russel's initial tasks, Dean Gurney's primary responsibility was to relieve the president of the burden of contacts with students.

These appointments at two major universities signaled the beginning of a trend. For the college growing into a large and complex university, the office of the president quickly ceased to be a one-man job. Those part-time assistants, usually professors, who served as librarian, bursar, or registrar had by 1900 turned into full-time administrative officers, and by the 1930s they were supervising large staffs. A 1936 study by Earl J. McGrath documents the trend. The author charts the growth from a median of three or four administrative officers in the 1880s to a median of nearly sixty for the larger universities by 1930. As noted previously in this chapter, the decades from 1890 to 1910 proved to be the turning point. The lines on McGrath's chart after 1890 turn upward abruptly, showing a doubling of these officers from an average of about 12 in that year to 30 in 1910.

What brought about this transformation of American universities into complex administrative systems, especially in contrast to the much simpler organization of European universities? Many determinants exerted influence, of course. In large part, administrative expansion responded to the need to coordinate and, to a degree, control the expansion of the academic structure. In part, it grew out of a relationship with the general society, unique to this country, which imposed on the university the task of securing financial support from both public and private sources and concurrently of attending to public relations. In part, the enlarged administration implemented an intricate credit system for student admissions and educational accounting.

Fundamentally, however, the administrative organization of universities resulted from the managerial role of the American college president, the coincidental result of the fact that early founders looked to the colleges of the English universities for their patterns. In doing this they carried over the concept of a permanent headship, designated in the English colleges as *warden, master, provost, president,* or *rector* (Cowley, 1971, Ch. 11, p. 10; Davis, 1961, p. 304).[9] In contrast to the English custom of election by the fellows of the college, the presidents in this country from the very beginning have been appointed by governing boards. Thus, the presidents of the early colleges had responsibilities as executives for boards. For the first two centuries this constituted a relatively simple and personal, almost paternal, relationship with student and teachers. When, after the Civil War, colleges ceased to be small and universities appeared with expanded enrollments, academic fragmentation, and diversified relationships with the external society, presidents found their responsibility elaborated and their need for staff assistance imperative.

By 1900 it could be said that the general administration had developed something like its full measure of force in American higher education. In 1902, President Nicholas Murray Butler assumed the presidency of Columbia complete with clerical staff, abetted by well-established offices for the registrar and bursar (Veysey, 1965, p. 307). Probably typical of its times, the University of North Carolina administration included a registrar, bursar, librarian, and part-time secretary for the university. The office of alumni secretary was not unknown by 1900 (McGrath, 1936). Although largely a product of this century, business officers commonly served as bursars or collectors of fees. By the turn of the century, librarians had established themselves on a full-time basis and had begun to employ assistants — in contrast with the rudimentary condition of these services 40 years previously. The first press bureau appeared at the University of Wisconsin in 1904 (Seller, 1963, p. 3). The office of registrar was nearly universal. The office of vice-president, usually assigned to handle specific functions such as university relations, academic affairs, medical affairs, or similar constellations of administrative services, had appeared in some numbers by the First World War.

Concurrently, presidents turned to the title of *dean* to further delegate their academic responsibilities. By 1900 this title was used for the heads of professional schools, especially medicine and law, and of schools or divisions of arts and sciences. The office of dean served in smaller colleges to designate the "second in command." In an 1896 reorganization at Cornell. for example, President Schurman appointed deans of academic affairs and of graduate studies. All the universities and two-thirds of the colleges included in the McGrath study bad academic deans by 1900. The designation of the title of dean for student affairs also has precedent in the late nineteenth century. At Harvard, Eliot's appointment of Dean Gurney, as noted above, was a response to the pressures of his responsibilities for students. Similar appointments were made at Swarthmore, Oberlin, and Chicago in the 1890s. The same forces that had fragmented the unitary curriculum of the early colleges in support of specialized knowledge made the orientation of faculty members more intellectual and pushed into secondary or tertiary importance their concern with students. Into this void came the forerunners of contemporary student personnel services. Deans of women began to meet annually in 1903; directors of student unions appeared in 1914; the National Association of Deans of Men was organized in 1917.

In summary, then, the organizational structure of American universities was etched clearly enough by the first decade of this century. Its two mainstreams flowed to and from the offices of presidents: one an academic route to deans and thence to departmental chairmen; the other a managerial hierarchy. Whatever the organizational charts designated, as early as 1910 it had become apparent that initiative on the academic side had begun to rest heavily at the departmental level.

Twentieth-Century Expansion

If the late nineteenth century constitutes the formative years of American higher education, the present century has been an era of growth and consolidation. During the decades following the Civil War, colleges began their search for a personality appropriate to the times and to their position in society. As the years of maturity approached, each found its particular role in what has become a spectrum from small, unitary schools to large, complex universities which set the pace and pattern for the whole system. Diversity became the pervasive quality of the new era-diversity among institutions and within the major universities.

Expansion in this century has led to colleges and universities that number faculty members in the hundreds and thousands and students in the thousands and tens of thousands. Society's commitment to send youth to college as a major preparation for adult roles is evident in the steady increase from 52,000 students in 1869 to 2,650,000 in 1949 to more than double this by the 1970s. The less than 2 percent of the age group who attended college at the close of the Civil War has grown to more than 40 percent and approaches 50 percent. This expansion in numbers has carried with it a similar expansion in functions. By the early 1960s Clark Kerr, then president of the University of California, could comment that his university employed more people "than IBM . . . in over a hundred locations, counting campuses, experiment stations, agricultural and urban extension centers, and projects abroad involving more than fifty countries." He pointed to "nearly 10,000 courses in its catalogues; some form of contact with nearly every industry. nearly every level of government, nearly every person in its region" (Kerr, 1966, pp. 7-8). The "multiversity" has proved to be the ultimate outcome for the "new university" of 70 years ago.

Since 1900 no radical departures have altered the form of university organization or changed in any substantial way its function. In the retrospect of the last 60 years, the major thrusts that have characterized this era are the following: first, the expansion in numbers of both personnel and of units of the administrative structure, both academic and managerial; second, the consolidation of departmental control over academic matters; and, third, the diffusion of participation in government with a concurrent lessening of the influence of boards and presidents.

Administrative Expansion

Aside from the study by McGrath (1936) and a recent article by David R. Witmer (1966), little documentation exists to delineate the specifics of administrative expansion in this century. But the outward manifestations are obvious. What university of any size today lacks that imposing administration building located near the center of the campus? Within its walls dozens and even hundreds of clerks, typists, secretaries, bookkeepers, accountants, staff assistants, and a variety of administrative officers labor diligently over correspondence and reports, accounts and records, and a variety of managerial services — frequently in a high degree of efficient isolation from the, classroom, laboratory, and library across the campus. In addition, one finds a plethora of service positions ranging from dietitians and delivery men to personnel for institutional research.

Paralleling the managerial services, the academic organization has had its own expansion of new functions and offices appended to departments and professional schools. It takes only a quick glance at the telephone directory of a major university to spot such activities as the animal facilities, athletic publicity and promotion, black studies program, carbon research, program in comparative literature, council for international studies, continuing education division, cooperative urban extension center, and creative aft center at the top of the alphabet through to technical research services, theater program, upward bound project, urology studies, and urban studies council at the bottom. Each of these activities has its director or head who reports to a chairman, a dean, or a vice-president. Each has a professional staff of one to a dozen individuals aided by secretaries and research assistants. The totality presents a bewildering complex of functions requiring administrative coordination and control.

As one looks over charts for the period, what stands out clearly is the steady, inexorable increase in administrative personnel and services paralleling the increase in numbers of students and facility members.

Departmental Influence

Specialization of knowledge has its counterpart in specialization of departments. But more than this it has led to what amounts to a monopoly of the expert. This specialization has left the university-wide administrators, and at times deans as well, unable to do more than respond to initiative on matters of personnel facilities, teaching, curriculum, and research. Authors Paul L. Dressel and Donald J. Reichard (1970, p. 387)[10] observed in their historical overview that the department "has become a potent force, both in determining the stature of the university and in hampering the attempts of the university to improve its effectiveness and adapt to changing social and economic requirements." As early as 1929 a study of departments in small colleges demonstrated that they exercised a major influence in matters related to teaching, curriculum, schedule, and promotion (Reeves & Russell, 1929). More recent studies confirm the trend toward departmental autonomy and control over its own affairs (Caplow & McGee, 1958), evidenced by what David Riesman (1958) has called an academic procession in which the less prestigious institutions have followed the leadership of the major, prestigious universities.

This departmental autonomy has come as a logical outgrowth of size and specialization and of the pressing necessity to delegate and decentralize if major administrators were not to find themselves overwhelmed. A new kind of professor, the specialist and expert and man of consequence in society, has replaced the teacher and has augmented his (the specialist's) influence with a national system of professional and disciplinary societies. Together they have set the standards and the values, both oriented to productive scholarship, that dominate the universities.

Diffusion of Government

Following hard on the downward shift of academic power, governing boards have withdrawn extensively from active involvement in university affairs. This condition was incipient in 1905, as noted by James B. Munroe, industrialist and trustee at Massachusetts Institute of Technology. The trustees, he observed then, "find less and less opportunity for usefulness in a machine so elaborate that any incursion into it by those unfamiliar may do infinite harm — (Munroe, 1913). Fifty years later, in the same vein, the 1957 report on The Role of Trustees of Columbia University, (Columbia University, 1957) stated flatly that, while governing boards may hold final legal authority, their actual role in government leaves them removed from the ongoing affairs of their institutions. And as Trustee Ora L. Wildermuth, secretary of the Association of Governing Boards of State Universities, commented in 1949: If a governing board contents itself with the selection of the best president available and with him develops and determines the broad general principles . . . and then leaves the administration and academic processes to the administrative officers and the Faculty, it will have done its work well." It serves best to select a president, hold title to property, and act as a court of last appeal, he summarized (Wildermuth, 1949, p. 238).

Pressing up from a departmental base, faculty members have moved into governmental affairs via the formalization of a structure of senates, councils, and associated committees. Evidence supports the contention that by 1910 professors were not hesitant to refer to their "rightfully sovereign power" (Veysey, 1965, p. 392). President Harper of Chicago formally stated in his decennial report that it was a "firmly established policy of the Trustees that the responsibility for the settlement of educational questions rests with the Faculties" (Bogert, 1945, p. 81). During the first half of this century the precedent of the major universities slowly carried over to other institutions. In 1941 a survey of 228 colleges and universities by the AAUP (American Association of University Professors) Committee T on College and University Government led to the comment that "in the typical institution the board of trustees appointed the president, the president appointed deans, and the deans in turn designated executives. . . . Consultation concerning personnel and budget . . . took place between administrative and teacher personnel through departmental executives — ("The Role of Faculties . . ." 1948). A decade later, however, the same committee reported an increase in faculty communication with trustees, participation in personnel decisions, influence on personnel policies, consultation about budgetary matters, and control of academic programs ("The Place and Function . . . ." 1953). By the late 1960s the basic position of the AAUP had the strength of general tradition; in the eyes of a new breed of faculty radicals it had become a conservative force. In essence, the AAUP's position was based upon five principles: (1) that faculties have primary responsibility over educational policies; (2) that they concur through established committees and procedures in academic personnel matters; (3) that they participate actively in the selection of presidents, deans, and chairmen; (4) that they are consulted on budgetary decisions; and (5) that appropriate agencies for this participation have official standing.

Precedents for student involvement in university and college government (distinct from extracurricular campus activities) have gained a new force, although their roots lie deep in the history of higher education. Professor Cowley (1964, Ch. 11, p. 16) has described the abortive two-year "House of Students" at Amherst in 1828 as a legislative body concerned with security on campus, study hours, and similar matters. In this century, something of the same spirit has appeared sporadically. At Barnard during the academic year 1921-22, students carried out a sophisticated analysis of the curriculum. At Dartmouth in 1924, a committee of 12 seniors submitted a critical review of the education program. At Harvard in 1946, following the publication of the faculty report General Education in a Free Society (Harvard Committee, 1946), students published an equally formidable document. Overall, as Cowley (1964, Ch. 11, p. 47) observes, "American students have continuously and sometimes potently affected the thinking and actions of professors, presidents, and trustees." Historically their influence has been an informal one. Their drive for direct participation on the governing councils and boards of colleges and universities generated real potency only during the late 1960s.[11] Its effectiveness remains conjectural, although the evidence suggests that the student drive for participation will tend to dissipate further the influence of boards and presidents.

Alumni have maintained their traditional voice in government, although one can perceive an undermining of the spirit of alma mater and the significance of financial contributions so long associated with their institutional commitments. This participation was substantiated by a 1966 survey of 82 public and private universities and colleges which reported that 31 of the institutions have elected alumni trustees and an additional 24 have trustees nominated by alumni. Nearly all had alumni on their boards, however.[12] Cornell University's situation is typical of private institutions. In a 1966 letter the president of the Alumni Association noted that 'a trustee is not required to be an alumnus of the University unless he is elected by the alumni. At present, however, of the 40 members, 35 are alumni." In retrospect, then, higher education is moving into the final decades of the twentieth century with a pattern of organization similar in its major dimensions to that with which it entered the century. The question readily comes to mind whether this form will continue to prove effective.

Conclusion

That the American university, the hallmark of the American system of higher education, has flourished as an institution uniquely fitted to its times stands without question. Its commitment to the expansion of knowledge and its application are emulated throughout the world. Similarly, its organizational arrangements have grown out of and suited well its particular kind of educational enterprise. Inevitably governing boards and presidents had to delegate as institutions expanded. That they did so in a manner that enhanced the effectiveness of the academic endeavor has proved to be no minor achievement. Departments, in turn, have served well by translating the essence of specialized knowledge into workable organizational forms. Student personnel administrators, in their turn, have filled that void between individual and organization left by the impersonalism inherent in a faculty pre-eminently concerned with the extension of knowledge. A faculty governing structure has given an organizational channel to the exercise of professorial influence, in turn an academically essential counterbalance to the authority of governing boards and external constituencies. In sum, universities have proved an effective organizational means by which scholarship and learning could flourish within the confines of large, complex organizations.

Yet, as the decade of the 1970s unfolds, a sense of uncertainty about just how well universities do perform has begun to settle over the campuses of the nation. Students in large universities, and even to a degree in smaller institutions, find themselves caught in a complex of increasingly impersonal relationships and an educational endeavor which enhances advanced study and research more than student learning. Both influences tend to dull any sense of intellectual awakening or of personal meaning for life on the part of students. Most faculty cling hard to the traditional fields of knowledge and to specialization despite a societal need for synthesis and application of what is known. As, historically, cultures and nations in their greatest flowering have begun to show their inherent weaknesses, so the university in the last few decades has provided evidence of its limitations. The changing nature of the social order, as it too reaches a pinnacle of scientific-technological achievement, amplifies these weaknesses.

A historical survey such as this would be inadequate indeed if it did not at least suggest some clues to the future. In conclusion, therefore, we note three pervasive organizational inadequacies. One can be attributed to size and complexity, a second to specialization and departmentalization, and the third to the shifting pattern of institutional government. All were incipient but generally underway as higher education emerged from the First World War.

The size and complexity of United States universities seem to dictate that they have become large bureaucracies. Actually, however, one finds two bureaucracies. On the one hand, over the past 50 years faculties have created a hierarchy of departments, schools, and senates or executive councils well larded with a variety of permanent and temporary committees. This bureaucracy claims rights of control over the totality of the academic function. On the other hand, administrators have formed a separate hierarchy to grapple with the immense tasks of management of essential yet supportive services which maintain the university, not the least of which are budget and finance. The lines of relationship between the two bureaucracies have become tenuous. The different attitudes and values associated with each have driven a psychological wedge between faculty members and administrators. Faculty remain committed to a traditional ideal of the university as an integrated community, at the same time giving constant evidence that they fail to grasp its real operational nature and managerial complications. Administrators find their managerial tasks so consuming that they become forgetful of the nature of the academic enterprise.

The second evidence of dysfunction stems from the nature of the department as the organizational unit for disciplinary and professional specialization. The commitment to specialization energizes centrifugal forces that tend to push faculty loyalties out from the universities. Thus the university is often merely a base, temporary or permanent, from which the scholar pursues his primary concern with research activities. Specialization has produced a similar tendency toward fragmentation of the academic organization. While exercising a dominant influence on instruction, curriculum, research, and other academic matters, schools and departments show a low regard for university values and a high concern for disciplinary and professional values. Despite many evidences to the contrary during the student disruptions of the last few years, this condition is reinforced by academic condescension toward administrators, who are viewed as servants rather than leaders of the professorate. It reflects what one might call a faculty schizophrenia which categorizes administrators as minions while condemning them for failure to stand firmly as defenders of the academic faith in times of crisis.

At times this divergency threatens an atrophy in leadership for large universities in an era when leadership is of utmost importance. The remedy, however, inevitably must lie beyond the bounds of organizational factors. Forms of government serve only as well as they are supported in the general values and commitments of those affected by them. Any rectification of this condition, therefore, must stem from deep within the higher education enterprise. In particular, there must be some resolution of the conflict between the clear and direct rewards that accompany achievement in scholarship and research and the nominal recognition, despite societal expectation, accorded to the education of students. From this base line one moves into explorations of reward systems that conform to stated purposes. One also has to reflect upon organizational systems that prove responsive to changing conditions as against those that support existing arrangements.

The third problem — the shifting power in institutional government — was anticipated in 1903 by President Schurman of Cornell when he characterized his role as that of a mediator. Sixty years later Clark Kerr made the same observation with greater force. Presidential deference to faculty expertise in academic affairs is only one facet of the situation, however. The history of university organization in the twentieth century has been an account of the disintegration of the traditional form of government conceived in terms of formal authority granted to governing boards, which have exercised it through the president as executive officer.

The diffusion of government by means of dissipation of boards and presidential influence and dispersion of operating control to departments, administrative offices, and faculty governing bodies has been accompanied by the intrusion of external forces. Professional and disciplinary associations, accrediting agencies, agencies of the federal government for all institutions and state executive offices for public ones — all have tended to bypass presidents and boards. It appears that higher education has experienced one of those historic circles. Governing boards today serve much the way the original visitors or overseers did. What is lacking is a new corporation in the sense of a controlling or managerial council to fill the vacuum. As one English observer phrased it, organizationally American universities have tended to become "confederations of largely autonomous departments." It adds up to what he has characterized as "the hole in the centre" (Shils, 1970).

As universities enter the decade of the 1970s, the pressures on the established organization are evidenced in student dissent and the public reaction to it. The movement toward decentralization of control over educational and administrative functions has begun to come up against external demands for more forceful central authority to the end not only of "law and order" but of a "more efficient use of resources." Mass higher education and the possibility of almost universal higher education exacerbate the problems. More fundamentally, one finds growing evidences of academic inadequacies in the face of the need for new kinds of education and scholarship. These must relate to the role of the university in a society pressed by ecological and social dislocation stemming from scientific and technological achievement. One readily suspects that the organizational forms effective in 1900 may serve but poorly for the year 2000.

Reprinted by permission from The University as an Organization, edited by James A. Perkins, 1973, McGraw-Hill Book Company, pp. 15-37. Copyright © 1973 by The Carnegie Foundation for the Advancement of Teaching.

Notes

[1] These arrangements for the College of William and Mary were stated in a manner that led to conflicts between the two boards during its early years, although essentially they remained in effect until it became a state institution shortly after 1900. At Harvard, however, practice nullified the apparent intent of the 1650 charter, so that by the eighteenth century the immediate governing council (the Corporation) had passed into the hands of external members. The practice was disputed from time to time by tutors until an 1825 vote of the Overseers finally and formally stated that "the resident instructors of Harvard University" did not have any exclusive right to be chosen members of the Corporation (Quincy, 1860, vol. 2, p. 324).

[2] Yale historians apparently have tended to credit Clap with a successful defense. Recent investigation of this incident by Professor W. H. Cowley, however, discloses that a visitation was made the following year, about which one of the visitors later observed that "we touch'd them so gently, that till after ye Assembly, they never raw they were taken in, that we had made ourselves Visitors, & subjected them to an Annual Visitation" (a point made in correspondence with this author).

[3] This precedent has undergone modification in more recent decades as state budget bureaus, civil service commissions, and coordinating boards have intruded directly into the internal affairs of public institutions.

[4] Exceptions to these rights do exist, particularly in connection with the control of property and the borrowing of monies. Frequently special corporations are set up within the control of state universities to handle private funds. Actual practice varies among the states, some of which limited the powers of boards in the founding legislation.

[5] In recent decades the growth in academic status and influence of the disciplines and professional departments and schools has further strengthened faculty power within institutions. The status associated with productive scholarship and research has given faculty members a greatly improved position vis-á-vis administration in internal affairs, a condition documented by Theodore Caplow and Reece J. McGee in their classic study, *The Academic Marketplace*, 1958.

[6] Amherst in 1874, Dartmouth in 1875, Rutgers in 1881, Princeton in 1900, Columbia in 1908, Brown in 1914. (In the 1865 modification of its charter, Harvard adopted a plan whereby alumni gained the right to elect all new members to the Board of Overseers, the body with ultimate responsibility for that institution.)

[7] Little attention is given, unfortunately, to the uniquely significant role of the governing board in this country as the agency that both has protected internal autonomy and intellectual freedom and has served as a force to keep institutions relevant to the general society. This history badly needs doing. Despite

occasional intrusions into internal affairs and matters related to academic freedom, the governing board has served as a point of balance for that essential dualism between institutional and academic autonomy and public accountability which has characterized American higher education. Current forces pressing for greater internal participation on the one hand and increased public control on the other need tempering by the experience of the past in this connection.

[8] For example, Harvard established 12 divisions, each including one or more departments, in 1891; Chicago had 26 departments in three faculties in 1893; Cornell, Yale, Princeton, Johns Hopkins, and Syracuse, among others, all reveal the trend toward departmentalization during the decade of the 1890s (Forsberg & Pearce, 1966).

[9] Actually, the first head of Harvard had the title of master and that of Yale, rector. The Harvard custom lasted two years. that at Yale about forty. Both colleges shifted to the title of president.

[10] This report anticipated a more complete study by Dressel, Marcus, and Johnson entitled The Confidence Crisis, Jossey-Bass, Inc., San Francisco, 1970.

[11] In his 1970 book, Should Students Share the Power? Earl J. McGrath reports a survey of existing practice, noting that more than 80 percent of 875 institutions admit some students to membership in at least one policy-making body. In the same year the University of Tennessee admitted students to its trustee committees. A House bill submitted in 1969 in the Massachusetts legislature proposed an elected student member of each of the governing boards of public universities.

[12] Conducted by Howard University with the sponsorship of the American Alumni Council. The questionnaire was mailed to 112 institutions, from which 82 usable responses were received.

Emerging Developments in Postsecondary Organization Theory and Research: Fragmentation or Integration

MARVIN W. PETERSON

ABSTRACT: Developments in theory and research on postsecondary institutions as organizations are proceeding in many different directions, threatening to fragment this critical area of research. This article examines the major developments and identifies dilemmas in theory development research methods, organizational behavior context, relating theory to practice, and identifying professional colleagues. These areas need to be understood and addressed to assure the continued, integrated development of postsecondary organization theory and research.

* * *

Reflecting on the emerging developments in organization theory and research in postsecondary education over the past decade suggests a major concern: There is a substantial tension between the current tendency to fragment and proliferate knowledge about organizational behavior in postsecondary education and the need to integrate it. Opening this topic brings to mind a few past warnings by some astute observers of colleges and universities.

In commenting on universities, Alfred North Whitehead (1928) said, "the heart of the matter is beyond all regulation" (p. 638).

Frederick Rudolph (1962) concludes his history of the *American College and University* with the observation that change in higher education is best typified as "drift, reluctant accommodation, and belated recognition that, while no one was looking, change had in fact taken place" (p. 491).

In a more current practical observation, Kingman Brewster (1965) suggests "the real trouble with attempting to devise a strategy, let alone a plan, for a university is that basically we (faculty) are all anarchists—significant thought, art, and action must have creativity. Creativity by definition defies predictions plan" (p. 45).

For those of us who think our work in postsecondary organizational behavior can make a difference, these observations should give reason to pause. Yet it is precisely these complexities and the variety of students, learning and research styles, faculty and administrative behavior, academic and administrative structures, external demands and pressures, and institutional roles, missions, structures, processes, and characteristics that challenge us to understand the patterns of organizational behavior in these institutions with their strong fragmenting tendencies. The organizing challenge is to preserve the positive aspects of that variety and richness while assuring that we accomplish our mutual educational and academic purposes and to make each college or university more effective. The dilemma is not whether to organize, but how to organize, to what degree, and for what purpose. The challenge of postsecondary organizational theory and research is to try to understand what holds together these fascinating institutions as organizations and what makes them more effective.

An Image of Adolescence

Before examining some of the recent developments and the dilemmas they raise, it is useful to recall that this is still an emerging scholarly arena. For example, the larger field of organizational behavior is almost entirely a post World War II phenomenon. It has grown rapidly as an interdisciplinary arena of study and has spawned graduate degree programs, departments, schools, and professional associations of scholars and practitioners. It has also produced an extensive literature and some highly sophisticated journals on organizational theory, research, and application. Indeed, Pfeffer (1982) describes it as a "thicket."

Although not yet of thicket proportions, the literature on organizational theory and research in postsecondary education is also growing rapidly. Using a human "developmental" rather than a "thicket" image, one might mark 1963 as the beginning of "infancy" of our interest in postsecondary organizational theory and research. In separate articles, McConnell (1963) of Berkeley and Henderson (1963) of Michigan decried the paucity of literature and research about the organization and administration of higher education. In the decade following, numerous practical and conceptual writings and some serious research efforts emerged.

By 1974, one might describe the area as past "early childhood" and entering "pre-adolescence." In that year, a comprehensive review of the research literature on "Organization and Administration in Higher Education" for Volume II of *Review of Research in Education* highlighted some of the theoretical and conceptual bases of the research, assessed the sophistication of the research, and attempted to identify major gaps (Peterson, 1974). An initial list of 500 publications was quickly reduced to less than 200, which were research based. That review noted that the quantity of research had increased substantially after 1970, that it was attracting researchers from several social science fields who were doing some excellent work, and that most major issues of the late 1960's and early 1970's were receiving attention. However, major concerns were noted and recommendations focused on the following:

1. The limited development or use of theoretical models or concepts from related disciplines and the need for greater emphasis in this area.
2. Studies were too often exploratory case studies or descriptive surveys. Longitudinal, before and after, field experiments, and comparative studies were almost nonexistent. Studies used exploratory as a rationale for avoiding conceptualization and/or quantification. Even quantitative surveys seldom used bivariate statistical analyses and ignored multivariate or causal path approaches, even when data might have allowed. There was a need for greater sophistication in research strategy, design, and methodology.
3. Replication studies and use of reliably constructed instruments on different populations to extend generalizability of any findings had seldom occurred and was needed.
4. Since the most sophisticated theoretical formulations and sophisticated designs came from scholars with disciplinary backgrounds, a professional network for involving them was needed.

The most recent decade has been one of substantial progress. Research that examines the organizational behavior of colleges and universities at the individual, group or process, organization, and interorganization of organization environment level has expanded both in quantity and sophistication. A formal review such as the one 10 years ago would be extensive. This paper only examines the high points and scans the major theoretical, methodological, and application developments and dilemmas that face us today. The current stage seems to be one of "advanced adolescence"—maturing rapidly, capable of extremes of sophistication and foolishness, and alternately confident and uncertain. The current high level of productivity is generating a wide array of theoretical, methodological, and application activities that create a tension that can either lead to proliferation and fragmentation or a new synthesis and integration.

As an "adolescent," the research area is struggling with problems of identity and commitment—what is the field? Where are developments in postsecondary organizational theory and research methods going and do we want to go there? It is struggling with the issue of relevance—are we dealing with important issues and relating theory to practice (or vice-versa) in constructive ways? Also, it is struggling with the issue of legitimacy—what professional peer group provides intellectual criticism and guidance to direct these efforts? An overview of developments in five areas—theory, research, content, relation to practice, and peers—poses some interesting images and dilemmas to stimulate discussion about where we should go.

Because organizational behavior has few bounds, these comments focus primarily on organizational level phenomenon, that is, where the entire college or university or major segment of it is dealt with as an organization. Also, because the literature is growing rapidly, the attempt is not to summarize what we have learned but rather to ask: How is the area developing?

On Theory Development

Since the 1974 review that found limited use of theoretical concepts and models in higher education, the area has exploded. At that time there were three basic models of organization (six, if one includes their derivatives): bureaucracy or formal-rational and goal models; collegial and professional community models; and political and public bureaucracy models. These were basically internally oriented and used to analyze the pervading governance issues. In the intervening decade, conceptual discussions and research in postsecondary education now includes open systems, environmental contingency, organizational life cycle, and strategic models that reflect the increased concern for external developments and forces. Task-technology and information or resource models reflect our growing concern with the impact those changes have on us. The list now includes a variety of emergent social system models. Temporary adaptive, loosely coupled, organized anarchy, and social network models reflect primarily internal models that attempt to account for some of the postsecondary education special characteristics. The cultural model, which Peters and Waterman (1982) have popularized, has also reemerged in higher education. Clark's (1970) *Distinctive Colleges* and Riesman, Gusfeld, and Gamson's (1970) study of *Academic Values and Mass Education* introduced us to the concern for culture 15 years ago. More recently, Dill (1982) has examined our changing institutional value systems at professional meetings, and researchers like Bess have been challenging us at professional meetings to examine the larger values that postsecondary institutions and educators should address. Closely related to the study of organizational cultures and values are proponents of the natural study of organizational phenomenon—an antimodel perspective. Finally, there are interorganizational models: Systems of organizations, organizational networks, organizational ecology, and industry models are being used to examine broader patterns of relationships among postsecondary organizations. (See Table I.)

The list is not comprehensive and includes only organizational level models. The intent is not to examine each model; rather, the character of the list itself prompts some observations and raises issues about where we are going in the expansion of models and frameworks.

First, and perhaps most important, the pre-1974 models are what Pfeffer (1982) classified as "internal, purposive" models; they focus on a managed set of activities that impact on the organizations' performance—they see organizations as self directed. The recent models give more credence to technology, the environment, or the emergent social structure as the major determinants of action. (The distinction between "internal, purposive" and "emergent and social structure" will be discussed later.)

Second, as it did a decade ago, the list consists primary of "borrowed" models. Admittedly, many have been distorted or modified to fit our postsecondary context, but only two—Cohen and March's (1974) model of organized anarchy and Weick's (1976) loosely coupled notion—were generated primarily to reflect the postsecondary context. Even those, however, have roots in other settings because neither are new concepts. It is ironic that in postsecondary education, which many argue is unique, so little attention is given to theory generation and so much reliance is placed on borrowing models from institutional settings. Clearly, theory generation deserves greater attention.

Table I

Some Organizational Models in Postsecondary Education

Internal purposive:	Formal-rational/goal
	Collegial/professional community
	Political/public bureaucracy
Environmental:	Open systems
	Contingency
	Strategic
	Life cycle
Technology:	Task/techno-structure
	Information system/resource models
Emergent social systems:	Temporary adaptive
	Organized anarchy
	Loosely coupled
	Social networks
	Organizational culture/values
	Organizational learning
	Natural/anti-models
Interorganizational:	Systems of organizations
	Organizational networks
	Ecology models
	Industry model

A third observation on the list of models has to do with the fragmented nature of the models themselves and with how one deductively builds theory.[1] Borrowing models has led to a multitude of models that focus on different phenomenon. The models also vary in normative, analytic, or predictive purpose and often have different assumptions about explanatory forces (e.g., internal or external, guided or emergent). The concern is that little attention has been given either to *mapping* the organizational territory covered by these borrowed theories or to *examining* comparatively the nature of each model. The need to relate our theoretical models to organizational phenomenon (the territory) to identify gaps is noted by Bess (1983) in his edited volume of *Review of Higher Education*.

The direct comparison of models dealing with a similar phenomenon is also useful to highlight their differing perspectives and content. Baldridge's (1971) comparison of bureaucratic, collegial, and political models over a decade ago covered the organizational and governance models in vogue at the time. More recently, we have many limited comparisons of models (or submodels) or concepts that focus on only one level or type of organizational phenomenon—for example, Cameron's (1984) comparison of four models of organizational adaption (population ecology, life cycles, strategic choice, and symbolic action) in the *Journal of Higher Education*. But many questions remain. For example, how does the loose-coupling model compare with a social network model? Is a coupling element the same as or different from a linkage element? Mapping our theories in relation to organizational phenomenon and analytic comparison of models offers useful ways of reducing fragmentation and/or discovering overlaps; however, a comprehensive scheme for comparing all our models still needs considerable conceptual thought and effort.

The final observation is our failure to examine the "appropriateness" or "adequacy" of each of our borrowed models or constructs, evidently because they appear to be intuitively logical or seem to make sense. In much of the conceptual literature and research, writers have a tendency to become advocates of the model they are discussing. They seldom ask critical analytic questions. Is the model an analytic framework, a normative theory, or an explanatory or predictive theory? Does the model satisfy simple criteria for a good theory? Five come to mind (Pfeffer, 1982, p. 38). First, is there "clarity" in the phenomenon being examined and definition of key concepts and variables? Are conceptual and operational definitions of variables clear? For example, one still sees influence defined and measured in different ways, yet discussed without recognizing the differences. Second, is the model "parsimonious" in the number of variables it contains (or loaded with inexplicable contingencies)? Third, does the theory have a "logical coherence"? For example, Weick (1976) proposed "loose-coupling" as an idea and an analytic perspective that was yet to be defined, evaluated, and developed. However, several researchers have discussed it as if it were already an explanatory theory rather than challenging it (Lutz, 1982). Fourth, do we ask if the model exhibited exhibited "consistency" with real data and whether the conditions or "contingencies" are present? For example, organizational anarchy is a popular way of explaining some of our less predictable behavior but others have questioned its usefulness when "organizational slack," one of its key assumptions, is declining or not present. In a recent analysis of the review and reorganization of the biological sciences at Berkeley, Trow (1984) suggests it is not as useful as a more rational paradigm.

A fifth criterion for theory is "refutability." Do we attempt to refute or disconfirm our models? It prompts comments at two levels. First, as research has accumulated using some of these models or their key concepts, there has not been an inductive, balanced, and systematic examination of the convergent or divergent evidence for or against a particular model. Because so much organizational research in higher education is problem oriented, the research reviews have focused on categorizing the research around issues addressed, patterns of descriptive findings, types of institutions studied, methods used, and so forth—not on evidence converging with or diverging with a model or its prediction. There are few scholarly outlets for reviews of this nature, and it also appears that critical, comparative analysis of research findings is not a high priority that postsecondary organizational researchers have emphasized. Many review articles and even entire books report only findings and insights supporting their argument for their model and do not systematically weigh the counter evidence. An exemplary exception is the research on attrition in which several careful research scholars have examined quantitative studies in a systematic and balanced fashion around theoretical frameworks (Pascarella & Terenzini, 1979; Tinto, 1982). But even this group has not used meta-analysis to statistically test the convergence of predictions and theory across studies.

The second concern about refuting or disconfirming the research models is that although organizational research is now more likely to be theoretically or conceptually oriented and to develop hypothesis, it is often based on one model. The studies are designed either to support or not support the theory. Seldom do we use what Platt (1964) referred to in *Science* as "strong inference"—testing different models or competing hypotheses in the same study. Although she did not use statistical tests, Chaffee's (1984) recent study comparing adaptive vs. interpretive strategies in institutions that had suffered decline is one example of this approach.

This abbreviated overview of the organizational theories and models portrays it as a *muddled* arena and highlights one of our developmental dilemmas. Should postsecondary organizational research focus on theory *generation* that can more adequately reflect the uniqueness of higher education? Should it focus on *systematic synthesis* of the many theoretical models and extensive research to establish if there is more convergence or less fragmentation than appears? Should it focus on systematic model *testing*, which is the most convincing way to establish results but which is time consuming, expensive, and of limited practical interest? I shall return to the dilemmas later.

On Research Developments

In 1974, postsecondary organizational research was characterized as primarily descriptive surveys or exploratory case studies. Although these are still present, research strategies, methods, and techniques have also expanded and become more sophisticated. Before noting some of the changes, it is useful to note what has not changed. There is still little or no use of experimental research strategies and primary emphasis remains on field research. Few longitudinal, pre-post, or quasi-experimental designs are noted. Some simulation strategies have been tried, but mostly in quantitative computer simulations. Cohen, March, and Olsen's (1972) test of their organized anarchy model and the many resource flow and forecasting simulations developed in the mid-1970's are most notable. Interestingly, behavioral simulations that have been used to model organizational behavior in other professional settings have received little use. The changes, on the other hand, are most instructive and are a product of our changing models, the conditions affecting higher education, and our increasing research sophistication.

First, comparative case studies that combine both structured qualitative and quantitative methods appear to be used more often. This enhances the opportunity to validate variables and causal patterns, enhances generalizability, and in some instances allows sophisticated statistical comparisons and even multivariate analysis. Mortimer's (1979) studies of resource decline processes emphasize content analysis of documents and interviews from several institutions, whereas Baldridge's (1979) study of the impact of management systems in several liberal arts colleges uses both qualitative and quantitative approaches for making comparisons.

Second, more large survey studies now incorporate institutional characteristics along with individual survey results and have led to enriched analysis examining the effects of individual and organizational variables. Baldridge's (1978) extensive study of governance in the mid to late 1970's, which produced numerous studies of different governance issues, is an example. Both the comparative case studies and large-scale surveys have on occasion used complex index building and even causal path modeling.

Third, there has been some increase in the use of standardized data bases of institutional characteristics for secondary analysis in large-scale studies. Birnbaum's (1983) study of changing patterns of institutional diversity and Zammuto's (1984) study of shifting patterns of liberal arts colleges and their enrollment are examples that draw on the HEGIS data base for an ecological analysis of our institutions.

Fourth, out of the renewed emphasis on organizational culture and the models reflecting less formal, more emergent phenomenon (loose-coupling, organized anarchy, natural models, etc.) has come a substantial interest in less structured qualitative methods. Strategies such as content analysis of documents and interviews, use of unobtrusive measures, and ethnographic and phenomenological approaches appear to be used more frequently.

Large-scale studies that combine a thorough synthesis of research, carefully develop models and variables, employ institutional surveys with comparative case studies, and use both quantitative and qualitative methods are still rare. Cameron's (1983) current series of studies of effectiveness, Chaffee's (1984) studies of strategic management, and Peterson's (1978) study of the impact of black students on predominantly white colleges are examples. Such studies are expensive, time consuming, and require long-term commitments. Unfortunately, funding for such large-scale research has declined and is seldom available.

These observations on research strategies and methods highlight the fact that organizational research in higher education is becoming a complex "methodological maze" that is increasingly sophisticated and raises the second dilemma: Do we emphasize larger scale *quantitative* studies that yield greater generalizability and potential for statistical modeling but are expensive and uncertain, or *intensive qualitative* studies that may be more helpful in generating new theory and new ideas?

Table II

Two Cultures of Organizational Theory and Research		
Paradigm:	Traditional, Conservative or Social Fact	Cultural, Radical, or Social Definition
Elements of Reality:	Objective	Subjective
View of Knowledge:	Positivism	Interpretive
Causation:	Predictive	Diagnostic, Final Cause
Content Focus:	Structures, Patterns	Emergent Processes, Dynamics
Use of Theory:	Variance Testing	Process or Developmental
Research Design:	Planned	Audit
Methodology:	Reductionist	Wholistic
Measurement:	Quantitative	Qualitative

Organizational Behavior: The Contextual Debate

The previous theoretical and methodological dilemmas are a reflection of a debate that has been raging in the larger realm of organizational behavior for the past 5 years. Since the advances in postsecondary education have both been borrowed from and lag the developments in organizational behavior, it can be useful to examine that debate briefly. In an exaggerated form, it can be posed as a dialectic between two extreme positions or paradigms, as an argument about basic philosophical and metaphysical assumptions: What constitutes reality in organizations (the ontological issue)? How do we gain knowledge about them (the epistemological issue)? What are our assumptions about causation (the teleological dimension)? (See Table II.)

Stated simply: The first is variously called the "Traditional," "Conservative," or "Social Fact" paradigm (Cummings, 1981; March, 1982; Meryl, 1981). It views organizational elements as objective, accepts them as positive facts, and is concerned with predicting events. The major focus is on structures, observable behaviors and organizational elements, and respondents' attitudes and self reports. Theories are posed in terms of how one set of variables varies with others, and the concern is to test them. The methodologies are primarily reductionist and quantitative in nature.

The second, the "Cultural," "Radical," or "Social Definition" paradigm views organizational elements as those that are subjective and must be interpreted, primarily by the organizational actors themselves. It is more concerned with diagnosis or final causes. The major focus is on emergent processes and dynamics. Theories are process theories, and the concern is mostly with development of theory. However, some supporters of this view reject the notion of any theoretical models and recommend describing or auditing the phenomenon under study. The methodologies tend to be more wholistic, viewing the entire context of organizational behavior and making more extensive use of qualitative research methods.

Setting aside the externally oriented and technological organizational models noted earlier, the distinction, although not as clear or sharp, has emerged in our postsecondary models. For example, prior to 1974 the formal-rational, political, and collegial models more closely fit the traditional paradigm. They all suggest that objective phenomenon can be used to explain events and that institutions can be managed or intentionally directed if one understands the formal, political, or collegial patterns. All have been the basis of research using primarily statistical or other forms of objective analysis based on survey data of attitude and perceptions, on measures of individual and institutional characteristics, and on content of documents and structured interviews.

On the other hand, the more recent models such as social networks, loose-coupling, organizational learning, and examining institutions as cultures reject the more intentional and rational assumptions of the traditional models, and they often criticize their failure to account for much of what happens in higher education. These models choose to focus on understanding how people in higher education interpret events, how they are influenced by the setting and the content of events, and how they ascribe meaning to them. The focus is on the examination and diagnosis of behavior and how processes emerge or are shaped. Their methodologies tend to rely more on ethnography (intensive, anthropological case studies), in-depth interviews and participant observations, and phenomenological investigation.

Naturally, these two positions are extremes, and many of the discussions of theory, research, and methodology in postsecondary education either incorporate or acknowledge both perspectives. Nonetheless, the intensity of the debate that mirrors the two previous dilemmas does suggest a potential third one for the development of organizational theory and research in postsecondary education: Will these *dialectical views* continue as two potentially *divisive paradigms* or will there be an *accommodation*?

Theory to Practice

The second topic on our developmental agenda is the "relevance" issue, the relationship of theory and research to practice. Because organizational research on postsecondary education has often been heavily practice oriented, the topic is important. However, several changes appear to be reshaping this interface.

First, the tendency to be responsive to current practical issues continues and often leads to extremely descriptive research. Fortunately, the recent research on retrenchment or decline and on effectiveness (e.g., Cameron, 1983; Mortimer, 1979) have resisted this criticism by examining issues that are not ephemeral and by placing the problem in a sound conceptual framework. Given postsecondary education's current pressures, researchers need to weigh the temptation for visible, descriptive studies and give equal attention to research on important longer-term issues.

Second, there is an increasing administrative research capacity and sophistication in higher educational institutions. This can reduce the pressure on scholars for immediate useful studies. It can also provide faculty members interested in postsecondary organizational and administrative issues with greater opportunity to synthesize research and to translate it to knowledgeable administrators. This is a potentially useful development and is reflected in the increasing array of monograph series such as the *ASHE/ERIC Research Reports*, the *New Directions* series from Jossey-Bass, and other association publications that provide opportunities for synthesis around current and practical issues.

Third, the increased emphasis on conceptual models and more complicated array of research strategies and methods previously noted may tend to make postsecondary organizational research either less useful or more difficult for administrators to comprehend. This makes the translation and dissemination of research results to practitioners more critical than it has been in the past. It is my observation that the issue of research utilization is getting less emphasis by postsecondary organizational researchers than in the past just when the need may be increasing. This issue, which has become a central concern to institutional researchers, is the topic of a recent *New Directions for Institutional Research* volume (Lindquist, 1981).

Fourth, closely related to the previous points is the tendency of current organizational research efforts to adopt an approach in which the researcher is viewed as neutral or noninvolved. In courses and literature on higher and postsecondary research design that I have reviewed, applied research techniques related to the practice of institutional research, policy analysis, and evaluation are approached largely from the perspective of a neutral researcher. Little attention is given to strategies of action research or organizational development where the researcher participates with the actors. Almost no attention is given to advocacy research. Yet many graduate students in postsecondary education enter administrative careers requiring such skills. However, scholars have recently made such contributions. For example, Gamson's (1984) *Varieties of Liberal Education* was based on her experience as a FIPSE project coordinator in which she assisted project institutions in designing and carrying out evaluations. Victor Baldridge has recently directed a project to design, implement, and evaluate attrition reduction programs in several schools in which he adopted a more active research role. Clifton Conrad, Robert Blackburn, and Robert Berdahl among others have participated in advocacy research roles for U.S. Department of Justice Investigations of desegregation in Louisiana The point is that strategies of research involvement as well as dissemination may be called for in this theory to practice interface.

These observations suggest the fourth dilemma: Are researchers to become more isolated or more involved? The key issue is not so much, the interest in theoretical versus practical problems, but whether the postsecondary organizational researcher should emphasize roles as neutral or uninvolved experts who conceptualize and design, as intermediaries who translate and disseminate, or as involved research-practitioners or advocates.

Professional Peers

The final developmental topic is concerned with defining the legitimate professional colleagues and mentors in postsecondary organizational theory and research to whom one looks for criticism and guidance. Individuals who have done the conceptual writing and research are identifiable. However, there are still few programmatic efforts or organizations concentrating primarily on postsecondary organizational studies. Associations like AERA and ASHE do not have a formal special interest group devoted to this area alone. There is not a single postsecondary journal or monograph series with this focus, although all give it attention in special sections or special publications. In light of the fragmenting tendencies of the theory and research and absence of professional foci, a few brief comments on professional peers are appropriate.

First, the previous theory to practice discussion suggests a dilemma in the identification of peers. Are they other scholars or administrators? Clearly, other scholars should be a source of critical scholarly interchange. But what of administrators? Are we allies or increasingly aliens as our previous theory-practice dilemma hints? Off campus, a few postsecondary organizational researchers have found colleagues and rewards in institutional membership associations (e.g., AGB, ACE, etc.) and the other administrative associations (e.g., AIR, AAUA, etc.). On campus, administrators can be a source of stimulation in problem identification and provide access to applied projects, data, local resources, opportunities for dissemination, and even influence. One increasingly finds senior administrators with some organizational theory or research expertise. Many institutions have an expanded institutional research and planning staff who have applied research assignments. Unfortunately budget pressures often make administrators reluctant to have their own faculty probing sensitive and often conflicting events and issues.

Second, among scholarly colleagues one also has some peer choices. In the field of education, the network of postsecondary researchers as noted is still embryonic or loosely coupled. On campus, other education school faculty are accessible, but the numbers interested in organizational concepts and research issues are limited and often have a heavy practitioner orientation. Educational statistics and research faculty often focus on or emphasize individual and small group level phenomenon rather than organizations as the unit of analysis.

Outside of education, more faculty are involved in organization behavior, both on and off campus, they are but not as interested in Postsecondary education. As in any interdisciplinary field, one has the choice of an association-based disciplinary group (e.g., ASA's Organization Section), another professional school unit (e.g., a department of organization behavior in a business school), or a less clearly defined interdisciplinary network. As an example of the network, an "organizational behavior seminar" at the University of Michigan involves about 25 faculty from Law, Business, Education, Social Work, Engineering, Public Policy, Sociology, Psychology, Public Health, Political Science, and so on, and meets occasionally to share someone's research or to interact with an invited outside scholar. Interestingly, while many of the members have known each other for years, it did not become organized until a visiting scholar who had met us individually invited us all to lunch.

The point is that the sources of professional peers are numerous, but they are still ill defined as a resource for the criticism, guidance, and collaboration that are so useful in furthering this area of study. Stimulating such a network is probably a valuable activity, but involves basic choices about orientation and membership: practitioners or scholars; education lists, professionals, or disciplinarians. Resolving this dilemma may influence the direction on many of the previous dilemmas.

Dilemmas Revisited

This overview suggests there is a great deal of potential fragmentation in the rapidly developing area of postsecondary organizational theory and research highlighted by these five dilemmas. Further development may involve answering all five of them with a resounding, "Yes."

There is a *muddled array of models*. Yet we need to emphasize further theory "development" to find better ways to understand postsecondary education's uniqueness. The newer emergent models offer useful examples. But there is also a need to encourage theory and research "synthesis" to clarify the theories and constructs, to examine more critically the applicability of the borrowed models, and to see what has been learned conceptually as well as about practice. And there is a need to pursue more rigorous "testing" of individual models and the comparative testing of competing explanations to confirm or refute them, rather than continuing to advocate them.

The *methodological maze* that is necessary to understand the complexity of organizational behavior in any setting will continue to be many faceted. There is a need to continue the emphasis on large-scale comparative and survey research strategies and to utilize "quantitative" techniques and multivariate or causal analysis to enhance the generalizablity of our findings and to test our competing theories. But there is also a need to expand efforts in using the more intensive, "qualitative" strategies and methods to give construct validity to the quantitative variables, to examine the causal assumptions in the theories, and to generate new insights or models for more extensive examination.

It is useful not only to emphasize both paradigms but also to seek an integration to avoid becoming embroiled in an extended and exaggerated *philosophical dialectic*. The different models and theories and different research strategies and methods each need to be examined in relation to criteria for sound theory and methodology and to be used as appropriate to the purpose, problem, and setting of the research project. Sensitive manipulation and open-minded interpretation of quantitative approaches and causal models can lead to the refutation of existing models and the suggestion of questions for intensive qualitative exploration. Examples that merge the two paradigms are the combined use of survey and comparative case studies employing both qualitative and quantitative approaches in large studies such as the NCHEMS research on effectiveness and decline and the use of grounded theory in more focused studies such as Richardson, Fisk, and Okun's (1983) study of literacy.

Clearly, the theory-practice or relevance dilemma is a product of the conflict between our expanded efforts in research and theory development and the urgent demands of postsecondary education today. There is a need for good "conceptualizers and designers" to place the practical findings in a broader context and to guide the development of explanatory frameworks. We need "translators" who can effectively disseminate the extensive array of theoretical and research literature. We also need "practitioner researchers" who can involve subjects in the research process and not just do research on practical problems. More importantly, we need more balanced attention to the range of methods from theory development and critique, to strategies of dissemination and utilization of research, and to research approaches that stress research involvement.

Rogers and Gamson (1982) have a recent article on "Evaluation as a Developmental Process." In a chapter of *Black Students on White Campuses* (Blackburn, Gamson, & Peterson, 1978), the authors discuss the use of an interracial team in the study of a sensitive social issue. There is a need to analyze and share our insights into how to do organizational research in postsecondary education. In these examples and in the theory to practice and professional roles discussion, the thesis is that, in the establishment of a "peer" group of colleagues and mentors, form follows function—it may be timely to bring colleagues together around some of the developmental issues in postsecondary organization theory and research.

Such efforts may determine whether postsecondary organizational theory and research survives its adolescent dilemmas and grows to wholesome, integrated maturity or becomes more fragmented and stifles its development.

Notes

[1]For an excellent discussion of theory development in organizations, see Larry Mohr's *Explaining Organizational Behavior* (Jossey-Bass, 1982) and Jeffrey Pfeffer's *Organizations and Organization Theory* (Pitman, 1982).

[2]Two useful sources on nonquantitative research methods are *Administrative Science Quarterly*, Vol. 27, 1982, which is devoted to articles on qualitative methods, and a recent NDIR monograph by Kuhns and Martorana on *Qualitative Methods in Institutional Research* (1984).

[3]Clifton Conrad's article discussing grounded theory in the *Review of Higher Education* (1982).

References

Baldridge, J.V. *Power and Conflict in the University*. San Francisco: Jossey-Bass, 1971.

————. *Policy Making and Effective Leadership*. San Francisco: Jossey-Bass, 1978.

Baldridge, J.V. & Tierney, M. *New Approaches to Management*. San Francisco: Jossey-Bass, 1979.

Bess, J. "Maps and Gaps in the Study of College and University Organization." *Review of Higher Education*, 1983, 6; 239–251.

Birnbaum, R. *Maintaining Diversity in American Higher Education*. San Francisco: Jossey-Bass, 1983.

Blackburn, R., Gamson, Z., & Peterson, M. "Chronology of the Study and First Steps." In M. Peterson, et al. (Eds.), *Black Students on White Campuses*. Ann Arbor: Institute for Social Research, University of Michigan, 1978.

Brewster, K., Jr. "Future Strategy of the Private University." *Princeton Alumni Weekly*, 1965; 45–46.

Cameron, K. *A Study of Organizational Effectiveness and its Predictors*. Unpublished manuscript, 1983.

————. "Organizational Adaptation and Higher Education." *Journal of Higher Education*, 1984, 55, (2); 122–144.

Chaffee, E. "Successful Strategic Management in Small Private Colleges." *Journal of Higher Education*, 1984, 55, (2); 212–241.

Clark, B. *The Distinctive Colleges*. Chicago: Aldine, 1970.

Cohen, M., & March, J. *Leadership and Ambiguity*. New York: McGraw-Hill, 1974.

Cohen, M., March, J., & Olsen, J. "A Garbage Can Model of Organizational Choice." *Administrative Science Quarterly*, 1972, 17, 1–25.

Conrad, C. "Grounded Theory: An Alternative Approach to Research in Higher Education." *Review of Higher Education*, 1982, 5 (4); 239–249.

Cummings, L.L. "Organizational Behavior in the 1980's." *Decision Sciences*, 1981, 12; 265–377.

Dill, D. "The Structure of the Academic Profession: Toward a Definition of Ethical Issues." *Journal of Higher Education*, 1982, 3; 255–267.

Gamson, Z. *Varieties of Liberal Educational*. San Francisco: Jossey-Bass, 1984.

Henderson, A. "Improving Decision-Making Through Research." In G. Smith (Ed.), *Current Issues in Higher Education*. Washington, DC: AAHE, 1963.

Kuhns, E., & Martorana, S.V. (Eds.). "Qualitative Methods in Institutional Research." In *New Directions for Institution Research*. San Francisco: Jossey-Bass, 1982.

Lindquist, J. (Ed.). "Increasing the Use of Institutional Research." In *New Directions for Institutional Research*. San Francisco: Jossey-Bass, 1981.

Lutz, F. "Tightening up Loose Coupling in Organizations of Higher Education." *Administration Science Quarterly*, 1982, 27; 653–669.

March, J. *Handbook of Organizations*. Chicago: Rand McNally, 1965.

————. Emerging Developments in the Study of Organizations." *Review of Higher Education*, 1982, 6; 1–18.

McConnell, T.R. "Needed: Research in College and University Organization and Administration." In T. Lunsford (Ed.), *Study of Academic Organizations*. Boulder, CO: Western Institute Commission on Higher Education, 1963.

Meryl, L. "A Cultural Perspective on Organizations: The Need for and Consequences of Viewing Organizations as Culture-Bearing Milieux." *Human Systems Management*, 1981, 2; 246–258.

Mohr, L. *Exploring Organizational Behavior*. San Francisco: Jossey-Bass, 1982.

Mortimer, K. *The Three R's of the Eighties: Reduction, Reallocation, and Retrenchment*, (ERIC/AAHE Research Reports, No. 4). Washington, DC: AAHE, 1979.

Pascarella, E.T., & Terenzini, P. "Interaction Effects in Spady's and Tinto's Conceptual Models of College Dropout." *Sociology of Education*, 1979, 52; 197–210.

Peters, T., & Waterman, R. *In Search of Excellence*. New York, Harper and Row, 1982.

Peterson, M., et al. *Black Students on White Campuses*. Ann Arbor: Institute for Social Research, University of Michigan, 1978.

————. "Organization and Administration in Higher Education: Sociological and Social-Psychological Perspectives." In F. Kerlinger (Ed.), *Review of Research in Education*, Vol. II. Itasca, IL: Peacock, 1974.

Pfeffer, J. *Organizations and organization theory*. Marshfield, MA: Pitman, 1982.

Platt, J.R. Strong inference. *Science*, 1964, 146, (3642); 347–353.

Richardson, R., Fisk, E., & Okun, M. *Literacy in the Open Access College*. San Francisco: Jossey-Bass, 1983.

Riesman, D., Gusfeld, J., & Gamson, Z. *Academic Values and Mass Education*. Garden City, NY: Doubleday, 1970.

Rogers, T., & Gamson, Z. "Evaluation as a Developmental Process." *Review of Higher Education*, 1982, 5, 225–238.

Rudolph, F. *The American College and University: A History*. New York: Knopf, 1962.

Tinto, V. "Limits of Theory and Practice in Student Attrition." *Journal of Higher Education*, 1982, 6; 687–700.

Trow, M. "Reorganizing the Biological Sciences at Berkeley." *Change*, 1984, 28; 44–53.

Weick, K. "Educational Organizations as Loosely Coupled Systems." *Administrative Science Quarterly*, 1976, 21(1); 1–19.

Whitehead, A.M. "Universities and Their Functions." *Atlantic Monthly*, 1928, 141 (5); 638–644.

Zammuto, R. "Are the Liberal Arts an Endangered Species?" *Journal of Higher Education*, 1984, 55, (2); 184–211.

Alternative Models of Governance in Higher Education

J. VICTOR BALDRIDGE, DAVID V. CURTIS, GEORGE P. ECKER, AND GARY L. RILEY

Organizations vary in a number of important ways: they have different types of clients, they work with different technologies, they employ workers with different skills, they develop different structures and coordinating styles, and they have different relationships to their external environments. Of course, there are elements common to the operation of colleges and universities, hospitals, prisons, business firms, government bureaus, and so on, but no two organizations are the same. Any adequate model of decision making and governance in an organization must take its distinctive characteristics into account.

The chapter deals with the organizational characteristics and decision processes of colleges and universities. Colleges and universities are unique organization, differing in major respects from industrial organizations, government bureaus, and business firms.

Distinguishing Characteristics of Academic Organizations

College and universities are complex organizations. Like other organizations they have goals, hierarchical systems and structures, officials who carry out specified duties, decision-making processes that set institutional policy, and a bureaucratic administration that handles routine business. But they also exhibit some critical distinguishing characteristics that affect their decision processes.

Goal Ambiguity

Most organizations are goal-oriented, and as a consequence they can build decision structures to reach their objectives. Business firms want to make a profit, government bureaus have tasks specified by law, hospitals are trying to cure sick people, prisons are in the business of "rehabilitation."

By contrast, colleges and universities have vague, ambiguous goals and they must build decision processes to grapple with a higher degree of uncertainty and conflict. What is the goal of a university? This is a difficult question, for the list of possible answers is long: teaching, research, service to the local community, administration of scientific installations, support of the arts, solutions to social problems. In their book *Leadership and Ambiguity*, Cohen and March comment:

> Almost any educated person could deliver a lecture entitled "The Goals of the University." Almost no one will listen to the lecture voluntarily. For the most part, such lectures and their companion essays are well-intentioned exercises in social rhetoric, with little operational content. Efforts to generate normative statements of the goals of the university tend to produce goals that are either meaningless or dubious [Cohen and March, 1974, page 195].

Goal ambiguity, then, is one of the chief characteristics of academic organizations. They rarely have a single mission. They rarely have a single mission. On the contrary, they often try to be all things to all people. Because their existing goals are unclear, they also find it hard to reject new goals. Edward Gross (1968) analyzed the goals of faculty and administrators in a large number of American universities and obtained some remarkable results. To be sure, some goals were ranked higher than others, with academic freedom consistently near the top. But both administrators and faculty marked as important almost every one of forty-seven goals listed by Gross!

Not only are academic goals unclear, they are also highly contested. As long as goals are left ambiguous and abstract, they are readily agreed on. As soon as they are concretely specified and put into operation, conflict erupts. The link between clarity and conflict may help explain the prevalence of meaningless rhetoric in academic policy statements and speeches. It is tempting to resort to rhetoric when serious content produces conflict.

Client Service

Like schools, hospitals, and welfare agencies, academic organizations are "people-processing" institutions. Clients with specific needs are fed into the institution from the environment, the institution acts upon them, and the clients are returned to the larger society. This is an extremely important characteristic, for the clients demand and often obtain significant input into institutional decision-making processes. Even powerless clients such as schoolchildren usually have protectors, such as parents, who demand a voice in the operation of the organization. In higher education, of course, the clients are quite capable of speaking for themselves—and they often do.

Problematic Technology

Because they serve clients with disparate, complicated needs, client-serving organizations frequently have problematic technologies. A manufacturing organization develops a specific technology that can be segmented and routinized. Unskilled, semiskilled, and white collar workers can be productively used without relying heavily on professional expertise. But it is hard to construct a simple technology for an organization dealing with people. Serving clients is difficult to accomplish, and the results are difficult to evaluate, especially on a short-term basis. The entire person must be considered; people cannot be separated easily into small, routine, and technical segments. If at times colleges and universities do not know clearly *what* they are trying to do, they often do not know *how* to do it either.

Professionalism

How does an organization work when its goals are unclear, its service is directed to clients, and its technology is problematic? Most organizations attempt to deal with these problems by hiring expertly trained professionals. Hospitals require doctors and nurses, social welfare agencies hire social workers, public schools hire teachers, and colleges and universities hire faculty members. These professionals use a broad repertoire of skills to deal with the complex and often unpredictable problems of clients. Instead of subdividing a complicated task into a routine set of procedures, professional work requires that a broad range of tasks be performed by a single employee.

Sociologists have made a number of important general observations about professional employees, wherever they may work:

1. Professionals demand *autonomy* in their work. Having acquired considerable skill and expertise in their field, they demand freedom from supervision in applying them.

2. Professionals have *divided loyalties*. They have "cosmopolitan" tendencies and loyalty to their peers at the national level may sometimes interfere with loyalty to their local organization.
3. There are strong tensions between *professional values* and *bureaucratic expectations* in an organization. This can intensify conflict between professional employees and organizational managers.
4. Professionals demand *peer evaluation* of their work. They believe that only their colleagues can judge their performance, and they reject the evaluations of others, even those who are technically their superiors in the organizational hierarchy.

All of these characteristics undercut the traditional norms of a bureaucracy, rejecting its hierarchy, control structure, and management procedures. As a consequence, we can expect a distinct management style in a professional organization.

Finally, colleges and universities tend to have *fragmented* professional staffs. In some organizations there is one dominant professional group. For example, doctors are the dominant group in hospitals. In other organizations the professional staff is fragmented into subgroups, none of which predominates. The faculty in a university provides a clear example. Burton R. Clark comments on the fragmented professionalism in academic organizations:

> The internal controls of the medical profession are strong and are substituted for those of the organization. But in the college or university this situation does not obtain; there are twelve, twenty-five, or fifty clusters of experts. The experts are prone to identify with their own disciplines, and the "academic profession" overall comes off a poor second. We have wheels within wheels, many professions within a profession. No one of the disciplines on a campus is likely to dominate the others. . . The campus is not a closely knit group of professionals who see the world from one perspective. As a collection of professionals, it is decentralized, loose, and flabby.
>
> The principle is this: where professional influence is high and there is one dominant professional group, the organization will be integrated by the imposition of professional standards. Where professional influence is high and there are a number of professional groups, the organization will be split by professionalism. The university and the large college are fractured by expertness, not unified by it. The sheer variety supports the tendency for authority to diffuse toward quasi-autonomous clusters [Clark, 1963, pages 37, 51].

Environmental Vulnerability

Another characteristic that sets colleges and universities apart from many other complex organizations is environmental vulnerability. Almost all organizations interact with their social environment to some extent. But though no organization is completely autonomous, some have considerably greater freedom of action than others. The degree of autonomy an organization has vis-a-vis its environment is one of the critical determinants of how it will be managed.

For example, in a free market economy, business firms and industries have a substantial degree of autonomy. Although they are regulated by countless government agencies and constrained by their customers, essentially they, are free agents responsive to market demands rather than to government control. At the other extreme, a number of organizations are virtually "captured" by their environments. Public school districts, for example, are constantly scrutinized and pressured by the communities they serve.

Colleges and universities are somewhere in the middle on a continuum from "independent" to "captured." In many respects they are insulated from their environment. Recently, however, powerful external forces have been applied to academic institutions. Interest groups holding conflicting values have made their wishes, demands, and threats well known to the administrations and faculties of academic organizations in the 1970's.

What impact does environmental pressure have on the governance of colleges and universities? When professional organizations are well insulated from the pressures of the outside environment, then professional values, norms, and work definitions play a dominant role in shaping the character of the organization. On the other hand, when strong external pressure is applied to colleges and universities, the operating autonomy of the academic professionals is seriously reduced. The faculty and administrators lose some control over the curriculum, the goals, and the daily operation of the institution. Under these circumstances, the academic professionals are frequently reduced to the role of hired employees doing the bidding of bureaucratic managers.

Although colleges and universities are not entirely captured by their environments, they are steadily losing ground. As their vulnerability increases, their governance patterns change significantly.

"Organized Anarchy"

To summarize, academic organizations have several unique organizational characteristics. They have ambiguous goals that are often strongly contested. They serve clients who demand a voice in the decision-making process. They have a problematic technology, for in order to serve clients their technology must be holistic and adaptable to individual needs. They are professionalized organizations in which employees demand a large measure of control over institutional decision processes. Finally, they are becoming more and more vulnerable to their environments.

The character of such a complex organizational system is not satisfactorily conveyed by the standard term "bureaucracy." Bureaucracy carries the connotation of stability or even rigidity; academic organizations seem more fluid. Bureaucracy implies distinct lines of authority and strict hierarchical command; academic organizations have blurred lines of authority and professional employees who demand autonomy in their work. Bureaucracy suggests a cohesive organization with clear goals; academic organizations are characteristically fragmented with ambiguous and contested goals. Bureaucracy does adequately describe certain aspects of colleges and universities, such as business administration, plant management, capital outlay, and auxiliary services. But the processes at the heart of an academic organization — academic policy making, professional teaching, and research — do not resemble the processes one finds in a bureaucracy. Table 1-1 summarizes the differences between the two types of organizations.

TABLE 1-1

Organizational Characteristics of Academic Organizations and More Traditional Bureaucracies		
	Academic organizations (colleges and universities)	Traditional bureaucracies (government agency, industry)
Goals	Ambiguous, contested, inconsistent	Clearer goals, less disagreement
Client service	Client-serving	Material-processing, commercial
Technology	Unclear, nonroutine, holistic	Clearer, routinized, segmented
Environmental	Predominantly professional	Predominantly nonprofessional
relations	Very vulnerable	Less vulnerable
Summary image	"Organized anarchy"	"Bureaucracy"

Perhaps a better term for academic organizations has been suggested by Cohen and March. They describe the academic organization as an "organized anarchy" — a system with little central coordination or control:

> In a university anarchy each individual in the university is seen as making autonomous decisions. Teachers decide if, when, and what to teach. Students decide if, when, and what to learn. Legislators and donors decide if, when, and what to support. Neither coordination...nor control [is] practiced. Resources are allocated by whatever process emerges but without explicit accommodation and without explicit reference to some superordinate goal. The "decisions" of the system are a consequence produced by the system but intended by no one and decisively controlled by no one [Cohen and March, 1974, pages 33-34].

The organized anarchy differs radically from the well-organized bureaucracy or the consensus-bound collegium. It is an organization in which generous resources allow people to go in different directions without coordination by a central authority. Leaders are relatively weak and decisions are made by individual action. Since the organization's goals are ambiguous, decisions are often by-products of unintended and unplanned activity. In such fluid circumstances, presidents and other institutional leaders serve primarily as catalysts or facilitators of an ongoing process. They do not so much lead the institution as channel its activities in subtle ways. They do not command, but negotiate. They do not plan comprehensively, but try to apply preexisting solutions to problems.

Decisions are not so much "made" as they "happen." Problems, choices, and decision makers happen to come together in temporary solutions. Cohen and March have described decision processes in an organized anarchy as

> sets of procedures through which organizational participants arrive at an interpretation of what they are doing and what they have done while they are doing it. From this point of view an organization is a collection of choices looking for problems, issues and feelings looking for decision situations in which they might be aired, solutions looking for issues for which they might be the answer, and decision makers looking for work [Cohen and March, 1974, page 81].

The imagery of organized anarchy helps capture the spirit of the confused organizational dynamics in academic institutions: unclear goals, unclear technologies, and environmental vulnerability.

Some may regard "organized anarchy" as an exaggerated term, suggesting more confusion and conflict than really exist in academic organizations. This is probably a legitimate criticism. The term may also carry negative connotations to those unaware that it applies to specific organizational characteristics rather than to the entire campus community. Nevertheless, "organized anarchy" has some strong points in its favor. It breaks through the traditional formality that often surrounds discussions of decision making, challenges our existing conceptions, and suggests a looser, more fluid kind of organization. For these reasons we will join Cohen and March in using organized anarchy" to summarize some of the unique organizational characteristics of colleges and universities: (1) unclear goals, (2) client service, (3) unclear technology, (4) professionalism, and (5) environmental vulnerability.[1]

Models of Academic Governance

Administrators and organization theorists concerned with academic governance have often developed images to summarize the complex decision process: collegial system, bureaucratic network, political activity, or participatory democracy. Such models organize the way we perceive the process, determine how we analyze it, and help determine our actions. For example, if we regard a system as political, then we form coalitions to pressure decision makers. If we regard it as collegial, then we seek to persuade people by appealing to reason. If we regard it as bureaucratic, then we use legalistic maneuvers to gain our ends.

In the past few years, as research on higher education has increased, models for academic governance have also proliferated. Three models have received widespread attention, more or less dominating the thinking of people who study academic governance. We will examine briefly each of these models in turn: (1) the bureaucracy, (2) the collegium, and (3) the political system. Each of these models has certain points in its favor. They can be used jointly to examine different aspects of the governance process.

The Academic Bureaucracy

One of the most influential descriptions of complex organizations is Max Weber's (1947) monumental work on bureaucracies. Weber discussed the characteristics of bureaucracies that distinguish them from less formal work organizations. In skeleton form he suggested that bureaucracies are networks of social groups dedicated to limited goals and organized for maximum efficiency. Moreover, the regulation of a bureaucratic system is based on the principle of "legal rationality," as contrasted with informal regulation based on friendship, loyalty to family, or personal allegiance to a charismatic leader. The hierarchical structure is held together by formal chains of command and systems of communication. The bureaucracy as Weber described it includes such elements as tenure, appointment to office, salaries as a rational form of payment, and competency as the basis of promotion.

BUREAUCRATIC CHARACTERISTICS OF COLLEGES AND UNIVERSITIES

Several authors have suggested that university governance may be more fully understood by applying the bureaucratic model. For example, Herbert Stroup (1966) has pointed out some characteristics of colleges and universities that fit Weber's original description of a bureaucracy. They include the following:

1. Competence is the criterion used for appointment.
2. Officials are appointed, not elected.
3. Salaries are fixed and paid directly by the organization, rather than determined in "free-fee" style.
4. Rank is recognized and respected.
5. The career is exclusive; no other work is done.
6. The style of life of the organization's members centers on the organization.
7. Security is present in a tenure system.
8. Personal and organizational property, are separated.

Stroup is undoubtedly correct in believing that Weber's paradigm can be applied to universities, and most observers are well aware of the bureaucratic factors involved in university administration. Among the more prominent are the following.

1. The university is a complex organization under *state charter*, like most other bureaucracies. This seemingly innocent fact has major consequences, especially as states increasingly seek to exercise control.
2. The university has a *formal hierarchy*, with offices and a set of bylaws that specify the relations between those offices. Professors, instructors, and research assistants may be considered bureaucratic officers in the same sense as deans, chancellors, and presidents.
3. There are *formal channels of communication* that must be respected.
4. There are definite *bureaucratic authority relations*, with certain officials exercising authority over others. In a university the authority relations are often vague and shifting, but no one would deny that they exist.
5. There are *formal policies and rules* that govern much of the institution's work, such as library regulations, budgetary guidelines, and procedures of the university senate.
6. The bureaucratic elements of the university are most vividly apparent in its *"people-processing"* aspects: record keeping, registration, graduation requirements, and a

multitude of other routine, day-to-day activities designed to help the modern university handle its masses of students.

7. *Bureaucratic decision-making processes* are used, most often by officials assigned the responsibility for making routine decisions by the formal administrative structure. Examples are admissions procedures, handled by the dean of admissions; procedures for graduation, routinely administered by designated officials; research policies, supervised by specified officials; and financial matters, usually handled in a bureaucratic manner by the finance office.

WEAKNESSES IN THE BUREAUCRATIC MODEL

In many ways the bureaucratic model falls short of encompassing university governance, especially if one is primarily concerned with decision-making processes. First, the bureaucratic model tells us much about authority — that is, legitimate, formalized power —but not much about informal types of power and influence, which may take the form of mass movements or appeals to emotion and sentiment. Second, it explains much about the organization's formal *structure* but little about the dynamic *processes* that characterize the organization in action. Third, it describes the formal structure at one particular time, but it does not explain changes over time. Fourth, it explains how policies may be carried out most efficiently, but it says little about the critical process by which policy is established in the first place. Finally, it also ignores political issues, such as the struggles of various interest groups within the university.

The University Collegium

Many writers have rejected the bureaucratic model of the university. They seek to replace it with the model of the "collegium" or "community of scholars." When this literature is closely examined, there seem to be at least three different threads running through it.

A DESCRIPTION OF COLLEGIAL DECISION MAKING

This approach argues that academic decision making should not be like the hierarchical process in a bureaucracy. Instead there should be full participation of the academic community, especially the faculty. Under this concept the community of scholars would administer its own affairs, and bureaucratic officials would have little influence (see Goodman, 1962). John Millett, one of the foremost proponents of this model, has succinctly stated his view:

> I do not believe that the concept of hierarchy is a realistic representation of the interpersonal relationships which exist within a college or university. Nor do I believe that a structure of hierarchy is a desirable prescription for the organization of a college or university....
>
> I would argue that there is another concept of organization just as valuable as a tool of analysis and even more useful as a generalized observation of group and interpersonal behavior. This is the concept of community....
>
> The concept of community presupposes an organization in which functions are differentiated and in which specialization must be brought together, or coordination, if you will, is achieved not through a structure of superordination and subordination of persons and groups but through a *dynamic of consensus* [Millett. 1962, pages 234-235].

A DISCUSSION OF THE FACULTY'S PROFESSIONAL AUTHORITY

Talcott Parsons (1947) was one of the first to call attention to the difference between "official competence," derived from one's office in a bureaucracy, and "technical competence," derived from one's ability to perform a given task. Parsons concentrated on the technical competence of the physician, but others have extended this logic to other professionals whose authority is based on what they *know* and can *do*, rather than on their official position. Some examples are the scientist in industry, the military adviser, the expert in government, the physician in the hospital, and the professor in the university.

The literature on professionalism strongly supports the argument for collegial organization. It emphasizes the professional's ability to make his own decisions and his need for freedom from organizational restraints. Consequently, the collegium is seen as the most reasonable method of organizing the university. Parsons, for example, notes (page 60) that when professionals are organized in a bureaucracy, "there are strong tendencies for them to develop a different sort of structure from that characteristic of the administrative hierarchy...of bureaucracy. Instead of a rigid hierarchy of status and authority there tends to be what is roughly, in formal status, a company of equals."

A UTOPIAN PRESCRIPTION FOR OPERATING THE EDUCATIONAL SYSTEM

There is a third strand in the collegial image. In recent years there has been a growing discontent with our impersonal contemporary society. The multiversity, with its thousands of students and its huge bureaucracy, is a case in point. The student revolts of the 1960's and perhaps even the widespread apathy of the 1970's are symptoms of deeply felt alienation between students and massive educational establishments. The discontent and anxiety this alienation has produced are aptly expressed in the now-famous sign worn by a Berkeley student: "I am a human being — do not fold, spindle, or mutilate."

As an alternative to this impersonal, bureaucratized educational system, many critics are calling for a return to the "academic community." In their conception such a community, would offer personal attention, humane education, and "relevant confrontation with life." Paul Goodman's *The Community of Scholars* (1962) still appeals to many who seek to reform the university. Goodman cites the need for more personal interaction between faculty and students, for more relevant courses, and for educational innovations to bring the student into existential dialogue with the subject matter of his discipline. The number of articles on this subject, in both the mass media and the professional journals, is astonishingly large. Indeed, this concept of the collegial academic community is now widely proposed as one answer to the impersonality and meaninglessness of today's large multiversity. Thus conceived, the collegial model functions more as a revolutionary, ideology and a utopian projection than a description of actual governance processes at any university.

WEAKNESSES IN THE COLLEGIAL MODEL

Three themes are incorporated in the collegial model: (1) decision making by consensus, (2) the professional authority of faculty members, and (3) the call for more humane education. These are all legitimate and appealing. Few would deny that our universities would be better centers of learning if we could somehow implement these objectives. There is a misleading simplicity about the collegial model, however, that glosses over many realities.

For one thing, the *descriptive* and *normative* visions are often confused. In the literature dealing with the collegial model it is often difficult to tell whether a writer is saying that the university is a collegium or that it ought to be a collegium. Discussions of the collegium are frequently more a lament for paradise lost than a description of reality. Indeed, the collegial image of round-table decision making is not an accurate description of the processes in most institutions.

Although at the department level there are many examples of collegial decision making, at higher levels it usually exists only in some aspects of the committee system. Of course, the proponents may be advocating a collegial model as a desirable goal or reform strategy. This is helpful, but it does not allow us to understand the actual workings of universities.

In addition, the collegial model fails to deal adequately with the problem of *conflict*. When Millett emphasizes the "dynamic of consensus," he neglects the prolonged battles that precede consensus, as well as decisions that actually represent the victory of one group over another. Proponents of the collegial model are correct in declaring that simple bureaucratic rule making is not the essence of decision making. But in making this point they take the equally indefensible position that major decisions are reached primarily by consensus. Neither extreme is correct, for decisions are rarely made by either bureaucratic fiat or simple consensus.

The University as a Political System

In *Power and Conflict in the University* (1971), Baldridge posed a "political" model of university governance. Although the other major models of governance — the collegial and the bureaucratic — have valuable insights to offer, we believe that further insights can be gained from this model. It grapples with the power plays, conflicts, and rough-and-tumble politics to be found in many academic institutions.

BASIC ASSUMPTIONS OF A POLITICAL MODEL

The political model assumes that complex organizations can be studied as miniature political systems. There are interest group dynamics and conflicts similar to those in cities, states, or other political entities. The political model focuses on policy-forming processes, because major policies commit an organization to definite goals and set the strategies for reaching those goals. Policy decisions are critical decisions. They have a major impact on an organization's future. Of course, in any practical situation it may be difficult to separate the routine from the critical, for issues that seem minor at one point may later be decisive, or vice versa. In general, however, policy decisions bind an organization to important courses of action.

Since policies are so important, people throughout an organization try to influence them to reflect their own interests and values. Policy making becomes a vital target of interest group activity that permeates the organization. Owing to its central importance, then, the organization theorist may select policy formation as the key for studying organizational conflict and change, just as the political scientist often selects legislative acts as the focal point for his analysis of a state's political processes. With policy formation as its key issue, the political model operates on a series of assumptions about the political process.

1. To say that policy making is a political process is not to say that everyone is involved. On the contrary, *inactivity* prevails. Most people most of the time find the policy-making process an uninteresting, unrewarding activity. Policy making is therefore left to the administrators. This is characteristic not only of policy making in universities but of political processes in society at large. Voters do not vote; citizens do not attend city council meetings; parents often permit school boards to do what they please. By and large, decisions that may have a profound effect on our society are made by small groups of elites.

2. Even people who are active engage in *fluid participation*. They move in and out of the decision-making process. Rarely do people spend much time on any given issue. Decisions, therefore, are usually made by those who persist. This normally means that small groups of political elites govern most major decisions, for they invest the necessary time in the process.

3. Colleges and universities, like most other social organizations, are characterized by fragmentation into *interest groups* with different goals and values. When resources are plentiful and the organization is prospering, these interest groups engage in only minimal conflict. But they are likely to mobilize and try to influence decisions when resources are tight, outside pressure groups attack, or internal groups try to assume command.

4. In a fragmented, dynamic social system *conflict* is natural. It is not necessarily a symptom of breakdown in the academic community. In fact, conflict is a significant factor in promoting healthy organizational change.

5. The pressure that groups can exert places severe *limitations on formal authority* in the bureaucratic sense. Decisions are not simply bureaucratic orders but are often negotiated compromises between competing groups. Officials are not free simply to issue a decision. Instead they must attempt to find a viable course acceptable to several powerful blocs.

6. *External interest groups* exert a strong influence over the policy-making process. External pressures and formal control by outside agencies — especially in public institutions — are powerful shapers of internal governance processes.

THE POLITICAL DECISION MODEL VERSUS THE RATIONAL DECISION MODEL

The bureaucratic model of organizational structure is accompanied by a rational model of decision making. It is usually assumed that in a bureaucracy the structure is hierarchical and well organized, and that decisions are made through clear-cut, predetermined steps. Moreover, a definite, rational approach is expected to lead to the optimal decision. Graham T. Allison has summarized the rational decision-making process as follows:

1. *Goals and objectives.* The goals and objectives of the agent are translated into a "payoff" or "utility" or "preference" function, which represents the "value" or "utility" of alternative sets of consequences. At the outset of the decision problem the agent has a payoff function which ranks all possible sets of consequences in terms of his values and objectives. Each bundle of consequences will contain a number of side ef-fects. Nevertheless, at a minimum, the agent must be able to rank in order of prefer-ence each possible set of consequences that might result from a particular action.

2. *Alternatives.* The rational agent must choose among a set of alternatives displayed before him in a particular situation. In decision theory these alternatives are represented as a decision tree. The alternative courses of action may include more than a simple act, but the specification of a course of action must be sufficiently precise to differentiate it from other alternatives.

3. *Consequences.* To each alternative is attached a set of consequences or outcomes of choice that will ensue if that particular alternative is chosen. Variations are generated at this point by making different assumptions about the accuracy of the decision maker's knowledge of the consequences that follow from the choice of each alternative.

4. *Choice.* Rational choice consists simply of selecting that alternative whose consequences rank highest in the decision maker's payoff function [Allison, 1971, pages 29-30].

The rational model appeals to those who regard their actions as essentially goal-directed and rational. Realistically, however, we should realize that the rational model is more an ideal than an actual description of how people act. In fact, in the confused organizational setting of the university, political constraints often undermine the force of rationality. A political model of decision making requires us to answer some new questions about the decision process:

The first new question posed by the political model is *why* a given decision is made at all. The formalists have already indicated that "recognition of the problem" is one element in the process, but too little attention has been paid to the activities that bring a particular issue to the forefront. Why is *this* decision being considered at *this* particular time? The political model insists that interest groups, powerful individuals, and bureaucratic processes are critical in drawing attention to some decisions rather than to others. A study of "attention cues" by which issues are called to the community's attention is a vital part of any analysis.

Second, a question must be raised about the right of any person or group to make the decisions. Previously the *who* question was seldom raised, chiefly because the decision literature was developed for hierarchical organizations in which the focus of authority could be easily defined. In a more loosely coordinated system however, we must ask a prior question: Why was the legitimacy to make the decision vested in a particular person or group? Why is Dean Smith making the decision instead of Dean Jones or why is the University Senate dealing with the problem instead of the central administration? Establishing the right of authority over a decision is a political question, subject to conflict, power manipulation, and struggles between interest groups. Thus the political model always asks tough questions: Who has the right to make the decision? What are the conflict-ridden processes by which the decision was located at this point rather than at another? The crucial point is that often the issue of *who* makes the decision has already limited, structured, and pre-formed *how* it will be made.

The third new issue raised by a political interpretation concerns the development of complex decision networks. As a result of the fragmentation of the university, decision making is rarely located in one official; instead it is dependent on the advice and authority of numerous people. Again the importance of the committee system is evident. It is necessary to understand that the committee network is the legitimate reflection of the need for professional influence to intermingle with bureaucratic influence. The decision process, then, is taken out of the hands of individuals (although there are still many who are powerful) and placed into a network that allows a *cumulative buildup* of expertise and advice. When the very life of the organization clusters around expertise, *decision making is likely to be diffused, segmentalized, and decentralized.* A complex network of committees, councils, and advisory bodies grows to handle the task of assembling the expertise necessary for reasonable decisions. Decision making by the individual bureaucrat is replaced with decision making by committee, council, and cabinet. Centralized decision making is replaced with diffuse decision making. The process becomes a far-flung network for gathering expertise from every corner of the organization and translating it into policy [Baldridge, 1971, page 190].

The fourth new question raised by the political model concerns alternative solutions to the problem at hand. The rational decision model suggests that all possible options are open and within easy reach of the decision maker. A realistic appraisal of decision dynamics in most organizations, however, suggests that by no means are all options open. The political dynamics of interest groups, the force of external power blocs, and the opposition of powerful professional constituencies may leave only a handful of viable options. The range of alternatives is often sharply limited by political considerations. Just as important, there is often little time and energy available for seeking new solutions. Although all possible solutions should be identified under the rational model, in the real world administrators have little time to grope for solutions before their deadlines.

In *Power and Conflict in the University*, Baldridge summed up the political model of decision making as follows:

First, powerful political forces — interest groups, bureaucratic officials, influential individuals, organizational subunits — cause a given issue to emerge from the limbo of ongoing problems and certain "attention cues" force the political community to consider the problem. Second, there is a struggle over locating the decision with a particular person or group, for the location of the right to make the decision often determines the outcome. Third, decisions are usually "preformed" to a great extent by the time one person or group is given the legitimacy to make the decision; not all options are open and the choices have been severely limited by the previous conflicts. Fourth, such political struggles are more likely to occur in reference to "critical" decisions than to "routine" decisions. Fifth, a complex decision network is developed to gather the necessary information and supply the critical expertise. Sixth, during the process of making the decision political controversy is likely to continue and compromises, deals, and plain head cracking are often necessary to get any decision made. Finally, the controversy is not likely to end easily. In fact, it is difficult even to know when a decision is made, for the political processes have a habit of unmaking, confusing, and muddling whatever agreements are hammered out.

This may be a better way of grappling with the complexity that surrounds decision processes within a loosely coordinated, fragmented political system. The formal decision models seem to have been asking very limited questions about the decision process and more insight can be gained by asking a new set of political questions. Thus the decision model that emerges from the university's political dynamics is more open, more dependent on conflict and political action. It is not so systematic or formalistic as most decision theory, but it is probably closer to the truth. Decision making, then, is not an isolated technique but another critical process that must be integrated into a larger political image [Baldridge, 1971, pages 191-192].

It is clear that a political analysis emphasizes certain factors over others. First, it is concerned primarily with problems of goal setting and conflicts over values, rather than with efficiency in achieving goals. Second, analysis of the organization's change processes and adaptation to its environment is critically important. The political dynamics of a university are constantly changing, pressuring the university in many directions, and forcing change throughout the academic system. Third, the analysis of conflict is an essential component. Fourth, there is the role of interest groups in pressuring decision makers to formulate policy. Finally, much attention is given to the legislative and decision-making phases — the processes by which pressures and power are transformed into policy. Taken together these points constitute the bare outline for a political analysis of academic governance.

The revised political model: an environmental and structuralist approach. Since the political model of academic governance originally appeared in *Power and Conflict in the University*, we have become aware that it has several shortcomings. For this reason we offer a few observations about some changes in emphasis, a few corrections in focus.

First, the original political model probably underestimated the impact of routine bureaucratic processes. Many, perhaps most, decisions are made not in the heat of political controversy but according to standard operating procedures. The political description in *Power and Conflict in the University* was based on a study of New York University. The research occurred at a time of extremely high conflict when the university was confronted with two crises, a student revolution and a financial disaster. The political model developed from that study probably overstresses the role of conflict and negotiation as elements in standard decision making, since those were the processes apparent at the time. Now we would stress that it is important to consider routine procedures of the governance process.

Second, the original political model, based on a single case study, did not do justice to the broad range of political activity that occurs in different kinds of institutions. For example, NYU is quite different from Oberlin College, and both are distinctive institutions compared to local community colleges. Many of the intense political dynamics observed in the NYU study may have been exaggerated in a troubled institution such as NYU, particularly during the heated conflicts of the late 1960's.

Third, we want to stress even more strongly the central role of environmental factors. The NYU analysis showed that conflict and political processes within the university were linked to environmental factors. But even more stress on the environmental context is needed.

Finally, as developed in *Power and Conflict in the University*, the political model suffered from an "episodic" character. That is, the model did not give enough emphasis to long-term decision-making patterns, and it failed to consider the way institutional structure may shape and channel political efforts. Centralization of power, the development of decision councils, long-term patterns of professional autonomy, the dynamics of departmental power, and the growth of unionization were all slighted by the original model. There are other important questions concerning long-term patterns: What groups tend to dominate decision making over long periods of time? Do some groups seem to be systemically excluded from the decision-making process? Do different kinds of institutions have different political patterns? Do institutional characteristics affect the morale of participants in such a way that they engage in particular decision-influencing activities? Do different kinds of institutions have systematic patterns of faculty participation in decision making? Are decision processes highly centralized in certain kinds of institutions?

Finally, we are not substituting the political model for the bureaucratic or collegial model of academic decision making. In a sense, they each address a separate set of problems and, taken together, they often yield complementary interpretations. We believe, however, that the political model has many strengths, and we offer it as a useful tool for understanding academic governance. See Table 1-2 for a comparison of the three decision-making models.

Images of Leadership and Management Strategies

Thus far we have made two basic arguments: (1) colleges and universities are unique in many of their organizational characteristics and, as a consequence, it is necessary to create new models to help explain organizational structure, governance, and decision making; and (2) a political model of academic governance offers useful insights in addition to those offered by the bureaucratic and collegial models. In this section we will suggest that some alternative images of leadership and management style are needed to accommodate the unique characteristics of academic organizations.

Table 1-2

	Three Models of Decision Making and Governance		
	Bureaucratic	Collegial	Political
Assumptions about structure	Hierarchical bureaucracy	Community of peers	Fragmented, complex professional federation
Social	Unitary: integrated by formal system	Unitary: integrated by peer consensus	Pluralistic: encompasses different interest groups with divergent values
Basic theoretical foundations	Weberian bureaucracy, classic studies of formal systems	Professionalism literature, human-relations approach to organization	Conflict analysis, interest group theory, community power literature
View of decision-making process	"Rational" decision making; standard operating procedures	Shared collegial decision: consensus, community participation	Negotiation, bargaining, political brokerage, external influence
Cycle of decision making	Problem definition; search for alternatives; evaluation of alternatives; calculus; choice; implementation	As in bureaucratic model, but in addition stresses the involvement of professional peers in the process	Emergence of issue out of social context; interest articulaion ; conflict; legislative process; implementation of policy; feedback

Leadership Under the Bureaucratic Model

Under the bureaucratic model the leader is seen as a hero who stands at the top of a complex pyramid of power. The hero's job is to assess problems, propose alternatives, and make rational choices. Much of the organization's power is held by the hero. Great expectations are raised because people trust the hero to solve their problems and to fend off threats from the environment. The image of the authoritarian hero is deeply ingrained in most societies and in the philosophy of most organization theorists.

We expect leaders to possess a unique set of skills with emphasis on problem-solving ability and technical knowledge about the organization. The principles of "scientific management," such as Planning, Programming, Budgeting Systems (PPBS) and Management by Objectives, are often proposed as the methods for rational problem solving. Generally, schools of management, business, and educational administration teach such courses to develop the technical skills that the hero-planner will need in leading the organization.

The hero image is deeply imbedded in our cultural beliefs about leadership. But in organizations such as colleges and universities it is out of place. Power is more diffuse in those organizations; it is lodged with professional experts and fragmented into many departments and subdivisions. Under these circumstances, high expectations about leadership performance often cannot be met. The leader has neither the power nor the information necessary to consistently make heroic decisions. Moreover, the scientific management procedures prescribed for organizational leaders quickly break down under conditions of goal ambiguity, professional dominance, and environmental vulnerability — precisely the organizational characteristics of colleges and universities. Scientific management theories make several basic assumptions: (1) the organization's goals are clear; (2) the organization is a closed system insulated from environmental penetration; and (3) the planners have the power to execute their decisions. These assumptions seem unrealistic in the confused and fluid world of the organized anarchy.

Leadership Under the Collegial Model

The collegial leader presents a stark contrast to the heroic bureaucratic leader. The collegial leader is above all the "first among equals" in an organization run by professional experts. Essentially, the collegial model proposes what John Millett calls the "dynamic of consensus in a community of scholars." The basic role of the collegial leader is not so much to command as to listen, not so much to lead as to gather expert judgments, not so much to manage as to facilitate, not so much to order but to persuade and negotiate.

Obviously, the skills of a collegial leader differ from those required by the scientific management principles employed by the heroic bureaucrat. Instead of technical problem-solving skills, the collegial leader needs professional expertise to ensure that he is held in high esteem by his colleagues. Talent in interpersonal dynamics is also needed to achieve consensus in organizational decision making. The collegial leader's role is more modest and more realistic. He does not stand alone, since other professionals share the burden of decision making with him. Negotiation and compromise are the bywords of the collegial leader; authoritarian strategies are clearly inappropriate.

Leadership Under the Political Model

Under the political model the leader is a mediator or negotiator between power blocs. Unlike the autocratic academic president of the past, who ruled with an iron hand, the contemporary president must play a political role by pulling coalitions together to fight for desired changes. The academic monarch of yesteryear has almost vanished. In his place is not the academic hero but the academic statesman. Robert Dahl has painted an amusing picture of the political maneuvers of Mayor Richard Lee of New Haven, and the same description applies to academic political leaders:

> The mayor was not at the peak of a pyramid but rather at the center of intersecting circles. He rarely commanded. He negotiated, cajoled, exhorted, beguiled, charmed, pressed, appealed, reasoned, promised, insisted, demanded, even threatened, but he most needed support and acquiescence from other leaders who simply could not be commanded. Because the mayor could not command, he had to bargain [Dahl, 1961, page 204].

The political interpretation of leadership can be pressed even further, for the governance of the university more and more comes to look like a "cabinet" form of administration. The key figure today is not the president, the solitary giant, but the political leader surrounded by his staff, the prime minister who gathers the information and expertise to construct policy. It is the "staff," the network of key administrators, that makes most of the critical decisions. The university has become much too complicated for any one man, regardless of his stature. Cadres of vice-presidents, research men, budget officials, public relations men, and experts of various stripes surround the president, sit on the cabinet, and help reach collective decisions. Expertise becomes more critical than ever and leadership becomes even more the ability to assemble, lead, and facilitate the activities of knowledgeable experts.

Therefore, the president must be seen as a "statesman" as well as a "hero-bureaucrat." The bureaucratic image might be appropriate for the man who assembles data to churn out routine decisions with a computer's help. In fact, this image is fitting for many middle-echelon officials in the university. The statesman's image is much more accurate for the top administrators, for here the influx of data and information gives real power and possibilities for creative action. The statesman is the innovative actor who uses information, expertise, and the combined wisdom of the cabinet to plan the institution's future; the bureaucrat may only be a number manipulator, a user of routine information for routine ends. The use of the cabinet, the assembly of expertise, and the exercise of political judgment in the service of institutional goals — all this is part of the new image of the statesman leader which must complement both the hero leader and the collegial leader.

Table 1-3 presents a summary and comparison of the three basic images of leadership and management we have just described.

Table 1-3

Images of Leadership and Management Under Three Models of Governance			
	Bureaucratic	Collegial	Political
Basic leadership image Leadership skills	Hero Technical problem-solving skills	"First among equals" Interpersonal dynamics	Statesman Political strategy, interpersonal dynamics, coalition management
Management Expectation	"Scientific management" Very high: people believe the hero-leader can solve problems and he tries to play the role	Management by consensus Modest: leader is developer of consensus among professionals	Strategic decision making Modest: leader marshalls political action action, but is constrained by the counter efforts of other groups

Summary

Colleges and universities are different from most other kinds of complex organizations. Their goals are more ambiguous and contested, they serve clients instead of seeking to make a profit, their technologies are unclear and problematic, and professionals dominate the work force and decision-making process. Thus colleges and universities are not standard bureaucracies, but can best be described as "organized anarchies" (see Cohen and March, 1947).

What decision and governance processes are to be found in an organized anarchy? Does the decision process resemble a bureaucratic system, with rational problem solving and standard operating procedures? Does it resemble a collegial system in which the professional faculty participate as members of a "community of scholars"? Or does it appear to be a political process with various interest groups struggling for influence over organizational policy? Each image is valid in some sense; each image helps complete the picture. Finally, we question the standard image of leadership and management. Classic leadership theory, based on a bureaucratic model, suggests the image of the organizational leader as a hero who uses principles of scientific management as the basis for his decisions. We have suggested that the leader's image should be that of the academic statesman, and that management should be considered a process of strategic decision making.

The research reported in this paper was supported by the Stanford Center for Research and Development in Teaching, by funds from the National Institute of Education (contract no. NE-C-00-3-0062).

Notes

[1] Our list of characteristics of an organized anarchy extends Cohen and March's, which contains (1) and (3), plus a characteristic called "fluid participation."

References

Allison, Graham T. *Essence of Decision.* Boston: Little, Brown, 1971.

Baldridge, J. Victor. *Power and Conflict in the University.* New York: John Wiley, 1971.

Clark, Burton R. "Faculty Organization and Authority." *The Study of Academic Administration,* edited by Terry Lunsford. Boulder, Colo.: Western Interstate Commission for Higher Education, 1963. Reprinted as chapter 4 in this volume.

Cohen, Michael D., and March, James G. *Leadership and Ambiguity: The American College President.* New York: McGraw-Hill, 1974.

Dahl, Robert. *Who Governs?* New Haven, Conn.: Yale University Press, 1961.

Goodman, Paul. *The Community of Scholars.* New York: Random House, 1962.

Gross, Edward, and Grambsch, Paul V. *Changes in University Organization, 1964-1971.* New York: McGraw-Hill, 1974.

Gross, Edward. *University Goals and Academic Power.* Washington, D.C.: Office of Education, 1968.

Millett, John. *The Academic Community.* New York: McGraw-Hill, 1962.

Parsons, Talcott. "Introduction." *The Theory, of Social and Economic Organization,* by Max Weber. New York: Free Press, 1947.

Stroup, Herbert. *Bureaucracy in Higher Education.* New York: Free Press, 1966.

Weber, Max. *The Theory of Social and Economic Organization.* New York: Free Press, 1947.

The Organizational Saga in Higher Education

Burton R. Clark

An organizational saga is a collective understanding of a unique accomplishment based on historical exploits of a formal organization, offering strong normative bonds within and outside the organization. Believers give loyalty to the organization and take pride and identify from it. A saga begins as strong purpose, introduced by a man (or small group) with a mission, and is fulfilled as it is embodied in organizational practices and the values of dominant organizational cadres, usually taking decades to develop. Examples of the initiation and fulfillment of sagas in academic organizations are presented from research on Antioch, Reed, and Swarthmore.[1]

* * *

Saga, originally referring to a medieval Icelandic or Norse account of achievements and events in the history of a person or group, has come to mean a narrative of heroic exploits, of it unique development that has deeply stirred the emotions of participants and descendants. Thus a saga is not simply a story but a story that at some time has had a particular base of believers. The term often refers also to the actual history itself, thereby including a stream of events, the participants, and the written or spoken interpretation. The element of belief is crucial, for without the credible story, the events and persons become history; with the development of belief, a particular bit of history becomes a definition full of pride and identity for the group.

Introduction

An *organizational saga* is a collective understanding of unique accomplishment in a formally established group. The group's definition of the accomplishment, intrinsically historical but embellished through retelling and rewriting, links stages of organizational development. The participants have added affect, an emotional loading, which places their conception between the coolness of rational purpose and the warmth of sentiment found in religion and magic. An organizational saga presents some rational explanation of how certain means led to certain ends, but it also includes affect that turns a formal place into a beloved institution, to which participants may be passionately devoted. Encountering such devotion, the observer may become unsure of his own analytical detachment as he tests the overtones of the institutional spirit or spirit of place.

The study of organizational sagas highlights nonstructural and nonrational dimensions of organizational life and achievement. Macroorganizational theory has concentrated on the role of structure and technology in organizational effectiveness (Gross, 1964; Litterer, 1965, March, 1965; Thompson, 1967; Price, 1968; Perrow, 1970). A needed corrective is more research on the cultural and expressive aspects of organizations, particularly on the role of belief and sentiment at broad levels of organization. The human-relations approach in organizational analysis, centered largely on group interaction, showed some awareness of the role of organization symbols (Whyte, 1948: ch. 23), but this conceptual lead has not been taken as a serious basis for research. Also, in the literature on organizations and purposive communities, "ideology" refers to unified and shared belief (Selznick, 1949; Bendix, 1956; Price, 1968: 104-110; Carden, 1969); but the concept of ideology has lost denotative power, having been stretched by varying uses. For the phenomenon discussed in this paper, "saga" seems to provide the appropriate denotation. With a general emphasis on normative bonds, organizational saga refers to a unified set of publicly expressed beliefs about the formal group that (a) is rooted in history, (b) claims unique accomplishment, and (c) is held with sentiment by the group.

To develop the concept in this paper, extreme cases and exaggerations of the ideal type are used; but the concept will be close to reality and widely applicable when the phenomenon is examined in weak as well as strong expression. In many organizations, even some highly utilitarian ones, some segment of their personnel probably develop in time at least a weak saga. Those who have persisted for some years in one place will have had at minimum, a thin stream of shared experience, which they elaborate into a plausible account of group uniqueness. Whether developed primarily by management or by employees, the story helps rationalize for the individual his commitment of time and energy for years, perhaps for a lifetime, to a particular enterprise. Even when weak, the belief can compensate in part for the loss of meaning in modern work, giving some drama and some cultural identity to one's otherwise entirely instrumental efforts. At the other end of the continuum, a saga engages one so intensely as to make his immediate place overwhelmingly valuable. It can even produce a striking distortion, with the organization becoming the only reality, the outside world becoming illusion. Generally the almost complete capture of affect and perception is associated with only a few utopian communities, fanatical political factions, and religious sects. But some formal rationalized organizations, as for example business and education, can also become utopian, fanatical, or sectarian.

Organizational sagas vary in durability. They can arise quickly in relatively unstructured social settings, as in professional sports organizations that operate in the volatile context of contact with large spectator audiences through the mass media. A professional baseball or football team may create a rags-to-riches legend in a few months' time that excites millions of people. But such a saga is also very fragile as an ongoing definition of the organization. The story can be removed quickly from the collective understanding of the present and future, for successful performance is often unstable, and the events that set the direction of belief can be readily reversed, with the great winners quickly becoming habitual losers. In such cases, there seems to be an unstable structural connection between the organization and the base of believers. The base of belief is not anchored within the organization nor in personal ties between insiders and outsiders, but is mediated by mass media, away from the control of the organization. Such sagas continue only as the organization keeps repeating its earlier success and also keeps the detached followers from straying to other sources of excitement and identification.

In contrast, organizational sagas show high durability when built slowly in structured social contexts; for example, the educational system, specifically for the purposes of this paper, three liberal arts colleges in the United States. In the many small private colleges, the story of special performance emerges not in a few months but over a decade or two. When the saga is firmly developed, it is embodied in many components of the organization, affecting the definition and performance of the organization and finding protection in the webbing of the institutional parts. It is not volatile and can be relegated to the past only by years of attenuation or organizational decline.

Since the concept of organizational saga was developed from research on Reed, Antioch, and Swarthmore, three distinctive and highly regarded colleges (Clark, 1970), material and categories from their developmental histories are used to illustrate the development of a saga, and its positive effects on organizational participation and effectiveness are then considered.[2]

Development of Saga

Two stages can be distinguished in the development of an organizational saga, initiation and fulfillment. Initiation takes place under varying conditions and occurs within a relatively short period of time: fulfillment is related to features of the organization that are enduring and more predictable.

Initiation

Strong sagas do not develop in passive organizations tuned to adaptive servicing of demand or to the fulfilling of roles dictated by higher authorities (Clark, 1956, 1960). The saga is initially a strong purpose, conceived and enunciated by a single man or a small cadre (Selznick, 1957) whose first task is to find a setting that is open, or can be opened, to a special effort. The most obvious setting is the autonomous new organization, where there is no established structure, no rigid custom, especially if a deliberate effort has been made to establish initial autonomy and bordering outsiders are preoccupied. There a leader may also have the advantage of building from the top down, appointing lieutenants and picking up recruits in accord with his ideas.

Reed College is strongly characterized by a saga, and its story of hard-won excellence and nonconformity began as strong purpose in a new organization. Its first president, William T. Foster, a thirty-year-old, high-minded reformer, from the sophisticated East of Harvard and Bowdoin went to the untutored Northwest, to an unbuilt campus in suburban Portland in 1910, precisely because he did not want to be limited by established institutions, all of which were, to his mind, corrupt in practice. The projected college in Oregon was clear ground, intellectually as well as physically, and he could there assemble the people and devise the practices that would finally give the United States an academically pure college, a Balliol for America.

The second setting for initiation is the established organization in a crisis of decay. Those in charge, after years of attempting incremental adjustments (Lindblom, 1959), realize finally that they must either give up established ways or have the organization fail. Preferring that it survive, they may relinquish the leadership to one proposing a plan that promises revival and later strength, or they may even accept a man of utopian intent. Deep crisis in the established organization thus creates some of the conditions of a new organization. It suspends past practice, forces some bordering groups to stand back or even to turn their backs on failure of the organization, and it tends to catch the attention of the reformer looking for an opportunity.

Antioch College is a dramatic example of such a setting. Started in the 1860's, its first sixty years were characterized by little money, weak staff, few students, and obscurity. Conditions worsened in the 1910's under the inflation and other strains of World War I. In 1919 a charismatic utopian reformer, Arthur E. Morgan, decided it was more advantageous to take over an old college with buildings and a charter than to start a new one. First as trustee and then as president, he began in the early 1920's an institutional renovation that overturned everything: as president he found it easy to push aside old, weak organizational structures and usages. He elaborated a plan of general education involving an unusual combination of work, study, and community participation; and he set about to devise the implementing tool. Crisis and charisma made possible a radical transformation out of which came a second Antioch, a college soon characterized by a sense of exciting history, unique practice, and exceptional performance.

The third context for initiation is the established organization that is not in crisis, not collapsing from long decline, yet ready for evolutionary change. This is the most difficult situation to predict, having to do with degree of rigidity. In both ideology and structure, institutionalized colleges vary in openness to change. In those under church control, for example, the colleges of the more liberal Protestant denominations have been more hospitable than Catholic colleges, at least until recently, to educational experimentation. A college with a tradition of presidential power is more open to change than one where the trustees and the professors exert control over the president. Particularly promising is the college with a self-defined need for educational leadership. This is the opening for which some reformers watch, the sound place that has some ambition to increase its academic stature, as for example, Swarthmore College.

Swarthmore began in the 1860s, and had become by 1920 a secure and stable college, prudently managed by Quaker trustees and administrators and solidly based on traditional support from nearby Quaker families in Pennsylvania, New Jersey, and Maryland. Such an organization would not usually be thought promising for reform, but Frank Aydelotte, who became its president in 1920, judged it ready for change. Magnetic in personality, highly placed within the élite circle of former Rhodes scholars, personally liked by important foundation officials, and recommended as a scholarly leader, he was offered other college presidencies, but he chose Swarthmore as a place open to change through a combination of financial health, liberal Quaker ethos, and some institutional ambition. His judgment proved correct, although the tolerance for his changes in the 1920's and 1930's was narrow at times. He began the gradual introduction of a modified Oxford honors program and related changes, which resulted in noteworthy achievements that supporters were to identify later as "the Swarthmore saga" (Swarthmore College Faculty, 1941).

Fulfillment

Although the conditions of initiation of a saga vary, the means of fulfillment are more predictable. There are many ways in which a unified sense of a special history is expressed; for example, even a patch of sidewalk or a coffee room may evoke emotion among the believers; but one can delimit the components at the center of the development of a saga. These may center, in colleges, on the personnel, the program, the external social base, the student subculture, and the imagery of the saga.

PERSONNEL

In a college, the key group of believers is the senior faculty. When they are hostile to a new idea, its attenuation is likely; when they are passive, its success is weak; and when they are devoted to it, a saga is probable. A single leader, a college president, can initiate the change, but the organizational idea will not be expanded over the years and expressed in performance unless ranking and powerful members of the faculty become committed to it and remain committed even after the initiator is gone. In committing themselves deeply, taking some credit for the change and seeking to ensure its perpetuation, they routinize the charisma of the leader in collegial authority. The faculty cadre of believers helps to effect the legend, then to protect it against later leaders and other new participants who, less pure in belief, might turn the organization in some other direction.

Such faculty cadres were well developed at Reed by 1925, after the time of its first two presidents; at Antioch, by the early 1930's, after Morgan, disappointed with his followers, left for the board of directors of the new TVA; and at Swarthmore, by the 1930's, and particularly, by 1940, after Aydelotte's twenty years of persistent effort. In all three colleges, after the departure of the change agent(s), the senior faculty with the succeeding president, a man appropriate for consolidation, undertook the full working out of the experiment. The faculty believers also replaced themselves through socialization and selective recruitment and retention in the 1940's and 1950's. Meanwhile, new potential innovators had sometimes to be stopped. In such instances, the faculty was able to exert influence to shield the distinctive effort from erosion or deflection. At Reed, for example, major clashes between president and faculty in the late 1930's and the early 1950's were precipitated by a new change-oriented president, coming in from the outside, disagreeing with a faculty proud of what had been done, attached deeply to what the college had become, and determined to maintain what was for them the distinctive Reed style. From the standpoint of constructing a regional and national model of purity and severity in undergraduate education, the Reed faculty did on those occasions act to create while acting to conserve.

PROGRAMS

For a college to transform purpose into a credible story of unique accomplishment, there must be visible practices with which claims of distinctiveness can be supported; that is, unusual courses, noteworthy requirements, or special methods of teaching. On the basis of seemingly unique practices, the program becomes a set of communal symbols and rituals, invested with meaning. Not reporting grades to the students becomes a symbol, as at Reed, that the college cares about learning for learning's sake; thus mere technique becomes part of a saga.

In all the three colleges, the program was seen as distinctive by both insiders and outsiders. At Swarthmore it was the special seminars and other practices of the honors program, capped by written and oral examination by teams of visiting outsiders in the last days of the senior year. At Antioch it was the work-study cycle, the special set of general education requirements, community government, and community involvement. At Reed it was the required freshman lecture-and-seminar courses, the junior qualifying examination, and the thesis in the senior year. Such practices became central to a belief that things had been done so differently, and so much against the mainstream, and often against imposing odds, that the group had generated a saga.

SOCIAL BASE

The saga also becomes fixed in the minds of outside believers devoted to the organization, usually the alumni. The alumni are the best located to hold beliefs enduringly pure, since they can be as strongly identified with a special organizational history as the older faculty and administrators and yet do not have to face directly the new problems generated by a changing environment or students. Their thoughts can remain centered on the past, rooted in the days when, as students, they participated intimately in the unique ways and accomplishments of the campus.

Liberal alumni, as those of Reed, Antioch, and Swarthmore here, seek to conserve what they believe to be a unique liberal institution and to protect it from the conservative forces of society that might change it — that is, to make it like other colleges. At Reed, for example, dropouts as well as graduates were struck by the intellectual excellence of their small college, convinced that college life there had been unlike college life anywhere else, and they were ready to conserve the practices that seemed to sustain that excellence. Here too, conserving acts can be seen for a time as contributing to an innovation, protecting the full working out of a distinctive effort.

STUDENT SUBCULTURE

The student body is the third group of believers, not overwhelmingly important but still a necessary support for the sage. To become and remain a saga, a change must be supported by the student subculture over decades, and the ideology of the subculture must integrate with the central ideas of the believing administrators and faculty. When the students define themselves as personally responsible for upholding the image of the college, then a design or plan has become an organizational saga.

At Antioch, Reed, and Swarthmore, the student subcultures were powerful mechanisms for carrying a developing saga from one generation to another. Reed students, almost from the beginning and extending at least to the early 1960's, were great believers in the uniqueness of their college, constantly on the alert for any action that would alter it, ever fearful that administration or faculty might succumb to pressures that would make Reed just like other colleges. Students at Antioch and Swarthmore also offered unstinting support for the ideology of their institution. All three student bodies steadily and dependably transferred the ideology from one generation to another. Often socializing deeply, they helped produce the graduate who never quite rid himself of the wish to go back to the campus.

IMAGERY OF SAGA

Upheld by faculty, alumni, and students, expressed in teaching practices, the sage is even more widely expressed as a generalized tradition in statues and ceremonies, written histories and current catalogues, even in an "air about the place" felt by participants and some outsiders. The more unique the history and the more forceful the claim to a place in history, the more intensely cultivated the ways of sharing memory and symbolizing the institution. The saga is a strong self-fulfilling belief; working through institutional self-image and public image, it is indeed a switchman (Weber, 1946), helping to determine the tracks along which action is pushed by men's self-defined interests. The early belief of one stage brings about the actions that warrant a stronger version of the same belief in a later period. As the account develops, believers come to sense its many constituent symbols as inextricably bound together, and the part takes its meaning from the whole. For example, at Antioch a deep attachment developed in the 1930's and 1940's to Morgan's philosophy of the whole man and to its expression in a unique combination of work, study, community participation, and many practices thought to embody freedom and nonconformity. Some of the faculty of those years who remained in the 1940's and 1950's had many memories and impressions that seemed to form a symbolic whole: personnel counselors, folk dancing in Red Square, Morgan's towering physique, the battles of community government, the pacifism of the late 1930's, the frequent dash of students to off-campus jobs, the dedicated deans who personified central values. Public image also grew strong and sharp, directing liberals and radicals to the college and conservatives to other places. The symbolic expressions themselves were a strong perpetuating force.

Conclusion

An organizational saga is a powerful means of unity in the formal place. It makes links across internal divisions and organizational boundaries as internal and external groups share their common belief. With deep emotional commitment, believers define themselves by their organizational affiliation, and in their bond to other believers they share an intense sense of the unique. In an organization defined by a strong sage, there is a feeling that there is the small world of the lucky few and the large routine one of the rest of the world. Such an emotional bond turns the membership into a community, even a cult.

An organizational saga is thus a valuable resource, created over a number of years out of the social components of the formal enterprise. As participants become ideologues, their common definition becomes a foundation for trust and for extreme loyalty. Such bonds give the organization a competitive edge in recruiting and maintaining personnel and helps it to avoid the vicious circle in which some actual or anticipated erosion of organizational strength leads to the loss of some personnel, which leads to further decline and loss. Loyalty causes individual to stay with a system, to save and improve it rather than to leave to serve their self-interest elsewhere (Hirschman, 1970). The genesis and persistence of loyalty is a key organizational and analytical problem. Enduring loyalty follows from a collective belief of participants that their organization is distinctive. Such a belief comes from a credible story of uncommon effort, achievement, and form.

Pride in the organized group and pride in one's identity as taken from the group are personal returns that are uncommon in modern social involvement. The development of sagas is one way in which men in organizations increase such returns, reducing their sense of isolation and increasing their personal pride and pleasure in organizational life. Studying the evocative narratives and devotional ties of formal systems leads to a better understanding of the fundamental capacities of organizations to enhance or diminish the lives of participants. The organization possessing a saga is a place in which participants for a time at least happily accept their bond.

Burton R. Clark is a professor of sociology at Yale University.

Notes

[1] Revised version of paper presented at the 65th Annual Meeting of the American Sociological Association, September, 1970, Washington, D.C. I wish to thank Wendell Bell, Maren L. Carden, Kai Erikson, and Stanley Udy for discussion and comment. Parts of an early draft of this paper have been used to connect organizational belief to problems of governance in colleges and universities (Clark, 1971).

[2] For some discussion of the risks and tensions associated with organizational sagas, particularly that of success in one period leading to later rigidity and stagnation, see Clark (1970: 258-261). Hale (1970) gives an illumination discussion of various effects of a persistent saga in a theological seminary.

References

Bendix, R., *Work and Authority in Industry*. New York: John Wiley, 1956.

Carden, M. L., *Oneida: Utopian Community to Modern Corporation*. Baltimore: The Johns Hopkins Press, 1960.

Clark, B. R., *Adult Education in Transition: A Study of Institutional Insecurity*. Berkeley: University of California Press, 1956.

————.*The Open Door College. A Case Study*. New York: McGraw-Hill, 1960.

————.*The Distinctive College: Antioch, Reed, and Swarthmore*. Chicago: Aldine, 1970.

————."Belief and loyalty in college organization," *Journal of Higher Education*, 1971, XLII, 6: 499-515.

Gross, B. M., *The Managing of Organizations*. (2 vols.) New York: Free Press, 1964.

Hale, J. R. *The Making and Testing of an Organizational Saga: A Case-Study of the Lutheran Theological Seminary at Gettysburg, Pennsylvania, with Special Reference to the Problem of Merger, 1959-1960*. Unpublished Ed.D. dissertation, Columbia University, 1970.

Hirschman, A. O., *Exit, Voice, and Loyalty*. Cambridge, Mass.: Harvard University Press, 1970.

Lindblom, C. E. "The science of 'muddling through.'" *Public Administration Review*, 1950 19: 79-88.

Litterer, J. A.*The Analysis of Organizations*. New York: John Wiley, 1965.

March, J. G. (ed.), *Handbook of Organizations*: Chicago: Rand McNally, 1965.

Perrow, C. *Organizational Analysis*. Belmont, California: Wadsworth, 1970.

Price, J. L. Organizational Effectiveness: An Inventory of Propositions. Homewood, Illinois: Richard D. Irwin, 1968.

Selznick, P. *TVA and the Grass Roots*. Berkeley: University of California Press, 1949.

————.Leadership in Administration. New York: Harper & Row, 1957.

Swarthmore College Faculty. *An Adventure in Education: Swarthmore College Under Frank Aydelotte*. New York: Macmillan, 1941.

Thompson, J. D. Organizations in Action. New York: McGraw-Hill, 1967.

Weber, M. *From Max Weber: Essays in Sociology*. Translated and edited by H. H. Gerth and C. Wright Mills. New York: Oxford, 1946.

Whyte, W. F. *Human Relations in the Restaurant Industry*. New York: McGraw-Hill, 1948.

The Professional Bureaucracy

Henry Mintzberg

Prime Coordinating Mechanism:	Standardization of skills
Key Part of Organization:	Operating core
Main Design Parameters:	Training, horizontal job specialization, vertical and horizontal decentralization
Contingency Factors:	Complex, stable environment, nonregulating, non-sophisticated technical system, fashionable

We have seen evidence at various points in this book that organizations can be bureaucratic without being centralized. Their operating work is stable, leading to "predetermined or predictable, in effect, standardized" behavior (our definition of bureaucracy in Chapter 3), but it is also complex, and so must be controlled directly by the operators who do it. Hence, the organization turns to the one coordinating mechanism that allows for standardization and decentralization at the same time, namely the standardization of skills. This gives rise to a structural configuration sometimes called *Professional Bureaucracy*, common in universities, general hospitals, school systems, public accounting firms, social work agencies, and craft production firms. All rely on the skills and knowledge of their operating professionals to function; all produce standard products or services.

The Basic Structure

The Work of the Operating Core

Here again we have a tightly knit configuration of the design parameters. Most important, *the Professional Bureaucracy relies for coordination on the standardization of skills and its associated design parameter, training and indoctrination. It hires duly trained and indoctrinated specialists—professionals—for the operating core, and then gives them considerable control over their own work.* In effect, the work is highly specialized in the horizontal dimension, but enlarged in the vertical one.

Control over his own work means that the professional works relatively independently of his colleagues, but closely with the clients he serves. For example, "Teacher autonomy is reflected in the structure of school systems, resulting in what may be called their structural looseness. The teacher works alone within the classroom, relatively hidden from colleagues and superiors, so that he has a broad discretionary jurisdiction within the boundaries of the classroom" (Bidwell, 1965, pp. 975-976). Likewise, many doctors treats their own patients, and accountants maintain personal contact with the companies whose books they audit.

Most of the necessary coordination between the operating professionals is then handled by the standardization of skills and knowledge, in effect, by what they have learned to expect from their colleagues. ". . . the system works because everyone knows everyone else knows roughly what is going on" (Meyer quoted in Weick, 1976, p. 14). During an operation as long and as complex as open-heart surgery, "very little needs to be said [between the anesthesiologist and the surgeon] preceding chest opening and during the procedure on the heart itself: lines, beats and lights on equipment are indicative of what everyone is expected to do and does—operations are performed in absolute silence, particularly following the chest-opening phase" (Gosselin, 1978). The point is perhaps best made in reverse, by the cartoon that shows six surgeons standing around a patient on the operating table with one saying, "Who opens?" Similarly, the policy and marketing courses of the management school may be integrated without the two professors involved ever having even met. As long as the courses are standard, each knows more or less what the other teaches.

Just how standardized complex professional work can be is illustrated a paper read by Spencer (1976) before a meeting of the International Cardiovascular Society. Spencer notes that "Becoming a skillful clinical surgeon requires a long period of training, probably five or more years" p. 1178). An important feature of that training is "repetitive practice" to evoke an "automatic reflex" (p. 1179). So automatic, in fact, that Spencer keeps a series of surgical "cookbooks" in which he lists, even for "complex" operations, the essential steps as chains of thirty to forty symbols on a single sheet, to "be reviewed mentally in sixty to 120 seconds at some time during the day preceding the operation" (p. 1182).

But no matter how standardized the knowledge and skills, their complexity ensures that considerable discretion remains in their application. No two professionals—no two surgeons or teachers or social workers—ever apply them in exactly the same way. Many judgments are required, as Perrow (1970) notes of policemen and others:

> There exist numerous plans: when to suspend assistance, when to remove a gun from its holster, when to block off an area, when to call the FBI, and when remove a child from the home. The existence of such plans does not provide a criterion for choosing the most effective plan . . . Instead of computation the decision depends upon human judgment. The police patrolman must decide whether to try to disperse the street corner gang or call for reinforcements. The welfare worker must likewise decide if new furniture is an allowable expense, and the high school counselor must decide whether to recommend a college preparatory or vocational program. Categories channel and shape these human judgments but they do not replace them (p. 216).

Training and indoctrination is a complicated affair in the Professional Bureaucracy. The initial training typically takes place over a period of years in a university or special institution. Here the skills and knowledge of the profession are formally programmed into the would-be professional. But in many cases that is only the first step, even if the most important one. There typically follows a long period of on-the-job training, such as internship in medicine and articling in accounting. Here the formal knowledge is applied and the practice of the skills perfected, under the close supervision of members of the profession. On-the-job training also completes the process of indoctrination, which began during the formal teaching. Once this process is completed, the professional association typically examines the trainee to determine whether he has the requisite knowledge, skills, and norms to enter the profession. That is not to say, however, that the individual is examined for the last time in his life, and is pronounced completely full, such that "After this, no new ideas can be imparted to him," as humorist and academic Stephen Leacock once commented about the Ph.D., the test to enter the profession of university teaching. The entrance examination only tests the basic requirements at one point in time; the process of training continues. As new knowledge is generated and new skills develop, the professional upgrades his expertise. He reads the journals, attends the conferences, and perhaps also returns periodically for formal retraining.

The Bureaucratic Nature of the Structure

All of this training is geared to one goal—the internalization of standards that serve the client and coordinate the professional work. In other words, *the structure of these organizations is essentially bureaucratic, its coordination—like that of the Machine Bureaucracy—achieved by design, by standards that predetermine what is to be done.* How bureaucratic is illustrated by Perrow's (1970) description of one well-known hospital department:

> . . . obstetrics and gynecology is a relatively routine department, which even has something resembling an assembly (or deassembly?) line wherein the mother moves from room to room and nurse to nurse during the predictable course of her labor. It is also one of the hospital units most often accused of impersonality and depersonalization. For the mother, the birth is unique, but not for the doctor and the rest of the staff who go through this many times a day (p. 74).

But the two kinds of bureaucracies differ markedly in the source of their standardization. *Whereas the Machine Bureaucracy generates its own standards—its technostructure designing the work standards for its operators and its line managers enforcing them—the standards of the Professional Bureaucracy originate largely outside its own structure, in the self-governing associations its operators join with their colleagues from other Professional Bureaucracies.* These associations set universal standards which they make sure are taught by the universities and used by all the bureaucracies of the profession. *So whereas the Machine Bureaucracy relies on authority of a hierarchical nature—the power of office—the Professional Bureaucracy emphasizes authority of a professional nature—the power of expertise* (Blau, 1967–68). Thus, although Montagna (1968) found internal as well as external rules in the large public accounting firms he studied, the latter proved more important. These were imposed by the American Institute of Certified Public Accountants and included an elaborate and much revised code of ethics, a newly codified volume of principles of accounting, and revised auditing standards and procedures.

> These rules serve as a foundation for the firms' more specific internal rules, a few of which are more stringent, others of which merely expand on the external rules. Nearly to a man, the total sample [of accountants questioned] agreed that compared with internal rules, the external rules were the more important rules for their firms and for the profession as a whole (p. 143).

Montagna's findings suggest that the other forms of standardization are difficult to rely on in the Professional Bureaucracy. The work processes themselves are too complex to be standardized directly by analysts. One need only try to imagine a work study analyst following a cardiologist on his rounds or observing a teacher in a classroom in order to program their work. Similarly, the outputs of professional work cannot easily be measured, and so do not lend themselves to standardization. Imagine a planner trying to define a cure in psychiatry, the amount of learning that takes place in the classroom, or the quality of an accountant's audit. Thus, Professional Bureaucracies cannot rely extensively on the formalization of professional work or on systems to plan and control it.

Much the same conclusion can be drawn for the two remaining coordinating mechanisms. Both direct supervision and mutual adjustment impede the professional's close relationships with his clients. That relationship is predicated on a high degree of professional autonomy—freedom from having not only to respond to managerial orders but also to consult extensively with peers. In any event, the use of the other four coordinating mechanisms is precluded by the capacity of the standardization of skills to achieve a good deal of the coordination necessary in the operating core.

The Pigeonholing Process

To understand how the Professional Bureaucracy functions in its operating core, it is helpful to think of it as a repertoire of standard programs—in effect, the set of skills the professionals stand ready to use—which are applied to predetermined situations, called contingencies, also standardized. As Weick (1976) notes of one case in point, "schools are in the business of building and maintaining categories" (p. 8). The process is sometimes known as *pigeonholing*. In this regard, *the professional has two basic tasks: (1) to categorize the client's need in terms of a contingency, which indicates which standard program to use, a task known as diagnosis, and (2) to apply, or execute, that program.* Pigeonholing simplifies matters enormously. "People are categorized and placed into pigeonholes because it would take enormous resources to treat every case as unique and requiring thorough analysis. Like stereotypes, categories allow us to move through the world without making continuous decisions at every moment" (Perrow, 1970, p. 58). Thus, a psychiatrist examines the patient, declares him to be manic-depressive, and initiates psychotherapy. Similarly, a professor finds 100 students registered in his course and executes his lecture program; faced with 20 instead, he runs the class as a seminar. And the management consultant carries his own bag of standard acronymical tricks—MBO, MIS, LRP, PERT, OD. The client with project work gets PERT, the one with managerial conflicts, OD. Simon (1977) captures the spirit of pigeonholing with his comment that "The pleasure that the good professional experiences in his work is not simply a pleasure in handling difficult matters; it is a pleasure in using skillfully a well-stocked kit of well-designed tools to handle problems that are comprehensible in their deep structure but unfamiliar in their detail" (p. 98).

It is the pigeonholing process that enables the Professional Bureaucracy to decouple its various operating tasks and assign them to individual, relatively autonomous professionals. Each can, instead of giving a great deal of attention to coordinating his work with his peers, focus on perfecting his skills. As Spencer (1976) notes in the case of vascular surgery, "with precise diagnosis and expert operative technique excellent results could almost always be obtained" (p. 1177).

The pigeonholing process does not deny the existence of uncertainty in servicing a client. Rather, it seeks to contain it in the jobs of single professionals. As Bidwell (1965) notes, "The problem of dealing with variability in student abilities and accomplishments during a school year . . . is vested in the classroom teacher, and one important component of his professional skill is ability to handle day-to-day fluctuations in the response to instruction by individual students and collectively by the classroom group" (p. 975). The containment of this uncertainty—what Simon characterizes as unfamiliarity in detail in the job of the single professional—is one of the reasons why the professional requires considerable discretion in his work.

In the pigeonholing process, we see fundamental differences among the Machine Bureaucracy, the Professional Bureaucracy, and the Adhocracy. The Machine Bureaucracy is a single-purpose structure: presented with a stimulus, it executes its one standard sequence of programs, just as we kick when tapped on the knee. No diagnosis is involved. In the Professional Bureaucracy, diagnosis is a fundamental task, but it is circumscribed. The organization seeks to match a predetermined contingency to a standard program. Fully open-ended diagnosis—that which seeks a creative solution to a unique problem-requires a third structural configuration, which we call Adhocracy. No standard contingencies or programs exist in that structure.

Segal (1974) refers to these three as "chain-structured," "mediatively-structured," and "adaptively-structured" organizations. The chain-structured organization relates to only a small part of the environment and accepts inputs only at one end; once ingested, these are processed through a fixed sequence of operations. The mediatively-structured organization—our Professional Bureaucracy—is designed "to channel external dissimilarity into uniform organizational categories" (p. 215). Segal cites the example of the welfare department:

> A glance at the telephone numbers individuals must call to initiate contact with the welfare department indicates that the potential client cannot simply need help, he must need help as defined by the organization—aging, adoption, children in trouble, landlord-tenant complaints, etc. (p. 215).

In other words, the welfare department leaves part of the diagnosis to the client. The adaptively-structured organization, or Adhocracy, "is not structured to screen out heterogeneity and uncertainty" (p. 217). It adapts to its client's individual problem rather than trying to fit it into one of its own categories. Segal provides an example of each of these three types of organizations from the field of mental health:

1. The chain-structured custodial unit responds to the pressure in the environment to keep mental patients out of the public eye and in physical captivity. The chain-structured custodial unit is thus designed to achieve the singular purpose of custodial behavior.
2. The individual treatment structure responds to other pressure in the environment by arranging its units and care to help each patient to fit into a *category* of behavior defined by society. This facility is thus categorically responsive as staff attempts to change patients' behavior so that it fits their own standards of "normality."
3. The adaptively-structured milieu treatment ward responds to a more relativistic environmental pressure. In this instance, units and roles are arranged so that the very definition of normality is a product of interaction between staff and patients (p. 218).[1]

It is an interesting characteristic of the Professional Bureaucracy that its pigeonholing process creates an equivalence in its structure between the functional and market bases for grouping. *Because clients are categorized—or, as in the case of the welfare recipients above, categorize themselves—in terms of the functional specialists who serve them, the structure of the Professional Bureaucracy becomes at the same time both a functional and a market-based one.* Two illustrations help explain the point. A hospital gynecology department and a university chemistry department can be called functional because they group specialists according to the knowledge, skills, and work processes they use, or market-based because each unit deals with its own unique types of clients—women in the first case, chemistry students in the second. Thus, the distinction between functional and market bases for grouping breaks down in the special case of the Professional Bureaucracy.

Focus on the Operating Core

All the design parameters that we have discussed so far—the emphasis on the training of operators, their vertically enlarged jobs, the little use made of behavior formalization or planning and control systems—suggest that *the operating core is the key part of the Professional Bureaucracy. The only other part that is fully elaborated is the support staff, but that is focused very much on serving the operating core.* Given the high cost of the professionals, it makes sense to back them up with as much support as possible, to aid them and have others do whatever routine work can be formalized. For example, universities have printing facilities, faculty clubs, alma mater funds, building and grounds departments, publishing houses, archives, bookstores, information offices, museums, athletics departments, libraries, computer facilities, and many, many other support units.

The technostructure and middle line of management are not highly elaborated in the Professional Bureaucracy. In other configurations (except Adhocracy), they coordinate the work of the operating core. But in the Professional Bureaucracy, they can do little to coordinate the operating work. The need for planning or the formalizing of the work of the professionals is very limited, so there is little call for a technostructure (except, as we shall see, in the case of the nonprofessional support staff). In McGill University, for example, an institution with 17,000 students and 1200 professors, the only units that could be identified by the author as technocratic were two small departments concerned with finance and budgeting, a small planning office, and a center to develop the professors' skills in pedagogy (the latter two fighting a continual uphill battle for acceptance).

Likewise, the middle line in the Professional Bureaucracy is thin. With little need for direct supervision of the operators, or mutual adjustment between them, the operating units can be very large, with few managers at the level of first-line supervisor, or, for that matter, above them. The McGill Faculty of Management at the time of this writing has fifty professors and a single manager, its dean.

Thus, Figure 19–1 shows the Professional Bureaucracy, in terms of our logo, as a flat structure with a thin middle line, a tiny technostructure, and a fully elaborated support staff. All these features are reflected in the organigram of McGill University, shown in Figure 19-2.

Figure 19–1

The Professional Bureaucracy

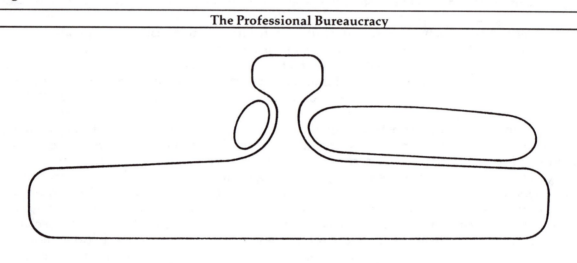

Decentralization in the Professional Bureaucracy

Everything we have seen so far tells us that *the Professional Bureaucracy is a highly decentralized structure, in both the vertical and horizontal dimensions.* A great deal of the power over the operating work rests at the bottom of the structure, with the professionals of the operating core. Often each works with his own clients, subject only to the collective control of his colleagues, who trained and indoctrinated him in the first place and thereafter reserve the right to censure him for malpractice.

The professional's power derives from the fact that not only is his work too complex to be supervised by managers or standardized by analysts, but also that his services are typically in great demand. This gives the professional mobility, which enables him to insist on considerable autonomy in his work. The professional tends to identify more with his profession than with the organization where he practices it. Thus, Perrow (1965, p. 959) talks of the "stronger grip" of the medical profession on its members than the specific hospital, while

Beyer and Lodahl (1976) note in academia that "Many faculty members receive an important part of their rewards—recognition—from their scientific communities, and this reward is only secondarily reinforced by their universities" (p. 124). In these organizations, even "promotion is

Figure 19–2

Organigram of McGill University (circa 1978, used permission)

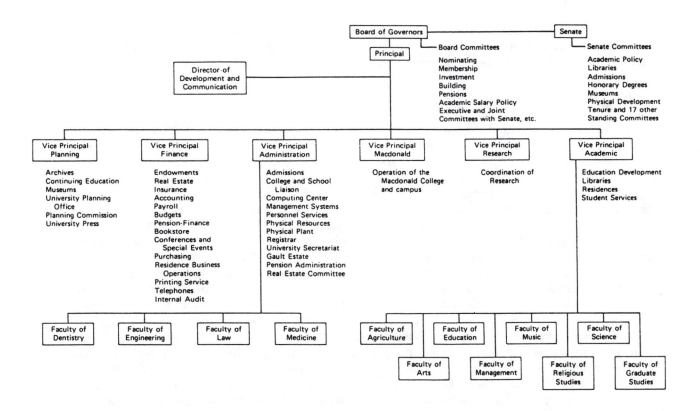

not related to the climbing of an administrative ladder but to professional progress, or the ability to handle more and more complex professional problems" (SIAR, 1975, p. 62). Thus, when the professional does not get the autonomy he feels he requires, he is tempted to pick up his kit bag of skills and move on.

One is inclined to ask why professionals bother to join organizations in the first place. There are, in fact, a number of good reasons. For one thing, professionals can share resources, including support services, in a common organization. One surgeon cannot afford his own operating theater, so he shares it with others, just as professors share laboratories, lecture halls, libraries, and printing facilities. Organizations also bring professionals together to learn from each other, and to train new recruits.

Some professionals must join the organization to get clients. The clients present themselves to an organization that houses many different kinds of professionals, depending on it to diagnose their problem and direct them to the individual professional who can best serve them.

Thus, while some physicians, have their private patients, others receive them from the hospital emergency department or from in-patient referrals. In universities, students select the department where they wish to study—in effect, diagnosing their own general needs—but that department, in turn, helps direct them into specific courses given by individual professors.

Another reason professionals band together to form organizations is that the clients often need the services of more than one at the same time. An operation requires at least a surgeon, an anesthesiologist, and a nurse; an MBA program cannot be run with less than about a dozen different specialists. Finally, the bringing together of different types of professionals allows clients to be transferred between them when the initial diagnosis proves incorrect or the needs of the client change during execution. When the kidney patient develops heart trouble, that is no time to change hospitals in search of a cardiologist. Similarly, when a law student finds his client needs a course in moral ethics, or an accountant finds his client needs tax advice, it is comforting to know that other departments in the same organization stand ready to provide the necessary service.

The Administrative Structure

What we have seen so far suggests that the Professional Bureaucracy is a highly democratic structure, at least for the professionals of the operating core. In fact, *not only do the professionals control their own work, but they also seek collective control of the administrative decisions that affect them*, decisions, for example, to hire colleagues, to promote them, and to distribute resources. Controlling these decisions requires control of the middle line of the organization, which professionals do by ensuring that it is staffed with "their own." Some of the administrative work the operating professionals do themselves. Every university professor, for example, carries out some administrative duties and serves on committees of one kind or another to ensure that he retains some control over the decisions that affect his work. Moreover, full-time administrators who wish to have any power at all in these structures must be certified members of the profession, and preferably be elected by the professional operators or at least appointed with their blessing. What emerges, therefore, is a rather democratic administrative structure. The university department chairmen, many of them elected, together with the deans, vice-presidents, and president—all of them necessarily academics—must work alongside a parallel hierarchy of committees of professors, many of them elected, ranging from the departmental curriculum committee to the powerful university senate (shown with its own subcommittees in Figure 19–2). This can be seen clearly in Figure 19–3, the organigram of a typical university hospital. The plethora of committees is shown on the right side, reporting up from the medical departments through the Council of Physicians and Dentists directly to the Board of Trustees, bypassing the managerial hierarchy entirely. (Notice also the large number of support services in the organization and the relative absence of technocratic units.)

The nature of the administrative structure—which itself relies on mutual adjustment for coordination—indicates that the liaison devices, while uncommon in the operating core, are important design parameters in the middle line. Standing committees and ad hoc task forces abound, as was seen in Figure 19-3; a number of positions are designated to integrate the administrative efforts, as in the case of the ward manager in the hospital; and some Professional Bureaucracies even use matrix structure in administration.

Because of the power of their operators, Professional Bureaucracies are sometimes called "collegial" organizations. In fact, some professionals like to describe them as inverse pyramids, with the professional operators at the top and the administrators down below to serve them— to ensure that the surgical facilities are kept clean and the classrooms well supplied with chalk. Thus comments Amitai Etzioni (1959), the well-known sociologist:

Figure 19–3

Organigram of a University Hospital

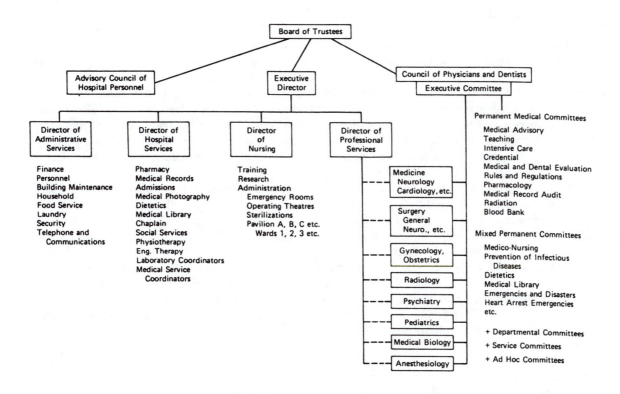

. . . in professional organizations the staff-expert line-manager correlation, insofar as such a correlation exists at all, is reversed... Managers in professional organizations are in charge of secondary activities; they administer *means* to the major activity carried out by experts. In other words, if there is a staff-line relationship at all, experts constitute the line (major authority) structure and managers the staff. . . . The final internal decision is, functionally speaking, in the hands of various professionals and their decision-making bodies. The professor decides what research he is going to undertake and to a large degree what he is going to teach; the physician determines what treatment should be given to the patient (p. 52).

Etzioni's description may underestimate the power of the *professional* administrator—an issue we shall return to shortly—but it seems to be an accurate description of the nonprofessional one, namely the administrator who manages the support units. For the support staff—often much larger than the professional one, but charged largely with doing nonprofessional work—there is no democracy in the Professional Bureaucracy, only the oligarchy of the professionals. Support units, such as housekeeping or kitchen in the hospital, printing in the university, are as likely as not to be managed tightly from the top. They exist, in effect, as machine bureaucratic constellations within the Professional Bureaucracy.

What frequently emerge in the Professional Bureaucracy are parallel administrative hierarchies, one democratic and bottom up for the professionals, and a second machine bureaucratic and top down for the support staff. As Bidwell (1965) notes: "The segregation of professional and nonprofessional hierarchies in school systems presumably permit this differentiation of modes of control" (p. 1016; see also Blau, 1967-68).

In the professional hierarchy, power resides in expertise; one has influence by virtue of one's knowledge and skills. In other words, a good deal of power remains at the bottom of the hierarchy, with the professional operators themselves. That does not, of course, preclude a pecking order among them. But it does require the pecking order to mirror the professionals experience and expertise. As they gain experience and reputation academics move through the ranks of lecturer, and then assistant, associate, and full professor; and physicians enter the hospital as interns and move up to residents before they become members of the staff.

In the nonprofession hierarchy, power and status reside in administrative office; one salutes the stripes, not the man. The situation is that Weber originally described: "each lower office is under the control and supervision of a higher one" (cited in Blau, 1967–68, p. 455). Unlike the professional structure, here one must practice administration, not a specialized function of the organization, to attain status.

But "research indicates that a professional orientation toward service and a bureaucratic orientation toward disciplined compliance with procedures are opposite approaches toward work and often create conflict in organizations" (Blau, 1967–68, p. 456). Hence, these two parallel hierarchies are kept quite independent of each other. The two may come together at some intermediate level, as when a university dean oversees both the professional and secretarial staff. But often, as shown in Figure 19–4, they remain separate right up to the strategic apex. The hospital medical staff, as shown in Figure 19–3, does not even report to the executive director—the chief executive officer—but directly to the board of trustees. (Indeed, Charns [1976] reports that 41 percent of physicians he surveyed in academic medical centers claimed they were responsible to no one!)

Figure 19–4

Parallel Hierarchies in the Professional Bureaucracy

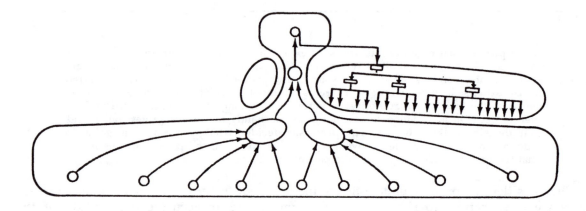

The Roles of the Professional Administrator

Where does all this leave the administrators of the professional hierarchy, the executive directors and chiefs of the hospitals and the presidents and deans of the universities? Are they as powerless as Etzioni suggests? Compared with their peers in the Simple Structure and the Machine Bureaucracy, they certainly lack a good deal of power. But that is far from the whole story. While the professional administrator may not be able to control the professionals directly, he does perform a series of roles that gives him considerable indirect power in the structure.

First, *the professional administrator spends much time handling disturbances in the structure*. The pigeonholing process is an imperfect one at best, leading to all kinds of jurisdictional disputes between the professionals. Who should teach the statistics course in the MBA program, the mathematics department or the business school? Who should perform mastectomies in hospitals, surgeons who specialize in operations or gynecologists who specialize in women? Seldom, however, can a senior administrator impose a solution on the professionals or units involved in a dispute. Rather the unit managers—chiefs, deans, or whoever—must sit down together and *negotiate* a solution on behalf of their constituencies. Coordination problems also arise frequently between the two parallel hierarchies, and it often falls to the professional administrator to resolve them.

Second, *the professional administrators—especially those at higher levels—serve key roles at the boundary of the organization, between the professionals inside and interested parties—governments, client associations, and so on—on the outside*. On one hand, the administrators are expected to protect the professionals' autonomy, to "buffer" them from external pressures. "The principal is expected to 'back the teacher up' —support her authority in all cases of parental 'interference' " (Melcher, 1976, p. 334). So, too, the executive director of the hospital is supposed to keep the government or the trustees from interfering in the work of the physicians. On the other hand, the administrators are expected to woo these outsiders to support the organization, both morally and financially. "...teachers consider it a prime responsibility of the administrator to secure for them the greatest possible amount of resources" (Hills, quoted in Melcher, 1976, p. 333), as do professors in universities and physicians in hospitals. Thus, the external roles of the manager—maintaining liaison contacts, acting as figurehead and spokesman in a public relations capacity, negotiating with outside agencies— emerge as primary ones in the job of the professional administrator.

Some view the roles professional administrators are called upon to perform as signs of weakness. Like Etzioni, they see these people as the errand boys of the professionals, or else as pawns caught in various tugs of war—between one professional and another, between support staffer and professional, between outsider and professional. In fact, however, these roles are the very sources of administrator power. Power is, after all, gained at the locus of uncertainty. And that is exactly where the professional administrators sit. The administrator who succeeds in raising extra funds for his organization gains a say in how these are distributed. Similarly, the one who can reconcile conflicts in favor of his unit or who can effectively buffer the professionals from external influence becomes a valued—and therefore powerful—member of the organization. The professionals well know that "Without the 'superb politician,' metropolitan school systems, urban governments, universities, mental hospitals, social work systems, and similar complex organizations would be immobilized" (Thompson, 1967, p. 143).

Ironically, *the professional becomes dependent on the effective administrator*. The professional faces a fundamental dilemma. Frequently, he abhors administration, desiring only to be left alone to practice his profession. But that freedom is gained only at the price of administrative effort—raising funds, resolving conflicts, buffering the demands of outsiders. That leaves the professional two choices: to do the administrative work himself, in which case he has less time to practice his profession, or to leave it to administrators, in which case he must surrender some of his power over decision making. And that power must be surrendered, it should further be noted, to administrators who, by virtue of the fact that they no longer wish to practice the profession, probably favor a different set of goals. Damned if he does and damned if he doesn't. Take the case of the university professors oriented to research. To ensure the fullest support for research in his department, he should involve himself in committees where questions of the commitment to teaching versus research are decided. But that takes time, specifically time away from research. What is the use of spending time protecting what one has no time left to do. So the professor is tempted to leave administration to full-time administrators, those who have expressed a disinterest in research by virtue of seeking full-time administrative office.

We can conclude that *power in these structures does flow to those professionals who care to devote the effort to doing administrative instead of professional work*—a considerable amount of power, in fact, to those who do it well, especially in complex professional organizations, such as the modern hospital (Perrow, 1967). *But that, it should be stressed, is not laissez-faire power: the professional administrator keeps his power only as long as the professionals perceive him to be serving their interests effectively.* The managers of the Professional Bureaucracy may be the weakest among those of the five structural configurations, but they are far from impotent. *Individually, they are usually more powerful than individual professionals*—the chief executive remaining the single most powerful member of the Professional Bureaucracy—even if that power can easily be overwhelmed by the *collective* power of the professionals.

Strategy Formulation in the Professional Bureaucracy

A description of the strategy formulation process in the Professional Bureaucracy perhaps best illustrates the two sides of the professional administrator's power. At the outset it should be noted that strategy takes on a very different form in these kinds of organizations. Since their outputs are difficult to measure, their goals cannot easily be agreed upon. So *the notion of a strategy—a single, integrated pattern of decisions common to the entire organization—loses a good deal of its meaning in the Professional Bureaucracy.*

Given the autonomy of each professional—his close working relationships with his clients, and his loose ones with his colleagues—it becomes sensible to think in terms of a personal strategy for each professional. In many cases, each selects his own clients and his own methods of dealing with them—in effect, he chooses his own product-market strategy. But professionals do not select their clients and methods at random. They are significantly constrained by the professional standards and skills they have learned. That is, the professional associations and training institutions outside the organization play a major role in determining the strategies that the professionals pursue. Thus, to an important extent all organizations in a given profession exhibit similar strategies, imposed on them from the outside. These strategies—concerning what clients to serve and how—are inculcated in the professionals during their formal training and are modified as new needs emerge and the new methods developed to cope with them gain acceptance by the professional associations. In medicine, for example, researchers develop new forms of treatment and test them experimentally. They publish their results in the medical journals, these publications leading to more experimentation and elaboration until the methods are considered sufficiently safe to pass into standard practice—that is, to become part of the repertoire of programs of all hospitals. And this whole process is overseen by the professional associations, which pass judgments on acceptable and unacceptable practices, and through whose journals, newsletters, conferences, and training programs information on new practices is disseminated. This control of strategy can sometimes be very direct: in one of the McGill studies, a hospital that refused to adopt a new method of treatment was, in effect, censured when one of the associations of medical specialists passed a resolution declaring failure to use it tantamount to malpractice.

We can conclude, therefore, that *the strategies of the Professional Bureaucracy are largely ones of the individual professionals within the organization as well as of the professional associations on the outside.* Largely, but not completely. There are still degrees of freedom that allow each organization within the profession to adapt the basic strategies to its own needs and interests. There are, for example, mental hospitals, women's hospitals, and veterans' hospitals; all conform to standard medical practice, but each applies it to a different market which it has selected.

How do these organizational strategies get made? It would appear that *the Professional Bureaucracy's own strategies represent the cumulative effect over time of the projects, or strategic "initiatives," that its members are able to convince it to undertake*—to buy a new piece of equipment in a hospital, to establish a new degree program in a university, to develop a new specialty department in an accounting firm. Most of these initiatives are proposed by members of the operating core—by "professional entrepreneurs" willing to expend the efforts needed to negotiate the acceptance of new projects through the complex administrative structure (and if the method is new and controversial, through outside professional associations as well, and also through outside funding agencies if the project is an expensive one). A proposal for a new Ph.D. program in management at McGill University was worked out by an ad hoc committee and then approved within the Faculty of Management by its Graduate Program Committee, Academic Committee, and Faculty Council; from there it went to the Executive Committee and the Council of the Faculty of Graduate Studies; then it moved on to the Academic Policy Committee of the Senate of the University and then to the full Senate itself; from there it went to the University Programs Committee of the Quebec government Ministry of Education and then into the Ministry itself, and then back and forth between these bodies and the university administration a few more times until it was finally approved (as a joint program of four universities).

What is the role of the professional administrator in all this? Certainly far from passive. As noted earlier, administration is neither the forte nor the interest of the operating professional (for good reason, as should be clear from the example above!). So he depends on the full-time administrator to help him negotiate his project through the system. For one thing, the administrator has time to worry about such matters—after all, administration is his job; he no longer practices the profession. For another, the administrator has a full knowledge of the administrative committee system as well as many personal contacts within it, both of which are necessary to see project through it. The administrator deals with the system every day; the professional entrepreneur may promote only one new project in his entire career. Finally, the administrator is more likely to have the requisite managerial skills, for example, those of negotiation and persuasion.

But the power of the effective administrator to influence strategy goes beyond helping the professionals. Every good manager seeks to change his organization in his own way, to alter its strategies to make it more effective. In the Professional Bureaucracy, this translates into a set of strategic initiatives that the administrator himself wishes to take. But in these structures— in principle bottom up—the administrator cannot impose his will on the professionals of the operating core. Instead, he must rely on his informal power, and apply it subtly. Knowing that the professionals want nothing more than to be left alone, the administrator moves carefully— in incremental steps, each one hardly discernible. In this way, he may achieve over time changes that the professionals would have rejected out of hand had they been proposed all at once.

To conclude, we have seen again that while the weak administrator of the Professional Bureaucracy may be no more than the errand boy of the professionals, the strong one—a professional himself, politically adept and fully aware of the power system of his organization—can play a major role in changing its strategies.

Conditions of the Professional Bureaucracy

This third structural configuration appears wherever the operating core of an organization is dominated by skilled workers—professionals—who use procedures that are difficult to learn yet are well defined. This means an environment that is both complex and stable—complex enough to require the use of difficult procedures that can be learned only in extensive formal training programs, yet stable enough to enable these skills to become well defined, in effect, standardized. Thus, the environment is the chief contingency factor in the use of the Professional Bureaucracy.

In contrast, the factors of age and size are of less significance. Larger professional organizations tend to be somewhat more formalized (Holdaway et al., 1975; Bidwell, 1965, p. 1017)[2] and to have more fully developed staff support structures (Bidwell, 1965, p. 977). But that does not preclude the existence of small Professional Bureaucracies, or, for that matter, of young ones as well. The Machine Bureaucracy has a start-up time because the standards need to be worked out within the organization. Thus, it passes through a period of Simple Structure before its procedures become routinized. In the Professional Bureaucracy, in contrast, the skilled employees bring the standards into the organization with them when they join. So there is little start-up time. Put a group of doctors in a new hospital or a group of lawyers in a new law office and in no time they are functioning as if they had been there for years. Size would seem to be a relatively minor contingency factor for the same reason, and also because the professionals to a large extent work independently. One accountant working on his own adheres to the same professional standards as 2000 working in a giant firm. Thus, Professional Bureaucracies hardly pass through the stage of Simple Structure in their formative years.

Technical system is an important contingency factor, at least for what it is not in the Professional Bureaucracy—neither highly regulating, sophisticated, nor automated. The professional operators of this structural configuration require considerable discretion in their work. It is they who serve the clients, usually directly and personally. So the technical system cannot be highly regulating, certainly not highly automated. As Heydebrand and Noell (1973) point out, the professional resists the rationalization of his skills—their division into simply executed steps—because that makes them programmable by the technostructure, destroys his basis of autonomy, and drives the structure to the machine bureaucratic form.

Nor can the technical system be sophisticated. That would pull the professional into a closer working relationship with his colleagues and push him to a more distant one with his clients, driving the organization toward another structural configuration—the adhocratic form. The surgeon uses a scalpel, the accountant a pencil. Both must be sharp, but are otherwise simple and commonplace instruments; yet both allow their users to perform independently what can be exceedingly complex functions. More sophisticated instruments—such as the computer in the accounting firm or the coronary care unit in the hospital—reduce the professional's autonomy by forcing him to work in multidisciplinary teams, as he does in the Adhocracy. These teams are concerned in large part with the design, modification, and maintenance of the equipment; its operation, because that tends to be regulating, and often automated, impersonalizes the relationship between the professional and his clients. Thus, *in the pure form of the Professional Bureaucracy, the technology of the organization—its knowledge base—is sophisticated but its technical system—the set of instruments it uses to apply that knowledge base-is not.*

Thus, the prime example of the Professional Bureaucracy is the *personal service organization,* at least the one with complex, stable work. Schools and universities, consulting firms, law and accounting offices, social work agencies all rely on this structural configuration as long as they concentrate not on innovating in the solution of new problems, but on applying standard programs to well-defined ones. The same is true of hospitals, at least to the extent that their technical systems are simple. (In those areas that call for more sophisticated equipment—apparently a growing number, especially in teaching institutions—the hospital is driven toward a hybrid structure, with characteristics of the Adhocracy. The research function would also seem to drive it, and the university as well, toward the same hybrid, research being oriented more than clinical practice and teaching to innovation.[3] The same effect results from dynamic environmental conditions—again increasingly common in teaching hospitals. But all these forces are strongly mitigated by the hospital's overriding concern with safety. Only the tried and true can be used on regular patients. Institutions entrusted with the lives of their clients have a natural aversion to the looser, organic structures such as Adhocracy.)

A good deal of the service sector of contemporary society in fact applies standard programs to well-defined problems. Hence, the Professional Bureaucracy structure tends to predominate there. And with the enormous growth of this sector in the last few decades, we find that the Professional Bureaucracy has emerged as a major structural configuration.

So far, all of our examples have come from the service sector. But Professional Bureaucracies are found in manufacturing too, notably where the environment demands work that is complex yet stable, and the technical system is neither regulating nor sophisticated. This is the case of the *craft enterprise*, an important variant of the Professional Bureaucracy. Here the organization relies on skilled craftsmen who use relatively simple instruments to product standard outputs. The very term "craftsman" implies a kind of professional who learns traditional skills through long apprentice training and then is allowed to practice them free of direct supervision. Craft enterprises seem typically to have tiny administrations—no technostructures and few managers, many of whom, in any event, work alongside the craftsmen.

Many craftsmen were eliminated by the Industrial Revolution. Their jobs—for example, the making of shoes—were rationalized, and so control over them passed from the workers who did them to the analysts who designed them. Small craft enterprises metamorphosed into large Machine Bureaucracies. But some craft industries remain, for example, fine glasswork and handmade pottery, portrait photography, and gastronomic cuisine.[4] In fact, as these examples indicate, the term "craft" has today come to be associated with functional art, handmade items that perform a function but are purchased for their aesthetic value.

There is at least one major industry that has remained largely in the craft stage, and that is construction. In a paper entitled "Bureaucratic and Craft Administration of Production: A Comparative Study," Stinchcombe (1959–60) contrasts mass production and construction firms, describing the latter much as we have described Professional Bureaucracy. He notes that professionalization of the labor force in the construction industry serves the same functions as bureaucratic administration in mass production industries" (p. 169). In construction, "work processes [are] governed by the worker in accordance with the empirical lore that makes up craft principles" (p. 170). As a result, few clerks are needed (20 percent of the administrative personnel, versus 53 percent in mass production, where they are used, Stinchcombe explains, to effect machine bureaucratic control), the communication system is less formalized, and less emphasis is placed on the hierarchy of authority. Stinchcombe also cites another study of the construction industry that noted "the low development of distinctly bureaucratic production control mechanisms, such as cost accounting, detailed scheduling, regularized reporting of work process, and standardized inspection of specific operations" (p. 182).[5]

The markets of the Professional Bureaucracy are often diversified. As noted earlier, these organizations often bring together groups of professionals from different specialties who serve different types of clients. The hospital includes gynecologists to serve women, pediatricians to serve children, and so on, while the university has its philosophy professors to teach those interested in general knowledge and its management professors for those in search of specific career skills. Hypothesis 11 would lead us to the conclusion that such market diversity encourages the use of the market basis for grouping the professionals. In fact, we have already seen this to be the case (although we also saw that the market basis for grouping turns out to be equivalent to the functional one in Professional Bureaucracies, as a result of the way in which professional services are selected).

Sometimes the markets of Professional Bureaucracies are diversified geographically, leading to a variant we call the *dispersed professional bureaucracy*. Here the problem of maintaining loyalty to the organization becomes magnified, since the professionals do their autonomous work in remote locations, far from the administrative structure. The Royal

Canadian Mounted Police, for example, were dispersed across the Canadian west and north late last century to bring order to what were then lawless districts of the country. Once sent out, each Mountie was on his own. The same situation exists today in intelligence (spy) agencies, forest ranger services, and international consulting firms. As a result, these organizations must rely extensively on training and indoctrination, especially the latter. The employees are selected carefully, trained extensively, and indoctrinated heavily—often by the organization itself—before they are sent out to the remote areas to perform their work. Thus, even on their own, the Mounties carried the norms and skills of the R.C.M.P. with them and so served it resolutely. Moreover, the employees of the dispersed professional bureaucracy are frequently brought back to the central headquarters for a fresh dose of indoctrination, and they are often rotated in their jobs to ensure that their loyalty remains with the organization and does not shift to the geographical area they serve. The U.S. Forest Rangers, for example, are recruited largely from the forestry schools—having already demonstrated a commitment to forests and a love of the outdoors—and are then further trained and indoctrinated, and, once on the job, are rotated from post to post. Both the rotation and indoctrination "facilitate communication between headquarters and the field by keeping loyalties and career interests centrally directed" as well as keeping "the foresters independent of private interests in the regions or communities in which they serve . . ." (Wilensky, 1967, pp. 59–60; see also Kaufman, 1960).

This chapter has stressed the role of training in the Professional Bureaucracy more than indoctrination. Indoctrination only emerged as important in this last variant. But there is another variant, the *missionary organization*—common in religious orders, charitable foundations (Sills, 1957), and the like, and sometimes found also in business firms (Perrow, 1970, pp. 166–170)—where indoctrination replaces training as the key design parameter. Because this organization has an attractive mission, and perhaps a distinguished history as well, its members also share a strong ideology—a set of norms about the goals and strategies the organization pursues. The members may come by this naturally, or they may have been indoctrinated into the ideology when they first joined. In any event, because every member of the organization can be trusted to pursue its main goals and strategies, there can be an extensive decentralization to the level of the single individual, resulting in a structure that in some ways resembles the Professional Bureaucracy.

The Professional Bureaucracy is also occasionally found as a hybrid structure. In our discussion of hospitals earlier, we alluded to a possible combination with characteristics of the Adhocracy which we can call the *professional bureaucracy/adhocracy*. Another hybrid—the *simple professional bureaucracy*—occurs when highly trained professionals practicing standard skills nevertheless take their lead from a strong, sometimes even autocratic, leader, as in the Simple Structure. Consider, for example, the following description of a symphony orchestra, an organization staffed with highly skilled musicians who play standard repertoires:

> An orchestra is not a democracy but a dictatorship. The interpretation and presentation of this complex repertoire cannot be pieced together as a kind of consensus among the musicians.

> Such a system has been tried out, notably in Russia in the 1920's, but the famous conductorless orchestra, Persimfans, lasted only a few years. There were countless long rehearsals while the musicians argued about the treatment of every passage, and any one of the members was given the democratic right, in turn, to lay down his instrument and listen to the effect from the hall.

> It was finally decided that it would be much more efficient, and less costly, to allow one man of recognized ability to impose his ideas upon the rest of the orchestra, a conclusion the rest of the European orchestras had reached more than a century earlier...

I think it was one of Szell's musicians who was quoted as saying: "He's a sonovabitch, but he makes us play beyond ourselves."[6]

Finally, we might note briefly the effects of the contingency factors of power, notably fashion and the influence of the operators. Professionalism is a popular word among all kinds of identifiable specialists today; as a result, *Professional Bureaucracy is a highly fashionable structure*—and for good reason, since it is a very democratic one. Thus, it is to the advantage of every operator to make his job more professional—to enhance the skills it requires, to keep the analysts of the technostructure from rationalizing those skills, and to establish associations that set industry-wide standards to protect those skills. In these ways, the operator can achieve what always escapes him in the Machine Bureaucracy—control of his work and the decisions that affect it.

Some Issues Associated with Professional Bureaucracy

The Professional Bureaucracy is unique among the five structural configurations in answering two of the paramount needs of contemporary men and women. It is democratic, disseminating its power directly to its workers (at least those who are professional). And it provides them with extensive' autonomy, freeing them even of the need to coordinate closely with their peers, and all of the pressures and politics that entails. Thus, the professional has the best of both worlds: he is attached to an organization, yet is free to serve his clients in his own way, constrained only by the established standards of his profession.

As a result, professionals tend to emerge as responsible and highly motivated individuals, dedicated to their work and the clients they serve. Unlike the Machine Bureaucracy that places barriers between the operator and the client, this structure removes them, allowing a personal relationship to develop. Here the technical and social systems can function in complete harmony.

Moreover, *autonomy allows the professionals to perfect their skills, free of interference.* They repeat the same complex programs time after time, forever reducing the uncertainty until they get them just about perfect, like the Provençal potter who has spent his career perfecting the glazes he applies to identical pots. The professional's thought processes are "convergent"— vascular surgeon Spencer (1976) refers to them as deductive reasoning. Spencer quotes approvingly the bridge aficionado who stood behind champion Charles Goren during a three-day tournament and concluded: "He didn't do anything I couldn't do, except he didn't make any mistakes" (p. 1181). That captures nicely the secure feelings of professionals and their clients in Professional Bureaucracies. The Provençal potter expects few surprises when he opens his kiln; so, too, do Dr. Spencer's patients when they climb on to his operating table. They know the program has been executed so many times—by this surgeon as well as by the many whose experiences he has read about in the journals—that the possibility of mistakes has been minimized. Hospitals do not even get to execute new programs on regular patients until they have been thoroughly tested and approved by the profession. So the client of the Professional Bureaucracy can take satisfaction in the knowledge that the professional about to serve him will draw on vast quantities of experience and skill, will apply them in a perfected, not an experimental procedure, and will likely be highly motivated in performing that procedure.

But in these same characteristics of democracy and autonomy lie all the major problems of the Professional Bureaucracy. For *there is virtually no control of the work outside the profession, no way to correct deficiencies that the professionals themselves choose to overlook.* What they tend to overlook are the major problems of coordination, of discretion, and of innovation that arise in these structures.

Problems of Coordination

The Professional Bureaucracy can coordinate effectively only by the standardization of skills. Direct supervision and mutual adjustment are resisted as direct infringements on the professional's autonomy, in one case by administrators, in the other by peers. And standardization of work processes and of outputs are ineffective for this complex work with its ill-defined outputs. But *the standardization of skills is a loose coordinating mechanism at best, failing to cope with many of the needs that arise in the Professional Bureaucracy.*

There is, first of all, the need for coordination between the professional and the support staff. To the professional, that is simply resolved: he gives the orders. But that only catches the support staffer between two systems of power pulling in different ways, the vertical power of line authority above him, and the horizontal power of professional expertise to his side.

Perhaps more severe are the coordination problems between the professionals themselves. Unlike Machine Bureaucracies, Professional Bureaucracies are not integrated entities. They are collections of individuals who join to draw on the common resources and support services but otherwise want to be left alone. As long as the pigeonholing process works effectively, they can be. But that process can never be so good that contingencies do not fall in the cracks between the standard programs. The world is a continuous intertwined system. Slicing it up, although necessary to comprehend it, inevitably distorts it. Needs that fall at the margin or that overlap two categories tend to get forced —artificially—into one category or another. In contemporary medicine, for instance, the human body is treated not so much as one integrated system with interdependent parts, as a collection of loosely coupled organs that correspond to the different specialties. For the patient whose malady slots nicely into one of the specialties, problems of coordination do not arise. For others —for example, the patient who falls between psychiatry and internal medicine—it means repeated transfers in search of the right department, a time-consuming process when time is critical. In universities the pigeonholing process can be equally artificial, as in the case of the professor interested in the structure of production systems who fell between the operations and organizational behavior departments of his business school and so was denied tenure.

The pigeonholing process, in fact, emerges as the source of a great deal of the conflict of the Professional Bureaucracy. Much political blood is spilled in the continual reassessment of contingencies, imperfectly conceived, in terms of programs, artificially distinguished.

Problems of Discretion

The assumption underlying the design of the Professional Bureaucracy is that the pigeonholing process contains all of the uncertainty in single professional jobs. As we saw above, that assumption often proves false to the detriment of the organization's performance. But even where it works, problems arise. For it focuses all the discretion in the hands of single professionals, whose complex skills, no matter how standardized, require the exercise of considerable judgment. That is, perhaps, appropriate for professionals who are competent and conscientious. Unfortunately not all of them are; and *the professional bureaucratic structure cannot easily deal with professionals who are either incompetent or unconscientious.*

No two professionals are equally skilled. So the client who is forced to choose among them—to choose in ignorance, since he seeks professional help precisely because he lacks the specialized knowledge to help himself—is exposed to a kind of Russian Roulette, almost literally so in the case of medicine, where single decisions can mean life or death. But that is inevitable: little can be done aside from using the very best screening procedures for applicants to the training schools.

Of greater concern is the unconscientious professional—the one who refuses to update his skills after graduation, who cares more for his income than his clients, or who becomes so enamored with his skills that he forgets about the real needs of his clients. This last case represents a means-ends inversion common in Professional Bureaucracies, different from that found in Machine Bureaucracies but equally serious. In this case, the professional confuses the needs of his clients with the skills he has to offer them. He simply concentrates on the program that he favors —perhaps because he does it best or simply enjoys doing it most —to the exclusion of all the others. This presents no problem as long as only those clients in need of that favorite program are directed his way. But should other clients slip in, trouble ensues. Thus, we have the psychiatrists who think that all patients (indeed, all people) need psychoanalysis, the consulting firms prepared to design the same planning system for all their clients, no matter how dynamic their environments, the professors who use the lecture method for classes of 500 students or 5, the social workers who feel the compulsion to bring power to the people even when the people do not want it.

Dealing with this means-ends inversion is impeded by the difficulty of measuring the outputs of professional work. When psychiatrists cannot even define the words "cure" or "healthy," how are they to prove that psychoanalysis is better for manic-depressives than chemical therapy would be? When no one has been able to measure the learning that takes place in the classroom, how can it be demonstrated with reliability that lectures are better or worse than seminars or, for that matter, than staying home and reading. That is one reason why the obvious solution to the problems of discretion—censure by the professional association—is seldom used. Another is that professionals are notoriously reluctant to act against their own, to wash their dirty linen in public, so to speak. In extreme cases, they will so act—certain behavior is too callous to ignore. But these instances are relatively rare. They do no more than expose the tip of the iceberg of misguided discretion.

Discretion not only enables some professionals to ignore the needs of their clients; it also encourages many of them to ignore the needs of the organization. Professionals in these structures do not generally consider themselves part of a team. To many, the organization is almost incidental, a convenient place to practice their skills. They are loyal to their profession, not to the place where they happen to practice it. But the organization has need for loyalty, too—to support its own strategies, to staff its administrative committees, to see it through conflicts with the professional association. Cooperation, as we saw earlier, is crucial to the functioning of the administrative structure. Yet, as we also saw earlier, professionals resist it furiously. Professors hate to show up for curriculum meetings; they simply do not wish to be dependent on each other. One can say that they know each other only too well!

Problems of Innovation

In these structures, major innovation also depends on cooperation. Existing programs can be perfected by individual specialists. But new ones necessarily cut across existing specialties—in essence, they require a rearrangement of the pigeonholes—and so call for interdisciplinary efforts. As a result, the reluctance of the professionals to work cooperatively with each other translates itself into problems of innovation.

Like the Machine Bureaucracy, the Professional Bureaucracy is an inflexible structure, well suited to producing its standard outputs but ill-suited to adapting to the production of new ones. All bureaucracies are geared to stable environments; they are performance structures designed to perfect programs for contingencies that can be predicted, not problem solving ones designed to create new programs for needs that have never before been encountered.

The problems of innovation in the Professional Bureaucracy find their roots in convergent thinking, in the deductive reasoning of the professional who sees the specific situation in terms of the general concept. In the Professional Bureaucracy this means that new problems are forced into old pigeonholes. The doctoral student in search of an interdisciplinary degree—for, after all, isn't the highest university degree meant to encourage the generation of new knowledge—

inevitably finds himself forced back into the old departmental mode. "It must be a D.B.A. or a D.Ed.; we don't offer educational administration here." Nowhere are the effects of this deductive reasoning better illustrated than in Spencer's (1976) comments that "All patients developing significant complications or death among our three hospitals ... are reported to a central office with a narrative description of the sequence of events, with reports varying in length from a third to an entire page," and that six to eight of these cases are discussed in the one-hour weekly "mortality-morbidity" conferences, including presentation of it by the surgeon and "questions and comments" by the audience (p. 1181). An "entire" page and ten minutes of discussion for cases with "significant complications"! Maybe enough to list the symptoms and slot them into pigeonholes; hardly enough even to begin to think about creative solutions. As Lucy once told Charlie Brown, great art cannot be done in half an hour; it takes at least forty-five minutes!

The fact is that great art and innovative problem solving require *inductive* reasoning, that is, the induction of new general concepts or programs from particular experiences. That kind of thinking is *divergent*—it breaks away from old routines or standards rather than perfecting existing ones. And that flies in the face of everything the Professional Bureaucracy is designed to do.

So it should come as no surprise that Professional Bureaucracies and the professional associations that control their procedures tend to be conservative bodies, hesitant to change their well-established ways. Whenever an entrepreneurial member takes up the torch of innovation, great political clashes inevitably ensue. Even in the Machine Bureaucracy, once the managers of the strategic apex finally recognize the need for change, they are able to force it down the hierarchy. In the Professional Bureaucracy, with operator autonomy and bottom-up decision making, and in the professional association with its own democratic procedures, power for strategic change is diffuse. Everybody must agree on the change, not just a few managers or professional representatives. So change comes slowly and painfully, after much political intrigue and shrewd maneuvering by the professional and administrative entrepreneurs.

As long as the environment remains stable, the Professional Bureaucracy encounters no problem. It continues to perfect its skills and the given system of pigeonholes that slots them. But dynamic conditions call for change—new skills, new ways to slot them, and creative, cooperative efforts on the part of multidisciplinary teams of professionals. And that calls for another structural configuration, as we shall see in Chapter 21.

Dysfunctional Responses

What responses do the problems of coordination, discretion, and innovation evoke? Most commonly, those outside the profession—clients, nonprofessional administrators, members of the society at large and their representatives in government—see the problems as resulting from a lack of external control of the professional, and his profession. So they do the obvious: try to control the work with one of the other coordinating mechanisms. Specifically, they try to use direct supervision, standardization of work processes, or standardization of outputs.

Direct supervision typically means imposing an intermediate level of supervision, preferably with a narrow "span of control"—in keeping with the tenets of the classical concepts of authority—to watch over the professionals. That may work in cases of gross negligence. The sloppy surgeon or the professor who misses too many classes can be "spoken to" or ultimately perhaps fired. But specific professional activities—complex in execution and vague in results— are difficult to control by anyone other than the professionals themselves. So the administrator detached from the work and bent on direct supervision is left nothing to do except engage in bothersome exercises. As in the case of certain district supervisors who sit between one Montreal school board and its schools and, according to the reports of a number of principals, spend time telephoning them at 4:59 on Friday afternoons to ensure they have not left early for the weekend. The imposition of such intermediate levels of supervision stems from the assumption that professional work can be controlled, like any other, in a top-down manner, an assumption that has proven false again and again.

Likewise, the other forms of standardization, instead of achieving control of the professional work, often serve merely to impede and discourage the professionals. And for the same reasons—the complexity of the work and the vagueness of its outputs. Complex work processes cannot be formalized by rules and regulations, and vague outputs cannot be standardized by planning and control systems. Except in misguided ways, which program the wrong behaviors and measure the wrong outputs, forcing the professionals to play the machine bureaucratic game—satisfying the standards instead of serving the clients. Back to the old means-ends inversion. Like the policeman in Chicago who described to Studs Terkel (1972) the effects of various such standards on his work:

> My supervisor would say, "We need two policy arrests, so we can be equal with the other areas." So we go out and hunt for a policy operator . . . .
>
> A vice officer spends quite a bit of time in court. You learn the judges, the things they look for. You become proficient in testifying. You change your testimony, you change the facts. You switch things around 'cause you're trying to get convictions . . . .
>
> Certain units in the task force have developed a science around stopping your automobile. These men know it's impossible to drive three- blocks without committing a traffic violation. We've got so many rules on the books. These police officers use these things to get points and also hustle for money. The traffic law is a fat book. He knows if you don't have two lights on your license plate, that's a violation. If you have a crack in your windshield, that's a violation. If your muffler's dragging, that's a violation. He knows all these little things.
>
> So many points for a robbery, so many points for a man having a gun. When they go to the scene and the man with the gun has gone, they'll lock up somebody anyway, knowing he's not the one. The record says, "Locked up two people for UUW"—unlawful use of weapons. The report will say, "When we got there, we saw these guys and they looked suspicious." They'll get a point even if the case is thrown out of court. The arrest is all that counts (pp. 137–140).

Graphic illustrations of the futility of trying to control work that is essentially professional in nature. Similar things happen when accountants try to control the management consulting arms of their firms—"obedience is stressed as an end in itself because the CPA as administrator is not able to judge the non-accountant expert on the basis of that expert's knowledge" (Montagna, 1968: 144). And in school systems when the government technostructure believes it can program the work of the teacher, as in that of East Germany described proudly to this author by a government planner, where each day every child in the country ostensibly opens the same book to the same page. The individual needs of the students—slow learners and fast, rural and urban—as well as the individual styles of the teachers have to be subordinated to the neatness of the system.

The fact is that complex work cannot be effectively performed unless it comes under the control of the operator who does it. Society may have to control the overall expenditures of its Professional Bureaucracies—to keep the lid on them—and to legislate against the most callous kinds of professional behavior. But too much external control of the professional work itself leads, according to Hypothesis 14, to centralization and formalization of the structure, in effect driving the Professional Bureaucracy to Machine Bureaucracy. The decision-making power flows from the operators to the managers, and on to the analysts of the technostructure. The effect of this is to throw the baby out with the bathwater. Technocratic controls do not improve professional-type work, nor can they distinguish between responsible and irresponsible behavior—they constrain both equally. That may, of course, be appropriate for organizations in which responsible behavior is rare. But where it is not—presumably the majority of cases—*technocratic controls only serve to dampen professional conscientiousness.* As Sorensen and Sorensen (1974) found, the more machine bureaucratic the large public accounting firms, the more they experienced conflict and job dissatisfaction.

Controls also upset the delicate relationship between the professional and his client, a relationship predicated on unimpeded personal contact between the two. Thus, Cizanckas, a police chief, notes that the police officer at the bottom of the pecking order in the "paramilitary structure" is more than willing, in turn, to vent his frustration on the lawbreaker" (paraphrased by Hatvany, 1976, p. 73). The controls remove the responsibility for service from the professional and place it in the administrative structure, where it is of no use to the client. It is not the government that teaches the student, not even the school system or the school itself; it is not the hospital that delivers the baby, not the police force that apprehends the criminal, not the welfare department that helps the distraught family. These things are done by the individual professional. If that professional is incompetent, no plan or rule fashioned in the technostructure, no order from an administrator can ever make him competent. But such plans, rules, and orders can impede the competent professional from providing his service effectively. At least rationalization in the Machine Bureaucracy leaves the client with inexpensive outputs. In the case of professional work, it leaves him with impersonal, ineffective service.

Furthermore, the incentive to perfect, even to innovate—the latter weak in the best of times in professional bureaucracy—can be reduced by external controls. In losing control over their own work, the professionals become passive, like the operators of the Machine Bureaucracy. Even the job of professional administrator—never easy—becomes extremely difficult with a push for external control. In school systems, for example, the government looks top-down to the senior managers to implement its standards, while the professionals look bottom-up to them to resist the standards. The strategic apex gets caught between a government technostructure hungry for control and an operating core hanging on to its autonomy for dear life. No one gains in the process.

Are there then no solutions to a society concerned about its Professional Bureaucracies? Financial control of Professional Bureaucracies and legislation against irresponsible professional behavior are obviously necessary. But beyond that, must the professional be left with a blank check, free of public accountability? Solutions are available, but they grow from a recognition of professional work for what it is. *Change in the Professional Bureaucracy does not sweep in from new administrators taking office to announce major reforms, nor from government technostructures intent on bringing the professionals under control. Rather, change seeps in, by the slow process of changing the professionals—changing who can enter the profession, what they learn in its professional schools (ideals as well as skills and knowledge), and thereafter how willing they are to upgrade their skills.* Where such changes are resisted, society may be best off to call on the professionals' sense of responsibility to serve the public, or, failing that, to bring pressures on the professional associations rather than on the Professional Bureaucracies.

Notes

[1]For an excellent related example—a comparison of the prison as a Machine Bureaucracy (custodial-oriented) and as a Professional Bureaucracy (treatment-oriented)—see Cressey (1958; or 1965, pp. 1044-1048). Van de Ven and Delbecq (1974) also discuss this trichotomy in terms of "systematized" programs, which specify both means and ends in detail, "discretionary" programs, which specify ends and a repertoire of means but require the operator to select the means in terms of the ends, and "developmental" programs, for highly variable tasks, which may specify general ends but not the means to achieve them.

[2] Boland (1973) finds them also to be more democratic, which seems to stem from their being more formalized: "The faculty in the larger institutions are much more likely to develop a strong faculty government. Those in the smaller institutions, on the other hand, are more often subject to the decrees of

administrative officials" (p. 636). This seems akin to the situation Crozier described, where the operators of large bureaucratic organizations force in rules to protect their interests. But that seems to work more to the operators' advantage in Professional rather than in Machine Bureaucracies, in the former case the rules setting up the means for true self-government, in the latter, serving only to protect the workers from the arbitrary whims of their bosses.

[3]However, Kuhn's (1970) description of the practice of scientific research gives the distinct impression that most of the time —namely during periods of what he calls "normal" science, when the researchers are essentially elaborating and perfecting a given "paradigm"—the professional bureaucratic structure might be equally appropriate. Only during scientific "revolutions" should the adhocratic one clearly be more relevant.

[4]Restaurants can be viewed as falling into the manufacturing or service sectors, depending on whether one focuses on the preparation of the food or on the serving of it.

[5]Stinchcombe also ascribes some of these structural characteristics to the dynamic nature of the construction industry's environment, which pushes the firms to adopt the organic features of Simple Structure or Adhocracy.

[6] From "MSD Crisis Plus ça change" by E. McLean, Canada Wide Feature Service in the Montreal Star, December 4, 1976. Used with permission.

Performance and Paralysis: The Organizational Context of the American Research University

Daniel Alpert

Introduction: Universities in Transition

> Organizationally the university is, in fact, one of the most complex structures in modern society; it is also increasingly archaic. It is complex because its formal structure does not describe either actual power or responsibilities; it is archaic because the functions it must perform are not and cannot be discharged through the formal structure provided in its charter.
>
> James A. Perkins [35, p. 3]

> [Organizational] learning cannot proceed effectively without maps which can be used to relate errors to features within the organization. Maps. . . are organized pictures which show how the features of the system have been placed in some sort of pattern which illuminates the interdependence among the parts of the system.
>
> Chris Argyris and Donald A. Schön, [2, p. 159]

Despite a record of remarkable performance since World War II, American universities have been facing increasingly hard times in the 1970s and 1980s. The current period of economic retrenchment has called into sharp focus the question of the nation's commitment to its institutions of higher education and equally serious questions regarding the responsibilities of universities to society. Retrenchment has also revealed within the academy serious problems relating to management and governance, on the one hand, and identity and purpose on the other. The symptoms of trouble include loss of confidence in the future, decline in faculty morale, and a slowdown of the infusion of talented young recruits into graduate study. Paradoxically, these problems have intensified at the same time that corporations declare their entry into the "knowledge business" as a new growth industry, and technological revolutions in computers and telecommunications herald the arrival of the "information age."

In the early 1970s, a study by Lanier and Anderson [28, p. 77] for the American Council on Education found "massive evidence of widespread retrenchment in higher education." Since then, universities have experienced continuing financial restraints but have dealt with each subsequent cutback as a short-term crisis. In 1981, Robert Barak [5, p. 213] observed that "little has changed since 1976. Higher education still desperately needs an ongoing and continuous strategic approach to management." And Herman Neibuhr, Jr. of Temple University concurs: "Retrenchment may be a short range solution to avoid deficits, but it is hardly a strategy to pursue until the year 2000" [33, p. 16]. But the perceived need for long-range strategies is in marked contrast to the short-term, belt-tightening tactics that have dominated academic responses to retrenchment for more than a decade.

Any organization confronting a period of retrenchment is faced with a central dilemma: should it respond by increasing organizational efficiency or should it embark on innovative efforts to improve effectiveness? As these terms are defined by Pfeffer and Salancik [38, p. 11], "organizational efficiency is an *internal* standard of performance. . . The question whether what is being done should be done is not posed, but only how well it is being done. Efficiency is measured by the ratio of resources utilized to output produced." In contrast, "the effectiveness of an organization is its ability to create acceptable outcomes and actions . . . [it] is an *external* standard of how well an organization is meeting the demands of the various groups and organizations that are concerned with its activities." The efficiency-effectiveness dilemma has been phrased in terms of organizational learning by Argyris and Schön [2, pp. 18–26] as follows: Does the situation call for "singleloop" organizational learning, that is, retaining the existing norms, goals, and structures and doing better the things we are now doing? Or does it call for "double-loop" learning, that is, reformulating the norms, goals, and structures and embarking in innovative directions to create acceptable outcomes? Petrie and Alpert [37] define the central problem of retrenchment in higher education as the necessity to choose sensibly between these alternatives. Whetten [58] argues persuasively that the single-loop search for greater efficiency has dominated academic responses to retrenchment because of our greater ability to measure efficiency and the difficulty of conclusively settling debates over goals and priorities. Argyris and Schön [2] assert that the tendency to limit organizational learning to single-loop learning is so strong that new organizational maps and new theories that govern organizational actions—what they call "theories-in-use"—are required even to postulate alternative strategies.

Not surprisingly, the difficulties associated with retrenchment have most often been framed in financial terms, and in some ways, this approach to defining the problems makes them simpler to handle: financial problems cannot indefinitely be deferred or ignored, and the language is widely understood. Furthermore, budget shortages do not suggest failures of leadership and do not of themselves call for major modification of internal goals or ways of doing things; if money could somehow be found, the organization could go about its business as usual. In short, financial difficulties are attributable to changes in the external economic environment, an arena in which universities are presumed to have little control. But to many observers (e.g., Boyer and Hechinger [11], Mingle and Associates [31], Richman and Farmer [41]) the cutbacks associated with recent retrenchment are coincident with significant, longer term structural and attitudinal changes in the society, which themselves constitute demands for changes in higher education. In this view, the financial crunch of the past fifteen years is a symptom as well as a problem—a symptom of difficulties that reside not in the financial environment but in the way universities respond. To these thoughtful observers, retrenchment is partly an indication that our universities are not sufficiently adaptive or responsive to the needs of society.

Faced with retrenchment, the dominant tendency within academic institutions has been to deal with each budget reduction as though it were unique to the institution in question, to contend among departments in a zero-sum game for the limited available resources, and to seek to maintain the status quo. In the absence of clear lines of authority or consensus among equals, even a minimal cutback (a few percent) can reduce a highly regarded campus to a state of sharp confrontation, low morale, and serious discontent. The resulting impasse constitutes what Yarmolinsky calls "institutional paralysis": "One of the more remarkable things about universities . . . Is that, with a few honorable exceptions, they have managed to survive, and even to prosper, without developing any conscious process for making institutional choices" [59, p. 61]. Institutional paralysis is a result, Yarmolinsky argues, of "four major disfunctions within the body politic. . . . no one group in the university has all the factors necessary for institutional change: the concern, the status, the authority, and the equipment to achieve institutional change" [59, p. 61]. In his view, the system of governance is hopelessly inadequate, and he proposes some significant organizational changes. In the opinion of Eric Ashby, another astute observer of the academic scene, institutional paralysis is also attributable to serious differences among academics regarding the purposes of the enterprise. More than a decade ago, he warned that "the gravest single problem facing American higher education is [the] alarming disintegration of consensus about purpose . . . [This grave threat] requires a reevaluation of the relation between universities and American society" [4, p. 104]. To deal with this problem, he proposed an internal "restoration of consensus within the academic community about the rights and responsibilities of universities in society . . ." [4, p. 105].

Despite the cogency of these observations, little attention has been given to these and similar exhortations for change—either in the governance of universities or in the formulation of their purposes. That such powerfully stated concerns have been largely ignored in academic deliberations of the past decade may be a symptom in itself—perhaps a symptom that Yarmolinsky is correct in his assertion that none of the constituencies has the capacity to effect change. Perhaps their admonitions have been disregarded because Yarmolinsky and Ashby did not place the problems in an organizational context that would suggest a workable process for corrective action. In any event, exhortations to the academic community-at-large must necessarily go unheeded if each of the individual constituencies believes they are addressed to someone else.

These circumstances add weight to the need for appropriate organizational models, which are needed in any complex organization to aid in the framing of institutional problems and in identifying the system domain in which they should be addressed. In the case of the university, the problems are obfuscated and made even more intractable because the formal organizational chart of the university is such a poor representation of reality. Hence, students of academic organizational behavior have for some time found it necessary to develop alternative models as a framework for investigation, Among the models that have been described in the organizational literature are the collegial model, the bureaucratic model, the political model, and the organized anarchy model, each emphasizing different aspects of the university, as suggested metaphorically by their names (for a survey, see Garvin [22] or Richman and Farmer [411]. However, as Garvin points out, most of them share a key drawback: "they focus exclusively on internal decision-making rules and procedures, while paying little attention to the environment in which universities operate" [22, p. 4]. Garvin [22, p. 21] has proposed a utility maximizing model, using an economic approach that pays special attention to the motivation and goals of the key actors. Richman and Farmer [41] describe the university in terms of an open-systems approach [25], which takes into account the external environment. Each of these models has merit and, in many ways, they are complementary. But because they are typically process models, focusing on different actors in the academic community, the relationships among the models is unclear. They provide little insight into the structural relationships within the university and do not clearly define the interdependence among the parts of the overall system.

This article presents a new descriptive model, a matrix model, that was developed in an attempt to portray the organizational structure and practices of the university and to locate organizational problems in a problem-solving space. The motivation for creating a new map arose from an ongoing study of universities' responses to retrenchment (for other reports of this inquiry, see Whetten [57] and Petrie and Alpert [37]) that identified many paradoxes, incongruities, and inconsistencies not only in the rhetoric used to describe the problem issues but in the underlying structures and theories-in-use. The matrix model is intended to portray in concise and visual terms some key features of the organization, mission, and inner workings of the university while also describing its relationships with the external environment. This model is not based on new theories of organizational behavior or on new data relating to the operational characteristics of the institutions. Rather, it is intended to portray and make sense of various features of organizational behavior that have been observed by others; it incorporates or is compatible with many key features of the models mentioned above. The matrix model takes as its reality the modern comprehensive research university as described by such authorities as Kerr [26], Perkins [35], Jencks and Riesman [24], and Cohen and March [15]. Although it could be modified to include most of the 240 institutions offering the Ph.D., the model is specifically focused on the 100 or so leading universities that confer more than 95 percent of these degrees and are identified as "research universities" in *A Classification of Institutions of Higher Education (Revised Edition 1976)* issued by the Carnegie Foundation for the Advancement of Teaching.

This presentation starts with a simple linear model of the university, as proposed by Alpert [37], and then the matrix model is developed. Initially generated as an organizational map of a given campus, the matrix model has also evolved as a descriptive model of the American university system as an interdependent whole. Next, the matrix model is utilized to provide a context for some major dissonances and incongruities in the academic enterprise that have been highlighted by retrenchment and to suggest directions for organizational learning. Special attention is given to changing expectations and demands and the need for addressing the different and often conflicting purposes of the overall university system. Finally, the need for new maps for the future university is discussed and some observations about settings for creating them are offered.

A Linear Model of the University

> It is generally agreed that institutions of higher learning are best understood as collections of fundamentally autonomous units rather than in terms of a central authority, or conception of a whole, to which they are subordinate. Departments were . . . designed to avoid curricular chaos and to shift power from the president to the faculty.
>
> Elizabeth Coleman [16, p. 48]

Figure 1

Linear Model of the University

Structure
$$U = \boxed{d_1} + \boxed{d_2} + \boxed{d_3} + \boxed{d_4} + \boxed{d_5} + \cdots + \boxed{d_n}$$

Quality
$$Q = \boxed{q_1} + \boxed{q_2} + \boxed{q_3} + \boxed{q_4} + \boxed{q_5} + \cdots + \boxed{q_n}$$

Mission
$$M = \boxed{m_1} + \boxed{m_2} + \boxed{m_3} + \boxed{m_4} + \boxed{m_5} + \cdots + \boxed{m_n}$$

The idea of a matrix model of the modern research university started with a "linear model" used by Petrie and Alpert [37, p. 107] to describe the university's structure, its internally perceived mission, and many aspects of its organizational behavior under conditions of budgetary restraint. As shown in Figure 1, the linear model embodies Coleman's description. It portrays the university as a set of autonomous academic departments and professional schools, each represented by a separate rectangle and tied together by its institutional identity, geographic location, administration, support services, and board of trustees. It is a classic example of a "loosely coupled" organization as described by Weick [56]; in its basic structure, the whole is identical to the sum of its departmental parts.

The linear model goes beyond the portrayal of organizational structure; it symbolizes the perceived institutional mission as well. The basic departmental mission is considered to be "the pursuit of excellence," interpreted by most faculty members and administrators as the successful, self-directed search for new knowledge in the many areas of specialization of the comprehensive research university. The assessment of academic quality is identified with the quality of the research in the various disciplines and professional fields and is carried out through the process of peer group evaluation. The most prevalent measure of departmental quality has come to be its prestige among peer groups, that is, its comparative standing in a national ordering assembled by colleagues in the discipline [12, 18, 43]. For many academics, the improvement of prestige has become the departmental mission itself [22]. Given these perceptions, the mission of the university is seen as the sum of its departmental missions and the quality of the institution is seen as the separately measured quality of its departments. In both structure and mission, therefore, the whole of the university has come to be viewed as the sum of its individual departmental parts. As a result, the proposed responses to external crises are largely restricted to those which can be handled with the available resources, personnel, and motivation of the individual units.

The next section identifies the connections that relate the departments to external stakeholders, giving added insights about institutional behavior. However, even in the absence of a description of the external environment, the linear model serves to portray many of the characteristics of the modern research university, some of which are:

1. The department has become the key unit of academic life; it is virtually autonomous in such important functions as appointments and selection of areas of research emphasis, setting standards for individual faculty performance, and establishing curricular and degree requirements for students.
2. The decentralized organizational structure and the project system for the support of research are well-suited to the scientific research activities of the university; they have helped to make American academic scientists the world-leaders in almost every discipline.
3. Due to the autonomy of departments and the lack of shared goals, retrenchment has been accompanied by an increase in competition for scarce resources among departments and a resulting loss of faculty morale.
4. The faculty senate has lost status and effectiveness as a factor in campus governance.

The linear model helps to explain the very different organizational responses of the university under conditions of growth and of retrenchment. During the growth period of the 1950s and 1960s, the increasingly decentralized system of governance was highly adaptive. Change took place by enlarging the institution, keeping the old structure intact and adding new academic units under the stimulus of readily available federal research funds and the rapid growth in student enrollments. Academic units were added to accommodate new research activities, developed by outstanding faculty members with entrepreneurial instincts; at the same time, many existing departments also grew substantially. New programs, departments, and institutes were seen as contributors to the prestige of the institution, and there was relatively little opposition to their formation, provided they did not directly compete with existing units. Proposals to add units were often based on the availability of new sources of external funding and did not call for existing units to give up their claims on resources. The period of growth was accompanied by greatly increased responsibilities for the individual professor, especially the successful scientific researcher. Faculty members became entrepreneurs, assuming responsibilities for proposal-writing and project management, recruiting graduate assistants, completing annual reports, consulting in Washington, and sitting on peer review panels—all in addition to previous commitments to teaching undergraduates and guiding graduate students. Given the academic reward system, recognition of research by one's peers in the discipline had a much higher priority than concerns about the internal governance of the campus. In any event, the successful professor felt much too busy to sit through tedious faculty senate meetings on issues of minor import. Thus, for individual as well as institutional reasons, the system of faculty participation in the governance of the overall university atrophied.

In times of retrenchment, slack is reduced and competition among units increases; maintaining support for one department implies reducing support for others. In the absence of consensus on priorities or of effective mechanisms for making institutional choices, there are few alternatives for the various departments but to dig in and protect their political turf. Thus, the decentralization that was highly adaptive during a period of expansion becomes maladaptive in times of retrenchment. To reduce or eliminate programs in times of retrenchment is far more difficult than to add them in times of growth.

The linear model of the university helps to clarify some of the dilemmas of current university life, providing insights into such issues as:

1. why faculty members define the overall mission of the university solely in terms of their individual departmental missions and consider adaptation to change possible only in the same terms;
2. why proposed changes, budgetary or otherwise, justified in the larger campus interest, are perceived primarily in terms of departmental interests;
3. why the accepted mechanisms for assessing departmental performance severely limit modification of structure or change in institutional priorities;
4. why the expectations of external stakeholders, to whom the university is presented (by the administration) as a single organization with clearly defined institutional structure and goals, are often at odds with the expectations of faculty members.

At the same time, the linear model has inherent limitations. It says little about the relationship of the university to the external environment; the linear model does not illuminate the external mechanisms for the evaluation of internal performance nor does it differentiate between sources of financial support and how these affect the mission and governance of the university. By looking inward to the university campus, the linear model suffers from one of the limitations experienced by the universities themselves; that is, it highlights internal barriers to change without providing insights into external constraints. The next section expands the linear model to include the roles of institutions and actors external to the local campus and their effects on its administration, governance, and mission.

The Matrix Model

> To understand the behavior of an organization you must understand the context of that behavior—that is, the ecology of the organization.... No organization is completely self-contained or in complete control of the conditions of its own existence.
>
> Jeffrey Pfeffer and Gerald R. Salancik [38, p. 1; 19]

A matrix is constructed by presenting in one diagram the linear models for the n leading universities in the nation ($U_1, U_2, U_3, \ldots U_n$). As shown in Figure 2, each linear representation is placed above the other, and the departments at the various universities are aligned one above the other, so that all anthropology departments, for example, are in the same column. Thus any given department, d_{ij}, is located on a row corresponding to a specified university (U_i) and in a column corresponding to a specified discipline (D_j). It is immediately apparent that each department has special relationships with the other departments in its own row, which represents the campus community, and with the other departments in its own column, which represents the disciplinary community. Each of these, the horizontal and the vertical communities, may be viewed as a loosely coupled system, with significantly different forms of coupling in the horizontal and vertical directions. The departments in a given row (campus) share the same institutional name, geographic location, board of trustees, and overall organizational identity, while the departments in a given column are coupled in other significant ways, for example, professional missions, research activities, and reward and recognition systems.

Figure 2

Matrix Model of the Research University

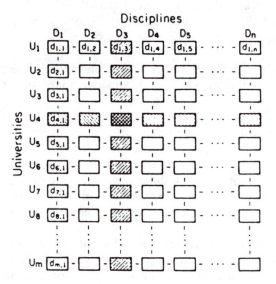

Historically, the increase in the relative influence of the disciplinary communities has been continuous since the turn of the century, as the mission of universities has shifted from the dissemination of known truths to the search for new knowledge [47, 54]. As Perkins has observed, "Before the nineteenth century, a primary rationale for scholarship or research was its impact on teaching. . . . Today teaching and research are missions with distinctive styles and different, often contradictory, requirements for organizational structure. The differences are important" [35, pp. 6–7]. The shift in emphasis from teaching to research as the primary institutional goal was accompanied by a related but different organizational change—a change which Jencks and Riesman [24] refer to as "the academic revolution"—the transfer of authority in academic matters from the president to the faculty. The emergence of the disciplinary communities as the arbiters of institutional life corresponds to the takeover by the professoriate of the dominant role in the governance of the university. This shift was accelerated by the entry of the federal government as a major source of funds allocated directly to individual researchers and handled by their departments. A principal consequence of the enlargement of the federal role was to hasten the decentralization of the individual university; the various departments became more independent of the internal administration and more dependent on the support of external constituencies.

The roles of the campus and disciplinary communities in the life of the typical department can readily be identified with the academic functions that the departmental staff is called on to carry out. Table 1 lists those functions and responsibilities that are primarily associated with one or the other of the two communities. By and large, the horizontal (campus) community addresses itself to the undergraduate teaching mission of the university, whereas the vertical (disciplinary) community addresses itself primarily to graduate education, research, and faculty selection and performance. The campus community was originally shaped and its structure defined by the teaching mission of the university. For alumni, for state legislators, and for many of its friends and benefactors, the teaching mission still represents the principal goal of the university as an educational institution. It is the campus community that relates and is meaningful to undergraduate students, student organizations, and student life. In the university of today, the disciplinary communities have assumed the central responsibilities not only for graduate and professional education, but also for setting the goals, justifying and selling research agendas to federal sponsors, allocating academic research grants, and implementing the peer review process for the rating of individual and departmental quality. To department heads, the disciplinary community establishes standards for faculty and departmental performance, manages the professional societies and refereed journals, and staffs the advisory panels controlling the dispersal of federal research funding. The sister departments in the disciplinary community constitute the sources of talent for graduate students and faculty recruits. To individual faculty members at comprehensive research universities, the national disciplinary community is typically more meaningful to their professional careers and more familiar in terms of culture and day-to-day contacts than are faculty members in the other departments on their own campus.

Table 1

Community Responsibilities and Activities	
Campus Community	Disciplinary Community
Undergraduate education	Graduate education and research
Student life	
Shared facilities: library, physical plant	Professional journals, meetings
Faculty appointments	Peer review system
Faculty security: tenure	Faculty mobility
Campus governance	Accreditation boards
Campus administration	Professional societies
Allocation of institutional funds	Allocation of research grants and contracts

If every university in the nation had the same number and identity of departments and professional schools, the representation of all universities in Figure 2 would be the same and the matrix would be completely symmetrical. Obviously, there are differences in the departmental make-up of comprehensive universities; in fact, the number of departments among research universities varies substantially, ranging from about fifty to more than a hundred. In the matrix diagram, the absence of a given department or professional school is indicated by a vacancy in the regular structure; if a given university does not have a department of astronomy or a school of agriculture, these units do not appear on the corresponding row of the matrix. The greatest variance among institutions lies in the number and identity of their professional schools, a factor which makes for differences in campus ambiance and stated mission. But the professional colleges themselves are aligned in national "disciplinary communities" that, like the departments of arts and sciences, are characterized more by their similarities than their differences. By and large, the basic linear array of departments fits sensibly into a matrix. As is evidenced by the various comparative assessments of graduate and professional programs, there are few among the major research universities that do not organize and identify their disciplines and professional departments in similar ways.

The similarity of departmental organization and goals is itself an indicator of the power exercised by the national disciplinary communities in setting the standards and scholarly goals of American universities. In a few recently established campuses, for example, the University of California at Santa Cruz and the University of Illinois at Chicago, there were at the outset significant departures from the norm, with unorthodox organizational structures intended to support a distinctive campus mission. After the first few years of operation, however, the pressures (both internal and external) to adopt more conventional structure and mission were inexorable; except for a few departures from standard nomenclature, both campuses today fit comfortably on the matrix diagram.

The significant influence of the disciplinary communities in the mission and composition of universities is enhanced by the activities of a number of professional, economic, and political institutions external to any given campus. Providing services and support to the academic community, they obviously belong in the matrix diagrams as extensions of the vertical (disciplinary) columns as shown schematically in Figure 3; they include: (1) federal agencies and private research foundations, (2) accrediting agencies, (3) national professional associations (e.g., American Psychological Association), (4) associations of practicing professionals (e.g., American Medical Association), (5) client organizations (e.g., the American Farm Bureau), and (6) national laboratories (e.g., the Fermilab high energy physics facility).

Since World War II, the federal sponsorship of academic research has played a crucial role in the strengthening of the disciplinary communities. In fact, the sponsoring agencies can be considered integral parts of the disciplinary communities. And the sponsors' contributions to academic research are reciprocated by the key roles that the disciplinary communities play in the management of the agencies. Academic researchers sit on advisory committees, carry out the peer review of grant proposals, and help to recruit the disciplinary colleagues who make up the agency staffs. Channeled through the vertical columns of the matrix, federal research support is allocated directly to individual principal investigators in the form of grants and contracts. Although the institution is allotted a share of the funding in the form of indirect costs, the central university administration is typically bypassed or plays only a minor role in a process that cumulatively defines the priorities, the staffing, and the research mission of the institution. In Washington, the allocation of federal funds among the many agencies and subdivisions is carried out in a complex political process involving the executive and legislative branches of government, the agencies themselves, and the intellectual leaders of the disciplines. With few exceptions, the central administrators of universities play a minor role in determining federal research policy or the allocating of federal funds to the various disciplines.

The supportive relationship of powerful external organizations to the disciplinary communities has its counterpart in a similar array of organizations that relate directly to the campus communities. As shown schematically in the horizontal communities of Figure 3, these external campus-related organizations include: (1) state governments, (2) students (tuition) and private donors, (3) alumni associations, (4) university foundations, and (5) councils of American educators and universities. Both the sources and uses of institutional funding are identified strongly with the undergraduate educational mission, especially at private universities, where student tuition and alumni giving comprise major portions of the overall budget. In public (state-supported) universities, the institutional funding from the state government is also identified with the undergraduate teaching function, though it may include support for graduate education and research as well. Institutional funds are not allocated directly to departments or individual faculty members but go to the campus and are dispensed through the office of the president or chancellor.

Figure 3

External Support Agencies and Associations. Disciplinary support in the vertical column; institutional support in the horizontal row.

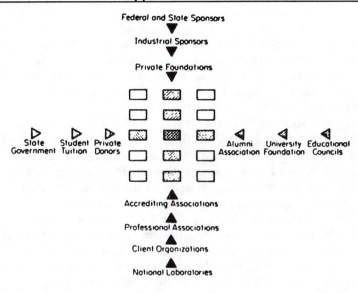

Figure 4 includes in the matrix both the horizontal and vertical groups of external organizations. The differences in the character of these external stake-holders are matched by the wide differences in the purposes of the academic activities with which they identify.

Figure 4

Matrix Model including External Agencies and Internal Cross-Disciplinary Research Units

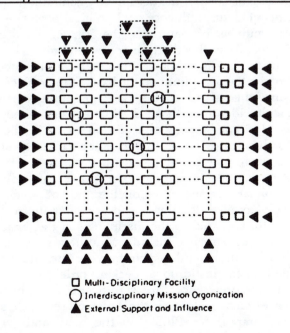

The Rating of Disciplinary Communities: Role of Intellectual Leaders

I have previously referred to the quality rating of academic departments and have commented on the importance of these ratings in the lives of the institutions. Carried out by the disciplinary communities, the comparative ratings of departments reflect their reputations for research excellence and have had an enormous effect on the internal organizational behavior of the universities [22, 37]. A department with a rating substantially above others on campus has great leverage in the internal competition for resources, appointments to key committees, and faculty perquisites such as lower teaching loads and higher salaries. Taken together, the various departmental ratings comprise an informal institutional rating, which represents the university's comparative standing among institutions.

In a matrix diagram such as Figure 4, it is possible, at least in principle, to identify each major university in the nation and, based on the published ratings of its departments, to arrange the universities in descending order of institutional excellence from top to bottom. Thus, the matrix diagram could be used as a convenient way of recording both the departmental and institutional ratings for every research university in the nation. The chart could also be used to identify the departments on a given campus that are well above or below the rating of the institution as a whole. That institutional ratings have not been formally published is due to certain ambiguities in the relation of institutional ratings to departmental ratings. If all departments were equally valued, the institutional rating would logically be derived by taking the average of the departmental ratings. In fact, however, the disciplines are not considered to be of equal importance to the status of a research university; a physics department rated twentieth in the nation typically has more status and power on its campus than a Spanish department rated tenth. That is to say, the disciplinary communities themselves vary in status and size just as do the campus communities. Although no comparable ranking among disciplines has been published or widely acknowledged, a survey of the nation's research campuses today would quickly reveal commonly held opinions of the relative status of corresponding departments.

In principle, then, just as the campus communities could be ordered along the vertical axis of the matrix in terms of prestige or quality, the disciplinary communities could be arranged along the horizontal axis in terms of status, affluence, and political power. An appraisal of the status of the disciplines reveals a number of features of the organizational behavior of universities and their leadership. Because it is the disciplinary communities that rate the campuses in terms of their contributions to the disciplines, it might be anticipated that it would be the campus communities who rate the disciplines on the basis of their perceived contributions to the campuses. In some measure, this is indeed the case; in setting curricular requirements, for example, the campus faculty identifies those disciplines considered most central. On some campuses, however, special circumstances of tradition or of intellectual or administrative leadership may lead to disparities between local departmental status and that of their national discipline: that is, there may be high status departments in disciplines that are weak or vice versa. To the extent that such variations exist, the campus communities can be said to affect the ratings of disciplinary communities on the "micro" level. But since internal and external factors are strongly coupled, there is a widespread pattern of similarity among the nation's campuses in the status accorded to the disciplines on the "macro" level. Currently, for example, the high status departments include computer science, electrical engineering, chemistry, business administration, and psychology—quite independent of whether the university is fifth or fiftieth in the institutional pecking order.

Although campus faculty preferences are significant, disciplinary status is even more strongly affected by such external factors as the level of research support available from federal agencies, the job market for Ph.D.s in the field, and "student consumerism"—undergraduate student preferences for degree programs (see David Riesman [42]). Disciplines or professions considered essential to the nation's defense posture, to its economic well-being, or to the health of its citizens are clearly favored for gaining access to federal research funding. Just as the values of the most prestigious campuses influence the goals of others, there is a strong tendency for the values of the most prestigious disciplines to be imposed on other disciplines; even for professional fields in which scholarly journals play a minimal role, departments are increasingly evaluated according to norms of scientific or scholarly publication.

The consideration of disciplinary status highlights the multiple roles of the intellectual leaders on the nation's campuses. They carry out political activities in Washington in addition to their primary roles as disciplinary leaders: (a) directing the research activities in their own laboratories, which set the standards of disciplinary research achievement in their fields, (b) writing proposals for grants and contracts for this research, and (c) implementing the peer review system, which determines which papers are published and which researchers will receive grants (and promotions). Because they play important roles on government advisory boards and on the boards of professional organizations that affect the federal allocation of funds to the various disciplines, the charisma and persuasiveness of the disciplinary intellectual leaders, as well as their connections to other powerful organizations, are critical to disciplinary status. As the various fields of research have expanded, these demands have increased accordingly; to put it mildly, the intellectual leaders of the nation are overloaded. In recognition of these realities, the outstanding intellectual leaders in many prestigious departments are spared—indeed protected from—the chores on the home campus (committee work and day-to-day participation in the campus governance process). It isn't that they are spared from chores as such; rather, they carry out these duties in the service of the disciplinary rather than the campus community. And because their contributions as researchers are greatly valued by the department, both in terms of internal leadership and maintaining external visibility, the leading researchers often receive special treatment in departmental assignments and perquisites. In fact, the intellectual leaders on the nation's campuses rarely have time enough to become involved in problems of curricular reform or institutional reorganization and are dragooned into campus budget administration only at times of crisis. Indeed, except during crises, there is a distinct separation of the preoccupations and concerns of intellectual leadership and administrative leadership. The intellectual leaders are primarily involved professionally with the activities of their disciplinary communities, while the administrators (presidents, deans, and faculty committee persons) are aligned with their responsibilities in the local campus community.

In partial summary, the matrix model describes the overall institutional complex that influences the policies and practices of a typical research university. The research universities include some 10,000 departments that are arrayed rather symmetrically in about 100 disciplinary communities on about 100 major research campuses and tied together in an interdependent national system.

By recognizing the importance and nationwide character of the disciplinary communities, the model calls attention to the fact that no American university is fully autonomous, able to set a course independent of the other universities in the nation. Many of the persons and institutions that determine the goals and assess the performance of a given university do not live on its campus or report to its board of trustees. In fact, the matrix diagram is simultaneously a portrayal of the entire assembly of institutions of higher education and a portrayal of any one of them. In other words, all of the universities in the nation comprise a single interconnected organism for higher education and research. Despite differences in the number or composition of departments and other academic units, the regularities and national dimensions of the matrix serve to explain the similarity of aspirations among research universities, whether they are public or private, whether they are in the top decible or the bottom. Because quality is defined primarily in terms of a single measure of research "excellence," the pressures for conformity to the disciplinary conventions and fashions are often greater for less distinguished universities than for those at the top. This pressure for conformity is in turn imposed on the individual faculty member. Because mobility and rewards are associated with climbing the departmental status ladder, individuals can be visible to disciplinary leaders only if they are turning out papers that are readily published and recognized as being in the mainstream of the discipline. In specifying the orthogonal roles of intellectual and administrative leaders on the nation's campuses, the matrix formulation calls attention to the complex issues of leadership and responsibility in the comprehensive university, the key features of which are hidden from view by formal organizational charts. (I will return to these issues in the discussion of the role of university presidents in the matrix model.)

As with any attempt to portray this highly complex organizational system, the matrix model has limitations. Because the model is intended to identify problems and to locate them in an organizational problem-solving space, it tends to highlight certain problematic situations, such as the fragmentation of the university community. The model is also biased toward emphasizing the forces encouraging conformity among universities; it does not adequately portray the ways in which universities differ in cultural traditions and ambiance, in disciplinary emphasis, or in functional emphasis. Furthermore, the model undoubtedly reflects my greater familiarity with state-supported, land-grant universities than with private universities, and some of the inferences or conclusions may not be generalizable for all categories of research universities. Despite these limitations, many features of the matrix model are applicable, not only to most research universities but to a wide variety of other universities and colleges. Even small liberal arts colleges, primarily oriented to undergraduate education, exhibit strong loyalties to the values of the research universities, particularly in their dependence on the disciplinary communities for measuring professorial performance, for providing faculty mobility, and for strengthening professional identity.

Relating Research to Other Campus Activities: Multidisciplinary Facilities and Interdisciplinary Mission Organizations

For the sake of clarity, I have postponed a brief discussion of academic organizational units that do not fit into the standard departmental matrix array, in particular, units involving faculty members from several departments in organized collaborative enterprises. I am not referring to the hierarchical groupings of departments into schools and colleges, typically headed by a dean or director. In some of the professional colleges strongly identified with a single profession (e.g., law, medicine, education), these officers play the same roles as department heads and their colleges are symbolized in the matrix model accordingly. In colleges made up of a number of quite different departments, the dean typically plays an intermediary role between the departments and the central administration. It does not detract from the importance of such deans in the university to say that they play a staff rather than a line role, providing administrative services to departments and acting as spokespersons for their faculties and departments in the president's office. Rather, I attend to those special academic units whose activities involve faculty members from a number of departments and start with a brief discussion of interdepartmental organizations, mostly oriented to research activities, though some such organizations are devoted to instruction, applied research, and/or public service.

Although the organizational literature often refers to all such units as "organizational research units" (ORUs), it is useful to distinguish between two classes of interdepartmental research units [1, 21]. The first, directed to serving the disciplinary research needs of faculty members in many departments, I refer to as "multidisciplinary facilities" (MDFs). The second, directed to addressing problems transcending the know-how and knowledge of any one discipline, I refer to as "interdisciplinary mission organizations' (IMOs). The management of MDFs is well understood in the academic community. One such facility, the central library, has been successfully managed in universities for centuries. Other examples are the various language and area centers, computer service organizations, electron microscope laboratories, and other major instrument facilities. Operated under guidelines and priorities established by an interdepartmental advisory committee, the MDF is so commonplace on the campus that some academics take it for granted that all interdepartmental activities can and should be governed in the same way. Because a prime goal of the MDF is to provide access to shared facilities by the participating faculty, administration of the MDF is typically assigned to a director, operating under guidelines specified by a representative committee made up of the various departmental clients. The MDF may be staffed by nonfaculty professionals to provide sophisticated services to its faculty clients. In some cases, the MDF includes a common building, offering contiguous offices or laboratories to encourage collaboration between individuals in different disciplines. However, the research goals are set, not by the organizational unit, but by the faculty investigators—acting individually or at most with a few colleagues working on related research problems. The problems under investigation are typically disciplinary in character, occasionally applying techniques developed in one discipline to the problems posed by another. In Figure 4, the MDFs are shown as shaded squares; they are part of the (horizontal) campus community and governed accordingly. Interestingly, some of the most prominent MDFs (e.g., libraries, computer service organizations) are common to most campuses; like their departmental counterparts, they have formed national organizations and may also be represented as vertical communities on the matrix chart.

Contrasting with MDFs, the successful management of interdisciplinary mission organizations runs contrary to traditional ways of doing things in academia. If the operating metaphor for managing the MDF is the faculty advisory committee, the corresponding metaphor for the management of IMO activities is the participating network or team. Since the IMO is typically utilitarian, problem-focused, and accountable to mission-oriented sponsors, success depends critically on the commitment, inventiveness, and breadth of problem-related experience of the participants rather than their expertise in specialized fields. It follows that the personnel composition of each IMO is unique to the campus on which it is located even when committed to the same goals as those on other campuses. Hence the IMOs are symbolically represented in Figure 4 as stippled circles and are randomly located among overlapping departments to reflect the variability in staffing and administration. Examples are the Center for Policy Alternatives at MIT, the Computer-based Education Research Laboratory at the University of Illinois at Urbana-Champaign, and the Center for Energy and Environmental Studies at Princeton University.

In a university setting focusing on individual faculty publication and relying on external peer group evaluation as the dominant means for assessing performance, it is not surprising that IMOs constitute anomalies in the scheme of things. In the first place, a central requirement for success is that the individual leaders of the interdisciplinary team must themselves be interdisciplinary persons. This requirement means that academic today is not a likely source of such leaders; when they do emerge, they may not be acknowledged as legitimate scholars by the disciplinary communities or promotion committees. Because project success depends on collaboration, invention, and concern with the solution of problems while promotion depends on individual scholarly (scientific) achievement and publication in refereed journals, interdisciplinary, problem-focused activity is dangerous territory for untenured faculty members. Hence, the staffing of IMOs is largely made up of nontenured professionals who do not aspire to professorial status. Furthermore, successful policy- or problem-oriented research must meet deadlines and serve real clients, which calls for a form of corporate accountability to the sponsor or client. These performance requirements are not well served by conventional procedures on such administrative matters as selection of leadership or personnel, tenure, performance evaluation, and so on.

Because the IMO does not figure prominently in the overall research university, academic innovation takes place largely within the boundaries of the existing departments. The department (or integrated professional school) is the largest organizational unit having the capacity to encourage collaboration or new directions among its faculty; it provides research facilities, financial and moral support, graduate students, and perhaps most significantly, the authority to select the new faculty recruits. On occasion, research problems of one discipline are attacked with instruments or methodologies that have been developed in other disciplines; in such cases, innovation depends on the individual faculty member who has the capacity and style for reaching across departmental lines. But the departmental structure is seen to be so "natural" that cross-disciplinary fields (such as biochemistry, geophysics, and bioengineering) that originate at the boundaries soon become formalized as new departments. As soon as this is accomplished, collaboration across departmental lines again depends on individuals' initiative.

In the research university, the research, educational, and public service missions are integrated at the level of the individual department and, most often, at the level of the individual professor. In the matrix model, the individual department is at the intersection between the disciplinary (research-oriented) community and the campus (undergraduate-oriented) community. Thus, the department is the nominal organizational structure for relating the research and educational missions. However, as Bess points out, "There are many who argue that the integrity of the university is preserved by interplay among the (research, education and public service) missions. What in fact takes place, however, is that instead of integration of the missions through organizational structure, the 'multiple-function' professional faculty member is expected personally to make the necessary connections" [6, p. 209]. The individual faculty member is also the principal source of initiatives for problems that do not fall within the perceived mission of any department. That cross-disciplinary programs have been initiated even during the years of retrenchment is a tribute to a small number of unorthodox academics whose personal dedication has overcome the general low level of institutional recognition or support. The typical organizational form in which such programs evolve is the informal network made up of self-selected individual faculty members with overlapping interests. Such recently developed interdepartmental programs as "Science, Technology, and Society" and "Women's Studies" are widely dispersed on the nation's campuses, but they face a double-bind situation making their long-term survival uncertain. Departmental status seems essential if they are to achieve program continuity, financial support, and a voice in the appointment and promotion of qualified faculty participants. On the other hand, departmental status is a hazard because the objectives of such programs call for collaborating with other departments rather than competing with them. Thus, program success may be antithetical to the coordinative role; in the development of initiatives transcending departmental lines, the research university depends on dedicated (and often unconventional) individual faculty members rather than organizational structure or administrative leadership.

Role of the President's Office in the Matrix Model

Even the astute Daniel Moynihan exhibits serious confusion about the nature of academic leadership and the role of administrators in the modern university. In his widely quoted article, "State vs. Academe: Nationalizing the Universities" [32], he spells out some of the negative consequences of federal involvement in sponsoring of academic research. Moynihan bemoans the growth of federal influence on the academic mission and makes the significant point that "no money was made available for the universities to do with as they thought best." In particular, he has some scorching things to say about the failure of university presidents a decade or two ago to foresee this predicament: "It was at least possible [between 1957 and 1972] for the universities to have negotiated a distinctive relationship between themselves and the national government. . . . That this was not done involved a profound failure of leadership" [32, p. 33].

Moynihan has leveled valid and serious criticism at the federal contract with universities, but by assuming that the presidents of American universities had the power suggested by their position at the top of the formal organization chart, Moynihan ignores the reality of the circumstances. If the university presidents of the 1950s and early 1960s had followed Moynihan's prescription and demanded from the federal government direct institutional support for their campuses, they would have come into direct confrontation with faculties who were well along in the process of relegating the administrators to secondary roles in the research enterprise and making use of the project support system to do so. As indicated previously, the principal effect of the exponential growth of federal support was not to centralize the management of the university in Washington, as Moynihan avers, but to further remove the president from a significant role in the management of the campus. The new contract with the federal agencies transferred power from the campus communities to the disciplinary communities, who did not seek and did not assume responsibility for the university as an institutional whole. By the late 1960s and early 1970s, many of the universities, led by the National Association of State Universities and Land-Grant Colleges, had become sufficiently concerned to lobby strongly in Congress for implementation of institutional grants to universities [3]. However, under the impetus of the Nixon administration, Congress chose in 1972 to enhance the federal subsidy to higher education, not in the form of direct institutional support but through scholarship aid and loans to students.

Moynihan's view of academic administration is consistent with the "great man" theory of academic administration—a view unusually prevalent among faculty members today [42]. Faced with unresolvable dilemmas of competing priorities and overly busy schedules, many faculty members acknowledge their own feeling of powerlessness and look upward in the organizational chart for institutional salvation. They take seriously the possibility of calling upon an all-knowing and all-powerful "great man" in the presidency who will "make the right decisions" and lead the university out of its troubles. More often than not, the goal they would have the president pursue is to persuade donors or legislators to new levels of financial commitment that would permit them to carry on as before and so remove by sheer charisma the baffling constraints exposed by retrenchment. Failing that, the "strong" departments would ask the "great man" to make the hard decisions (to eliminate the "weaker" programs) and the "weak" departments would have him maintain the integrity of the university by resisting the pressures of passing scholastic fads. The limited record of success has not perceptibly lessened the attractiveness of "great man" solutions to the university's problems.

Most of the university presidents in office today are able, perceptive, and articulate. They assume responsibility for a broad variety of tasks, they work painfully long hours, and they are concerned for the university and the integrity of its relationship to society. But as Cohen and March have observed, their influence on the activities of the campus is limited: "Compared to the heroic expectations he and others might have, the president has modest control over the events of college life. The contributions he makes can easily be swamped by outside events or the diffuse qualities of university decision making" [15, p. 2]. The matrix model reveals the basic dilemma of university presidents: they are expected to carry the burden of leadership for institutions that are separately accountable to individual legislatures and boards of trustees but governed as part of an inseparable and interdependent nationwide system of institutions. The ambiguities associated with this situation are exacerbated by the differences in accountability to sponsors and clients of the president and of the intellectual leaders of the campus. The president feels directly accountable not only to federal sponsors but also to the state legislature, students, parents, donors, and all other constituencies who provide institutional support for the campus. In contrast, faculty members generally tend to view their prime responsibilities in terms of national goals, contributing to the body of published scientific and scholarly knowledge, and educating future scientists and scholars.

The dilemmas of the president's role of accountability to external sponsors are matched by the dilemmas of his or her responsibilities within the university. As chief spokesperson for their universities, presidents are prominent in searching for funds; as chief budgetary officers, they are responsible for keeping the books balanced. The president is also expected to provide the necessary coordination between departmental and institutional goals and to balance the educational, public service, and research functions of the campus. But the discretionary funds and resources at the disposal of the president of a typical university are remarkably limited. Thus, lacking authority and legitimacy in matters of educational policy and divorced from initiatives in the research enterprise, the president's capacity for providing coordination among academic units and for revitalizing the institutional mission is, to say the least, limited. It is a "Catch-22" situation: the president lacks enough understanding of departmental problems to justify the extension of his or her power and also lacks the power to justify the expansion of his or her understanding.

Given these discordant views of the president's role, how should the president's office be symbolized in the matrix model? Two alternatives seem plausible:

1. the president as mediator and spokesperson for an array of semiautonomous academic units, providing administrative services to the campus as a whole under guidelines and legitimizing influence of the faculty senate and a variety of related faculty committees (note the similarity to the role of director of an MDF);
2. the president as leader of an interdisciplinary mission organization of faculty and staff from all colleges and departments and charged with the responsibility for making decisions—on his or her own, if necessary—regarding the overall campus mission (note the corresponding similarity to the role of leader of an IMO; undergraduate education was the original interdisciplinary mission).

Both of these representations of the president's office in the matrix model appropriately suggest responsibilities far exceeding authority and suggest accountability to internal as well as to external constituencies of the university. Which of these descriptions is most appropriate? It seems fair to say that in Kerr's comprehensive "multiversity" of the 1950s and early 1960s, the president was primarily a mediator/spokesperson, a provider of administrative services to the campus at large [26]. On occasion, however, even in those days, the president was called on to act as initiator and leader. Thus, it may be more appropriate to assert that the president is called on to play both roles, the mix depending on the size of the campus, the reputation and national stature of the faculty, and the makeup of institutional and disciplinary sources of funding. The president's role also depends on the economic environment. When retrenchment became a fact of life on the nation's campuses, the mediator/spokesperson role was inadequate for rapid-response cutback management, if only because the process was too time-consuming and revealed irreconcilable conflicts of purpose. Retrenchment thus provides opportunities, as well as demands, for the president to go beyond the symbolic role of leadership and, in concert with intellectual leaders and administrative leaders at other universities, to set the stage for organizational learning for the local campus as well as for the larger academic community.

Directions for Organizational Learning

> There is much urgent educational work to be done in the United States and the years ahead are no time for retreat or retrenchment.
>
> Howard R. Bowen [10, p. 154]

> The status quo is the only solution that cannot be vetoed.
>
> Clark Kerr [27, p. 30]

The major dissonances in governance and purpose forcefully articulated by Yarmolinsky and Ashby suggest the need for double-loop organizational learning, that is, reformulating the organizational structure as well as the norms of institutional behavior. Some further dissonances are here identified that are highlighted by the matrix model as characteristics of the national system of universities and suggest the need for organizational learning at the level of the overall enterprise as well as at the individual institution.

A first set of dissonances is associated with the growing awareness of the inadequacies of undergraduate education, in the preparation of students for life in a complex society. Perhaps these inadequacies are most apparent to university and college presidents. F. W. Wallin, president of Earlham College, is persuaded that "Our inherited concepts about education need significant revision, when information itself becomes a pivotal resource in society. . . . It is clear that in the future we and our universities will have to be more interdisciplinary, interprofessional and more interdepartmental [55, pp. 7–8]. Boyer and Hechinger advocate major new priorities for higher education: "The nation's schools, colleges, and universities have a special obligation to combat growing illiteracy about public issues. . . [America's colleges and universities] must perform for society an *integrative* function, seeking appropriate responses to life's most enduring questions, concerning themselves not just with information, but with wisdom" [11, pp. 48, 60]. Another former university president, Harlan Cleveland, wants us to educate students who can "put it all together" and who can relate 'hard' technologies to their soft impacts and implications" [14]. Still others want universities to deal with growing scientific and technological illiteracy; Rustum Roy, editor of the *Bulletin of Science, Technology, and Society*, offers the following statement: "In a world with increasing technological and scientific complexity, science literacy must be more than the understanding of a few basic principles in the biological or physical sciences. Rather, it must encompass the ability to apply an understanding of science principles, methodology, capabilities, and limitations to the wide range of decisions students will face both as citizens and as professionals" [46, p. 290].

But such exhortations, directed to the academic world at large, seldom address the organizational mechanisms through which reforms in instructional programs could be implemented. And they tend to beg the question about whether the faculties—including those in our most prestigious universities—are qualified to combat illiteracy about public policy or the role of science and technology in society. By the above criteria for science literacy, the large majority of science and engineering faculties (as well, of course, as humanities faculties) are scientifically illiterate. Education for citizenship is discussed as though all that were necessary would be a change in the curricular requirements imposed on students. But in an increasingly complex and interconnected world, literacy concerning public issues—and cultural literacy more broadly defined—calls for extensive learning by professors beyond their specializations. Most research-oriented professors are too busy to get involved, even if they recognize the need for it. On most campuses, there are a few dedicated individuals who have aspirations for redirecting educational programs across departmental boundaries, but they typically are denied sufficient organizational, financial, or moral support to translate these intentions into functional programs. In times of retrenchment, even less support is available. On occasion, the financial stimulus for new educational programs is provided by external foundations. All too often, however, a few faculty participants may embark on such a new interdisciplinary program only to see the system revert to "normal" soon after the external support dries up. In the absence of viable organizational mechanisms for supporting and maintaining the quality of interdisciplinary instruction, faculty initiatives that cross departmental lines frequently accomplish the exact opposite of what was intended. As I. I. Rabi once remarked about the efforts to promote general undergraduate education in the 1960s, "We are developing still another breed of specialists, called generalists."

The performance of the university as an educational institution is also limited by a lack of institutional commitment to research and development in the educational process itself. This paradoxical situation has been sharply criticized by Professor F. Reif, a member of the Group in Science and Mathematics Education at the University of California at Berkeley:

> ... the educational mode of the functioning of the university today is basically not very different from what it was 50 years.ago, all the talk of an impending educational revolution notwithstanding. Educational innovations are few in number and often marginal in their impact. Nor is this situation surprising, since the university, unlike any progressive industry, is not in the habit of improving its own performance by systematic investment in innovative research and development. Indeed, the resources allocated by the university to educational innovation are usually miniscule or nonexistent. . . . there is a tendency to view education narrowly as mere classroom teaching and thus to ignore important issues. . . . Is it too farfetched to suggest that the university should take education at least as seriously as the Bell Telephone Company takes communication? [40, p. 538]

In contrast, there has been a growing tendency for industrial corporations to take education seriously, not only as a profit-making venture but as an essential process in the development of their own management and personnel. In fact, Guzetta describes a "quiet revolution," embodied in the movement of traditionally nonteaching organizations into the arena of education, fulfilling demands to which "traditional educational institutions have been reticent in responding" [23, p. 10]. Thus, universities have not maintained their share of the market for advanced education. In certain fields, such as computer science and engineering, some industrial corporations are hiring recruits at the baccalaureate level and providing advanced professional training themselves.

A second major dissonance in the nation's universities is their adherence to an institutional rating game based on a single measure of departmental performance—peer assessment of disciplinary research achievement. Although the concept of an appropriate institutional mission unique to the individual campus is a popular rhetorical notion among educational administrators, the matrix model suggests that adherence to a standard departmental structure and a national system of evaluating university quality department-by-department enforces a remarkable conformity. Under conditions of retrenchment, this system tends to discourage diversity even further. On many of the campuses subjected to major cutbacks in the past few years, the departments threatened with serious reduction or discontinuance were often much the same. The "smaller but better university" is one that focuses a greater fraction of its resources on research in the high status disciplines and, as a result, resembles its sister institutions even more [50]. A university that depends entirely on external peer evaluation of its department, as the measure of its quality is not likely to modify its structure, merge departments, or establish new academic units. Nor is it likely to shift priorities from disciplinary research to other institutional functions.

An important consequence of the lack of diversity is a related dissonance involving the overall magnitude of the academic commitment to disciplinary research, both on an absolute basis and relative to educational activities, applied research, and public service. If the sole justification and function of the academic enterprise were the production of new knowledge in the existing disciplines, its current size is too large by at least an order of magnitude; most of the important advances in research are made by a small fraction of the faculty members associated with a small fraction of the nation's universities. Ernest Lynton, Commonwealth Professor at the Center for Studies in Policies and the Public Interest, University of Massachusetts, points out:

> With a quarter million full-time faculty members in institutions called universities, it is very difficult to maintain the position that all of them are scholars capable of significant original research. . . .

> There are tens of thousands of scholarly journals which each year carry literally hundreds of thousands of articles. Much of what is published is second rate and trivial. . . . Even in the more prestigious institutions, a substantial number of faculty in fact carries out little or no research. . . . Yet throughout that vast and heterogeneous array of institutions . . . there is but one accepted, valued and rewarded scholarly goal: To conduct original research and to publish it in scholarly refereed journals. [29, pp. 20–21]

The use of a single measure of institutional excellence assures that lesser institutions refusing to accept mediocrity as a permanent station in life will fight to enlarge the disciplinary research commitment of their faculty and thus to increase the size of each of the disciplinary research communities. This tendency exacerbates competition for limited research funds and offers little incentive to embark in new areas of basic or applied research or to develop new approaches to instruction.

A third major dissonance results from the operating premise within universities that successful professors, having achieved tenure as young scholars in their thirties, should be engaged in the same academic pursuits throughout their careers. The tenure system evolved in an academic enterprise geared for undergraduate education; it is distinctly at odds with the goals of the disciplinary communities oriented to maximizing the quality of the basic research enterprise. The disciplinary communities do not offer tenure or security. The peer review system rewards researchers on the basis of promise or past performance, but it makes no long-term commitment to the support of old warhorses. In times of retrenchment, the tenure system results in serious barriers to the hiring of younger faculty and places those who are appointed in competition with established scholars. We have noted the pressures on untenured faculty members to stay within the mainstream of their disciplines; similar pressures are placed on older faculty to run harder to maintain their departmental status. Because there are few avenues for tenured faculty to change careers, the resultant situation, observed by Bess, is that those faculty members who do not excel in research and are not rewarded for performance in other academic roles often lapse into self-serving, "satisficing" behavior [6, p. 28].

Administrators, keenly aware of the "deadwood" problem, seek to ease out unproductive older faculty—through early retirement and other means—and thus to maintain quality. But the process is fraught with ethical as well as practical problems associated with dismissing tenured faculty. By adhering to a single measure of performance, universities do not encourage older faculty members to develop competence and commitments in directions other than basic disciplinary research: for example, educating for citizenship, carrying out and managing applied research, or codifying and disseminating knowledge. By contrast, industrial laboratories have long recognized the value of career changes. Young industrial scientists may excel in basic research. but as they mature, they are often encouraged to address their knowledge and skills to applied problems and management, making greater contributions to the corporate mission and being rewarded accordingly. In the university, the single measure of academic performance limits the diversity of individual, as well as institutional, objectives.

At the heart of these dissonances is an unexamined assumption held by many academics, a widespread belief in the automatic benevolence of science and scholarly research. That is to say, the search for new knowledge is viewed as a good in itself, from which benefits to society flow automatically or as byproducts, including better education, technological innovation, greater industrial productivity, national well-being, and military supremacy. A corollary of this belief is another premise, identified by Churchman as equally untenable: "In the main basic science is a separable part of the total system of humanity" [13, p. 109]. This assumed separability, he goes on to explain, "is why basic research is deemed to be value free and apart from politics, and why we have to call on the researcher's peers to judge his excellence." These notions of separability and accountability only to ones peers are slowly being brought into explicit scrutiny by the academy under the impetus of the continuing inadequacies of federal funding and retrenchment imposed by state governments.

In response to the new realities, virtually every university in the nation has embarked on a search for added support from industrial corporations. Although this search has been largely motivated by the desire to maintain the status quo and to augment federal support for ongoing programs, the industrial connection at some universities is being reconsidered in the larger context of the relationships of universities to other institutions in society. The new realities of the past few years include the emergence of Japan as a leading industrial nation despite a secondary role in basic science. In a recent article [8], Harvard president Derek Bok presents the thesis that universities should assume a responsibility for the uses of science, for the "transfer" of science to society in the complex process of innovation. Bok is keenly aware of the potential conflicts of interest that may be inherent in the university-industry connection and the potential harm to institutional integrity. But he is also sensitive to the need for a transfer of knowledge between academic researchers and industry; he recognizes that research is not a separable enterprise. Bok's justification for university involvement in industrial development is presented in simple terms: ". . . Every institution that depends on public support should recognize a responsibility to serve society's legitimate needs" [8, p. 25]. This renewed commitment to public service, articulated in the language of the land-grant universities, comes from the president of one of the most independent of the nation's private universities.

A change in university-industry relationships is exemplified by the appearance on some of the nation's leading campuses of major research and development facilities dedicated to the encouragement of high-technology industry. These new facilities are not dedicated solely to a search for new knowledge but to developing an infrastructure for relating scientific advance and technological innovation. Recently organized examples are the Center for Integrated Systems at Stanford University, the Robotics Laboratory at Carnegie-Mellon University,. and the Whitehead Institute for Biomedical Research associated with MIT. It remains to be seen whether the new laboratories will be successful in relating basic academic research to new technological initiatives.

Roy [45] has his doubts; he proposes that the laboratories be managed directly by industrial corporations. And there is reason for concern; the recent record of universities in managing mission- or policy-oriented research is uninspired [44, 53] if not downright irresponsible, as Coleman concludes:

> The history of faculty-directed research on problems posed by government and foundations is one of deception and disappointment; deception by the university academic in transforming the client's problem to a problem that interested him (i.e., one that could gain him status in his discipline) and disappointment on the client's part when he received a research report which failed to address his problem or which, addressing it, failed to solve it.... The very structure which made these intellectual skills available—the autonomy of university faculty members, the absence of an organized chain of command—also incapacitates the faculty member for systematic and organized attack on the problems ... [17, p. 376]

The poor record is due, as previously indicated, to a worrisome lack of appreciation of the organizational and support mechanisms required for effectively carrying out problem-oriented research. Coleman attributes the difficulties to a serious "structural fault" of the university [17, pp. 375–85].

Potentially, IMOs for research and education could perform important "impedance matching" functions between the basic research activities of the academic community and the needs of a mission-oriented society. That is to say, IMOs could be structured as parallel organizations with authority comparable to that of departments—providing faculty participants with opportunities to serve both the disciplinary missions of their departments and the interdisciplinary missions (either education, public service, or research) of the special units and rewarding the individual faculty participant for successful performance in either. In practice, with a few notable exceptions such as the agricultural experiment stations, the interdisciplinary organizations have neither the prestige nor the authority to carry out a coordinating function among the various academic missions.

The matrix model highlights the inadequacy of organizational structures for relating the basic research mission to the other missions of the university. We have called attention to the fact that the responsibilities for coordinating and integrating the multiple functions and missions are typically assigned to individual faculty members. And because they are selected and rewarded for their attributes as specialized researchers, it is not surprising that some dimensions of the university's objectives are not adequately addressed. Bess points out that "since faculty are trained in graduate schools largely to perform research in their disciplines, they have little cross-disciplinary background, inclination, and understanding; little training in the pedagogical nuances needed in teaching; and inadequate awareness of skills in the organizational and administrative techniques" [6, p. 209]. Furthermore, faculty members are under increasing time pressures. The pressures on the individual affect morale; the focus on narrowly defined activities threatens the integrity of the collective mission.

It is interesting to contrast the organizational structures of universities with those widely adopted in other research and development and policy research organizations in the public or the private sector. At such organizations as A. D. Little, the Rand Corporation, or many innovative industrial laboratories, technical research personnel may be organized in departments corresponding to disciplinary backgrounds or areas of research activity. However, when the corporation is called on to carry out a novel development task or policy study, it creates a flexible and often temporary infrastructure designed to encourage collaboration and to assign accountability among a team of experts of differing backgrounds and skills. Such infrastructures are sometimes referred to in organizational literature [20] as "matrix organizations," but aside from the use of the term, there is no direct relationship to the matrix model presented here. In the "matrix organization," a set of systems managers (e.g., research and development project leaders) share or contend for resources controlled by a set of functional managers. As Sayles explains, "Organizational goals are, at once, multiple and conflicting and changing—and they need to reuse the same technical talent and technology for a multiplicity of end results. . . . [Matrix management introduces] structural imperatives that serve to maintain fluidity in the balance of power among the major subdivisions of the organization . . . and discourage the formation of rigid, exclusionary norms and suboptimal, vested-interest groups" [48, p. 16].

In their best-selling book, *In Search of Excellence* [361, Peters and Waterman express a strong aversion to the term "matrix organization" but advocate similar organizations with quite different labels, such as temporary structures, ad hoc groups, fluid organizations, shadow organizations, or skunk works. Such parallel organizations are not oriented to enhance organizational efficiency—to do better the things now being done—but to encourage innovation and collaboration toward novel goals. Whatever the nomenclature, such temporary groupings of key personnel and resources constitute organizational mechanisms aimed at achieving organizational effectiveness, defined previously as the ability to create acceptable outcomes and actions. We have noted that interdisciplinary mission (or "matrix") organizations are not altogether foreign to the campus. On some campuses, successful IMOs have been built around the personalities of unique individuals [44]. But these activities are idiosyncratic; by and large, universities have not acknowledged the need for mission-oriented organizations that transcend departmental lines, nor have they developed the leadership required to manage such activities. This lack severely limits their capacity to coordinate the efforts of faculty members on complex tasks, to effect changes in mission, and to integrate the various missions of the university.

Where Do We Wish To Go?

> There are three kinds of maps needed to help organizations learn for action. The first is a map of where the organization is; the second is a map of where it wishes to go; the third is a map of how to get there from here.
>
> Chris Argyris and Donald A. Schön [2, p. 160]

> No matter how much pressure is put on a person or social system to change through disconfirmation and the induction of guilt-anxiety, no change will occur unless members of the system feel it is safe to give up the old responses and learn something new.
>
> Edgar H. Schein [49, p. 77]

During the past decade, pervasive environmental changes have confronted all of the major institutions of American life. On the industrial scene, these changes have been so traumatic for many major industries—automobiles, steel, heavy industry, consumer electronics—that "double-loop" organizational learning has become a condition for survival. In universities, the changes in environment have been manifested as an extended period of retrenchment, imposing stresses on every dimension of the academic enterprise. Universities have responded primarily by single-loop organizational learning—making every effort to maintain the existing norms, goals, and structures—and doing with less support today the things that were being done yesterday. This article has presented an organizational map of the comprehensive research university as it is, and it has addressed the growing evidence that the norms, theories-in-use, and structures of the university may no longer be adequate to the missions they are intended to serve. The matrix model reveals that the problems facing universities are exacerbated by the divergent goals of the disciplinary and campus communities. As has been indicated, the intellectual leaders are predominantly oriented to basic research and to the goals and directives of federal agencies that sponsor it; they properly justify their activities in terms of contributions to national welfare. The administrative leaders play only a limited role in developing research initiatives on the home campus; they are, however, necessarily involved in the instructional programs and public service activities and accountable to the local and regional sponsors who represent the major sources of financial support for research universities. In fact, the federal government allocates for academic research and development only about $5 billion annually (for fiscal year 1983), providing less than 20 percent of the operating costs of the overall system of research universities. This support is clearly inadequate if the current priorities of research universities are to continue. That is to say, the major burden of financial support for research universities is assumed by stakeholders other than research agencies of the federal government, and much of the institutional support (including student tuition, state subsidies, and federal aid to students) is oriented to undergraduate education and public service rather than basic research. This offers a major dilemma that has not been confronted directly in the academic enterprise: science cannot be well served by inadequately funded universities, but given the current support mechanisms, universities will not be adequately funded if they default on their education and service missions.

The matrix model offers a starting point for universities wishing to redefine their roles in either the local or the national context. It reveals some of the features of both the internal and external environments that have constrained efforts to redefine organizational goals. Under pressures of retrenchment, many universities have been induced to reexamine their priorities on a campus-wide basis and to try to provide a rationale for the support of their individual campuses. By and large, however, they have proceeded as though the crisis were unique to their own campuses—as though the rest of the system would continue to function in a business-as-usual fashion. There have been relatively few efforts to reexamine the educational and research needs of the nation or the purposes of the national university system as a whole.

This article has suggested a particular need to reconsider the evaluation of institutional performance. Although inspired by the worthy motive of defining and achieving "excellence," the research universities of the nation have been led into a rating game that places far greater rewards on conformity than diversity, measuring performance primarily in terms of original research published in scholarly journals. This situation has served to impose the values and the mission of the outstanding research institutions on most of the other colleges and universities without providing, even in principle, for the justification or support of the overall research enterprise. A narrow definition of excellence has also served to impose the values of the most powerful disciplines on many of the less prestigious disciplines and professional schools and, in the process, has denigrated their intended purposes. At the same time, the national needs for undergraduate education and for advanced continuing education are not being adequately addressed, and little attention has been given to the local and regional needs for applied research and public service. Because it is highly unlikely that a single model of an educational institution can adequately serve the diversity of the educational and research needs, it seems necessary to develop alternative measures of excellence that will emphasize the individuality of the various campuses and, at the same time, will develop an image of the system of universities as complementary centers of learning. In reconceiving measures of excellence, a special responsibility falls on the leaders of the most prestigious universities, who educate the faculties and set the cultural climate for the enterprise as a whole.

Developing a new sense of purpose or a new approach to the evaluation of performance will call for new maps of the future university, either for the individual campus or for the nation's universities viewed as differentiated parts of an interconnected enterprise. How could the academic community go about designing maps of the future university? The matrix model has illuminated two significant barriers to addressing organizational problems of the university community in a systematic way. One barrier is the commitment to suboptimization along both of the axes of the matrix; some academic leaders do not even acknowledge the existence of problems except as they impinge directly on their own communities. A second barrier is a resulting lack of candor in discussing such problems: the presidents of our universities are subject to criticisms from so many constituencies, internal as well as external, that they find it difficult to discuss publicly substantive inadequacies in any dimension of performance. Similar vulnerabilities are experienced by faculty members, who are typically held accountable to their immediate departmental colleagues in formal deliberations regarding larger academic issues. Under these circumstances, a first step in organizational learning, either at the local or the national level, is the creation of a "safe place" for the candid discussion of matters that have been heretofore undiscussable. Some form of informal organization seems essential, transcending the governance structures of individual institutions and transcending the professional disciplinary and professional communities. In "The Management of Decline," Boulding suggested: "It may be indeed that a prime institutional need is the development of 'invisible colleges,' that is, small .groups of people with similar tasks who are in close, constant communication and operate as a 'discipline'. . . . The invisible college indeed is the social invention that gave rise to science" [9, p. 64].

Though informal networks rarely control access to major financial resources, they do provide access to a critical human resource—independent actors who think for themselves. Following World War II, an informal national network of academic scientists utilized their prominence in the war effort to establish a powerful national commitment to the support of basic scientific research. In the recent past, such interinstitutional networks have been created to deal with problems experienced by many campuses on such issues as codes of professional ethics in university-industry relations and modification of government regulations on accounting operations [19, 34, 51]. It is interesting to note that the public pronouncements of outcomes are often identified by the "safe place" (Pajaro Dunes, Asilomar) where the meetings of such networks were convened. The leading academic scholars and administrators in the nation are remarkably gifted; many of them have the stamina as well as the talent to perform multiple tasks in superlative fashion. They already participate in informal networks that transcend their campuses, and with the rapid development of computer-communications technologies, they will be in day-to-day contact on a world-wide scale. This article has argued the need for new maps for the future university, the design of which would call for interdisciplinary and interinstitutional networks, made up of self-selected participants on the nations' campuses and elsewhere, and the creation of "safe places" for contemplating and discussing these issues.

This article was stimulated by the author's participation in an ongoing series of seminar-workshops on organizational responses to retrenchment, sponsored by the Center for Advanced Study at the University of Illinois at Urbana-Champaign. Resource persons for specific issues in the series included an interesting,diversity of administrators, faculty members, legislators, and other stakeholders in the academic enterprise from this campus and elsewhere. The continuing inquiry was carried out by an informal, self-selected network of faculty members from various departments, including Stuart Albert, Richard Boland, Clark Bullard, Fred Coombs, Hugh Petrie; Sue Schneider, James Votruba, and David Whetten, to whom I am indebted for an introduction into the literature of organizational behavior and for many illuminating and provocative discussions.

References

Alpert, D. "The Role and Structure of Interdisciplinary and Multidisciplinary Research Centers." Paper presented at Conference of Graduate Schools meeting, Washington, D.C., 1969.

Argyris, C., and D. Schön. *Organizational Learning: A Theory of Action Perspective.* Reading: Addison-Wesley, 1978.

Arnold, C. K. "The Federal Role in Funding Education." *Change*, September 1982, 14; 39–43.

Ashby, E. *Any Person, Any Study: An Essay on Higher Education in the United States.* New York: McGraw-Hill, 1971.

Barak, R. J. "Program Evaluation as a Tool for Retrenchment." In *Challenges of Retrenchment,* edited by J. R. Mingle and Associates, pp. 212–25. San Francisco: Jossey-Bass, 1981.

Bess, J. L. *University Organization: A Matrix Analysis of the Academic Professions.* New York: Human Sciences Press, 1982.

Birnbaum, P. H. "Assessment of Alternative Management Forms in Academic Interdisciplinary Research Projects." *Management Science,* November 1977, 24; 272–84.

Bok, D. "Balancing Responsibility and Innovation." *Change,* September 1982, 14; 16–25.

Boulding, K. E. "The Management of Decline," *Change,* June 1975, 7; 8–9, 64.

Bowen, H. R. *The State of the Nation and the Agenda for Higher Education.* San Francisco: Jossey-Bass, 1982.

Boyer, E. L., and F. M. Hechinger. *Higher Education in the Nation's Service.* Washington, D.C.: Carnegie Foundation for the Advancement of Teaching, 1981.

Cartter, A. M. *An Assessment of Quality in Graduate Education.* Washington, D.C.: American Council on Education, 1966.

Churchman, C. W. "An Interdisciplinary Look at Science Policy in an Age of Decreased Funding." In *Research in the Age of the Steady-State University,* edited by D. J. Phillips and S. P. Shen, pp. 109–13. Boulder: Westview Press, 1982.

Cleveland, H. "What's Higher about Higher Education?" Paper presented at National Conference of the American Association for Higher Education, mimeographed, Washington, D.C., March 1981.

Cohen, M. D.. and J. G. March. *Leadership and Ambiguity. The American College President*. New York: McGraw-Hill, 1974.

Coleman, E. "'More' Has Not Meant 'Better' in the Organization of Academe." *Chronicle of Higher Education*, June 1981, 1; 48.

Coleman, J. S. "The University and Society's New Demands Upon It." In *Content and Context: Essays on College Education*, edited by C. Kaysen. New York: McGraw-Hill, 1973; 359–400.

Conference Board of Associated Research Councils. *An Assessment of Research Doctorate Programs in the United States*. 5 vols. Washington, D.C.: National Academy Press, 1982.

Culliton, B. J. "Pajaro Dunes: The Search for Consensus." *Science*, 9 April 1982, 216; 155–58.

Davis, S. M., and P. R. Lawrence. *Matrix*. Reading: Addison-Wesley, 1977.

Friedman, R. C., and R. S. Friedman. "The Role of Organized Research Units in Academic Science." Research report, Pennsylvania State University, June 1982.

Garvin, D. A. *The Economics of University Behavior*. New York: Academic Press, 1980.

Guzzetta, D. J. "Education's Quiet Revolution-Changes and Challenges." *Change*, September 1982, 14, 10–11, 60.

Jencks, C., and D. Riesman. *The Academic Revolution*. Garden City: Doubleday, 1968.

Katz, D., and R. L. Kahn. *The Social Psychology of Organizations*. 2nd ed. New York: Wiley and Sons, 1978.

Kerr, C. *The Uses of the University*. Cambridge: Harvard University Press, 1963.

————. "Postscript 1982." *Change*, October 1982, 14; 23–31.

Lanier, L. H., and C. J. Anderson. *A Study of the Financial Condition of Colleges and Universities; 1972–75*. Washington, D.C.: American Council on Education, 1975.

Lynton, E. A. "A Crisis of Purpose: Reexamining the Role of the University." *Change*, October 1983, 15; 18–23, 53.

Mingle, J. R., R. O. Berdahl, and M. W. Peterson. "Political Realities of Statewide Reorganization, Merger, and Closure." in *Challenges of Retrenchment*, edited by J. R. Mingle and Associates, pp. 273–97. San Francisco: Jossey-Bass, 1981.

Mingle, J. R., and Associates. *Challenges of Retrenchment*. San Francisco: Jossey-Bass, 1981.

Moynihan, D. P. "State vs. Academe: Nationalizing the Universities." *Harper's*, December 1980, 261; 31–40.

Niebuhr, H., Jr. "Strengthening the Human Learning System." *Change*, November/December 1982, 14; 16–21.

Norman, C. "Faculty v. OMB: One More Time." *Science*, 5 February 1982, 215; 642.

Perkins, J. A. *The University as an Organization*. New York: McGraw-Hill, 1973.

Peters, T. J., and R. H. Waterman, Jr. *In Search of Excellence*. New York: Harper and Row, 1983.

Petrie, H. G., and D. Alpert. "What is the Problem of Retrenchment in Higher Education?" *Journal of Management Studies*, January 1983, 20; 97–119.

Pfeffer, J., and G. R. Salancik. *The External Control of Organizations. A Resource Dependence Perspective*. New York: Harper and Row, 1978.

Phillips, D. I., and S. P. Shen. *Research in the Age of the Steady-State University*. Boulder: Westview Press, 1982.

Reif, F. "Educational Challenges for the University." *Science*, 3 May 1974, 184; 537–42.

Richman, B. M., and R. N. Farmer. *Leadership, Goals, and Power in Higher Education*. San Francisco: Jossey-Bass, 1974.

Riesman, D. *On Higher Education.* San Francisco: Jossey-Bass, 1980.

Roose, K. D., and C. J. Anderson. *A Rating of Graduate Programs.* Washington, D.C.: American Council on Education, 1970.

Rossini, F. A., and A. L. Porter. "Frameworks for Integrating interdisciplinary Research." *Research Policy,* 1979, 8; 70–79.

Roy, R. "Graduate Universities—A New Model."*Science,* December 1981, 214; 1297.

————. "STS: Core of Technological Literacy." *Bulletin of Science, Technology, & Society,* 1982, 2; 289–90.

Rudolph, F. *The American College and University: A History.* New York: Alfred A. Knopf, 1962.

Sayles, L. R. "Matrix Management: The Structure with a Future." *Organizational Dynamics,*Autumn 1976, 5; 2–17.

Schein, E. H. *Professional Education.* New York: McGraw-Hill, 1972.

Shapiro. H. T. "What Does 'Smaller But Better' Mean?" *University Record* (University of Michigan), April 1981, I; 1–3.

Shapiro, H. T., and R. Heller. "Circular A-21 Negotiations." *Science,* 216, 9 April 1982, 126.

Smith, B. L. R., and J. J. Karlesky. *The Universities in the Nation's Research Effort.* New Rochelle: Change Magazine Press, 1977.

Teich, A. H. "Research Centers and Non-Faculty Researchers: A New Academic Role.' in *Research in the Age of the Steady-State University,* edited by D. J. Phillips and S. P. Shen, Boulder: Westview Press, 1982; 91–108. .

Veysey, L. R. *The Emergence of the American University.* Chicago: University of Chicago Press, 1965.

Wallin, F. W. "Universities for a Small Planet—A Time to Reconceptualize Our Role; *Change,* March 1983, 15; 7–9.

Weick, K. E. "Educational Organizations as Loosely Coupled Systems." *Administrative Science Quarterly,* March 1976, 21; 1–19.

Whetten, D. A. "Sources, Responses, and Effects of Organizational Decline." In *The Organizational Life Cycle,* edited by J. R. Kimberley and R. H. Miles. San Francisco: Jossey-Bass, 1980; 342–74.

————. "Organizational Responses to Scarcity: Exploring the Obstacles to Innovative Responses to Retrenchment in Education," *Education Administrative Quarterly,* 17, Summer 1981, 80–97.

Yarmolinsky, A. "Institutional Paralysis." *Daedalus,* 2, Winter 1975, 61–67.

Educational Organizations as Loosely Coupled Systems

KARL E. WEICK

In contrast to the prevailing image that elements in organizations are coupled through dense, tight linkages, it is proposed that elements are often tied together frequently and loosely. Using educational organizations as a case in point, it is argued that the concept of loose coupling incorporates a surprising number of disparate observations about organizations, suggests novel functions, creates stubborn problems for methodologists, and generates intriguing questions for scholars. Sample studies of loose coupling are suggested and research priorities are posed to foster cumulative work with this concept.

* * *

Imagine that you're either the referee, coach, player or spectator at an unconventional soccer match: the field for the game is round; there are several goals scattered haphazardly around the circular field; people can enter and leave the game whenever they want to; they can throw balls in whenever they want; they can say "that's my goal" whenever they want to, as many times as they want to, and for as many goals as they want to; the entire game takes place on a sloped field; and the game is played as if it makes sense (March, personal communication).

If you now substitute in that example principals for referees, teachers for coaches, students for players, parents for spectators and schooling for soccer, you have an equally unconventional depiction of school organizations. The beauty of this depiction is that it captures a different set of realities within educational organizations than are caught when these same organizations are viewed through the tenets of bureaucratic theory.

Consider the contrast in images. For some time people who manage organizations and people who study this managing have asked, "How does an organization go about doing what it does and with what consequences for its people, processes, products, and persistence?" And for some time they've heard the same answers. In paraphrase the answers say essentially that an organization does what it does because of plans, intentional selection of means that get the organization to agree upon goals, and all of this is accomplished by such rationalized procedures as cost-benefit analyses, division of labor, specified areas of discretion, authority invested in the office, job descriptions, and a consistent evaluation and reward system. The only problem with that portrait is that it is rare in nature. People in organizations, including educational organizations, find themselves hard pressed either to find actual instances of those rational practices or to find rationalized practices whose outcomes have been as beneficent as predicted, or to feel that those rational occasions explain much of what goes on within the organization, Parts of some organizations are heavily rationalized but many parts also prove intractable to analysis through rational assumptions.

It is this substantial unexplained remainder that is the focus of this paper. Several people in education have expressed dissatisfaction with the prevailing ideas about organizations supplied by organizational theorists. Fortunately, they have also made some provocative suggestions about newer, more unconventional ideas about organizations that should be given serious thought. A good example of this is the following observation by John M. Stephens (1967: 9–11):

> (There is a) remarkable constancy of educational results in the face of widely differing deliberate approaches. Every so often we adopt new approaches or new methodologies and place our reliance on new panaceas. At the very least we seem to chorus new slogans. Yet the academic growth within the classroom continues at about the same rate, stubbornly refusing to cooperate with the bright new dicta emanating from the conference room...[These observations suggest that] we would be making a great mistake in regarding the management of schools as similar to the process of constructing a building or operating a factory. In these later processes deliberate decisions play a crucial part, and the enterprise advances or stands still in proportion to the amount of deliberate effort exerted. If we must use a metaphor or model in seeking to understand the process of schooling, we should look to agriculture rather than to the factory. In agriculture we do not start from scratch, and we do not direct our efforts to inert and passive materials. We start, on the contrary, with a complex and ancient process, and we organize our efforts around what seeds, plants, and insects are likely to do anyway....The crop, once planted, may undergo some development even while the farmer sleeps or loafs. No matter what he does, *some* aspects of the outcome will remain constant. When teachers and pupils foregather, some education may proceed even while the Superintendent disports himself in Atlantic City.

It is crucial to highlight what is important in the examples of soccer and schooling viewed as agriculture. To view these examples negatively and dismiss them by observing that "the referee should tighten up those rules," "superintendents don't do that." "schools are more sensible than that," or "these are terribly sloppy organizations" is to miss the point. The point is although researchers don't know what these kinds of structures are like but researchers do know they exist and that each of the negative judgments expressed above makes sense only if the observer assumes that organizations are constructed and managed according to rational assumptions and therefore are scrutable only when rational analyses are applied to them. This paper attempts to expand and enrich the set of ideas available to people when they try to make sense out of their organizational life. From this standpoint, it is unproductive to observe that fluid participation in schools and soccer is absurd. But it can be more interesting and productive to ask, how can it be that even though the activities in both situations are only modestly connected, the situations are still recognizable and nameable? The goals, player movements, and trajectory of the ball are still recognizable and can be labeled "soccer." And despite variations in class size, format, locations, and architecture, the results are still recognized and can be labeled "schools." How can such loose assemblages retain sufficient similarity and permanence across time that they can be recognized, labeled, and dealt with? The prevailing ideas in organization theory do not shed much light on how such "soft" structures develop, persist, and impose crude orderliness among their elements.

The basic premise here is that concepts such as loose coupling serve as sensitizing devices. They sensitize the observer to notice and question things that had previously been taken for granted. It is the intent of the program described here to develop a language for use in analyzing complex organizations, a language that may highlight features that have previously gone unnoticed. The guiding principle is a reversal of the common assertion, "I'll believe it when I see it" and presumes an epistemology that asserts, "I'll see it when I believe it." Organizations as loosely coupled systems may not have been seen before because nobody believed in them or could afford to believe in them. It is conceivable that preoccupation with rationalized, tidy, efficient, coordinated structures has blinded many practitioners as well as researchers to some of the attractive and unexpected properties of less rationalized and less tightly related clusters of events. This paper intends to eliminate such blindspots.

The Concept of Coupling

The phrase "loose coupling" has appeared in the literature (Glassman, 1973; March and Olsen, 1975) and it is important to highlight the connotation that is captured by this phrase and by no other. It might seem that the word coupling is synonymous with words like connection, link, or interdependence, yet each of these latter terms misses a crucial nuance.

By loose coupling, the author intends to convey the image that coupled events are responsive, *but* that each event also preserves its own identity and some evidence of its physical or logical separateness. Thus, in the case of an educational organization, it may be the case that the counselor's office is loosely coupled to the principal's office. The image is that the principal and the counselor are somehow attached, but that each retains some identity and separateness and that their attachment may be circumscribed, infrequent, weak in its mutual affects, unimportant, and/or slow to respond. Each of those connotations would be conveyed if the qualifier loosely were attached to the word coupled. Loose coupling also carries connotations of impermanence, dissolvability, and tacitness all of which are potentially crucial properties of the "glue" that holds organizations together.

Glassman (1973) categorizes the degree of coupling between two systems on the basis of the activity of the variables which the two systems share. To the extent that two systems either have few variables in common or share weak variables, they are independent of each other. Applied to the educational situation, if the principal-vice-principal-superintendent is regarded as one system and the teacher-classroom-pupil-parent-curriculum as another system, then by Glassman's argument if we did not find many variables in the teacher's world to be shared in the world of a principal and/or if the variables held in common were unimportant relative to the other variables, then the principal can be regarded as being loosely coupled with the teacher.

A final advantage of coupling imagery is that it suggests the idea of building blocks that can be grafted onto an organization or severed with relatively little disturbance to either the blocks or the organization. Simon (1969) has argued for the attractiveness of this feature in that most complex systems can be decomposed into stable subassemblies and that these are the crucial elements in any organization or system. Thus, the coupling imagery gives researchers access to one of the more powerful ways of talking about complexity now available.

But if the concept of loose coupling highlights novel images heretofore unseen in organizational theory, what is it about these images that is worth seeing?

Coupled Elements

There is no shortage of potential coupling elements, but neither is the population infinite.

At the outset the two most commonly discussed coupling mechanisms are the technical core of the organization and the authority of office. The relevance of those two mechanisms for the issue of identifying elements is that in the case of technical couplings, each element is some kind of technology, task, subtask, role, territory and person, and the couplings are task-induced. In the case of authority as the coupling mechanism, the elements include positions, offices, responsibilities, opportunities, rewards, and sanctions and it is the couplings among these elements that presumably hold the organization together. A compelling argument can be made that *neither* of these coupling mechanisms is prominent in educational organizations found in the United States. This leaves one with the question what *does* hold an educational organization together?

A short list of potential elements in educational organizations will provide background for subsequent propositions. March and Olsen (1975) utilize the elements of intention and action. There is a developing position in psychology which argues that intentions are a poor guide for action, intentions often follow rather than precede action, and that intentions and action are loosely coupled. Unfortunately, organizations continue to think that planning is a good thing, they spend much time on planning, and actions are assessed in terms of their fit with plans. Given a potential loose coupling between the intentions and actions of organizational members, it should come as no surprise that administrators are baffled and angered when things never happen the way they were supposed to.

Additional elements may consist of events like yesterday and tomorrow (what happened yesterday may be tightly or loosely coupled with what happens tomorrow) or hierarchical positions, like, top and bottom, line and staff, or administrators and teachers. An interesting set of elements that lends itself to the loose coupling imagery is means and ends. Frequently, several different means lead to the same outcome. When this happens, it can be argued that any one means is loosely coupled to the end in the sense that there are alternative pathways to achieve that same end. Other elements that might be found in loosely coupled educational systems are teachers-materials, voters-schoolboard, administrators-classroom, process-outcome, teacher-teacher, parent-teacher, and teacher-pupil.

While all of these elements are obvious, it is not a trivial matter to specify which elements are coupled. As the concept of coupling is crucial because of its ability to highlight the identity and separateness of elements that are momentarily attached, that conceptual asset puts pressure on the investigator to specify clearly the identity, separateness, and boundaries of the elements coupled. While there is some danger of reification when that kind of pressure is exerted, there is the even greater danger of portraying organizations in inappropriate terms which suggest an excess of unity, integration, coordination, and consensus. If one is nonspecific about boundaries in defining elements then it is easy—and careless—to assemble these ill-defined elements and talk about integrated organizations. It is not a trivial issue explaining how elements persevere over time. Weick, for example, has argued (1974: 363–364) that elements may appear or disappear and may merge or become separated in response to need-deprivations within the individual, group, and/or organization. This means that specification of elements is not a one-shot activity. Given the context of most organizations, elements both appear and disappear over time. For this reason a theory of how elements become loosely or tightly coupled may also have to take account of the fact that the nature and intensity of the coupling may itself serve to create or dissolve elements.

The question of what is available for coupling and decoupling within an organization is an eminently practical question for anyone wishing to have some leverage on a system.

Strength of Coupling

Obviously there is no shortage of meanings for the phrase loose coupling. Researchers need to be clear in their own thinking about whether the phenomenon they are studying is described by two words or three. A researcher can study "loose coupling" in educational organizations or "loosely coupled systems." The shorter phrase, "loose coupling," simply connotes things, "anythings," that may be tied together either weakly or infrequently or slowly or with minimal interdependence. Whether those things that are loosely coupled exist in a system is of minor importance. Most discussions in this paper concern loosely coupled systems rather than loose coupling since it wishes to clarify the concepts involved in the perseverance of sets of elements across time.

The idea of loose coupling is evoked when people have a variety of situations in mind. For example, when people describe loosely coupled systems they are often referring to (1) slack times—times when there is an excessive amount of resources relative to demands; (2) occasions when any one of several means will produce the same end; (3) richly connected networks in which influence is slow to spread and/or is weak while spreading; (4) a relative lack of coordination, slow coordination or coordination that is dampened as it moves through a system: (5) a relative absence of regulations; (6) planned unresponsiveness; (7) actual causal independence; (8) poor observational capabilities on the part of a viewer; (9) infrequent inspection of activities within the system; (10) decentralization; (11) delegation of discretion; (12) the absence of linkages that should be present based on some theory—for example, in educational organizations the expected feedback linkage from outcome back to inputs is often nonexistent; (13) the observation that an organization's structure is not coterminus with its activity; (14) those occasions when no matter what you do things always come out the same— for instance, despite all kinds of changes in curriculum, materials, groupings, and so forth the outcomes in an educational situation remain the same; and (15) curricula or courses in educational organizations for which there are few prerequisites—the longer the string of prerequisites, the tighter the coupling.

Potential Functions and Dysfunctions of Loose Coupling

It is important to note that the concept of loose coupling need not be used normatively. People who are steeped in the conventional literature of organizations may regard loose coupling as a sin or something to be apologized for. This paper takes a neutral, if not mildly affectionate, stance toward the concept. Apart from whatever affect one might feel toward the idea of loose coupling, it does appear a priori that certain functions can be served by having a system in which the elements are loosely coupled. Below are listed seven potential functions that could be associated with loose coupling plus additional reasons why each advantage might also be a liability. The dialectic generated by each of these oppositions begins to suggest dependent variables that should be sensitive to variations in the tightness of coupling.

The basic argument of Glassman (1973) is that loose coupling allows some portions of an organization to persist. Loose coupling lowers the probability that the organization will have to—or be able to—respond to each little change in the environment that occurs. The mechanism of voting, for example, allows elected officials to remain in office for a full term even though their constituency at any moment may disapprove of particular actions. Some identity and separateness of the element "elected official" is preserved relative to a second element, "constituency," by the fact of loosely coupled accountability which is measured in two, four, or six year terms. While loose coupling may foster perseverance, it is not selective in what is perpetuated. Thus archaic traditions as well as innovative improvisations may be perpetuated.

A second advantage of loose coupling is that it may provide a sensitive sensing mechanism. This possibility is suggested by Fritz Heider's perceptual theory of things and medium. Heider (1959) argues that perception is most accurate when a medium senses a thing and the medium contains many independent elements that can be externally constrained. When elements in a medium become either fewer in number and/or more internally constrained and/or more interdependent, their ability to represent some remote thing is decreased. Thus sand is a better medium to display wind currents than are rocks, the reason being that sand has more elements, more independence among the elements, and the elements are subject to a greater amount of external constraint than is the case for rocks. Using Heider's formulation metaphorically, it could be argued that loosely coupled systems preserve many independent sensing elements and therefore "know" their environments better than is true for more tightly coupled systems which have fewer externally constrained, independent elements. Balanced against this improvement in sensing is the possibility that the system would become increasingly vulnerable to producing faddish responses and interpretations. If the environment is known better, then this could induce more frequent changes in activities done in response to this "superior intelligence."

A third function is that a loosely coupled system may be good system for localized adaptation. If all of the elements in a large system are loosely coupled to one another, then any one element can adjust to and modify a local unique contingency without affecting the whole system. These local adaptations can be swift, relatively economical, and substantial. By definition, the antithesis of localized adaptation is standardization and to the extent that standardization can be shown to be desirable, a loosely coupled system might exhibit fewer of these presumed benefits. For example, the localized adaptation characteristic of loosely coupled systems may result in a lessening of educational democracy.

Fourth, in loosely coupled systems where the identity, uniqueness, and separateness of elements is preserved, the system potentially can retain a greater number of mutations and novel solutions than would be the case with a tightly coupled system. A loosely coupled system could preserve more "cultural insurance" to be drawn upon in times of radical change than in the case for more tightly coupled systems. Loosely coupled systems may be elegant solutions to the problem that adaptation can preclude adaptability. When a specific system fits into an ecological niche and does so with great success, this adaptation can be costly. It can be costly because resources which are useless in a current environment might deteriorate or disappear even though they could be crucial in a modified environment. It is conceivable that loosely coupled systems preserve more diversity in responding than do tightly coupled systems, and therefore can adapt to a considerably wider range of changes in the environment than would be true for tightly coupled systems. To appreciate the possible problems associated with this abundance of mutations, reconsider the dynamic outlined in the preceding discussion of localized adaptation. If a local set of elements can adapt to local idiosyncrasies without involving the whole system, then this same loose coupling could also forestall the spread of advantageous mutations that exist somewhere in the system. While the system may contain novel solutions for new problems of adaptation, the very structure that allows these mutations to flourish may prevent their diffusion.

Fifth, if there is a breakdown in one portion of a loosely coupled system then this breakdown is sealed off and does not affect other portions of the organization. Previously we, had noted that loosely coupled systems are an exquisite mechanism to adapt swiftly to local novelties and unique problems. Now we are carrying the analysis one step further, and arguing that when any element misfires or decays or deteriorates, the spread of this deterioration is checked in a loosely coupled system. While this point is reminiscent of earlier functions, the emphasis here is on the localization of trouble rather than the localization of adaptation. But even this potential benefit may be problematic. A loosely coupled system can isolate its trouble spots and prevent the trouble from spreading, but it should be difficult for the loosely coupled system to repair the defective element. If weak influences pass from the defective portions to the functioning portions, then the influence back from these functioning portions will also be weak and probably too little, too late.

Sixth, since some of the most important elements in educational organizations are teachers, classrooms, principals, and so forth, it may be consequential that in a loosely coupled system there is more room available for self-determination by the actors. If it is argued that a sense of efficacy is crucial for human beings, then a sense of efficacy might be greater in a loosely coupled system with autonomous units than it would be in a tightly coupled system where discretion is limited. A further comment can be made about self-determination to provide an example of the kind of imagery that is invoked by the concept of loose coupling.

It is possible that much of the teacher's sense of—and actual—control comes from the fact that diverse interested parties expect the teacher to link their intentions with teaching actions. Such linking of diverse intentions with actual work probably involves considerable negotiation. A parent complains about a teacher's action and the teacher merely points out to the parent how the actions are really correspondent with the parent's desires for the education of his or her children. Since most actions have ambiguous consequences, it should always be possible to justify the action as fitting the intentions of those who complain. Salancik (1975) goes even farther and suggests the intriguing possibility that when the consequences of an action are ambiguous, the stated *intentions* of the action serve as surrogates for the consequences. Since it is not known whether reading a certain book is good or bad for a child, the fact that it is intended to be good for the child itself becomes justification for having the child read it. The potential trade-off implicit in this function of loose coupling is fascinating. There is an increase in autonomy in the sense that resistance is heightened, but this heightened resistance occurs at the price of shortening the chain of consequences that will flow from each autonomous actor's efforts. Each teacher will have to negotiate separately with the same complaining parent.

Seventh, a loosely coupled system should be relatively inexpensive to run because it takes time and money to coordinate people. As much of what happens and should happen inside educational organizations seems to be defined and validated outside the organization, schools are in the business of building and maintaining categories, a business that requires coordination only on a few specific issues—for instance, assignment of teachers. This reduction in the necessity for coordination results in fewer conflicts, fewer inconsistencies among activities, fewer discrepancies between categories and activity. Thus, loosely coupled systems seem to hold the costs of coordination to a minimum. Despite this being an inexpensive system, loose coupling is also a nonrational system of fund allocation and therefore, unspecifiable, unmodifiable, and incapable of being used as means of change.

When these several sets of functions and dysfunctions are examined, they begin to throw several research issues into relief. For example, oppositions proposed in each of the preceding seven points suggest the importance of contextual theories. A predicted outcome or its opposite should emerge depending on how and in what the loosely coupled system is embedded. The preceding oppositions also suggest a fairly self-contained research program. Suppose a researcher starts with the first point made, as loose coupling increases the system should contain a greater number of anachronistic practices. Loosely coupled systems should be conspicuous for their cultural lags. Initially, one would like to know whether that is plausible or not. But then one would want to examine in more fine-grained detail whether those anachronistic practices that are retained hinder the system or impose structure and absorb uncertainty thereby producing certain economies in responding. Similar embellishment and elaboration is possible for each function with the result that rich networks of propositions become visible. What is especially attractive about these networks is that there is little precedent for them in the organizational literature. Despite this, these propositions contain a great deal of face validity when they are used as filters to look at educational organizations. When compared, for example, with the bureaucratic template mentioned in the introduction, the template associated with loosely coupled systems seems to take the observer into more interesting territory and prods him or her to ask more interesting questions.

Methodology and Loose Coupling

An initial warning to researchers: the empirical observation of unpredictability is insufficient evidence for concluding that the elements in a system are loosely coupled. Buried in that caveat are a host of methodological intricacies. While there is ample reason to believe that loosely coupled systems can be seen and examined, it is also possible that the appearance of loose coupling will be nothing more than a testimonial to bad methodology. In psychology, for example, it has been argued that the chronic failure to predict behavior from attitudes is due to measurement error and not to the unrelatedness of these two events. Attitudes are said to be loosely coupled with behavior but it may be that this conclusion is an artifact produced because attitudes assessed by time-independent and context-independent measures are being used to predict behaviors that are time and context dependent. If both attitudes and behaviors were assessed with equivalent measures, then tight coupling might be the rule.

Any research agenda must be concerned with fleshing out the imagery of loose coupling—a task requiring a considerable amount of conceptual work to solve a few specific and rather tricky methodological problems before one can investigate loose coupling.

By definition, if one goes into an organization and watches which parts affect which other parts, he or she will see the tightly coupled parts and the parts that vary the most. Those parts which vary slightly, infrequently, and periodically will be less visible. Notice, for example, that interaction data—who speaks to whom about what—are unlikely to reveal loose couplings. These are the most visible and obvious couplings and by the arguments developed in this paper perhaps some of the least crucial to understand what is going on in the organization.

An implied theme in this paper is that people tend to overrationalize their activities and to attribute greater meaning, predictability, and coupling among them than in fact they have. If members tend to overrationalize their activity, then their descriptions will not suggest which portions of that activity are loosely and tightly coupled. One might, in fact, even use the presence of apparent over-rationalization as a potential clue that myth making, uncertainty, and loose coupling have been spotted.

J.G. March has argued that loose coupling can be spotted and examined only if one uses methodology that highlights and preserves rich detail about context. The necessity for a contextual methodology seems to arise, interestingly enough, from inside organization theory. The implied model involves cognitive limits on rationality and man as a single channel information processor. The basic methodological point is that if one wishes to observe loose coupling, then he has to see both what is and is not being done. The general idea is that time spent on one activity is time spent away from a second activity. A contextually sensitive methodology would record both the fact that some people are in one place generating events and the fact that these same people are thereby absent from some other place. The rule of thumb would be that a tight coupling in one part of the system can occur only if there is loose coupling in another part of the system. The problem that finite attention creates for a researcher is that if some outcome is observed for the organization, then it will not be obvious whether the outcome is due to activity in the tightly coupled sector or to inactivity in the loosely coupled sector. That is a provocative problem of interpretation. But the researcher should be forewarned that there are probably a finite number of tight couplings that can occur at any moment, that tight couplings in one place imply loose couplings elsewhere, and that it may be the *pattern* of couplings that produces the observed outcomes. Untangling such intricate issues may well require that new tools be developed for contextual understanding and that investigators be willing to substitute nonteleological thinking for teleological thinking (Steinbeck, 1941: chapter 14).

Another contextually sensitive method is the use of comparative studies. It is the presumption of this methodology that taken-for-granted understandings—one possible "invisible" source of coupling in an otherwise loosely coupled system—are embedded in and contribute to a context. Thus, to see the effects of variations in these understandings one compares contexts that differ in conspicuous and meaningful ways.

Another methodological trap may await the person who tries to study loose coupling. Suppose one provides evidence that a particular goal is loosely coupled to a particular action. He or she says in effect, the person wanted to do this but in fact actually did that, thus, the action and the intention are loosely coupled. Now the problem for the researcher is that he or she may simply have focused on the wrong goal. There may be other goals which fit that particular action better. Perhaps if the researcher were aware of them, then the action and intention would appear to be tightly coupled. Any kind of intention-action, plan-behavior, or means-end depiction of loose coupling may be vulnerable to this sort of problem and an exhaustive listing of goals rather than parsimony should be the rule.

Two other methodological points should be noted. First, there are no good descriptions of the kinds of couplings that can occur among the several elements in educational organizations. Thus, a major initial research question is simply, what does a map of the couplings and elements within an educational organization look like? Second, there appear to be some fairly rich probes that might be used to uncover the nature of coupling within educational organizations. Conceivably, crucial couplings within schools involve the handling of disciplinary issues and social control, the question of how a teacher gets a book for the classroom, and the question of what kinds of innovations need to get clearance by whom. These relatively innocuous questions may be powerful means to learn which portions of a system are tightly and loosely coupled. Obviously these probes would be sampled if there was a full description of possible elements that can be coupled and possible kinds and strengths of couplings. These specific probes suggest, however, in addition that what holds an educational organization together may be a small number of tight couplings in out-of-the-way places.

Illustrative Questions For A Research Agenda

Patterns of Loose and Tight Coupling: Certification versus Inspection

Suppose one assumes that education is an intrinsically uninspected and unevaluated activity. If education is intrinsically uninspected and unevaluated then how can one establish that it is occurring? One answer is to define clearly who can and who cannot do it and to whom. In an educational organization this is the activity of certification. It is around the issues of certification and of specifying who the pupils are that tight coupling would be predicted to occur when technology and outcome are unclear.

If one argues that "certification" is the question "who does the work" and "inspection" is the question "how well is the work done," then there can be either loose or tight control over either certification or inspection. Notice that setting the problem up this way suggests the importance of discovering the distribution of tight and loosely coupled systems within any organization. Up to now the phrase loosely coupled systems has been used to capture the fact that events in an organization seem to be temporally related rather than logically related (Cohen and March, 1974). Now that view is being enriched by arguing that any organization must deal with issues of certification (who does the work) and inspection (how well is the work done). It is further being suggested that in the case of educational organizations there is loose control on the work—the work is intrinsically uninspected and unevaluated or if it is evaluated it is done so infrequently and in a perfunctory manner—but that under these conditions it becomes crucial for the organization to have tight control over who does the work and on whom. This immediately suggests the importance of comparative research in which the other three combinations are examined, the question being, how do these alternative forms grow, adapt, manage their rhetoric and handle their clientele. Thus it would be important to find organizations in which the controls over certification and inspection are both loose, organizations where there is loose control over certification but tight control over inspection, and organizations in which there is tight control both over inspection and over certification. Such comparative research might be conducted among different kinds of educational organizations within a single country (military, private, religious schooling in the United States), between educational and noneducational organizations within the same country (for example, schools versus hospitals versus military versus business organizations) or between countries looking at solutions to the problem of education given different degrees of centralization. As suggested earlier, it may not be the existence or nonexistence of loose coupling that is a crucial determinant of organizational functioning over time but rather the patterning of loose and tight couplings. Comparative studies should answer the question of distribution.

If, as noted earlier, members within an organization (and researchers) will see and talk clearly about only those regions that are tightly coupled, then this suggests that members of educational organizations should be most explicit and certain when they are discussing issues related to certification for definition and regulation of teachers, pupils, topics, space, and resources. These are presumed to be the crucial issues that are tightly controlled. Increasing vagueness of description should occur when issues of substantive instruction—inspection—are discussed. Thus, those people who primarily manage the instructional business will be most vague in describing what they do, those people who primarily manage the certification rituals will be most explicit. This pattern is predicted *not* on the basis of the activities themselves—certification is easier to describe than inspection—but rather on the basis of the expectation that tightly coupled subsystems are more crucial to the survival of the system and therefore have received more linguistic work in the past and more agreement than is true for loosely coupled elements.

Core Technology and Organizational Form

A common tactic to understand complex organizations is to explore the possibility that the nature of the task being performed determines the shape of the organizational structure. This straightforward tactic raises some interesting puzzles about educational organizations. There are suggestions in the literature that education is a diffuse task, the technology is uncertain.

This first question suggests two alternatives: if the task is diffuse then would not any organizational form whatsoever be equally appropriate *or* should this directly compel a diffuse form of organizational structure? These two alternatives are not identical. The first suggests that if the task is diffuse then any one of a variety of quite specific organizational forms could be imposed on the organization and no differences would be observed. The thrust of the second argument is that there is one and only one organizational form that would fit well when there is a diffuse task, namely, a diffuse organizational form (for instance, an organized anarchy).

The second question asks if the task in an educational organization is diffuse then why do all educational organizations look the way they do, and why do they all look the same? If there is no clear task around which the shape of the organization can be formed then why is it that most educational organizations do have a form and why is it that most of these forms look identical? One possible answer is that the tasks of educational organizations does not constrain the form of the organization but rather this constraint is imposed by the ritual of certification and/or the agreements that are made in and by the environment. If any of these nontask possibilities are genuine alternative explanations, then the general literature on organizations has been insensitive to them.

One is therefore forced to ask the question, is it the case within educational organizations that the technology is unclear? So far it has been argued that loose coupling in educational organizations is partly the result of uncertain technology. If uncertain technology does not generate loose coupling then researchers must look elsewhere for the origin of these bonds.

Making Sense in/of Loosely Coupled Worlds

What kinds of information do loosely coupled systems provide members around which they can organize meanings, that is, what can one use in order to make sense of such fleeting structures? (By definition loosely coupled events are modestly predictable at best.) There is a rather barren structure that can be observed, reported on, and retrospected in order to make any sense. Given the ambiguity of loosely coupled structures, this suggests that there may be increased pressure on members to construct or negotiate some kind of social reality they can live with. Therefore, under conditions of loose coupling one should see considerable effort devoted to constructing social reality, a great amount of face work and linguistic work, numerous myths (Mitroff and Kilmann, 1975) and in general one should find a considerable amount of effort being devoted to punctuating this loosely coupled world and connecting it in some way in which it can be made sensible. Loosely coupled worlds do not look as if they would provide an individual many resources for sense making—with such little assistance in this task, a predominant activity should involve constructing social realities. Tightly coupled portions of a system should not exhibit nearly this preoccupation with linguistic work and the social construction of reality.

Coupling as a Dependent Variable

As a general rule, any research agenda on loose coupling should devote equal attention to loose coupling as a dependent and independent variable. Most suggestions have treated loose coupling as an independent variable. Less attention has been directed toward loose coupling as a dependent variable with the one exception of the earlier argument that one can afford loose coupling in either certification or inspection but not in both and, therefore, if one can locate a tight coupling for one of these two activities then he can predict as a dependent variable loose coupling for the other one.

Some investigators, however, should view loose coupling consistently as a dependent variable. The prototypic question would be, given prior conditions such as competition for scarce resources, logic built into a task, team teaching, conflict, striving for professionalism, presence of a central ministry of education, tenure, and so forth, what kind of coupling (loose or tight) among what kinds of elements occurs? If an organization faces a scarcity of resources its pattern of couplings should differ from when it faces an expansion of resources (for instance, scarcity leads to stockpiling leads to decoupling). Part of the question here is, what kinds of changes in the environment are the variables of tight and loose coupling sensitive to? In response to what kinds of activities or what kinds of contexts is coupling seen to change and what kinds of environments or situations, when they change, seem to have no effect whatsoever on couplings within an organization? Answers to these questions, which are of vital importance in predicting the outcomes of any intervention, are most likely to occur if coupling is treated as a dependent variable and the question is, under what conditions will the couplings that emerge be tight or loose?

Assembling Loosely Connected Events

Suppose one assumes that there is nothing in the world except loosely coupled events. This assumption is close to Simon's stable subassemblies and empty world hypothesis and to the idea of cognitive limits on rationality. The imagery is that of numerous clusters of events that are tightly coupled within and loosely coupled between. These larger loosely coupled units would be what researchers usually call organizations. Notice that organizations formed this way are rather unusual kinds of organizations because they are neither tightly connected, nor explicitly bounded, but they are stable. The research question then becomes, how does it happen that loosely coupled events which remain loosely coupled are institutionally held together in one organization which retains few controls over central activities? Stated differently, how does it happen that someone can take a series of loosely coupled events, assemble them into an organization of loosely coupled systems, and the events remain both loosely coupled but the organization itself survives? It is common to observe that large organizations have loosely connected sectors. The questions are, what makes this possible, how does it happen? What the structure in school systems seems to consist of is categories (for example, teacher, pupil, reading) which are linked by understanding and legitimated exogenously (that is, by the world outside the organization). As John Meyer (1975) puts it, "the system works because everyone knows everyone else knows roughly what is to go on....Educational organizations are holding companies containing shares of stock in uninspected activities and subunits which are largely given their meaning, reality, and value in the wider social market." Note the potential fragility of this fabric of legitimacy.

It remains to be seen under what conditions loosely coupled systems are fragile structures because they are shored up by consensual anticipations, retrospections, and understanding that can dissolve and under what conditions they are resilient structures because they contain mutations, localized adaptation, and fewer costs of coordination.

Separate Intending and Acting Components

Intention and action are often loosely coupled within a single individual. Salancik (1975) has suggested some conditions under which dispositions within a single individual may be loosely coupled. These include such suggestions as follows. (1) If intentions are not clear and unambiguous, then the use of them to select actions which will fulfill the intentions will be imperfect. (2) If the consequences of action are not known, then the use of intention to select action will be imperfect. (3) If the means by which an intention is transformed into an action are not known or in conflict, then the coupling of action to intention will be imperfect. (4) if intentions are not known to a person at the time of selecting an action, then the relationships between action and intention will be imperfect. This may be more common than expected because this possibility is not allowed by so-called rational models of man. People often have to recall their intentions after they act or reconstruct these intentions, or invent them. (5) If there exists a set of multiple intentions which can determine a set of similar multiple actions, then the ability to detect a relationship between any one intention and any one action is likely to be imperfect. To illustrate, if there is an intention A which implies selecting actions X and Y, and there is also an intention B which implies selecting actions X and Y, then it is possible that under both presence and absence of intention A, action X will be selected. Given these circumstances, an observer will falsely conclude that this relationship is indeterminate.

The preceding list has the potential limitation for organizational inquiry in that it consists of events within a single person. This limitation is not serious *if* the ideas are used as metaphors or if each event is lodged in a different person. For example, one could lodge intention with one person and action with some other person. With this separation, then all of the above conditions may produce loose coupling between these actors but additional conditions also come into play given this geographical separation of intention from action. For example, the simple additional requirement that the intentions must be communicated to the second actor and in such a way that they control his actions, will increase the potential for error and loose coupling. Thus any discussion of separate locations for intention and action within an organization virtually requires that the investigator specify the additional conditions under which the intending component can control the acting component. Aside from the problems of communication and control when intention and action are separated there are at least two additional conditions that could produce loose coupling.

1. If there are several diverse intending components all of whom are dependent on the same actor for implementing action, then the relationship between any one intention and any one action will be imperfect. The teacher in the classroom may well be the prototype of this condition.
2. The process outlined in the proceeding item can become even more complicated, and the linkages between intention and action even looser, if the single acting component has intentions of its own.

Intention and action are often split within organizations. This paper suggests that if one were to map the pattern of intention and action components within the organization these would coincide with loosely coupled systems identified by other means. Furthermore, the preceding propositions begin to suggest conditions under which the same components might be at one moment tightly coupled and at the next moment loosely coupled.

Conclusion: A Statement of Priorities

More time should be spent examining the possibility that educational organizations are most usefully viewed as loosely coupled systems. The concept of organizations as loosely coupled systems can have a substantial effect on existing perspectives about organizations. To probe further into the plausibility of that assertion, it is suggested that the following research priorities constitute a reasonable approach to the examination of loosely coupled systems.

1. Develop Conceptual Tools Capable of Preserving Loosely Coupled Systems

It is clear that more conceptual work has to be done before other lines of inquiry on this topic are launched. Much of the blandness in organizational theory these days can be traced to investigators applying impoverished images to organizational settings. If researchers immediately start stalking the elusive loosely coupled system with imperfect language and concepts, they will perpetuate the blandness of organizational theory. To see the importance of and necessity for this conceptual activity the reader should reexamine the 15 different connotations of the phrase "loose coupling" that are uncovered in this paper. They provide 15 alternative explanations for any researcher who claims that some outcome is due to loose coupling.

2. Explicate What Elements Are Available in Educational Organizations for Coupling

This activity has high priority because it is essential to know the practical domain within which the coupling phenomena occur. Since there is the further complication that elements may appear or disappear as a function of context and time, this type of inventory is essential at an early stage of inquiry. An indirect benefit of making this a high priority activity is that it will stem the counterproductive suspicion that "the number of elements in educational organizations is infinite." The reasonable reply to that comment is that if one is precise in defining and drawing boundaries around elements, then the number of elements will be less than imagined. Furthermore, the researcher can reduce the number of relevant elements if he has some theoretical ideas in mind. These theoretical ideas should be one of the outcomes of initial activity devoted to language and concept development (Priority 1).

3. Develop Contextual Methodology

Given favorable outcomes from the preceding two steps, researchers should then be eager to look at complex issues such as patterns of tight and loose coupling keeping in mind that loose coupling creates major problems for the researcher because he is trained and equipped to decipher predictable, tightly coupled worlds. To "see" loosely coupled worlds unconventional methodologies need to be developed and conventional methodologies that are underexploited need to be given more attention. Among the existing tools that should be refined to study loose coupling are comparative studies and longitudinal studies. Among the new tools that should be "invented" because of their potential relevance to loosely coupled systems are nonteleological thinking (Steinbeck, 1941), concurrence methodology (Bateson, 1972: 180–201), and Hegelian, Kantian, and Singerian inquiring systems (Mitroff, 1974). While these latter methodologies are unconventional within social science, so too is it unconventional to urge that we treat unpredictability (loose coupling) as our topic of interest rather than a nuisance.

4. Promote the Collection of Thorough, Concrete Descriptions of the Coupling Patterns in Actual Educational Organizations

No descriptive studies have been available to show what couplings in what patterns and with what strengths existed in current educational organizations. This oversight should be remedied as soon as possible.

Adequate descriptions should be of great interest to the practitioner who wants to know how his influence attempts will spread and with what intensity. Adequate description should also show practitioners how their organizations may be more sensible and adaptive than they suspect. Thorough descriptions of coupling should show checks and balances, localized controls, stabilizing mechanisms, and subtle feedback loops that keep the organization stable and that would promote its decay if they were tampered with.

The benefits for the researcher of full descriptions are that they would suggest which locations and which questions about loose coupling are most likely to explain sizeable portions of the variance in organizational outcomes. For example, on the basis of good descriptive work, it might be found that both tightly and loosely coupled systems "know" their environments with equal accuracy in which case, the earlier line of theorizing about "thing and medium" would be given a lower priority.

5. Specify the Nature of Core Technology in Educational Organizations

A surprisingly large number of the ideas presented in this paper assume that the typical coupling mechanisms of authority of office and logic of the task do not operate in educational organizations. Inquiry into loosely coupled systems was triggered partly by efforts to discover what *does* accomplish the coupling in school systems. Before the investigation of loose coupling goes too far, it should be established that authority and task are not prominent coupling mechanisms in schools. The assertions that they are not prominent seem to issue from a combination of informal observation, implausibility, wishful thinking, looking at the wrong things, and rather vague definitions of core technology and reward structures within education. If these two coupling mechanisms were defined clearly, studied carefully, and found to be weak and/or nonexistent in schools, *then* there would be a powerful justification for proceeding vigorously to study loosely coupled systems. Given the absence of work that definitively discounts these coupling mechanisms in education and given the fact that these two mechanisms have accounted for much of the observed couplings in other kinds of organizations, it seems crucial to look for them in educational organizations in the interest of parsimony.

It should be emphasized that if it *is* found that substantial coupling within educational organizations is due to authority of office and logic of the task, this does not negate the agenda that is sketched out in this paper. Instead, such discoveries would (1) make it even more crucial to look for patterns of coupling to explain outcomes, (2) focus attention on tight and loose couplings within task and authority induced couplings, (3) alert researchers to keep close watch for any coupling mechanisms other than these two, and (4) would direct comparative research toward settings in which these two coupling mechanisms vary in strength and form.

6. Probe Empirically the Ratio of Functions to Dysfunctions Associated with Loose Coupling

Although the word "function" has had a checkered history, it is used here without apology— and without the surplus meanings and ideology that have become attached to it. Earlier several potential benefits of loose coupling were described and these descriptions were balanced by additional suggestions of potential liabilities. If one adopts an evolutionary epistemology, then over time one expects that entities develop a more exquisite fit with their ecological niches. Given that assumption, one then argues that if loosely coupled systems exist and if they have existed for sometime, then they bestow some net advantage to their inhabitants and/or their constituencies. It is not obvious, however, what these advantages are. A set of studies showing how schools benefit and suffer given their structure as loosely coupled systems should do much to improve the quality of thinking devoted to organizational analysis.

7. Discover How Inhabitants Make Sense Out of Loosely Coupled Worlds

Scientists are going to have some big problems when their topic of inquiry becomes low probability couplings, but just as scientists have special problems comprehending loosely coupled worlds so too must the inhabitants of these worlds. It would seem that quite early in a research program on loose coupling, examination of this question should be started since it has direct relevance to those practitioners who must thread their way through such "invisible" worlds and must concern their sense-making and stories in such a way that they don't bump into each other while doing so.

Karl E. Weick is a professor of psychology and organizational behavior at Cornell University.

This paper is the result of a conference held at La Jolla California, February 2–4, 1975 with support from the National Institute of Education (NIE). Participants in the conference were in addition to the author, W.W. Charters, Center for Education Policy and Management, University of Oregon; Craig Lundberg. School of Business, Oregon State University; John Meyer, Dept. of Sociology, Stanford University; Miles Meyers, Dept. of English. Oakland (Calif.) High School; Karlene Roberts, School of Business, University of California, Berkeley; Gerald Salancik, Dept. of Business Administration, University of Illinois and Robert Wentz, Superintendent of Schools, Pomona (Calif.) Unified School District. James G. March, School of Education, Stanford University, a member of the National Council on Educational Research, and members of the NIE staff were present as observers. This conference was one of several on organizational processes in education which will lead to a report that will be available from the National Institute of Education, Washington, D C. 20208. The opinions expressed in the paper do not necessarily reflect the position or policy of the National Institute of Education or the Department of Health, Education, and Welfare.

References

Bateson, Mary Catherine. *Our Own Metaphor*, New York: Knopf, 1972 .

Cohen, Michael D., and James G. March. *Leadership and Ambiguity*. Now York: McGraw-Hill, 1974.

Glassman, R. B. "Persistence and Loose Coupling in Living Systems." *Behavioral Science*, 1973, 18; 83–98.

Heider, Fritz. "Thing and medium." *Psychological Issues*, 1959, 1 (3); 1–34.

March, J. G., and J. P. Olsen, *Choice Situations in Loosely Coupled Worlds*. Unpublished manuscript, Stanford University, 1975.

Meyer, John W., *Notes on the Structure of Educational Organizations*. Unpublished manuscript, Stanford University, 1975.

Mitroff, Ian I., *The Subjective Side of Science*. Now York: Elsevier, 1974.

Mitroff, Ian I., and Ralph H. Kilmann, *On Organizational Stories: An Approach to the Design and Analysis of Organizations Through Myths and Stories*. Unpublished manuscript. University of Pittsburgh, 1975.

Salancik, Gerald R., *Notes on Loose Coupling: Linking Intentions to Actions*. Unpublished manuscript. University of Illinois, Urbana-Champaign, 1975.

Simon, H. A., 'The architecture of complexity." *Proceedings of the American Philosophical Society*, 106, 1969; 467–482

Steinbeck, John, *The Log from the Sea of Cortez*. New York: Viking, 1941.

Stephens, John M., *The Process of Schooling*. New York: Holt, Rinehart, and Winston, 1967.

Weick, Karl E., "Middle range theories of social systems." *Behavioral Science*, 1974, 19; 357–367.

Organizational Culture in the Study of Higher Education

ANDREW T. MASLAND

The pervasive influence of organizational culture has recently recaptured the attention of those who study organizations. Ouchi's *Theory Z* (1981), Pascale and Athos' *The Art of Japanese Management* (1981), and Deal and Kennedy's *Corporate Cultures* (1982) describe how organizational culture profoundly influences managerial behavior. This paper first defines organizational culture and briefly examines how the concept has been applied to colleges and universities. It then describes possible approaches and techniques for uncovering the influence of organizational culture. Finally, the paper explores why the study of organizational culture is relevant to researchers and practitioners. Thus, the paper defines and illustrates the application of a useful perspective on higher education.

The literature has previously recognized that there is more to organizations than formal structure. The classic elements of organizational design such as hierarchical structure, formalization, rationality, and specialization are important (Tosi, 1975), but they do not fully explain organizational behavior. Leadership, for example, can transform an organization with a formal structure of rules and objectives into an institution that is a "responsive, adaptive organism" (Selznick, 1957, p. 5).

Pettigrew (1979) expands upon Selznick's study of organizations. Pettigrew views leadership and values as one part of a concept he calls organizational culture. He defines organizational culture as "the amalgam of beliefs, ideology, language, ritual, and myth" (1979, p. 572). Pettigrew argues that an organization is a continuing social system and the elements of culture exert a powerful control over the behavior of those within it. Organizational culture induces purpose, commitment, and order; provides meaning and social cohesion; and clarifies and explains behavioral expectations. Culture influences an organization through the people within it.

The recent popular literature on Japanese management techniques highlights the influence of organizational culture. Pascale and Athos (1981) describe organizational culture as the glue that holds an organization together. It is a "bass clef" that conveys at a deep level what management really cares about. Theory Z (Ouchi, 1981) is a specific configuration of cultural beliefs and values. Ouchi asserts that this particular combination of cultural elements is largely responsible for the success of Japanese businesses. In contrast to Ouchi, Deal and Kennedy (1982) propose that a variety of corporate cultures can increase organizational effectiveness. A strongly articulated culture tells employees what is expected of them and how to behave under a given set of circumstances. The coherence of thought and action a strong culture produces thus enhances organizational success. Corporations with weak cultures do not have the sense of purpose and direction that is found in those with strong cultures, and are often less successful (Deal & Kennedy, 1982).

It is somewhat ironic that widespread interest in the interaction of culture and management grew out of studies of Japanese firms. As Chait (1982), Dill (1982), and Wyer (1982) note, traditional administrative practices common in American colleges and universities are similar to Japanese management styles. Shared governance and collegiality are participatory management. Academic departments, in discussions of future direction, quality control, and problem resolution, function like quality circles. Tenure traditionally provides the economic and psychological benefits of lifetime employment. Although colleges and universities have tong benefited from these managerial practices, they have not been identified as "organizational culture."

The concept of organizational culture is not new to higher education, however. Clark (1980) notes that the lofty doctrines associated with colleges and universities elicit almost religious emotions. He defines four cultural spheres that affect academic life in this way. They are (a) the cultures of specific academic disciplines, (b) the culture of the academic profession, (c) institutional cultures, and (d) the cultures of national systems of higher education. These four elements reflect academic structures. This paper focuses on the third category, the cultures of specific institutions.

The strength of institutional culture depends on several factors (Clark, 1980). Primary among them is the scale of the organization. Small organizations tend to have stronger cultures than do large organizations. Second is the tightness of the organization. Colleges with highly interdependent parts have stronger cultures than those with autonomous parts. Third is the age of the organization. As discussed below, culture develops over time and an institution with a long history simply has a larger foundation upon which to build its culture. Finally, the institution's founding influences the strength of its culture. A traumatic birth or transformation, like a long history, provides a stronger base upon which to build cultural values and beliefs. In colleges with stronger cultures there is greater coherence among beliefs, language, ritual, and myth. Weak cultures lack this coherence.

Clark's description of organizational saga is a classic embodiment of academic culture. Saga is a "collective understanding of unique accomplishment in a formally established group" (Clark, 1972, p. 179). It is a set of beliefs and values lied together in a story about the institution's past. A saga strengthens the bond between the organization and students, alumni, faculty, and staff. A saga shapes social reality on the campus and thus helps control behavior. According to Clark saga intensifies organizational commitment and feelings of membership in a special community. The trust and loyalty a saga produces are valuable resources in preserving organizational strength.

At the institutional level culture affects many aspects of campus life. There is a long history of interest in student culture and its effects (see, for example, Feldman & Newcomb, 1969; Becker, Geer, Hughes, & Strauss, 1961). Similar to the study of student culture is research on organizational climate—the atmosphere or style of life on a campus (Pace, 1968). A wide variety of instruments measure climate, but they classify institutions by standard typologies and are heavily influenced by psychological constructs. Organizational culture, on the other hand, focuses on the shared values, beliefs, and ideologies which are unique to a campus. Thus measures of climate do not illuminate culture.

Organizational culture also affects curriculum and administration. Masland (1982), for example, demonstrates that organizational culture influences how academic computing fits into an institution's curriculum. As might be expected, a college that values a traditional liberal arts education is less apt to introduce a technical computing major. On the other hand, a college that primarily teaches business and management will want to introduce its students to the practical applications of computing that support business decisions. Along somewhat similar lines, an organization's culture affects the management of computer resources. A belief that students should have free access to computer resources in the same way that they have unlimited library resources is part of some campus cultures. But when computer resources are scarce, allocating them among competing users is a difficult task. This problem would not arise if institutional values did not stress unlimited access to educational resources.

Thus, the literature on higher education has begun to apply the concept of organizational culture—the implicit values, beliefs, and ideologies of those within an organization. In particular, research demonstrates that in higher education culture can affect student life, administration, and curriculum.

While organizational culture is becoming more widely used and accepted, it is still difficult to find clear and succinct methods of uncovering an institution's culture. Typical of the means given for discovering organizational culture is this description.

> All one has to do to get a feel for how the different cultures of competing businesses manifest themselves is to spend a day visiting each. . . . There are characteristic ways of making decisions, relating to bosses, and choosing people to fill key jobs (Schwartz & Davis, 1981, p. 30).

Although this may be true, the advice is rather vague for the researcher who wants to study organizational culture. The difficulty in studying culture arises because culture is implicit, and we are all embedded in our own cultures. In order to observe organizational culture, the researcher must find its visible and explicit manifestations (Schein, 1981).

Windows on Organizational Culture

Fortunately, there are methods available which uncover manifestations of organizational culture. Each involves looking for a specific influence of culture at work and from that evidence deducing something about the culture itself. Examination of organizational history, for example, often illuminates culture and its influences because culture develops over time through the actions and words of organizational leaders. Cultural manifestations can also be seen in current actions. The methods used to make decisions, agendas of meetings, and personnel policy are common arenas for cultural influences. To understand an organization's culture one must pay close attention to the details of daily life. There are a number of windows on organizational culture that make it easier to see both past and present cultural influences. This article focuses on four in particular: saga, heroes, symbols, and rituals. While there are a variety of ways to "see" culture, these four are particularly helpful, in part because they are easy to understand and apply. These four windows are closely related and may seem redundant, yet there are subtle differences among them.

Saga like heroes: Symbols and rituals

Saga (Clark, 1972) is the first window on organizational culture in higher education. A saga usually has its roots in an organization's history, and it describes a unique accomplishment of the organization. An institution's saga codifies what sets a college apart from others. Key faculty members, students, and alumni usually support an institution's saga, as do unique academic program elements and images about the institution. Clark uses Antioch, Swarthmore, and Reed as examples of three colleges with strong sagas. He demonstrates how the sagas at these schools profoundly influence institutional life. At Reed College, for example, the saga dates from the school's founding in 1910 by William T. Foster. The first president established a college known for "hard-won excellence and nonconformity" (Clark, 1972, p. 180). Antioch's saga arose from the influence of reformer Arthur E. Morgan who completely restructured Antioch and launched a saga based on combining work, study, and community participation.

Heroes

Organizational heroes or Saints (Deal & Kennedy, 1982; Dill, 1982) are a second window on organizational culture. Heroes are people who are important to an organization and often represent ideals and values in human form. They may play a central role in an institution's saga because heroes are people who have made crucial decisions or who exemplify behavior suitable to the college. They are role models, set standards, and preserve what makes the organization unique. People in an organization tell stories about heroes and the examples they set. The stories about heroes are another way to see organizational culture. They are passed down to newcomers in an organization as examples of successful behavior in the past.

Often, a college's founder is an organizational hero. The examples of Reed and Antioch cited above illustrate such heroes. Another example is a small college that has always combined liberal arts with career-oriented programs for women. Its founder stated that he wanted to provide women with an education that would make them self-sufficient. The college does this, and it did so long before the current trend towards career education began. The school's founder set an example personnel at the college endeavor to follow. A hero at a business college provides a final illustration. He was a long-time faculty member and administrator who fought for accreditation from an important agency. His long battle demonstrated and validated the value college personnel place on excellence.

Symbols

Symbols are a third window on organizational culture. A symbol can represent implicit cultural values and beliefs, thus, making them tangible. Personnel can point to a symbol as a concrete example much the same way that a hero personifies cultural values. Symbols also can serve an important external function. While heroes and stories may only be known to those within an organization, the public may recognize organizational symbols.

The business college mentioned above provides an excellent example of how a symbol gives insight into culture. The college has fairly extensive computer resources. It uses them to introduce students to the techniques and knowledge they will need in tomorrow's business environment. The desire to do this stems in part from the value the college places on leadership and excellence in business education. The computer facilities are a symbol of this value.

Metaphor is another type of symbol that is helpful in understanding organizational culture. The language people use when they talk about an organization reveals its culture. As with other symbols, metaphors make explicit normally implicit cultural values and beliefs (Beaudoin, 1981). Because metaphors help express that which usually is difficult to verbalize, they are an excellent key for unlocking culture. Masland (1982) examined a college that described its computer facilities as "supermarket computing." This is a vivid metaphor that invokes an image of practicality and value in the institution's approach to computing.

Rituals

Rituals are another means of identifying cultural values, beliefs, and ideologies. Rituals are a useful tool for uncovering culture because they translate culture into action. They provide tangible evidence of culture. An outstanding teaching award ceremony, for example, can demonstrate to an academic community the strength of the institution's values. Is such a ceremony taken seriously and the recipient seen as receiving a great honor, or is it dismissed as meaningless? If the institution values excellence in teaching, the former is more likely than the latter. Rituals provide continuity with the past. They demonstrate that old values and beliefs still play a role in campus life. Rituals also provide meaning. In an organization with ambiguous goals and uncertain outcomes, the annual convocation ceremony may provide a sense of meaning and direction for personnel. This kind of ritual reinforces the institution's culture. Moreover, daily rituals of interaction between faculty and administrators illustrate the relative importance of each group and the ideologies surrounding their roles.

Collecting Cultural Data

Saga, heroes, rituals, and symbols are means of exploring an organization's culture. In a strong culture they work in unison and illustrate the culture. But the researcher still needs specific methodologies to learn about each window. The common techniques described below are useful ways of examining the four cultural windows and thus culture itself.

Interviews, observation, and document analysis are three basic techniques. Of the three, interviews may be the most important. According to Gorden (1975), interviews are the most effective means of gathering data on beliefs, attitudes, and values. But because culture is implicit interview questions cannot ask about culture directly. Instead the researcher should probe the four cultural windows discussed above. Asking respondents what makes their college distinct or unique, or what makes it stand apart from similar schools a prospective applicant might consider, uncovers organizational saga. Similar questions focus on the school's educational philosophy and what is unique about its academic mission. Respondents draw upon their understanding of the institution's saga when answering such questions. They disclose what the college means to them. They also refer to the symbols and rituals that represent this meaning in a more tangible form. Thus listening carefully to responses in an interview is an excellent means of uncovering manifestations of organizational culture.

Interviewees may also respond positively to questions about organizational heroes, although referring to them as heroes may be counterproductive. It can be helpful to ask respondents to describe who the organization remembers and why they are remembered. Questions about organizational heroes are closely connected to questions about institutional history. Because cultural values and beliefs become institutionalized slowly over a period of time, their influence on past events is often apparent. Interviews are an excellent means of gathering such data.

Members of various campus constituencies such as faculty, students, administrators, and staff should be included in the interview sample. Snowball sampling (Murphy, 1980), in which one respondent suggests others who might also have valuable information, is one useful sampling method. With such a sampling plan the investigator can locate those individuals who have the greatest knowledge of the college.

Observation, a second useful technique, can be used concurrently with interviews. It is not simply classical observation of decision makers at work, committee meetings, or faculty members' teaching. Rather, it is also observing from many sources what is important in daily life on the campus. Through observation one can learn which issues receive careful attention and close scrutiny. Such issues are often central to the organization's culture.

Observation is a valuable means of learning more about cultural symbols, rituals, and heroes. As an outsider, an observer often sees symbols to which community members have become habituated. Thus, the observer may recognize the implicit meaning and importance of symbols that an insider takes at face value. As with symbols, an outsider may see rituals that insiders do not notice. These are the small, daily rituals that illustrate the relative value placed on different people or positions in the organization. Moreover, the memories of heroes are often immortalized in paintings, statues, or buildings.

A third technique is analysis of written documents. Document analysis is a useful means of filling in the gaps interviews and observation leave. It is also a valuable addition because documents are not subject to problems of selective recall and reinterpretation in light of the contemporary situation (Murphy, 1980).

Document analysis is an efficient method of gathering background information on the college. It is well suited for collecting data on institutional history. Historical accounts provide past examples of cultural influences while also illuminating the development of values, beliefs, and ideologies. Presidential annual reports often reference particularly important or traumatic events and decisions. Similarly, reports of blue ribbon committees may contain information about organizational culture. Campus newspapers may refer to key events and decisions. Those that create controversy often come closest to important cultural values and beliefs. Document analysis is also a means of learning more about the college's curriculum and its relationship to the campus culture. Worth noting are the unique features of a curriculum and why they exist. Finally, documents often highlight important and continuing rituals such as convocations or award ceremonies.

Several types of documents lend themselves to cultural analysis. These can include, but are not limited to, official college publications, correspondence, minutes of meetings, campus newspapers, and college histories. Institutional mission statements, planning documents, and self-studies for accreditation may also be useful. While such documents may seem trite (Chait, 1979), they are part of an organization's culture. Particularly in an organization with a strong culture, a mission statement reflects the institution's culture.

In summary, the use of interviews, observation, and document analysis encourages triangulation (Denzin, 1970). Each technique can confirm, disconfirm, or modify data obtained using the other two. Differences among the data must be investigated and the reasons for inconsistencies uncovered. In organizations with a strong culture, data from each source should confirm the other two because written statements, actions, and oral descriptions all form a coherent whole. Discrepancies among the data sources may indicate a weak or fractured culture.

Analysis of Cultural Data

Qualitative data collected while investigating organizational culture are usually complex and voluminous. Analysis begins and is concurrent with data collection. While gathering information, researchers may begin to see themes and trends in what people say about the organization and what they observe. These preliminary findings are then tested and further explored as the data collection process continues.

A basic technique for analyzing cultural data is thematic analysis—finding the recurrent cultural themes in the data (Schatzman & Strauss, 1973). Using this approach, the analyst structures and codes the data in order to distill important aspects of the organizational culture. Once researchers discover the underlying themes, they must determine how the themes fit together. Gradually, the analyst refines the principal ideas that recur throughout and begins to develop the central "story line" on the institution's culture. On a campus with a strong culture the analytic process is relatively straightforward because the data are consistent. If the culture is weak, the themes will not be as strong and the data may show discrepancies.

Consistency in cultural images takes several forms. Each respondent often refers to the same organizational heroes. Trends or problems which reappear over the history of the organization point to important cultural elements. Rituals and symbols support the culture. The clarity of values and the ways in which people act on them will be apparent. Another key to analysis is to look for the repeated use of symbols and rituals. Those repeated in many different contexts point to fundamental cultural features (Ortner, 1973). Important parts of the organization's culture are often associated with several different symbols or rituals.

Why Study Organizational Culture?

Over the past decade the perspectives on academic governance have expanded from the bureaucratic model to include political concepts and those of organized anarchies (Baldridge, 1971; Cohen & March, 1974). The concept of organizational culture may also provide valuable insight into colleges and universities. On a theoretical level, cultural analysis is another tool for researchers. Understanding the culture of a particular institution may further explain campus management because culture appears to influence managerial style and decision practices. Analysis of culture may expose conflicting cultural elements which could lead to ineffective behavior and plans. It might also help explain variations in curriculum and resistance to curricular change. Additional empirical research is needed to explore this area.

There is another argument that makes the study of organizational culture appear even more central to higher education. Organizational culture is what Leifer (1979) calls an unobtrusive organizational control. Unobtrusive controls operate in conjunction with two other levels of control mechanisms. Explicit controls (such as formal regulations and direct comments) and implicit controls (such as specialization and hierarchy) also influence organizational life. But when explicit and implicit controls are weak, the unobtrusive forces such as organizational culture become more important. A college or university campus is the classic example of an organization with weak explicit and implicit control mechanisms (Cohen & March, 1974; March & Olsen, 1976). Thus, it seems all the more appropriate to study organizational culture in higher education in greater depth.

Organizational culture is also useful on a practical level. Exploration of organizational culture may help explain how an organization arrived at its current state. Culture may explicate past influences on decisions and actions. It may provide an underlying rationale for institutional development. This understanding can then provide a better foundation for administrators' decision making (Smith & Steadman, 1981).

Finally, as colleges and universities confront the challenges of the eighties, a better comprehension of organizational culture may be vital at a broader level. As institutions and systems of higher education expand, academic culture fragments (Clark, 1980; Dill, 1982). Larger institutions, increased autonomy of institutional units, and specialization within disciplines contribute to what Clark calls the move from an "integrated academic culture" to "the many cultures of the conglomeration" (1980, p. 25). If, as this paper suggests, culture is a critical element of institutional life and management, it deserves careful attention. In fact, Dill (1982) argues that administrators must "manage" academic cultures during these times of decline because an institution derives strength from its culture. Institutional culture relieves some of the pressures and strains that decline puts on the social fabric of an organization. It does this because culture is a force that provides stability and a sense of continuity to an ongoing social system such as a college or university. Managing a force such as culture is a difficult task at best. The first step is acknowledging culture's existence and trying to understand the cultures of individual campuses. The techniques outlined above are useful in this respect.

In conclusion, exploring organizational culture is another means of learning more about colleges and universities. Traditional approaches to studying governance and decision making provide useful insights into why and how higher education works the way it does. But the perspective of cultural influences supplements the traditional approaches. It may further explain the variations found among colleges and universities. Although organizational culture is difficult to identify and study, it is worth the effort. Further investigation of organizational culture is needed to uncover its specific influence on the college and university campus. Before this is possible, however, culture needs to become part of the common parlance of researchers in higher education.

References

Baldridge, J. V. . *Power and Conflict in the University*. New York: John Wiley, 1971.

Beaudoin, D. B. *Presidents' Metaphors and Educational Leadership*. Unpublished manuscript. Harvard University, Harvard Graduate School of Education, Cambridge, 1981.

Becker, H. S., Geer. B., Hughes, E. C., & Strauss, A. L. *Boys in White*. Chicago: University of Chicago Press, 1961.

Chait, R. P. Mission madness strikes our colleges. *The Chronicle of Higher Education*, 16 July 1979; p. 36.

Chait, R. P. Look who invented Japanese management! *AGB Reports*, 1982, March/April; pp. 3-7.

Clark, B. R. The organizational saga in higher education. *Administrative Science Quarterly*, 1972, 17; 179-194.

Clark, B. R. *Academic Culture*. Working Paper. IHERG-42, Yale University, Higher Education Research Group, March1980,.

Cohen, M. D., & March. J. G. *Leadership and ambiguity*. New York: McGraw-Hill, 1974.

Deal, T. E., & Kennedy, A. A. *Corporate Cultures*. Reading, MA: Addison-Wesley. 1982.

Denzin, N. K. *The Research Act: A Theoretical Introduction to Sociological Methods*. Chicago: Aldine Publishing, 1970.

Dill. D. D. The management of academic culture: Notes on the management of meaning and social integration. *Higher Education*, 1982, 11; 303-320.

Feldman, K. A., & Newcomb, T. M. *The Impact of College on Students*. San Francisco: Jossey-Bass, 1969.

Gorden, R. L. *Interviewing: Strategy, Techniques, and Tactics*. Homewood, IL: Dorsey Press, 1975.

Leifer, R. *The Social Construction of Reality and the Evolution of Mythology as a Means for Understanding Organizational Control Processes*. Paper presented at the international meeting of the Institute of Management Science, Honolulu, Hawaii, June 1979.

March, J. G., & Olsen, J. P. *Ambiguity and Choice in Organizations*. Bergen, Norway: Universitetsforlaget, 1976.

Masland, A. T. *Organizational Influences on Computer Use in Higher Education*. Unpublished doctoral dissertation, Harvard University. Cambridge, 1982.

Murphy, J. T. *Getting the Facts: A Field Guide for Evaluation and Policy Analysis*. Santa Monica, CA: Goodyear Publishing, 1980.

Ortner, S. B. On key symbols. *American Anthropologist*, 1973, 75; 1338-1346.

Ouchi, W. *Theory Z: How American Business Can Meet the Japanese Challenge*. Reading, MA: Addison-Wesley, 1981.

Pace, C. R. The measurement of college environments. In R. Tagiuri & G. H. Litwin (Eds.), *Organizational Climate* Boston: Harvard University, Division of Business Research, 1968; 127–147.

Pascale. R. T., & Athos, A. G. *The Art of Japanese Management*. New York: Simon & Schuster, 1981.

Pettigrew, A. M. "On Studying Organizational Cultures." *Administrative Science Quarterly*, 1979, 24; 570-581.

Schatzman, L., & Strauss, A. L. *Field Research: Strategies for a Natural Sociology*. Englewood Cliffs, NJ: Prentice Hall, 1973.

Schein, E. H. "Does Japanese Management Have a Message For American Managers." *Sloan Management Review*, 1981, 23(1); 55-68.

Schwartz, H., & Davis, S. M. "Matching Corporate Culture and Business Strategy." *Organizational Dynamics*, 1981, 10; 30-48.

Selznick, P. *Leadership in Administration*. New York: Harper & Row, 1957.

Smith, G. D., & Steadman, L. E. Present value of corporate history. *Harvard Business Review*, 1981, 59(6); 164–173.

Tosi, H. C. *Theories of Organization*. Chicago: St. Clair Press, 1975.

Wyer, J. C. "Theory Z—The Collegial Model Revisited: An Essay Review." *The Review of Higher Education*, 1982, 5(2); 111–117.

Organizational Culture in Higher Education: Defining the Essentials

William G. Tierney

Within the business community in the last ten years, organizational culture has emerged as a topic of central concern to those who study organizations. Books such as Peters and Waterman's *In Search of Excellence* [37], Ouchi's *Theory Z* [33], Deal and Kennedy's *Corporate Cultures* [20], and Schein's *Organizational Culture and Leadership* [44] have emerged as major works in the study of managerial and organizational performance.

However, growing popular interest and research activity in organizational culture comes as something of a mixed blessing. Heightened awareness has brought with it increasingly broad and divergent concepts of culture. Researchers and practitioners alike often view culture as a new management approach that will not only cure a variety of organizational ills but will serve to explain virtually every event that occurs within an organization. Moreover, widely varying definitions, research methods, and standards for understanding culture create confusion as often as they provide insight.

The intent for this article is neither to suggest that an understanding of organizational culture is an antidote for all administrative folly, nor to imply that the surfeit of definitions of organizational culture makes its study meaningless for higher education administrators and researchers. Rather, the design of this article is to provide a working framework to diagnose culture in colleges and universities so that distinct problems can be overcome. The concepts for the framework come from a year-long investigation of organizational culture in American higher education.

First, I provide a rationale for why organizational culture is a useful concept for understanding management and performance in higher education. In so doing, I point out how administrators might utilize the concept of culture to help solve specific administrative problems. The second part of the article considers previous attempts to define culture in organizations in general, and specifically, in colleges and universities. Third, a case study of a public state college highlights essential elements of academic culture. The conclusion explores possible avenues researchers might examine in order to enhance a usable framework of organizational culture for managers and researchers in higher education.

The Role of Culture in Management and Performance

Even the most seasoned college and university administrators often ask themselves, "What holds this place together? Is it mission, values, bureaucratic procedures, or strong personalities? How does this place run and what does it expect from its leaders?" These questions usually are asked in moments of frustration, when seemingly rational, well-laid plans have failed or have met with unexpected resistance. Similar questions are also asked frequently by members new to the organization, persons who want to know "how things are done around here." Questions like these seem difficult to answer because there is no one-to-one correspondence between actions and results. The same leadership style can easily produce widely divergent results in two ostensibly similar institutions. Likewise, institutions with very similar missions and curricula can perform quite differently because of the way their identities are communicated to internal and external constituents and because of the varying perceptions these groups may hold.

Institutions certainly are influenced by powerful, external factors such as demographic, economic, and political conditions, yet they are also shaped by strong forces that emanate from within. This internal dynamic has its roots in the history of the organization and derives its force from the values, processes, and goals held by those most intimately involved in the organization's workings. An organization's culture is reflected in what is done, how it is done, and who is involved in doing it. It concerns decisions, actions, and communication both on an instrumental and a symbolic level.

The anthropologist, Clifford Geertz, writes that traditional culture, "denotes a historically transmitted pattern of meanings embodied in symbols, a system of inherited conceptions expressed in symbolic forms by means of which [people] communicate, perpetuate, and develop their knowledge about and attitudes toward life" [25, p. 89]. Organizational culture exists, then, in part through the actors' interpretation of historical and symbolic forms. The culture of an organization is grounded in the shared assumptions of individuals participating in the organization. Often taken for granted by the actors themselves, these assumptions can be identified through stories, special language, norms, institutional ideology, and attitudes that emerge from individual and organizational behavior.

Geertz defines culture by writing, "Man is an animal suspended in webs of significance he himself has spun. I take culture to be those webs, and the analysis of it to be therefore not an experimental science in search of law, but an interpretive one in search of meaning" [25, p. 5]. Thus, an analysis of organizational culture of a college or university occurs as if the institution were an interconnected web that cannot be understood unless one looks not only at the structure and natural laws of that web, but also at the actors' interpretations of the web itself. Organizational culture, then, is the study of particular webs of significance within an organizational setting. That is, we look at an organization as a traditional anthropologist would study a particular village or clan.

However, not unlike traditional villagers, administrators often have only an intuitive grasp of the cultural conditions and influences that enter into their daily decision making. In this respect they are not unlike most of us who have a dim, passive awareness of cultural codes, symbols, and conventions that are at work in society at large. Only when we break these codes and conventions are we forcibly reminded of their presence and considerable power. Likewise, administrators tend to recognize their organization's culture only when they have transgressed its bounds and severe conflicts or adverse relationships ensue. As a result, we frequently find ourselves dealing with organizational culture in an atmosphere of crisis management, instead of reasoned reflection and consensual change.

Our lack of understanding about the role of organizational culture in improving management and institutional performance inhibits our ability to address the challenges that face higher education. As these challenges mount, our need to understand organizational culture only intensifies. Like many American institutions in the 1980s, colleges and universities face increasing complexity and fragmentation.

As decision-making contexts grow more obscure, costs increase, and resources become more difficult to allocate, leaders in higher education can benefit from understanding their institutions as cultural entities. As before, these leaders continue to make difficult decisions. These decisions, however, need not engender the degree of conflict that they usually have prompted. Indeed, properly informed by an awareness of culture, tough decisions may contribute to an institution's sense of purpose and identity. Moreover, to implement decisions, leaders must have a full, nuanced understanding of the organization's culture. Only then can they articulate decisions in a way that will speak to the needs of various constituencies and marshal their support.

Cultural influences occur at many levels, within the department and the institution, as well as at the system and state level. Because these cultures can vary dramatically, a central goal of understanding organizational culture is to minimize the occurrence and consequences of cultural conflict and help foster the development of shared goals. Studying the cultural dynamics of educational institutions and systems equips us to understand and, hopefully, reduce adversarial relationships. Equally important, it will enable us to recognize how those actions and shared goals are most likely to succeed and how they can best be implemented. One assumption of this article is that more often than not more than one choice exists for the decision-maker; one simple answer most often does not occur. No matter how much information we gather, we can often choose from several viable alternatives. Culture influences the decision.

Effective administrators are well aware that they can take a given action in some institutions but not in others. They are less aware of why this is true. Bringing the dimensions and dynamics of culture to consciousness will help leaders assess the reasons for such differences in institutional responsiveness and performance. This will allow them to evaluate likely consequences before, not after they act.

It is important to reiterate that an understanding of organizational culture is not a panacea to all administrative problems. An understanding of culture, for example, will not automatically increase enrollments or increase fund raising. However, an administrator's correct interpretation of the organization's culture can provide critical insight about which of the many possible avenues to choose in reaching a decision about how to increase enrollment or undertake a particular approach to a fund-raising campaign. Indeed, the most persuasive case for studying organizational culture is quite simply that we no longer need to tolerate the consequences of our ignorance, nor, for that matter, will a rapidly changing environment permit us to do so.

By advocating a broad perspective, organizational culture encourages practitioners to:

- consider real or potential conflicts not in isolation but on the broad canvas of organizational life;
- recognize structural or operational contradictions that suggest tensions in the organization;
- implement and evaluate everyday decisions with a keen awareness of their role in and influence upon organizational culture;
- understand the symbolic dimensions of ostensibly instrumental decisions and actions; and
- consider why different groups in the organization hold varying perceptions about institutional performance.

Many administrators intuitively understand that organizational culture is important; their actions sometimes reflect the points mentioned above, A framework for organizational culture will provide administrators with the capability to better articulate and address this crucial foundation for improving performance.

Thus far, however, a usable definition of organizational culture appropriate to higher education has remained elusive. If we are to enable administrators and policy makers to implement effective strategies within their own cultures, then we must first understand a culture's structure and components. A provisional framework will lend the concept of culture definitional rigor so that practitioners can analyze their own cultures and ultimately improve the performance of their organizations and systems. The understanding of culture will thus aid administrators in spotting and resolving potential conflicts and in managing change more effectively and efficiently. However, if we are to enable administrators and researchers to implement effective strategies within their own cultures, then we first must make explicit the essential elements of culture.

Cultural Research: Where Have We Been

Organizations as Cultures

Ouchi and Wilkins note: "Few readers would disagree that the study of organizational culture has become one of the major domains of organizational research, and some might even argue that it has become the single most active arena, eclipsing studies of formal structure, of organization-environment research and of bureaucracy" [34, pp. 457–58].

Researchers have examined institutions, organizations, and subunits of organization as distinct and separate cultures with unique sets of ceremonies, rites, and traditions [30, 32, 38, 49]. Initial attempts have been made to analyze leadership from a cultural perspective [3, 39, 43, 45]. The role of cultural communication has been examined by March [28], Feldman and March [22], and Putnam and Pacanowsky [41], Trujillo [50], Tierney [46], and Pondy [40]. Organizational stories and symbols have also been investigated [17, 18, 29, 47].

Recent findings indicate that strong, congruent cultures supportive of organizational structures and strategies are more effective than weak, incongruent, or disconnected cultures [7, 27]. Moreover, the work of numerous theorists [5, 26, 31, 42] suggests that there is an identifiable deep structure and set of core assumptions that may be used to examine and understand culture.

Colleges and Universities as Cultures

Numerous writers [11, 21] have noted the lack of cultural research in higher education. Dill has commented: "Ironically the organizations in Western society which most approximate the essential characteristics of Japanese firms are academic institutions. They are characterized by lifetime employment, collective decision making, individual responsibility, infrequent promotion, and implicit, informal evaluation" [21, p. 307]. Research in higher education, however, has moved toward defining managerial techniques based on strategic planning, marketing and management control.

Higher education researchers have made some attempts to study campus cultures. Initially, in the early 1960s the study of culture primarily concerned student cultures [2, 6, 12, 19, 35, 36]. Since the early 1970s Burton Clark has pioneered work on distinctive colleges as cultures [13], the role of belief and loyalty in college organizations [14], and organizational sagas as tools for institutional identity [15]. Recent work has included the study of academic cultures [1, 23, 24], leadership [8, 10, 48], and the system of higher education as a culture [4, 16]. Thus, a foundation has been prepared on which we can build a framework for studying culture in higher education.

A Cultural Framework: Where We Might Go

Anthropologists enter the field with an understanding of such cultural terms as "kinship" or "lineage." Likewise, productive research depends on our being able to enter the field armed with equally well defined concepts. These terms provide clues for uncovering aspects of organizational culture as they also define elements of a usable framework. Necessarily then, we need to consider what cultural concepts can be utilized by cultural researchers when they study a college or university. This article provides an initial attempt to identify the operative cultural concepts and terms in collegiate institutions.

The identification of the concepts were developed through the analysis of a case study of one institution. By delineating and describing key dimensions of culture, I do not presume to imply that all institutions are culturally alike. The intense analysis of one institution provides a more specific understanding of organizational culture than we presently have and presumably will enable researchers to expand upon the framework presented here.

Of the many possible avenues that exist for the cultural researcher to investigate, Table 1 outlines essential concepts to be studied at a college or university. That is, if an anthropologist conducted an in depth ethnography at a college or university and omitted any mention of institutional mission we would note that the anthropologist had overlooked an important cultural term.

Table 1

A Framework of Organizational Culture	
Environment:	How does the organization define its environment?
	What is the attitude toward the environment?
	(Hostility? Friendship?)
Mission:	How is it defined?
	How is it articulated?
	Is it used as a basis for decisions?
	How much agreement is there?
Socialization:	How do new members become socialized?
	How is it articulated?
	What do we need to know to survive/excel in this organization?
Information:	What constitutes information?
	Who has it?
	How is it disseminated?
Strategy:	How are decisions arrived at?
	Which strategy is used?
	Who makes decisions?
	What is the penalty for bad decisions?
Leadership:	What does the organization expect from its leaders?
	Who are the leaders?
	Are there formal and informal leaders?

Each cultural term occurs in organizational settings, yet the way they occur, the forms they take, and the importance they have, differs dramatically. One college, for example, might have a history of formal, autocratic leadership, whereas another institution might operate with an informal, consensually oriented leader. In order to illustrate the meaning of each term I provide examples drawn from a case study of a public institution identified here as "Family State College." The data are drawn from site visits conducted during the academic year 1984-85. Participant observation and interviews with a random sample of the entire college community lend "thick description" [25] to the analysis. Each example highlights representative findings of the college community.

Family State College

"The intensity of an academic culture," writes David Dill, "is determined not only by the richness and relevance of its symbolism for the maintenance of the professional craft, but by the bonds of social organization. For this mechanism to operate, the institution needs to take specific steps to socialize the individual to the belief system of the organization. . . The management of academic culture therefore involves both the management of meaning and the management of social integration" [21, p. 317]. Family State College offers insight into a strong organizational culture and exemplifies how administrators at this campus utilize the "management of meaning" to foster understanding of the institution and motivate support for its mission.

In dealing with its environment Family State College has imbued in its constituents a strong feeling that the institution has a distinctive purpose and that the programs reflect its mission. By invigorating old roots and values with new meaning and purpose, the president of Family State has largely succeeded in reconstructing tradition and encouraging a more effective organizational culture. As with all executive action, however, the utilization, strengths, and weaknesses of a particular approach are circumscribed by institutional context.

Environment

Founded in 1894, Family State College exists in a fading industrial town. The institution has always been a career-oriented college for the working class in nearby towns and throughout the state. "I came here," related one student, "because I couldn't afford going to another school, and it was real close by." Fifty percent of the students remain in the local area after graduation, and an even higher percentage (80 percent) reside in the state. In many respects the city of Family and the surrounding area have remained a relatively stable environment for the state college due to the unchanging nature of the working-class neighborhoods. An industrial arts professor explained the town-gown relationship: "The college has always been for the people here. This is the type of place that was the last stop for a lot of kids. They are generally the first generation to go to college and college for them has always meant getting a job."

When Family State's president arrived in 1976, he inherited an institution in equilibrium yet with a clear potential to become stagnant. The institution had low visibility in the area and next to no political clout in the state capital. Family State was not a turbulent campus in the late 1970s; rather, it was a complacent institution without a clear direction. In the past decade the institutional climate has changed from complacency to excitement, and constituents share a desire to improve the college.

The college environment provided rationales for change. Dwindling demand for teachers required that the college restructure its teacher-education program. A statewide tax that eliminated "nonessential" programs in high schools reduced the demand for industrial arts at Family State. New requirements by state hospitals brought about a restructured medical-technology program. The college's relationship to its environment fostered a close identification with its working-class constituency and prompted change based on the needs of a particular clientele.

Mission

Individuals spoke of the mission of the college from one of two angles: the mission referred either to the balance between career-oriented and liberal arts programs or to the audience for whom the college had been founded— the working class. Although people spoke about the mission of the college in terms of both program and clientele, the college's adaptations concerned programmatic change, not a shift in audience. That is, in 1965 the college created a nursing program that easily fit into the mission of the college as a course of study for working-class students. An industrial-technology major is another example of a program that responded to the needs of the surrounding environment and catered to the specified mission of the institution. Rather than alter or broaden the traditional constituency of the institution, the college tried to create new curricular models that would continue to attract the working-class student to Family State.

As a consequence, the college continues to orient itself to its traditional clientele— the working people of the area. The city and the surrounding area have remained a working-class region throughout the college's history; the town has neither prospered and become middle class nor has it faded into oblivion. Continuing education programs and the courtship of adult learners have broadened the clientele of the college while maintaining its traditional, working-class constituency.

The president frequently articulates his vision of the institutional mission in his speeches and writing. One individual commented: "When I first came here and the president said that 'we're number one' I just thought it was something he said, like every college president says. But after [you're here] awhile you watch the guy and you see he really believes it. So I believe it too." "We are number one in a lot of programs," said the president. "We'll go head to head with a lot of other institutions. Our programs in nursing, communication, and industrial technology can stack up against any other state college here. I'd say we're the best institution of this kind in the state."

Presidential pronouncements of excellence and the clear articulation of institutional mission have a two-fold import. First, institutional mission provides the rationale and criteria for the development of a cohesive curricular program. Second, the president and the other organizational participants have a standard for self-criticism and performance. All too often words such as "excellence" can be so vague that they have no measurable meaning. Family State however, can "stack up against any other state college." That is, rather than criterion-referenced performance measures such as standardized tests and achievement levels of incoming students, Family State College has standards of excellence that are consistent with the historic mission of state colleges.

Socialization

One individual who had recently begun working at the college noted: "People smiled and said hello here. It was a friendly introduction. People said to me, 'Oh, you'll really love it here.' It was that wonderful personal touch. When they hire someone here they don't want only someone who can do the job, but someone who will also fit in with the personality of the place." One individual also noted that, soon after he arrived, the president commented on how well he did his work but was worried that he wasn't "fitting in" with the rest of the staff. What makes these comments interesting is that they are about a public state college. Such institutions often have the reputation of being impersonal and bureaucratic, as opposed to having the "personal touch" of private colleges.

A student commented: "If a student hasn't gotten to know the president in a year then it's the student's damn fault. Everybody sees him walking around here. He's got those Monday meetings. He comes to all the events. I mean, he's really easy to see if you've got something you want to talk to him about. That's what's special about Family. How many places can a student get to know the president? We all call him 'Danny' (not to his face) because he's so familiar to us." The student's comment is particularly telling in an era of declining enrollments. One reason students come to the school, and one reason they stay at Family, is because the entire institution reflects concern and care for students as personified by the president's open door and the easy accessibility of all administrators.

Information

People mentioned that all segments of the institution were available to one another to help solve problems. Every Monday afternoon the president held an open house where any member of the college community could enter his office and talk to him. All segments of the community used the vehicle. As one administrator reported: "That's sacred time. The president wants to know the problems of the different constituencies. People seem to use it. He reflects through the open house that he really cares."

The president also believes in the power of the written word, especially with respect to external constituencies. It is not uncommon to read about Family State or the president in the local press. A survey done by the college discovered that the local citizenry had a positive, working knowledge of the president and the college. The president attends a multitude of local functions, such as the chamber of commerce and United Way meetings, and civic activities. He also invites the community onto the college campus.

Although mailings and written information are important vehicles for sharing information with external constituencies, oral discourse predominates among members of the institution. Internal constituencies appear well informed of decisions and ideas through an almost constant verbal exchange of information through both formal and informal means. Formal means of oral communication include task forces, executive council meetings, and all-college activities. At these gatherings individuals not only share information but also discuss possible solutions to problems or alternatives to a particular dilemma.

The president's communicative style percolates throughout the institution. Information from top administrators is communicated to particular audiences through weekly meetings of individual departments. One vice president described the process: "The president's executive staff meets once a week and we, in turn, meet with our own people. There's lots of give and take. The key around here is that we're involved in a process to better serve students. Open communication facilitates the process. God help the administrator or faculty member who doesn't work for students."

Informal channels of communication at Family State are an equally, if not more important means for sharing and discussing ideas as well as developing an esprit de corps. The president hosts several functions each year at his house near campus. He brings together disparate segments of the college community, such as different faculty departments, for a casual get-together over supper, brunch, or cocktails. "This is like a family," explained the president. "Too often people don't have the time to get together and share with one another food and drink in a pleasant setting."

It is not uncommon to see many different segments of the institution gathered together in public meeting places such as the cafeteria or a lounge. In discussions with faculty, staff, and administrators, many people showed a working knowledge of one another's tasks and duties and, most strikingly, the student body.

Throughout the interviews individuals consistently mentioned the "family atmosphere" that had developed at the college. As one individual noted: "Everything used to be fragmented here. Now there's a closeness."

Strategy

Family State's decision-making process followed a formal sequence that nevertheless accommodated informal activity. Initiatives often began at the individual or departmental level, as with proposals to create a new program. Eventually the new program or concept ended up in the College Senate—composed of faculty, students, and administration. A subcommittee of the senate decided what action should be taken and recommended that the idea be accepted or defeated. The senate then voted on the issue. Once it had taken action, the next step was presidential—accept the proposal, veto it, or send it back to the senate for more analysis. The final step was approval by the Board.

Formalized structures notwithstanding, a strictly linear map of decision analysis would be misleading. Most often the administration made decisions by widespread discussion and dialogue. "It's participative decision making," commented one individual. The president's decisions existed in concrete, but individuals saw those decisions as building blocks upon which further, more participative decisions were made. "The key around here," observed one administrator, "is that we're involved in a process to better serve students. Open communication facilitates the process."

Although, as noted, the college has adapted to its environment, the college did not rely solely on adaptive strategy. The president noted: "I don't believe that an institution serves its culture well if it simply adapts. The marketplace is narrow and changes quickly." Instead, the administration, particularly the president, has brought about change through an interpretive strategy based on the strategic use of symbols in the college and surrounding environment.

Chaffee defines interpretive strategy as ways that organizational representatives "convey meanings that are intended to motivate stakeholders" [9, p. 94]. Interpretive strategy orients metaphors or frames of reference that allow the organization and its environment to be understood by its constituents. Unlike strategic models that enable the organization to achieve goals or adapt to the environment, interpretive strategy proceeds from the understanding that the organization can play a role in creating its environment. Family State's president accentuates process, concern for the individual as a person, and the central orientation of serving students. He does so through several vehicles, foremost among them being communication with constituencies and the strategic use of space and time.

The president's use of space is an important element in his leadership style and implementation of strategy. He frequently extends his spatial domain beyond the confines of the college campus and into the city and surrounding towns. Conversely, invitations to the community to attend events at the college and utilize the library and other facilities have reduced spatial barriers with a city that otherwise might feel excluded. Informal gatherings, such as suppers at the president's house, or luncheons at the college, have brought together diverse constituencies that otherwise have little reason to interact with one another. Moreover, the president has attended to the physical appearance of the institution, making it an effective symbol to his constituencies that even the grounds demand excellence and care.

The president's symbolic use of space sets an example emulated by others. His open-door policy, for example, permeates the institution. Administrators either work in open space areas in full view of one another or the doors to their offices are physically open, inviting visits with colleagues, guests, or more importantly, students. The openness of the president's and other administrators' doors creates an informality throughout the college that fosters a widespread sharing of information and an awareness of decisions and current activities.

The president is also a visible presence on the campus. He spends part of every day walking throughout the institution for a casual inspection of the grounds and facilities. These walks provide a way for people to talk with him about matters of general concern and enable him to note something that he may not have seen if he had not walked around the campus. Administrators, too, interact with one another and with students not only in their offices but on the other's "turf." "The atmosphere here is to get to know students," said one administrator, "see them where they are, and not have a host of blockades so students feel as if they are not listened to."

The discussion of communication and space has made reference to time. The president continually integrates formal and informal interactions with his constituencies. According to his secretary and a study of the presidential calendar, about one and one-half hours per day are scheduled as "free time" that he uses as he sees fit—for reading, writing, or perhaps walking around the campus.

The president regularly schedules meetings with his executive circle or individuals such as the treasurer. The meetings revolve around both a mixture of formal agenda-like items and ideas or problems that either the president or his lieutenants feel they have. Although his schedule is generally very busy, it is not difficult to see the president. His secretary makes his appointments. She notes that if a faculty member or administrator asked to see the president, she would schedule an appointment when he was available in the very near future. Students, too, can see the president, but his secretary generally tries to act as a gatekeeper to insure that the students really need to see the president and not someone else.

Leadership

The president's awareness of patterns and styles of communication and his conscious use of time and place are perhaps best illustrated by a meeting we had during one of our site visits to Family State. We waited in the president's outer office with the director of institutional research.

The door swung open and the president walked out to greet us. He said: "I'm sorry for being late. I knew about your appointment and had planned to be back here on time, but I was walking around the campus for forty-five minutes, and just at the last minute I made a detour to check out the cafeteria, to see how things were going. I met a guy down there who works in the kitchen and he and I have always said we should play cribbage some time (he's a cribbage player) and wouldn't you know he had a board with him today and he asked me to play. So I did. He beat me too. So I wasn't doing anything very presidential in being late for you. I was just walking around the campus on this beautiful day, and playing cribbage in the kitchen with a friend."

The president's disclaimer notwithstanding, his actions are presidential in that they develop and reinforce an institutional culture. His effective use of symbols and frames of reference, both formally and informally, articulates the college's values and goals and helps garner support from faculty, students, staff, and the community. This should not imply, however, that presidents should necessarily spend their time walking around campus or playing cribbage with the kitchen help. What is effective at one institution is unlikely to work at another. Nevertheless, the role of symbolic communication that we witness on this campus, buttressed by tangible, constructive change, provides valuable clues about effectiveness and organizational culture.

Tying the Framework Together

People come to believe in their institution by the ways they interact and communicate with one another. The ongoing cultural norms of Family State foster an implicit belief in the mission of the college as providing a public good. In this sense, staff, faculty members, and administrators all feel they contribute to a common good—the education of working-class students. When individuals apply for work at Family State, they are considered not only on the basis of skill and qualifications but also on how they will fit into the cultural milieu. Socialization occurs rapidly through symbols such as open doors, the constant informal flow of communication punctuated by good-natured kidding, access throughout the organization, dedication to hard work, and above all, commitment to excellence for students. When people speak of their mission, they speak of helping people. Members of the college community work from the assumption that an individual's actions do matter, can turn around a college, and can help alter society.

Belief in the institution emerges as all the more important, given an unstable economic and political environment. The district in which the college resides has little political clout, and consequently the institution is not politically secure. Rapidly shifting employment patterns necessarily demand that the institution have program flexibility. Although the college has created programs such as medical technology and communication/media, it has not made widespread use of adaptive strategy.

"The strength of academic culture," states David Dill, "is particularly important when academic institutions face declining resources. During these periods the social fabric of the community is under great strain. If the common academic culture has not been carefully nurtured during periods of prosperity, the result can be destructive conflicts between faculties, loss of professional morale, and personal alienation" [21, p. 304]. Family State College exemplifies a strong organizational culture. Further, the academic culture nurtures academic excellence and effectiveness.

It is important to reiterate, however, that all effective and efficient institutions will not have similar cultures. The leadership exhibited by the president at Family State, for example, would fail miserably at an institution with a different culture. Similarly, the role of mission at Family State would be inappropriate for different kinds of colleges and universities. The rationale for a cultural framework is not to presume that all organizations should function similarly, but rather to provide managers and researchers with a schema to diagnose their own organizations.

In providing a provisional framework for the reader, I have neither intended that we assume the different components of the cultural framework are static and mutually exclusive, nor that an understanding of organizational culture will solve all institutional dilemmas. If we return to the Geertzian notion of culture as an interconnected web of relationships, we observe that the components of culture will overlap and connect with one another. In the case study, for example, the way the leader articulated organizational mission spoke both to the saga of the institution as well as its leadership.

How actors interpret the organizational "web" will not provide the right answers to simplistic choices. Rather, a cultural analysis empowers managers with information previously unavailable or implicit about their organization which in turn can help solve critical organizational dilemmas. As with any decision-making strategy, all problems cannot be solved simply because an individual utilizes a particular focus to an issue. For example, a specific answer to whether or not tuition should be raised by a particular percentage obviously will not find a solution by understanding culture. On the other hand, what kind of clientele the institution should have, or what its mission should be as it adapts to environmental change are critical issues that speak to the costs of tuition and demand cultural analysis.

Conclusion: Where Do We Go From Here?

Many possible avenues await the investigation of organizational culture. This article has provided merely the essential terms for the study of academic culture. A comprehensive study of organizational culture in academic settings will demand increased awareness of determinants such as individual and organizational use of time, space, and communication. In this case study, we observed the president's formal and informal uses of different cultural concepts. Individuals noted, for example, how they were well-informed of administrative decisions and plans primarily through informal processes. Evidence such as the president's casual conversations with administrators or walking around the campus were effective examples of the informal use of time. Further work needs to be done concerning the meaning and effective use of formality and informality with regard to time, space, and communication.

I have used the term "organizational culture" but have made no mention of its subsets: subculture, anticulture, or disciplinary culture. An investigation of these cultural subsets will provide administrators with useful information about how to increase performance and decrease conflict in particular groups. We also must investigate the system of higher education in order to understand its impact on individual institutions. For example, state systems undoubtedly influence the culture of a public state college in ways other than budgetary. A study of the influence of states on institutional culture appears warranted.

Each term noted in Table 1 also demands further explication and analysis. Indeed, the concepts presented here are an initial attempt to establish a framework for describing and evaluating various dimensions of organizational culture. Developing such a framework is an iterative process that should benefit from the insights of further research endeavors. An important research activity for the future will be the refinement and extension of this framework. The methodological tools and skills for such cultural studies also need elaboration.

By developing this framework and improving ways of assessing organizational culture, administrators will be in a better position to change elements in the institution that are at variance with the culture. This research will permit them to effect orderly change in the organization without creating unnecessary conflict. Moreover, the continued refinement of this framework will permit research to become more cumulative and will help foster further collaborative efforts among researchers.

WILLIAM G. TIERNEY is assistant professor and research associate at the Center of the Study of Higher Education at The Pennsylvania State University, 123 Willard Bldg., University Park, Pa. 16802.

References

Becher, T. "Towards a Definition of Disciplinary Cultures." *Studies in Higher Education*, 1981, 6; 109–22.

Becker, H. S. "Student Culture." in *The Study of Campus Cultures*, edited by Terry F. Lunsford, pp. 11–26. Boulder, Col.: Western Interstate Commission for Higher Education, 1963.

Bennis, W. "Transformative Power and Leadership." In *Leadership and Organizational Culture*, edited by T. J. Sergiovanni and J. E. Corbally, pp. 64–71. Urbana, Ill.: University of Illinois Press, 1984.

Bourdieu, P. "Systems of Education and Systems of Thought." *International Social Science Journal*, 1977, 19; 338–58.

Burrell, G., and G. Morgan. *Sociological Paradigms and Organizational Analysis*. London: Heinemann, 1979.

Bushnell, J. "Student Values: A Summary of Research and Future Problems." In *The Larger Learning*, edited by M. Carpenter, Dubuque, Iowa: Brown, 1960; 45–61.

Cameron, K. S. "Measuring Organizational Effectiveness in Institutions of Higher Education." *Administrative Science Quarterly*, 1987, 23; 604–32.

Chaffee, E. E. *After Decline, What? Survival Strategies at Eight Private Colleges*. Boulder, Col.: National Center for Higher Education Management Systems, 1984.

―――. "Three Models of Strategy." *Academy of Management Review*, 1985, 10; 89–98,

Chaffee, E. E., and W. G. Tierney. *Collegiate Culture and Leadership Strategy*. New York: MacMillan, forthcoming.

Chait, R. P. "Look Who Invented Japanese Management!" *AGB Quarterly*, 1982, 17; 3–7.

Clark, B. R. "Faculty Culture." In *The Study of Campus Cultures*, edited by Terry F. Lunsford, pp. 39–54. Boulder, Col.: Western Interstate Commission for Higher Education, 1963.

Clark, B. R. *The Distinctive College*, Chicago, Ill.: Aldine, 1970.

―――. "Belief and Loyalty in College Organization." *Journal of Higher Education*, 42, June 1971; 499–520.

―――. "The Organizational Saga in Higher Education." In *Readings in Managerial Psychology*, edited by H. Leavitt. Chicago, Ill.: University of Chicago Press, 1980.

Clark B. R., ed.) *Perspectives in Higher Education*. Berkeley, Calif.: University of California Press, 1984.

Dandridge, T. C. "The Life Stages of a Symbol: When Symbols Work and When They Can't." In *Organizational Culture*, edited by P. J. Frost, L. E Moore, M. R. Louis, C. C. Lundberg, and J. Martin, Beverly Hills, Calif.: Sage, 1985, 141–54.

Dandridge, T. C., 1. Mitroff, and W. F. Joyce. "Organizational Symbolism: A Topic to Expand Organizational Analysis." *Academy of Management Review*, 1980, 5; 77–82.

Davie, J. S., and A. P. Hare. "Button-Down Collar Culture." *Human Organization*, 1956, 14; 13–20.

Deal, T. E., and A. A. Kennedy. *Corporate Cultures: The Rites and Rituals of Corporate Life*. Reading, Mass.: Addison-Wesley, 1982.

Dill, D. D. "The Management of Academic Culture: Notes on the Management of Meaning and Social Integration." *Higher Education*, 1982, 11; 303–20.

Feldman, M. S., and J. G. March. "Information in Organizations as Signal and Symbol." *Administrative Science Quarterly*, 1981, 26; 171–86.

Freedman, M. *Academic Culture and Faculty Development*. Berkeley, Calif.: University of California Press, 1979.

Gaff, J. G., and R. C. Wilson. "Faculty Cultures and Interdisciplinary Studies." *Journal of Higher Education*, March 1971, 42; 186–201.

Geertz, C. *The Interpretation of Cultures*. New York: Basic Books, 1973.

Koprowski, E. J. "Cultural Myths: Clues to Effective Management." *Organizational Dynamics,*, 1983; 39–51.

Krakower, J. Y. *Assessing Organizational Effectiveness: Considerations and Procedures*. Boulder, Col.: National Center for Higher Education Management Systems, 1985.

March, J. G. "How We Talk and How We Act: Administrative Theory and Administrative Life." In *Leadership and Organizational Culture*, edited by T. J. Sergiovanni and J. E. Corbally, Urbana, Ill.: University of Illinois Press, 1984, 18–35.

Mitroff, I. I., and R. H. Kilmann. "Stories Managers Tell: A New Tool for Organizational Problem Solving." *Management Review*, 1975, 64; 18–28.

————. "On Organizational Stories: An Approach to the Design and Analysis of Organizations through Myths and Stories." In *The Management of Organization Design*, edited by R. H. Kilmann, L. R. Pondy, and D. P. Slevin, New York: North Holland, 1976, 189–207.

Mitroff, I. I., and R. Mason. "Business Policy and Metaphysics: Some Philosophical Considerations." *Academy of Management Review*, 1982, 7; 361–70.

Morgan, G., P. J. Frost, and L. R. Pondy. "Organizational Symbolism." *In Organizational Symbolism*, edited by L. R. Pondy, P. J. Frost, and T. C. Dandridge. Greenwich, Conn.: JAI Press, 1983.

Ouchi, W. G. "Theory Z: An Elaboration of Methodology and Findings." *Journal of Contemporary Business*, 1983, 11; 27–41.

Ouchi, W. G., and A. L. Wilkins. "Organizational Culture." *Annual Review of Sociology*, 1985, 11; 457–83.

Pace, C. R. "Five College Environments." *College Board Review*, 1960, 41; 24–28.

————. "Methods of Describing College Cultures." *Teachers College Record*, 1962, 63; 267–77.

Peters, T. J., and R. H. Waterman. *In Search of Excellence*. New York: Harper and Row, 1982.

Pettigrew, A. M. "On Studying Organizational Cultures." *Administrative Science Quarterly*, 1979, 24; 570–81.

Pfeffer, J. "Management as Symbolic Action: The Creation and Maintenance of Organizational Paradigms." *Research in Organizational Behavior*, 1981, 3; 1–52.

Pondy, L. R. "Leadership is a Language Game." In *Leadership: Where Else Can We Go*, edited by M. McCall and M. Lombardo, Durham, N.C.: Duke University Press, 1978, 87–99.

Putnam, L. L., and M. E. Pacanowsky, eds.) *Communication and Organizations: An Interpretive Approach*. Beverly Hills, Calif.: Sage, 1983.

Quinn, R. E., and J. Rohrbaugh. "A Competing Values Approach to Organizational Effectiveness." *Public Productivity Review*, 1981, 5; 122–40.

Schein, E. H. "The Role of the Founder in Creating Organizational Culture." *Organizational Dynamics*, 1983, 12; 13–28.

————. *Organizational Culture and Leadership*. San Francisco: Jossey-Bass, 1985.

Smircich, L., and G. Morgan. "Leadership: The Management of Meaning." *Journal of Applied Behavioral Science*, 1982, 18; 257–73.

Tierney, W. G. "The Communication of Leadership." Working paper. Boulder, Col.: National Center for Higher Education Management Systems, 1985.

————. "The Symbolic Aspects of Leadership: An Ethnographic Perspective." *American Journal of Semiotics*, in press.

————. *The Web of Leadership*. Greenwich, Conn.: JAI Press, forthcoming.

Trice, H. M., and J. M. Beyer. "Studying Organizational Cultures through Rites and Ceremonials." *Academy of Management Review*, 1984, 9; 653–69.

Trujillo, N. "'Performing' Mintzberg's Roles: The Nature of Managerial Communication." In *Communication and Organizations: An Interpretive Approach*, edited by L. L. Putnam and M. E. Pacanowsky. Beverly Hills, Calif.: Sage, 1983.

Understanding Academic Culture and Climate

MARVIN W. PETERSON AND MELINDA G. SPENCER

The current interest in organizational culture and climate makes these two complex and confusing concepts an important arena for institutional researchers to understand and to add to their research arsenal.

* * *

The optimist looked at the institutional research report on a rather mediocre, entering freshman class and commented, "What an interesting group of students. It will be an exciting challenge to see how much we can help their learning development," The pessimist retorted, "Another mediocre group of students. It's going to be difficult to teach them anything." Clearly these comments reflect two typical but different value sets regarding the central teaching-learning function of their institution and the purpose or meaning of that work. Those comments, heard and interpreted by others, no doubt set the tone for student and faculty attitudes and behavior toward each other and toward the teaching-learning process. The underlying values, beliefs, and meaning in the comments in part constitute the institution's *culture*. The resultant attitudes and behavior in part establish the *climate*. Implicitly we understand both concepts, but they are still among the most complex and confusing in the array of tools we use to research the dynamics of institutional behavior and to foster or manage improvement.

This volume may reflect the well-documented tension in organizational theory and research between rational, empirical, explicit approaches to understanding organizational behavior and the less rational, qualitative, intuitive approaches (Peterson, 1985). This paradigm shift reflects a longer-term debate in many disciplines (Lincoln, 1989) and is emerging in institutional research via topics such as qualitative methods, quality-improvement approaches, and the importance of context. Examination of the topic of culture and climate in institutional research reflects a conceptual and methodological shift toward the less rational, more intuitive side of the paradigm, adding a significant new set of concepts and tools to the analytic artillery. This chapter attempts to (1) clarify the concepts of organizational culture and climate and distinguish between them, (2) identify some of the conceptual approaches to culture and climate that raise some general research issues, and (3) identify some of the organizational research issues and institutional research implications of explicitly examining culture and climate.

An Emergent Phenomenon

Despite conceptual confusion and the "soft" nature of the constructs, organizational climate and culture have emerged as one of the most active arenas of scholarly and practical research conducted by individuals from a variety of disciplines. This interest is more than just an academic curiosity about paradigm shifts and a desire to create new models or research approaches. Rather, the concepts of culture and climate are proving useful as a way of understanding the complexities of organizational operations.

The concepts of organizational culture and climate, as they have evolved, perform several important functions. The highly visible and popular research on effective organizations has identified culture as a major factor in effectiveness (Tichy, 1983). Organizational climate has long been seen as an important concept related to individual performance (Blackburn and Pitney, 1988). Culture and climate provide members with and reflect their understanding of the purpose or meaning of their organization and their work. They provide a mechanism for attracting, selecting, and socializing new members. Often culture and climate provide a sense of organizational identity for members by providing them with a sense of what is unique or distinctive about their organization or how it differs from similar places. This organizational identity is not completely static and may mature or change over time. When communicated externally, this cultural identity can function to create an image and establish legitimacy with various outside constituencies. Finally, organizational culture and climate provide a reasonable framework for making sense of the nonrational and informal aspects of an organization that are not captured in formal documents and procedures, objective characteristics of its members, quantitative measures of resources and performance, or organizational charts.

Although the major interest and research activity related to culture and climate has occurred outside of higher education institutions, interest within is also expanding. Growing constituent demands for more accountability and for proof of educational improvement and the inadequacy of specific quantitative measures to reflect performance have increased faculty, administrator, and policymaker interest in developing alternative frameworks for evaluating organizational performance. The concept of culture represents a paradigm for providing a holistic perspective on organizational functioning. In an era of growing institutional competition for students and funding, an institutional image reflecting a positive culture and climate on a few key dimensions is often sought.

While research on culture in higher education is not new, its complex and elusive nature has limited attempts to study it comparatively. Major classic studies are mostly case studies of single institutions, for example, Lunsford (1963), Foote, Mayer, and Associates (1968), Clark (1970), and Riesman, Gusfield, and Gamson (1970). The distinctive nature and unique character of higher education institutions have long been recognized and accepted both within and outside higher education (Veysey, 1965; Martin, 1985). A few comprehensive studies of institutions conducted by Chaffee and Tierney (1988), Tierney (1988), and Peterson, Cameron, Jones, Mets, and Ettington (1986) suggest that the culture of an institution is pivotal in determining the success of organizational improvement efforts. (Two recent syntheses of organizational culture research in higher education are by Peterson, Cameron, Jones, Mets, and Ettington, 1986; and Kuh and Whitt, 1988. More-focused reviews are Cameron and Ettington, 1988; Chaffee and Tierney, 1988; and Tierney, 1988). There are numerous studies of subcultures and subclimates within institutions, such as the work by C. P. Snow (1959) and Burton Clark (1987).

Research on organizational climate, which was quite popular in the 1960s and 1970s, is far more extensive. Much of it has involved the design and development of instruments to measure student, faculty, and administrative views of a wide variety of organizational phenomena. Among those elements studied are organizational missions and goals (Clark, 1970; Davies, 1986), academic workplaces (Austin and Gamson, 1983), organizational functioning (Blau, 1973), academic images and reputations (Webster, 1985; Heverson, 1987), and student, faculty, and administrator environments (Feldman and Newcomb, 1969; Locke, Fitzpatrick, and White, 1983; Blackburn, Horowitz, Edington, and Klos, 1986). Much of this literature is descriptive or compares various institutions, rather than relating the culture and climate measures to other organizational variables (Peterson, Cameron, Jones, Mets, and Ettington, 1986). Even so, one is able to get a sense of the interrelatedness and interdependency of the various elements within the institutional environment.

Thus, although the higher education research on organizational culture and climate is not as extensive as in the larger field of organizational behavior, a significant groundwork has been laid. It is apparent from the findings outside of higher education that these concepts are linked to other important organizational variables (Deal and Kennedy, 1982; Peters and Waterman, 1982; Deming, 1986). Within higher education preliminary results suggest the same. More important, some of the current organizational processes and problems may benefit from research on these concepts.

Definitions, Dimensions, and Distinctions

Culture and climate are terms that have been used to describe somewhat abstract phenomena and that emanate from disciplines as diverse in interests as anthropology, sociology, psychology, linguistics, and organizational behavior (Ott, 1989). The two terms have been used to describe quite different levels of behavior (societies, nations, tribes, professions, social groups, organizations, subcultures/subclimates), often in different time frames (current context or historical evolution) and for both single-context and comparative purposes. Consequently, there are numerous subtleties and distinctions in the definitions, and often little common ground. Within higher education the terms environment, culture, and climate are often used interchangeably to describe a wide array of different organizational phenomena.

Definitions

From the perspective of institutional researchers, our primary concern is to focus on organizational behavior, especially that of major subgroups. For the purposes of this discussion, the term *environment* is the broadest concept, potentially including all internal and external, organizationally related phenomena. *Culture* and *climate* are seen as concepts describing a subset of the internal environment of an institution. While definitions of culture and climate vary, it is useful to define them in ways that capture their central essence and that circumscribe a set of phenomena important to understanding higher education institutions (see Table 1).

Culture, as a construct or concept, emanates primarily from anthropology, sociology, linguistics, and, more recently, studies of organizational behavior and psychology. It focuses on the deeply embedded patterns of organizational behavior and the shared values, assumptions, beliefs, or ideologies that members have about their organization or its work, Organizational culture is a holistic perspective. It may serve purposes that are (1) *instrumental*: social interpretation of what the organization *is* or *does*, a form of member control, or a mode of organizational adaptation to problems and challenges and (2) *interpretive*: a sense of what the organization *has*, a sense of meaning for members about the organization or their work (Peterson, Cameron, Jones, Mets, and Ettington, 1986). The major features of culture are that it (1) serves to emphasize an organization's unique or distinctive character, which provides a subordinate meaning to members, (2) is deeply embedded and enduring, and (3) is not malleable, changed primarily by cataclysmic events or through slower, intensive, and long-term efforts. As a holistic interpretation of the institution, culture is often captured in sagas about the organization (Clark, 1970), its heroic and revered figures (Deal and Kennedy, 1982), its often ritualistic or symbolic patterns and events (Zucker, 1988), and strongly held images, beliefs, or myths about the place (Koproski, 1983). For anyone familiar with colleges or universities, culture has face validity. It is the dominant behavioral or belief pattern that reflects or holds the institution together—a kind of "organizational glue."

Table 1

Primary Distinctions of Culture and Climate

Organizational Concept	Culture	Climate
Basis of concept	Deeply shared values, assumptions, beliefs, or ideologies of members	Common member perception of attitudes toward and feelings about organizational life
Primary conceptual sources	Anthropology, sociology, linguistics, and organizational behavior	Cognitive and social psychology and organizational behavior
Organizational perspective	Holistic primary emergent patterns	Pervasive, various organizational patterns, often focused on specific arenas
Major purposes of concept	Instrumental (Is): social interpretation, behavior control, and adaptation	Extrinsic: member control
	Interpretive (Has): metaphor or meaning	Intrinsic: member motivation
Primary elements or emphasis	Superordinate meaning	Common view of participants
Primary values or use	Identifies uniqueness in relation to other organizations	Comparison among organizations or over time
Major characteristics	Embedded or enduring	Current patterns or atmosphere
Nature of change	Cataclysmic or long-term and intensive efforts	More malleable, various direct or indirect means

Climate, as a construct or concept, emanates primarily from cognitive and social psychology and studies of organizational behavior. Although the terms climate and culture are often used interchangeably, the two can be usefully distinguished. Climate can be defined as the current common patterns of important dimensions of organizational life or its members' perceptions of and attitudes toward those dimensions. Thus, climate, compared to culture, is more concerned with current perceptions and attitudes rather than deeply held meanings, beliefs, and values (Hellrigel and Slocum, 1974).

The purposes served by organizational climate reflect its psychological base and individual-level focus as opposed to culture's more holistic approach. Climate is usually viewed as serving extrinsic purposes (member control) and intrinsic purposes (member motivation). The major features of climate are (1) its primary emphasis on common participant views of a wide array of organizational phenomena that allow for comparison among groups or over time, (2) its focus on current patterns of beliefs and behaviors, and (3) its often ephemeral or malleable character. Climate is pervasive, potentially inclusive of a broad array of organizational phenomena, yet easily focused to fit the researcher's or the administrator's interest. Again, the concept of organizational climate has face validity for anyone familiar with higher education. If culture is the "organizational value," climate is the "atmosphere," or "style." One interesting analogy suggests that culture is the meteorological zone in which one lives (tropical, temperate, or arctic) and climate is the daily weather patterns.

Dimensions

Several dimensions or variables are useful in examining both culture and climate. *Distinctiveness, content,* and *continuity* are three dimensions that contrast culture and climate. A focus on distinctiveness or uniqueness is key to understanding culture. Since culture is seen as an emergent pattern that reflects what the organization is or has, the focus is on those elements, such as behavioral patterns, values, beliefs, or ideologies, that make the institution unique (Schein, 1985). Comparison or contrast of institutions is thus based on and limited to content differences. Climate, on the other hand, focuses on common participant views of various organizational phenomena (Allaire and Firsirotu, 1984). This makes it possible to specify the phenomena and easier to compare changes in a specific arena of climate in a single institution over time or across various institutions or subgroups.

Since culture emphasizes an institution's uniqueness, it is difficult also to prescribe the content of culture a priori. Since colleges and universities are educational organizations, both the research literature and common sense suggest some broad categories of possible cultural elements, such as the governance pattern, philosophy of education, perspectives on teaching/learning, the nature of an educational or academic community, and the commitment to clientele. However, identification of the specific content of culture is critical to understanding its unique meaning to being able to contrast it with other institutions or subgroups, and to assessing its content change over time.

Climate, on the other hand, deals with more clearly focused elements. Thus, it is possible to prescribe the organizational phenomena one wishes to examine. Common categories are institutional goals and functioning, governance and decision patterns, teaching and learning processes, participant behaviors, effort, and interaction patterns, and work patterns or workplace dynamics. Unlike culture, the content of which cannot be easily specified, the options with climate are extensive, so it is important to identify the content of the climate one is examining.

Finally, on the dimension of continuity, culture, by definition, focuses on enduring patterns of embedded values, beliefs, and the like and is difficult to change. Climate, on the other hand, may be enduring but focuses on less embedded attitudes and behaviors. Consequently, climate is more likely to change than culture, and to change more rapidly.

Culture and climate also share four dimensions that are useful in clarifying the existence of the elements of culture or climate being examined. *Strength*, the degree to which culture or climate variables are valued and shape or control members' behavior, is important to understanding the effect of each variable and the ease with which it might be changed. Three dimensions that undergird strength are also useful in establishing the reliability and validity of its existence as a variable. Those are the *congruence* among the subelements of culture (related values, beliefs and so on) and climate (related perceptions or attitudes), the *clarity* or explicit nature of the content of the culture or climate variable, and the *consensus* among institutional members about the strength or importance of the variable.

Continuum, Complementary, or Contrast

Obviously, the confusion about culture and climate are the results of their multiple disciplinary sources; the different purposes and perspectives involved; their different emphases, uses, and characteristics; and some contrasting key dimensions, Yet, the dilemma remains: Are climate and culture merely a continuum ranging from a broad spectrum of attitudes and perceptions of organizational life (climate) to a cluster of those that are deeply embedded and valued (culture)? Are they two separate concepts focusing on similar phenomena that provide complementary views of an organization? Or, are culture and climate focusing on different phenomena and providing contrasting views of organizational life? This chapter cannot definitively answer these questions. In part, the answer depends on the content of the culture and climate on which one chooses to focus. More important, from the perspective of the institutional researcher, these definitions and dimensions suggest that both culture and climate can be distinguished and used to enhance our understanding of college and university environments.

Models of Culture and Climate

Use of the concepts of culture and climate to study colleges and universities has some interesting implications for research approaches and methodology. While there are many diverse and often nitpicking definitions and distinctions for both culture and climate and models of how to conceptualize each, it is possible to identify some of the more popular descriptive frameworks that may be useful to institutional researchers.

Cultural Models: Focusing Content

The numerous approaches and typologies for understanding and studying organizational culture can generally be grouped under the following four broad categories: geospatial; traditions, myths, artifacts, and symbolism; behavioral patterns and processes; and espoused versus embedded values and beliefs (see Figure 1). These define the organizational phenomena examined and affect research methodology.

Geospatial approaches focus on tangible and visible physical elements that have shared meaning within the culture. An example is the considerable attention in recent years given to the campus physical plant and architecture. Campus structures, styles, and patterns have often served as visible manifestations of deeper institutional beliefs or as signals of future institutional directions. The somewhat facetious "edifice complex" or preoccupation of many presidents and alumni with initiating major building projects is a well-known phenomenon within higher education (Thelin and Yankovich, 1985). However, the nature, location, condition, and design of campus structures, statues, sculptures, traffic patterns, and other construction can convey a wealth of information about the shared values and beliefs of the culture. Since these elements are relatively permanent, the role that they play within the campus culture, the shared meanings they convey, and the sense of the historical context and present status can make them critical elements in shaping or perpetuating cultural meaning. Descriptive studies of these elements are straightforward, but what they mean is a matter of interpretation, judgment, or opinion.

A second set of approaches focuses on the traditions, myths, and artifacts found within the organizations. As symbols these elements convey more than simple actions. A graduation ceremony, for example, symbolizes more than a simple graduation (Ott, 1989). The celebrations and major campus events, the heroes and villains of the institution, the major sagas of the institution's successes or failures, and the language and jargon used to describe them are all forms of institutional culture that can provide great insight into the past and current ideologies and assumptions that members hold important and that guide their actions. Studies of these phenomena can provide a broad range of information about the shared assumptions, values, and beliefs members hold about their organization, but they can also be time consuming to conduct. Often, these elements illustrate the idealized view of the institution, highlighting values and beliefs that are avowed but not necessarily practiced.

Behavioral patterns and processes comprise a third set of approaches for studying organizational culture. This category includes the manifest patterns of behavior that are present in the organization's operations, and that have been referred to as the "social architecture" of the organization (Jaccaci, 1989). These patterns and processes can be distinguished from other artifacts in that they involve behavioral activities with relatively standard content and form, sustained and repeated over time. They may be either formally defined by the organization or informally developed and supported by members within the organization. Because patterns and processes are manifested behaviors, studies of these elements can be relatively simple to execute (Sherkenback, 1988). However, determining the cultural impact of these elements requires careful consideration of the manifested processes, the subsequent reactions to them, and their meanings within the organization.

Figure 1

Conceptual Model of Organizational Culture

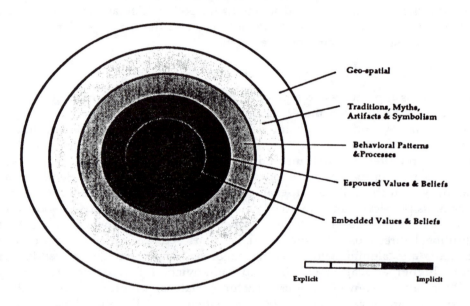

Note: *Adapted from Schein, 1985; Ott, 1989.*

A final set of approaches to considering organizational culture focuses on the values and beliefs that the members share about their organization. These may be explicitly stated, such as those found in mission statements and organizational charters, or implicitly held and revealed only through members' actions. While the espoused values and beliefs are often those that are widely communicated and that form the institutional identity, they often present the organization in its ideal, rather than actual, form. The implicit, or embedded, values and beliefs are those that members carry with them and that provide a real sense of the meaning of their organizational reality (Schein, 1985). It is this latter level of values and beliefs that actually guides members' daily actions. Studies of values and beliefs, while critical in determining the shared meanings that guide member and organizational behavior, are also the most difficult and time-consuming to conduct. The fact that these cultural values and beliefs often function in the unconscious of the individual, where they go unchallenged and unrecognized, makes them difficult to discern (Wilkins, 1983). Often, the researcher is forced to consider other elements within the culture and make an interpretive "leap of faith" regarding the values and beliefs that guide members' behavior.

Researching Culture

While each of these approaches reveals important information and provides insight into the institution, the picture that emerges is essentially incomplete. The culture of an organization is holistic and cannot be completely understood by limiting study to only one of these approaches to culture or one aspect of organizational functioning. Further, the meaning attached to the various elements within the culture is not always readily apparent nor can it be externally derived. Rather, the significance of these "culture bearing" elements can only be determined with qualitative methods within the context of the organization (Ouchi and Wilkins, 1988).

Climate Models: Focusing Content

The conceptual foundations for climate studies are also extensive. They include psychological concerns for attitude formation processes, expectancy theory, and cognitive process models of attitudes and perceptions, as well as sociological models addressing the formation and impact of norms, role modeling, group dynamics, and organizational socialization. For the purposes of this volume and most institutional researchers, three broad categories of climate help to delineate the conceptual content of climate research (Peterson, 1988).

Objective climate focuses on patterns of behavior or formal activity in an institution that can be observed directly and objectively. Certain practices and procedures, characteristics, and quantifiable patterns of behavior of academic management are examples. These fixed, prescribed patterns are relatively easy to identify and research. However, focusing on actual behavior requires observation and can be time consuming. In addition, patterns may not always be obvious. A major concern for researchers is whether objective patterns of behavior and those formally prescribed or required are similar or different, and whether these differences are critical and have dysfunctional consequences. While this research on objective climate is useful, it fails to get at the attitudes toward and perceptions and motivational consequences of organizational climate.

Perceived climate focuses on the cognitive images that participants have of how organizational life actually does function and how it should function. These perceptions may be accurate or inaccurate, but they represent reality from the perspective of participants. They shape norms that guide behavior and expectations and that may underscore motivation. Generally, research on perceived climate focuses on how participants view various institutional patterns and behaviors. Perceptions of institutional goals and functioning, governance and decision making, effort and participation, and workplace dynamics are commonly examined in higher education. Within this rubric, interview approaches, fixed-response instruments, and survey techniques are well-understood and commonly used methodologies. While useful, the critical issue in conducting perceived climate studies is to select from among the many aspects of organizational life that could be addressed and then to determine what to do with data that often present mixed results. The comparison of actual and ideal views reflecting the differences between perceived reality and expectations is often the most informative contrast.

Psychological or felt climate is the motivational, rather than perceptual, dimension that focuses on how participants feel about their organization and their work, These measures are the least used, yet potentially most constructive, climate dimensions. Unlike the objective and perceptual measures of climate, many motivational climate dimensions have been linked to individual and organizational performance measures. Examples include measures of members' loyalty and commitment, their morale and satisfaction, their beliefs about their quality of effort or involvement, and their sense of belonging. These dimensions are included in numerous studies of administrators, faculty, and students in higher education. While interviews, fixed-response instruments, and survey techniques are well understood, there are few well-designed psychological climate or motivational instruments that have been calibrated to fit faculty and administrators in higher education. Development of such instruments involves sophisticated research skills, can be expensive and time consuming, and is usually not a high priority for institutional research offices.

Some Organizational Research Issues

While these definitions, dimensions, distinctions, and models of culture and climate are helpful in bringing pertinent concepts into focus, and such research can provide insights that are useful to an institution of higher education, the resulting picture is still unclear. Research on culture and climate raises a set of broad organizational research issues that also need to be understood and addressed.

Holistic Versus Focused (Comprehensive or Specific)

In studying climate, the array of phenomena that can be addressed is unlimited. Within this framework, it is understood that the choice of a broad focus or specific focus needs to be addressed. However, the advantage of a cultural approach is its emphasis on a holistic view of the organization or unit under study. For a cultural approach to be most useful, it is not possible to focus on only one aspect of organizational functioning or on one type of content. Each aspect needs to be understood within a total context (Schein, 1985). A decision to conduct a cultural audit or study is an extensive and long-term endeavor, cutting across many organizational functions and levels of content suggested by the cultural model. Climate studies, however, can be either comprehensive or focused on specific organizational dimensions, depending on the purpose of the research.

Instrumental Versus Interpretive (Is or Has)

Studying culture places one in the center of a complex (and sometimes esoteric) argument that asks whether culture is something an organization is or has. The former perspective likens culture to an individual's personality interpretable only from the standpoint of its meaning to the participant. This perspective suggests that predefined research protocols, methods, and analytic approaches that attempt to analyze culture are not useful. Rather, research must be phenomenologically oriented, interpreting organizational culture through ethnographically thick descriptions of its context and meaning to its participants (Geertz, 1973). This type of research, while often insightful and fascinating, is not likely to prove fruitful to the overloaded institutional researcher seeking to improve some aspect of his or her institution. However, a more interpretive approach, which assumes culture is what an organization has, allows the researcher to apply his or her own interpretation to the pattern of functioning that is being described. In complex organizations, adopting a holistic perspective and examining multiple layers of cultural evidence can be a fruitless or confusing effort, as the results are open to very different interpretations.

Intrinsic Versus Extrinsic (Individual or Organization)

A slightly different issue in research on climate involves the question of whether climate is an intrinsic measure of participants' motivation or an extrinsic measure of organizational patterns that control member behavior. While the distinction of perceived (extrinsic) and psychological (intrinsic) climate is clear in principle, in practice it can be quite opaque. The administrative implications, however, are clear. Changing external controls to influence perceptions is much easier than changing individuals' motivation and involves very different change strategies.

Quantitative Versus Qualitative Methods (Distinctiveness and Insight Versus Reliability and Comparison)

Research on organizational climate can be approached systematically using either qualitative methods (interviews, observations, focus groups, document content analyses, and so on) or quantitative approaches (fixed-response instruments, survey sampling, and statistical analysis). The former offers significant insight on new emergent issues and organizational phenomena. The latter provides information that can be statistically compared and contrasted. However, when studying organizational culture, the primary methods are qualitative, involving ethnographically thick descriptions drawn from participant observation by the researcher, examination of institutional records and documents, and open-ended interviews. Even more structured attempts at case studies, triangulation of data, or use of grounded theory are primarily qualitative.

Some researchers have attempted to build institutional typologies for quantitatively measuring institutional culture. However, this approach requires the use of a prescribed set of dimensions and renders the identification of distinctive features of the culture less likely. For example, Cameron has attempted to classify institutions on an internal-external orientation and a member-control dimension of flexibility-rigidity that yields a fourfold classification of the organizational culture as market, clan, adhocracy, or hierarchy (Cameron and Ettington, 1988). As yet, the efficacy of such cultural typologies measured by quantitative instruments has not been proven in higher education. Thus, the researcher is left with the choice of either a qualitative approach that allows the institution's distinctive features to be identified but renders comparison to other institutions problematic or a quantitative approach that may be statistically reliable and allow cross-institution comparison but fails to capture the critical cultural or climate features.

Independent, Intervening, or Dependent (or All Three)

Another issue for studies of culture and climate is the question of whether these variables are (1) *independent*, affecting individual behavior and institutional functioning, (2) *intervening* between administrative action or strategy and performance, or (3) *dependent*. To even suggest such a distinction in culture studies assumes culture is instrumental, rather than interpretive, in nature. In most higher education research, culture has been studied for its own sake, and climate similarly or for institutional comparisons. Conceptually, climate and culture can be seen as all three types of variables. Consequently, it is important for researchers to consider carefully the research model and research questions they are attempting to answer.

Loose Coupling (Rationalizing Muddled Results)

While the notion of colleges and universities as loosely coupled organizations has been discussed, it is important to keep this notion in mind when addressing research on culture and climate. Both are "soft" variables. Climate is, by definition, a variable that is subject to change for many reasons. Culture, by definition, is enduring and not easily changed. Researchers and administrators focusing on culture and climate should not expect to see close relationships between their decisions or actions and changes in these variables. Rather, the two variables need to be examined over longer time frames and in light of other simultaneous changes that may affect them.

Paradox (a Researcher's Paradise)

One of the advantages of a cultural perspective is that it can force administrators to recognize that paradoxes existing within their institution are not always detrimental. A paradox is the simultaneous existence of two seemingly contradictory values or purposes ("We want to be an inner-city institution" and "We want to focus on excellence or quality"), The existence of seemingly contradictory views, if carefully documented, can be a focus for creative discussions and problem solving. But, if left unrecognized or unattended, those contradictions can lead to internal conflicts.

Subcultures/Climates (and How Many)

Most participants in higher education know their institutions are seldom monolithic and that important subunits or groups are quite different. Those differences are often critical in mitigating conflict, guiding broad participation, or stimulating productive competition or cooperation. Nowhere is this insight more important than in the study of organizational culture and climate. The literature on differing perceptions of administrators, faculty, and students and on the differences among disciplines and professions is extensive. Sensitivity to the potential existence of subcultures and subclimates is important for anyone doing research in this arena (and for tactful presentation of findings).

The Role of Institutional Research: Some Implications

Although the study of institutional culture and, to a lesser degree, climate have been of greater academic than practical interest, it is apparent that institutional researchers will be drawn into or influenced by research in this arena. While the research issues are clear, there are several roles or stances that institutional researchers can assume as the interest in and usefulness of these concepts continues to evolve and expand.

AWARENESS

Attempt to develop, unobtrusively, an understanding of important cultural and climate dimensions in our institutions of higher education. This can be done by reviewing past studies, doing some purposive exploration, or engaging key participants in focused discussions.

ESTABLISH CULTURAL CONTEXT

Try to define important dimensions of institutional culture and climate as context for other research studies to help convey what the dimensions mean and to aid in their interpretation.

BUILD BENCHMARKS

Since long-term research is needed and causal links are difficult to establish in culture and climate research, conduct a series of one-time investigations on important cultural or climate conditions to serve as benchmarks at a future date.

ACTIVE PROGRAM OF CULTURE/CLIMATE STUDIES

Although time consuming and often not of immediate concern, launching a series of studies geared toward important goals such as clarifying institutional image and improving the climate for undergraduate education can be a good way to make such studies useful and to learn about and improve the methodology. It may also be a way to involve a different group of faculty in institutional research.

CULTURE/CLIMATE CHANGE EXPERT

Managing or changing an institution's climate or culture usually involves administrative strategies not often practiced in colleges and universities. The institutional research office could be a repository of some of this expertise.

To summarize, each institution has its own culture and climate for the practice of institutional research—the value placed on systematic research on institutional dynamics, problems, and pressures. Perhaps the primary focus of the institutional research office could or should be to build a supportive culture and climate for conducting this research and systematically using it to improve the institution over time—for the sake of institutional research and the institution.

MARVIN W. PETERSON is director of the Center for the Study of Higher and Postsecondary Education and chair of the Program in Higher and Adult Continuing Education at the University of Michigan, Ann Arbor.

MELINDA G. SPENCER is a doctoral student in higher education at the University of Michigan, Ann Arbor.

References

Allaire, Y, and Firsirotu, M. E. "Theories of Organizational Culture." *Organizational Studies*, 1984, 5, 193–226.

Austin, A.E., and Gamson, Z. F. *Academic Workplace: New Demands, Heightened Tensions*. ASHE-ERIC Higher Education Report No. 10. Washington D.C.: Association for the Study of Higher Education, 1983.

Blackburn, R. T., Horowitz, S. M., Edington, D. W, and Klos, D. M. "University Faculty and Administrator Response to Stresses: Correlations with Health and Job/Life Satisfactions." *Research in Higher Education*, 1986, 25 (1), 31–41.

Blackburn, R. T., and Pitney, J. A. *Performance Appraisal for Faculty: Implications for Higher Education*. Ann Arbor: National Association for Research to Improve Postsecondary Teaching and Learning, University of Michigan, 1988.

Blau, P. M. *The Organization of Academic Work*. New York: Wiley, 1973.

Cameron, K. S., and Ettington, D. R. "The Conceptual Foundations of Organizational Culture." In J. C. Smart (ed.), *Higher Education: Handbook of Theory and Research*. Vol. 4. New York: Agathon, 1988.

Chaffee, E. E., and Tierney, W G. *Collegiate Culture and Leadership Strategies*. New York: American Council on Education and Macmillan, 1988.

Clark, B. R. *The Distinctive College: Antioch, Reed, and Swarthmore*. Chicago: Aldine, 1970.

Clark, B. R. *The Academic Life: Small Worlds, Different Worlds*. Princeton, NJ.: Princeton University Press, 1987.

Davies, G. K. "The Importance of Being General: Philosophy, Politics, and Institutional Missions Statements." In J. C. Smart (ed.), *Higher Education: Handbook of Theory and Research*. Vol. 2. New York: Agathon, 1986.

Deal, T. E., and Kennedy, A. A. *Corporate Cultures: The Rites and Rituals of Corporate Life*. Reading, Mass.: Addison-Wesley, 1982.

Deming, W E. *Out of the Crisis*. Cambridge, Mass.: Center for Advanced Engineering Study, Massachusetts Institute of Technology, 1986.

Feldman, K. A., and Newcomb, T. M. *The Impact of College on Students*. San Francisco: Jossey-Bass, 1969.

Foote, C., Mayer, H., and Associates. *The Culture of the University: Governance and Education*. San Francisco: Jossey-Bass, 1968.

Geertz, C. *The Interpretation of Cultures*. New York: Basic Books, 1973.

Hellriegel, D., and Slocum, J. W. Jr. "Organizational Climate: Measures, Research, and Contingencies." *Academy of Management Journal*, 1974, 17, 255–279.

Heverson, E. D. "Boosting Academic Reputations: A Study of University Departments." *Review of Higher Education*, 1967, 11, 177–197.

Jaccaci, A. T. "The Social Architecture of a Learning Culture." *Training & Development Journal*, 1989, 43 (11), 49–51.

Koproski, E. J. "Cultural Myths: Clues to Effective Management." *Organizational Dynamics*, 1983, 12 (2), 39–51.

Kuh, G. D., and Whitt, E. J. *The Invisible Tapestry: Culture in American Colleges and Universities.* ASHE-ERIC Higher Education Report No. 1. Washington, D.C.: Association for the Study of Higher Education, 1988.

Lincoln, Y. S. "Trouble in the Land: The Paradigm Revolution in the Academic Disciplines." In J. C. Smart (ed.), *Higher Education: Handbook of Theory and Research.* Vol. 5. New York: Agathon, 1989.

Locke, E. A., Fitzpatrick, W, and White, F. M. "Job Satisfaction and Role Clarity Among University and College Faculty." *Review of Higher Education*, 1983, 6, 343–365.

Lunsford, I. F. (ed.). *The Study of Campus Cultures.* Boulder, Colo.: Western Interstate Commission on Higher Education, 1963.

Martin, J. "Can Organizational Culture Be Managed?" In P. J. Frost, L. F. Moore, M. R. Louis, C. C. Lundberg, and J. Martin (eds.), *Organizational Culture.* Newbury Park, Calif.: Sage, 1985.

Ott, J. S. *The Organizational Culture Perspective.* Chicago: Dorsey, 1989.

Ouchi, W. G., and Wilkins, A. L. "Organizational Culture." In A. Westoby (ed.), *Culture and Power in Educational Organizations.* Philadelphia: Open University Press, 1988.

Peters, T. J., and Waterman, R. H. *In Search of Excellence: Lessons from America's Best-Run Companies.* New York: Harper & Row, 1982.

Peterson, M. W. "Emerging Developments in Postsecondary Organization Theory and Research: Fragmentation or Integration." *Education Researcher*, 1985, 14 (3), 5–12.

Peterson, M. W. "The Organizational Environment for Student Learning." In J. S. Stark and L. A Mets (eds.), *Improving Teaching and Learning Through Research.* New Directions for Institutional Research, no. 57. San Francisco: Jossey-Bass, 1988.

Peterson, M. W, Cameron, K. S., Jones, P., Mets, L. A., and Ettington, D. *The Organizational Context for Teaching and Learning: A Review of the Research Literature.* Ann Arbor: National Center for Research to Improve Postsecondary Teaching and Learning, University of Michigan, 1986.

Reisman, D., Gusfield, J., and Gamson, Z. F. *Academic Values and Mass Education: The Early Years of Oakland and Monteith.* New York: Doubleday, 1970.

Schein, E. H. *Organizational Culture and Leadership: A Dynamic View.* San Francisco: Jossey-Bass, 1985.

Sherkenback, W. W. *The Deming Route to Quality and Productivity: Road Maps and Roadblocks.* Washington, D.C.: CEEP Books, 1988.

Snow, C. P. *The Two Cultures and the Scientific Revolution.* New York: Cambridge University Press, 1959.

Thelin, J. R., and Yankovich, J. "Bricks and Mortar: Architecture and the Study of Higher Education." In J. C. Smart (ed.), *Higher Education: Handbook of Theory and Research.* Vol. 1. New York: Agathon, 1985.

Tichy, N. M. *Managing Strategic Change: Technical, Political, and Cultural Dynamics.* New York: Wiley, 1983.

Tierney, W G. "Organizational Culture in Higher Education." *Journal of Higher Education*, 1988, 59, 2–21.

Veysey, L. R. *The Emergence of the American University.* Chicago: University of Chicago Press, 1965.

Webster, D. S. "James McKeen Cattell and the Invention of Academic Quality Ratings, 1903–1910." *Review of Higher Education*, 1985, 8, 107–121,

Wilkins, A. L. "The Culture Audit: A Tool for Understanding Organizations." *Organizational Dynamics*, 1983, 12 (2), 24–38.

Zucker, L. G. "Where Do Institutional Patterns Come from? Organizations as Actors in Social Systems." In L. G. Zucker (ed.), *Institutional Patterns and Organizations: Cultures and Environment.* Cambridge, Mass.: Ballinger, 1988.

References

PART I

Alpert, Daniel (1985). "Performance and paralysis: The organizational context of the American research university." *The Journal of Higher Education*, 56(3): 241-281.

Baldridge, J.V.; Curtis, D.V.; Ecker, G.P.; & Riley, G.L. (1977). "Alternative models of governance in higher education." In G.L. Riley and J.V. Baldridge, *Governing academic organization*. Berkeley, CA: McCutchan Publishing Corporation.

Clark, Burton R. (1972). "The organizational saga in higher education." *Administrative Science Quarterly*, 17(2): 178-184.

Duryea, E.D. (1973). "Evolution of university organization." In J. Perkins, *The university as an organization*. New York: McGraw-Hill.

Masland, Andrew T. (1985). "Organizational culture in the study of higher education." *Review of Higher Education*, 8(2): 157-168.

Mintzberg, Henry. (1979). "The professional bureaucracy." In H. Mintzberg, *The structure of organizations*, pp. 348-379. Englewood Cliffs, NJ: Prentice-Hall.

Peterson, Marvin W. (1985). "Emerging developments in postsecondary organization theory and research: Fragmentation or integration." *Educational Researcher*, 14(3): 5-12.

Peterson, Marvin W. & Spencer, Melinda G. (1991). "Understanding organizational culture and climate." In W.G. Tierney (ed.), *Assessing academic climates and cultures*. New Directions in Institutional Research, No. 68. San Francisco: Jossey-Bass.

Tierney, William G. (1988). "Organizational culture in higher education: Defining the essentials." *Journal of Higher Education*, 59(1): 2-21.

Weick, Karl E. (1976). "Educational organizations as loosely coupled systems." *Administrative Science Quarterly*, 21(1): 1-19.

Suggested Additional References

PART I

Cameron, K.S., and D.R. Ettington. "The Conceptual Foundations of Organizational Culture". In J. Smart (ed.), *Higher Education: Handbook of Theory and Research*, Vol. VI. New York: Agathon Press, 1988.

Chaffee, E.E. "Organizational Concepts Underlying Governance and Administration." In M. Peterson and L. Mets (eds.), *Key Resources on Higher Education Governance, Management, and Leadership*. San Francisco: Jossey-Bass, 1987.

Cresswell, J.W., R.W. Roskins, and T.C. Henry. "A typology of multicampus systems". *Journal of Higher Education*, Vol. 56, 1985, pp. 26-37.

Lutz, F.W. "Tightening Up Loose Coupling in Organizations of Higher Education." *Administrative Science Quarterly*, Vol. 27, 1982, pp. 653-669.

McGuiness, A.C. "State Coordination and Governance of Higher Education 1987." *State Postsecondary Structures Handbook: 1988*. Denver, CO: Education Commission of the States.

Trow, M.A. "Reorganizing the Biological Sciences at Berkeley." *Change*, Vol. 15,1983, pp. 44-53.

Weick, K.E. "Contradictions in a Community of Scholars: The Cohesion-Accuracy Tradeoff." *Review of Higher Education*, Vol. 6, 1983, pp. 253-267.

PART II
GOVERNANCE AND MANAGEMENT PROCESSES

Statement on Government of Colleges and Universities

AMERICAN ASSOCIATION OF UNIVERSITY PROFESSORS
AMERICAN COUNCIL ON EDUCATION
ASSOCIATION OF GOVERNING BOARDS OF UNIVERSITIES
AND COLLEGES

Editorial Note. The Statement which follows is directed to governing board members, administrators, faculty members, students and other persons in the belief that the colleges and universities of the United States have reached a stage calling for appropriately shared responsibility and cooperative action among the components of the academic institution. The Statement is intended to foster constructive joint thought and action, both within the institutional structure and in protection of its integrity against improper intrusions.

It is not intended that the Statement serve as a blueprint for government on a specific campus or as a manual for the regulation of controversy among the components of an academic institution, although it is to be hoped that the principles asserted will lead to the correction of existing weaknesses and assist in the establishment of sound structure and procedures. The Statement does not attempt to cover relations with those outside agencies which increasingly are controlling the resources and influencing the patterns of education in other institutions of higher learning, e.g., the United States Government, the state legislatures, state commissions, interstate associations or compacts and other interinstitutional arrangements. However it is hoped that the Statement will be helpful to these agencies in their consideration of educational matters.

Students are referred to in this Statement as an institutional component coordinate in importance with trustees, administrators and faculty. There is, however, no main section on students. The omission has two causes: (1) the changes now occurring in the status of American students have plainly outdistanced the analysis by the educational community, and an attempt to define the situation without thorough study might prove unfair to student interests,[1] and (2) students do not in fact presently have a significant voice in the government of colleges and universities; it would be unseemly to obscure, by superficial equality of length of statement, what may be a serious lag entitled to separate and full confrontation. The concern for student status felt by the organizations issuing this Statement is embodied in a note "On Student Status" intended to stimulate the educational community to turn its attention to an important need.

This Statement, in preparation since 1964, is jointly formulated by the American Association of University Professors, the American Council on Education, and the Association of Governing Boards of Universities and Colleges. On October 12, 1966, the Board of Directors of the ACE took action by which the Council "recognizes the Statement as a significant step forward in the clarification of the respective roles of governing boards, faculties, and administrations," and "commends it to the institutions which are members of the Council." On October 29, 1966, the Council of the AAUP approved the Statement, recommended approval by the Fifty-

Third Annual Meeting in April, 1967, and recognized that "continuing joint effort is desirable, in view of the areas left open in the jointly formulated Statement, and the dynamic changes occurring in higher education." On November 18, 1966, the Executive Committee of the AGB took action by which that organization also "recognizes the Statement as a significant step forward in the clarification of the respective roles of governing boards, faculties and administrations," and "commends it to the governing boards which are members of the Association"

I. Introduction

This Statement is a call to mutual understanding regarding the government of colleges and universities. Understanding, based on community of interest, and producing joint effort, is essential for at least three reasons. First, the academic institution, public or private, often has become less autonomous; buildings, research, and student tuition are supported by funds over which the college or university exercises a diminishing control. Legislative and executive governmental authority, at all levels, plays a part in the making of important decisions in academic policy. If these voices and forces are to be successfully heard and integrated, the academic institution must be in a position to meet them with its own generally unified view. Second, regard for the welfare of the institution remains important despite the mobility and interchange of scholars. Third, a college or university in which all the components are aware of their interdependence, of the usefulness of communication among themselves, and of the force of joint action will enjoy increased capacity to solve educational problems.

II. The Academic Institution: Joint Effort

A. Preliminary Considerations

The variety and complexity of the tasks performed by institutions of higher education produce an inescapable interdependence among governing board, administration, faculty, students and others. The relationship calls for adequate communication among these components, and full opportunity for appropriate joint planning and effort.

Joint effort in an academic institution will take a variety of forms appropriate to the kinds of situations encountered. In some instances, an initial exploration or recommendation will be made by the president with consideration by the faculty at a later stage; in other instances, a first and essentially definitive recommendation will be made by the faculty, subject to the endorsement of the president and the governing board. In still others, a substantive contribution can be made when student leaders are responsibly involved in the process. Although the variety of such approaches may be wide, at least two general conclusions regarding joint effort seem clearly warranted: (1) important areas of action involve at one time or another the initiating capacity and decision-making participation of all the institutional components, and (2) differences in the weight of each voice, from one point to the next, should be determined by reference to the responsibility of each component for the particular matter at hand, as developed hereinafter.

B. Determination of General Educational Policy

The general educational policy, i.e., the objectives of an institution and the nature, range, and pace of its efforts, is shaped by the institutional charter or by law, by tradition and historical development, by the present needs of the community of the institution, and by the professional aspirations and standards of those directly involved in its work. Every board will wish to go beyond its formal trustee obligation to conserve the accomplishment of the past and to engage seriously with the future; every faculty will seek to conduct an operation worthy of scholarly standards of learning; every administrative officer will strive to meet his charge and to attain the goals of the institution. The interests of all are coordinate and related, and unilateral effort can lead to confusion or conflict. Essential to a solution is a reasonably explicit statement on general educational policy. Operating responsibility and authority, and procedures for continuing review, should be clearly defined in regulations.

When an educational goal has been established, it becomes the responsibility primarily of the faculty to determine appropriate curriculum and procedures of student instruction.

Special considerations may require particular accommodations: (1) a publicly supported institution may be regulated by statutory provisions, and (2) a church-controlled institution may be limited by its charter or bylaws. When such external requirements influence course content and manner of instruction or research, they impair the educational effectiveness of the institution.

Such matters as major changes in the size or composition of the student body and the relative emphasis to be given to the various elements of the educational and research program should involve participation of governing board, administration and faculty prior to final decision.

C. Internal Operations of the Institution

The framing and execution of long-range plans, one of the most important aspects of institutional responsibility, should be a central and continuing concern in the academic community.

Effective planning demands that the broadest possible exchange of information and opinion should be the rule for communication among the components of a college or university. The channels of communication should be established and maintained by joint endeavor. Distinction should be observed between the institutional system of communication and the system of responsibility for the making of decisions.

A second area calling for joint effort in internal operations is that of decisions regarding existing or prospective physical resources. The board, president and faculty should all seek agreement on basic decisions regarding buildings and other facilities to be used in the educational work of the institution.

A third area is budgeting. The allocation of resources among competing demands is central in the formal responsibility of the governing board, in the administrative authority of the president, and in the educational function of the faculty. Each component should therefore have a voice in the determination of short and long-range priorities, and each should receive appropriate analyses of past budgetary experience, reports on current budgets and expenditures, and short and long-range budgetary projections. The function of each component in budgetary matters should be understood by all; the allocation of authority will determine the flow of information and the scope of participation in decisions.

Joint effort of a most critical kind must be taken when an institution chooses a new president. The selection of a chief administrative officer should follow upon cooperative search by the governing board and the faculty, taking into consideration the opinions of others who are appropriately interested. The president should be equally qualified to serve both as the executive officer of the governing board and as the chief academic officer of the institution and the faculty. His dual role requires that he be able to interpret to board and faculty the educational views and concepts of institutional government of the other. He should have the confidence of the board and the faculty.

The selection of academic deans and other chief academic officers should be the responsibility of the president with the advice of and in consultation with the appropriate faculty.

Determinations of faculty status, normally based on the recommendations of the faculty groups involved, are discussed in Part V of this Statement; but it should here be noted that the building of a strong faculty requires careful joint effort in such actions as staff selection and promotion and the granting of tenure. Joint action should also govern dismissals; the applicable principles and procedures in these matters are well established.[2]

D. External Relations of the Institution

Anyone—a member of the governing board, the president or other member of the administration, a member of the faculty, or a member of the student body or the alumni—affects the institution when he speaks of it in public. An individual who speaks unofficially should so indicate. An official spokesman for the institution, the board, the administration, the faculty, or the student body should be guided by established policy.

It should be noted that only the board speaks legally for the whole institution, although it may delegate responsibility to an agent.

The right of a board member, an administrative officer, a faculty member, or a student to speak on general educational questions or about the administration and operations of his own institution is a part of his right as a citizen and should not be abridged by the institution.[3] There exist, of course, legal bounds relating to defamation of character, and there are questions of propriety.

III. The Academic Institution: The Governing Board

The governing board has a special obligation to assure that the history of the college or university shall serve as a prelude and inspiration to the future. The board helps relate the institution to its chief community: e.g., the community college to serve the educational needs of a defined population area or group, the church-controlled college to be cognizant of the announced position of its denomination, and the comprehensive university to discharge the many duties and to accept the appropriate new challenges which are its concern at the several levels of higher education.

The governing board of an institution of higher education in the United States operates, with few exceptions, as the final institutional authority. Private institutions are established by charters; public institutions are established by constitutional or statutory provisions. In private institutions the board is frequently self-perpetuating; in public colleges and universities the present membership of a board may be asked to suggest candidates for appointment. As a whole and individually when the governing board confronts the problem of succession, serious attention should be given to obtaining properly qualified persons. Where public law calls for election of governing board members, means should be found to insure the nomination of fully suited persons, and the electorate should be informed of the relevant criteria for board membership.

Since the membership of the board may embrace both individual and collective competence of recognized weight, its advice or help may be sought through established channels by other components of the academic community. The governing board of an institution of higher education, while maintaining a general overview, entrusts the conduct of administration to the administrative officers, the president and the deans, and the conduct of teaching and research to the faculty. The board should undertake appropriate self-limitation.

One of the governing board's important tasks is to ensure the publication of codified statements that define the over-all policies and procedures of the institution under its jurisdiction.

The board plays a central role in relating the likely needs of the future to predictable resources; it has the responsibility for husbanding the endowment; it is responsible for obtaining needed capital and operating funds; and in the broadest sense of the term it should pay attention to personnel policy. In order to fulfill these duties, the board should be aided by, and may insist upon, the development of long-range planning by the administration and faculty.

When ignorance or ill-will threatens the institution or any part of it, the governing board must be available for support. In grave crises it will be expected to serve as a champion. Although the action to be taken by it will usually be on behalf of the president, the faculty, or the student body, the board should make clear that the protection it offers to an individual or a group is, in fact, a fundamental defense of the vested interests of society in the educational institution.

IV. The Academic Institution: The President

The president, as the chief executive officer of an institution of higher education, is measured largely by his capacity for institutional leadership. He shares responsibility for the definition and attainment of goals, for administrative action, and for operating the communications system which links the components of the academic community. He represents his institution to its many publics. His leadership role is supported by delegated authority from the board and faculty.

As the chief planning officer of an institution, the president has a special obligation to innovate and initiate. The degree to which a president can envision new horizons for his institution, and can persuade others to see them and to work toward them, will often constitute the chief measure of his administration.

The president must at times, with or without support, infuse new life into a department; relatedly, he may at times be required, working within the concept of tenure, to solve problems of obsolescence. The president will necessarily utilize the judgments of the faculty, but in the interest of academic standards he may also seek outside evaluations by scholars of acknowledged competence.

It is the duty of the president to see to it that the standards and procedures in operational use within the college or university conform to the policy established by the governing board and to the standards of sound academic practice. It is also incumbent on the president to insure that faculty views, including dissenting views, are presented to the board in those areas and on those issues where responsibilities are shared. Similarly the faculty should be informed of the views of the board and the administration on like issues.

The president is largely responsible for the maintenance of existing institutional resources and the creation of new resources: he has intimate managerial responsibility for a large area of nonacademic activities, he is responsible for public understanding, and by the nature of his office is the chief spokesman of his institution. In these and other areas his work is to plan, to organize, to direct, and to represent. The presidential function should receive the general support of board and faculty.

V. The Academic Institution: The Faculty

The faculty has primary responsibility for such fundamental areas as curriculum, subject matter and methods of instruction, research, faculty status, and those aspects of student life which relate to the educational process. On these matters the power of review or final decision lodged in the governing board or delegated by it to the president should be exercised adversely only in exceptional circumstances, and for reasons communicated to the faculty. It is desirable that the faculty should, following such communication, have opportunity for further consideration and further transmittal of its views to the president or board. Budgets, manpower limitations, the time element and the policies of other groups, bodies and agencies having jurisdiction over the institution may set limits to realization of faculty advice.

The faculty sets the requirements for the degrees offered in course, determines when the requirements have been met, and authorizes the president and board to grant the degrees thus achieved.

Faculty status and related matters are primarily a faculty responsibility; this area includes appointments, reappointments, decisions not to reappoint, promotions, the granting of tenure, and dismissal. The primary responsibility of the faculty for such matters is based upon the fact that its judgment is central to general educational policy. Furthermore, scholars in a particular field or activity have the chief competence for judging the work of their colleagues; in such competence it is implicit that responsibility exists for both adverse and favorable judgments. Likewise there is the more general competence of experienced faculty personnel committees having broader charge. Determinations in these matters should first be by faculty action through established procedures, reviewed by the chief academic officers with the concurrence of the board. The governing board and president should, on questions of faculty status, as in other matters where the faculty has primary responsibility, concur with the faculty judgment except in rare instances and for compelling reasons which should be stated in detail.

The faculty should actively participate in the determination of policies and procedures governing salary increases.

The chairman or head of a department, who serves as the chief representative of his department within an institution, should be selected either by departmental election or by appointment following consultation with members of the department and of related departments: appointments should normally be in conformity with department members' judgment. The chairman or department head should not have tenure in his office; his tenure as a faculty member is a matter of separate right. He should serve for a stated term but without prejudice to re-election or to reappointment by procedures which involve appropriate faculty consultation. Board, administration, and faculty should all bear in mind that the department chairman has a special obligation to build a department strong in scholarship and teaching capacity.

Agencies for faculty participation in the government of the college or university should be established at each level where faculty responsibility is present. An agency should exist for the presentation of the views of the whole faculty. The structure and procedures for faculty participation should be designed, approved and established by joint action of the components of the institution. Faculty representatives should be selected by the faculty according to procedures determined by the faculty.

The agencies may consist of meetings of all faculty members of a department, school, college, division or university system, or may take the form of faculty-elected executive committees in departments and schools and a faculty-elected senate or council for larger divisions or the institution as a whole.

Among the means of communication among the faculty, administration, and governing board now in use are: (1) circulation of memoranda and reports by board committees, the administration, and faculty committees, (2) joint *ad hoc* committees, (3) standing liaison committees, (4) membership of faculty members on administrative bodies, and (5) membership of faculty members on governing boards. Whatever the channels of communication, they should be clearly understood and observed.

On Student Status

When students in American colleges and universities desire to participate responsibly in the government of the institution they attend, their wish should be recognized as a claim to opportunity both for educational experience and for involvement in the affairs of their college or university. Ways should be found to permit significant student participation within the limits of attainable effectiveness. The obstacles to such participation are large and should not be minimized: inexperience, untested capacity, a transitory status which means that present action does not carry with it subsequent responsibility, and the inescapable fact that the other components of the institution are in a position of judgment over the students. It is important to recognize that student needs are strongly related to educational experience, both formal and informal. Students expect, and have a right to expect, that the educational process will be structured, that they will be stimulated by it to become independent adults, and that they will have effectively transmitted to them the cultural heritage of the larger society. If institutional support is to have its fullest possible meaning it should incorporate the strength, freshness of view and idealism of the student body.

The respect of students for their college or university can be enhanced if they are given at least these opportunities: (1) to be listened to in the classroom without fear of institutional reprisal for the substance of their views, (2) freedom to discuss questions of institutional policy and operation, (3) the right to academic due process when charged with serious violations of institutional regulations, and (4) the same right to hear speakers of their own choice as is enjoyed by other components of the institution.

Notes

[1] Note: 1950, the formulation of the Student Bill of Rights by the United States National Student Association: 1956, the first appearance of *Academic Freedom and Civil Liberties of Students*, published by the American Civil Liberties Union: 1961, the decision in Dixon v. Alabama State Board of Education currently the leading case on due process for students: 1965, the publication of a tentative Statement on the Academic Freedom of Students, by the American Association of University Professors.

[2] See the 1940 *Statement of Principles on Academic Freedom and Tenure* and the 1958 *Statement on Procedural Standards in Faculty Dismissal Proceedings*. These statements have been jointly approved or adopted by the Association of American Colleges and the American Association of University Professors; the 1940 Statement has been endorsed by numerous learned and scientific societies and educational associations.

[3] With respect to faculty members, the 1940 *Statement of Principles on Academic Freedom and Tenure* reads: "The college or university teacher is a citizen, a member of a learned profession, and an officer of an educational institution. When he speaks or writes as a citizen, he should be free from institutional censorship or discipline, but his special position in the community imposes special obligations. As a man of learning and an educational officer, he should remember that the public may judge his profession and his institution by his utterances. Hence he should at all times be accurate, should exercise appropriate restraint, should show respect for the opinion of others. and should make every effort to indicate that he is not an institutional spokesman."

Process of Academic Governance

Kenneth P. Mortimer and T. R. McConnell

In Chapter One we identified two major themes for this book and a set of subthemes. The two major themes were the distribution of authority and the varied base for legitimate governance. We showed that a number of factors are important in the distribution of authority — among them the organizational level at which decisions are made; the constituents who are, or claim a right to be, involved in decisions; the issue under consideration; and the historical-cultural traditions under which the institution operates. In Chapter One we also argued that the dynamics of the shifting bases of legitimacy are closely related to a fundamental incompatibility between the bases of formal and of functional authority which Blau (1973) calls the incompatibility of bureaucracy and scholarship.

This concluding chapter will summarize the major points made in the book and offer suggestions that we believe will enhance the quality of academic decision making. This summary is organized under five policy dilemmas: the sharing of formal authority, the scope and form of constituent-group involvement in governance, the tension between centralization and decentralization, the meaning of consultation, and the balance between codification and discretion. Before beginning this discussion, we shall briefly recapitulate the changing context of postsecondary education in the 1970s and 1980s.

The Changing Context

During the quarter-century following World War II, American postsecondary education dealt with different problems from those it will face in the 1980s. From 1945 to 1970 or so, there was unprecedented growth and prosperity. During the 1960s, enrollments in postsecondary education tripled; during certain years of that decade, community colleges were founded at the rate of one a week. When Nelson Rockefeller became governor of New York and decided to support the development of the SUNY system, the major problem confronting academic administrators at SUNY was how to spend the money responsibly. Organizational changes, curriculum innovation, and enlarged academic units were all financed out of increasing enrollments and a growing economy, and a major issue was how to provide access for youth in an increasingly demanding and egalitarian-minded society.

The issues in the 1970s have changed substantially. The basic question being asked now is whether the nation can afford open admissions, expensive facilities that are used inefficiently, and numerous research-oriented public institutions. The abolition of the draft has made college attendance seem less necessary for many young men. The failure of a college education to guarantee a better job during a decline in economic growth has raised serious questions about whether four years in college are necessary for a fruitful life. Finally, it is apparent that the number of college-age youth will not increase at the prodigious rate of the 1950s and 1960s but will instead decrease in the 1980s.

These developments have raised uncomfortable questions for higher education. The pressure to prove effectiveness and efficiency has led to attempts to quantify educational outcomes that in fact are presently unmeasurable and intangible. The consequence has been to oversimplify the mission of colleges and universities. We pointed out in Chapter Seven that existing measures of change in college students are inadequate to identify the effects of a college education. Nor have attempts to relate exist to any of the "fuzzy" measures for change proved particularly enlightening. Yet, in the presumed interests of economy and efficiency, proponents of educational accountability continue to press for a justification of the cost of the educational outcomes actually attained.

Boards of trustees and faculties have long been at odds on a number of points, but faculties have become aware of this fact only during crises. Student disruptions in the late 1960s accentuated the tensions between trustees and others and strengthened faculty interest in collective bargaining.

The weakness of internal participatory mechanisms, such as faculty senates, have become more evident as internal politics have become more overt and the danger of external intervention have mounted. Internally, it has become increasingly apparent that the role of a senate is advisory rather than legislative. Furthermore, faculties are beginning to realize that senates are no help when the "enemy" is the legislature or the governor. Senates themselves probably cannot invent lobbying mechanisms to counteract these external agents.

To some extent, collective bargaining is a response by faculties to the forces cited above. Declining faculty purchasing power, due to increased living costs, and increasing aggressiveness by legislators and governors have led a number of faculties to adopt collective bargaining as a countervailing force to both internal and external pressures.

The influence of external agencies in college and university governance is growing. The legislative, judicial, and executive branches of local, state, and federal government are now enforcing their concepts of governance and accountability on colleges and universities. At the same time postsecondary education has lost its favored status in the competition for public monies and now must compete with other social needs for ever scarcer funds.

The increased influence of state coordination and system-level administration has moved many decisions further away from campus-based constituencies. Moreover, pressure from these external agents for the adoption of management techniques requires centralization of information as the basis for efficient control. We have little doubt that such centralization of information will continue to grow and will be a major factor in the redistribution of authority that is still in process — a redistribution that will tend to move decision making upward in the organization.

External agents are less reluctant to enter the decision-making process at its final stages than they have been in the past. For example, the courts and arbitrators exercise final review over many internal decisions. Court action on a single case will often dictate the university's future internal procedures. For example, should the United States Supreme Court decide that discriminatory practices are inherent in preferential admissions programs, institutions will have to revise their admissions policies.

Similarly, legislation that gives students access to their own records, such as the Buckley Amendment, has led colleges and universities to modify the way they keep student records. Indeed, the fact that students can examine any recommendation concerning themselves may well change the entire system of recommending students for employment. Few faculty members would be willing to share their confidential evaluations of student performance with the student.

Higher education is in the throes of a shift from informal and consensual judgments to authority based on formal criteria. Standardization, litigation, and centralization have become the watch-words of college and university governance. There have been changes in societal and legislative expectations about higher education, an increase in external regulation of colleges and universities, an increase in emphasis on managerial skills and the technocratic features of modern management, and a greater codification of internal decision-making procedures. These changes raise the question whether existing statements of shared authority provide adequate guidelines for internal governance.

Sharing of Formal Authority

In Chapter One we discussed the contrary between the bases of legitimacy of traditional governance patterns and those of collective bargaining. The concept of shared authority as traditionally developed in the literature and in the joint AAUP/ACE/AGB statement on college and university governance stresses mutual interdependence among internal constituents, including governing boards, faculties, administrators, and students. While we recognize that an academic community need not be of one mind on all basic educational issues, we think that the contrast between the traditional concepts of legitimacy and those embodied in collective bargaining in the industrial sector is so marked as to delineate different conceptions of governance.

To be more specific, we see three major flaws in shared authority as a concept and in the way it operates in colleges and universities: (1) it does not describe actual governance patterns in a majority of institutions, (2) it ignores the conflict of interest and adversary decision-making practices inherent in a major new governance structure, collective bargaining, and (3) it takes little account of the external forces we discuss in Chapters Seven through Nine. Below we consider these points in more detail.

Infrequency in Practice

Surveys and case studies throughout this book show that shared authority is not the dominant pattern of governance in most institutions, even on issues of high salience to faculty members. In some prestigious, or "elite," institutions, such as the University of California at Berkeley, faculties seem to prefer a separation of jurisdictions to genuine shared authority. In community colleges, emerging state and regional universities and colleges, and many independent liberal arts colleges, the principles of shared authority have only begun to penetrate — and institutions of these types account for about 80 percent of American colleges and universities.

Conflict of Interest

The practice of shared authority is—or should be—built on shared values that can give rise to consensus. In other words, there must be some degree of agreement about shared goals and the controlling values of the institution before consensus on a given issue can be achieved. A basic conclusion from our analysis of senates, collective bargaining, and faculty relations with administrators, students, and trustees is that the formal authority of trustees and administrators is inescapable. The legal authority of lay governing boards is a well-established American tradition (Duryea, 1973, pp. 19-23), and although it has undergone some erosion, it is in remarkably good health. The major pressure for the redistribution of authority is an attempt to get trustees and their delegates to share this formal authority with faculty, students, and others. The grounds for sharing the authority to govern are inherent in the purposes of the institution — the acquisition, testing, and transmission of knowledge by specialized professionals. Thus, Finkin (1976, pp. 391-392) argues that "in contrast to the assumptions governing blue-collar industrial employment, the system of structured professional influence in faculty-status decisions in higher education assumes, first, that management's practical authority to decide is shared with the faculty and, second, that the correctness of the judgment rests largely on subjective assessments."

Recognizing that there should be limits on formal authority, we take the position that in major processes of governance, joint involvement is preferable to segmental decision making and constitutes the most reasonable means of balancing the seemingly disparate requirements of formal and functional authority. The joint AAUP/ACE/AGB statement, reviewed in Chapter One, places great emphasis on the *primary responsibility* of faculties over such matters as curriculum and faculty status, and defines the concept of primary responsibility as the ability to take action that has the force of legislation and can be overruled only in rare instances and for compelling reasons. This preoccupation with primary responsibility for academic decisions is accompanied by the view that other decisions, in contrast, require joint endeavor.

In our view, "academic" issues, such as faculty status, and "fiscal" issues, such as the reassignment of vacant positions due to retirement, termination, or the phasing out of existing programs, are inescapably interdependent, and more emphasis should therefore be placed on the principle of joint endeavor. The concept of primary responsibility overemphasizes faculty or student *control* and ignores the legitimate concerns of other groups. For example, a decision to hire or retain a faculty member involves more than a determination of the individual's professional competence. These other considerations include, for example, balance among different schools of thought within a discipline; affirmative action standards; balance within an academic unit among teaching, research, and service; and the salary to be offered. We think it unrealistic for the faculty to argue that such considerations are irrelevant to particular decisions and therefore that these decisions require little, if any, administrative participation. It is equally unrealistic for the administration to argue that fiscal matters related to academic affairs are adequately decided without faculty participation.

In sum, we argue that those concerned with college and university governance should eschew the search for separate areas of authority and look for ways to enhance joint involvement. This search can, of course, be conducted through collective bargaining as well as such more traditional structures as senates and committees.

Collective bargaining, however, docs seem to require more formalized arrangements than are customary. The most important implication for administrators and trustees is that should adversary patterns of governance and a conflict-of-interest mentality *dominate* bargaining relations, the board of trustees can no longer serve as a court of last resort in resolving internal disputes. Under bargaining the board is a party to the dispute, not a final arbiter.

We therefore think it incumbent on the national associations, particularly the AAUP, to be more specific about whether the joint statement's emphasis on the mutual interdependence of academic constituents can be reconciled with certain features of collective bargaining as it has developed in business and industry. We noted these features in Chapter Three and showed some of the difficulties in their application to traditional academic relationships. Industrial practice must obviously be modified in academic institutions, and the AAUP could profitably speak to this point.

Closed-System Framework

Another basic weakness of the joint statement on shared authority is its almost exclusive focus on internal affairs. It does state that mechanisms for faculty involvement should exist at all appropriate levels — but it mentions the system level only in a footnote. Future revisions of the joint statement should pay more serious attention to both system- and state-level relations with faculty, administrators, and students. It is important to ask such questions as these: Does the AAUP wish to retain its emphasis on primary responsibility at the system level? What principles, in the AAUP's opinion, ought to govern relations between consultative mechanisms at the campus and system levels?

Our point is simply that many — probably most — of the threats to departmental, college, and campus autonomy and patterns of governance are generated by external forces and developments.

Constituent Participation in Governance

The first six chapters of this book emphasize relations among the various internal constituencies that take part in governance or claim a right to. We have consistently avoided extensive discussions of *whether* the faculty and students should take part; we have assumed that the appropriate question is the form and scope that their participation should take. We argued that the legitimacy and effectiveness of faculty senates are threatened by their unrepresenta-tiveness and their inability to act quickly and decisively in times of crisis. Faculty unions are often presented as an alternative or supplement to senates, but we see no evidence that they are any more representative of the faculty than senates are. Many unions limit participation in their internal governance to dues-paying members, who usually make up less than half the fac-ulty. Garbarino (1975, p. 106) estimates that the average union membership in 1971 was 30 per-cent of those eligible and that the figure may have risen to 50 percent by 1974. The problem of representativeness remains, and the question of who actually speaks for the faculty or students will continue to be important for some time. In Chapters Five and Eight we showed that repre-sentativeness is a problem for trustees and state governing and coordinating boards as well.

Administrators, we believe, bear the responsibility for seeking out and hearing representative views. When campus political factions control senate or union machinery (or both), a truly concerned administration must look for ways to make sure that minority factions and less vocal points of view are heard and considered. In some situations this effort will require the judicious appointment of those representing diverse views to influential committees. In other cases administrators will have to work more subtly to make sure that such individuals or groups are consulted about important matters.

We realize that this advice may cause administrators in unionized institutions some difficulty, since legally they must deal exclusively with the union on terms and conditions of employment. Nevertheless, we believe that administrations should not surrender their means of communication with the faculty to the exclusive domain of the union. Avoiding doing so will require leadership of the highest order and faculty/administration relations built on trust and a shared sense of institutional purpose.

Whether traditional mechanisms like senates will continue under collective bargaining depends on institutional politics, traditions of faculty involvement in governance, and the amount of trust between the parties. Regardless of the eventual outcome, the horizontal dimension — that is, the representativeness of internal governance — will continue to be a question of major importance.

The major debate over the *form* of constituent-group involvement continues to be over the appropriateness of collective bargaining. We suspect that by 1980 or 1985 the various implications of bargaining will be more apparent. Like most researchers, we find it difficult, if not impossible, to isolate the impact of bargaining from the impact of other developments, such as affirmative action, fixed enrollments, job-security pressures, legislative oversight, and judicial intervention. There is, however, a basic question whose joint consideration by administrators and faculty members might aid in the process of accommodation: What general purposes should govern an approach to bargaining?

As far as possible, all tactical questions should be analyzed against the general purposes to be achieved. If the parties wish to preserve campus autonomy, as opposed to system-wide decision making, they should probably go to great lengths to resolve disputes at the campus level or below rather than have solutions imposed from above. If they want to enhance individual autonomy, they should probably avoid negotiating a centralized workload policy.

The reality of bargaining and living with a contract will quickly impose the contract's character on faculty/administration relations. If relations have been acrimonious historically, bargaining will probably not change that. Without explicit attention to major purposes, however, there is real danger that the process will control the substance of faculty/administration interactions.

The Centralization/Decentralization Dilemma

We pointed out in Chapters Eight and Nine that the discussion of the vertical distribution of authority tends to concentrate on how to reconcile society's legitimate concern for accountability with higher education's claim to autonomy. Furthermore, within institutions there is great concern about the authority of system-level administrators and faculty organizations over those at the campus level. Each level of the organizational hierarchy is concerned about its relations with higher and lower levels.

In Chapter Six we urged that the delegation or the assumption of authority be coupled with accountability. In coming years we expect to see more emphasis on periodic review of the wisdom with which delegated authority has been used. There should be rigorous and detailed discussion of the mechanisms and procedures for periodic review of delegated authority throughout the institution and the system.

In summary, the sharing of formal authority, the scope and form of internal participation in governance, and the vertical distribution of authority should be characterized by full and open consultation with an emphasis on joint endeavor. Consultation and joint effort should be built on a high degree of trust. Trust can be encouraged by an emphasis on process, which we shall now discuss.

The Consultation Process

We propose that ensuring adequate consultation has six elements: consultation should occur early in the decision-making process; the procedures for consultation should be uniform and fair to all parties; there must be adequate time to formulate a response to the request for consultation; information relevant to the decision should be freely available; the advice rendered must be adequately considered and feedback given; and the decision, when made, should be communicated to the consulting group.

Early Consultation

In Chapter One we divided the decision-making process into six stages. We do not insist that these stages are the only ones to be considered. The point we think important is that consultation should occur before alternatives are formulated, positions rigidified, and courses charted.

It is important that the groups with an interest in the problem being decided have a chance to consider the formulation of alternatives as well as the phrasing of the issues well before the alternatives become rigidified. A typical faculty complaint is that the administration asks for consultation only after deciding on a course of action. It is *not* consultation, as defined here, for the trustees or administration to inform interested parties that there will be a new program or policy and then to ask for help in implementing it. The principle of early consultation requires that issues be phrased in general terms at the initial stage of discussion. The next task is joint formulation of the specific questions that the consultation is to address. For example, many institutions are currently reexamining tenure policies because the declining growth rate and limited mobility of the faculty portend a fairly stable professoriate in the coming decades. Some of the alternatives being considered are quotas, more rigid criteria for tenure, and abolition of tenure in favor of term contracts. These alternatives are actually prematurely identified solutions to some rather ill-defined problems. Early consultation among constituent groups should concentrate on the institution's current tenure practices, the implications of a high tenure ratio if one seems likely, and how possible changes in tenure policies might affect academic affairs. For example, what evidence is there that a highly tenured faculty would be more resistant to curricular innovation than a less tenured one? If the basic problem turns out to be receptiveness to new ideas, the issue is much broader than tenure policy, and this fact should be recognized.

Early consultation is a vital step in building and maintaining the sense of legitimacy so necessary to effective academic governance.

Joint Formulation of Procedures

Uniform and fair procedures are equally important. An institutional document that we studied at Fresno State College had a statement that illustrates our basic concern about uniform and fair procedures for consultation. The statement can be paraphrased as follows: The consultative body has a right to be consulted about the procedures through which consultation is to be conducted.

Although we were critical of what we viewed as overly rigid consultative procedures at Fresno, we believe that an agreement over appropriate processes is a vital part of relations built on trust and joint endeavor. Such questions as these are pertinent: Is a faculty committee being asked for informal advice, or is a written committee report expected? Should the committee deliberate only among its own members, or should it hold public hearings and consult widely before rendering advice? Should the committee seek to arrive at a consensus, or should it transmit a range of acceptable alternatives? More specifically, should a search committee for an academic administrator name a number of acceptable candidates or one candidate? If more than one is to be named, should the committee rank the candidates or otherwise express a preference? Answers to such questions should be jointly agreed on as part of the committee's charge.

The process of collective bargaining will, of course, almost *require* some agreement about procedures. In many cases, the first round of negotiations includes an attempt to write down, for the first time, procedures for arriving at certain decisions. The federal government's affirmative action guidelines, in effect, require some concentration on search-and-screen procedures for faculty and administrative appointments. In short, colleges and universities almost have to *have* such procedures "on the books." We believe they should be jointly formulated and clear to all.

Time to Formulate Responses

A common source of irritation for participants in college and university governance is a request for advice that has to be given immediately. Many such requests are legitimate, especially when a crisis threatens the stability of the campus. Too often, however, they merely reflect sloppy planning or inadequate anticipation of problems.

But it is not unreasonable for deadlines to be placed on requests for consultation. Faculty committees are fond of deliberating for one or two years before rendering a decision or giving advice, and that is not generally necessary or desirable.

The most glaring violations of this principle of adequate-time to formulate a response occur when administrators ask for advice or appoint committees just before the summer break. Faculty members and students may not be available in the summer, and administrators, most of whom are on twelve-month appointments, tend to formulate their own proposals or solutions over the summer. When the fall term begins, faculty and students are confronted with solutions they had little part in formulating. The calendar requires advanced planning so that the summer months are not used to avoid the requirements of adequate consultation.

Availability of Information

The persons considering alternatives should have free access to the information they need. Few limitations need be placed on the availability of information relevant to the problem under consideration. Some restraints, however, may be appropriate. For example, the confidentiality of personnel records may be necessary to protect the legitimate privacy of faculty and staff.

We urge that those who would restrict the free flow of information in academic affairs be prepared to justify that limitation. Some of the previous practices of restricting financial information have been obviated or overruled by state "sunshine" laws. The budgets of public institutions have become public documents, and often the only remaining question is how much detail is made available — as seen, for example, in the privacy of individual salaries within the structure of published salary scales.

Of course, other exceptions to the free flow of information exist. Administrators may ask for independent and confidential evaluations of operating units and for independent judgments of individual faculty members being considered for promotion. The confidentiality of such reviews is a controversial question under collective bargaining. Some faculty unions continue to argue for completely open personnel files and an opportunity for faculty members to rebut criticisms of their performance. Yet confidentiality lies at the heart of peer review systems. If peer review is to operate effectively, faculty colleagues must be assured that their evaluations will be confidential. Those who would unwisely restrict access to relevant information threaten the basic attitude of trust and cooperation needed for effective governance.

Adequate Feedback

A basic principle of consultation that is most often ignored is that adequate response must be forthcoming after advice has been rendered. Administrators are responsible for giving serious consideration to reports and memoranda from faculty, students, and other groups. Indeed, if our previous comments are carefully considered, committee or task force reports will not contain any basic surprises for administrators but, rather, will be the product of collaborative discussion and debate. Ideally, administrative veto would rarely be necessary.

The feedback stage of the consultation process gives the administration a unique opportunity to continue the debate over the important policy matters in a particular decision. Administrators should make it clear that their failure to accept or to immediately implement a report from the faculty or students does not necessarily mean that the report has been rejected. Part of the feedback may well be a statement that the report is adequate or even outstanding, but that it does not now have a high priority in institutional development.

There are times, of course, when the failure to implement or accept a report does mean its total rejection. We believe that it is then appropriate for the administrator to meet with the committee and explain why the report is unacceptable. During such discussions it should be determined whether the entire series of recommendations is unsatisfactory or whether only one or two recommendations are unacceptable.

Sometimes a committee recommendation cannot be accepted because of financial considerations or because the administration is privy to information or viewpoints not shared by the committee. Those who restrict the flow of relevant or decisive information bear the responsibility for justifying the restriction. Administrators and trustees who argue that recommendations are unacceptable for reasons unknown to the committee that prepared a report may be taxing the committee's sense of trust and hence of legitimacy. Frequently resorting to decisive but private information will not inspire wholehearted consultation or participation in decision making.

There is considerable debate over appropriate means for providing adequate feedback. For example, administrators are traditionally reluctant to provide reasons in writing when faculty members are denied tenure, since such written statements can be interpreted as "charges" if the case eventually gets to court. As in our more general comments above, we urge that this particular problem of adequate feedback be the subject of joint discussion among constituencies.

Communication of the Decisions

It seems obvious that when decisions are made, they should be publicized, adequately communicated, or both, but the point is too often ignored. The deliberation over making or implementing decisions should include discussion of how to communicate them to the academic community. Negative decisions on tenure are, of course, a matter of record, and the individual candidate is quite normally informed. It is less common for administrators to inform a faculty committee that its recommendations on tenure or promotion will be denied and why.

We believe an institution that adopts these six principles of consultation among faculty members, administrators, trustees, and students will be taking a significant first step toward creating and maintaining a sense of trust and legitimacy in academic governance. Discussion, debate, and even conflict over the *substance* of particular educational decisions is to be expected, but it should be possible to reach agreement on the processes by which decisions should be made. This emphasis on process can be a significant force in legitimating academic governance; it should enlighten the discussion about roles and responsibilities.

A major argument against greater emphasis on process is that it would increase the codification of rules and procedures and thus the inflexibility of academic governance at the expense of administrative discretion. Discretion, like decentralization, has acquired the status of an abstract but desirable goal for administrators. The final section of this chapter will look at the need for discretion in governance within the limits placed by our previous discussion of the consultative process.

In Defense of Discretion

One basic issue throughout this book has been the degree to which the conduct of academic affairs should be formalized and standardized. A good many forces exert pressure for increased codification of the decision-making process. Collective bargaining tends to make the terms and conditions of faculty employment into a legally binding agreement between managers and the managed. The push for behavioral objectives in instruction or management by objectives in administration is an attempt to codify behaviors or other outcomes for which individuals can be held accountable; the questionable assumptions underlying these techniques are that codification of objectives is both possible and desirable and that, once stated, the objectives can be measured. New managerial technologies such as information systems and program budgeting require the standardization and routinization of data bases. Finally, the pressure for increased accountability from external agents requires that institutions pay more attention to formalizing internal affairs. Legislatures are demanding reports on faculty workload, the executive branch of government is demanding quantitative measures of institutional productivity that can be compared across institutions, and faculty members are being pressed to show that they have made identifiable contributions to student performance.

To some extent, codification is an attempt to limit discretion in academic governance. The discretion thus limited is usually administrative, but some effort is also directed at the discretion allowed faculty members and students when performing managerial functions. For example, much of the debate about making faculty evaluation more objective is an attempt to modify what some consider the arbitrary and capricious nature of professional judgment. The effort to restrict subjective appraisals is an attempt to eliminate the opportunity for faculty members to use discretion in making judgments about the professional worth of their colleagues.

The pressure to limit discretion is so severe that a new attempt needs to be made for justifying its responsible practice in university affairs. The dilemma need not be stated in absolute terms — that codification should replace discretion. In fact, the question is one of degree — how much discretion and for what purposes?

Davis (1969) has written an illuminating essay on the concept of discretionary justice as it applies to legal affairs. The basic question of his essay is "What can be done that is not now done to minimize injustice from the exercise of discretionary authority?" (p. 1). His answer is that society needs to eliminate much unnecessary discretionary action and that we should do more than we have been doing to confine, to structure, and to check necessary discretionary power. He nevertheless takes the position that "the goal is not the maximum degree of confining, structuring, and checking; the goal is to find the optimum degree for each power in each set of circumstances" (pp. 3-4). In keeping with our earlier contingency approach, we can see that Davis is arguing for a situation-specific view of discretion: the amount necessary depends on the situation.

In Davis' terms, an administrator has discretion whenever the effective limits on his power leave him free to choose among courses of action or inaction. Inaction may be a significant option; the failure to act can have consequences as important as those that a decision to do something can have.

Administrative or faculty discretion is exercised not merely in the final disposition of cases or problems but in the major steps involved in the decision-making process. These interim steps are far more numerous than the final decision to accept or not to accept a recommendation. The discretion to initiate, to consult, to review, to accept, or to veto can be an important part of university governance. Discretion is not limited to making substantive choices. It extends to the procedures for decision making — the methods, forms, timing, and degree of emphasis, as well as many other subsidiary factors. The point is that discretion is an integral part of administrative and faculty involvement in academic governance.

Many areas of discretion that are not now guided by rules could be. The prevalence of discretion in these areas may well be due to administrative and faculty reluctance to codify the traditions of operation, the feeling that many decisions should be made as close to the operational level as possible, or the belief that extensive specification would too greatly limit the freedom of competent administrators. For example, as we pointed out in the discussion of decentralization in Chapter Nine, the authority of department heads under the same dean often varies. Colleges and universities often prefer to leave the responsibility and authority of department heads to the discretion of the dean. Codifying their prerogatives might strengthen the hands of some department heads vis-á-vis the faculty, but it might hamper the performance of others who operate on functional authority and in whom faculty members have greater confidence and to whom faculty members are disposed to grant more discretion as a means of expediting departmental business.

Some aspects of governance are uncodified because no one knows how to formulate adequate rules. This is especially so in the area that colleges and universities call professional judgment. It is hard to formulate rules for arriving at professional judgments of the quality of a colleague's work except in rather general terms. Some progress has been made in means of student appraisal of teaching. Evaluating a faculty member's research, however, is a far more difficult process to standardize.

Many areas of discretion are left uncodified because discretion is preferred to any rules that might be formulated. That is, individualized justice is often better, or thought to be better, than the results that a formal procedure could produce. For example, many colleges and universities do not attempt to define faculty workload; they prefer to leave it to individual negotiations between department heads and faculty members. Most universities prefer to let each faculty member decide how many doctoral dissertations he or she will supervise, even if inequalities in faculty load result. Department heads in many universities have the discretion to adjust teaching loads so that particular faculty members may concentrate on research or creative activity as desirable. We believe such discretion is in the interests of the faculty and of society as well.

Since colleges and universities *must* continue to undertake tasks for which no one is able to prepare regulations in advance, the use of discretion in academic governance will not and should not be severely restricted. We believe that discretion is an indispensable tool for the individualization of administrative justice. Discretion is and will continue to be a main source of creativity in the administration of colleges and universities.

Nevertheless, we agree with Davis (p. 25) that every consideration that supports discretion may be coupled with a warning about its dangers. Discretion is a tool for positive ends only when properly used — as an axe can be used for mayhem or for splitting firewood.

What is necessary is a thorough analysis of academic government directed toward identifying areas in which the exercise of trustee, administrative, or faculty discretion is necessary to preserve basic academic and educational values. The approach to this analysis should be characterized by a high degree of openness, To quote Davis (p. 98), "The seven instruments that are most useful in the structuring of discretionary power are open plans, open policy statements, open rules, open findings, open reasons, open precedents, and fair informal procedures. The reason for repeating the word open is a powerful one: openness is a natural enemy of arbitrariness and a natural ally in the fight against injustice. We should enlist it much more than we do."

We hasten to add also that discretion is susceptible to many kinds of abuse, including, at the worst, flagrant discrimination, favoritism, and caprice. Consequently, discretion may be highly damaging to the basic trust, collaboration, and cooperation so crucial in the conduct of academic affairs. It is essential, therefore, for faculty members — and, in appropriate instances, students — to have clearly understood and fully accessible avenues for the adjudication and possible redress of grievances. Furthermore, as pointed out in Chapter Six, the exercise of authority — certainly discretionary authority and decision making — must be coupled with accountability. In discussing presidential discretion (Chapter Six) we noted that President Brewster of Yale has proposed that a regular procedure be established for periodic reappraisal of the administrator's competence and the community's confidence in his or her integrity. This might be accomplished by term appointments accompanied by appraisal of performance in preparation for reappointment. This policy is appropriate not only for presidents and other central administrative officers but also for deans, department heads, and heads of research institutes.

The legitimacy of university and college governance based on mutual trust and cooperation among constituencies is more important, we believe, than the form or structure for participation in university affairs. We have emphasized the importance of educational planning as a device for interaction and debate among the various groups that should be represented in university affairs. Planning is essential, but the need for legitimacy in governance puts increased emphasis on who can be trusted to perform the planning function. If the tone of faculty/trustee/administration relations is characterized by adversariness and a conflict-of-interest mentality, then the open information so crucial to effective planning will not be available. When relations are highly adversarial, information becomes a political tool to be shared or withheld according to political advantage. We hope it is clear that such relations are not part of a system of joint participation in governance. Such a system, we hope, will somehow survive the advent of collective bargaining and the overt redistribution of influence, power, and authority that colleges and universities are experiencing.

The Processes of Choice

MICHAEL D. COHEN AND JAMES G. MARCH

The Basic Ideas

When we look at universities as they struggle with the problems of reorganization, reform, choice, and survival, we are struck by one quite consistent theme: Decision opportunities are fundamentally ambiguous stimuli (Cohen, March, Olsen, 1972).[1] Although organizations can often be viewed as vehicles for solving well defined problems and as structures within which conflict is resolved through bargaining, they are also sets of procedures through which organizational participants arrive at an interpretation of what they are doing and what they have done while doing it. From this point of view, an organization is a collection of choices looking for problems, issues and feelings looking for decision situations in which they might be aired, solutions looking for issues to which they might be the answer, and decision makers looking for work.

Such a view of organizational choice focuses attention on the ways in which the meaning of choice changes over time. It calls attention to the strategic effects of timing (in the introduction of choices and problems), the time pattern of available energy, and the impact of organizational structure on these.

A key to understanding the processes within organizations is to view a choice opportunity[2] as a garbage can into which various problems and solutions are dumped by participants. The mix of garbage in a single can depends partly on the labels attached to the alternative cans; but it also depends on what garbage is being produced at the moment, on the mix of cans available, and on the speed with which garbage is collected and removed from the scene.

Although we may imagine that choice opportunities lead first to the generation of decision alternatives, then to an examination of the consequences of those alternatives, then to an examination of the consequences in terms of objectives, and finally to a decision, such a model is often a poor description of what actually happens. In a garbage can situation, a decision is an outcome (or an interpretation) of several relatively independent "streams" within an organization.

We will limit our attention to the interrelations among four such streams:

1. *Problems.* Problems are the concern of people inside and outside the organization. They arise over issues of lifestyle; family; frustrations of work; careers; group relations within the organization; distribution of status, jobs, and money; ideology; or current crises of mankind as interpreted by the mass media or the nextdoor neighbor. All require attention. Problems are, however, distinct from choices; and they may not be resolved when choices are made.
2. *Solutions.* A solution is somebody's product. A computer is not just a solution to a problem in payroll management, discovered when needed. It is an answer actively looking for a question. The creation of need is not a curiosity of the market in consumer products; it is a general phenomenon of processes of choice. Despite the dictum that you cannot find the answer until you have formulated the question well, you often do not know what the question is in organizational problem solving until you know the answer.

3. *Participants.* Participants come and go. Since every entrance is an exit somewhere else, the distribution of entrances depends on the attributes of the choice being left as much as it does on the attributes of the new choice. Substantial variation in participation stems from other demands on the participants' time (rather than from features of the decision under study).

4. *Choice opportunities.* These are occasions when an organization is expected to produce behavior that can be called a decision. Opportunities arise regularly, and any organization has ways of declaring an occasion for choice. Contracts must be signed; people hired, promoted, or fired; money spent, and responsibilities allocated.

Although not completely independent of each other, each of the streams can be viewed as independent and exogenous to the system. Attention will be concentrated here on examining the consequences of different rates and patterns of flows in each of the streams and different procedures for relating them.

The properties of universities as organized anarchies make the garbage can ideas particularly appropriate to an understanding of organizational choice within higher education. Although a college or university operates within the metaphor of a political system or a hierarchical bureaucracy, the actual operation of either is considerably attenuated by the ambiguity of college goals, by the lack of clarity in educational technology, and by the transient character of many participants. Insofar as a college is correctly described as an organized anarchy, a college president needs to understand the consequences of a garbage can decision process.

Implications of the Ideas

Elsewhere (Cohen, March, Olsen, 1972) we have detailed the development of these basic ideas into a computer simulation model that has been run under conditions simulating a variety of different organizational structures. This garbage can model of choice operates under each of the hypothesized organization structures to assign problems and decision makers to choices, to determine the energy required and effective energy applied to choices, to make such choices and resolve such problems as the assignments and energies indicate are feasible.

For each run of the model we have computed five simple summary statistics to describe the process:

1. *Decision style.* Within a garbage can process, decisions are made in three different ways:
   a. By *oversight.* If a choice is activated when problems are attached to other choices and if there is energy available to make the new choice quickly, it will be made without any attention to existing problems and with a minimum of time and energy.
   b. By *flight.* In some cases, choices are associated with problems (unsuccessfully) for some time until a choice "more attractive" to the problems comes along. The problems leave the choice, and thereby make it possible to make the decision. The decision resolves no problems (they having now attached themselves to a new choice).
   c. By *resolution.* Some choices resolve problems after some period of working on them. The length of time may vary greatly (depending on the number of problems). This is the familiar case that is implicit in most discussion of choice within organizations. Some choices involve both flight and resolution (i.e., some problems leave, the remainder are solved). We have defined these as resolution, thus slightly exaggerating the importance of that style; As a result of that convention, the three styles are mutually exclusive and exhaustive with respect to any one choice. but the same organization may use any one of them on different choices. Thus, we can describe the decision-making style of the organization by specifying the proportion of completed choices that are made in each of these three ways.

2. *Problem activity.* We wish to find some measure of the degree to which problems are active within the organization. Such a measure should reflect something like the degree of conflict within the organization or the degree of articulation of problems. We have taken the number of time periods that each problem is active and attached to some choice, and added them together to obtain the total time periods for all problems.

3. *Problem latency.* A problem may be active but not attached to any choice. It may be recognized and accepted by some part of the organization but may not be considered germane to any available choice. Presumably an organization with relatively high problem latency will exhibit somewhat different symptoms from one with low latency. We have measured problem latency by taking the total number of periods that each problem is active but not attached to a choice and added them together to obtain the total time periods for all problems.

4. *Decision-maker activity.* To measure the degree of decision-maker activity in the system, we require some measure that reflects decision-maker energy expenditure, movement, and persistence. We have computed the total number of times that any decision maker shifts from one choice to another.

5. *Decision difficulty.* We want to be able to characterize the ease with which a system makes decisions. Because of the way in which decisions can be made in the system (see the above discussion of decision style), that is not the same as the level of problem activity. We have used, as a measure, the total number of periods that each choice is active, and we added them together to obtain the total number of periods for all choices.

These summary statistics,[3] along with a more intensive look at the individual histories of the simulations, reveal eight major properties of garbage can decision processes.

First, resolution of problems is not the most common style for making decisions except under conditions where flight is severely restricted or under a few conditions of light load. In each of our cases there were 20 problems and 10 choices. Although the mean number of choices not made was only 1.0, the mean number of problems not solved was 12.3. Decision making by flight and oversight is a major feature of the process in general. The behavioral and normative implications of a decision process that appears to make choices in large part by the flight of problems or by oversight may be particularly important for university presidents to consider.

Second, the process is thoroughly and generally sensitive to variations in load. An increase in the net energy load on the system generally increases problem activity, decision-maker activity, decision difficulty, and the uses of flight and oversight. Problems are less likely to be solved, decision makers are likely to shift from one problem to another more frequently, choices are likely to take longer to make and to be less likely to resolve problems.

Third, decision makers and problems tend to *track* each other through choices. Both decision makers and problems tend to move together from choice to choice. As a result, decision makers may be expected to feel that they are always working on the same problems in somewhat different contexts, mostly without results. Problems, in a similar fashion, meet the same people wherever they go with the same result.

Fourth, there are some important interconnections among three key aspects of the "efficiency" of the decision processes we have specified. The first of these is problem activity—the amount of time unresolved problems are actively attached to choice situations. Problem activity is a rough measure of potential for decision conflict in the organization. It assesses the degree of involvement of problems in choices. The second aspect is problem latency—the amount of time that problems spend activated but not linked to choices. The third aspect is decision time—the persistence of choices. Presumably, a good organizational structure would keep both problem activity and problem latency low through rapid problem solution in its choices. In the garbage can process we never observe this. Some structures reduce the number of unresolved problems active in the organization but at the cost of increasing the latency period of problems and (in most cases) the time devoted to reaching decisions. Other structures decrease problem latency, but at the cost of increasing problem activity and decision time.

Fifth, the decision-making process is frequently sharply interactive. Although some phenomena associated with the garbage can are regular and flow through nearly all the cases (for example, the effect of overall load), other phenomena are much more dependent on the particular combination of structures involved. In fact, the process is one that often looks capricious to an observer. Many of the outcomes are produced by distinct consequences of the particular time phasing of choices, problems, and participant availability.

Sixth, important problems are more likely to be solved than important ones. Early-arriving problems are more likely to be resolved than later ones. The system, in effect, produces a queue of problems in terms of their importance—to the strong disadvantage of late-arriving, relatively unimportant problems, particularly when load is heavy. This queue is the result of the operation of the model. It was not imposed as a direct assumption.

Seventh, important choices are much *less* likely to resolve problems than are unimportant choices. Important choices are made by oversight and flight. Unimportant choices are made by resolution. The differences are substantial. Moreover, they are not connected to the entry times of the choices. We believe this property of important choices in a garbage can decision process can be naturally and directly related to the phenomenon in complex organizations of "important" choices that often appear to just "happen."

Eighth, although a large proportion of the choices are made, the choice failures that do occur are concentrated among the most important and least important choices. Choices of intermediate importance are virtually always made.

In a broad sense, these features of the decision-making process provide some clues to how organizations survive when they do not know what they are doing. Much of the process violates standard notions of how decisions ought to be made. But most of those notions are built on assumptions that cannot be met under the conditions we have specified. When objectives and technologies are unclear, organizations are charged to discover some alternative decision procedures that permit them to proceed without doing violence to the domains of participants or to their model of an organization. It is a difficult charge, to which the process we have described is a partial response.

At the same time, the details of the outcomes clearly depend on features of the organizational structure. The same garbage can process results in different behavioral symptoms under different levels of load on the system or different designs of the structure of the organization. These differences raise the possibility of predicting variations in decision behavior in different organizations. In the next section we consider one possible application of such an approach to the domain of higher education.

Garbage Cans and Universities

Although there is great variability among colleges and universities, we think the model's major attributes have fairly general relevance to decision making in higher education. University decision making frequently does not "resolve" problems. Choices are likely to be made by flight or oversight. University decision processes appear to be sensitive to changes in load. Active decision makers and problems seem often to track one another through a series of choices without appreciable progress in solving problems. Important choices seem particularly likely not to solve problems.

What we see, both in the model and in actual observations of universities, are decisions whose interpretations continually change during the process of resolution. Problems, choices, and decision makers arrange and rearrange themselves. In the course of these arrangements the meaning of a choice can change several times—if the "meaning" of a choice is understood as the mix of problems that are discussed in the context of that choice.

Problems are often solved, but rarely by the choice to which they are first attached. A choice that might, under some circumstances, be made with little effort becomes an arena for many problems. As a result, it becomes almost impossible to make—until the problems drift off to another arena. The matching of problems, choices, and decision makers is partly controlled by content, "relevance," and competence; but it is also quite sensitive to timing, the particular combinations of current garbage cans, and the overall load on the system.

In order to consider a more specific application of the model, we have attempted to examine the events associated with one kind of adversity within organizations—the reduction of organizational slack.

Slack is the difference between the resources of the organization and the combination of demands made on it. Thus, it is sensitive to two major factors: (1) the money and other resources provided to the organization by the external environment; and (2) the consistency of the demands made on the organization by participants. It is commonly believed that organizational slack has been reduced rather substantially within American colleges and universities over the past few years. If we can establish some possible relations between changes in organizational stack and the key structural variables within the model, we should be able to show the consequences of slack reduction in a garbage can decision-making process.

Elsewhere (Cohen, March, Olsen, 1972) we have outlined ways in which we can tie the variable in the model to some features (particularly size and wealth) of universities. With this specification, we can use the garbage can model to predict the differences we would expect to observe among several types of schools. The results with respect to our five basic outcome statistics can be found in Table 28. They suggest that under conditions of prosperity, as we have defined them, overt conflict (problem activity) will be substantially higher in poor schools than in rich ones, and decision time will be substantially longer. Large, rich schools will be characterized by a high degree of problem latency. Most decisions will resolve some problems.

Table 28 also shows the effects of adversity on our four types of schools according to the garbage can model. By examining the first stage of adversity, some possible reasons for discontent among presidents of large, rich schools can be seen. In relation to other schools they are not seriously disadvantaged. The large, rich schools have a moderate level of problem activity, a moderate level of decision by resolution. In relation to their earlier state, however, large, rich schools are certainly deprived. Problem activity and decision time have increased greatly; the proportion of decisions which resolve problems has decreased from 68 percent to 21 percent; administrators are less able to move around from one decision to another. In all these terms. the relative deprivation of the presidents of large, rich schools is much greater, in the early stages of adversity, than that of administrators in other schools.

The large, poor schools are in the worst absolute position under adversity. They have a high level of problem activity, a substantial decision time,[4] a low level of decision-maker mobility, and a low proportion of decisions being made by resolution. But along most of these dimensions, the change has been less for them.

The small, rich schools experience a large increase in problem activity, an increase in decision time, and a decrease in the proportion of decisions by resolution as adversity begins. The small, poor schools seem to move in a direction counter to the trends in the other three groups. Decision style is little affected by the onset of stack reduction, problem activity, and decision time decline; and decision-maker mobility increases. Presidents of such organizations might feel a sense of success in their efforts to tighten up the organization in response to resource contraction.

The application of the model to this particular situation among American colleges and universities clearly depends upon a large number of assumptions. Nevertheless, the derivations from the model have some face validity as description of some aspects of recent life in American higher education.

Table 28

Effects of adversity on four types of colleges and universities operating within a garbage can decision process

Type of school type of situation	Decision-style proportion resolution	Outcome			
		Problem activity	Problem latency	Decision-maker activity	Decision time
Large, rich universities					
Good times	0.68	0	154	100	0
Bad times. early	0.21	210	23	58	34
Bad times, late	0.65	57	60	66	14
Large, poor universities					
Good times	0.38	210	25	66	31
Bad times, early	0.24	248	32	55	38
Bad times, late	0.31	200	30	58	28
Small, rich colleges					
Good times	1.0	0	0	100	0
Bad times, early	0	310	0	90	20
Bad times, late	1.0	0	0	100	0
Small, poor colleges					
Good times	0.54	158	127	15	83
Bad times, early	0.61	101	148	73	52
Bad times, late	0.62	78	151	76	39

The model also makes some predictions of future developments. As adversity continues, the model predicts that all schools, and particularly rich schools, will experience improvement in their position. Among large, rich schools decision by resolution triples, problem activity is cut by almost three-fourths, and decision time is cut more than one-half. Small, rich schools return to the performance levels of good times. If the model has validity, a series of articles in the magazines of the next decade detailing how President X assumed the presidency of rich school Y and guided it to peace and progress (short decision time, decisions without problems, low problem activity) can be expected.

Conclusion

We have tried to translate a set of observations made in the study of some university organizations into a model of decision making in what we have called organized anarchies— that is, in situations which do not meet the conditions for more classical models of decision making in some or all of three important ways: preferences are problematic, technology is unclear, or participation is fluid. The garbage can process, as it has been observed, is one in which problems, solutions, and participants move from one choice opportunity to another in such a way that the nature of the choice, the time it takes, and the problems it solves all depend on a relatively complicated intermeshing of the mix of choices available at any one time, the mix of problems that have access to the organization, the mix of solutions looking for problems, and the outside demands on the decision makers.

A major feature of the garbage can process is the partial decoupling of problems and choices. Although we think of decision making as a process for solving problems, that is often not what happens. Problems are worked upon in the context of some choice, but choices are made only when the shifting combinations of problems, solutions, and decision makers happen to make action possible. Quite commonly this is after problems have left a given choice arena or before they have discovered it (decisions by flight or oversight).

Though the specification of the model is quite simple, the interaction within it is rather complex, so that investigation of the probable behavior of a system fully characterized by the garbage can process and our specifications requires computer simulation. We acknowledge immediately that no real system can be fully characterized in this way. Nonetheless, the simulated organizations exhibit behaviors that can be observed some of the time in almost all organizations and frequently in some, such as universities. The garbage can model is a possible step toward seeing the systematic interrelatedness of organizational phenomena that are familiar, even common, but that have generally been regarded as isolated and pathological. Measured against a conventional normative model of rational choice, the garbage can process does seem pathological, but such standards are not really appropriate since the process occurs precisely when the preconditions of more "normal" rational models are not met.

It is clear that the garbage can process does not do a particularly good job of resolving problems. But it does enable choices to be made and problems sometimes to be resolved even when the organization is plagued with goal ambiguity and conflict, with poorly understood problems that wander in and out of the system, with a variable environment, and with decision makers who may have other things on their minds. This is no mean achievement.

We would argue that there is a large class of significant situations within universities in which the preconditions of the garbage can process probably cannot be eliminated. Indeed in some, such as pure research, they should not be eliminated. The great advantage of trying to see garbage can phenomena together as a process is the possibility that that process can be understood, that organization design and decision making can take account of its existence, and that, to some extent, it can be managed.

Notes

[1]This chapter draws heavily on work we have done jointly with Johan Olsen.

[2]Choice opportunity may be defined as an occasion on which an organization is expected to produce a decision.

[3]For a discussion of alternative measures, see Cohen, March, and Olsen (1972).

[4] We have some indirect supporting evidence of an unobtrusive sort. Our original letter requesting cooperation in our studies was mailed to all 42 colleges at the same time. We have recorded the number of days later that an answer was dated in the responding president's office. Since the letters were all mailed (airmail) from California, some of the variation in response time was a function of variation in the time required to deliver the original letter. Most, however, is due to "processing" time in the college or university involved. Forty-one of the 42 colleges responded. The mean and median number of days required for a response from these 41 are shown below for each type of school:

Type of school	Rich		Poor	
	Mean	Median	Mean	Median
Large	20.6	20	44.8	42
Medium	16.3	15	24.7	17
Small	24.1	16	32.9	21

Response times are impressively slow (they ranged from 1 to 78 days), but slowest of all among the large, poor institutions. We might observe also that the one institution from which no reply was received was a large, poor one. The fastest response was from a "president" who reported that since our source book was published his college and gone out of business.

The Management of Academic Culture: Notes on the Management of Meaning and Social Integration

David D. Dill

Abstract: This article is concerned with the management of the symbolic life of academic organizations, an area strangely neglected in discussions of academic management. The adoption by higher education of the techniques of market-based businesses comes at a time when these businesses are being criticized for lack of attention to organizational culture. Academic institutions may best be understood as value-rational organizations grounded in strong cultures described as ideologies and belief systems. Some thoughts on the management of academic culture, on the management of meaning and social integration, are developed.

* * *

No community, no organization, no institution...can exist for long without a belief or set of beliefs so deeply and widely held that it is more or less exempt from ordinary demands that its goodness or rightness be demonstrable at any given moment. . . [But] dogma and faith unsupported by the bonds of structure are, as comparative religion teaches us, notoriously fragile. Robert Nisbet (pp. 23, 40)

Introduction

We are members of academic communities, but we manage academic organizations. When we seek to give meaning to the term "academic community" we speak of symbolic context: the distinctive history and traditions of our particular university, past sacrifices by notable faculty members on the behalf of academic freedom. When we seek to give meaning to the term "academic management" we speak of rational processes: goal setting, evaluation, cost analysis. A necessary condition for the management of academic organizations is the assumption that they are academic communities; the faculty are committed to a common set of beliefs. Yet academic managers do not discuss the actions by which a common set of beliefs can be maintained. We assume a common academic culture; we do not manage it.

The strength of academic culture is particularly important when academic institutions face declining resources. During these periods the social fabric of the community is under great strain. If the common academic culture has not been carefully nurtured during periods of prosperity, the result can be destructive conflicts between faculties, loss of professional morale, and personal alienation.

The basic argument to be presented is that academic institutions possess distinctive cultures which are developed and sustained by identifiable actions of the community members. These actions include the presentation of symbolic events, such as honoring a distinguished researcher, which emphasize the core values of the institution; this process will be termed "the management of meaning." These actions also include designing structural bonds, such as the joint appointment of faculty members, which help transmit the core values of the institution; this process will be termed the management of social integration. The techniques of managing meaning and social integration are the undiscussed skills of academic management.

To understand the relevance of these skills we must first explore three interrelated phenomena: first, the part culture plays in models of management; second, the traits which distinguish universities from other organizations and make the management of culture of particular importance; third, the reasons for the decline of the existing academic culture. From this discussion we can begin to develop the threads of a distinctive process critical to maintaining academic institutions—the management of academic culture.

The Trends in Management: Academic

Many academic institutions in the United States are confronting the issue of survival. To the issues of financial stress which dominated the 1970s—soaring fuel costs, rapid inflation, inadequate budgeting and investment strategies, decreased federal support for research—has been added the decline in available numbers of traditional age students. Recent policy decisions to cut federal support for student loan funds can further decrease, dramatically, student enrollments, thereby intensifying the competition between institutions.

The response to this on the part of academic institutions has been conventional. If academic institutions are engaged in a competitive market—competing for scarce financial resources from multiple and shifting supporters, competing for able students and faculty, competing for social prestige—then it is argued they should adopt the managerial techniques of market-based businesses: strategic planning, marketing, and management control. Strategic planning refers to the organization defining its distinctive competence in such a way that it occupies a special niche in the market and is thereby assured of resources necessary for survival. Marketing refers both to discerning the needs of the market place and advertising the institution's distinctive competence to potential customers and supporters. Management control refers to accounting mechanisms such as cost and workload analyses which assure that critical resources are used to attain the strategic plans.

There is ample evidence in the United States that this is indeed the trend of events. The survival of academic institutions will depend upon the application of the skills of American management once extolled by Servan-Schreiber in *The American Challenge* (1968). The Institute for Educational Management at Harvard University, which provides continuing education for provosts, chancellors, and deans of distinguished institutions, emphasizes these skills. Contemporary books on academic management argue that only through this type of managerial attention may academic institutions survive (Anthony and Herzlinger, 1980; Balderston, 1975; Mayhew, 1979). Continuing education, pamphlets, and consulting enterprises in these areas abound. The trend in the management of academic organizations is clearly towards the adoption of the tools of management originally developed in the business sector.

The Trend in Management: Business

The trends in business management tend to be flowing in the other direction. Many American business corporations are also confronting the issue of survival. A mounting criticism of these corporations is that they have focused so heavily on a management orthodoxy of market driven behavior and strict management controls that they are managing American corporations to economic decline (Hayes and Abernathy, 1980). As the competitive advantage that American business enjoyed since World War II has eroded, numerous observers are arguing the superiority of European and particularly Japanese management methods. Now Servan-Schreiber has written *The World Challenge* (1981), which addresses the managerial advantage of other countries with emphasis on Japan. Recent American publications such as *Japan as Number One* (Vogel, 1979), *Theory Z* (Ouchi, 1981), and *The Art of Japanese Management* (Pascale and Athos, 1981) dissect Japanese management techniques and urge their adoption in the United States.

While Japanese organizations employ similar techniques of strategic planning, marketing and management control as those used by American businesses and currently advocated for adoption by universities, they also emphasize several "soft" techniques of management traditionally under-represented in the American management literature (Pascale and Athos, 1981). These soft techniques address the management of human resources with particular attention to:

1. procedures for recruiting, socializing and training personnel;
2. the cultural style of organization visible in various traditions and ceremonies;
3. the values or meanings in which the work of the organization is grounded.

In this sense, Japanese organizations "make meaning" for their workers, and design the organization to enhance interdependence and personal development. Consequently, it is argued, Japanese organizations are highly productive and command uncommon loyalty and commitment from their workers.

Similarly, Ouchi (1981) argues that the high commitment and effectiveness of Japanese workers derives from certain distinctive structural characteristics of the organizations. Lifetime employment, for example, is more common in Japanese business. The promotion of personnel is less frequent and status distinctions between employees are not as pronounced. The evaluation of personnel is more informal, decision making is consensual and collective, and personnel are regularly rotated. Explicit use is made of symbols such as key promotions and public meetings to express the critical values of the organization.

Each of these writers suggest that while these management techniques are consistent with Eastern cultural traditions, they are not solely dependent upon Japanese or oriental culture for their success. IBM is consistently cited as one American company which has created uncommon commitment to the firm by emphasizing the management of human resources, the culture of the organization, and techniques which enhance the contact and communication between personnel (Pascale and Athos, 1981). IBM makes substantial use of a system of basic beliefs—respect for the individual, customer service, and excellence—and a set of supporting fundamental principles. These core values are maintained by stressing an attitude of ascetic conformity (e.g., required white shirts), a common symbol system (.e.g., the THINK signs), and a stress on an interdependent social life (e.g., a rich program of recreation for employees and families). Partially as a result of these managerial techniques, which are remarkably similar to those employed in Japanese organizations such as Matsushita Corporation, IBM is regarded as possessing a distinctive identity, high employee loyalty, and as one of the most effective of Western organizations.

In summary, there are three critical points to this brief review of management trends. First, the long-term effectiveness of the tools advocated for adoption by academic organizations—strategic planning, marketing and management control—is being seriously questioned within the business community. (This is particularly true in the case of market-driven planning and financial controls.) Second, increased attention is being given to the management of Japanese organizations. Ironically the organizations in Western society which most approximate the essential characteristics of Japanese firms are academic institutions. That is, they are also characterized by life-time employment, collective decision making, individual responsibility, infrequent promotion, and implicit, informal evaluation (Ouchi, 1981). Third, the Japanese management techniques place particular emphasis on the development of human resources and the maintenance of an organizational culture.

Organizational Culture

The most striking aspect of this recent work on Japanese organizations is its stress on the symbolic features of organizational life. The writers direct attention to social activities within Japanese organizations which eventually generate purpose, commitment, and order for organizational members. This phenomenon has been termed organizational culture, the system of "publicly and collectively accepted meanings operating for a given group at a given time" (Pettigrew, 1979, p. 574). For individuals to function in any organized setting, they must have some continuing sense of the reality in which they work. It is the expressive social fabric surrounding them that gives meaning to the individual tasks and objectives they pursue.

Organizational culture, then, is the shared beliefs, ideologies, or dogma of a group which impel individuals to action and give their actions meaning. Because of the distinctive nature of academic institutions, organizational culture plays a significant role in their functioning.

The Nature of Universities

The philosopher William James once said that any difference that is a difference should make a difference. What is the difference, if any, about universities as organizations which should be taken into account in their management? Satow (1975) has argued that organizations dominated by professionals must be viewed as "value-rational" organizations, in which members have absolute belief in the values of the organization for their own sake, independent of the values' prospects for success. The very authority of the enterprise therefore rests on obedience to a set of values or ideological norms. For example, the legitimacy of rules and regulations within academic institutions is determined by their consistency with the goals of academic ideology. When professional commitment to these norms (e.g., the pursuit of truth), comes into conflict with bureaucratic rules (e.g., government requirements that researchers obtain the consent of their subjects) priority is given to ideology (e.g., many researchers ignore the regulations in conducting their research). The notion that even academic organizations are grounded in an ideology, or dogma, has been neatly described by Madden (in Nisbet, 1971, p. viii-ix):

> Every institutionalization of human activity is grounded on an unquestioned (not unquestionable!) faith which must be maintained in order to sustain the institution itself and the human function it embodies. If dogma seems the opposite of scholarship, which should be based upon the principle of open inquiry, then consider the case of science, an institution unquestionably devoted to inquiry. Every scientific inquiry is an act of faith in the worth of inquiry itself, every testing of an hypothesis is an act of faith in the idea that not only positive but even negative findings produce knowledge. Every inquiry must stabilize its premises in order even to locate its problems. These are parts of the dogma of science, and in fact of scholarship in general, including the humanities.

Satow further suggests that value-rational organizations are not only identified by their ideologies, but bound together by them. For example: selection of staff is based in part on their ideological commitment, for instance, schools of thought in economics; performance evaluation of faculty members is not dependent upon a set of standards to which behavior can be compared as in bureaucratic organizations, but upon flexible professional judgments based on shared tradition; policy is not determined hierarchically, but collegially, and premised upon common values and beliefs. Thus the nature of the enterprise, both its pattern of authority and its basic techniques of social organization, vary from market-based businesses.

Clark (1981) has suggested that the ideology or culture of academic organizations is much more complex than that of other organizations. Ideologies, or systems of belief, permeate academic institutions at at least three different levels: the culture of the enterprise, the culture of the academic profession at large, and the culture of academic discipline.

In Western society the culture of the academic enterprise has been powerful in terms of tradition and symbolic life. Through the language of titles and degrees, the specified curriculum and examinations which form the *rites de passage* of student life, and the characteristic organization of facilities, colleges, deans and chancellors, western universities can trace a direct lineal relationship to medieval universities, thereby providing the powerful symbol of ageless continuity to academic work (Haskins, 1957). Because the foundings of many European and American universities were supported by various religious groups, the search for truth and the transmission of knowledge have been historically associated with the sacred, and the reverence still awarded these centers of learning cannot fully be explained by their contemporary secular importance.

Certain institutions—in the United States, often smaller private colleges—have developed a particularly intense and localized form of enterprise culture, which Clark has termed a saga: "a collective understanding of current institutional character that refers to an historical struggle and is embellished emotionally and loaded with meaning to the point where the organization becomes very much an end-in-itself" (Clark, 1981, pp. 12-13). In this sense the common institutional tradition and shared symbols provide meaning and reward to organizational members, engendering commitment, loyalty, and uncommon effort.

The second level of culture is that of the collected academic profession. In Europe, the academic profession or guild has a substantial history, although its contemporary basis for meaning and identity has been eroded by the autonomy of faculties and chairs and the absence of any national system of professional identification. In the United States the development of the American Association of University Professors (AAUP) in the second decade of this century came in response to the strong and suppressive administrative groups at various institutions which were antagonistic to the emerging scholarly and scientific ideology in support of free inquiry. The AAUP therefore attempted to foster the shared identity of an academic profession grounded in a common dogma and articulated in the symbol of academic freedom and the ritual of tenure. The AAUP employed the symbolic activities of traditional religious organizations: the identification and celebration of martyrs (dismissed faculty), excommunication (the AAUP "blacklist" of offending institutions), the liturgical study group (AAUP chapter meetings), and the codification of gallant effort (the written history of the AAUP). The conduct of the AAUP was informed by scientific and scholarly values; the guidelines for an AAUP institutional investigation read like the methodological imputations of the field researcher. The result of these efforts was an influential group of believers who were successful in altering the bylaws and contracts of many institutions to a form consistent with that of a value-rational organization.

Finally, we can also speak of the cultures or distinctive ideologies of the academic disciplines (Becher, 1981). These systems of shared belief clearly evoke the greatest meaning, commitment, and loyalty from contemporary academics. It is a culture with its own symbols of status and authority in the forms of professional awards, research grants, and publications, its ritualistic behavior at professional meetings, and its distinguishing articles of faith. For example, Becher (1981, p. 115) describes physicists as possessing a strong common identity and a "shared, 'almost religious,' belief in the unity of nature." Because this faith is developed during the intense socialization of graduate work, and because it is so central to the belief systems of adherents, it is rarely recognized as such until a paradigmatic shift occurs in a theoretical perspective, or methodological given. A shift, for example, from a qualitative-comparative method to a highly quantitative approach. At these times the intensity of the clash in belief systems within the discipline itself dramatizes the value systems at work beneath the surface of the field. These clashes would do justice to any conflict between religious sects over basic faith.

The difference that makes a difference, then, about academic institutions is that they are value-rational organizations whose members are committed to, and find meaning in, specified ideologies. These ideologies are manifest in a symbolic life or culture at the level of the enterprise, the profession, and discipline. Given the contemporary attention to the means by which Japanese managers create and maintain the culture of their organizations, one would expect that academic administrators would have a comparable skill in presenting and nurturing the ideologies or belief systems of their organizations. In fact, discussion and attention to the management of meaning, and the mechanisms of social structure necessary to maintain a common culture are as absent in American academic organizations as in American business corporations.[1] This is because both the overall strength of academic culture and the skills for managing it have declined.

The Decline of Academic Culture

Viewed from the perspective of value-rational organizations, the decline of academic institutions in the West cannot be attributed only to inattention to modern skills of management such as strategic planning, marketing and management control. Some portion of the decline must be attributed to the loss of a unifying system of belief, of a center of personal and collective identity, or of what Robert Nisbet has termed the "Degradation of the Academic Dogma" (Nisbet, 1971). Ideology or culture is not self-preserving. It requires the exercise of symbolic management and certain forms of social organization to keep it alive. In reviewing Clark's (1981) analysis of academic belief systems, it becomes obvious that the cultures which once commanded loyalty and gave meaning to the enterprise and the profession at large have been dissipated.

This decline or degradation can be attributed to the steady erosion of an enterprise culture originally based upon sectarian religious beliefs and to two other interrelated phenomena:

1. the rapid growth of systems of higher education;
2. an orientation toward the individual, discipline-based, career.

These latter two phenomena have produced faculty members who are socially and psychologically independent of the enterprise and the profession. One example of this change is evident in language. Faculty members who a generation ago would define themselves in terms of their institution—"I am a member of the Harvard faculty"—now identify themselves in terms of their field—"I am a sociologist, currently at Harvard."

In the United States the loss of meaning of enterprise culture has been relatively rapid. In only a hundred years we have moved from colleges and universities with the symbols and traditions of required chapel, a liberal education heavily based upon religious and moral precepts, and baccalaureate services at graduation, to secular institutions which retain many of these symbols and rituals but have discarded the underlying religious faith which gave these symbols meaning. In its place, we have adopted a faith in disciplinary ideology. But at the enterprise level we have failed to develop a corresponding culture rich enough in symbol and ritual to provide a unifying sense of belief. While even public universities possessed some religious rituals, the secular commitment to the separation of church and state inevitably led to their demise as significant symbols. The rapid growth of individual institutions, notably public institutions, further attenuated the bonds of enterprise culture. Commitment and loyalty to institution, a sense of shared belief, tended to remain strong only at those private colleges which retained a religious identity, substituted a secular version of distinctive purpose in the form of a saga or were capable, as were Harvard, Yale and a few other private research universities, of creating an institution-wide belief system dedicated to the academic dogma.

Similar to the decline of enterprise culture has been the decline of the academic profession as a unifying belief system. The rapid growth of American higher education was not constrained as in other countries by centralized traditions as to what constituted an appropriate discipline or field, or as to what institutions were eligible to offer advanced degrees. As a result, fields, disciplines, and Ph.D. recipients proliferated so rapidly after World War II as to eliminate the shared traditions, the identification to a common calling, the sense of a single profession which the AAUP attempted to establish at the turn of the century. At that time it was feasible to develop a professional identity through the mechanism of a collective association. The professoriate was small in size and the number of doctoral-granting universities limited in number. The disciplinary associations were in their early stages of development. Finally, the actions by some administrators to dismiss outspoken faculty members presented a sufficient threat against survival of the profession to galvanize faculty into developing a common culture of meaning and importance. Today the AAUP is a collective bargaining agent, one of several in the United States, and its moral force for the academic profession has withered. Similarly, the shared identity and meaning of an academic profession among faculty members in the United States has also disappeared.

Nisbet (1971) suggests that the principal reason for this decline in enterprise culture, and the culture of the profession at large, is the identification of the faculty members with the culture of the discipline. But a more useful conception is the identification of individual faculty members with their *professional careers* (Blankenship, 1977). Specific organizational conditions of the last several decades have provided status and prestige directly to the individual faculty member and have thereby compromised the authority of the faculties at all levels—discipline, enterprise, profession—to maintain the norms of academic culture by conferring conventional status. These organizational conditions were byproducts of the rapid growth of higher education and high social investment in scholarly and scientific work: easy promotion brought about by an insufficient supply of able faculty members; frequent movement between institutions; relatively plentiful funds to promote individual involvement in professional associations; ready access to grants, leaves, and research funds; and sharp gains in salary. In a time of academic decline, these conditions which fostered identification with an individual career are changing to conditions which will make the individual career rewards less attractive. Under these circumstances we can anticipate substantial numbers of faculty members choosing early retirement should that option be made available.

An additional problem is that of isolation. The focus on an individual career draws the faculty member toward increasing specialization, particularly in research. This specialization results in declining involvement in institutional requirements for teaching, counselling and administration, and a lessening of social ties with disciplinary and institutional colleagues. Recent research on professionals suggests that a decline in satisfaction from interpersonal contacts in professional life may produce professional non-involvement and a search for satisfaction in areas unrelated to the core activities of the professional craft (Korman et al., 1981). Thus contemporary reports of "burn out," of loss of professional commitment and satisfaction, of declining motivation for professional work, may be related to the erosion of academic culture at all levels.

Before turning to a discussion of the management of academic culture, let us review the argument to this point. Under pressure to survive, academic institutions, particularly in the United States, are adopting the management techniques of market-based businesses. At the same time, these techniques are being criticized within the business community as insufficient, and attention has been drawn to the emphasis of Japanese organizations on organizational culture. Not only do academic organizations possess several key traits of Japanese organizations, e.g., lifetime employment, but they are organizations in which organizational culture plays a dominant role. Furthermore, critical segments of the academic culture—the culture of the profession and the culture of the enterprise—have fallen into decline, while the culture of the discipline has strengthened. The primary meaning for academics has thus become not profession, not institution, but their professional career, and external conditions may decrease the meaningfulness of that orientation as well. Academic managers therefore face the real potential of alienation at the level of the profession, the enterprise and the discipline.

The techniques of increasing commitment and providing meaning in academic life are the same at the level of the discipline, the enterprise and the academic profession. These techniques, the mechanisms of coordination and control in professional organizations, are the meaning of symbol systems and the extent of social integration (Blankenship, 1977).

As Figure 1 suggests, the meaning of symbol systems and the extent of social integration are mutually related. Each directly affects identification with the academic discipline/ enterprise/profession. To increase commitment and involvement in academic life, we might explore the means of increasing the meaning of symbol systems and increasing social integration. We might explore the management of academic culture.

Figure 1

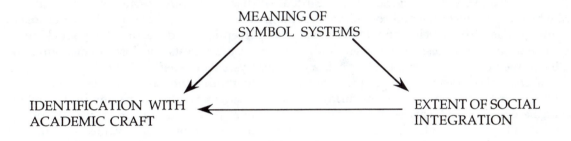

The Management of Academic Culture: Meaning

The Management of Academic Culture: Meaning

To begin to talk about the management of meaning, we must become more specific about the concept of organizational culture. The nurturance of the symbolic life of academic organizations requires attending to the symbolism of concrete social events and occasions, to the constructions which faculty members place upon publicly expressed academic life (Geertz, 1973). To do this we need to view culture as composed of the more specific components: myth, symbol, and ritual (Pettigrew, 1979).

Myth is to be defined, not as false belief, but as the distinctive history of an institution or group embodied in written documents, reminiscences, legends and the physical properties of a place. Myths help to anchor the present in the past, and provide meaning which legitimates the social practices of academic life. Symbols are those "objects, acts, relationships or linguistic formations that stand ambiguously for a multiplicity of meanings, evoke emotions, and impel men to action" (quoted in Pettigrew, 1979, p. 574). The term ritual has come to mean ceremonies devoid of meaning. As used here, however, a ritual is a patterned sequence of social activity which expresses and articulates meaning. While the management of myth, symbol, and ritual can occur at any level of the academic belief system—enterprise, profession at large, or discipline—the following discussion will focus on enterprise culture.

Many academic administrators have an exquisite sense of myth and are skilled in its presentation and maintenance. This requires insuring that the history of an institution or group is not forgotten, that it is rewritten, read and known, that individuals who embody that history in their lives are visible and active in the community, and that traditional ceremonies of the community are scrupulously maintained. The management of myth would require that additions to the physical) home of the community are tied to and reinvest the myth, and that any public activity is an opportunity to proclaim and celebrate the myth.

Academic institutions abound with symbols. An example is liberal education. Liberal education is symbolic in that it cannot be tangibly grasped, defined or specified. It is an ideology which serves the purpose of providing a unifying belief among individuals whose primary belief systems are anchored in their disciplines. The symbol of liberal education is thereby a critical component of enterprise academic culture: the belief in liberal education suggests that members of the academic community have a meaningful purpose in working together, that they are in fact a community.

The symbol of liberal education is supported by ritual, the formal attempts to define it. These attempts invariably occur after major shocks to the social fabric of society and to the worth of the academic dogma. Thus the general education program emerged at Columbia after World War I and the Harvard Report on general education after World War II. Most recent attempts to strengthen and define liberal education occurred after the campus disruptions of the Vietnamese War and the racial crisis. In this sense, the outcome of the ritual—the curriculum defined—is relatively meaningless. It is the ritual of discipline-wide discussion of a symbolic idea which creates meaning and commitment to the institution as a whole. By the same token, the emerging sense of cynicism about this ritual, the perception of departmental politicking to sustain enrollments necessary for their budget base, also suggests the loss of meaning, the decline in the power of this symbol to create a common system of belief.

If a chancellor, dean, or department head were to think seriously about the creation of meaning, or more responsibly, the nurturing of existing academic culture, what myths or symbols should be emphasized? This is the critical issue, and one for which corporate and industrial examples offer little insight. It is this selection and heightening of critical values which is at the heart of the creative dimension of leadership. It can only be said, that the values chosen for emphasis must be necessary conditions to the core technologies of academic life: research, scholarship and teaching. In this sense it is obvious that the major symbols and supporting rituals of American universities—athletic valor and team play—important as they may be for creating meaning among alumni and financial supporters, do little to strengthen academic culture. The celebration of academic values such as honesty, sustained curiosity, the communication of knowledge, and continued intellectual growth should be necessary conditions for any vital academic culture.[2] Vital in the sense that the myths, symbols and rituals comprising the culture would preserve the distinctive identity of the academic craft, specify the behaviors necessary to the sustenance of the craft, and provide meaning to these behaviors. While many academic institutions possess rituals such as founding day, or graduation, what myths, symbols and rituals exist which draw institution-wide attention to critical academic values, which celebrate and help sustain them? What proportion of the expressive lives of academic administrators is spent in symbolic activity of this type?

One difficulty with academic symbols and their supporting rituals is that they are often abstract.[3] They do not immediately communicate with the everyday behaviors of academic life. One means of animating symbols, which helps to communicate their meaning to academic life as it is lived, is the canonization of exemplars. Saints are individuals who in harsh or extreme circumstances have personified values necessary for the community to function, thereby earning our respect, our adoration and emulation. Who might be saints to serve as vital symbols for the contemporary academic community? Individuals who have made substantial contributions to knowledge with little or no research support, individuals whose dedication to teaching and scholarship has been marked by self-sacrifice and disinterest in worldly goods, individuals who have resisted the suppression of knowledge, individuals who have made dramatic and significant shifts in fields in the latter stages of their careers, and so on. The selection, canonization and celebration of faculty exemplars in the life of an academic institution becomes a powerful symbol in time of stress and hardship as to the values of the enterprise essential to survival. People as symbols provide meaning in work, because identification with the symbol offers courage to the organizational members to live through difficult periods.

A final means of managing symbolic life is through the ritual of the guild. A guild is a sworn brotherhood of persons following a common craft and seeking to preserve the distinctive identity of that craft. In this sense the AAUP, the faculty of a given institution, and particularly the faculty of a specific discipline, can be viewed as guilds. The decline of the AAUP and the faculty of an institution as guilds can then be understood as the loss of a common identity. If we wish to strengthen the culture of the enterprise, to nurture a system of belief of potential meaning, we might consider the formation of guilds. Guilds provide a powerful means of socialization, communication and cameraderie. The meetings and activities of a guild satisfy needs for affiliation and provide the sense of involvement in an activity of long-term importance.

How might the structure of the guild be employed to manage meaning? One example is teaching. Teaching is a distinctive characteristic of the academic craft in which all members engage. But which member of the community act to superintend or preserve teaching, act to maintain faith in the importance of teaching, act to define the necessary values in teaching which distinguish the "sacred" from the "profane"? Where is the academic guild of teachers? Occasionally the university acts to honor great teachers by identifying them, offering an award, and celebrating their gifts. Often, too, universities debase their basic values by conferring this status in the form of a cash award or salary increase, rather than in symbolically meaningful terms. Following their celebration, these great teachers are then ignored by the organization and play no special role in the life of the academic community. An alternative scenario might be to induct each individual into a formal guild of the elect; to assign to that guild the authority and responsibility of selecting future members; to provide the guild with distinctive facilities and perquisites; to involve the guild in means to improve teaching on a campus such as dispensing funds for innovation in teaching; to request that the guild oversee the orientation of new faculty members to the campus; and to encourage the guild to hold distinctive ceremonies and activities which maintain belief in the importance of teaching. A comparable guild could be developed for research and scholarship which might serve as an antidote to the current system which confers status in the form of faculty chairs with high salaries; a system which builds no community of scholars dedicated to the preservation of the craft, but superintends belief in financial remuneration as the ultimate reward for the pursuit of knowledge.

In summary, one aspect of the management of academic culture involves the management of meaning. Some important tools in the management of meaning, include the nurturance of myth, the identification of unifying symbols, the ritual observance of symbols, the canonization of exemplars, and the formation of guilds. These are critical managerial tools in value-rational organizations, because it is through shared beliefs and traditions that such organizations can be coordinated and controlled and professional loyalty, commitment, and identity can be maintained.

The Management of Academic Culture: Social Integration

The intensity of an academic culture is determined not only by the richness and relevance of its symbolism for the maintenance of the professional craft, but by the bonds of social organization. These bonds are created by the mechanism of collegial communication with feedback about professional activity (Hage, 1974). For this mechanism to operate the institution needs to take specific steps to socialize the individual to the belief system of the organization, and promote joint activities between colleagues from throughout the enterprise. The decline of academic culture is thus partially traceable to the rapid growth of academic communities, the isolation of specialities, and the inattention given to the process of social organization necessary to nurture academic culture. The management of academic Culture therefore involves both the management of meaning and the management of social integration.

One example of this inattention to social integration can be seen in the development of new fields. During periods of rapid growth organizations frequently grow by adoption rather than extension. Adoption entails the appointment of a specialist in the new field who subsequently makes independent critical decisions about additional staff. If the new staff is socialized at all, it is within the department or field, rarely to institutional norms. Development of the curriculum, definition of degrees and the process of teaching and research, are carried out in isolation from other colleagues, responsive at best to broadly stated institutional policies or to distant mechanisms of review. The potential for conflict over time with basic institutional beliefs becomes obvious. This was frequently experienced during the 1970s in new professional programs, or new fields such as ethnic studies, where faculty members did not fully subscribe to the ideology of the parent institution and as a result issues of quality control and academic integrity became a continuing source of debate. By contrast, some more selective institutions grew by extension. For example, the recently developed School of Organization and Management at Yale University was begun around a core of professors from existing disciplines already on the campus. Selection of new faculty members frequently required joint appointment to an existing discipline thus assuring that traditional academic values of the institution were observed in the definition of new positions. While broad searches for new faculty members were conducted, new appointments were most typically made from a small-core of selective graduate schools where students had been intensely socialized to academic values consistent with those of Yale University. Thus the techniques of extension: growth around a faculty core already committed to the academic culture, selection of new appointees by emphasizing harmony between their socialization and institutional belief systems, and appointment of new recruits who subscribe to existing disciplinary ideologies, all tend to insure the strength of the academic culture and the maintenance of academic norms.

The intensive socialization of new students to a college or department is a matter of course. Intensive socialization of faculty members to the traditions and values of the institution is much more rare. The assumption has been that prior socialization in graduate training has been appropriate and sufficient. Given the growth and fragmentation of academic systems, this traditional assumption may no longer be valid. If one instead wished to consider socialization to the values of the enterprise, there are several ways this might be accomplished: by particular rituals such as social occasions with older, prestigious faculty drawn from across the institution (e.g., the aforementioned guilds); the gift of a history of the institution to all new faculty members; programs nominally introducing new appointees to teaching and research support services provided by the institution, but which also include substantial inculcation to institutional values and tradition. The most powerful socialization device, one institutionalized by Japanese organizations, in the "Sempai-Kohai" (senior-junior) relationship, is that of mentoring (Pascale and Athos, 1981). The mentoring process in this sense focuses not on technical skill, but on norms and values which the mentor possesses and which the new appointee will learn. To be effective in an academic context, mentors might be assigned to new faculty from senior faculty in a related but separate discipline, thereby providing vertical (across ranks) and horizontal (across fields) integration, and avoiding conflict with peer evaluation.

In addition to the process of socialization are the organizational policies and procedures which promote interdepartmental communication or vertical and horizontal integration. In academic organizations these might include: extradepartmental faculty involvement in the definition of new positions; the requirement of extradepartmental faculty participation in faculty search committees, encouragement of joint appointments; systematic encouragement of joint research and teaching through targeted funding; and the requirement of outside department members on doctoral committees. There is nothing exceptional about these suggestions, although an analysis of the policies and practices of many academic institutions will reveal that such practices have steadily deteriorated, and that contemporary academic management is noticeably inattentive to the principles of vertical and horizontal social integration.

Ouchi (1981) has argued that Japanese organizations have promoted interdependence and organizational loyalty by minimizing specialized career paths. Frequent rotation is a specific means employed by Japanese industries to lessen the isolation of specialization. Recognizing that faculty members often broaden perspective over their careers, from highly specialized inquiry in their early years to issues of greater scope in later life, we might adapt the technique of rotation to one of "internal sabbaticals" in which faculty members are released from present duties and reappointed in different but related departments or fields at the same institution for a specified period of time.

The maintenance of academic culture depends to a substantial extent upon careful management of the technique of social organization critical for sustaining common belief systems. These techniques involve an emphasis on socialization and policies which promote organization-wide communication principally through joint activities featuring vertical and horizontal integration. These facets of social organization coupled with a strongly shared system of belief are the primary methods of coordination and control in value-rational organizations.

Conclusion

The major perspective of this article has been that while the techniques of market-based bureaucrats may aid the short-term survival of academic organizations, they may do little to increase the productivity, commitment and loyalty of the professional staff. Indeed, these techniques may clash substantially with the core ideologies of academic life. The revival of academic institutions in a time of diminishing resources must also address the management of academic culture: the nurturing of the expressive life of academic institutions and the strengthening of social integration.

The notion that academic culture can be managed may suggest an over-weaning confidence in the capacity of managers. Certainly self-conscious efforts at social engineering have a dubious track record. It is wise to be modest about what can be accomplished. The major thesis of this article, however, has not been to argue for the creation of new systems of value in academic life, but to maintain existing ones. The issue is not whether academic culture should be managed. The issue is whether those with the principal responsibility of superintending academic values have focused on the appropriate means of accomplishing the task.

Given the distinctive nature of academic organization the maintenance of the expressive aspects of academic community deserves much more attention than it has received in discussions of academic management. The nurturance of the symbolic life of academic organizations and the distinctive skills of social organization necessary for their coordination and control are unique skills of academic management which must be rediscovered and accentuated or they will be lost. To begin, we must first discuss the management of academic culture not as anthropologists, sociologists, educators, theologians, or journalists, but seriously.

This is a revised version of a paper originally presented at the Fifth International Conference on Higher Education, University of Lancaster, 2 September 1981. I am indebted to Philip Altbach, Tony Becher, Zelda Gamson, and the members of Study Group Six for their constructive criticisms of the original paper.

David D. Dill is at the School of Education, University of North Carolina, U.S.A.

Notes

[1]James G. March, an astute observer of academic organizations has recently argued that the management of symbols is an underemphasized aspect of administration. See, James G. March, "How We Talk and How We Act," David D. Henry, Lecturer in Higher Education, University of Illinois, September, 1980.

[2]For some thinking about values which may be necessary conditions for effective university teaching, see the special issue on "Ethics and the academic profession," *Journal of Higher Education* May/June, 1982.
[3]I am indebted to the Reverend Robert W. Duncan for his creative thinking on these issues.

References

Anthony, R. N. and Herzlinger, R. E. *Management Control in Nonprofit Organizations.* Homewood, Ill: Irwin, 1980.

Balderston, F. E. *Managing Today's University.* San Francisco: Jossey-Bass, 1975.

Becher, T. "Towards a Definition of Disciplinary Cultures," *Studies in Higher Education*, 1981, 6; 109-122.

Blankenship, R. L. "Toward a Theory of Collegial Power and Control," in Ralph Blankenship, (ed.) *Colleagues in Organization* New York: John Wiley, 1977.

Clark, B. R. "Belief," March (unpublished paper), 1981.

Geertz, C. *The Interpretation of Cultures.* New York: Basic Books, 1973.

Hage, H. *Communication and Organizational Control.* New York: John Wiley, 1974.

Hayes, R. H. and Abernathy, W. J. "Managing Our Way to Economic Decline," *Harvard Business Review*, 1980, 58; 67-77.

Haskins, C. H. *The Rise of Universities.* Ithacca, New York: Cornell University, 1957.

Korman, A. K., Wittig-Berman, U. and Lang, D. "Career Success and Personal Failure: Alienation in Professionals and Managers." *Academy of Management Journal*, 1981, 24; 242-260.

Mayhew, L. B. *Surviving the Eighties.* San Francisco: Jossey-Bass, 1979.

Nisbet, R. *The Degradation of the Academic Dogma.* New York: Basic Books, 1971.

Ouchi, W. G. *Theory Z.* Reading, Mass: Addison-Wesley, 1981.

Pascale, R. T. and Athos, A. G. *The Art of Japanese Management.* New York: Simon and Schuster, 1981.

Pettigrew, A. M. "On Studying Organizational Cultures," *Administrative Science Quarterly*, 1979, 24; 570-581.

Satow, R. L. "Value-Rational Authority and Professional Organizations: Weber's Missing Type," *Administrative Science Quarterly*, 1975, 20; 526-531.

Servan-Schreiber, J. *The American Challenge.* New York: Atheneum, 1968.

Servan-Schreiber, J. *World Challenge.* New York: Simon and Schuster, 1981.

Vogel, E. F. *Japan as Number One.* New York: Harper and Row, 1979.

The Latent Organizational Functions of the Academic Senate: Why Senates Do Not Work But Will Not Go Away

ROBERT BIRNBAUM

Academic senates[1] are generally considered to be the normative organizational structure through which faculty exercise their role in college and university governance at the institutional level [1]. Although no complete census is available, analysis of data in past studies [23, 25] suggest that senates may exist in one or another form on between 60 to 80 percent of all campuses.

With the advent of faculty collective bargaining in the late 1960s, concern was expressed that senates, unable to compete with the more adversarial and aggressive union, might disappear on many campuses [35]. Not only has this prediction proven to be false [5, 6], but there is evidence that the proportion of institutions with senates has increased over the past decades [3].

This growth is somewhat perplexing in view of the stream of criticisms that increasingly has been directed against the senate structure. It has been called weak, ineffective, an empty forum, vestigial, unrepresentative, and inept [2, 12, 24, 33, 35, 38]. Its detractors have referred to it as "slowly collapsing and becoming dormant" [24, p. 61] and "purely ceremonial" [7]. In a 1969 national study, 60 percent of faculty respondents rated the performance of their campus senate or faculty council as only "fair" or "poor" [11]. A more recent consideration of faculty governance has stated that "traditional structures do not appear to be working very well. Faculty participation has declined, and we discovered a curious mismatch between the agenda of faculty councils and the crisis now confronted by many institutions" [12, p. 12.].

These negative evaluations of faculty governance structures are not new. A trenchant observer in 1918 [47, p. 186] noted the administrative use of faculty "committees-for-the-sifting-of-the-sawdust" to give the appearance, but not the reality, of participation, and called them "a nice problem in self-deception, chiefly notable for an endless proliferation" (p. 206).

There is not complete agreement that the senate has no real instrumental value. Blau's [9] finding of a negative correlation between senate participation and educational centralization at over one hundred colleges and universities, for example, led him to state that "an institutionalized faculty government is not mere window dressing but an effective mechanism for restricting centralized control over educational programs, in accordance with the professional demands of the faculty. Formal institutionalization of faculty authority fortifies it" (p. 164). Another supporter of the senate [21], after reviewing the literature, reported that the senate continued to be "a useful mechanism for campus-wide faculty participation" (p. 26) at certain types of research universities and elite liberal arts colleges in some governance areas, although it was less useful in others. But despite the support of a small number of observers, the clear weight of evidence and authoritative opinion suggests that, except perhaps in a small number of institutions with particular characteristics, the academic senate does not work. Indeed, it has been suggested that it has never worked [2]. Yet it survives and, in many respects, thrives.

After citing a litany of major criticisms of the senate and proposing reasons for its deficiencies, Lieberman [30, p. 65] added, "what is needed is not so much a critique of their inherent weaknesses, but an explanation of their persistence in spite thereof." Similarly, Hobbs [22], in looking at the functions of university committees, suggested that rather than focusing attention on recommending ways in which these committees might be made more effective, greater attention should be given to examining their roles in university organization. This article will conduct such an examination by considering the roles that senates are presumed to play—and the roles they actually play—within four alternative organizational models that consider the senate as part of bureaucratic, collegial, political, or symbolic organizational systems.

Manifest and Latent Functions

The manifest functions of an organizational structure, policy, or practice can be thought of as those for which behavior leads to some specified and related achievement. Institutional processes that usually lead to expected and desired outcomes should be expected to persist. Often, however, organizations engage in behavior that persists over time even though the manifest function is clearly not achieved. Indeed, such behavior may persist even when there is significant evidence that the ostensible function *cannot* be achieved. There is a tendency to label such organizational behavior as irrational or superstitious and to identify an institution's inability to alter such apparently ineffectual behavior as due to "inertia" or "lack of leadership."

Merton's [36] concept of functional analysis suggests an alternative explanation. Some practices that do not appear to be fulfilling their formally intended functions may persist because they are fulfilling unintended and unrecognized latent functions that are important to the organization. As Merton describes it, functional analysis examines social practices to determine both the planned and intended (manifest) outcomes and the unplanned and unintended (latent) outcomes. This is particularly useful for the study of otherwise puzzling organizational behavior because it "clarifies the analysis of seemingly irrational social patterns. . . , directs attention to theoretically fruitful fields of inquiry. . . , and precludes the substitution of naive moral judgments for sociological analysis" (p. 64-66, 70). In particular, it points towards the close examination of persistent yet apparently ineffective institutional processes or structures to explore the possibility that they are meeting less obvious, but still important, organizational needs. "We should ordinarily (not invariably) expect persistent social patterns and social structures to perform positive functions which are at the time not adequately fulfilled by other existing patterns and structures" [36, p. 72]. The senate may do more than many of its critics believe, and "only when we attend to all the functions and their social contexts can we fully appreciate what it is that the senate does" [42, p. 174].

This article shall examine two major questions. First, and briefly, what are the manifest functions of the academic senate that its critics claim appear not to be fulfilled, and what organizational models do they imply? Second, and at greater depth, what may be the latent functions of the academic senate that may explain its growth and persistence despite its failure to meet its avowed purposes, and how do these functions relate to organizational models?

The Manifest Functions of the Academic Senate

In general, those who criticize the senate have not clearly articulated the criteria they have employed, and their analyses tend to be narrative and anecdotal with no explicit conceptual orientation. Their comments and conclusions, however, suggest that they evaluate the senate implicitly using the three traditional models of the university as a bureaucracy, as a collegium, and as a political system.

Probably the most prevalent implicit model is that of the university as bureaucracy. In his study of the effectiveness of senates (which is one of the few studies to specify desired outcomes) Millett established eight criteria that "would provide some reasonable conclusions

[handwritten marginalia: Millett's criteria]

about the contributions and the effectiveness of campus-wide governance to the process of institutional decision making" [38, p. xiv]. These included the extent to which senates clarified institutional purpose, specified program objectives, reallocated income resources, and developed new income sources, as well as the extent to which they were involved in issues such as the management of operations, degree requirements, academic behavior, and program evaluation. The identification of the senate's role in decision making and the emphasis upon goal-setting, resource allocation, and evaluation suggest an implicit view of the senate as an integral part of a hierarchical, rational organization. This bureaucratic orientation is also seen in one of the two "modal" university committee types identified by Hobbs [22]. This type, among other characteristics, meets often, has a decision-making function, records minutes, prepares written reports for administrative officers, and has a clear sense of task. Other analysts have also used language that either explicitly or metaphorically identifies the senate in bureaucratic terms. Senates are needed to deal with "the full range of academic and administrative matters" [12, p. 13], their purpose "approximates that of the college's management" [24, p. 126], and they assist "the discovery and employment of techniques to deal with deficit spending, with increasing enrollments, with healing the wounds resulting from student dissent, with curriculum expansion, with faculty salary increases in a tight budget, with parking, and so forth" [41, p. 40].

[handwritten marginalia: bureaucratic model]

A second model implicitly views the senate as part of a political system. In this model the senate is seen as a forum for the articulation of interests and as the setting in which decisions on institutional policies and goals are reached through compromise, negotiation, and the forming of coalitions. Senates serve as a place for campus politicians to exercise their trade, which in its worst sense may identify them as "poorly attended oratorical bodies" [24, p. 127] and in the best sense means that they can "provide a forum for the resolution of a wide range of issues involving the mission and operation of the institution" [1, p. 57]. Given the significant differences that typify the interest groups that make up its constituencies, the senate enables participants to deal with inevitable conflict as they "engage one another civilly in dispute" [22, p. 242].

[handwritten marginalia: Political model]

The model of the university as collegium is less explicitly identified in analyses of the senate than the other two models, but it appears to be recognized through constant references in the literature to the concept of collegiality. The senate in this view would be a forum for achieving Millett's [37] goal of a dynamic of consensus.

[handwritten marginalia: Collegial model]

Depending upon the organizational assumptions used, an observer might consider the senate to be effective in governance either (a) to the extent that it efficiently considered institutional problems and, through rational processes, developed rules, regulations, and procedures that resolved them, or (b) to the extent that, perceived as fully representative of its constituencies, it formulated and clarified goals and policies, or (c) to the extent that, through interaction in the senate forum, it developed shared values leading to consensus. But senates often appear to do none of these things well. From the bureaucratic perspective they are slow and inefficient, from a political position they are oligarchical and not representative, and from a collegial viewpoint faculty interactions may be as likely to expose latent conflict as to increase feelings of community [39].

[handwritten marginalia: senate as result an questionable]

These alternative organizational models suggest a range of activities, processes, and outcomes as the manifest functions of the senate. Because these functions do not appear to be performed adequately, the senate has been judged to be ineffective. In many ways the senate appears to be a solution looking for problems. Millett, for example, provides a list of eight specific problems and questions raised by student activism in the 1960s (such as the role of higher education in defense research, or the role of higher education in providing community service to the disadvantaged) to which appropriately comprised senates were presumably an answer. He found that there was "very little evidence that organs of campus-wide governance, after they were established, were particularly effective in resolving these issues"[38, p. 200]. Because its manifest functions are not being fulfilled, the persistence of the senate suggests that it is filling important latent functions. What might some of these be?

The Latent Functions of the Academic Senate

THE SENATE AS SYMBOL

In addition to whatever effects they may have upon outcomes, organizational structures and processes also often have symbolic importance to participants [20]. Academic senates may fill a number of important symbolic purposes. We will consider three: the senate may symbolize institutional membership in the higher education system, collective and individual faculty commitment to professional values, and joint faculty-administration acceptance of existing authority relationships.

Faculty participation in governance is generally accepted as an essential characteristic of "mainstream" colleges and universities. Since 1950 there has been a significant increase in the types and kinds of institutions that many consider only marginally identified with higher education. These include, for example, community colleges with strong administrative hierarchies, unselective state colleges with traditions rooted in teacher education and the paternalistic practices of school systems, and small and unselective independent institutions with authoritarian presidents. By establishing an academic senate structure that was more typical of the system to which they aspired than it was of the one from which they developed, an institution could suggest the existence of faculty authority even when it did not exist. This structural symbol of a faculty voice could support a claim to being a "real" college.

The development of a senate can also symbolize a general faculty commitment to substantive values. The most visible and public matters of faculty concern at some institutions have been related to faculty collective bargaining, which has tended to focus upon employee issues that in many ways were similar to those of other workers. Particularly in the public sector, but sometime in the private sector as well, faculty emphasis upon salary, working conditions and other mundane matters has eroded in the minds of the public their claim to professional status. Creating a senate may be a response to that erosion, symbolizing a commitment to professional values and faculty concern for more purely academic matters. This helps to legitimate the institution's desire to be treated differently than other organizations and the faculty's claim to be treated differently than other groups of workers. Through a senate, the faculty can symbolically endorse such desirable attributes or outcomes as increased quality, standards, and integrity even though (or perhaps because) they cannot define either the problems or their solutions in operational terms. The senate may thus serve as a forum through which, individually and collectively, faculty may symbolically embrace values in lieu of actual behavior. Within the senate, academics who have never had controversial new ideas can publicly defend academic freedom, and those without scholarly interests can argue for reduced teaching loads to encourage research. In this way even faculty who cannot do so through the publication of scholarship or research, can publicly display their academic *bona fides*.

Senates may also serve as symbols of campus authority relationships. A major criticism directed against the senate is that it exists at the pleasure of the administration and board of trustees [3, 30]. Because of this, its authority has been described as "tenuous" [39, p. 26]. However, the fact is that although trustees have rejected senate recommendations, they have not abolished senates (except in rare circumstances involving the introduction of faculty collective bargaining). Indeed, administrations support senates and believe them to be even more "effective" than do faculty members [23]. Why should both the faculty and the administration continue to support the senate structure? It is obvious that faculty would wish to maintain senates because they are a symbol of administrative acceptance of the idea of faculty participation in governance. Administrators may support senates because voluntary faculty participation in such bodies is a tacit acknowledgement by the faculty that they recognize and accept the ultimate legal authority of the administration and board. The senate is thus a symbol of cooperation between faculty and administration. As in other organizational settings, parties may cooperate in perpetuating an already established structure even when the objective utility of the structure is agreed by the parties to be of little value [17]. The continued existence of the senate therefore is not only a visible manifestation of the ability of the parties to cooperate but also reflects an intent to further increase cooperative activities.

The symbolic value of the senate is so strong that even those like Millett [38] who after study have concluded that the senate is ineffective when evaluated against specific criteria, continue to support it. Even if it doesn't work in terms of its ostensible aims, it may be preferable that an institution have a nonfunctioning senate than that it have no senate at all.

THE SENATE AS STATUS PROVIDER

Cohen and March [13] have suggested that "most people in a college are most of the time less concerned with the content of a decision than they are with eliciting an acknowledgment of their importance within the community. . . . Faculty members are more insistent on their right to participate in faculty deliberations than they are on exercising that right" (pp. 201–2). In an analogous vein, the existence of a senate certifies the status of faculty members by acknowledging their right to participate in governance, while at the same time not obligating them to do so. The vigorous support of faculty for a strong and active voice in campus governance, coupled with their reluctance to give the time that such participation would require [16, 18], should therefore not be surprising.

The senate also offers a route of social mobility for older and less prestigious faculty locals whose concern for status based on traditional norms is frustrated by a lack of scholarly achievement [27]. Participation in committee affairs and opportunities it brings to work with higher status administrators provides a local means for enhancing their own importance.

In addition to certifying the status of participants in general, providing an opportunity for individuals to serve as senator is a means of conferring status that protects the institution from two quite different, but potentially disruptive, elements: informal leaders and organizational deviants.

Universities are normative organizations that rely upon the manipulation of symbols to control the behavior of their members [19]. Unlike organizations characterized by control through coercive or utilitarian power, normative organizations tend to have more "formal leaders" (those who influence others both through their personal power and through the organizational positions they hold) and fewer informal leaders (personal power only) or officials (positional power only). Formal leadership provides a relatively effective means of exercising power in a decentralized and loosely coupled system. By the same token, the development of informal leaders can be dysfunctional by facilitating the development of semiautonomous subgroups that can diminish the formal leader's influence.

Formal leaders cannot prevent the development of informal leaders, but in normative organizations "to the degree that informal leaders arise. . . , the tendency is to recruit them and gain their loyalty and cooperation by giving them part-time organizational positions. . . . The tendency is for the informal leaders to lose this status within the given organization and for control to remain largely in the hands of the formal leaders" [19, p. 64]. Membership in a prestigious body such as a senate with presumed quasi-administrative responsibilities can be used towards the same end "of providing alternative channels of social mobility for those otherwise excluded from the more conventional avenues for 'social advancement' " [36, p. 76]. Senate membership provides legitimate organizational roles in which informal leaders can participate and have their status confirmed while at the same time preventing them from disrupting ongoing organizational structures and processes.

There is a second group of campus participants whose activities, if not channelled through a legitimate structure such as a senate, might prove disruptive to the organization. They are the institutional deviants, often highly vocal persons with a single-minded devotion to one or another cause. Senates offer these deviant faculty a legitimized opportunity to vent their grievances and solicit potential support. Election of such persons may sometimes lead administrators to discount the senate as "nonrepresentative" and may be seen by them as yet another example of senate weakness. On the other hand, the need for even deviants to allocate attention means that time spent acting in the relatively stable environment of the senate is time they do not have available for participating in relatively more vulnerable settings, such as the department. The senate may thus serve as a system for absorbing the energies of potentially disruptive faculty members. Because the senate, like the administration, is subject to overload, it can attend to only a small number of items at any one time. The difficulty of convincing senate colleagues of the justice of their position is more likely to reduce aspirations of deviants than would be constant rebuffs by administrators or departmental colleagues; if a faculty member cannot convince his or her colleagues, how can the administration possibly be convinced?

THE SENATE AS GARBAGE CAN AND DEEP FREEZE

Sometimes a college or university can use rational processes to make choices and solve problems when it is called upon to make a decision. However, this becomes difficult when unexpectedly other people become involved in the decision process, new problems are introduced, and new solutions are proposed. These independent streams of participants, problems, and solutions may somehow become attached to each other, often by chance, just as if they were all dumped into a large container, leading to what has been referred to as "garbage can decision making" [15]. Choices become more difficult as they become increasingly connected with "garbage" (that is, with problems, potential solutions, or new participants who, at least to the decision maker, appear irrelevant). Choices become easier if they can be made either before these irrelevant matters become attached to them (decision making by oversight), or after these irrelevant matters can be made to leave the choice (decision making by flight). Because of the essential ambiguity of the college and university processes, any choice point can become a garbage can. One of the latent functions of the senate may be to function as a structural garbage can, and the inability of the senate to make speedy decisions may increase its effectiveness in this role by putting some problems into an organizational "deep freeze."

An administrator who wishes to make a decision but finds it difficult to do so because irrelevant problems have become associated with it, can refer those irrelevant problems to the senate. The decision can then be made by flight while the attention of participants is directed elsewhere.

The deliberate speed of the senate makes it possible for many problems that are referred to it to resolve themselves over time with no need for any specific action. This kind of outcome is shown by the disparaging statement of one faculty member: "The committees [of the senate] report, but usually it has taken so long to 'study the issue' that the matter is long since past" [3, p. 80].

Other issues, particularly those that deal with goals and values and thus might be divisive if an attempt were made to resolve them, may be referred to the senate with the justifiable expectation that they will absorb a significant amount of energy and then will not be heard of again. Still, the senate debate has an important outcome even if it does not lead to taking action. Through the presentation of alternative positions and arguments, participants come to realize that an issue whose resolution initially appeared to be self-evident and therefore enjoying wide support is in fact complex and contentious. As the attractiveness of simplistic solutions is reduced, aspirations are modified and potential conflict is therefore managed.

THE SENATE AS ATTENTION CUE

The number of problems available in a university searching for decision opportunities and forums in which they can be resolved, although perhaps finite in number, is at any specific time far greater than can be acted upon. Administrative attention is in comparatively short supply, and as administrators "look for work" they must decide to which of many different potential attention cues they should pay attention. This is a nontrivial issue, because the ability of problems, solutions, decision makers, and choice opportunities to become coupled through temporal rather than through logical relationships makes it exceptionally difficult for an administrator to know on an *a priori* basis what is most important. In the absence of a calculus or an algorithm that permits administrators to predict how important any specific problem may prove to be, they must rely on heuristics (such as "oil the squeaky wheel") to indicate when an item may have reached a level of concern sufficient to require administrative attention. There are many sources of such cues: a telephone call from a state legislator or an editorial in the local paper or student press are examples. So too is discussion and action (potential or actual) by the senate. As Mason [33] and others have commented, senate agendas "tend to be exceedingly crowded...[and] even if a senator has succeeded in placing a policy-question in the agenda 'it will not be reached until the meeting has gone on so long that the member's one overwhelming desire is to go home' " [p. 75]. As a result, not every item that is proposed for the senate agenda actually gets on it, and not every item that gets on it is attended to. The presence of a specific item on an agenda that becomes the subject of extended discussion and possible action therefore signifies that it is of unusual importance and worth an investment of administrative time. By the same token, a matter proposed to the senate but not considered by it can be used as a justification for administrative indifference. The senate thus operates in the university in a manner similar to that of a public agency before a budget subcommittee. When there are no more than the usual level of complaints, no action need be taken. But when "an agency shouts more loudly than usual, subcommittee members have a pretty good idea that something is wrong" [46, p. 154].

Because most items which someone wants discussed by the senate are never acted upon, the use of the senate as an attention cue is an efficient way of allocating attention. It relieves the administration of responsibility for dealing with every problem, establishes a rationale for a system of priorities, provides a justification for inattention to some items, and maintains the symbolic relationship of administration responsiveness to faculty concerns.

THE SENATE AS PERSONNEL SCREENING DEVICE

Universities constantly have to fill administrative positions, and it is often less disruptive institutionally as well as desirable financially to do so with faculty members. However, not every faculty member is acceptable, and at least two characteristics not often found in combination are desirable: a person should have the confidence of faculty colleagues and should also be sympathetic to the administrative point of view. The senate provides a forum in which such persons can be more easily identified and evaluated.

Election to the senate itself provides strong (although not absolutely reliable) evidence of acceptability to faculty colleagues, and working with administrators in preparing reports or other committee assignments allows senators to demonstrate through the equivalent of on-the-job participation their commitment to administrative values.

Anecdotal evidence indicates that administrators are often selected from among faculty "committeemen," [27, p. 83], and case study material [34] has shown how the intimate involvement of faculty committee members with administrative officers in policy formulation has meant that "many senate committee members have moved easily and naturally into regular administrative positions" [34, p. 103]. Of course, persons selected for administrative positions because they perform well in the kinds of ideological and noninstrumental debates of the senate may turn out not to be the most effective institutional leaders [13].

THE SENATE AS ORGANIZATIONAL CONSERVATOR

More attention has traditionally been given to the presumed negative consequences of the university's acknowledged resistance to change than to the potentially positive aspects of maintaining the ongoing system. From a functional perspective, ongoing organizational processes and structures exist in an equilibrium that is a response to and a resultant of a number of forces operating upon and within the institution. As with any open system, the university is homeostatic in nature and tends to react to the instability caused by change by responding in a manner that returns it to its former state. The senate, by inhibiting the propensity to change that increasingly characterizes the administration, serves as a major element in this homeostatic process of organizational conservation.

Administrators in general, and presidents in particular, usually do not wish to change the university in dramatic ways, and the processes through which they are selected and socialized tend to make their roles conservative [13]. Yet they occupy boundary positions in the organization and find themselves exposed, as faculty members are not, to the demands of the external environment as well as those of the organization. In that external environment there are a number of factors that implicitly or explicitly pressure university administrators to become more intrusive in organizational life [see, for example, 24]. Administrators may attempt to introduce new institutional policies in response to regulations enacted or proposed by state agencies, calls for accountability by external study groups, or potential fiscal emergencies based on worse-case scenarios. These policies almost always seek to increase administrative authority. Faculty are less likely to be directly influenced by such pressures and therefore less likely to be persuaded that dramatic action is required. By opposing such administrative initiatives, senates act not only as "an effective mechanism for restricting centralized control over academic programs" [9, p. 164], but also serve as a constraint upon an ambitious administration [18].

In addition to external pressures, there are powerful, if less obvious, reasons for increased administrative activism, and these reasons are related to the increased availability of institutional information. The movement toward the "management" of higher education has, among other things, led to complex systems for the collection and analysis by administrators of previously inaccessible institutional data. These data illuminate anomalies, inequities, and nonstandard practices that must then be justified or abolished and therefore provoke administrative intervention. But as Trow [43] has pointed out, it is precisely the obscurity caused by bad data collection that may permit the diversity and innovation upon which institutional quality is based. The senate's ability to resist administrative initiatives can therefore be seen, at least in some cases, as protecting the institution from making changes based upon measurable but ultimately unimportant factors and thus preserving those enduring organizational and institutional qualities that are beyond routine measurement.

In addition to the increased quantity of data, there are also changes in the processes through which data reach administrators in executive positions, as well as in the speed with which they move through the organization. In the past, data might eventually have come to administrative attention after having first been passed through and manipulated by a series of committees and long after corrective administrative measures could be applied. Today these same data may be transmitted directly to the president from a state coordinating board, often with a time lag measured in weeks rather than years. The effect on a university can be similar to that in other social systems characterized by "symptoms of communication failures based on a superabundance of information, inadequately assimilated, rather than its scarcity" [Douglas Cater, cited in 31, p. 1]. Today administrators may face an endless and often real-time stream of data calling for corrective action before there is time to plan, consult, or fully consider.

The existence of a senate reduces administrative aspirations for change and increases the caution with which the administration acts. This not only protects much of value within the organization but also prevents the unwitting disruption of ongoing but latent systems through which the university keeps the behavior of organizational participants within acceptable bounds. The senate thus is the structure through which, in Clark Kerr's [26] terms, the faculty serve as the institution's balance wheel, "resisting some things that should be resisted, insisting on more thorough discussion of some things that should be more thoroughly discussed, delaying some developments where delay gives time to adjust more gracefully to the inevitable. All this yields a greater sense of order and stability" (p. 100).

THE SENATE AS RITUAL AND AS PASTIME

Senates usually meet on a regular schedule, follow a standard agenda format, involve the same core of participants, and engage in their activities under stipulated rules of order. In an organization typified by ambiguity, it is often comforting to engage in scheduled and structured activities in which the behaviors of others can be generally predicted. The senate thus serves as a ritual, a "formality of procedure or action that either is not directed towards a pragmatic end, or if so directed, will fail to achieve the intended aim" [10, cited in 32, p. 164]. The identification of the senate as "theatrical and debate-oriented " [24, p. 127] underscores its ritualistic qualities.

The rituals of senates serve a number of important organizational functions. Among other things, it helps stabilize and order the organization, it provides assurances that mutually expected interactions will occur, and it reduces anxiety [32]. Senates also provide organizational participants with opportunities for engaging in acceptable behavior when faced with ambiguous or uncertain stimuli. When one doesn't know what else to do, participating in senate debate can appear to be a contribution towards solutions and can enable faculty members to "pretend that they are doing something significant" [3, p. 80].

Ritual provides participants with a sense of membership and integration into an organization and into a profession. For others, however, the senate may be enjoyed purely as a pastime. It is a place where one can meet friends, engage in political intrigues, gossip about the administration, and complain about parking—all common forms of faculty recreation. It is also a place where speeches can be made, power can be displayed, nits can be picked, and the intricacies of Robert's Rules of Order can be explored at infinite depth. Those faculty who do enjoy such things have a vested interest in perpetuating the senate, for without it a forum for their involvement would be lost.

THE SENATE AS SCAPEGOAT

The best-laid plans of institutions often go awry. To some extent, this may be due to cognitive limits to rationality that suggest that only a small proportion of potentially important variables may be attended to at any given time. Equally as important may be the organizational characteristics of colleges and universities as decentralized and loosely coupled systems [44]. In such systems it is often difficult to predict events, and intentions, actions, and outcomes may be only modestly related. Even the power of the president, usually considered the single most influential person in the institution, is severely circumscribed.

When plans are not enacted or goals not achieved, organizational constituents search for reasons. In order to meet psychological needs, these reasons must of course blame others and not oneself; and in order to meet political needs, these reasons must be specific rather than conceptual. A president is unlikely to blame an institutional failure on weak presidential performance, and a board of trustees is not likely to accept a president's argument that a certain task cannot be performed because it is beyond the capabilities of a loosely coupled system. On the other hand, Boards can understand a president's assertion that a specific act was made difficult or impossible because of opposition by the senate and may even entertain a claim that it would be impossible to implement a program because of the likelihood of future senate opposition. In the same way, faculty members at the department or school level can argue against considering a new policy on the grounds that the senate would not approve it and can blame the senate when a program supported by the senate breaks down when implemented at lower organizational levels.

Cause and effect relationships are extremely difficult to assess in the equivocal environment of the college or university. The actions (or lack thereof) of a structure such as the senate, which has high visibility and an ambiguous charge, can plausibly be blamed for deficiencies of all kinds in institutional operation. An academic department can use the senate as a scapegoat for its own unwillingness to make the difficult choices necessary to strengthen its departmental curriculum as easily as a politically incompetent president can accuse it of scuttling a major policy initiative. In these and in similar cases, the senate helps the participants "make sense" of an exceptionally complex system while at the same time preserving their self-images of acumen and professional competence.

Academic Senates in Symbolic Organizational Systems

This article began by discussing the perceived shortcomings of senates when traditional organizational models of the bureaucracy, collegium, and political system are used to assess their effectiveness. It then suggested a number of important latent functions that senates may play. Let us now consider these latent functions in the context of newer models that view organizations as symbolic or cultural systems.

Our world is too complex, equivocal, and confusing to be understood completely, and people must find ways of simplifying and interpreting it if they are to function effectively. There are many ways in which the world can be interpreted, and organizations can be seen as groups of people who interact regularly in an attempt to construct and understand reality, to make sense of ambiguous events, and to share meanings in distinctive ways. Through their regular interactions they develop a culture, which may be defined as "the values or social ideals and the beliefs that organizational members come to share. These values or beliefs are manifested by symbolic devices such as myths, rituals, stories, legends, and specialized language" [40, p. 344].

Within the context of these cultural inventions, people decide what is important, take indeterminate relationships and develop them into coherent beliefs about cause and effect, and retrospectively make sense of events that were too equivocal to be understood as they occurred. A major organizational model built upon these ideas is that of the "organized anarchy," an institution characterized by problematic goals, unclear technology and fluid participation. "The American college or university is a prototypical organized anarchy. It does not know what it is doing. Its goals are either vague or in dispute. Its technology is familiar but not understood. Its major participants wander in and out of the organization. These factors do not make the university a bad organization, or a disorganized one; but they do make it a problem to describe, understand, and lead" [13, p. 3].

An organized anarchy is a loosely coupled system in which individuals and subunits within the organization make essentially autonomous decisions. Institutional outcomes are a resultant of these only modestly interdependent activities and are often neither planned nor predictable. It is difficult in such an environment to make inferences about cause and effect, to determine how successful one is, or even to be certain in advance whether certain environmental changes or evolving issues will turn out to be important or trivial. In this situation of great ambiguity, people spend more time in sense making than in decision making [45] and in engaging in activities that verify their status. The decoupling of choices and outcomes makes symbolic behavior particularly important, and particular choices, problems, solutions, and participants often become associated with one another because of their temporal, rather than their logical relationships.

Organized anarchies need structures and processes that symbolically reinforce their espoused values, that provide opportunities for individuals to assert and confirm their status, and that allow people to understand to which of many competing claims on their attention they should respond. They require a means through which irrelevant problems and participants can be encouraged to seek alternative ways of expressing themselves so that decision makers can do their jobs. They should also be able to "keep people busy, occasionally entertain them, give them a variety of experiences, keep them off the streets, provide pretexts for storytelling, and allow socializing" [45, p. 264].

Given these requirements, the issue of the "success" of the academic senate can be seen from a completely different perspective. Questions concerning its rationality, efficiency, ability to resolve important issues, representatives, and community-building effectiveness, which may be important under other models, are of less consequence here. If one uses notions of symbolic or cultural systems to consider a college or university as an organized anarchy, academic senates may be effective indeed. This may be the reason they have survived and prospered even though they have not fulfilled the manifest purposes that their charters claim. If senates did not exist, we would have to invent them.

It's time to say something nice about senates. The concept of organized anarchy appears to capture a significant aspect of the role of the senate on many campuses but certainly not of all senates on all campuses at all times. There are many examples of senates that have taken responsibility for resolving a specific problem and have done so in a timely and efficient manner. There are senates in which important institutional policy has been determined and through whose processes of interaction faculty have developed shared values and increased feelings of community. Given the comments of observers of the senate, however, these appear to be exceptional rather than common occurrences.

Those who observe the workings of senates and find them deficient should be particularly careful in making recommendations for change, because these changes might affect not only performance of manifest functions but their important latent functions as well. This is particularly true when making recommendations based upon normative and ultimately moral concepts such as "shared authority" or "representativeness." Merton [36, p. 71] warned that "since moral evaluations in a society tend to be largely in terms of the manifest consequences of a practice or code, we should be prepared to find that analysis in terms of latent functions at times runs counter to prevailing moral evaluations. For it does not follow that the latent functions will operate in the same fashion as the manifest consequences which are ordinarily the basis of these judgments."

Anyone who recommends that senates change or be eliminated in favor of some other organizational structure should carefully consider their latent functions. As a general principle, "any attempt to eliminate an existing social structure without providing adequate alternative structures for fulfilling the functions previously fulfilled by the abolished organization is doomed to failure [and] is to indulge in social ritual rather than social engineering" [36, p. 81]. Functional analysis also enables us to evaluate more clearly warnings such as that senates are "ineffective because faculty [are] not active participants. If faculty do not become involved in...senate...affairs, the ominous predictions about the demise of faculty governance may come true" [4, p. 345-46]. To the extent that the organized anarchy model is an appropriate one, the future of the senate in governance is unlikely to be related to increased faculty involvement.

Presented at the Annual Meeting of the Association for the Study of Higher Education, San Diego, California, 14–17 February 1987.

The project presented or reported herein was prepared pursuant to a grant from the Office of Educational Research and Improvement/Department of Education (OERI/ED). However, the opinions expressed herein do not necessarily reflect the position or policy of the OERI/ED, and no official endorsement by the OERI/ED should be inferred.

Robert Birnbaum was professor of higher education at Teachers College, Columbia University, when this article was written. He is currently professor of higher education at the University of Maryland, College Park, and project director at the National Center for Postsecondary Governance and Finance.

Notes

[1] The term "academic senate" is used in this article to identify a formal, representative governance structure at the institutional level that may include only faculty (a "pure" senate), or one that, in addition to a faculty majority, may also include representatives of other campus constituencies, such as administrators, academic staff members, and/or students (a "mixed" senate), as defined by the Report of the AAHE Task Force on Faculty Representation and Academic Negotiations [1, p. 34].

References

American Association for Higher Education. *Faculty Participation in Academic Governance*. Washington, D.C.: American Association for Higher Education, 1967.

Baldridge, J. V. "Shared Governance: a Fable about the Lost Magic Kingdom". *Academe*, 1982, 68; 12–15.

Baldridge, J. V., D. V. Curtis, G. Ecker, and G. L. Riley. *Policy Making and Effective Leadership*. San Francisco: Jossey-Bass, 1978.

Baldridge, J. V., and F. R. Kemerer. "Academic Senates and Faculty Collective Bargaining." *Journal of Higher Education*, July/August 1976, 47; 391–411.

Baldridge, J. V., F. R. Kemerer, and Associates. *Assessing The Impact of Faculty Collective Bargaining*. Washington, D.C.: American Association for Higher Education, 1981.

Begin, J. P. "Faculty Collective Bargaining and Faculty Reward Systems." In *Academic Rewards in Higher Education*, edited by L. Becker. Cambridge: Ballinger, 1979.

Ben-David, J. *American Higher Education: Directions Old and New*. New York: McGraw-Hill, 1972.

Berry, M. F. "Faculty Governance." In *Leadership for Higher Education*, edited by R. W. Heyns. Washington, D.C.: American Council on Education, 1977.

Blau, P. M. *The Organization of Academic Work*. New York: John Wiley and Sons, 1973.

Burnett, J. H. "Ceremony, Rites, and Economy in the Student System of an American High School." *Human Organization*, 1969, 28; 1–10.

Carnegie Commission on Higher Education. *Governance of Higher Education: Six Priority Problems*. New York: McGraw-Hill, 1973.

Carnegie Foundation for the Advancement of Teaching. "A Governance Framework for Higher Education." *Educational Record*, 1983, 64; 12–18.

Cohen, M. D. and J. G. March. *Leadership and Ambiguity: The American College President*. New York: McGraw-Hill, 1974.

——. "Decisions, Presidents, and Status." In J. G. March and J. P. Olsen, *Ambiguity and Choice in Organizations*, 2d ed, Bergen: Universitetsforlaget, 1979.

Cohen, M. D., J. G. March, and J. P. Olsen. "A Garbage Can Model of Organizational Choice." *Administrative Science Quarterly*, 1972, 17; 1–25.

Corson, J. J. *Governance of Colleges and Universities*. New York: McGraw-Hill, 1960.

Deutsch, M. *The Resolution of Conflict: Constructive and Destructive Forces*. New Haven: Yale University Press, 1973.

Dykes, A. R. *Faculty Participation in Academic Decision Making*. Washington, D.C.: American Council on Education, 1968.

Etzioni, A. *Modern Organizations*. Englewood Cliffs, N.J.: Prentice-Hall, 1964.

Feldman, M. S. and J. G. March. "Information in Organizations as Signal and Symbol." *Administrative Science Quarterly*, 1981, 26; 171–86.

Floyd, C. E. *Faculty Participation in Decision Making: Necessity or Luxury?* Washington, D.C.: Association for the Study of Higher Education, 1985.

Hobbs, W. C. "Organizational Roles of University Committees." *Research in Higher Education*, 1975, 3; 233–42.

Hodgkinson, H. L. *The Campus Senate: Experiment in Democracy*. Berkeley: Center for Research and Development in Higher Education, 1974.

Keller, G. *Academic Strategy: The Management Revolution in American Higher Education*. Baltimore: The Johns Hopkins University Press, 1983.

Kemerer, F. R., and J. V. Baldridge. *Unions on Campus*. San Francisco: Jossey-Bass, 1975.

Kerr, C. *The Uses of the University*. Cambridge, Mass.: Harvard University Press, 1964.

Ladd, E. C., Jr., and S. M. Lipset. *Professors, Unions, and American Higher Education*. Washington, D.C.: American Enterprise Institute for Public Policy Research, 1973.

Lee, B. A. *Collective Bargaining in Four-Year Colleges*. Washington, D.C.: American Association for Higher Education, 1978.

————. "Contractually Protected Governance Systems at Unionized Colleges." *Review of Higher Education*, 1982, 5; 69–85.

Liberman, M. "Representational Systems in Higher Education." In *Employment Relations in Higher Education*, edited by S. Elam and M. H. Moskow. Washington, D.C.: Phi Delta Kappa, 1969.

Magarrell, J. "The Social Repercussions of an 'Information Society'." *Chronicle of Higher Education*, 1980, 20; 1, 10.

Masland, A. T. "Simulators, Myth, and Ritual in Higher Education." *Research in Higher Education*, 1983, 18; 161–77.

Mason, H. L. *College and University Government: A Handbook of Principle and Practice*. New Orleans: Tulane University, 1972.

McConnell, T. R. "Faculty Government." In *Power and Authority*, edited by H. L. Hodgkinson and L. R. Meeth. San Francisco: Jossey-Bass, 1971.

McConnell, T. R., and K. P. Mortimer. *The Faculty in University Governance*. Berkeley: Center for Research and Development in Higher Education, 1971.

Merton, R. K. *Social Theory and Social Structure*, rev. ed. Glencoe, Ill.: The Free Press, 1957.

Millett, J. D. *The Academic Community*. New York: McGraw-Hill, 1962.

————. *New Structures of Campus Power*. San Francisco: Jossey-Bass, 1978.

Mortimer, K. P., and T. R. McConnell. *Sharing Authority Effectively: Participation, Interaction and Discretion*. San Francisco: Jossey-Bass, 1978.

Smircich, L. "Concepts of Cultural and Organizational Analysis." *Administrative Science Quarterly*, 1983, 28; 339–58.

Stone, J. N., Jr. "Achieving Broad-Based Leadership." In *Leadership for Higher Education*, edited by R. W. Heyns. Washington, D.C.: American Council on Education, 1977.

Tierney, W. G. "Governance by Conversation: An Essay on the Structure, Function, and Communicative Codes of a Faculty Senate." *Human Organization*, 1983, 42; 172–77.

Trow, M. "The Public and Private Lives of Higher Education." *Daedalus*, 1975, 104; 113–27.

Weick, K. E. "Educational Organizations as Loosely Coupled Systems." *Administrative Science Quarterly*, 1976, 21; 1–19.

————. *The Social Psychology of Organizing*, 2nd ed. Reading, Mass.: Addison-Wesley, 1979.

Wildavsky, A. *The Politics of the Budgetary Process*, 2nd ed. Boston: Little, Brown, 1974.

Veblen, T. *The Higher Learning in America*. New York: Sagamore Press, 1957. (Originally published in 1918.)

High Faculty Morale: What Exemplary Colleges Do Right

R. EUGENE RICE AND ANN E. AUSTIN

Fifteen and twenty years ago, the lives of college faculty were a source of public fascination. Professors then scored near the top in prestige ratings. Their struggles with the challenges of intellect and passion were chronicled in novels and film—the subject of admiration, envy, and *resentment*.

In this decade, public attention has shifted from fascination to concern. The most thorough, recent assessment of the American professoriate is subtitled "a national resource imperiled" (Bowen and Schuster). Ernest Boyer's *College* depicts many faculty as disspirited and restless, burdened with "a low-grade frustration." Morale among faculty is said to be eroded by enrollment declines, budget cuts, and retrenchment—and nowhere more so than among liberal arts faculty.

In response to this development, the Council of Independent Colleges appointed a Taskforce on the Future of the Academic Workplace in Liberal Arts Colleges and launched a major study of faculty morale and the organizational conditions that affect it. To the surprise of many, a national survey of over 4,000 faculty in 140 colleges revealed that the morale and satisfaction of faculty in small liberal arts colleges had *not* deteriorated as dramatically as expected.

In an effort to identify organizational factors that support faculty morale, ten colleges in the study with high scores on satisfaction and morale scales were selected for a series of indepth case studies. Even among the faculty of these schools, the survey's open-ended questions revealed the critical stance expected of faculty—and the occasional chronic grump. The site visits, however, found the faculties of these ten colleges deeply committed to their work and enthusiastically supportive of their institutions' distinctive missions. The extensive reports on the site visits, compiled by teams of individuals noted nationally for their work on faculty issues, revealed levels of satisfaction and morale even higher than expected.

The ten liberal arts colleges characterized by this particular kind of excellence are:

1. Eastern Mennonite
2. College of Notre Dame
3. Gordon
4. Greenville
5. Lenoir-Rhyne
6. Nebraska Wesleyan
7. Saint Scholastica
8. Simpson
9. Smith
10. William Jewell

What are the sources of faculty morale and satisfaction at these ten colleges? We found four key features.

First, they all have *distinctive organizational cultures* that are carefully nurtured and built upon.

Second, they each have strong, *participatory leadership* that provides direction and purpose while conveying to faculty the empowering conviction that the college is theirs.

Third, all of the colleges have a firm sense of *organizational momentum*—they are institutions "on the move." A number are marked by what Burton Clark has called "a turn-around saga."

Finally, the faculty of these ten colleges have an unusually compelling *identification with the institution* that incorporates and extends the other three characteristics contributing to high morale.

These four primary features are complemented by a cluster of secondary elements that were also found to be important contributors to high faculty morale and satisfaction.

Our identification of organizational factors contributing to faculty morale is based, primarily, on data drawn from the case studies. These observations are confirmed, too, by survey data from the sample of 140 colleges, and by a comparison of "high morale" colleges (top one-third of the sample) with "low morale" colleges (bottom one-third).

Distinctive Organizational Culture

Long before the field of organizational behavior became enamored with the symbolic in the functioning of American corporations, leaders of liberal arts colleges were quite aware of the power and significance of organizational culture in the life of an institution. Indeed, most liberal arts colleges were *founded* to capture and perpetuate a distinctive culture.

Recently, however, pragmatic concerns about basic survival, about market share and "competitive edge," has led many private colleges to move away from the distinctive cultural missions that gave to these organizations their *raisons d'être*. The single most important hallmark of the ten colleges identified by this study is that each has a clearly articulated mission and carries forward a distinctive culture.

These are colleges with strong, penetrating cultures. They share with most other liberal arts colleges several intrinsic advantages that strengthen culture: their relatively small size, interdependent parts, and a long history—they have traditions on which to build. What is special about these cultures, however, is their coherence. They say what they do, in very clear terms—then, do what they say. A coherent culture permeates the fabric of the institution; you hear the same stories—the college lore—whether talking to the chairman of the board, a mathematics professor, a freshman, or the campus police.

The majority of these colleges are religious in character, with cultural roots in firm theological soil; they know where they came from. This sense of history shapes their present and informs their planning.

These colleges stand out from others, too, in that their particularity—their distinctive values and commitments—is combined with an openness, a genuine respect for difference. Cultural particularity can undermine faculty morale and satisfaction if it erodes academic freedom and discourages the critical thinking and dissent required for the intellectual and ethical development of students in a liberal arts context. Cultural distinctiveness is not enough; it is that delicate balance between particularity and openness that makes these colleges special.

As the study of corporate cultures has shown, distinctive organizational cultures need not be explicitly religious. Eastern Mennonite, Nebraska Wesleyan, St. Scholastics, and William Jewell have ties to religious communities that are clear, direct, and assiduously nurtured. Smith, on the other hand, has forged its uniqueness out of the challenge of providing a distinguished education for motivated and intellectually oriented women, at a time when many other selective women's colleges have become co-educational. Its resolute focus on the education of women is balanced, again, by a strong emphasis on diversity and the honoring of dissent.

The power of organizational culture is made evident and reinforced through events and structures that are heavily laden with the symbolic—the stories that are told, the people honored, the ceremonies and rituals, the personnel policies, even the architecture. Particularly indicative are the rituals, architecture, and student focus. Here is what we found.

Ritual

Greenville College has a series of ceremonial events running through the academic year that rehearse and underscore core commitments that sustain the college. These begin with an annual fall fellowship that includes faculty, staff, and spouses, and lasts for three days at an off-campus site. Faculty refer to it as a high point in the year's activities—an event that bonds members of the community together. Following commencement, Greenville has an Ivy Cutting Ceremony that goes back to the turn of the century. The graduates assemble in a large circle linked together by strands of ivy. Following a brief presentation, the president, in the center of the circle, cuts the ivy between each member—symbolizing the movement of the class away from the campus and into the world, with each retaining a part of that which bound them together in a common circle.

Across all ten colleges with high faculty morale, we found ceremonies and rituals that had retained their vitality, or that had been revived and infused with new meaning.

Architecture

Decisions to restore or replace important buildings on a campus can be enormously divisive; they can also be opportunities to make a significant cultural statement.

At Simpson College, the decision to save and restore College Hall, the oldest building on campus, took on symbolic proportions that went well beyond considerations of cost and design. Following considerable struggle among various constituencies of the college, the beautifully restored 1869 building now contributes to the recovery of historical perspective on the campus. The roots of the institution are celebrated in rooms dedicated to the memories of Bishop Matthew Simpson, founder of the College, and George Washington Carver, Simpson's most famous alumnus. The recognition of Carver, particularly, underscores the institution's commitment to social justice and an inclusive pluralism. These historic rooms are adjacent to the Admissions Office, tying the orientation of new students to a special set of values and to a particular sense of historical community.

At Eastern Mennonite College, the main campus building was destroyed by fire several years ago. The architecture of the newly built campus center, standing in the middle of the college grounds, recalls the silhouette of traditional Anabaptist barns. Inside, on the first floor, frequently visited college offices surround a large, comfortable gathering place. Symbolically and practically, interior spaces bring people together in a manner consistent with the spirit of collegiality, cooperation, and consensus permeating the college.

At several of these colleges, buildings on campus are named after faculty members, known to generations of students, whose lives exemplify core values of their institution. This contrasts with the more usual practice of naming buildings after contributors. As a symbolic gesture, it gives dignity to the faculty role and is a clear statement of institutional priorities.

Focus on Students

The cultures of these colleges includes a commitment to the student—the development of the whole person—that becomes a pivot point around which everything else turns. For faculty, this cultural priority makes the role of teachers and their relationship to students of unequivocally primary importance. While faculty in other institutions struggle with the competing demands of multiple roles and ambiguous standards of evaluation—particularly around the relationship between research and teaching—the faculty of these colleges know that their vocation is teaching and that this role is central to their institution. Disciplinary research, community service, and governance activities are valued, but are valued in relation to this primary agenda.

Notion of Community

The concept of community plays a large role in the self-understanding of these colleges; at most of them, the family metaphor is invoked frequently and without embarrassment. The community, or "family," is not, however, an end in itself, for that parochial condition would lead to a crippling localism and faculty stagnation. In each case the community spirit serves a larger purpose—defined in a variety of distinctive ways—to educate undergraduates and prepare them to take their place in a broader world.

Participatory Leadership

At the start of the study, we assumed that strong, effective leadership would be a key contributor to faculty morale. In accordance with research on academic leadership, we assumed that a variety of leadership approaches would work, but that what was important was managerial competence. We expected that some deans and presidents would be participatory in their leadership styles and others would be more hierarchical—relying for legitimacy on their capacities to be effective and productive.

This assumption was not supported by the case studies. Every one of the ten colleges with high morale and satisfaction had a leadership that was aggressively participatory, in both individual style and organizational structure. In addition, our survey data indicate that faculty at high-morale colleges perceive the decision-making climate to be more participatory than do their colleagues at low-morale colleges. In every one of the ten decision-making areas about which we inquired, faculty in high-morale colleges report greater involvement.

Strong Leadership/Flat Hierarchy

The case studies reveal what on the surface appears to be a contradiction. Our exemplary colleges have at the same time forceful leadership and an organizational structure that minimizes hierarchical distinctions. The powerful influence of the president on the life of the college was a topic raised frequently in campus interviews. At William Jewell, Simpson, Gordon, and Nebraska Wesleyan, the presidents were commended for almost singlehandedly turning the institutions around. Strong deans were given credit for holding colleges together in difficult times.

At the same time, most of these colleges have intentionally structured a flat hierarchy. In the religiously affiliated schools, a common theme, comfortably articulated, is that of "administrator as servant." At Eastern Mennonite this orientation is firmly embedded in the Anabaptist history of the college; brotherhood, service, and humility are institutionalized in a school where leadership is shared and decision making is largely consensual. At Greenville, the Faculty Handbook explicitly states that "the distinction between instruction and administration is meant to be only those of function and suggests no hierarchy of value related to the respective duties of each group." The site visitors to Greenville concluded: "It is not the great leader but the teaching faculty/administration 'family' that sets the tone for the institution."

Empowering Leaders

Presidents and deans in the ten colleges know how to empower others. In these institutions, power is not seen as a zero-sum game. In Rosabeth Kanter's terms, "power begets power." Those in positions of influence give power away. They share authority, and in so doing empower others and enhance the effectiveness of their organizations as a whole.

In a number of the colleges, the president and dean serve as a team in complementary roles. Often the president articulates the values, vision, and dream for the college and, in denominational colleges, is frequently a prominent spiritual leader. The dean serves to translate values and vision into the daily workings of the college. Such deans, we observed, take a personal approach, moving about campus and maintaining close contact with faculty. Also, during the site visits, faculty often commented on the capacity of the dean to recognize the accomplishments of faculty and to express gratitude.

The combined work of the administrative team at each of these colleges does much to foster collegewide commitment, and often, consensus.

Willingness to Share Information

The respect for faculty, and the sense of trust that permeates these institutions, is fostered by the sharing of important information. Detailed data and the complexities of institutional decisions are communicated in open forums. Faculty are heard on critical issues and know the details when they debate with administrators or among themselves. This depth of faculty understanding mitigates against polarization. Much of this has to do with the small size of these faculties and their willingness to meet frequently—some would say, incessantly—as a faculty-of-the-whole. Even in institutions where faculty salaries are exceptionally low (and this is true of several of these colleges), there is confidence that, given the resources available, good-faith efforts are being made to improve matters.

Faculty Leadership and Trustees

Colleges with low morale tend to have faculty who are institutionally disengaged. The ten exemplary colleges discussed here, by contrast, have faculty members who take major leadership roles in their institutions and who are actively involved in making key decisions. Individually, these faculty leaders are frequently strong people with impressive, charismatic qualities, who often become mentors to younger faculty and administrators, as well as to students.

Faculty leadership in these colleges, however, is more than a matter of individual disposition; it is a structural phenomenon. At Smith College a Faculty Council consisting of five faculty members—representing the principal governance committees—meets regularly with the board of trustees, the president, and the dean of the faculty. At Simpson, the chairs of the budget, educational policy, and personnel committees serve as representatives to the board.

At these colleges, the relationship of faculty to the board of trustees is particularly telling. The sense of faculty "ownership" of the institution is a corporative reality. In some of these institutions, the connection with board members extends beyond formal roles; trustees are regarded as part of the community and interact with faculty in ways that are open and direct, unmediated by the administration.

Authority, Not Domination

Georg Simmel, the German social theorist, made a distinction between authority and domination: Authority is embedded in communities of mutuality and interdependence, while domination is hierarchically bureaucratic, impersonal, and alienating. The ten exemplary colleges have leaders who have authority but do not "dominate," in Simmel's sense. The terms most often used to describe administration-faculty relationships across the ten campuses are telling: trusting, open, fair, integrity, respect for one another, caring, a "truthful" atmosphere, lack of antagonism, concerned, personal, responsible, and accessible.

Organizational Momentum

It is hardly a surprise that organizational culture and leadership should matter to faculty morale and satisfaction; what is striking in the case studies is that all ten colleges exhibit a sense of momentum; they are colleges "on the move." And this sense of momentum appears to relate directly to individual faculty satisfaction and group morale.

Much has been written recently about faculty who see themselves as "stuck" in mid-career. Faculty members can be full professors at the age of forty and have no place to go, in their own college or elsewhere—stuck in the same place and with the same colleagues for the next thirty years.

Our study found that an individual's sense of career momentum can be related to institutional momentum. The faculty in the ten colleges we studied have relatively high morale in part because they are in *colleges* where there is a sense of momentum. When faculty we interviewed were asked about their own vitality or that of colleagues, they frequently would turn to discuss the vitality of their institutions, to the sense of motion that permeated their colleges. At William Jewell, for instance, the college was seen as "on the upswing"; at St. Scholastica, the president was given credit for the sense of "forward motion"; and at Lenoir-Rhyne, regular reference was made to the rise in quality and the new academic standards.

"Turnaround Saga"

Several of the colleges report a "turn-around saga": They faced adversity, overcame the challenge, and are now moving forward. The story repeated frequently at Simpson reminds one of the Phoenix myth. Shirley Clark, the head of our visiting team, reports that the president emerged "as the popular organizational leader-hero who played a central role in setting the college on its feet financially, raising faculty salaries, (and) restoring and extending traditions to increase the sense of community. . ." In the words of Simpson faculty, "now we're poised, ready to break out"; "this is a place that believes in itself again"; "the school has momentum"; and "we're a good school getting better all the time."

Collective Projects

The momentum in several of these colleges has been sustained by carefully designed projects that either accentuated the direction in which the institution was moving or ventured into areas that are academically nontraditional. William Jewell and Lenoir-Rhyne chose the traditional route, developing programs that called for a new emphasis on academic excellence and the raising of standards. The College of Notre Dame, St. Scholastica, Simpson, and Smith introduced innovative programs that drew into the college new student populations. Both strategies involved faculty and rallied their support, introduced new opportunities for growth and change, and moved the institutions ahead through a collective academic effort.

Identification with the Institution

The fourth institutional characteristic that correlates with high faculty morale focuses on faculty members themselves and builds upon the other three: That is, faculty at all ten colleges have an unusually strong identification with their institutions.

Particularly striking is the congruence between individual faculty members' commitments and goals and those of the college. Much of this has to do with the distinctiveness of these colleges and the ability of their leaders to articulate that distinctiveness and build it into everyday operations at the college.

Selection Process

This inordinately strong identification with the institution begins with the way faculty are recruited for appointment to the college. In most of the ten, one finds an elaborate process of mutual selection. Faculty are recruited not merely into an educational institution, but into a community with defined values and goals. Great care is taken to articulate the culture and goals of the college and to explore the match between applicant and institution. The time spent on campus by the candidate is extensive and intense, usually involving not only meetings with faculty but a classroom presentation to students, a session with the president, and, frequently, time with faculty spouses.

Faculty are often selected from among those already well acquainted with the college and its values. At the College of Notre Dame, for instance, 38 percent of the present college staff–faculty and administrators—are graduates of the institution. Joseph Katz, the leader of that case study team, reports:

> Several faculty whom we talked with described their joining the college as faculty as 'coming home.' The team did not get the impression that so large a percentage of graduates among the faculty led to intellectual or social inbreeding. It seems instead to have infused fresh vitality into the spirit of community, and the graduates bring back to the college the fruits of their lives, work, and studies in other settings in other parts of the country.

Collaboration and Focused Support, Not Competition

The identification of faculty with the colleges in these case studies is enhanced by minimizing competition and emphasizing collaboration. Survey data show that the cultures of high-morale colleges are perceived as more collaborative than individualistic. Faculty at high-morale colleges are encouraged to work collaboratively with each other and with administrators.

Faculty can afford to identify with these colleges because each offers an environment in which individuals are encouraged and supported rather than constantly threatened with potential job loss. This contrasts with the experience of faculty in many other colleges, particularly in periods of unpredictable enrollments and retrenchment. Because the leadership in these colleges is participatory in style and the decision making collaborative, there is reason for faculty to believe that the institutions are theirs and they will not be cut loose without warning by unseen hands.

Faculty also identify with these institutions because these colleges offer reward systems that minimize competing loyalties. In so many colleges and universities today, the academic profession is torn by the competing demands of disciplinary, institutional, and external responsibilities. In the colleges under study, some faculty make contributions to their disciplines, but their disciplinary careers do not compete for time with their institutional careers—the priorities are clear. The same can be said for their external careers—their consulting with outside agencies. This work is also valued, but primarily in relation to the faculty members' responsibility to students and the college.

Because of its peculiar distinctiveness, Smith College is difficult to fit into any list of generalized statements about academic institutions. It has a faculty known for its intellectual diversity and that takes pride in its capacity to articulate conflicting points of view. Smith has dealt creatively, however, with the professional tensions built into careers of faculty in a highly selective institution. Teaching, scholarship, and service are thoughtfully balanced in a tenure and promotion process for which the faculty have full responsibility.

As the other nine colleges on our "exemplary" list attempt to sustain their momentum by pressing for higher standards and an agenda of "academic excellence" as it is traditionally understood (e.g., more faculty research, publications, and "national visibility"), the high faculty morale and satisfaction that they presently enjoy could be threatened. The governance and faculty evaluation processes developed over time at Smith could stand as instructive models for them.

Other Factors Contributing to Faculty Satisfaction and Morale

The case studies provide a wealth of information about other ways of supporting faculty morale and satisfaction.

It is clear, for example, that *faculty development programs* can make a significant difference. The "growth contract" developed and refined at Gordon College is a striking case in point.

We also found that a *broader definition of scholarship* has emerged in these colleges. This view of scholarship emphasizes keeping current in the discipline and incorporating new knowledge into teaching on a regular basis. While some faculty pursue research that leads to publication, there is an expectation that research and scholarship will be embedded in a primary commitment to translate and integrate new knowledge into good teaching. This definition of scholarship allows individuals to build on their own strengths, and it supports the central mission of the colleges.

Other factors important at these colleges include various *institutional policies* that sustain faculty morale and satisfaction. At several of the colleges, policies are tailored for faculty at different career stages and ages. In addition, a sense of *colleagueship* is found in these colleges that is very important in making faculty feel good about their work and their institutions.

Finally, a number of the colleges have a special *tie to the local community* that enhances faculty satisfaction and morale. For example, faculty at Lenoir-Rhyne are highly respected in the community of Hickory, North Carolina. They are seen as contributing to the quality of life, not only in the college, but in the local community as well. This special relationship, while contributing to the college and the town, enriches the lives of individual faculty members.

Concerns and Questions

As the major organizational factors related to morale emerged through the study, so too did several questions.

Colleges such as those we've discussed should be alert that their strong cultures—focused on teaching and close, committed communities—do not lead to a neglect of the concerns and issues regnant in the wider world of higher education and in the disciplines. Also, excellence in pursuing "broader definitions of scholarship" requires vigilance among faculty if they are to stay current in their fields.

A number of these colleges aspire to move higher in the pecking order of liberal arts colleges. One wonders, when they then turn to a greater emphasis on traditional research, whether such aspiration will undermine the key cultural values that presently contribute high morale.

Finally, the relationship between organizational momentum and faculty morale is particularly intriguing because of the questions it raises: How can organizational momentum be sustained? Will faculty morale decline if a college experiences a loss in momentum? Can "momentum" continue without growth?

Reflection on these questions reminds us of John Gardner's statement: "The only stability is stability in motion." Much of what Robert Waterman writes about in his new book, *The Renewal Factor,* can be found in the ten exemplary colleges. Perhaps this study has identified institutions with a special capacity for self-renewal. What we can be sure of, however, is that faculty renewal and institutional renewal will be inexorably linked.

Conclusion

In research on the industrial workplace, the relationship between job satisfaction and productivity is not immediately evident; satisfied workers are not always the most productive. In the liberal arts college, however, where the primary focus is on student learning and the development of the student in a wholistic sense, the satisfaction of faculty—indeed, the *excitement* of faculty about their work—is critical to the achievement of educational goals.

Another response to the question about the relationship between faculty morale and student learning is suggested in Parker Palmer's article on community and ways of knowing in the September/October, 1987 *Change*. Palmer articulates what has become a groundswell in higher education; an important epistemological shift is taking place in the discussion of how students learn, moving away from individualistic, objectivist (distancing) ways of knowing, to a recognition of the relational nature of knowledge.

Following upon William Perry's work on cognitive and ethical development, and some of the new scholarship in women's and ethnic studies, there is growing awareness of the strong connection between the power of community and the quality of learning. The importance of the relationship between human context and the making of meaning, between the knower and the known—self and world–must be acknowledged.

The small liberal arts college is the ideal place for this kind of connected learning, precisely because students are not objectified and treated as things. At its best, the liberal arts college is furthest from an educational assembly line; it is a learning community, to which morale and commitment are central.

Shared Governance and External Constraints

ROBERT O. BERDAHL

The topic of shared governance and external constraints will probably produce some terrain already familiar to many, but I was told long ago in graduate days at Berkeley that people sometimes require more to be reminded than informed. So if I can bring together into a coherent context some things the reader may know in bits and pieces and apply them to the issue of shared governance, perhaps a contribution will have been made.

For example, if, in the discussion of shared governance, one asks what are the relative shares for the faculty, students, trustees, and administrators, this raises the obvious issue of what substantive domain is to be shared. Clearly, if the university or college has fewer powers of self-governance than it used to have, then the debate about these respective roles should reflect that reduced terrain and be realistic rather than purely theoretical.

If external donors or the courts or state governments or federal bureaucratic offices now have the power of control, not even to mention the murky terrain of influence, then the internal debate about respective roles of shared governance should recognize that fact. I use the word "recognize" rather than "accept," because to understand that the domain of autonomy is somewhat reduced from its earlier, broader scale does not mean that one has to accept the legitimacy of the reduction. Rather, as I will later argue, these matters need to be examined almost individually, with balanced judgments made as to whether a particular movement of power from campus to external sources is legitimate from the standpoint of the public interest and not only because the academy would resist it in order to keep maximum control. Those are very tough and difficult judgments to make, and I shall conclude by suggesting that there is a monitoring role for all parties in shared governance and that monitoring cannot be left only to the senior administration and the board of trustees.

It is typically professorial to pause for some definitions, but it should be helpful to clarify some basic concepts before I consider how specific pieces of autonomy have gone here and there. For example, I find it fortuitous that three different studies—the Carnegie Commission's study (1973), *Governance of Higher Education;*[1] a book I wrote for the American Council on Education in 1971, *Statewide Coordination of Higher Education;*[2] and a book by Frank Newman published in 1987, *Choosing Quality: Reducing Conflict Between the State and the University*[3]—all have used some parallel terms. While they do not overlap completely, the parallels are close enough and interesting enough to suggest a common framework. The three of us—Carnegie, Newman, and Berdahl, if you will—talk about something that I called academic freedom, that the Carnegie Commission called intellectual independence, and that Newman discusses in the area of so-called ideological intrusions. All refer to the areas of political, social, and religious orthodoxy and the need to prevent some external agent (in the earlier days, as Walter Metzger has pointed out, it could be the board of trustees itself, but more recently it might be a state legislator or a wealthy donor) from finding that some faculty member has offended an element of orthodoxy, thereby creating tensions between the academy and society.

A second layer is the area of autonomy, and in my 1971 study I broke it down between "procedural autonomy" and "substantive autonomy." The Carnegie Commission used the words "academic independence" for the substantive side and "administrative independence" for the procedural side. Frank Newman has put in parallel terms of "political intrusions" for the substantive side and "bureaucratic intrusions" for the procedural side.

I will not dwell any further on these definitional matters, but I will use, for want of better terms, my own vocabulary of academic freedom and procedural and substantive autonomy to look at relations between the university and external societies.

For many years I have been greatly stimulated by a fine essay by Walter Metzger. In fact, a former colleague at Buffalo and I liked it so much that we put it into a book of readings called *Higher Education in American Society*.[4] The Metzger essay is "Academic Freedom in De-localized Academic Institutions." In it, he contrasts the relatively simpler environment of the typical college in 1915, at the time that the American Association of University Professors (AAUP) emerged and gave us its definition of academic freedom with the highly complex and interdependent world of current academic institutions.

In 1915 a so-called localized college had fairly distinct physical boundaries with the adjoining town, ruled more or less in loco parentis over its relatively small student body drawn from, perhaps, 2 percent of the college-age cohort, and exercised quite arbitrary powers over those students. It had a relatively straightforward curriculum taught by a faculty whose primary responsibility was teaching, with perhaps incidental research. It made relatively few demands on society in terms of either appropriations or other needs, and gave relatively modest direct service to society, not being heavily involved in gross national product or defense efforts. As a consequence, it had considerable autonomy. Although one does not want to look back with glowing eyes to a rosy period that never was, compared to today the powers of self-governance were certainly greater then. Since the college was not part of a multicampus system, it usually had a local board of trustees. There were few intruding statewide boards; the federal government played no particular role at all; and there were few, if any, faculty unions.

Therefore, as Metzger's essay points out, the issues of academic freedom or autonomy were very different from those we now confront. In fact, he says,

> One of the most important of the transformations has been the flow of decisional power from authorities on the campus to those resident outside. Richer, larger, more complex than ever before, the typical modern institution of higher learning is less self-directive than ever before. It has become, to coin a word, de-localized, with the consequences we are just beginning to perceive. De-localization has not been a single process, but a congeries of processes all working in the same direction and achieving a common end. The engulfing of many universities by the central city with the result that everything they do in the way of land use becomes imbued with political implications and ensnarled in municipal law. . . . The growth of bureaucratized philanthropy is a principal source of academic innovation. The subordination of judgment of admissions officers, the legislative judgments concerning civil rights, the involvement of universities in social welfare, and, thus, with clients it can serve but not control, may be considered other forces. So, too, the integration of public higher education[5] the assault by the courts on the principle of extraterritoriality and the enlargement of federal influence due to federal sponsorship of research and, of course, access for students in affirmative action.

Metzger's final point in his essay was that academe had been overly focused on traditional notions of academic freedom, and that, as a consequence, autonomy issues were neglected.

> No process of de-localization unless it threatened the well-being of professors was presumed to violate academic freedom and...without a violation of academic freedom, no insult to the university seemed to cause broad alarm. The autonomy and the integrity of the university, these heavenly things on earth, are not contained in that philosophy.[6]

So Metzger urged that the 1915 definition be broadened. What his essay did not have time to do was to examine the areas of autonomy, whether procedural or substantive, in their sensitive relationships with all the different external constituencies.

I will try an exercise in what Eric Ashby, in Great Britain, called the "ecology of higher education" by looking at some of the environmental elements and trying to suggest examples of the kinds of problems that emerge. Some are in the area of what we call influence, those legitimate pushes and pulls in a democratic society, in which pluralistic forces operate. A university or college can claim no immunity from those forces and, in fact, that lack of immunity is probably healthier for them. Nevertheless, they require scrutiny and evaluation. In other areas it is mandatory authority that has moved elsewhere, and one must comply unless one is convinced that the move is illegitimate; then one can counterattack either through the courts or the political process.

I start with town and gown and move further out. First come our good friends, the alumni, who, on the one hand, support alma mater with their money, their enthusiasm, and their volunteer efforts. But on occasion, their enthusiasm can go too far, particularly in such areas as intercollegiate athletics, where there have been instances of gross interference with campus decisions and priorities. We have all read relevant headlines in the newspapers. In the *Chronicle of Higher Education* there is a nearly unending series of horror stories about alumni with misplaced zeal trying to get the campus to do things differently than perhaps the academic or administrative participants in shared governance would accept. At Michigan State an open conflict broke out between the alumni association and the university's board, and a power confrontation nearly developed.

As a further example, the president of the University of Kentucky had to deal with Governor John Y. Brown, who, under alumni influence, wanted to help the president choose the next football coach. One could continue down that street with a whole host of anecdotes, but the point is that a university that thinks it can govern itself will learn that the alumni that it has roused to fervor in the support of alma mater may be a mixed blessing. Not only do they give money and support, but sometimes they want to help control the academy's decisions.

The same is true with donors, whether very powerful single individuals or foundations. Father Timothy S. Healy, President of Georgetown University, with some embarrassment, decided a few years after the fact to return to Muammar al Qaddafi and Libya a substantial gift for the establishment of a chair or an institute of Middle Eastern studies when, obviously, Libya was not going to permit any candidates of the Hebrew faith to be seriously considered for appointment. Clearly, that kind of conditional gift would violate some of the basic academic norms about holding open searches for the best-qualified candidates, even for endowed chairs. That kind of limitation could not be accepted with any self-respect and so the gift was ultimately returned—and should probably not have been accepted in the first place, one says with the wisdom of hindsight.

One also thinks of John Silber at Boston University, who was chided for having said, when confronted with criticism about admitting the sons of wealthy Middle Eastern sheikhs to Boston University, that there was a long and honorable historical precedent for the selling of indulgences. So the academy must handle the issue of wealthy donors ready to contribute money if only the academy will move in directions the donors desire. Since it is very hard to turn down money, it must be difficult to make such decisions, but those issues have to be faced.

I have already mentioned foundations. Basically, I think they have had a positive overall impact when they stimulated us to innovation and change in ways that we might not have attempted if left alone. Nevertheless, there is an element of inducing or, if you will, seducing the academy to move in directions that certain foundations feel are priority areas. And so again, in defining autonomy, you must consider the extent to which an academy is pulled off its true course, as defined from inside, by the lure of substantial amounts of money.

Accreditation is, I think, also basically benign; yet, some specialized groups can penetrate far into academe and lay down particular requirements for compliance that reach deep into autonomy. A doctoral student of mine at the University of Maryland wrote her dissertation about the process whereby the University of Baltimore achieved AACSB (American Association of Colleges of Schools of Business) accreditation. There were many detailed requirements about full-time/part-time faculty, and faculty with terminal qualifications were required to teach certain percentages of the total student enrollment (they had to switch faculty from day to night courses, and shift the faculty with terminal degrees into the big sections so that they would cover a larger percentage of students). Many things that academe traditionally thought were a matter of internal governance have clearly been delivered piecemeal to different specialized accrediting groups—business here, social work there, nursing there, dentistry there, library science there, architects there, chemistry there—need I go on? The point is that, little by little, academe has given a finger and a toe until the body has shrunk considerably.

I think the motivation of individual specialized accrediting processes is to improve the quality of higher education, and the demands they make of academe are efforts to improve each particular program. Nevertheless, from the standpoint of governance and determining, as a matter of internal decision-making, the balance among the various programs and the priorities for future growth or retrenchment—an increasingly tough agenda item for governance to confront—those priorities are obviously distorted because some players have external leverage on the academy through these specialized accrediting ultimatums. So again, in our definition of autonomy, we must take that into consideration.

I also look at collective bargaining as another external actor. I know that the membership of the faculty union comes from inside and so "we" are "they," but the center of gravity of the union in the legal sense is external to the academy. Thus even though, like a wealthy foundation or an accreditation visit, the motives of the process may be benign—looked at dispassionately in terms of the governance issue—a faculty union is still external to the academy. In defining autonomy, one must consider the fact that a union might bring into the collective-bargaining agreement certain matters that go far beyond wages, retirement plans, and health benefits, and include teaching loads, faculty/student ratios, and many other things that earlier were considered the heart of academe. I would therefore urge that faculty and staff unions be considered among the potential players in a redefinition of autonomy.

Then there are state governments, the area in which I personally have done the most work. The role of state government has expanded enormously since the 1960s. There are now statewide boards in forty-seven of the fifty states, and even little pretenses of them in the other three. The states create the legal framework within which universities must operate. In the public sector the government either appoints or elects members of the boards of trustees. There is the obvious issue of state appropriations of tax dollars and the coordination and regulation framework in which states are increasingly influencing, if not controlling, institutional role and mission, saying that a given institution should become a certain type of institution and that it does not have the freedom to become anything that it and its trustees aspire for it to be. There is also program approval power that says that, before an institution can establish a new academic program, it must pass through certain layers of approval. There is budget review and, increasingly now in state governments, a domain of accountability called "performance audit," in which state governments are no longer content to have appropriations generated by input analysis.

Input analysis involves questions such as the following: How many students do you expect and how do they translate into full-time-equivalent enrollment? How many new faculty positions does that new full-time-equivalent student count justify? How many new square feet of classroom will you need in the capital plant? Those were input factors that were relatively easier to handle in the old days of formula budgeting; but now in state government there is an increasing desire and even insistence directed not just toward higher education but toward public policy in general, and state governments begin to evaluate the output, the product, the performance. Many states have performance audit staffs, connected either with the state auditor or sometimes with specialized groups called, as in Virginia, the joint legislative audit and review commission. These are no longer green-eyeshade accountants who come in to audit the books for compliance with legality or efficiency. They get into questions of effectiveness that raise normative value considerations. These multidisciplinary teams are drawn from economics, public administration, and social psychology, and include statisticians and accountants; they ask some very tough questions about what the public agency in question is doing. And when they turn to us in the academy, we are not yet very ready to answer "We are producing quality graduates." "How do you know they are quality graduates?" "Well, we know because we are doing it." This answer is not good enough, and I anticipate an increasingly complex agenda between the university and the state government about how good we are at doing what we say we are doing.

Alongside that is a more attractive element of state government that intrudes little on autonomy. This is called incentive funding, in which incentive is placed out front in the form of dollars ("green carrots") for certain categorical programs. For example, the Funds for Excellence program in Virginia is a small fund for the improvement of postsecondary education that does some very interesting things with colleges. The program generates its own proposals to improve the general education scores of students in the first two years, or to make the engineering curriculum better, or to institute writing across the curriculum, or to get computers into the humanities. The projects are quite interesting, and I find that kind of agenda between the academy and state government to be fairly upbeat and in strong contrast to something like mandatory testing, which is imposed from the state down.

Frank Newman's 1987 book, *Choosing Quality*, covers the state government role in considerable detail. He gives little unidentified anecdotes on ideological intrusions, political intrusions, and bureaucratic intrusions, page by page, and it is quite interesting to read what is still going on in all three of those domains. State governments have become less intrusive because of ideological motives, impinging less in the area of academic freedom, and that is good news. But in the two other domains—the bureaucratic or procedural, as I call it, or, as Newman calls it, the substantive political area—there is still plenty to worry about. We want to keep looking at academic freedom, but, in the meantime, all these other agenda items have come up in the area of autonomy (or bureaucratic or procedural controls). We want to monitor them as well, because they affect academe and they certainly affect the debate about shared governance.

In the federal government, one of the three main elements of activity, particularly since World War II, has been to create the research process that Metzger mentioned; there the agenda is not one of any mandatory control, except that institutions have to subject themselves to the requirements of funding agencies if they want a share of their monies. Clark Kerr's book *The Uses of the University*[7] says that the three main impacts of the federal grant university have been to emphasize research over teaching, graduate programs over undergraduate, and science over humanities. To the extent that those three general influences have been pervasive in the flow of federal money, the academy must take that into consideration and decide whether it can go along with those three influences and whether it retains any countervailing forces with which to try to strengthen undergraduate education, humanities, and teaching.

I see those countervailing forces on the horizon. Right now state governments are concentrating on improving the quality of undergraduate education, and they are trying to drag the faculty, kicking and screaming, back into the classroom. There I see the state government as countervailing some of the federal influences, which makes for an interesting set of interplays in our federal-state relations. But the federal research domain has those pervasive influences, and there are also some bureaucratic controls at the federal level. Research universities fought against some of the more incredibly nitpicking requirements of compliance, as in an A95 directive in which the university would have to account for a faculty member's time throughout the whole week in order to know how much of it to charge to a given federal contract, to determine whether that person was spending an hour on teaching or research or public service. It gets ludicrous because, when you read a book, it is for several purposes, and it is kind of silly to overdo that kind of detailed requirement.

There was a committee out of the academy that negotiated with the national government about such regulations and, to give the Reagan administration credit, their deregulation orientation has led them to back off a little and that has been welcome.

Another aspect of federal programs has been to broaden access, and there it has had a basically benign impact on higher education. There are institutions like Grove City and Hillsdale College, which do not want to tangle with the federal government even through student access. In an effort to stay clear of federal jurisdiction, there have been some court cases like the Grove City case and others in which some campuses did not want to allow the federal subsidies to students to bring the campus under federal jurisdiction. Most of us, though, have not had that problem, and we gladly welcome students with Pell grants, with work-study, and with federal loans. Many colleges are probably now dependent on the continuation of those federal programs for their survival.

The third domain of the federal program since World War II has been that of social justice and affirmative action. There, of course, one finds the academy entangled deeply in federal jurisdiction, particularly through the court system. In the *Regents of the University of California v. Bakke* case in California, a white student denied admission to the medical school at the University of California—Davis claimed that the quota system for minorities denied him equal protection under the law—a kind of exercise in reverse discrimination. Enormous legal hassles can develop over the admissions process and the hiring of faculty and staff. In 1977 in *Adams v. Califano* (430 F. Supp. 118), some courts in the fourteen southern states had made major decisions that affected what campuses could do by way of new programs, the enhancement of the predominantly black colleges, including even consent decrees that students, trustees, and faculty of other races would be brought in. Again, one probably welcomes this as a necessary reaction to academe's own neglect of a moral agenda, but in terms of autonomy and the governing process, you have to realize that those decisions are no longer made only on campus. I said earlier that I was going to speak of things my audience already knew. This is one such thing, but when we add that dimension to all the others I have mentioned, it means that the academy now governs itself far, far less than it used to do.

In loco parentis tended to disappear long ago (and probably well it should have), and the courts have gone far in examining procedural due process. Have students accused of some disciplinary transgression been allowed careful due process inside the academy? The old days of the dean of students arbitrarily suspending or expelling some students have long since gone, and the college student personnel officers now need a good legal counsel to guide them. But normally, on substantive matters, the courts have deferred to academe, just as they have traditionally deferred to the political branches of government. In Missouri a woman named Horowitz was dropped by a medical school in her third year because her clinical work was considered unsatisfactory, although she received A's in most of her courses. She said, "I'm not going to practice medicine. I want my M.D. just to do research." She sued the University of Missouri, claiming they had treated her unfairly because she was getting A's in her nonclinical work. The university had brought in a second group of medical personnel from outside to judge her clinical work, and the second group had also found her wanting. The court's attitude was, "We're not going to touch it. If the medical faculty thinks she's not qualified, we're not going to substitute our judgment for theirs."

In a recent case in California, however, a court determined, if I read *The Washington Post* correctly, that the University of California agricultural extension program and research program had not conformed to the spirit or the letter of the Morrill Land Grant Act of 1862 and the Second Land Grant Act because too much of its research helped agribusiness and not enough helped the small family farmer. Evidently there was some language in the original land grant law (which, to be truthful, I have never read paragraph by paragraph) urging universities to do research on agriculture and help society without distinguishing between small family farmers and agribusiness (which in 1862 probably did not exist). But here we have the court intervening to examine a university's research program and deciding substantively, "It's not the right kind of program." Now, I don't know if that will be appealed. Interestingly enough, if the *Post* can be believed, the U. S. Department of Agriculture sided with the University of California, deciding that it had conformed to the land grant act and that it was a public interest group in California, like Nader's Raiders, that was representing the consumer or the small farm family business that had taken the university to court. If that were to go through, we might find—and I want to be cautiously speculative here—that the courts will not be as reticent as historically they seem to have been in second-guessing the substance of academic judgment. If that were to be true, we would have to reopen the question of relations between the academy and the courts which, until now, had been largely confined to due process issues.

University autonomy, then, is not what it used to be. It was never total, but the bits and pieces lost here and there on the road toward a system of mass access to higher education have been cumulatively substantial. Is the price too high? That is a very subjective judgment that needs an answer. I am willing to say no. I have had the privilege of attending two conferences in 1986 and 1987 with British colleagues on access and quality in higher education, and the generalization, to oversimplify our discussion, was that the British were very good on quality in their universities but were found wanting on access. They themselves said so. They said it was a tragedy in their society that higher education was being confined to such a relatively small proportion of their population, and that many potentially talented young men and women were not being allowed the opportunity to develop their talent. So they felt they had quality and needed access.

We may have achieved more in the area of access, although we still have an unfinished agenda in terms of certain disadvantaged students, but there are a lot of quality problems. Would I surrender some of our access for higher quality? No, I am optimistic enough to think we can have both. Just as the British are trying to expand their quality system of higher education, so I think we can improve the quality of our broadened system. But I would not return to the halcyon days of the localized institution of 1915 even though, in some ways, it looks rather attractive—Mr. Chips in his small academy teaching a few students across a kind of Mark Hopkins log.

We must have a broader system of access. There are numbers of students who present complexity for the curriculum, complexity for the faculty, and cost to the state and the nation, and with this complexity and those costs come issues of accountability that will require the sharing of power, not only on campus through governance but off campus through a very complicated governance system.

We must redefine the shared governance turf. I would urge that, as part of its role in shared governance, the faculty not only look at internal campus matters but appoint a faculty committee that, as a matter of course, monitors the institution's external relations. Its purpose should not be to second-guess every act that the senior administration or board of trustees performs, because they have to be left alone to get on with their business and, as full-time people, will be able to bring more resources to bear than amateur faculty members spending part of their time on a committee. But I would urge that a faculty committee take the commanding heights of policy surveillance and stay in touch with what is going on—for example, monitoring the campus's policy about accepting or rejecting gifts. Is anybody looking at that policy? Is anyone looking at the accreditation process? Is there a proper balance between specialized accrediting and the demands it makes, or does the academy need to stand on its hind legs and say, "Enough! Back off a little!"? On relations with state government, are the particular powers between the academy and the state capital about right, or has the state attempted to go too far and, if so, how does the academy form alliances in society to get the state government to back off? (On occasion this has happened. The State University of New York prompted the federal government to appoint a national blue-ribbon commission to investigate SUNY control by state government. After the commission issued a powerful report, the state backed off somewhat.) So it is not totally unthinkable, although I would have to tell you that achieving a slight reversal in the encroachment of some external constituency on academe does not come easily.

The AAUP, with which I have had some previous association, has a Committee R that deals with state and federal policies; it is important that the faculty also be aware of this dimension of campus autonomy as well as our concern with academic freedom. And the faculty senate, if it is a self-respecting body, ought to have some standing committee that monitors those issues and, on occasion when they are concerned about possible abuse, speaks to the proper administrative or trustee sources.

Notes

[1] Carnegie Commission on Higher Education, *Governance of higher Education* (New York: McGraw-Hill, 1973).

[2] R. O. Berdahl, *Statewide Coordination of Higher Education* (Washington, D.C.: American Council on Education, 1971).

[3] F. Newman, *Choosing Quality* (Denver: Education Commission of the States, 1987).

[4] P. G. Altbach and R. O. Berdahl, eds., *Higher Education in American Society* (Buffalo, N.Y.: Prometheus Books, 1981).

[5] In which Metzger means moving into formal public systems, with authority strongly moved off campus.

[6] Walter Metzger, "Academic Freedom in De-localized Academic Institutions," in Altbach and Berdahl, *Higher Education in American Society*, p. 63.

[7] C. Kerr, *Uses of the University* (Cambridge, Mass.: Harvard University Press, 1982).

Three Models of Strategy[1]

ELLEN E. CHAFFEE

Three models of strategy that are implicit in the literature are described—linear, adaptive, and interpretive. Their similarity to Boulding's (1956) hierarchical levels of system complexity is noted. The strategy construct is multifaceted, and it has evolved to a level of complexity almost matching that of organizations themselves.

***

Researchers and practitioners have used the term *strategy* freely—researchers have even measured it—for over two decades. Those who refer to strategy generally believe that they are all working with the same mental model. No controversy surrounds the question of its existence; no debate has arisen regarding the nature of its anchoring concept.

Yet virtually everyone writing on strategy agrees that no consensus on its definition exists (Bourgeois, 1980; Gluck, Kaufman, & Walleck, 1982; Glueck, 1980; Hatten, 1979; Hofer & Schendel, 1978; Lenz, 1980b; Rumelt, 1979; Spender, 1979; Steiner, 1979). Hambrick (1983) suggested that this lack of consistency is due to two factors. First, he pointed out, strategy is multidimensional. Second, strategy must be situational and, accordingly, it will vary by industry.

The literature affirms Hambrick's assessment that strategy is not only multidimensional and situational but that such characteristics are likely to make any consensus on definition difficult. Strategy also suffers from another, more fundamental problem; that is, the term strategy has been referring to three distinguishable mental models, rather than the single model that most discussions assume. Beyond reflecting various authors' semantic preferences, the multiple definitions reflect three distinct, and in some ways conflicting, views on strategy. This paper seeks to analyze the ways strategy has been defined and operationalized in previous treatises and studies. It highlights those aspects of strategy on which authors in the field appear to agree and suggests three strategy models that are implicit in the literature.

Strategy: Areas of Agreement

A basic premise of thinking about strategy concerns the inseparability of organization and environment (Biggadike, 1981; Lenz, 1980a). The organization uses strategy to deal with changing environments. Because change brings novel combinations of circumstances to the organization, the substance of strategy remains unstructured, unprogrammed, nonroutine, and nonrepetitive (Mason & Mitroff, 1981; Mazzolini, 1981; Miles & Cameron, 1982; Narayanan & Fahey, 1982; Van Cauwenbergh & Cool, 1982). Not only are strategic decisions related to the environment and nonroutine, but they also are considered to be important enough to affect the overall welfare of the organization (Hambrick, 1980).

Theorists who segment the strategy implicitly agree that the study of strategy includes both the actions taken, or the content of strategy, and the processes by which actions are decided and implemented. They agree that intended, emergent, and realized strategies may differ from one another. Moreover, they agree that firms may have both corporate strategy ("What businesses shall we be in?") and business strategy ("How shall we compete in each business?"). Finally, they concur that the making of strategy involves conceptual as well as analytical exercises. Some authors stress the analytical dimension more than others, but most affirm that the heart of strategy making is the conceptual work done by leaders of the organization.

Beyond these general factors, agreement breaks down. Yet the differences in point of view are rarely analyzed. Only the existence of multiple definitions of strategy is noted and, as in Mintzberg (1973), definitions are sometimes grouped by type. Analysis reveals that the strategy definitions in the literature cluster into three distinct groups.

Three Models of Strategy

The name assigned to each model of strategy represents its primary focus. Although these descriptions represent a collective version of similar views, each model also includes many variations of its central theme. Moreover, as will be shown later, the three models are not independent. However, for present purposes, the three models will be treated according to their independent descriptions in the literature.

Model I: Linear Strategy

The first model to be widely adopted is linear and focuses on planning. The term linear was chosen because it connotes the methodical, directed, sequential action involved in planning. This model is inherent in Chandler's definition of strategy.

> Strategy is the determination of the basic long-term goals of an enterprise, and the adoption of courses of action and the allocation of resources necessary for carrying out these goals (1962, p. 13).

According to the linear view, strategy consists of integrated decisions, actions, or plans that will set and achieve viable organizational goals. Both goals and the means of achieving them are results of strategic decision. To reach these goals, organizations vary their links with the environment by changing their products or markets or by performing other entrepreneurial actions. Terms associated with the linear model include strategic planning, strategy formulation, and strategy implementation.

The linear model portrays top managers as having considerable capacity to change the organization. The environment is, implicitly, a necessary nuisance "out there" that is composed mainly of competitors. Top managers go through a prototypical rational decision making process. They identify their goals, generate alternative methods of achieving them, weigh the likelihood that alternative methods will succeed, and then decide which ones to implement. In the course of this process, managers capitalize on those future trends and events that are favorable and avoid or counteract those that are not. Because this model was developed primarily for profit-seeking businesses, two of its important measures of results are profit and productivity.

Several assumptions that underlie the linear model are not made explicit in most discussions, but they nonetheless follow from the authors' tendency to emphasize planning and forecasting. For example:

> Conceptually, the process [of strategic planning] is simple: managers at every level of a hierarchy must ultimately agree on a detailed, integrated plan of action for the coming year; they [start] with the delineation of corporate objectives and [conclude] with the preparation of a one- or two-year profit plan (Lorange & Vancil, 1976, p. 75).

If a sequential planning process is to succeed, the organization needs to be tightly coupled, so that all decisions made at the top can be implemented throughout the organization. This tight coupling assumption enables intentions to become actions. A second assumption arises from the time-consuming and forward-looking nature of planning. In other words, though decisions made today are based on beliefs about future conditions, they may not be implemented until months, even years, from now. In order to believe that making such decisions is not a waste of time, one must assume either that the environment is relatively predictable or else that the organization is well-insulated from the environment. Also, most authors explicitly assume that organizations have goals and that accomplishing goals is the most important outcome of strategy.

Major characteristics of the linear model and the names of several authors whose definitions of strategy are consistent with this model are listed in Table 1. Note that though the authors' definitions of strategy constitute grounds for classifying them in the model, nearly all authors extend their discussions of strategy into areas that are relevant to more than one model.

Table 1

	Summary of Linear Strategy
Variable	**Linear Strategy**
Sample definition	"...determination of the basic long-term *goals* of an enterprise, and the adoption of courses of *action* and the allocation of *resources* necessary for carrying out *these goals*" (Chandler, 1962, p. 13, italics added).
Nature of strategy	Decisions, actions, plans
	Integrated
Focus for strategy	Means, ends
Aim of strategy	Goal achievement
Strategic behaviors	Change markets, products
Associated terms	Strategic planning, strategy formulation and implementation
Associated measures	Formal planning, new products, configuration of products or businesses, market segmentation and focus, market share, merger/acquisition, product diversity
Associated authors[2]	Chandler, 1962
	Cannon, 1968
	Learned, Christensen, Andrews, & Guth, 1969
	Gilmore, 1970
	Andrews, 1971
	Child, 1972
	Drucker, 1974
	Paine & Naumes, 1974
	Glueck, 1976
	Lorange & Vancil, 1976
	Steiner & Miner, 1977

As the dates in these citations suggest, interest in the linear model waned in the mid-1970s. Ansoff and Hayes (1976) suggested that the emphasis moved away from the linear model as the strategic problem came to be seen as much more complex. Not only does it involve several dimensions of the managerial problem and the process, but also technical, economic, informational, psychological, and political variables as well. The model that arose next is labeled here the adaptive model of strategy.

Model II: Adaptive Strategy

Hofer's definition typifies the adaptive model of strategy, characterizing it as

> concerned with the development of a viable match between the opportunities and risks present in the external environment and the organization's opportunities (1973, p. 3).

The organization is expected continually to assess external and internal conditions. Assessment then leads to adjustments in the organization or in its relevant environment that will create "satisfactory alignments of environmental opportunities and risks, on the one hand, and organizational capabilities and resources, on the other" (Miles & Cameron, 1982, p. 14).

The adaptive model differs from the linear model in several ways. First, monitoring the environment and making changes are simultaneous and continuous functions in the adaptive model. The time lag for planning that is implicit in the linear model is not present. For example, Miles and Snow (1978) portray strategic adaptation as recurring and overlapping cycles with three phases: the entrepreneurial phase (choice of domain), the engineering phase (choice of technology), and the administrative phase (rationalizing structure and process, and identifying areas for future innovation).

Second, the adaptive model does not deal as emphatically as the linear model with decisions about goals. Instead, it tends to focus the manager's attention on means, and the "goal" is represented by coalignment of the organization with its environment. Third, the adaptive model's definition of strategic behaviors goes beyond that of the linear model to incorporate not only major changes in products and markets, but also subtle changes in style, marketing, quality, and other nuances (Hofer, 1976a; Shirley, 1982).

A fourth difference follows from the relative unimportance of advance planning in the adaptive model. Thus, as might be expected, strategy is less centralized in top management, more multifaceted, and generally less integrated than in the linear model. However, top managers in the adaptive model still assume overall responsibility for guiding strategy development.

Finally, in the adaptive model the environment is considered to be a complex organizational life support system, consisting of trends, events, competitors, and stakeholders. The boundary between the organization and its environment is highly permeable, and the environment is a major focus of attention in determining organizational action. Whether taken proactively or reactively, action is responsive to the nature and magnitude of perceived or anticipated environmental pressures.

In sum, the adaptive model relies heavily on an evolutionary biological model of organizations. The analogy is made explicit in the following passage:

> As a descriptive tool, strategy is the analog of the biologist's method of "explaining" the structure and the behavior of organisms by pointing out the functionality of each attribute in a total system (or strategy) designed to cope with or inhabit a particular niche. The normative use of strategy has no counterpart in biology (as yet!), but might be thought of as the problem of designing a living creature . . . to exist within some environment . . . (Rumelt, 1979, pp. 197-198).

Table 2

Variable	Adaptive Strategy
Summary of Adaptive Strategy	
Sample definition	"...concerned with the development of a viable match between the opportunities and risks present in the external environment and the organization's capabilities and resources for exploiting those opportunities" (Hofer, 1973, p. 3).
Nature of strategy	Achieving a "match"
	Multifaceted
Focus for strategy	Means
Aim of strategy	Coalignment with the environment
Strategic behaviors	Change style, marketing, quality
Associated terms	Strategic management, strategic choice, strategic predisposition, strategic design, strategic fit, strategic thrust, niche
Associated measures	Price, distribution policy, marketing expenditure and intensity, product differentiation, authority changes, proactiveness, risk taking, multiplexity, integration, futurity, adaptiveness, uniqueness
Associated authors[3]	Hofer, 1973
	Guth, 1976
	Hofer & Schendel, 1978
	Litschert & Bonham, 1978
	Miles, Snow, Meyer, & Coleman, 1978
	Miller & Friesen, 1978
	Mintzberg, 1978
	Dill, 1979
	Steiner, 1979
	Rumelt, 1979
	Hambrick, 1980
	Bourgeois, 1980
	Snow & Hambrick, 1980
	Quinn, 1980
	Jemison, 1981
	Kotler & Murphy, 1981
	Green & Jones, 1981
	Hayman, 1981
	Jauch & Osborn, 1981
	Gluck et al., 1982
	Chakravarthy, 1982
	Hatten, 1982
	Shirley, 1982
	Camillus, 1982
	Miles & Cameron, 1982
	Galbraith & Schendel, 1983

As interest in strategy as adaptation increased so, too, did attention to the processes by which strategy arises and is carried out. Beginning with Mintzberg's (1973) modes of strategy making, a number of discussions have been presented to deal with the social, political, and interactive components of strategy (Fahey, 1981; Ginter & White, 1982; Greenwood & Thomas, 1981; Guth, 1976; Hofer, 1976b; E. Murray, 1978; J. Murray, 1978-79; Narayanan & Fahey, 1982; Tabatoni & Jarniou, 1976). Each of the authors dealt with organizational processes in the adaptive strategy model.

Adaptive strategy rests on several assumptions. The organization and its environment are assumed to be more open to each other than is implied in the linear model. The environment is more dynamic and less susceptible to prediction in the adaptive model. It consists of competitors, trends, and—of increasing importance—stake-holders. Rather than assuming that the organization must *deal with* the environment, the adaptive model assumes that the organization must *change with* the environment.

The adaptive model attempts to take more variables and more propensity for change into account that does the linear model. Table 2 lists terms that reflect this complexity, along with those authors whose strategy definitions fit the adaptive model. It also outlines the characteristics of the model. A number of authors using the adaptive model suggest that it can successfully handle greater complexity and more variables than the linear model. However, opinion is mounting that the situation is complex in other ways.

To meet this need, a third model of strategy is emerging.

Model III: Interpretive Strategy

Development of interpretive strategy parallels recent interest in corporate culture and symbolic management outside the strategy literature (Dandridge, Mitroff, & Joyce, 1980; Deal & Kennedy, 1982; Feldman & March, 1981; Meyer & Rowan, 1977; Peters, 1978 Peters & Waterman, 1982; Pfeffer, 1981; Smircich & Morgan, 1982; Weick & Daft, 1983). The parameters of the emerging interpretive model of strategy are still unclear. However, a recurring theme suggests that the model is based on a social contract, rather than an organismic or biological view of the organization (Keeley, 1980) that fits well with the adaptive model. The social contract view portrays the organization as a collection of cooperative agreements entered into by individuals with free will. The organization's existence relies on its ability to attract enough individuals to cooperate in mutually beneficial exchange.

The interpretive model of strategy further assumes that reality is socially constructed (Berger & Luckmann, 1966). That is, reality is hot something objective or external to the perceiver that can be apprehended correctly or incorrectly. Rather, reality is defined through a process of social interchange in which perceptions are affirmed, modified, or replaced according to their apparent congruence with the perceptions of others.

Strategy in the interpretive model might be defined as orienting metaphors or frames of reference that allow the organization and its environment to be understood by organizational stakeholders. On this basis, stakeholders are motivated to believe and to act in ways that are expected to produce favorable results for the organization. "Metaphors" is plural in this definition because the maintenance of social ties in the organization precludes enforcing agreement on a single interpretation (Weick & Daft, 1983).

Pettigrew (1977) provided an early example of the interpretive model by defining strategy as the emerging product of the partial resolution of environmental and intraorganizational dilemmas. Although his emphasis on the political and processual nature of strategy might be considered compatible with the adaptive model, he offered several innovative contributions. Among them are: (1) his interest in the management of meaning and symbol construction as central components of strategy and (2) his emphasis on legitimacy, rather than profit, productivity, or other typical goals of strategy.

Van Cauwenbergh and Cool (1982) defined strategy broadly as calculated behavior in nonprogrammed situations. They went on to posit middle management's central position in the strategy formulation process, as well as to point out that managing the organizational culture is a powerful tool in the hands of top management. The authors concluded by suggesting that their views differed from the traditional strategy literature in three ways: (1) organizational reality is incoherent in nature, not coherent; (2) strategy is an organization-wide activity, not just a top management concern; and (3) motivation, not information, is the critical factor in achieving adequate strategic behavior. Congruent with these authors' interest in organizational culture, Dirsmith and Covaleski dealt with what they called strategic norms, or

> institutional level action postures...that serve to guide acceptable behavior. [S]trategic norms involve the establishment of maps of reality or images held of organizations and environments (1983, p. 137).

The new themes in these writings suggest a strategy model that depends heavily on symbols and norms. Hatten (1979) saw this change as moving from the goal orientation of the linear model to a focus on desired relationships, such as those involving sources of inputs or customers. He envisaged a new theory of strategy that was oriented toward managerial perceptions, conflict and consensus, as well as the importance of language. The relatively few entries in Table 3 indicate that the model is too new to have become well-developed.

Table 3

Summary of Interpretive Strategy	
Variable	Interpretive Strategy
Sample definition	Orienting metaphors constructed for the purpose of conceptualizing and guiding individual attitudes of organizational participants
Nature of strategy	Metaphor
	Interpretive
Focus for strategy	Participants and potential participants in the organization
Aim of strategy	Legitimacy
Strategic behaviors	Develop symbols, improve interactions and relationships
Associated terms	Strategic norms
Associated measures	Measures must be derived from context, may require qualitative assessment
Associated authors[4]	Pettigrew, 1977
	Van Cauwenbergh & Cool, 1982
	Dirsmith & Covaleski, 1983
	Chaffee, 1984

Rather than emphasizing *changing with* the environment, as is true of the adaptive model, interpretive strategy mimics linear strategy in its emphasis on *dealing with* the environment. There is, however, an important difference. The linear strategist deals with the environment by means of organizational actions that are intended to affect relations instrumentally, but the interpretive strategist deals with the environment through symbolic actions and communication.

Interpretive strategy, like adaptive strategy, assumes that the organization and its environment constitute an open system. But in interpretive strategy the organization's leaders shape the attitudes of participants and potential participants toward the organization and its outputs; they do not make physical changes in the outputs. This attitude change seeks to increase credibility for the organization or its output. In this regard, interpretive strategy overlaps with the adaptive model. For example, when an adaptive strategist focuses on marketing to enhance product credibility, the strategist's behavior could be classified as interpretive. Because strategy is multifaceted, however, examining marketing in combination with other strategic moves permits surer classification into either the adaptive or interpretive model.

A final noteworthy distinction between the adaptive and interpretive models relates to the ways in which each conceptualizes complexity. Adaptive strategy arose from and attempts to deal with structural complexity, notably conflicting and changing demands for organizational output. Interpretive strategy emphasizes attitudinal and cognitive complexity among diverse stakeholders in the organization.

Each of the three models may be summarized briefly. In linear strategy, leaders of the organization plan how they will deal with competitors to achieve their organization's goals. In adaptive strategy, the organization and its parts change, proactively or reactively, in order to be aligned with consumer preferences. In interpretive strategy, organizational representatives convey meanings that are intended to motivate stakeholders in ways that favor the organization. Each model provides a way of describing a certain aspect of organizational functioning to which the term *strategy* has been applied. By analogy, one would have three descriptions of a single phenomenon if a geologist, a climatologist, and a poet were to model the Grand Canyon.

One value of diverse models, whether they relate to strategy or the Grand Canyon, is that they provide options. In future development of strategy, one might delineate the circumstances under which one model of strategy is more appropriate than the others. However, before such delineation is warranted, the models and their interrelationships require further theoretical attention.

As noted earlier, the three strategy models may not be independent of one another, although so far they have been treated separately in both the literature cited and this discussion. The basis for suggesting that the models are interrelated is that they show some similarity to a well-known hierarchy of systems in which each level incorporates the less complex levels that precede it (Boulding, 1956). If the strategy models were analogous to the systems hierarchy, the relationships among the models would also be hierarchical. The systems hierarchy has certain similarities to the three strategy models. Certain characteristics at each set of system levels match those of one of the strategy models. Furthermore, similarities between each level of systems and one of the strategy models suggest that an organization that functions at a given level in the systems hierarchy will benefit from using the corresponding model of strategy.

Therefore, relating the strategy models to the systems hierarchy makes three contributions toward elaborating on the strategy construct. First, it suggests a means of ordering and interrelating the disparate, more narrowly focused definitions of strategy in the existing literature. Second, discrepancies between system levels and strategy models suggest areas in which the models could profitably be developed. Third, the analogy provides a bridge for moving from a survey of theoretical literature to its implications for practice.

The Hierarchy of Strategy Models

Boulding (1956) developed a nine-level hierarchical framework that was keyed to all classes of systems, including human systems. At the most basic level were three classes that Pondy and Mitroff (1979) grouped together under the metaphor of a machine. In the highest of the three machine classes, a control mechanism regulates system behavior according to an externally prescribed target or criterion. Information flows between the regulator and the system operator. Linear strategy shows similar properties in that the executive is expected to control the organization according to predetermined goals and to change the goals when circumstances warrant.

The three intermediate classes constitute the biological set, the highest of which is the internal image system. At this level, because the system has differentiated receptors, it is imbued with detailed awareness of its environment. Awareness is organized into an image, but the system is not self-conscious. Other characteristics of the biological set include its having the same internal differentiation as the environment, as well as its having a generating mechanism that produces behavior. Adaptive strategy corresponds to the biological level, in that the model calls for the organization to scan, anticipate, and respond to various elements in its environment.

Boulding's most complex set of system levels is the cultural set. It consists of the symbol processing level, in which the system is a self-conscious user of language, and the multicephalous level, a collection of individuals acting in concert and using elaborate systems of shared meaning. Boulding's third level in the cultural set is transcendental, not fully specified. The cultural set is analogous to interpretive strategy. Weick and Daft (1983) place interpretation at level 6, the highest biological level, but they identify interpretation as a cultural phenomenon. Wherever it is placed, interpretive strategy, like the cultural level of systems, emphasizes the importance of symbol manipulation, shared meaning, and cooperative actions of individuals. Although the emphases are the same, interpretive strategy is not as fully developed as its correspondence to the cultural level might imply.

Each level in Boulding's hierarchy subsumes those that preceded it. If the same were true of the strategy models, then adaptive strategy would incorporate linear strategy, and interpretive strategy would incorporate both alternative and linear strategies. Although the evolution of the strategy construct proceeded sequentially through the hierarchy, beginning at the machine level kind recently reaching the cultural level, the shift from each level to the next abandoned, rather than incorporated, the preceding level(s). Boulding's cultural level is more complex than his biological level precisely because it builds on the base of the machine and biological levels. Interpretive strategy ignores linear and adaptive strategy. Dealing with stakeholder attitudes is not inherently more complex than dealing with consumer preferences, nor is conveying productive interpretations necessarily more complex than achieving coalignment with the environment. No interpretive strategist has evaluated the extent to which linear and adaptive strategy are subsumed in the "higher" model. Moreover, the adaptive strategists have largely ignored the linear model.

Some hints at relating the three models have appeared in the literature. For example, Weick and Daft (1983) suggested that one criterion of effective interpretation is detailed knowledge of the particulars of the environment (adaptive model) so that the phenomenon to be interpreted may be seen in context. Another paper implied that the models constitute a series of stages through which the organization itself moves over time as it becomes more sophisticated and adept at strategic management (Gluck et al., 1982). The authors stated that organizations start with financial and forecast-based planning (linear model), then shift to strategic analysis (adaptive model), and finally achieve strategic management (interpretive model). Cummings (1983) outlined two major themes in the literature: management by information (linear/adaptive) and management by ideology (interpretive). Cummings argued that both themes must be integrated to achieve an instrumental organization that serves the purpose of its participants. But he did not explain in operational terms how integration occurs. In the only empirical study that relates directly to the strategy models, Chaffee (1984) found that organizations recovering from decline used adaptive strategy but it was their use of interpretive strategy that differentiated them from organizations unable to recover. However, like Cummings and like Gluck and his colleagues, Chaffee did not deal with how or why the two models were integrated in organizational functioning.

It is important to integrate each lower level model with models that represent more complex systems because organizations exhibit properties of all levels of system complexity. Adaptive and interpretive strategies that ignore less complex strategy models ignore the foundations on which they must be built if they are to reflect organizational reality. Furthermore a comprehensive interpretive strategy probably requires some planning as would fit with a linear strategy and some organizational change as would fit with an adaptive strategy; and a viable adaptive strategy may well require some linear planning. But rather than building toward a sophisticated construct that equals the complexities for which it is intended, strategists have selected three key themes and treated them separately. Each may have value as far as it goes, but none integrates all levels of complexity and options for action that are inherent in an organization.

Finding three models of strategy holds implications for organizations, for managers, and for future development of the strategy construct. Even at this point, without deepening the adaptive and interpretive models to include lower levels of complexity, the analysis specifies three diverse ways of viewing the organizational problem and three classes of potential solutions. The models may be used conceptually to examine an organizational situation and consider alternatives for coping with it. For example, a manager might consider whether predictions about the declining demand for a product are: (a) based on firm evidence that will provide sufficient lead time for a planning task force to convene and generate alternatives to deal with the decline, (b) fundamental shifts in consumer preferences that could be addressed by modifying the product or replacing it with another, or (c) symptomatic of a loss of confidence among the buying public that could be remedied by better marketing to build legitimacy.

Futhermore, strategic decision making may profit from an analysis of a given situation's level of complexity. If an organization or a problem exhibits characteristics that are predominantly mechanistic, a linear strategy is called for. Adaptive strategies can be applied when issues of supply and demand are especially salient. Complex interpretive strategies may be reserved for situations in which modifying the attitudes of organizational stakeholders is the primary key to success.

The full value of strategy cannot be realized in practical terms, however, until theorists expand the construct to reflect the real complexities of organizations. Each successive level of strategy should incorporate those that are less complex. Then researchers can examine the ways this construct behaves in real organizations. Ultimately, the construct may emerge as a unitary merger of the three models, such as an interpretive model that incorporates adaptive and linear strategy. Or it may emerge as a hierarchy of three models: a mechanistic linear model; a biological adaptive model incorporating both linear strategy; and a cultural interpretive model, incorporating both linear and adaptive strategy. Theoreticians also may find value in still greater model differentiation. Perhaps this can be done by specifying a hierarchy that contains a model of strategy for each of Boulding's nine levels of system complexity.

Whatever the end products may be—and whether or not they finally relate to Boulding's hierarchy—it is time for strategy theoreticians and researchers to begin putting the pieces together. During the past 20 years, the strategy literature has greatly evolved. Today, in fact, it has almost arrived at the point at which it is capable of reflecting the actual level of complexity at which organizations operate. The way is now open to capitalize, both theoretically and empirically, on the richness of that complexity.

Ellen Earle Chaffee is Director of the Organizational Studies Division, National Center for Higher Education Management Systems, Boulder.

Notes

[1] The research reported here was supported by a contract (#400–83–0009) from the National Institute of Education. An abbreviated version was presented at the annual meeting of the Academy of Management, Boston, 1984, and appears in the Proceedings of the meeting. The author is grateful to Jane Dutton for several excellent suggestions.

[2] Classified by their *definitions* of strategy. Classification is not intended to imply that authors omit discussion of topics relevant to other models.

[3] Classified by their *definitions* of strategy. Classification is not intended to imply that authors omit discussion of topics relevant to other models.

[4] Classified by their *definitions* of strategy. Classification is not intended to imply that authors omit discussion of topics relevant to other models.

References

Andrews, K. R. *The concept of corporate strategy.* Homewood, IL: Irwin, 1971.

Ansoff, H. I., & Hayes, R. L. "Introduction." In H. I. Ansoff, R. P. Declerck, & R. L. Hayes (Eds.), *From strategic planning to strategic management.* New York: Wiley, 1976; 1–12.

Berger, P., & Luckmann, T. *The social construction of reality.* New York: Doubleday, 1966.

Biggadike, E. R. "The contributions of Marketing to Strategic Management." *Academy of Management Review,* 1981, 6; 621–632.

Boulding, K. E. "General Systems Theory—The Skeleton of Science." *Management Science,* 1956, 2; 197–208.

Bourgeois, L. J.. Ill. Strategy and Environment: A Conceptual Integration." *Academy of Management Review,* 1980, 5; 25–39.

Camillus, J. C. "Reconciling Logical Incrementalism and Synoptic Formalism—An Integrated Approach to Designing Strategy Planning Processes." *Strategic Management Journal,* 1982, 3; 227–283.

Cannon, J. T. *Business strategy and policy.* New York: Harcourt Brace Jovanovich, 1968.

Chaffee, E. E. "Successful Strategic Management in Small Private Colleges." *Journal of Higher Education,* 1984, 55; 212–241.

Chakravarthy, B. S. "Adaptation: A Promising Metaphor for Strategic Management." *Academy of Management Review,* 1982, 7; 35–44.

Chandler, A. D., Jr. *Strategy and Structure.* Cambridge, MA: MIT Press, 1962.

Child, J. "Organizational Structure, Environment, and Performance: The Role of Strategic Choice." *Sociology,* 1972, 6; 1–22.

Cummings, L. L. "The Logics of Management." *Academy of Management Review.* 1983, 8; 532–538.

Dandridge, T. C,, Mitroff, I., & Joyce, W. F. "Organizational Symbolism: A Topic to Expand Organizational Analysis. *Academy of Management Review,* 1980, 5; 77–82.

Deal, T. E., & Kennedy, A. A. *Corporate cultures: The rites and rituals of corporate life.* Reading, MA: Addison-Wesley, 1982.

Dill, W. R. "Commentary.' In D. E. Schendel & C. W. Hofer (Eds.), *Strategic management: A new view of business policy and planning.* Boston: Little, Brown, 1979; 47–51.

Dirsmith, M. W., & Covaleski, M. A. "Strategy, External Communication and Environment Context." *Strategic Management Journal*, 1983, 4; 137–151.

Drucker, P. F. *Management: Tasks, responsibilities, practices*. New York: Harper & Row, 1974.

Fahey, L. "On Strategic Management Decision Processes. *Strategic Management Journal*, 1981, 2; 43–60.

Feldman, M., & March, J. G. "Information in Organizations as Signal and Symbol." *Administrative Science Quarterly*, 1981, 26; 171–186.

Galbraith, C., & Schendel, D. "An Empirical Analysis of Strategy Types." *Strategic Management Journal*, 1983, 4; 153–173.

Gilmore, F. F. "Formulating Strategy in Smaller Companies." *Harvard Business Review*, 1970, 49(5); 71–81.

Ginter, P. M., & White, D. D. "A Social Learning Approach to Strategic Management: Toward a Theoretical Foundation." *Academy of Management Review*, 1982, 7; 253–261.

Gluck, F., Kaufman, S., & Walleck, A. S. "The Four Phases of Strategic Management." *Journal of Business Strategy*, 1982, 2(3), 9–21.

Glueck, W. F. *Business Policy: Strategy Formation and Management Action*. New York: McGraw-Hill, 1976.

————. *Strategic Management and business policy*. New York: McGraw-Hill, 1980.

Green, J., & Jones, T. "Strategic Development as a Means of Organizational Change: Four Case Histories," *Long Range Planning*, 1981, 14(3); 58–67.

Greenwood, P., & Thomas, H. "A Review of Analytical Models in Strategic Planning." *Omega*, 1981, 9(4); 397–417.

Guth, W. D. "Toward a Social System Theory of Corporate Strategy." *Journal of Business*, 1976, 49; 374–388.

Hambrick, D. C. "Operationalizing the Concept of Business-Level Strategy in Research." *Academy of Management Review*, 1980, 5; 567–575.

————. "Some Tests of the Effectiveness and Functional Attributes of Miles and Snow's Strategic Types." *Academy Management Journal*, 1983, 26; 5–25.

Hatten, K. J. "Quantitative Research Methods in Strategic Management." In D. E. Schendel & C. W. Hofer (eds.), *Strategic management: A New View of Business Policy and Planning*. Boston: Little, Brown, 1979; 448–467.

Hatten, M. L. "Strategic Management in Not-For-Profit Organizations." *Strategic Management Journal*, 1982, 3; 89–104.

Hayman, J. *Relationship of Strategic Planning and Future Methodologies*. Paper presented at the 1981 Annual Convention of the AREA, Los Angeles, 1981.

Hofer, C. W. "Some Preliminary Research on Patterns of Strategic Behavior." *Academy of Management Proceedings*, 1973; 46–59.

————. *Conceptual Scheme for Formulating a Total Business Strategy*. Boston: HBS Case Services, 1976a.

Hofer, C. W., "Research on Strategic Planning: A Survey of Past Studies and Suggestions for Future Efforts. *Journal of Economics and Business*, 1976b, 28; 261–286.

Hofer, C. W., & Schendel, D. *Strategy Formulation: Analytical Concepts*. St. Paul, MN: West, 1978.

Jauch, L.R., & Osborn, R. N. "Toward an Integrated Theory of Strategy." *Academy of Management Review*, 1981, 6; 491–498.

Jemison, D. B. "The Contributions of Administrative Behavior to Strategic Management." *Academy of Management Review*, 1981, 6; 633–642.

Keeley, M. "Organizational Analogy: A Comparison of Organismic and Social Contract Models." *Administrative Science Quarterly*, 1980, 25; 337–362.

Kotler, P., & Murphy, P. E. "Strategic Planning for Higher Education." *Journal of Higher Education*, 1981, 52; 470–489.

Learned, E. P., Christensen, C. R., Andrews, K. R., & Guth, W. R. *Business Policy*. Homewood, IL: Irwin, 1969.

Lenz, R. T. "Strategic Capability: A Concept and Framework for Analysis," *Academy of Management Review*, 1980a, 5; 225–234.

————. "Environment, Strategy, Organization Structure and Performance: Patterns in One Industry." *Strategic Management Journal*, 1980b, 1; 209–226.

Litschert, R. J., & Bonham, T. W. "Conceptual Models of Strategy Formulation." *Academy of Management Review*, 1978, 3; 211–219.

Lorange, P., & Vancil, R. F. "How to Design a Strategic Planning System." *Harvard Business Review*, 1976, 54(5); 75–81.

Mason, R. O., & Mitroff, I. I. *Challenging Strategic Planning Assumptions*. New York: 1981.

Mazzolini, R. "How Strategic Decisions are Made." *Long Range Planning*, 1981, 14(3); 85–96.

Meyer, J. W., & Rowan, B. "Institutionalized Organizations: Formal Structure as Myth and Ceremony." *American Journal of Sociology*, 1977. 83; 340–363.

Miles, R. E., & Snow, C. C., *Organizational Strategy, Structure, and Process*." New York: McGraw-Hill, 1978.

Miles, R. E., Snow, C. C., Meyer, A. D., & Coleman, H. J., Jr. "Organizational Strategy, Structure, and Process." *Academy of Management Review*, 1978, 3; 546–563.

Miles, R. H., & Cameron, K. S. *Coffin Nails and Corporate Strategies*. Englewood Cliffs, NJ: Prentice-Hall, 1982.

Miller, D. & Friesen, P. "Archetypes of Strategy Formulation." *Management Science*, 1978, 24; 253–280.

Mintzberg, H. "Strategy-Making in Three Modes." *California Management Review*, 1973, 16(2); 44–53.

————. "Patterns in Strategy Formation." *Management Science*, 1978, 24; 934–948.

Murray, E. A. "Strategic Change as a Negotiated Outcome." *Management Science*, 1978, 24; 960–972.

Murray, J. A. "Toward a Contingency Model of Strategic Decision." *International Studies of Management and Organization* 1978–79, 8; 7–34.

Narayanan, V. K., & Fahey, L. "The Micro-Politics of Strategy Formulation." *Academy of Management Review*, 1982, 7; 25–34.

Paine, F. T., & Naumes, W. *Strategy and Policy Formation: An Integration Approach*. Philadelphia: Saunders, 1974.

Peters, T. J. "Symbols, Patterns, and Settings: An Optimistic Case for Getting Things Done." *Organizational Dynamics*, 1978, 7(2); 3–23.

Peters, T. J., & Waterman, R. H., Jr. *In Search of Excellence: Lessons From America's Best-Run Companies*. New York: Harper & Row, 1982.

Pettigrew, A. M. Strategy Formulation as a Political Process." *International Studies of Management and Organization*, 1977, 7; 78–87.

Pfeffer, J. "Management as Symbolic Action: The Creation and Maintenance of Organizational Paradigms." In L. L. Cummings & B. M. Staw (Eds.), *Research in Organizational Behavior*. Greenwood, CT: JAI Press, 1981; 1–52.

Pondy, L. R., & Mitroff, I. I. Beyond Open System Models of Organization." In B. M. Staw (Ed.), *Research in Organizational Behavior*. Greenwood, CT: JAI Press, 1979; 3–39.

Quinn, J. B. *Strategies for Change: Logical Incrementalism*. Homewood, IL: Irwin, 1980.

Rumelt, R. P. Evaluation of Strategy: Theory and Models." In D. E. Schendel & C. W. Hofer (Eds.), *Strategic Management: A New View of Business Policy and Planning*. Boston: Little, Brown, 1979; 196–212.

Shirley, R. C. Limiting the Scope of Strategy: A Decision Based Approach." *Academy of Management Review*, 1982, 7, 262–268.

Smircich, L., & Morgan, G. Leadership: The Management of Meaning." *Journal of Applied Behavioral Science*, 1982, 18(3); 257–273.

Snow, C. C., & Hambrick, D. C. "Measuring Organizational Strategies: Some Theoretical and Methodological Problems." *Academy of Management Review*, 1980, 5; 527–538.

Spender, J. C. "Commentary." In D. E. Schendel & C. W. Hofer (Eds.), *Strategic Management: A New View of Business Policy and Planning*. Boston: Little, Brown, 1979; 383–404.

Steiner, G. A. *Strategic Planning*. New York: Free, Press. 1979.

Steiner, G. A., & Miner, J. B. *Management Policy and Strategy*. New York: Macmillan, 1977.

Tabatoni, P., & Jarniou, P. "The Dynamics of Norms in Strategic Management." In H. I. Ansoff, R. P. Declerck, & R. L. Hayes (Eds.), *From Strategic Planning to Strategic Management*. London: Wiley, 1976; 29–36.

Van Cauwenbergh, A., & Cool, K. "Strategic Management in a New Framework." *Strategic Management Journal*, 1982, 3; 245–265.

Weick, K. E., & Daft, R. L. "The Effectiveness of Interpretation Systems." In K. S. Cameron & D. A. Whetten (Eds.), *Organizational Effectiveness: A Comparison of Multiple Models*. New York: Academic Press, 1983; 71–93.

Strategic Planning for Higher Education

PHILIP KOTLER AND PATRICK E. MURPHY

At least one demographic impact will be positive. Institutions will be compelled to become more introspective and analytical, to undertake long-range planning. something they did not have to do in good times. They will be forced to set priorities and develop strategies, overcome institutional inertia and make long-overdue choices—for example, to identify areas of growing student interest and create new programs to replace those for which demand may have fallen off. A consumer orientation will benefit higher education. [17, p. 23]

* * *

If colleges and universities are to survive in the troubled years ahead, a strong emphasis on planning is essential. The type of planning that appears to be most appropriate for the future is "strategic" market planning. It is one of the most revolutionary commercial sector developments in the last ten years and promises to be a potent tool for use in nonprofit organizations.

Most colleges and universities are not set up with a strategic planning capacity. They are basically good at *operations*, that is, efficiently doing the same things day after day. Patterns of operation were traditionally established to meet the environmental conditions and opportunities; the schools' manner of conducting their affairs are likely to persist long after these procedures have lost their effectiveness in new environments.

Organizational leaders—boards, major administrators, and faculty representatives—are the only ones who can modify organizations through time as the environments change. Yet few collegiate leaders are able and willing to focus systematically on change. They are largely taken up in today's operations and results. Making changes in the goals, strategies, and organizational systems usually occur as reactions to crisis events rather than as thoughtful adaptations in advance of crises.

The general notion of planning, however, is not new to higher education. For some time, many institutions have undertaken three major levels of planning. The first level refers to the *budgeting and scheduling process*. All schools are forced to do this level of planning. A second level encompasses *short-range planning*. Major areas of concern here involve recruiting of students, physical plant decisions. development efforts, and program (curricular) modifications. The majority of colleges and universities are engaged, to some degree, in short-range planning. *Long-range planning* represents the third level. This type of planning utilizes both quantitative and qualitative assessments of the external environment to determine institutional priorities and strategies. Specifically, devising the school's mission and deciding about long-range program additions or deletions are usually part of the long-range planning process.[1] Other than in the area of "exigency" planning, most planning documents do not serve as a blueprint or become institutionalized [15]. Only a few schools presently seem to be effectively using long-range planning in their organization.

Figure 1

Strategic Planning Process Model

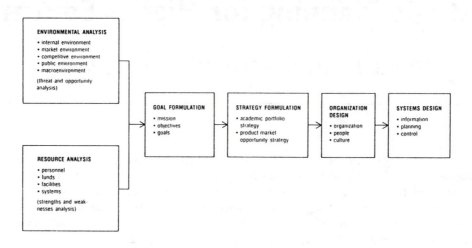

Strategic planning should not be confused with any of the planning levels currently used in higher education. It takes a long-run approach, but the focus is much more comprehensive and strategic than traditional long-range planning. *Strategic planning is defined as the process of developing and maintaining a strategic fit between the organization and its changing marketing opportunities.*

This definition suggests the appropriate steps that a college or university can take to improve itself (see Fig. 1). First, the institution must carry out a careful analysis of its *environment*, both today's and tomorrow's probable one. Then it must review its major *resources* as providing a key to what it can accomplish. The environment and resource analyses allow the organization to formulate new and appropriate *goals* that it wishes to pursue for the planning horizon. Goal formulation is followed by *strategy development* in which the most cost effective strategy is chosen for reaching the goals. The strategy will undoubtedly indicate certain changes that the institution must make in the *organization structure* if it is to implement the strategy. Finally, attention is turned to improving the organization's *systems* of information, planning, and control to permit carrying out the strategy effectively. When these components are aligned, they promise improved performance.

The strategic planning process should be completed at each major institutional level. First, the president and vice-presidents should undertake strategic planning as it affects the college or university as a whole. Then each dean (e.g., liberal arts school, business school, music school) should formulate strategic plans that impact the future of that college. In turn, each department chairperson can carry out strategic planning for the department. If a university operates branches in different locations, each branch should also utilize strategic techniques.

The president should begin the strategic planning process by setting parameters and stating organizational assumptions. This procedure is hierarchical in the context that overall goals are generally set at the top. As mentioned above, each dean and department chairperson would develop a strategic plan and send it up to the high level administrators. Then, the top administrators would examine all plans. There would likely be more than one iteration to this process. In fact, it may take on a negotiation flavor. The strategic planning process is a sequential one where the goals and broad assumptions go from the top down, but the detailed plans come from the bottom up.

Obviously, strategic planning procedures in higher education do not precisely parallel the process in a business setting. Since academic institutions are characterized by a high concentration of professionals and usually a significant amount of organizational inflexibility, planning is more democratized. The faculty senate or other faculty representatives have a crucial role to play in the planning endeavors of most colleges and universities. Therefore, administrators do not simply select the most cost-effective strategy, as business managers do, because they must consider a variety of organizational and behavioral constraints.

The stages of the strategic planning process for an academic institution will be examined using Beloit College as an example. Beloit is a nine-hundred student liberal arts college situated in southern Wisconsin. Its enrollment dropped substantially in the mid-1970s, and the administrators instituted several major changes at the school that helped to ensure the school's long-term viability. These alterations can be analyzed using the formal strategic planning procedure.[2]

Environmental Analysis

The first step in strategic planning is to carefully analyze the environment, because the environment keeps changing and calls for new organizational strategies. The major questions in an environmental audit are: (1) What are the major trends in the environment?; (2) What are the implications of these trends for the organization?; and (3) What are the most significant opportunities and threats? These questions must be examined for each major part of the organization's environment:

- *internal environment* (board of directors, administrators, faculty, and staff)
- *market environment* (traditional students, nontraditional students, alumni, source of funds, employers, and graduate schools)
- *public environment* (financial, media, government, activist, local, and general public)
- *competitive environment* (direct, type, and generic)
- *macroenvironment* (demographic, economic, technological, political, and cultural).

The aim is to produce a documented picture of the most significant environmental developments around which the organization must formulate its future goals, strategies, structures, and systems. For example, Fox [7] conducted an in-depth analysis of the macroenvironment. She described several key trends, along with their implications for colleges and universities.

For any trend analysis of an environment to be maximally useful, it should be converted into an opportunities—threats audit. A useful exercise for academic planners is to draw out several major opportunities and threats from the trend information. Threat analysis will first be described, then opportunity-analysis.

Threat Analysis

Every institution of higher education must establish some early warning system to identify and evaluate threats. A threat is defined as follows: "An *environmental threat* is a challenge posed by an unfavorable trend or specific disturbance in the environment that would lead, in the absence of purposeful action, to the stagnation, decline, or demise of an organization or one of its programs." Not all threats warrant the same attention or concern. Administrators should assess each threat according to two dimensions: (1) its potential *severity* as measured by the amount of money or prestige the organization would lose if the threat materialized and (2) its *probability* of occurrence.

Beloit College detected the following threats in the environmental analysis:

1. In the market environment, they found that most of their student body came from northern and eastern states where the college age population is projected to decline most severely in the future.
2. In the public environment, they determined that the local Beloit community was rather apathetic toward the college and might not support student employment or cooperate with class projects in the future.
3. In the competitive environment, Beloit officials felt that their direct competitors were private, prestigious, well-known institutions such as Carleton (Minnesota), Grinnell (Iowa), and Oberlin (Ohio). It was felt that these institutions might become much more aggressive in recruiting students in the 1980s.
4. In the macroenvironment, Beloit is a private school with a high tuition, and the economic environment represents a threat to them.

Table 1(A) shows an evaluation of these threats. The most serious threats—those that Beloit must monitor and be prepared to effectively respond to—are those with a severe impact and high probability (1 and 4). It can ignore threats that are low in both severity and probability, such as threat 2. Beloit should monitor, but need not prepare contingency plans, for threats such as action by competitors (3). By identifying and classifying threats, this college has a better system for knowing which environmental developments to monitor, plan for, or ignore.

Opportunity Analysis

Opportunity analysis can be potentially more important than threat analysis. By managing its threats successfully, an institution of higher education stays intact, but does not grow. But by managing its opportunities successfully, the school can make great strides forward. A marketing opportunity is defined as follows: "A *marketing opportunity* is an attractive area of relevant action in which a particular organization is likely to enjoy superior competitive advantages." Not all opportunities are equally attractive. An opportunity can be assessed in terms of two basic dimensions: (1) its potential *attractiveness* as measured by the amount of revenue or other results that an organization might value and (2) the *probability* that the institution will be successful in developing the opportunity.

Table 1

Threat and Opportunity Matrix		

A. Threat Matrix

Potential Severity	Probability of Occurrence	
	High	Low
High	1.4	3
Low		2

B. Opportunity Matrix

Potential Attractiveness	Probability of Success	
	High	Low
High	1.3	
Low	2	2

Beloit College officials determined that several marketing opportunities were open to them.

1. In a survey of employers, Beloit found that the demand for liberal arts graduates with some emphasis in applications areas was strong.
2. In the public environment, they detected that there was still strong sentiment on the part of legislators and public officials for public scholarship aid for small colleges.
3. In the competitive environment, Beloit noted that its location was reasonably close to a major metropolitan area (Chicago) and not perceived to be too distant from eastern cities.
4. In the macroenvironment, the school found that there was a local demand for self-improvement courses by the Beloit citizens.

These opportunities can be evaluated using the dimensions of attractiveness and probability shown in Table 1(B). The strongest opportunities seem to be 1 and 3. Opportunity 2 would be helpful to the college but would not make a major difference. Similarly, the school has neither the inclination nor a large enough faculty to move into the self-improvement area (opportunity 4).

Resource Analysis

Following the environmental analysis, the institution should undertake an analysis of its resource position. The purpose is to identify the major resources that the organization has (its *strengths*) and lacks (its *weaknesses*). The theory is that an organization should pursue goals, opportunities, and strategies that are suggested by, or congruent with, its strengths and avoid those where its resources would be too weak.

An institution should conduct a *resources audit* as part of this strategic planning process step. The major resources listed in Figure 1 are people, money, and facilities. The people are the faculty, administrators, and staff of the school. Beloit officials found in the resources audit that the school had an excess of faculty members given their enrollment. Therefore, it was advisable to cut the faculty by one-third, from 120 to 80 members. Although this was an arduous and unpleasant task, the move was necessitated by the severity of the situation. The quality of teaching was recognized as a strength to the institution. The monetary aspect of the resources audit includes financial strength and the ability to gain government, foundation, and alumni support, and funding for daily operations. Beloit found that its monetary situation could not be categorized as a weakness or strength. It fell into a middle range. Facilities and environment encompasses the physical plant and the geographics as well as the social environment of the school. Beloit administrators believe that its size and pleasant small-city campus are definite strengths. However, the location in the snowbelt is perceived as somewhat of a weakness. Of course, Beloit and other schools must more fully catalog internal, tangible as well as intangible strengths and weaknesses.

As a clue to developing goals, the college or university should pay closest attention to its distinctive competencies. *Distinctive competencies are those resources and abilities in which the organization is especially strong.* If a small college happens to have a strong foreign language program, it might want to consider such opportunities as starting an international studies program or an evening noncredit language program. Institutions of higher education will find it easiest to work from their strengths, although this carries the risk of over-developing their strengths rather than trying to build up a more balanced set of strengths. Furthermore, a distinctive competence may not be enough if the organization's major competitors possess the same distinctive competence. The school should pay attention primarily to those strengths in which it possesses a *differential advantage*, that is, it can out perform competitors on that dimension. For example, Georgetown University not only has an excellent international studies program, but its location in Washington, D.C., gives it a differential advantage in pursuing preeminence in this area of study.

In evaluating its strengths and weaknesses, the administration should not rely exclusively on its own perceptions, but it could initiate an *image study* of how the institution is perceived by its significant publics. For example, the provost may think the college has a fine reputation in the hard sciences, but an image study among high school counselors may reveal that they think the strength of the college is primarily in its humanities offering. A school should study how different key publics—students, parents, business firms, and others—perceive its strengths and weaknesses. The findings may reveal that the college has certain strengths and weaknesses it was not aware of, and others that it has exaggerated.

Goal Formulation

The environment and resource analyses are designed to provide the necessary, background and stimulus to administrative thinking about the basic institutional objectives and goals. Every organization at its inception is clear about its objectives. However, as the environment changes and presents new challenges, presidents and boards should review and reassess the basic mission, objectives, and goals. At some schools a review will convince participants in the planning process that the current goal structure is still clear, relevant, and effective. Other colleges and universities will find their goals clear but of diminishing appropriateness to the new environment and resource situation, while some will discover that their goals are no longer clear and that the organization is drifting.

The purpose of developing a clear set of institutional goals is precisely to keep the organization from drifting into an uncertain future. The institution needs to have a clear picture of what kind of organization it wants to look like at the end planning period. It needs to know what it wants to accomplish this year, the next year, and several years after. Goals enable the school officials to determine what they should be doing, develop effective plans, create targets for individuals' performances, and evaluate results. Without goals, whatever the organization does or achieves can be considered acceptable; there is no standard for planning or control.

The issue of institutional goals breaks into two distinct steps, namely, determining (1) what the current goals are and (2) what the goals should be. Even the image of the current goals will differ from person to person and group to group in the organization. The president may see the primary goal as upgrading the quality of the student body. the vice-president of admissions may see the primary goal as increasing the size of the student body, and the vice-president of finance may see the primary goal as increasing the percentage of nonscholarship students. The faculty as a whole may pursue the goal of a reduced teaching load to permit more time for research, whereas the administration may adopt the goal of an increased teaching load to reduce the cost of education. To define the current goals requires interviewing many individuals and groups as to what they think the institution's and their goals are (i.e., goal inventories). The resulting data will show that the school is really a coalition of several groups each giving and seeking different things from the organization.

Determining what the goals of the organization should be is an even harder task. In principle, the president or the board can unilaterally set new goals for the college for the next decade. Increasingly, however, top administrators usually find it appropriate to involve other groups (such as faculty and alumni) in the process of goal formulation. Their insights may not only be valuable, but goals are more likely to be embraced and supported because of their involvement in the process.

In carrying out the process of goal formulation, a useful step is to distinguish among three independent but related concepts, namely mission, objectives, and goals. This procedure involves establishing, first, the mission of the institution; second, the long and short-run objectives; and third, the specific current goals. The three terms are defined as follows: "Mission is the basic purpose of an organization, that is, what it is trying to accomplish; objective is a major variable that the organization will emphasize, such as student enrollment, alumni giving, reputation; and goal is an organizational objective that is made specific with respect to magnitude, time, and responsibility."

Mission

An institution of higher education exists to accomplish something in the larger environment, that is, its purpose or mission. A useful way to examine a school's mission is to answer the following questions [6]. What is our business? Who is the customer? What is our value to the customer? What will our business be? What should our business be? These simple-sounding questions are among the most difficult the college or university will ever have to answer. Successful organizations continuously raise these questions and try to answer them thoughtfully and thoroughly.

Consider these questions, for example, as they would face Beloit College. What is Beloit's business? The easy answer is that Beloit is in the *educational business*. But so is Harvard, Vassar, Indiana University, Oakton Community College, and Oral Roberts University. Beloit has to define a particular concept or brand of education if it is to stand out. Consider some possibilities. Is Beloit in the *intellectual training business* so that its students are highly knowledgeable and perceptive about the world they live in? Is Beloit in the *personal growth business* where it aims to help its students develop their total personhood—intellectually, emotionally, and socially" Is Beloit in the *college fun and games business* where it aims to give students the "best time of their lives" before becoming adults? Each definition implies a different customer and a different way of rendering value to the customer.

A growing number of schools are deciding to write formal *mission statements* to gain the needed clarity. They realize that defining the mission is critically important because it affects everything else. A well worked out mission statement provides the institution with a shared sense of opportunity, direction, significance, and achievement. The mission statements acts as an "invisible hand" that guides a college or university's diverse personnel to work independently and yet collectively toward the realization of the organization's goals.

Unfortunately, it is not easy to write a meaningful mission statement. The planning committee may have to meet many times and interview many people before it can prepare a meaningful one. The time is not wasted because in the process it may discover much about the institution and its latent opportunities. An effective mission statement should be *market-oriented, feasible, motivating,* and *specific* [13 pp. 75-76].

After evaluating its goals in light of market realities, Beloit's mission statement was altered to include career preparation as well as intellectual training. The key phrase that was added stated: "An awareness of the available career options together with the skills to perceive those options." This addition to Beloit's mission statement should serve it for many years.

Objectives

The mission statement describes the institutional commitments rather than the specific objectives and goals it will pursue in the coming period. Therefore, each institution has to move toward developing major objectives and goals for the coming period separate from but consistent with its mission statement. Ideally, the same type of thoughtful study that led to the mission statements will also characterize the objectives and goals setting process.

For every type of institution, there is always a potential set of relevant objectives, and the task is to make choices among them. For example, the objectives of interest to a college are: increased national reputation, improved classroom teaching, higher enrollment, higher quality students, increased efficiency, larger endowment, improved student social life, improved physical plant, lower operating deficit, and so on. The institution cannot successfully pursue all of these objectives simultaneously because of a limited budget and various tradeoffs, such as between increased cost efficiency and improved classroom teaching. In any given year, therefore, institutions will choose to emphasize certain objectives and either ignore others or treat them as constraints. For example, if Beloit's enrollment were to fall, Beloit would likely make increased enrollment a paramount objective subject to not letting student quality fall below a certain level. Thus, an institution's major objectives can vary from year to year depending on the administration's perception of the major problems, or opportunities, that the school faces at that time.

Goals

Next, an institution's objectives for the coming year should be restated in operational and measurable form, called *goals*. The objective "increased enrollment" must be turned into a goal, such as "increasing enrollment of the next academic year class by 15 percent." A goal statement permits the college or university to think about the planning, programming, and controlling aspects of pursuing that objective. Such questions arise as: Is a 15 percent enrollment increase feasible? What strategy would be used? What resources would it take? What activities would have to be carried out? Who would be responsible and accountable? All of these critical questions must be answered when deciding whether to adopt a proposed goal.

Typically, the institution will be evaluating a large set of potential goals at the same time and examining them for their consistency and priorities. The school may discover that it cannot simultaneously achieve "a 15 percent enrollment increase" and "a 10 percent increase in student quality," given its limited marketing budget. In this case, the planning committee may make adjustments in the target levels or target dates, or drop certain goals altogether in order to arrive at a meaningful and achievable set of goals.[3]

Strategy Formulation

After an institution formulates its mission and goals, it must determine strategies that will help it achieve its goals. The college may discover that it cannot find a feasible strategy to deliver an enrollment increase. If so, the planners will have to return to the goal formulation stage to reconsider its goals before determining a final set of strategies.

In developing feasible strategies, the organization should undertake two tasks. First, it should devise an *academic portfolio strategy*, that is, decide what to do with its current major products (programs). Second, it should develop a *product/market opportunity strategy*, that is, decide what new products and markets to add. Although these strategies are discussed sequentially, they probably, should be conducted concurrently and evaluated with respect to one another.

Academic Portfolio Strategy

Once institutional and marketing objectives and goals are set, the administration should examine its current academic portfolio. Just as investors review their portfolio periodically, so must a college or university evaluate its academic programs from time to time. In the 1960s colleges and universities continued to add courses and programs to satisfy demand, because there was enough budget to support all departments. However, in the 1970s many schools began to experience a financial crunch. Administrators were forced to identify the stronger programs and maintain full support for them, while taking funds out of their weaker programs.

Industry also experienced financial stringency in recent years, and many companies have examined their product line with a product portfolio tool developed by the Boston Consulting Group. Each product is either classified as a *star* (high market growth, high market share);

cash cow (low growth, high share); *question mark* (high growth, low share), or *dog* (low growth, low share) [1]. Stars are to be *built*, cash cows *maintained*, questions marks *built or dropped*, and dogs *dropped*. This tool has proven to be quite successful in the corporate setting. These characterizations have been applied to analyze British and U. S. universities [5, 16].

Table 2 suggests an alternative portfolio evaluation tool that we feel academic planners can better utilize. The two primary dimensions of this portfolio are *centrality* to the institutional mission and the *quality level* of the program. The third dimension, *market viability*, is shown in the table in parentheses. Academic programs were chosen as the unit for analysis in this illustration, but schools in a multiunit system or specific courses could also be utilized. Three levels (high, medium, and low) exist for all three dimensions. High quality is equated with national eminence, medium quality with average national strength, and low quality, means that the program is judged to be mediocre or poor. The levels within the centrality dimension are self-explanatory. A judgment on the levels within market viability should be evident from the information collected in the environmental analysis section.

Table 2

Academic Portfolio Evaluation Tool			
	Centrality		
Quality	High	Medium	Low
High	Psychology (MV-H)* Decision: Build Size Build quality		Home Economics (MV-H) Decision: Build size Hold quality
Medium		Geography (MV-M) Decision: Hold size Hold quality	
Low	Philosophy (MV-L) Decision: –Reduce size		Classical Languages (MV-L) Decision: Reduce size or terminate

*(MV-H. M. L.) = Market Value   High, Medium, or Low

There are many possible ways to judge the quality of an institution's various programs. Outside experts (faculty from other schools) may be asked to evaluate the research productivity of the department and content of the courses. Alternately, the percentage of graduates who go on to graduate school or are employed by national firms may be a surrogate measure of quality. Some independent agency's findings can also be utilized to measure quality.

The school shown in Table 2 has a strong liberal arts tradition. (The school shown in the table is hypothetical.) Psychology and philosophy are judged to be high on the centrality, scale, but philosophy is low in quality and market viability. The strategies that the higher education planner can use to deal with the academic programs are to *build, hold, reduce,* or *terminate*. Since the home economics department scores high on the quality and market viability dimensions, a plausible strategy would be to hold quality and build size. On the other hand. the philosophy department that is central to the university's mission, but is low in quality and market viability, should probably be reduced in size while building its quality.

Because classical languages is low on all scales, it should probably be terminated as a department. Certain courses, though, may remain a part of another program.

A number of institutions have been evaluating their programs in recent years. The academic portfolio evaluation procedure represents a more systematic approach to handling these difficult program decisions. Application of the portfolio analysis resulted in Northwestern University's recent reduction in the size of its geography department.

Product/Market Opportunity Strategy

A formidable challenge facing colleges and universities revolves around how they will maintain enrollment, if not grow, in the future. The strategic planning process formally addresses this issue. Table 3 depicts the opportunity matrix using products (programs) and markets as the variables. (See earlier definition of marketing opportunity.)

Table 3

Product Market Opportunity Strategy

| Markets | Products | | |
	Existing	Modified	New
Existing	1. Market Penetration	4. Product Modification short courses evening program weekend program new delivery system	7. Product Innovation new courses new departments new schools
Geographical	2. Geographical Expansion new areas of city new cities foreign	5. Modification for Dispersed Markets programs offered on military bases or at U.S. firms based abroad	8. Geographic Innovation

New	3. New Markets
	
	A. Individual
	   senior citizens
	   homemakers
	   ethnic minorities
	B. Institutional
	   business firms
	   social agencies
		6. Modification for New Markets
		
		A. Individual
		   senior citizens
		
		B. Institutional
		   business
		   government
			9. Total Innovation
			
			new courses
			new departments
			new schools

Cell number one is labeled *market penetration*. Under this strategy the institution seeks to gain larger numbers of students similar to those enrolled by relying on existing programs. Possibly, a state university in a large city with a low market share may utilize this strategy. Heavy promotion (i.e., increasing recruiting budget) would be essential to making this strategy work. However, given future demographics, this strategy would be inadequate for most schools.

Geographic expansion of existing programs allows institutions to discover new market opportunities for current courses (cell 2). This strategy is being implemented by many colleges and universities. Some hold classes in grade or high schools in their towns. Southern Methodist University of Dallas is offering courses in their MBA program in Houston. Similarly, Antioch College has established campuses in foreign countries. Significant geographic expansion may not be feasible for many institutions, however, because of resource requirements.

A third possible opportunity exists for schools interested in expanding existing products to *new markets*. Colleges and universities have been increasing their recruiting of nontraditional student groups, such as senior citizens, homemakers, and ethnic minorities. Women are being more directly served by larger numbers of institutions. Furthermore, educational opportunity programs on many campuses aim to attract more minority students. Finally, large business firms and some social agencies are inviting colleges to present courses on their premises to their employees.

Programs can be *modified* to appeal to existing markets (cell 4). Addition of evening programs for schools in large cities is an obvious possibility. Weekend programs can attract students not able to attend regular classes. For example, Alverno College, a private women's school in Milwaukee, instituted a weekend college and drew large numbers of housewives and employed women. A fine illustration of a new delivery system is Adelphi University's offering of courses on a commuter train between New York and several suburban locations. Administrators are constrained only by their imagination in developing these potential opportunities.

The fifth cell is named *modification for dispersed markets*. Colleges such as the University of Maryland that offer courses and programs for members of the armed forces both domestically and abroad are examples of this approach. Industrial firms with large pockets of concentrated overseas employment may represent an untapped market.

Product *modification for new markets* (cell 6) may be a more realistic avenue for growth of colleges and universities. It seems that to successfully penetrate the retired market may require a restructuring of courses and registration procedures. Specifically, the time period may need to be shorter, with less reading required, more comfortable seats, and possibly books with larger print. Iowa State has instituted "Elder-college" for retired adults. Similarly, business firms and government agencies may be relatively attractive markets for courses in sharpening communications skills. However, the English and speech departments would probably have to develop new courses to meet these particular needs.

The seventh opportunity category shown in Table 3 is labeled *product innovation*. Here, new courses, departments, or schools are developed for existing markets. Realistically, few schools, other than those located in the sunbelt, will be expanding in the future. An example of this strategy, though, was recently employed by the University of Houston, which purchased a downtown junior college and expanded it into a four-year school.

Geographic innovation can be accomplished by using technological breakthroughs. For instance, Illinois Bell has developed an electronic blackboard that allows a professor to write on a blackboard in one location and have it transmitted over telephone lines to a distant city. With the advent of home computers, interactive television, and other new media technologies, it will be possible to offer courses to a national audience.

The final category, *total innovation*, refers to offering new products for new markets. The "university without walls" that offers specialized programs for groups such as government agencies is an example. Competition for traditional higher education may increasingly come from corporate schools modeled after McDonald's Hamburger University. However, the notion of total innovation may not be a viable growth opportunity for most traditional institutions of higher education.

The product market opportunity matrix essentially helps the administration imagine new options in a systematic way. The hard work then begins when the various opportunities have to be evaluated according to their centrality, cost, market viability. and other appropriate criteria. Once the long-range strategy formulation is complete, the short-term step is to develop a marketing strategy for these market or product opportunities [12].

Organization Design

The purpose of strategy formulation is to develop strategies that can be carried out by the institution to achieve its goals. This presumes that the organization is capable of carrying out the strategies. It must have the structure, people, and culture to successfully implement each strategy. For example, if a college plans to build its reputation in the hard sciences, it will need a faculty that is strong in certain disciplines. Clearly, an organization's chosen strategies require certain structures to succeed. Most organization theorists believe that "structure should follow strategy" [3]. However, organizational structures in higher education are often hard to change, and growth opportunities are limited because of the need to satisfy internal constituents.

Under dynamic strategic planning, not only is it necessary to transform the organizational structure if required by the strategic thrust, but it may also be necessary to retrain or change some of the people who occupy sensitive positions in the organization. Thus, if a private college decides to change its fund raising strategy from reliance on wealthy donors to foundations, the vice-president of development who is used to "old-boy-network" fund raising may need retraining in "foundation grantpersonship" or be replaced with a foundation-oriented development vice-president.

In adopting a new strategic posture, the school may also have to develop a plan for changing the "culture" of the organization. Every organization has a culture, that is, its people share a certain way of looking at things. Colleges have an "academic culture," one that prizes academic freedom, highmindedness, abstract theorizing, and so on. The academic culture is often an outspoken critic of the "business culture" (profit as a worthwhile end) and the "marketing culture" (that institutions have to serve and satisfy their publics). College presidents who attempt to have their faculties improve their teaching, spend more time with students, develop new courses for nontraditional markets, and so on, often encounter tremendous resistance. With the growing shortage of students, the challenge facing the president is to develop a marketing orientation with the faculty in which everyone sees his or her job as sensing, serving, and satisfying markets. Changing the culture of an organization is a mammoth task, but one that may be essential if the organization is to survive in the new environment [2].

Systems Design

The last major step in strategic planning is to design or upgrade the systems that the organization needs to develop and carry out the strategies that will achieve its goals in the new environment. The three principal systems needed by an organization to be effective at strategic market planning are discussed below. They should be viewed as co-equal and interacting.

Marketing Information System

The job of effectively running an institution calls for a great amount of information about students, alumni, competitors, publics, and the larger macroenvironmental forces (demography, economy, politics, technology, and culture). This information can be obtained through student enrollment analysis, marketing intelligence, and marketing research. The information, if it is to be useful, must be accurate, timely, and comprehensive.

Marketing Planning System

Many organizations gather information but fail to use it in a disciplined fashion. More and more colleges and universities are becoming convinced of the benefits of operating a formal planning system in which long-term and annual goals, strategies, marketing programs, and budgets are developed at a regular time each year. The planning discipline calls for a planning staff, planning resources, and a planning culture if it is to be successful. It is our contention that discipline is essential if the organization hopes to achieve optimal marketplace results.

Marketing Control System

Plans are only useful if they are going to be implemented and monitored. The purpose of a marketing control system is to measure the ongoing results of a plan against the plan's goals and to take corrective action.[4] The corrective action may be to change the goals or plans or the implementation in light of new circumstances. If strategic planning is to have an impact in institutions of higher education, control systems must be instituted.

Conclusion

This article outlined the framework necessary for achieving a strategic planning posture in higher education. However, the implementation of this process was not explicitly addressed. Other authors have provided specific timetables for carrying out this procedure [9, 10].

The most important benefit of strategic planning for higher education decision makers is that it forces them to undertake a more market-oriented and systematic approach to long-range planning. The future that appears to hold many threats for most colleges and universities should become less imposing with the judicious use of strategic planning.

Philip Kotler is Harold T. Martin Professor of Marketing, Northwestern University. Patrick E. Murphy is associate professor of marketing, Marquette University.

Notes

[1]For a discussion of the increasing role of the public policymakers in academic planning, see [8].

[2] The authors would like to express their appreciation to Zeddie P. Bowen, provost of Beloit College, for providing information about his school. For more discussion on Beloit's planning see [14].

[3] For an advanced example of goal setting used at Stanford University see [11].

[4] For another approach to this subject see [4].

References

Abell, D. F., and J. S. Hammond, *Strategic Market Planning: Problems and Analytical Approaches.* Englewood Cliffs. N.J.: Prentice-Hall, 1979.

Caren. W. L., and F. R. Kemerer. "The Internal Dimensions of Institutional Marketing." *College and University*, (Spring 1979), 173–88.

Chandler, A. D. *Strategy and Structure.* Cambridge, Mass.: MIT Press, 1962.

Cranton, P. A., and L. H. Legge. "Program Evaluation in Higher Education." *Journal of Higher Education*, 49 (September/October 1978). 464–71.

Doyle, P.. and J. E. Lynch. "A Strategic Model for University Planning." *Journal of the Operations Research Society*, (July 1979). 603–9.

Drucker, P. *Management: Tasks, Responsibilities, Practices.* Chapter 7. New York: Harper & Row. 1973.

Fox, K. F. A. *Attracting a New Market to Northwestern's Undergraduate Programs: Older Women Living on the North Shore.* Evanston, Ill.: Program on Women, Northwestern University, 1979.

Fuller, B. "A Framework for Academic Planning." *Journal of Higher Education*, 48 (January/February 177), 65–77.

Gaither, G. H. "The Imperative to Plan in Higher Education." *North Central Association Quarterly,* (Fall 1977), 347–55.

Hollowood. J. R. "College and University Strategic Planning." Working paper. Cambridge, Mass.: Arthur D. Little, August 1979.

Hopkins. D. P., J. C. Larreche, and W. F. Massy. "Constrained Optimization of a University Administrator's Preference Function." *Management Science,* (December 1977), 365–77.

Kotler, P. *Marketing for Nonprofit Organizations.* Englewood Cliffs, N.J.: Prentice-Hall, 1975.

———. *Principles of Marketing.* Englewood Cliffs, N.J.: Prentice-Hall, 1980.

May, R. B. "One College's Struggle May Aid Other Schools Worried About Slump." *The Wall Street Journal,* (January 10, 1979), 1.

Moore, M. A. "On Launching Into Exigency Planning." *Journal of Higher Education,* 49 (November/ December 1978), 620–38.

Newbould, G. N. "Product Portfolio Diagnosis for U. S. Universities." *Akron Business and Economic Review,* (Spring 1980), 39–45.

Stewart, I. R., and D. G. Dickason. "Hard Times Ahead." *American Demographics,* June 1979.

The Role of Rationality in University Budgeting

ELLEN E. CHAFFEE

Rational decision making is generally conceded to be a normative ideal, but not susceptible to practice. It is thought to be unrealistic because rational theory prescribes an ordered sequence of events that cannot be followed in real decisions, and because it requires powers of search and comprehension that human beings do not have for most decision problems of typical complexity (Cyert and March, 1963; Cyert, Simon, and Trow, 1956; George, 1975; Nutt, 1976; Simon, 1955, 1976).

Because of such implementation problems, actual decision processes are rarely described as rational. However, in at least one case, participants in and observers of an annual decision process that reoccurred for almost 10 years believed that it was rational (George, 1980; Poulton, 1979). The process was allocation of general funds to academic departments at Stanford University during the 1970s. The purpose of this study is to test whether Stanford's budget decision process in the 1970s was rational.

The literature on decision making is vast, having sizable components within such varied disciplines as economics, operations research, political science, psychology, social psychology, sociology, business policy, and organizational behavior. Therefore, the term "rational decision making" might properly evoke images of diverse levels of analysis (individual, collective, group, and organization), several categories of operational variables (such as decision rules, organizational structure, longitudinal processes, or cognitive functions), and a host of definitions of rationality, ranging from the formal, precise, technical version of the economist to the vague connotations of sensibility and reasonableness of the layperson (see, for example, Diesing, 1962, Garfinkel, 1960, and March, 1978).

Specifically, this is a study of the decision process used by an organization. The purpose is to determine the extent to which that process conformed to a selected theory of rational choice. Because it is a study of decision *process*, several steps in decision making and patterns of interaction among participants over time will be examined. The phenomenon is dynamic, not static. Because it is a study of *organizational* decision making, the cognitive processes of a single individual are not the focus; rather, I will examine the nature of the interactions among several individuals, their inputs to a decision maker, and his choices. Because it is a study of *rational choice*, it is rational theory that directs the identification of the stages and interaction patterns in the organization. The theory selected is a behavioral model, called bounded rationality, proposed by Simon (1955, 1976, 1979). Simon developed bounded rationality as a realistic alternative to economic rationality.

Literature Review

Many organization-level theories of decision making have been proposed. Political science provides models of partisan mutual adjustment (Lindblom, 1959), multiple advocacy (George, 1975), and governmental politics (Allison, 1971), among others. Collegiality is widely known, its parameters for higher education described by Millett (1962). The bureaucratic model, first presented by Weber (1947), has come to have two connotations. Weber's ideal type was essentially the rational model, institutionalized in an efficient, hierarchical structure. However, Allison differentiated the rational model from what he called the organizational process model, and it was the latter which he traced back to Weber's work (1971, p. 298). Following Allison, the bureaucratic model will here refer to the use of standard patterns of organizational behavior whose rather mechanical outputs constitute decisions. Finally, one of the newer models is organized anarchy (Cohen and March, 1974).

These models can be clustered by type, with headings such as rational, political, bureaucratic, consensual, or loosely coupled systems. It is the rational class of models that is of interest here.

Rational Decision Making

Classic economic rationality underlies the theory of the firm, asserting two basic assumptions: that firms have a specific goal (profit maximization) and that firms operate with perfect knowledge of alternatives and consequences (Cyert and March, 1963, p. 8). Nutt (1976) calls the economic model "normative decision theory," listing these as its key assumptions: goals are known, needed information is obtainable, adequate resources are available, prediction is feasible, effects are judged according to criteria, and cause-effect relations are known (p. 86). This version of rationality is criticized for two major problems: the motivational and cognitive assumptions of the theory are unrealistic, and the firm in theory is much less complex than the firm in practice (Cyert and March, 1963, p. 8).

Simon relaxed some of these assumptions in creating bounded rationality, primarily by allowing the choosing organism to select a satisfactory alternative rather than the single best alternative. Nutt's version of Simon's theory is called behavioral decision theory, with these assumptions: goals are inferrable through domain decisions; alternatives cannot be completely known; some predictions can be made, but not all of them; and resources interact with decision processes (1976, p. 86). This model describes what "skillful decision makers often *try* to do when grappling with complex decisions" (Nutt, 1976, p. 89). March comments that bounded rationality has come to be widely recognized "both as an accurate portrayal of much choice behavior and as a normatively sensible adjustment to the costs and character of information gathering and processing by human beings" (1978, p. 589). The references that support March's statement, however, are not studies of organizational decision processes; they are studies from mathematics and operations research.

Empirical Studies

The rational actor model proposed by Allison (1971) is based on Simon's bounded rationality. Allison defined rational decision making to consist of four elements: goals, alternatives, consequences, and selection of those alternatives whose consequences rank highest among the decision maker's values. Allison used these elements to examine rationality and two other models through a qualitative, historical analysis of the Cuban missile crisis. Later Weil (1975) used two of Allison's models for a study of North Vietnamese foreign policy, combining quantitative and qualitative analyses.

Other studies of rational decision making at the organizational level of analysis have used other models of rationality. Cyert et al., (1956) used a case analysis of the decision to buy electronic data processing hardware to illustrate (1) the inadequacies of the classic rational decision model and (2) that an unstructured decision process could be programmed. Carter (1971) used the behavioral theory of the firm that was proposed by Cyert and March (1963) to study six top-level corporate planning decisions. The Cyert and March model was combined with

Cohen and March's organized anarchy (1974) in a study of university budget decision making under stress (Rubin, 1977). Personnel decision making in public agencies was studied quantitatively on the basis of participant survey data by Nalbandian and Klinger (1980). These authors equated rationality with computational strategy, which is expected when participants agree on organizational goals and on the means to achieve them (Thompson, 1967). Skok (1980) produced a study of state budget decision making that compared incrementalism with rational-comprehensive budgeting, defining the latter as zero-based, data-influenced choice.

In three previous university budget studies, the authors regressed each department's share of the annual operating budget (or a similar measure) on each department's score for a quantitative variable that represented a decision model (Pfeffer and Salancik, 1974; Hills and Mahoney, 1978; Pfeffer and Moore, 1980). In one case, for example, the authors used student credit hours as a measure of the bureaucratic model (a term which they used interchangeably with the rational model) and faculty representation on university policy committees as a measure of the political model. This approach is based on the fact that each decision model has a rule by which one alternative is chosen rather than another. In the rational-bureaucratic model, the inferred rule is automatic fair-share allocation based on workload; in the political model, the rule is to allocate more resources to more powerful parties. The present study is based on the premise that the decision rule approach provides insufficient evidence to infer a complex decision model.

The only common element in these studies is that they dealt with what each called rational decision making at the organizational level of analysis. They differ substantially in the kinds of decisions they examined, the kinds of organizational settings they used, the ways they defined rationality, and their empirical methods. Only two (Allison, 1971; Weil, 1975) explicitly tested, as this study does, for the extent to which a rational decision model generally characterized patterns in organizational processes with respect to a specific decision. The others examined the extent to which selected rational behaviors (search for information, computation, choice criteria) were used. Allison and Weil shared a single major finding: decisions do not correspond neatly to a single decision model: they vary both within and across levels of analysis.

Research Method

The two major methodological problems in studying organizational decision processes are (1) participants are not a good source of retrospective data with regard to what they did and why, and (2) the target is a moving one — a process that unfolds over time and is composed of diverse elements. With regard to the first problem, Nisbet and Wilson (1977) reviewed a large number of studies, concluding that individuals have little or no ability to report their cognitive preferences accurately. What is reported is usually based on some implicit theory or on past behavior, not on true preferences. The study of rational decision making depends in part upon matching choice behavior with prior preferences. So the fact that there is a weak correlation between reported self-insight and objective choices (Slovic and Lichtenstein, 1971), and that the theories in people's heads frequently do not match the theories they act upon (Argyris and Schon, 1978; Van Maanen, 1979) is a problem: how does one identify true prior preferences, rather than post-hoc justifications? The problem is confounded by the normative value of rational decision making: people are likely to bias their preference list toward the appearance of rationality because it is widely preferred.

A research method that is variously called policy capturing (Slovic and Lichtenstein, 1971), judgment analysis (Rohrbaugh, 1978), or multiattribute theory (Huber, 1974) helps solve this problem. Respondents are presented with hypothetical choices. The choices are set up so that analyzing the responses allows one to see the tradeoffs made and thereby infer the preference function of the respondent. In the case of budget research, where real decisions have measurable outcomes, hypothetical problems are not required. If the implicit tradeoff characteristics of the alternatives can also be measured, policy-capturing research can use actual field data. This was the approach used in the three previous university budget studies cited above (Pfeffer and Salancik, 1974; Hills and Mahoney, 1978; Pfeffer and Moore, 1980). Viewing the organization anthropomorphically, the method of previous budget studies tested the organization's value structure by policy capturing, asking the question, "Did the organization allocate resources by a bureaucratic decision rule, or by a political decision rule?"

Policy capturing is used as part of the Stanford test, but the decision maker determines the decision model variables; they are not intrinsic in the model itself. In the rational model, unlike the bureaucratic and political models, the decision rule is to maximize a set of values that cannot be inferred generically. Therefore, before policy capturing can be used here, a specific set of budget-related values held at Stanford during the 1970s must be identified.

Policy capturing does not solve the second problem, how to analyze the stages and events of the dynamic decision process. First, the stages as they are prescribed by theory must be identified; then a method or methods must be devised for determining whether Stanford exhibited those behaviors. As previously stated, I will use the stages of bounded rationality from Simon (1955), but as operationalized by Allison, who notes that his model is more stringent and closer to economic rationality than is Simon's (1971, p. 288). The Allison model is, in fact, similar to a description of economic rationality in Cyert et al. (1956).

The stages are outlined in Table 1. The elements that must be present for rational decision making are goals that are known before the decision is made, an extensive set of alternatives from which to choose, consequences that are reasonably well understood, and a choice that satisfies the preferences. Implicit in this list is a chronological order, requiring primarily that goals be available early and that deliberation on alternatives and consequences precede choice.

Table 1

Criteria to Test for the Rational Model at Stanford	
Rational Model Decision Element	Criterion
Goals Known, a priori preference function consistent the	Stanford's provost had and expressed a set of budget allocation priorities throughout 1970s.
Alternatives Search for means to desired ends expenditure	The provost considered a wide range of alternatives, making his selections simultaneously rather than sequentially.
Consequences Likelihood of producing desired outcomes	The provost considered all the expenditure alternatives with information about their costs and benefits.
Choice Select the maximizing alternative that	The provost chose expenditure alternatives enacted his set of budget allocation priorities.

Next, the research method required observable criteria for these stages, which are also presented in Table 1. If these criteria are satisfied by various kinds of evidence, to be discussed below, then the Stanford budget process is inferred to exhibit the corresponding elements of the rational model. Operationally, the study required that the provost, who directed Stanford's budget process, show evidence of a consistent set of budget allocation priorities throughout the decade of the study (prior goals); that he show evidence of considering a wide range of expenditure alternatives simultaneously rather than sequentially (extensive alternatives with opportunity for tradeoff analysis); that he make budget decisions himself, with information for each request about its likely effects and costs (understood consequences); and that his choices be consistent with his prior goals (satisficing choice).

An eclectic research method is required to handle the diversity in these criteria. The approach amounts to triangulation (Webb et al., 1966; Denzin, 1978; Campbell and Fiske, 1959) in which the convergence of two methods ". . . enhances our belief that the results are valid and not a methodological artifact" (Bouchard, 1976, p. 268). Wherever possible, the strategy was to use multiple methods for analyzing the multiple traits of the rational model. In addition, simply having divided the rational model into four separately tested elements ensures four tests for the model.

There are two major concerns in triangulation. One is how to recognize when evidence has converged, given the likelihood that evidence will be ambiguous or necessarily incomplete. The other is assigning relative weights or values to pieces of evidence (Jick, 1979). Is one document more convincing than another because of its source? Is content analysis more persuasive than survey results? Such concerns must be dealt with as a matter of judgment.

The study focused on allocations of general funds in the operating budget to 38 academic departments at Stanford during 1970 through 1979. The provost and primary decision maker was William F. Miller. The departments were members of the Schools of Humanities and Sciences, Engineering, and Earth Sciences, excluding only the departments in those schools that did not exist for the entire 10-year period. Four other schools at Stanford were excluded because none of the four was subdivided into academic departments and two of the four received funds in a special budget process that was unlike the one under study.

Results

Criterion 1: Goals

The first criterion required that the provost have a consistent set of priorities regarding what he was interested in funding from the operating budget, and that he express it early in his term and consistently throughout the 1970s.[1] In a 1972 report, Miller listed these "principal elements that enter a decision about the future of a program":

1. Academic importance
2. Student interest
3. Possibility for excellence in the program
4. Funding potential (1972b, p. 3).

These items are reiterated as four necessary conditions of a program in the draft of a document on the budget process prepared by Miller's vice provost, Raymond F. Bacchetti (letter to Miller, 26 July 1972). In a 1975 letter, Miller identified them as the four criteria he had often expressed for establishment of a program (6 January 1975). Miller used two of the four in both internal and public justifications for eliminating the department of architecture (3 June 1975, 20 July 1975). Later, he called the four items fundamental criteria for judging academic programs (1978). Miller explicitly applied the four criteria to his annual budget decisions both in the "Operating Budget Guidelines" (1975) and in a later interview (25 July 1980). Although there is some indication that Miller intended to use two of the four criteria, academic importance and funding potential, less for budget decisions and more for decisions about starting or terminating a program (1978, 1980), he generally seems to have intended these four criteria to guide his decisions about allocating general funds in the operating budgets. This frequent and consistent reiteration appears to satisfy the first criterion for the rational model.

Criterion 2: Alternatives

Second, in a rational process the provost would simultaneously consider a wide array of spending alternatives every year. The key terms to be tested are "simultaneously" and "wide array." The test is simplified by the fact that the chronology of budgeting events each year remained essentially the same throughout Miller's term of office.

In a memo to the president, Miller stated his intention to "form a protocol here that will require the studies within each of the Schools of enrollment, retirement, etc." (5 October 1971). A memo to Miller from Vice Provost Bacchetti (29 February 1972) outlines a chronology of events for operating budget decisions. This same chronology is reiterated in the 1973 and 1974 protocol letters from Miller to the deans (4 October 1973, 21 October 1974) and in every edition of the annual booklet called "Operating Budget Guidelines" published from 1973 through 1980. The annual sequence of events was remarkably stable throughout the decade; the question is, did it allow for simultaneous consideration of a wide array of alternatives?

Each of these chronologies shows an 18-month sequence of events. Within that sequence is a four-month "protocol process." Each year the provost wrote to the deans describing apparent constraints on the budget and posing detailed questions about the school's plans. He then met with them individually to discuss their wishes and his convictions, and each dean wrote a budget letter detailing his requests. Since the provost decided all across-the-board rates of increase outside of the process described here (for example, 7% on faculty salaries, 5% on travel), these deans' requests dealt with special items requiring increases greater than the incremental changes.

The vice provost then prepared a detailed list of all such requests for the provost's consideration. This list and the documentation provided by the deans gave the provost the opportunity to consider alternative expenditures simultaneously. Furthermore, there is evidence that the provost rejected attempts to bring requests forward for a decision at some other time when tradeoff values could not have been considered (Miller, 23 November 1971, 13 October 1972).

Whether the provost had a wide range of alternatives to consider is a matter of judgment. Each dean probably screened out many requests from departments so that the provost never saw them. However, the provost certainly had many alternatives. In the seven years for which complete sets of dean's budget letters could be found, 284 requests for funds were made on behalf of the 38 departments in the study. Averaging 40.6 requests per year, the provost had just over one request per department per year with a mean of $9255 per request. These figures assume some proportion when viewed in terms of the rate at which they were funded. Documentation of the provost's decisions was available for the last four years of the study. During that time, the provost had 156 requests. He authorized general funds in 97 (62%) of the cases, but full funding for only 36 requests (23%). The provost therefore had four times as many alternatives as he thought merited full funding, and 1.6 times as many as he thought merited any general funds.

The evidence for simultaneous decisions is unequivocal. The evidence for quantity of alternatives shows that he had many more than he could or would fund, but this is not a criterion that allows for unequivocal assessment.

Criterion 3: Consequences

The third criterion deals with the quality of information available to the provost: Was it sufficient to allow him to relate requests to his preferences through some understanding of causes and effects?

Miller was quite clear in his expectation that deans' budget letters would provide him with objective information. "In all the reviews ... reliance will be placed heavily upon systematic evidence and carefully considered judgments. . . . Unsupported views and anecdotal evidence of value will be of little assistance. . . ." (21 October 1974). In 1978, Miller asked for "supporting argument and where relevant and available, documentation" for each budget request in the deans' letters (15 October 1978). These letters were not Miller's only source of information, however: "Though we have both been working on the 1975-6 budget since at least last May, the transmittal of the accompanying protocol begins the more formal and focused budget process" (Miller, 21 October 1974). Still, the deans' budget letters ought to have summarized the information for each request, if the deans responded to the provost's charge.

When requests affecting multiple departments are consolidated, the deans wrote 165 rationales for expenditure requests in the last seven years of the period. Content analysis was applied to each rationale, using a six-item dichotomous-choice questionnaire. Scoring involved answering yes (1) or no (0) as to whether the dean's rationale:

1. Included explicit reference to meeting some goal or objective
2. Documented the need to solve the problem or meet the goal
3. Referred to alternative means of meeting the need, other than the means proposed
4. Defined results expected if the request is funded
5. Showed that the recommended solution has the most favorable cost-benefit ratio
6. Explicitly identified the value(s) that would be expressed by funding the request

The consistent theme of relating causes with desirable effects, which is central to the rational model, is readily apparent in these items. Summing the number of "yes" answers yielded a score between zero and six for each request rationale. The scores of four raters yielded an intraclass correlation for the reliability of average ratings of .59, significant at $p < .03$. The scores of the rater with the highest interrater correlations were used for the following analysis.

The mean score for the 165 requests in this analysis was 3.15, with a mode of 4.0. Most scores (69%) were either 3 or 4, out of a total of 6 possible points. According to these results, the deans gave the provost some or most, but not all, of the information he needed when they wrote their budget letters.

While the evidence is not strong, it is impressive when viewed in context. The writing styles of deans are idiosyncratic, as are their reasoning styles. There is considerable evidence in the letters that deans and provost communicated both orally and in writing about these requests in forums other than those evaluated in this analysis. If these deans' rationales for special increases provide as much information as the scores indicate, the provost is in a good position to choose rationally among them, especially when dealing with the satisficing decision rule of behavioral rationality rather than the optimizing rule of economic rationality.

Criterion 4: Choice

With reasonable confirmation of the first three criteria, the analysis proceeded to a policy-capturing regression for the fourth: whether the provost's choices were consistent with his goals. A regression equation of the form

$$\text{Decision result} = \text{preference}_1 + \text{preference}_2 + \ldots + \text{preference}_n$$

was needed. The left side of the equation, decision result, is the allocated general funds for the operating budget of each academic department for each of 10 years. That is the outcome of the budget decision process. Specifically, the endogenous variable is each department's proportional share of general funds each year. Expressing the budget as a proportion nets out the effects of inflation and across-the-board adjustments (Pfeffer and Moore, 1980). The budget share variable will change from one year to the next only if a decision is made that some departments will receive relatively more or less than others receive. Therefore, the variable measures the results of the provost's decisions regarding the deans' special requests.

As preference variables, the provost's list included academic importance, student interest, potential for excellence, and funding potential. The ideal regression equation would include one measure for each. Neither academic importance nor funding potential proved susceptible to measurement, however. The former is not explicated fully enough in Miller's writings to allow for a sufficiently concrete definition, and the latter, Miller acknowledges, is difficult to extricate from a ring of circular reasoning (1978). Omitting these two variables does not bias a policy-capturing regression, however, when the rational model is not the economic version in which a full set of ordered preferences is expected. If Miller chose according to any one or more of these four goals, he satisfied the behavioral model of rationality. Therefore, the regression equation will be estimated using measures of two of his goals.

The measure for student interest is students' registration for courses in the department. A strict test of the contribution of this goal is achieved by defining the measure as *changes* in the number of instructional units taught by the department (lagged one year to allow those changes to be known to the decision makers). The correlation between instructional units and budget shares before Miller took office was already high, r= .77, so defining the variable as changes in instructional units tests the provost's decisions without allowing him the benefit of historical correlation. For each of the 10 years in the study, student interest is defined as the number of student instructional units taught in the year when the budget was decided, minus the number taught in the previous year.

The provost's priority on excellence cannot be measured as directly, but a reasonable approximation can be developed from the results of a study of faculty from 15 of the Stanford departments in this study (Washburn, 1980). The study found that faculty are well aware of the national rank of their departments. In addition, service on university committees was the most frequent response when faculty were asked, "What accomplishments bring a local reputation for excellence to a department?" Finally, two of the top three responses to that question and another about what most affects administrators' judgments of department strength had to do with research: popular discoveries, important research, external research funding, and amount of research done.

Three measurable elements that are likely to contribute to the provost's assessment of excellence have been identified: national rank, committee representation, and research funding. While it is true that these elements might represent an entirely different concept on another campus,[2] the Washburn study of Stanford faculty supports them as components of perceived excellence on that campus.

National rank data were collected from ratings published in Roose and Andersen (1969) and Ladd and Lipset (1979), with only minor discrepancies between the two surveys in their placement of Stanford departments. Committee representation was each department's proportional share of members on 11 major university-wide policy committees. Unlike rank, which was constant over time, committee representation and research funds varied each year. Research funds were each department's proportional share of total grants and contracts received by all 38 departments that year. However, the number of departments for the remainder of the analysis reduces to 24, since 14 were in disciplines for which no national ranks were calculated.

Combining these three measures through factor analysis accomplishes two purposes: it allows assessment of the extent to which the three items seem to be measuring a single underlying construct and, if factor analysis does yield only one factor, it creates a single measure of one goal of the provost. Using one variable per concept conforms to standard regression practice.

The results of factor analysis are presented in Table 2. The three measures do yield a single factor in which each variable makes a nearly identical contribution to the concept and 41% of the total variance in the three variables is accounted for. The results support the idea that these three variables are components of a single factor, here called reputation rather than excellence because we are dealing with *perceived* excellence. The factor scores are used in the following regression to represent the provost's priority on excellence.

Table 2

Factor Analysis for Reputation[a]		
	Factor Loading	Est. Communality
Share of grants and contracts	.64924	.24395
Share of committee members	.63929	.23880
National rank[b]	−.63474	.23638

Eigenvalue: 1.2331

[a] Pooled cross sections (24 departments, 10 years).
[b] National rank is inversely scored.

Time series budget equations are plagued by serial correlation: most of each year's budget for an academic department (budget share$_t$) is explained by its budget in the previous year (budget share$_{t-1}$). In order to correct for serial correlation, the regression was estimated using generalized least squares (GLS) rather than ordinary least squares (OLS). GLS requires one additional variable in the regression equation, a lagged endogenous (dependent) variable, budget share in the previous year. This variable serves several critical purposes: (1) it provides data by which the GLS algorithm can calculate and correct for serial correlation; (2) it controls for the budget base, which is the assumed starting point in virtually all budgeting; and in so doing (3) it makes the equation dynamic, as is the process it models. What is left for the model variables to explain, after controlling for the relative size of last year's budget, is the relative *change* in this year's budget that *is not due to the base and across-the-board changes.*

The results of the policy-capturing regression were:

$$\text{budget share}_t = .001 + .93 \text{ budget share}_{t-1} + .0008 \text{ reputation factor} + .12E\text{-}6 \text{ change in instructional units}$$

where $R^2 = .9517$. Additional technical data are provided in Table 3.

The significance tests used here do not rely on estimates of standard error because the study deals with a population, so it incorporates no sampling error. However, section Ill of Table 3 reports the results of two tests to assess the contributions of each of the two substantive variables. First, does the variable's absence from the equation significantly reduce the overall power of the equation (R^2) to predict budget adjustments? If so, the variable makes a significant unique contribution to the equation. Second, does the variable make a significant contribution to R^2 after controlling for previous year's budget? If so, the total contribution of the variable is not fully absorbed by its contribution to the budget of the previous year.

As section III of Table 3 shows, the F statistic for both tests and both variables is significant at $p < .01$. In summary, the regression equation shows that after controlling for incrementalism (budget share at t-1), the two variables representing the provost's priorities add significantly to explained variance. Their F statistics are large, but the regression coefficients are small. Together, the priority variables add less than .01 to R^2.

Table 3

Policy-Capturing Regression for Criterion Four

I. Regression equation

$\text{Budget}_t = .001 + .93 \text{ budget}_{t-1} + .0008 \text{ reputation} + .12E\text{-}6 \text{ units change} \quad R^2 = .9517146$

II. Variables

	Mean	Std. Dev.	Budg$_{t-1}$	Reput.	Units chg.
				Correlations	
Budget share$_t$	.033	.015	.97	.62	−.03
Budget share$_{t-1}$	.033	.015		.61	−.06
Reputation	−.96E-7	.82			−.03
Units change	−37.89	1,732.17			

III. Tests for significance of contribution to R^2

Full model variables	Restricted model	Variable tested	R^2_{fm}	R^2_{rm}	F
Unique contribution:					
Budget share$_{t-1}$	Budget share$_{t-1}$	Reputation	.951715	.94683	23.87*
Reputation	Units change				
Units change					
Budget share$_{t-1}$	Budget share$_{t-1}$	Units change	.951715	.94838	16.30*
Reputation	Reputation				
Units change					
Total contribution:					
Budget share$_{t-1}$	Budget share$_{t-1}$	Reputation	.948379	.94368	21.57*
Reputation					
Budget share$_{t-1}$	Budget share$_{t-1}$	Units change	.946831	.94368	14.04*
Units change					

*Significant at p < .01.

The policy-capturing regression supports the fourth criterion of the rational model. The provost did allocate general funds to these departments in ways that were consistent with his goals.

Summary

The evidence in support of a rational decision process is substantial, but not unequivocal. It is strong for a consistent a priori set of preferences, for simultaneous selection among a wide array of alternatives, and for at least a satisficing choice among alternatives. However, the argument for rationality would be more convincing if academic importance and funding potential had been less ambiguous, if they had had measures, and if their measures had yielded significant regression coefficients.

These results supplement those of three earlier budget studies (Pfeffer and Salancik, 1974; Hills and Mahoney, 1978; Pfeffer and Moore, 1980) by attending to multiple facets of the rational model. At Stanford, budgeting not only acknowledged the reasonableness of workload as a criterion for resource allocation, as was shown in the earlier studies. It also incorporated a judgment criterion (reputation for excellence) and a number of procedural aspects of rationality.

Discussion

The extent to which the Stanford process conforms to the rational model is surprising, given the relative completeness of the test procedure and given the widely held opinion that budgeting is inherently a political process. As multifaceted and theoretically based as this test has been, however, its results cannot be called complete, partly because of the gaps in the evidence, but mostly because other models were not tested. Allison (1971) and Weil (1975) found that their cases exhibited features of two or three models simultaneously. Although other models were not applied to Stanford budgeting, the bureaucratic model is apparent in Stanford's reliance on the budget base and its routinization of the protocol process. It may have been an astute political move, motivating thinly disguised political responses, for the provost to state his four budget criteria with such all-purpose generality. Support for the collegial model might be found in the high frequency of face-to-face conferences among diverse individuals that preceded any final budget decisions. But whatever else may also be happening, the process shows substantial signs of procedural and substantive rationality.

This finding addresses an implicit debate in organizational management on the feasibility of rational decisions. Adherents of the position that rational decision making is feasible include institutional researchers, operations researchers, decision analysts, systems engineers, and others whose work produces information on optimal choice. Virtually all of the planning literature advocates rational plans and assumes rational implementation. On the other hand, many social scientists and practicing administrators assert that, in fact, rationality plays at best a limited role in decision making. They point out that most decisions of any import involve diverse, conflicting contenders and goals, some of which must be satisfied regardless of rational optimality.

Stanford's budgeting shows that bounded rationality is feasible, at least as one facet of a multifaceted process. Furthermore, a number of observers in this case believed that rationality was the dominant model, including a professor of political science who has written about decision models and whose position as a faculty member and political scientist suggests that he might have been among the most skeptical (George, 1980). What this study has not addressed is the larger issue beyond feasibility of the rational model — its utility.

Many at Stanford, administrators and faculty, took considerable pride in the budget process and invested a great deal in it. Yet with less than 6% of the total variance in 10 years of budget data left to explain after accounting for the budget base, it may be hard to believe that any effort above a minimal level is justifiable. One explanation for the discrepancy is that, although this latitude for change may not be much, it's all there is. That is, since so much of the budget is virtually fixed, especially in the short run, the small portion that is free to vary assumes tremendous importance. It is a critical tool for achieving important organizational changes, albeit slowly. This suggests that when the organization sets goals early and holds to them for a number of years, as rational decision makers can do, directed change has time to evolve. When goals are unspecified or change frequently, major new directions may not have time or sufficient impetus to appear.

Another explanation for heavy investment in budget decision making is its potential for symbolic value. Regardless of decision model, differential allocations among departments signal organizational priorities and subunit worth or power, even if the differences in allocations are small. The emerging literature on the symbolic value of management (Pfeffer, 1981; Feldman and March, 1981) is relevant to this issue. When the affected parties are scientists, scholars who value objectivity, the best — perhaps the only — way to minimize discontent about unequal budgets or refusals to fund important new ventures may be to ensure that they believe the process by which those decisions were made was rational. So, regardless of whether a rational process produces better decisions, it may be more comfortable, more acceptable, less contentious for an organization like a major research university than any other process. Rational reasons for rejecting a request make sense in that context, and the expected form for presenting and considering expenditure requests is seen as reasonable and fair.

The utility of any organizational decision model may be more heuristic than explanatory or prescriptive. The models seem to be neither mutually exclusive nor exhaustive as event descriptors. A single decision process may show signs of two or more models simultaneously. None of the models, including rationality, can function effectively as a categorical pigeon hole.

Rather than accepting any normative process, decision makers are probably better served by using decision models to understand the parts of the processes they use, for example, political jockeying for position, bureaucratic channels for review, and a collegial summary session. Such awareness can reaffirm their preference for some current behaviors as well as pinpoint areas of discomfort and identify possible alternative behaviors. Once the normative push behind any preferred model is abandoned, participants are free to mix and match model elements to suit the situation.

Conclusion

Rational decision making is probably neither normative nor, in most constructions, unrealistic. It is found in organizations but, like other decision models, neither emphatically nor alone. Through a rational process, Stanford did effectively implement a sustained attempt to match marginal resources with preferred priorities. To the extent that this kind of match is desirable in an organization, a rational process is suitable.

The most useful approach both to studying and using decision models is to decompose them into their constituent parts. For the researcher, this allows a multifaceted examination of the process and therefore a more complete understanding about how and where the model fits the data. For the decision maker, it permits a more refined understanding of the decision process. It can also shift the focus from rearranging an entire process so that it will conform to a single desired model to ensuring that each stage of the process is designated to be most suitable for its purposes.

This research was supported in part by the Bush Foundation and by the Institute for Research on Educational Finance and Governance at Stanford.

Notes

[1] The various communications and reports of William F. Miller referred to in the text are listed below:

Letter to Richard W. Lyman, President. Stanford, Calif., 5 October 1971.

Letter to Edward E. Shaw, Executive Assistant to the Vice President and Provost. Stanford, Calif., 23 November 1971.

Hallmarks of excellence. The Campaign for Stanford. Stanford. Calif.. 1972. (a) Reflections on university management in a period of dynamic equilibrium. Stanford annual financial report. Stanford, Calif., 1972. (b)

Letter to Messrs. R. M. Brown, J. E. W. Sterling, R. E. Guggenhime, F. H. Merrill. Stanford, Calif., 13 October 1972.

General protocol letter to the deans. Stanford, Calif., 4 October 1973.

General protocol letter to the deans. Stanford, Calif., 21 October 1974.

Letter to James L. Gibbs, Dean of Undergraduate Studies. Stanford, Calif., 6 January 1975.

Letter to Dean William Kays, School of Engineering. Stanford, Calif., 3 June 1975.

Statement on the closing of the Stanford Program in Architecture. Stanford, Calif., 20 July 1975.

Institutional policy secting: a dynamic view. Stanford, Calif, 1978.

Interview, Menlo Park, Calif., 25 July 1980.

[2] In fact, student credit hours were used in the three previous budget studies as a rational-bureaucratic measure, and representation on university committees was used as a political measure (Pfeffer and Salancik, 1974; Hills and Mahoney, 1978; Pfeffer and Moore, 1980). Equations in each of the three studies were exactly replicated using Stanford data, and the Stanford results were consistent with the results of the earlier studies (details are available from the author). At issue, then, is whether use of the two variables is justifiable in a test of the rational model when they have been used previously as proxies for other models.

Since previous authors did not distinguish between rational and bureaucratic decision making, use of student credit hours to represent one component of rationality at Stanford is more specific, but still compatible with its use in the earlier studies. But committee membership was used to represent political decision making in those studies, and it represents rational decision making at Stanford. Its revised use in the Stanford context is justified on two grounds.

First, the concepts of power (political model) and excellence (rational model) are so broad and vague that the variables require some form of corroboration to verify that they are appropriate proxies, Both Pfeffer and Salancik (1914) and Pfeffer and Moore (1980) corroborated committee representation as a power variable by showing its high correlation with an interview-based measure of departmental power on each campus. One of the weaknesses of the Hills and Mahoney (1978) study is that it used uncorrelated measures to represent power (Pfeffer and Moore, 1980, p. 639). The Stanford interpretation of committee membership as an indicator of excellence is corroborated by the Washburn (1980) study, cited in the text. Serving on committees evidently carries a different meaning at Stanford than at Illinois or California.

Second, committee membership joins two other verified proxies for excellence in a single, cohesive factor (Table 2). The Washburn (1980) study provides empirical grounds upon which to label that factor "excellence," although this study uses the more conservative term, "reputation." The Washburn findings and the factor results are mutually reinforcing, both supporting the use of committee membership as a valid proxy for excellence at Stanford.

References

Allison, G. T. *Essence of Decision: Explaining the Cuban Missile Crisis.* Boston: Little, Brown, 1971.

Argyris, C.. and Schon, D. *Organizational Learning: A Theory of Action Perspective.* Reading, Mass.: Addison-Wesley, 1978.

Bouchard, T. J., Jr. "Unobtrusive Measures: An Inventory of Uses." *Sociological Methods and Research,* 1916, 4; 267-300.

Campbell, D. T., and Fiske, D. W. "Convergent and Discriminant Validation by the Multitrait-Multimethod Matrix." *Psychological Bulletin,* 1959, 56; 81-105.

Carter, E. E. "The Behavioral Theory of the Firm and Top-Level Corporate Decisions." *Administrative Science Quarterly,* 1971, 16; 413-428.

Cohen, M. D., and March, J. G. *Leadership and Ambiguity: The American College President.* New York: McGraw-Hill, 1974.

Cyert, R. M., and March, J. G. *A Behavioral Theory of the Firm.* Englewood Cliffs, N.J.: Prentice-Hall, 1963.

Cyert, R. M., Simon, H. A. and Trow, D. B. "Observations of a Business Decision." *Journal of Business,* 1956, 29; 233-248.

Denzin, N. K. *The Research Act* (2nd ed.). New York: McGraw-Hill, 1978.

Diesing, P. *Reason in Society: Five Types of Decisions and Their Social Conditions.* Urbana, Ill.: University of Illinois Press, 1962; Greenwood Press, 1976.

Feldman, M. S., and March, J. G. "Information in Organizations as Signal and Symbol." *Administrative Science Quarterly,* 1981, 26, 171-186.

Garfinkel, H. "The Rational Properties of Scientific and Common Sense Activities." *Behavioral Science,* 1960, 5; 72-83.

George, A. *Toward a More Soundly Based Foreign Policy.* Washington, D.C.: Government Printing Office, 1975.

George, A. *Seminar. Institute for Research on Educational Finance and Governance at Stanford,* Stanford, Calif., 24 June 1980.

Hills, F. S., and Mahoney, T. A. "University Budgets and Organizational Decision Making." *Administrative Science Quarterly,* September 1978; 454-465.

Huber, G. P. "Multi-Attribute Utility Models: A Review of Field and Field-Like Studies." *Management Science,* 1974, 20; 1393-1402.

Jick, T. D. "Mixing Qualitative and Quantitative Methods: Triangulation in Action." *Administration Science Quarterly,* 1979, 24; 603-611.

Ladd, E. C., Jr., and Lipset, S. M. *1977 Survey of the American Professoriate.* Storrs, Conn.: University of Connecticut, 1979.

Lindblom, C. E. "The Science of 'Muddling Through.' " *Public Administration Review,* 1959, 19; 78-88.

March, J. G. "Bounded Rationality, Ambiguity, and the Engineering of Choice." *The Bell Journal of Economics,* 1978, 9; 587-608.

Millett, J. D. *The Academic Community.* New York: McGraw-Hill, 1962.

Nalbandian, J. and Klinger, D. E. "Integrating Context and Decision Strategy: A Contingency Theory Approach to Public Personnel Administration." *Administration and Society,* 1980, 12; 178-202.

Nisbet, R. E., and Wilson, T. "Telling More Than We Can Know: Verbal Reports on Mental Processes." *Psychological Review,* 1977, 132; 231-259.

Nutt, P. C. "Models for Decision Making in Organizations and Some Contextual Variables Which Stipulate Optimal Use." *Academy of Management Review,* 1976, 2; 84-98;

Operating budget guidelines for 1975-76. Stanford University, 1975.

Pfeffer, J. "Management as Symbolic Action: The Creation and Maintenance of Organizational Paradigms." In *Research in Organizational Behavior,* L. L. Cummings and B. M. Staw (Eds.). Greenwich, Conn.: JAI Press, 1981.

Pfeffer, J. and Moore, W. "Power and Politics in University Budgeting: A Replication and Extension." *Administrative Science Quarterly,* 1980, 25; 637-653.

Pfeffer, J. and Salancik, G. R. "Organizational Decision Making as a Political Process: The Case of a University Budget." *Administrative Science Quarterly,* 1974, 19; 135-151.

Poulton, N. L. *Impacts of Planning Activities in Research Universities: A Comparative Analysis of Five Institutional Experiences.* Doctoral dissertation, University of Michigan, 1979.

Rohrbaugh, J. "Judgment Analysis as Policy Formation: A New Method for Improving Public Participation." *Public Opinion Quarterly,* 1978, 42; 521-532.

Roose, K. D., and Andersen, C. J. *A Rating of Graduate Programs.* Washington, D.C.: American Council on Education, 1969.

Rubin, I. "Universities in Stress: Decision Making Under Conditions of Reduced Resources." *Social Science Quarterly,* 1977, 38; 242-254.

Simon, H. A. "A Behavioral Model of Rational Choice." *Quarterly Journal of Economics,* 1955, 69; 99-118.

Simon, H. A. "Rational Choice and the Structure of the Environment." *Psychological Review,* 1976, 63; 129-138.

Simon, H. A. "Rational Decision Making in Business Organizations." *American Economic Review,* 1979, 69; 493-513.

Skok, J. E. "Budgetary Politics and Decision Making: Development of an Alternative Hypothesis for State Government." *Administration and Society,* 1980, 11; 445-460.

Slovic, P., and Lichtenstein, S. "Comparison of Bayesian and Regression Approaches to the Study of Information Processing in Judgment." *Organizational Behavior and Human Performance*, 1971, 6; 649-744.

Thompson, J. D. *Organizations in Action*. New York: McGraw-Hill, 1967.

Van Maanen, J. "The Fact of Fiction in Organizational Ethnography." *Administrative Science Quarterly*, 1979, 24; 539-550.

Washburn, W. *Standards of Departmental Excellence: An Investigation of the Criteria used for Judging Excellence by Elected Departmental Faculties of a Research University*. Doctoral dissertation, Stanford University, 1980.

Weber, Max. *The Theory of Social and Economic Organizations*, trans. by A. M. Henderson. ed. by Talcott Parsons. Glencoe, Ill.: Free Press, 1947.

Webb, E. J., Campbell, D. T., Schwartz, R. D., and Sechrest, L. *Unobtrusive Measures: Non-Reactive Research in the Social Sciences*. Chicago: Rand McNally, 1966.

Weil, H. M. "Can Bureaucracies be Rational Actors? Foreign Policy Decision Making in North Vietnam." *International Studies Quarterly*, 1975, 19; 432-468.

Power and Centrality in the Allocation of Resources in Colleges and Universities

JUDITH D. HACKMAN

This work proposes a research-based theory about how colleges and universities allocate resources among units. The pivotal concept of centrality (how closely a unit's purposes match those central to the organization) affects how four other theoretical concepts interact: internal resource allocations, environmental power, institutional power, and resource negotiation strategies. A unit's environmental power, gained by its relative ability to acquire external resources needed by the institution, and a unit's institutional power combine with resource negotiation strategies to explain about half of the variance in internal resource allocations. The theory is developed from interviews at six varied institutions and is supported by analyses of data obtained from questionnaires completed by administrators of a state university, a liberal arts college, and a comprehensive college.

Whether the times are good or bad, some departments and offices in colleges and universities gain in institutional resources while other units lose. The purpose of this research is to work toward a practical theory of resource allocations that will explain such gains and losses in times of financial difficulty. It is hoped that these ideas eventually can be extended to universities and colleges when they are not under financial stress and then to organizations outside of academia. The intent is to offer insight into questions such as the following: (1) What factors most strongly affect the amount of money and space that a department or office acquires in the institution? (2) How does the allocation of resources differ between units central to the purposes of the institution and those units that are peripheral? and (3) What budget negotiation strategies help departments and offices increase their share of available resources?

Proposed Theory and Background

Although much of the proposed theory has evolved from the study described here, it also relates to and draws on previous studies about resource allocations and organizational power (Perrow, 1970; Hickson et al., 1971; Hinings et al., 1974; Pfeffer and Salancik, 1974; Salancik and Pfeffer, 1974; Hills and Mahoney, 1978). The theory rests on the basic assumption that colleges and universities are open systems in interaction with their environment (Katz and Kahn, 1978; Miller, 1978). From the environment these institutions bring in essential resources (such as students, faculty, staff, money, and other kinds of support), and in return they contribute services and products (especially educated students and knowledge). The proposed theory is based on five concepts: centrality, resource allocations, environmental power, institutional power, and resource allocation strategies.

Centrality

Centrality, the pivotal concept in this research, is defined as how closely the purposes of a unit match the central mission of its institution. Although centrality is defined as a continuum, for research purposes it is useful to characterize units as core or peripheral.

CORE UNITS

Core units are those whose functions are essential to the central mission of an institution. Without the core, the organization would have another overall purpose. The particular departments or offices viewed as core units vary among different institutions of higher education and differ over time within particular institutions. As an institution adapts to its environment, what is central changes continuously, although often imperceptibly.

For research universities, central activities are usually teaching and research by faculty members. Core units are primarily academic departments and schools but may also include research centers and institutes. Smaller institutions and those that focus primarily on teaching less frequently have research units.

PERIPHERAL UNITS

Peripheral units are the noncentral parts of the institution. They vary widely in size and mission, both within an individual college or university and from one institution to another. Included in this category are most administrative and support offices, as well as specialized units such as conference centers and summer camps. The roles of various kinds of peripheral units in colleges and universities have been described by various authors (Gulko, 1972; Ikenberry and Friedman, 1972; Bowen, 1977; Collier, 1978).

Resource Allocations

Resource allocations, the dependent variable in the proposed theory, is the relative share of internal institutional resources acquired by a unit, especially money, space, and campus location. A major assumption is that core and peripheral units acquire institutional resources in different ways. The present research focuses on one important aspect of resource allocations — the relative *change* in a unit's share of the general budget. This emphasis accords with Hills and Mahoney (1978: 458), who state that "subunit budgeting tends toward incremental budgeting rather than comprehensive budgeting, suggesting that investigation of budgeting criteria ought to focus on incremental budgets rather than total budgets."[1]

Environmental and Institutional Power

Two of the five proposed concepts refer to forms of unit power, the essential but elusive concept that many social scientists have at some time studied (Weber, 1947; Lasswell and Kaplan, 1950; Simon, 1953. French and Raven, 1977; Emerson, 1962; Gamson, 1968; Perrow, 1970; Hickson et al., 1971; Hinings et al., 1974; Pfeffer and Salancik, 1974; Salancik and Pfeffer, 1974). The form of power studied here is relational power among intraorganizational units within institutions that are open systems. The focus is on how power influences decision making in colleges and universities, especially critical decisions about resource allocations to academic departments and nonacademic offices.

Although much of the literature stresses unilateral power, the present research (like much of the research cited below) follows Emerson's (1962) view of power as a relational condition. According to Emerson, we understand the power of a unit or an individual when we know its relationship to the object of that power. The power of one unit over a second equals the dependence of the second unit on the first. Power therefore is relative from relationship to relationship and even from situation to situation.

Applying Emerson's work to colleges and universities gives, for any one department or office, a full set of different power relationships across all of the other units in the institution. The power of a unit vis à vis the rest of the institution equals the dependence of the organization on that unit. Dependence, from Emerson's (1962) perspective, is (1) directly proportional to the criticality of the resources that the unit controls and (2) inversely proportional to the substitutability of the unit for acquiring these resources, that is, the availability of those resources from other units.

Until recently, most research on power in work organizations examined power among hierarchical levels or interpersonal power. In reviewing literature for his study of functional group power among departments in industrial firms, Perrow (1970: 84) found "only a single study that asks survey questions regarding the power of functional *groups*." In the past decade there has been more research at the unit level. Hickson et al. (1971) and Hinings et al. (1974) proposed and studied a strategic-contingencies theory of intraorganizational power that examined structural rather than personal sources of power in subunits of work organizations. More closely related to the present study is the research of Hills and Mahoney (1978) and the work of Salancik and Pfeffer, who investigated power and resource allocations among academic departments in universities (Pfeffer and Salancik, 1974; Salancik and Pfeffer, 1974).

ENVIRONMENTAL POWER

The proposed concept of environmental power follows Emerson's view of power and is consistent with Pfeffer and Salancik's (1974: 470) finding that "power accrues to those departments that are most instrumental in bringing in or providing resources which are highly valued by the total organization." Environmental power is the relative ability of a unit to bring in outside resources that are critically needed by the institution. A unit realizes this form of power when the rest of the institution recognizes both the organization's motivational investment in the resources that the unit can acquire (criticality) and the relative ability of the unit to bring in needed resources from the environment (substitutability). The research examined the relative ability of a unit to obtain environmental resources such as those listed in Table 1, each weighted by how critical the resource was to the institution as a whole.

INSTITUTIONAL POWER

Institutional power is the unit's relative influence within the institution, independent of its environmental power. Variables examined that were potentially related to internal institutional power are listed in Table 1.

Table 1

Variables Examined for Three Concepts		
Environmental Power	**Institutional Power**	**Resource Negotiation Strategies**
1. Student recruitment and retention	1. Historical power within institution	1. Focusing on needs of total institution
2. Faculty recruitment and retention	2. Length of time in institution	2. Focusing on needs of division
3. Recruitment and retention of other expertise	3. Visibility within institution	3. Focusing on needs of unit
4. Prestige	4. Visibility outside institution	4. Focusing on needs of unit members
5. Ability to cope with current societal needs and problems	5. Visibility with board of trustees	5. Presenting lowest feasible budget
6. Overall outside financial support	6. Number of full-time-equivalent employees	6. Overstating budget needs
7. Federal government support	7. Percentage of faculty relative to managerial and professional staff	7. Omitting important items
8. Foundation support	8. Number of students served	8. Including budget request for innovative programs
9. Business and industry support	9. Interaction with central administration	
10. Alumni support	10. Number of times monthly that unit director talks with central administration	
11. Community support	11. Support of president	
12. State support	12. Ease of direct access to president	
13. State legislature support	13. Support of dean or director	
	14. Legal commitments from institution	

Resource Negotiation Strategies

Resource negotiation strategies are strategies used by unit heads to acquire resource allocations, particularly in negotiating budgets. In the present study, the strategies surveyed included how much a unit head used each of the strategies listed in Table 1 in negotiating the unit's annual budget allocation.

Research Design

The study focused on four groups of institutional units, formed by relating the two key concepts of centrality to the dependent variable, resource allocations: peripheral losers, peripheral gainers, core losers, and core gainers. The study was conducted in two phases. The first emphasized theory development, using a modified grounded-theory methodology of interviews, document collection, and relevant literature review (Glaser and Strauss, 1967; Conrad, 1978). The second phase provided provisional testing and theory refinement based on more detailed case investigation and survey techniques.

In the first phase, top administrators were asked to identify and discuss institutional units that fell into each of the four groups and to explore why and how the units lost or gained budget allocations. In the second phase, questionnaires given to heads of units in each group asked them to describe their units on scales reflecting the five theoretical concepts. Analyses of these qualitative and quantitative data made it possible to explore the resource patterns of the four groups and thereby lay a foundation for further theory development.

Methods

Participating Institutions

Table 2 characterizes the six institutions that took part in the research and lists the numbers and kinds of participants from each. The institutions ranged from a small, religious undergraduate women's college to a state university with several graduate and professional schools; from a well-known liberal arts college with a national student body to institutions that were primarily regional in enrollment.

Table 2

				Interviews		Completed questionnaires‡			
				Phase 1		Phase 2		Phase 2	
						Division heads	Department heads	Division heads	Department heads
Type of Institution	Size 1979-80	Highest degree	Pres	Vice Pres.	Other	N	N	N(%)	N(%)
State university	14,200	Doctorate	Pres	Academic Admin & Bus Development Student	Pres Asst. (2) Acad. Asso. V.P. (2)	8	3	11(92)	17(65)
Liberal arts college	2,700	Doctorate	Pres.	Academic Admin & Bus		3	3	2(67)	14(70)
Comprehensive college	3,800	Master's	Pres	Admin & Bus	Pres Asst			4(57)	24(89)
Women's college	550	Bachelor's	Pres	Academic Admin & Bus Student					
Technical university	7,250	Master's	—	Academic Admin & Bus External					
Regional university	9,750	Doctorate	—	Administrative Business Development Student	Planning Dir				
Total			4	16	6	11	6	17(77%)‡	55(75%)‡

*Most analyses of questionnaire data reported in this paper combine responses from heads of departments such as academic chairs and office directors and from deans and division heads
‡Two additional questionnaires were returned too late for inclusion in data analyses for a total return of 74(77 .9%)

All six institutions were located in New England, and all were accredited by the New England Association of Schools and Colleges. All of them had budgetary problems, although the levels of their financial stress varied. And although the details of budgeting differed, all began the annual budget process with requests from the departments that then moved up through division heads and deans to final decisions at the central administrative level. A few of the institutions had tried zero-based budgeting, but in practice their budgets had been primarily incremental, with occasional selective reductions and increases.

Phase 1

In the first phase of the research, preliminary interviews were conducted with 26 key administrators centrally involved in budgetary decisions at each of the institutions, and relevant documents were collected. The major goal was to tap the experience of knowledgeable persons in order to develop the theory and to clarify questions for Phase 2. Administrators were asked (1) to describe the annual budgetary process of their institution and (2) to discuss resource allocation experiences for four specific units that they identified as fitting each of the four groups (the designations for the four groups were not used during data collection), defined as follows:

Core gainers: Units central to the institution that have had an increase in their relative share of the budget in recent years.

Core losers: Units central to the institution that have had a decrease in their relative share of the budget.

Peripheral gainers: Units not central to the institution that have had an increase in their relative share of the budget.

Peripheral losers: Units not central to the institution that have had a decrease in their relative share of the budget.

Phase 1 interviews were transcribed, and their contents were coded and tallied. This analysis contributed to the theory development and to the design of Phase 2 questionnaires.

Phase 2

This phase of the study concentrated on the state university, the liberal arts college, and the comprehensive college. For these three institutions, 95 budgetary units were categorized as fitting into one of the four groups. In Phase 2, the identification of budgetary gainers and losers during the Phase 1 interviews was verified by a second administrator at each institution. Academic units were categorized as "core" and all other units as "peripheral." Because the central purpose of colleges and universities is to educate students (and in research institutions to extend knowledge through research), treating academic departments as core units sufficiently matched the definition of centrality.[2] Questionnaires were mailed to the 95 unit heads (chairs of academic departments, office directors, and also some division directors and deans); 74 questionnaires were returned, for a completion rate of 77.9 percent. (Two of the 74 arrived too late for the data analysis.) Second visits to two of the three Phase 2 institutions made it possible to examine additional institutional documents and to interview 17 unit heads, most of whom also answered the questionnaire.

DEVELOPMENT OF PHASE 2 QUESTIONNAIRE

The Phase 2 questionnaire, developed from Phase 1 of the study, covered several topics, including: (1) the institutional budgetary process, (2) areas emphasized by the administration, and (3) the unit's internal resource allocations, environmental power, institutional power, and budgetary strategies. Most of the questions were forced-choice and asked respondents to indicate their best answer. Open-ended questions were placed throughout the questionnaire to solicit additional categories for the proposed concepts and to develop the theory further. Two essentially identical instruments were used, one with wording adapted to heads of divisions and the other to heads of departments and offices.

Two questions were combined to measure a unit's environmental power. The first one examined a unit's "substitutability" (its relative ability to bring in each of the 13 environmental resources listed in Table 1) by asking, "On each of the following items, how do the contributions of your budgetary unit compare with those of other similar units?" Responses were given on a 5-point scale, where 1 = Much Lower than Most Similar Units and 5 = Much Higher. The second question measured "criticality" (the importance of each of the 13 resources to the institution) by asking, "How important do you believe each of the outside resources are to the future health and viability of your campus?" on a 5-point scale, where 1 = Not Important and 5 = Very important. These importance ratings were used to weight the contribution responses in developing indices of environmental power.

For a unit's institutional power, respondents were asked, "To the best of your knowledge, please indicate how your unit compares with other similar budgetary units in the institution on each of the following characteristics," and a 5-point scale was used, where 1 = Much Lower and 5 = Much Higher. Items were the 14 categories listed in Table 1 for institutional power and a general item on "present power within the institution."

For resource negotiation strategies, respondents were asked to indicate on a 5-point scale, where 1 = Very Little or Not at All and 5 = Very Much, "How much do you use each of the following strategies when you prepare your unit's annual budget?" Items were the eight categories listed in Table 1.

CENTRALITY AND RESOURCE ALLOCATIONS

For the analyses of questionnaire responses, each of these concepts was represented as a dichotomous variable, depending on the group into which a unit fell.

Results

Results are presented separately for each of the five propositions, which follow:

Proposition 1. A unit's centrality crucially affects the internal resources allocated to it by the institution.
1. Because core units are central to the mission of the institution, they gain internal institutional resources when they strengthen themselves.
2. Because peripheral units are not part of the core, they gain internal institutional resources when they contribute to the institution.

Proposition 2. A unit's environmental power interacts with its centrality to affect the internal resources it is allocated.
1. Core units gain internal institutional resources when they can obtain critical resources from the environment for their own use (e.g., students and academic prestige).
2. Peripheral units gain internal institutional resources when they can obtain resources critically needed by the total institution (e.g., financial resources in times of financial stress).

Proposition 3. A unit's institutional power also affects the internal resources it is allocated.

Proposition 4. The resource negotiation strategies used by the head of a unit interact with unit centrality to affect the internal resources it is allocated.

1. Core units fare better in obtaining internal institutional resources when their strategies emphasize unit needs.
2. Peripheral units fare better in obtaining internal institutional resources when their strategies emphasize institutional needs.

Proposition 5. Because environmental power, institutional power, and resource negotiation strategies are not highly correlated, their combined effect on resource allocations is greater than any of the concepts considered alone.

Proposition 1

The centrality variable proved analytically useful in the Phase 2 provisional statistical testing of the theory and also meaningful to the 26 top administrators interviewed in Phase 1. When asked to name four units fitting the four research groups, they readily identified "central" (core) and "noncentral" (peripheral) units that were gaining and losing resources on their campuses. They most frequently cited academic units as core units, although, in accordance with the idea that centrality is a continuum, a few academic units were described as peripheral or not close to the mission of a particular institution. Some of the units named most frequently in the four groups were:

Core gainers: computer science, business, and engineering
Core losers: teacher education, fine arts, and languages
Peripheral gainers: development, admissions, and administrative computing
Peripheral losers: student affairs, counseling, and the physical plant

The administrators' views about core and peripheral units demonstrated the intuitive usefulness of the centrality concept. Virtually all who were interviewed in Phase 1 stressed that academic goals were central to their institution, frequently making statements such as, "The central mission of the institution is the academic mission."

For most, peripheral units were defined by their optional and vulnerable nature. If they contributed to the overall organization, they were safe, but they were among the first to be scrutinized when funds became limited. Two respondents described their views of peripherality as follows.

> I say it's noncentral because if you ... had to cut out anything because you didn't have the money for them, I would be cutting out the noncentral units, and that's how I define them. (A vice president for administration and business.)

> [I define a noncentral program] as a program of worth, but if it became a budgetary or programmatic burden on the institution, it could be eliminated without affecting the integrity of the basic academic mission. [By burden, I mean] that the existence of the program causes us to have to cut back the level of support for academic core programs. (Another vice president for administration and business.)

> Documents from the two institutions that had developed written budget reallocation plans in recent years explicitly used the concept of centrality as a primary criterion for determining areas to reduce. Their top administrators recalled the use of this criterion:

> Certainly there are [central and noncentral units], and part of the rebalancing plan calls for looking at those things that are so-called peripheral programs and determining whether they are in some ways central to the mission; or, if they are indeed peripheral, they become of lower priority — things that we look at first to cut. (An administrator at the state university.)

> [When] we started talking about programs, we tried to divide them between core and peripheral. [Interviewer: You used those words?] Yes, we did. [Interviewer: I have been

> concerned that the word "peripheral" would be seen as pejorative.] Well, I'll tell you, it had pejorative connotations here . . . . People didn't like us using those terms one bit, but we used them anyway . . . . Four peripheral programs, when we began saying we were constrained, became [the] first target. (An administrator at the liberal arts college.)

Centrality also proved to be a key concept in the analyses of questionnaire responses. As the results for Propositions 2 and 5 demonstrate, numerous relationships that otherwise would have been obscured were clarified when core and peripheral units were analyzed separately. Both the interview and questionnaire responses supported Proposition 1.

Proposition 2

In the Phase 1 semistructured interviews, top administrators were asked how and why the departments and offices they named gained or lost resources. Analyses of their transcribed responses revealed, first of all, that the ability to bring in external resources was by far the predominant explanation of why programs had grown, and a decrease in such power was the major reason for decline. For example, a vice president at one of the regional institutions stated, "The key driving forces here are enrollment in the departments and the ability to generate outside related funds."

Second, the tally of responses for the four research groups showed different patterns for core and peripheral units. Most frequently mentioned for core units was the ability to attract and retain students, for example:

> The losses have been in the language and literature departments ... largely because it was thought that there simply was not a significant enough student demand. We should be putting our eggs where there is a demand. (An academic vice president.)

> For ongoing central academic programs, the budget responsibility is very much a function of perceived or real market potential, and that word is used without apology in this institution .... Programs that are healthy, of course, this is the real side of it, come in and say, "We doubled our enrollments ... we want something new. " And that will be responded to. (Another academic vice president.)

For peripheral units it was the ability to bring in financial resources. As one administrator said, "They'll either have to pay their own way and increase by getting their own revenues, or they will shrink."

Questionnaire responses confirmed and extended these findings. Multivariate analyses of questionnaire data showed that the external resources that related significantly to internal resource allocations differed for the core and peripheral units.

Two separate indices were created from answers to the environmental power questions to summarize how environmental power interacted with centrality and resource allocations. The Appendix lists the specific questionnaire items that composed each of the indices, gives their correlations with budgetary change, and describes the derivation of the indices. The core unit index is called "tapping external academic resources." because of its items. Core gainers were distinguished from core losers by their success in acquiring such needed academic external resources as students, academic prestige, and their ability to help students cope with current societal needs and problems. The peripheral unit index is called "tapping external financial resources." At least in current times of financial stress, the peripheral gainers, in contrast to peripheral losers, acquire internal budget resources by attracting much-needed financial support.

Table 3 gives results of multiple regression analyses that explored the relationships among centrality, budget allocations, environmental power, and institutional power. Considering environmental power alone, the core index "tapping external academic resources" accounted for 28.6 percent of the variance in budget change among the 39 core respondents, and the peripheral index "tapping external financial resources accounted for 19.8 percent of budget change variance among the 33 peripheral unit heads.[3]

Table 3

	Stepwise Multiple Regressions of Environmental Power and Institutional Power on the Budgetary Change of Core and Peripheral Units		
	Explained Variance(%)		F-ratio
Independent variables	Unit heads*	Adjusted for population+	
Environmental power index alone			
Core units	28.62	6.7	14.844**
Peripheral units	19.8	17.2	7.649*
Institutional power index alone			
Core units‡	41.3	38.0	12.663**
Peripheral units‡	38.1	34.0	9.224**

*$p < .01$; **$p < .001$
*$N = 39$ for core units, $N = 33$ for peripheral units,
‡Takes into account smaller sample size.
‡Multiple correlation = .64 for core units, .62 for peripheral units.

Proposition 3

In the Phase 1 interviews, aspects of institutional power were mentioned much less frequently than explanations of environmental power. Respondents did, however, mention some internal factors that influenced gains and losses in budget allocations, especially the importance of support from top administrators, such as the president or a dean. For example:

> That program was developed by the Dean. The faculty efforts had started many years ago, at least ten years ago. We had some modest reputation; we had the expertise here; but he put the whole thing together. It was his idea; he marketed it, he sold it. (An academic vice president talking about a scientific research unit.)

> I guess the success of that program will depend on the continued success of that advocate. If the individual loses interest or moves on, the budget ultimately will probably be eliminated or moved into some other responsibility area. (An administrator talking about a student service unit.)

> Sports have increased because we expanded the football program and the president decided to emphasize it. (An administrator at the technical university.)

> The film program could be a real winner, but not enough resources are allocated. It sits by itself and doesn't have a champion. If it were moved under the Dean of Arts and Sciences, then I think it would most likely get some money. (An administrator at the regional university.)

Analysis of the questionnaire items for institutional power followed the same procedures used for environmental power. Two summary indices of the institutional power questionnaire items were derived (Appendix). Here, too, the goal in constructing the indices was to compute summary scores that would distinguish between gainers and losers separately for core and for peripheral units.

In the two regression analyses reported in Table 3, institutional power was added second, after environmental power. For core units, institutional power added 12.7 percent in explained budgetary change variance, making a total of 41.3 percent. For peripheral units, institutional power added 18.3 percent, for a total of 38.1 percent. When these findings were adjusted for the population, taking into account the sample size (39 core respondents, 33 peripheral respondents), environmental power and institutional power explained 38 percent for core and 34 percent for peripheral unit heads.

In contrast to environmental power, the relationship between institutional power and budget allocations appears fairly similar for core and peripheral units. For both, all of the positive items measured aspects of a unit's present internal ties to the organization, whether through administrative support, constituent service, or general visibility.

Contrary to original expectations, perceptions of past power actually weighed negatively on both indices. Longevity and a unit's self-perceived power five years earlier both correlated negatively with budget gains. It may well be that in times of financial stress and change (both in higher education and in the general society), longevity and past institutional power are outweighed by the need to attend to present concerns. The nature of the relationship between environmental power and institutional power remains unclear. For peripheral units, no significant correlation between the two power variables ($r = -.03$) was found for the institutions in this study. For core units, the .37 correlation showed a connection, although causal directions could not be determined.

Proposition 4

Although this is the most tentative of the five propositions, there were some useful findings about resource negotiation strategies. First, analysis of the interview responses and questionnaire comments generated a number of additional strategies (Hackman, 1983) that should be explored in future research. Second, multiple regressions with the eight strategy categories from the questionnaire added to environmental power and institutional power showed increased explanations of variance in resource allocations. For core department and office unit heads (excluding heads of divisions and schools), 60.1 percent ($p < .001$) of the variance was explained; for peripheral department and office unit heads, 42.5 percent ($p < .10$) was explained. The most provocative finding was that "focusing on unit needs" loaded high on the core unit regression, supporting the conclusion that core units benefit when they help themselves. For peripheral units, "focusing on institutional needs" was high, supporting the idea that peripheral units gain when they contribute to the total institution.

Proposition 5

Two separate stepwise regressions were run to examine the unique and combined contributions of environmental and institutional power: one for core respondents and one for peripheral respondents (Table 3). Environmental and institutional power were virtually independent of each other for peripheral units; the two peripheral power indices correlated -.03. Even for the two core-unit indices, with a correlation of .37, their combination improved upon either considered alone. The correlations of environmental power with resource allocations was .54 for core units and .44 for peripheral units; the correlation of institutional power with resource allocations was .53 for core units and .41 for peripheral units.

For core respondents (Table 3), the combined environmental and institutional power indices explained 41.3 percent of the variance in budgetary change, with a multiple correlation of .64. The environmental power index alone explained 28.6 percent of the variance, and the institutional power index alone explained 28 percent. For peripheral respondents, the combined indices accounted for 38.1 percent of budgetary change, a multiple correlation of .62. Separately, the variance explained was 19.8 percent for environmental power, 17 percent for institutional power.

A second way to examine the combined power indices is shown in the contingency table in Figure 1. Each index was divided into high and low scores. All of the respondents with high-high scores on both the environmental and institutional power indices were budgetary gainers, and all but one of the low-low were losers. For both core and peripheral respondents, several respondents fell on the diagonal of mixed scores.

Figure 1

Contingency table for high and low environmental and institutional power indices showing losers and gainers for core (C) and peripheral (P) units.

		ENVIRONMENTAL POWER					
		LOW			HIGH		
INSTITUTIONAL POWER	LOW	10C	Losers	2p	4C	Losers	7P
		1C	Gainers	0P	5C	Gainers	2P
							BG
	HIGH	3C	Losers	8P	0C	Losers	0P
		3C	Gainers	6P	13C	Gainers	8P

An additional set of regressions that added resource negotiation strategies (and because of the different content in strategy questions excluded division heads) showed even higher values for explained variance (60.1 percent for 29 core department heads, 42.5 percent for 25 peripheral department heads) (Hackman, 1983).

Discussion and Conclusions

Provisional Testing

Although the purpose of this research was to develop rather than to test a theory of resource allocations in colleges and universities, the initial results are quite promising. The study has demonstrated that a unit's centrality interacts with its environmental power and resource negotiation strategies to affect the internal resource allocations that it acquires from the organization. In addition, a unit's institutional power separately influences its internal resource allocations.

A number of built-in checks and balances support the study's validity and potential for replication. The two-phase study design offers some mutually substantiating findings. Subjective interview responses are reflected in answers to quantified questionnaires; top administrators usually agree with heads of departmental and divisional units; and qualitative analyses are supported by quantitative statistics. Although the proposed theory requires additional testing and elaboration, it is possible to explore its potential contributions.

Relation to Past and Future Research

An important test of a theory's usefulness is its ability to integrate information that previously may have seemed confused and complex. Although it is not claimed that the proposed theory can make sense out of all the related literature, there are connections with past research, and it makes potential contributions that improve understanding. First, how does the present research and the proposed theory connect with previous work on power among organizational units? Second, which of the many organizational views of higher education institutions are supported by the research results? Third, what does the proposed theory suggest about budgeting theory and practice? And fourth, what is most unique about the research findings of this study?

PREVIOUS RESEARCH ON POWER AMONG INTRAORGANIZATIONAL UNITS

Although the present study followed a somewhat different methodology from that of Salancik and Pfeffer's (1974) research on academic departments, the findings about environmental power accord with their conclusions.

The present work also proposes the following ideas in the effort to understand power among intraorganizational units in colleges and universities: In addition to environmental power, there may be a second, sometimes unrelated internal institutional power that contributes to a unit's ability to acquire internal resources. For peripheral units, there was virtually no (-.03) correlation between the two power variables. Resource negotiation strategies are a third factor identified as affecting and adding to an explanation of internal resource allocations. Finally, the present research differs from that of Salancik and Pfeffer in its consideration of nonacademic as well as academic units. Power dynamics for core (academic) units were found to be quite different from those for peripheral units.

The present research was conducted without reference to the strategic-contingencies theory of intraorganizational power proposed by Hickson et al. (1971) and further tested by Hinings et al. (1974). It is useful, therefore, to compare the two theories. Strategic-contingencies theory includes several concepts closely related to those in the present study. Both theories emphasize structural sources of power rather than personality factors of individuals as explanations of power differences (Hinings et al., 1974: 23); both consider organizations as open systems, and both follow Emerson's (1962) notion that the power of a unit is related to the dependency of other units upon it.

As in the present work, the strategic-contingencies theorists emphasize the importance of centrality, but they define it as the degree to which a unit's activities are linked to the work-flow of other units. Another difference is their treatment of power as the dependent variable, to be predicted from measures of (1) substitutability, (2) uncertainty, (3) coping with uncertainty, and (4) centrality (place in workflow of units). In the present research, the dependent variable is not power itself, but rather a result of its exercise — the allocation of internal resources.

The two sets of concepts are clearly related. That they were developed quite separately provides a certain level of validation for the present research. Further work is required to identify the meaningful similarities and differences between the proposed theory and that of other theories of power among intraorganizational units.

ORGANIZATIONAL THEORY

Institutions of higher education have been variously characterized: as organized anarchies (Cohen and March, 1974), as collegial communities (Goodman, 1962; Millett, 1962), as academic bureaucracies (Stroup, 1966), as open systems (Pfeffer and Salancik, 1974), as increasingly centralized institutions (Mortimer and McConnell, 1978), and as political organizations (Baldridge, 1971; Pfeffer and Salancik, 1974; Pfeffer, 1977; Hills and Mahoney, 1978). At least for the study of resource allocations, the results of this study support the view of colleges and universities as political organizations that operate as open systems in interaction with the environment.

Open systems. The value of the open-systems perspective is demonstrated by analyses of one of the theory's key concepts, environmental power. Multiple regressions of questionnaire data from unit heads show that this variable accounts for about one-fourth of the variance in budget allocations. Similarly, central administrators who were interviewed for the study spontaneously and repeatedly used this notion to explain why particular budgetary units had gained or lost in recent years.

Political organizations. The very consideration of budgetary allocations and budgetary strategies is de facto a political issue, if we accept Harold Lasswell's classic definition of politics, "Who gets what, when, and where." This study has been about who (which budgetary units) gets what (budgetary gains or losses), when (in recent years), and how (with what environmental and institutional power, using what budgetary strategies). The definition of environmental power draws heavily on Emerson's (1962) and Pfeffer and Salancik's (1974) views of power, which link political behavior directly to systems theory.

Two other key concepts add support to the political view of colleges and universities: Institutional power is defined as the strength of a unit's influence within the organization, demonstrated by such measures as support from the president, number of students served, visibility, and overall internal power ratings. The addition of institutional power to environmental power ratings increases the explanation of resource allocation variance in the data to about two-fifths. And the further addition of resource negotiation strategies, another political concept, raises the statistical explanation even higher.

BUDGETING THEORY AND PRACTICE

Much of the debate on this topic concerns the possibilities and usefulness of rational versus political views of budgeting, of technique and analysis versus politics (Caruthers and Orwig, 1979). The present study reinforces the conclusion of others (e.g., Wildavsky, 1979) that budgeting is a political exercise. At the same time, the analytical results suggest that there may also be an inherent rationality in budgeting, even for institutions whose budget methods are largely incremental. Although there are efforts at some of the six institutions to extract rational justifications for budget requests and, in some cases, to use planning models and information planning systems, the budgeting rationality referred to here is something different from particular budgeting or planning techniques.

The significant relation of environmental power to resource allocations suggests the possibility of a rational link between budget decisions and the needs of an institution, a link that may be stronger in times of financial stress than in periods in which there is more budgetary slack. Accurate data about the relative ability of units to attract critical outside resources could be a useful tool both for central budget decision makers and (especially when "favorable" to their units) for unit heads.

UNIQUE CONTRIBUTIONS

The importance of centrality in understanding how organizations allocate resources is the most distinctive finding of the present study. Differences between core and peripheral units are the cornerstone of the proposed theory. Any future research should clarify the concept of centrality and refine the understanding of how to measure what is a core and what is a peripheral program. Second, the power indices identified for core and peripheral units should be tested and revised. Of all the findings, the power indices are the most likely to have been affected by the particularities of participating institutions and individuals.

IMPLICATIONS FOR PRACTITIONERS

Finally, it is tempting to look for practical guidelines from the present research, although the findings must be replicated to increase the reliability of any suggestions. Because the study focuses on resource allocations among budgetary units, the most logical implications are for budgetary unit heads. One interpretation is that unit strategists should determine first whether their programs are primarily core or peripheral and then develop their cases accordingly. It appears that core programs will gain internal resources when they acquire environmental resources that contribute to their own purposes — because, in fact, their needs are most often allied with the mission of the organization. In contrast, peripheral programs will benefit internally when they focus on broader institutional needs and bring in external resources that contribute to the whole.

The dynamics of the proposed theory are especially visible during times of economic stress, when the external resources most needed by colleges and universities are financial. The present findings suggest that during these times, peripheral units such as admissions and development offices, which bring in tuition and gifts, will gain in internal resources — particularly if they focus their resource negotiation strategies on the needs of the total institution. Core units, in contrast, will increase when they attract external academic resources, such as students and academic prestige, to their particular departments. Core units gain when they help themselves; peripheral units gain when they help the total institution. And, the administrators of all these units gain when they better understand the complexity of the resource allocation process.

I wish to thank the following people for their support and assistance: Richard L. Alfred, Elizabeth Fagerberg, Zelda Gamson, J. Richard Hackman, Robert L. Kahn, James L. Miller, Jr., Marvin W. Peterson, and Beverly Waters. The anonymous reviewers and the editors of ASQ also gave very helpful comments on an earlier version of the paper.

Notes

[1] The term "subunit" is used interchangeably with "unit" in the literature on resource allocations and intraorganizational power.

[2] Future research should explore the entire continuum of centrality, including non-academic units that may be considered core by some observers and academic units that are closer to the peripheral pole.

[3] For all of the analyses of resource allocations, the questionnaire respondents are heads of units with relatively extreme gains or losses. Analyses of units across the full spectrum of budget change might show somewhat different results.

References

Baldridge, J. Victor. *Power and Conflict in the University Research in the Sociology of Complex Organizations.* New York: Wiley, 1971.

Bowen, Howard Rothmann. *Investment in Learning: The Individual and Social Value of American Higher Education.* San Francisco: Jossey-Bass, 1977.

Caruthers, J. Kent, and Melvin D. Orwig. *Budgeting in Higher Education.* Washington, DC: AAHE/ERIC, 1979.

Cohen, Michael P., and James G. March. *Leadership and Ambiguity: The American College President.* New York: McGraw-Hill, 1974.

Collier, D. J. "Program Classification Structure," 2d ed. *Technical Report 106.* Boulder, CO: NCHEMS, 1978.

Conrad, Clifton F. "A grounded theory of academic change." *Sociology of Education,* 1978, 51; 101-112, .

Emerson, R. E. "Power-dependence relations." *American Sociological Review,* 1962, 27; 31-41.

French, John R. P., Jr., and Bertram Raven. "The bases of social power." in Barry M. Staw (ed.), *Psychological Foundations of Organizational Behavior.* Santa Monica. CA: Goodyear, 1977; 257-265.

Gamson, W. *Power and Discontent.* Homewood, IL: Dorsey, 1968.

Glaser, Barney G., and Anselm L. Strauss. *The Discovery of Grounded Theory: Strategies for Qualitative Research.* Chicago: Aldine, 1967.

Goodman, Paul. *The Community of Scholars.* New York: Random House, 1962.

Gulko, Warren W. "Program Classification Structure." *NCHEMS Technical Report 27.* Boulder. CO: WICHE, 1972.

Hackman, Judith Dozier. "Power and Peripherality: Developing a Practical Theory of Resource Allocations in Colleges and Universities." Unpublished Ph.D. dissertation, University of Michigan, Ann Arbor, 1983.

Hickson, D. J., C. R. Hinings, C. A. Lee, R. E. Schneck, and J. M. Pennings. "A Strategic Contingencies' Theory of Intraorganizational Power." *Administrative Science Quarterly*. 1971, 16; 216-229.

Hills, Frederick S., and Thomas A. Mahoney. "University Budgets and Organizational Decision Making." *Administrative Science Quarterly*, 1978, 23; 454-465.

Hinings, C. R., D. J. Hickson, J. M. Pennings, and R. E. Schneck. "Structural Conditions of Intraorganizational Power." *Administrative Science Quarterly*, 1974, 19; 22-44.

Ikenberry, Stanley O., and Renee C. Friedman. *Beyond Academic Departments: The Story of Institutes and Centers*. San Francisco: Jossey-Bass, 1972.

Katz, Daniel, and Robert L. Kahn. *The Social Psychology of Organizations*, 2d ed. New York: Wiley, 1978.

Lasswell, Harold D., and Abraham Kaplan. "Power and Society: A Framework for Political Inquiry." *Yale Law School Studies*, 2. New Haven, CT: Yale University Press, 1950.

Miller, James G. *Living Systems*. New York: McGraw-Hill, 1978.

Millett, John David. *The Academic Community*. New York: McGraw-Hill, 1962.

Mortimer, Kenneth P., and T. R. McConnell. *Sharing Authority Effectively*. San Francisco: Jossey-Bass, 1978.

Perrow, Charles. "Departmental Power and Perspectives in Industrial Firms." in Mayer N. Zald (ed.), *Power in Organizations*. Nashville. TN: Vanderbilt University Press, 1970; 59-85.

Pfeffer, Jeffrey. "Power and Resource Allocation in Organizations." In Barry M. Staw and Gerald R. Salancik (eds.), New Directions in Organizational Behavior. Chicago: St. Clair Press, 1977; 235-265.

Pfeffer, Jeffrey, and Gerald R. Salancik. "Organizational Decision Making as a Political Process: The Case of a University Budget." *Administrative Science Quarterly*, 1974, 19; 135-151.

Salancik, Gerald R., and Jeffrey Pfeffer. "The Bases and Uses of Power in Organizational Decision Making: The Case of a University." *Administrative Science Quarterly*, 1974, 19; 453-473.

Simon, Herbert. "Notes on the Observation and Measurement of Political Power." *Journal of Politics*, 1953, 15; 500-516.

Stroup, Herbert Howitt. *Bureaucracy in Higher Education*. New York: Free Press, 1966.

Weber, Max. Theory of Social and Economic Organizations. New York: Oxford University Press, 1947.

Wildavsky, Aaron. The Politics of the Budgetary Process, 3d ed. Boston: Little.,Brown, 1979.

Appendix: Peripheral and Core Indices of Environmental and Institutional Poww and Correlations with Resource Allocations*

Variable	Correlation	Variable	Correlation
Environmental power		Institutional power	
Core index		*Core index*	
Prestige	.56	Power of unit in the institution	
Ability to cope with current		at present	.41
societal needs	.36	Number of students served	.38
Recruitment and retention of		Support of president for unit	.33
students	.19	Institution's legal commitments	
Support from alumni	−.21	to unit	−.25
		Number times talk with central	
		administrators per month	−.22
		Visibility of unit in the institution	.16
		Visibility of unit outside the	
		institution	.16
		Length of time in the institution	−.14
		Number of full-time-equivalent	
		people in unit	−.14
Peripheral index		*Peripheral Index*	
Support from federal government	.40	Length of time in the institution	−.39
Ability to cope with current		Visibility of unit in the institution	.34
societal needs	−.35	Power of unit in the institution	
Support from foundations	.21	at present	.32
Prestige	−.15	Visibility of unit to board of trustees	.25
Support from business and industry	.14	Number times talk with central	
Recruitment and retention of students	−.13	administrators per month	.16

Index scores were averages of the variables listed above, as measured by related questionnaire items (shown in Table 1). For the two institutional power indices, these were the means of the items that asked how a unit compares with other similar budgetary units in the institution on each of the listed variables. For the two environmental power indices, index scores were weighted means of substitutability times institutional criticality for the listed variables. Substitutability was measured by items that asked how the unit's contribution of a resource compared with other similar units; institutional criticality was the average of all respondents in an institution to items that asked about the importance of each resource to the institution.

Index construction followed five steps: (1) one-way anovas were computed on all relevant power items (listed in Table 1) between gainers and losers, separately for core and for peripheral respondents; (2) items were chosen for each index using a rule that required higher significance levels for items with more missing data; (3) missing data were replaced with average group ratings; (4) items that correlated negatively were inverted; and (5) the modified scores were then averaged to compute the four indices.

Organizational Adaptation and Higher Education

KIM S. CAMERON

The recent report of the National Commission on Excellence in Education [46] concluded that "the educational foundations of our society are presently being eroded by a rising tide of mediocrity that threatens our very future as a nation and a people. What was unimaginable a generation ago has begun to occur—others are matching and surpassing our educational attainments." The explicit objective of the commission's report was to generate reform of our educational system in fundamental ways and to renew the nation's commitment to schools and colleges of high quality throughout the length and breadth of our land."

A variety of recommendations were made in the report, which called for innovation and adaptation on the part of educational institutions. These recommendations focused both on elementary and secondary schools and on colleges and universities. However, before educational institutions can implement these recommendations, they must become both knowledgeable and adept at instituting organizational change. They will need to become effective at implementing innovation, reform, and adaptation. One purpose of this special issue of the *Journal of Higher Education* is to point out ways in which reforms, innovations, and adaptations can and have occurred successfully. Hopefully, these articles will contribute to the renewal of America's educational institutions in general and of liberal arts colleges in particular.

Our focus in this issue is mainly on liberal arts colleges, for reasons pointed out in the *Introduction*, and on the concept of adaptation, as opposed to innovation or reform, for reasons that will become clear later. This article reviews what is known about organizational adaptation and points out types of adaptation that will be needed in institutions of higher education in the future. The focus is a conceptual one, and specific adaptive actions taken by institutions are not reviewed. Rather, the purpose is to give the reader a framework within which to comprehend adaptation in educational organizations.

In the first section, major conceptual approaches to organizational adaptation are reviewed. The second section discusses the probable environment that institutions of higher education are likely to face in the future that will require adaptation. The third section discusses some adaptive strategies and institutional characteristics that will be needed by colleges and universities if they are to remain effective.

Section 1: Approaches to Organizational Adaptation

"Organizational adaptation" refers to modifications and alterations in the organization or its components in order to adjust to changes in the external environment. Its purpose is to restore equilibrium to an imbalanced condition. Adaptation generally refers to a process, not an event, whereby changes are instituted in organizations. Adaptation does not necessarily imply reactivity on the part of an organization (i.e., adaptation is not just waiting for the environment to change and then reacting to it) because proactive or anticipatory adaptation is possible as well. But the emphasis is definitely on responding to some discontinuity or lack of fit that arises between the organization and its environment.

This kind of organizational change is not the same as "planned change," or what is often called Organization Development (OD). Adaptation focuses on changes motivated by the external environment; OD focuses on changes motivated from within the organization. OD is generally oriented toward changes in individual attitudes and behaviors and in the organization's culture; adaptation is more concerned with organization-level change (see, e.g., [12]). Goodman and Kurke [23] differentiated adaptation and planned change in the following ways:

> Planned organizational change deals with the basis of change; adaptation deals with the conditions or sources of change. Planned organizational change focuses primarily on change within the organization, but the adaptation literature focuses primarily on populations of organizations, and on organization-environment interfaces, and on changes within an organization that are environmentally dictated. The planned organization literature emphasizes the process of actually creating change rather than writing about the processes of change (adaptation literature). The planned organizational change literature is devoted to methods and techniques, but the adaptation literature is devoted to theorizing about the change processes or outcomes. [23, p. 4]

This article, and this issue in general, focuses on the process of adaptation because of the pervasive influence of the external environment on liberal arts colleges. Several articles in this issue (e.g., Zammuto, Pfnister, Martin) point out the threats that face liberal arts colleges because of changing environments. Most observers agree that environmental turbulence and complexity have greatly accelerated in recent years (see [58, 59, 41, 52]) and that the ability of organizations to cope with those changes is being stretched. As Toffler noted:

> I gradually came to be appalled by how little is actually known about adaptivity, either by those who call for and create vast changes in our society, or by those who supposedly prepare us to cope with those changes. Earnest intellectuals talk bravely about "educating for change," or "preparing people for the future." But we know virtually nothing about how to do it. In the most rapidly changing environment to which man has ever been exposed, we remain pitifully ignorant of how the human animal copes. [58, p. 2]

Toffler's observation, that little is known about adaptation, is beginning to be rectified somewhat on the organization level. The body of literature on organizational adaptation is relatively new (most of it has appeared since 1970), but it has nevertheless become quite extensive. In fact, it is so extensive that a summary of it must, of necessity, be selective and abridged. Therefore, in this first section, general themes are discussed and examples are used, but a comprehensive survey is not attempted.

One way to organize the conceptual approaches to organizational adaptation is to use a continuum anchored on one end by the assumption that managers have *no* power to influence the adaptability and long-term survival of their organizations. On the other end of the continuum is the assumption that managers have *complete power* to create adaptability and to ensure long-term survival. Figure 1 summarizes the major approaches to organizational adaptation on the basis of this continuum. These approaches to adaptation are briefly explained below.

Approaches Assuming Little or No Managerial Influences

Aldrich [2], Aldrich and Pfeffer [3], Hannan and Freeman [24], Birnbaum [8], McKelvey [39], and others have proposed and elaborated a "population ecology" or "natural selection" view of organizational adaptation. The population ecology approach to adaptation focuses on changes in environmental "niches" (i.e., subunits of the environment that support organizations). Two types of "niche" change can occur that lead to organizational adaptation. One is a change in the size of the niche, or the amount of resources available to organizations. The other is a change in the shape of the niche, or the type of organizational activities supported. Zammuto and Cameron [68] pointed out what adaptations are required of populations of organizations when faced with these different types of changes in environmental niches. For example, when a population of organizations encounters a change in niche shape (e.g., certain organizational activities are no longer supported), generalist organizations—those involved in a wide range of activities—are most adaptative. Successful adaptation requires becoming more diversified. On the other hand, when populations of organizations encounter changes in niche size (e.g., fewer resources are available), specialist organizations —those that are especially good at a narrow range of activities—are most adaptative. Successful adaptation requires organizations to specialize.

The population ecology approach suggests that adaptation is meaningful only if viewed from the population level of analysis (i.e., single organization changes are largely irrelevant). According to advocates, this level of analysis is important because of the many constraints and inertias inhibiting managerial action in organizations (i.e., formal structure, past history, norms, policies, and so on). The only meaningful change occurs as major shifts among entire populations of organizations, not as minor adjustments in existing organizational forms. The environment is viewed as such a powerful and pervasive force that it selects those organizational forms (or adaptations) that are to persist and other organizational forms die out. (For example, Hannan and Freeman [24] suggest that unstable environments select generalist organizations and stable environments select specialist organizations.)

The process is considered to be much like biological selection theories. The fittest species— those that evolve characteristics that are compatible with the environment—survive while other species become extinct. Most organizations adapt, therefore, not because of intelligent or creative managerial action but by the random or evolutionary development of characteristics that are compatible with the environment. Managerial discretion and influence is neither present nor relevant.

Figure 1

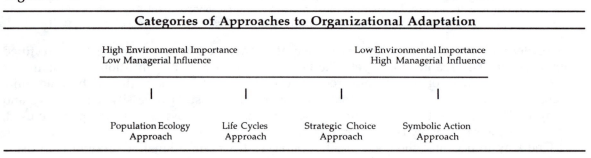

Categories of Approaches to Organizational Adaptation

High Environmental Importance Low Managerial Influence		Low Environmental Importance High Managerial Influence	
Population Ecology Approach	Life Cycles Approach	Strategic Choice Approach	Symbolic Action Approach

Another approach to adaptation that emphasizes evolutionary change and the powerful role of the environment but that allows for more managerial discretion is the "life cycles" approach to adaptation (see [13, 14, 51] for reviews). Single organizations are the preferred units of analysis, and they are assumed to progress through at least four sequential stages of development. At each stage, unique organizational features develop in order to overcome certain general problems encountered by all organizations. Without direct managerial intervention to alter this natural evolution, organizational adaptations tend to follow a predictable sequence. Cameron and Whetten summarized the sequence as follows:

> Organizations begin in a stage, labelled "creativity and entrepreneurship," in which marshalling resources, creating an ideology, and forming an ecological niche are emphasized. [The problem faced by the organization in this stage is to build legitimacy and acquire the resources needed to survive.] The second stage, the "collectivity" stage, includes high commitment and cohesion among members, face-to-face communication and informal structures, long hours of dedicated service to the organization, and an emerging sense of collectivity and mission. The organizational emphasis is on internal processes

and practices, rather than on external contingencies. [The problem faced by the organization is mobilizing the work force and building interdependence.] In the third stage, "formalization and control," where procedures and policies become institutionalized, goals are formalized, conservatism predominates, and flexibility is reduced. The emphasis is on efficiency of production. [The organizational problem in this stage is coordinating and stabilizing the work force and improving efficiency.] The fourth stage emphasizes "elaboration of structure" where decentralization, domain expansion, and renewed adaptability occur, and new multipurpose subsystems are established. (The organizational problem is overcoming rigidity and conservatism and expanding to meet new constituency demands.] [13, p. 527]

In each new stage of development, certain problems are encountered that are overcome by progressing on to the next life-cycle stage. That is, organizations encounter similar issues as they develop over time, and adaptation occurs by acquiring characteristics of the next life-cycle stage. This new stage solves the issues encountered in the previous stage but also generates issues that motivate further life-cycle development. Therefore, this approach to adaptation assumes that there is a natural tendency in organizations to follow a life-cycle pattern of development.

Two assumptions modify this approach and make it less deterministic than the population ecology view. The first assumption is that managers can speed up, slow down, or even abort this sequential development by their actions. That is, they can cause an organization to stay in an early stage for a long time, to move through the sequence very rapidly, or to go out of business before ever reaching subsequent stages. Second, these stages are most typical of the early history of organizations. After the fourth stage is reached, organizations may recycle through the sequence again as a result of unusual environmental events, leadership turnover, organizational membership changes, and so on. Managerial action can help determine which stage is returned to after stage 4 (see [14]).

Approaches Assuming Substantial Managerial Influence

On the other end of the continuum are approaches to adaptation that consider the decisions and actions of managers, not the external environment, to be the most important causes of organizational adaptation. They emphasize that managers can choose which environment the organization operates in, they can control and manipulate the environment, they can scan and thereby predict in advance environmental events, and so on. In short, organizations are not assumed to be at the mercy of an immutable environment; rather, they can act and influence their environment. The diverse literature on adaptation resulting from managerial action is organized into two major categories for the purpose of review. Several different models of adaptation are subsumed under each category.

One major category of adaptation models is the "strategic choice" approach [17, 3, 5]. A sampling of the different models summarized by this approach includes the "resource dependence" model [49], the "political economy" model [61], the "strategy-structure" model [16], and models by Miles and Snow [40], Miles and Cameron [42], March [35], and Miller and Friesen [43]. Whereas these authors recognize the importance of external environmental influences and the need for a fit between environment and an organization's structure and process [31], a variety of strategies are available to managers that can modify the environment and determine the success or failure of adaptation. As Chamberlain stated:

> Organizations are obviously not pushed and pulled and hauled by market forces which overwhelm them; rather, they demonstrably choose to follow a certain course of action which differs from other courses which they might have chosen and which, indeed, some of their number do elect to follow. Discretion is present. How important it is in the end result is still a moot point, but at least there is no basis for pretending that it has no effect. [15, p. 47]

The strategic choice approach is illustrated by Miles and Cameron [42], who found that organizations adapted very successfully to an extremely turbulent and hostile environment by implementing three types of strategies in sequence: "domain defense" strategies (designed to enhance the legitimacy of the organization and buffer it from environmental encroachment), "domain offense" strategies (designed to expand in current areas of expertise and exploit weaknesses in the environment), and "domain creation" strategies (designed to minimize risk by diversifying into safer or less turbulent areas of the environment). (See Cameron [11]) for a discussion of these strategies in higher education organizations.)

Miles and Snow [40] suggested that organizations develop a particular orientation—a "strategic competence"—that leads them to implement these various types of strategies at different times and in different ways. For example, "prospector" organizations are inclined to be "first in," to implement strategies early and innovatively. "Analyzer" organizations are inclined to wait for evidence that the strategy will be successful before implementing new adaptations. "Defenders" seek for stability and are slow to adapt. "Reactors" implement strategies sporadically and are often unable to follow through with a consistent adaptive response. Miles and Snow [40] and Snow and Hrebiniak [57] have found empirical evidence linking these strategic orientations to effective adaptation under varying environmental conditions.

Miller and Friesen [43] studied thirty-six organizations and 135 different organizational adaptations in order to identify how organizations adapted over time. They used historical case studies so a longitudinal time-frame could be observed. Evidence for the strategic choice approach was found as they identified several major "archetypes of organizational transition." The most prominent archetypes among successful organizations were entrepreneurial revitalization, scanning and troubleshooting, consolidation, centralization and boldness, and decentralization and professionalization. These authors concluded that "there do not appear to be a very great number of common transition types" [43, p. 288]. That is, only a few major adaptation strategies implemented by managers are typical of a large variety of organizations.

One major issue that permeates the strategic choice approach is whether adaptations are implemented incrementally (i.e., small, piecemeal changes are put into place by managers) or in a revolutionary way (i.e., major shifts occur affecting many organizational elements). On the one hand, some writers suggest that organizations adapt by "muddling through" or by implementing "a succession of incremental changes" [32]. Change occurs without requiring major aberrations from the routine. As March put it:

> Managers and leaders propose changes, including foolish ones; they try to cope with the environment and to control it; they respond to other members of the organization; they issue orders and manipulate incentives. Since they play conventional roles, organizational leaders are not likely to behave in strikingly unusual ways. And if a leader tries to march toward strange destinations, an organization is likely to deflect the effort. Simply to describe leadership as conventional and constrained by organizational realities, however, is to risk misunderstanding its importance. Neither success nor change requires dramatic action. The conventional, routine activities that produce most organizational change require ordinary people to do ordinary things in a competent way. [35, p. 575]

On the other hand, Miller and Friesen [44] represent those who argue that adaptation occurs in a revolutionary way. They point out that organizations possess a great deal of momentum, or inertia, that serves to inhibit alterations or reforms. Past strategies, structures, goals, political coalitions, myths and ideologies, and so on contribute to that momentum, so that major adjustments in a substantial part of the organization have to be made in order for adaptation to occur.

> Organizational adaptation is likely to be characterized by periods of dramatic revolution in which there are reversals in the direction of change across a significantly large number of variables of strategy and structure. Revolutions that display reversals for a high proportion of variables occur with very significantly high frequency. These major reorientations seem to take place because many excesses or deficiencies have developed during periods of pervasive momentum or because a new strategy requires realignments among many variables. Thus there follows a myriad of structural and strategic reversals. [44, pp. 593, 612]

The second category of adaptation models on this end of the continuum is called the "symbolic action" approach [48, 47, 18, 7]. It differs from the strategic choice approach by focusing on change in symbols, interpretations, and stories as opposed to change in structure and technology. The logic of this approach is that organizations are glued together mainly by the presence of common interpretations of events, common symbols, common stories or legends, and so on or by a "social construction of reality" [7]. Social construction of reality means that the interpretation of reality in an organization is a product of social definition. Shared meanings are much more important than are events themselves. Part of the socialization process in organizations is giving members access to these common meanings. The role of the manager, in turn, is to create, manipulate, or perpetuate these meanings so that they are accepted in the organization and thereby influence organizational behavior. Pfeffer summarized this perspective in the following way:

> The activity of management is viewed as making what is going on in the organization meaningful and sensible to the organizational participants, and furthermore developing a social consensus and social definition around the activities being undertaken. Management involves more than labeling or sense making—it involves the development of a social consensus around those labels and the definition of activity. [48, p. 21]

Organizational adaptation comes about through the use of a variety of strategies involving language, ritual, and symbolic behavior designed to modify organization members' shared meanings. Weick [65] referred to this as "enacting" the external environment. Several of the more prominent methods of adaptation in this approach are as follows:

1. *Interpreting history and current events.* "The effectiveness of a leader lies in his ability to make activity meaningful for those in his role set—not to change behavior but to give others a sense of understanding what they are doing and especially to articulate it so they can communicate about the meaning of their behavior. . . . If in addition the leader can put it into words, then the meaning of what the group is doing becomes a social fact. . . . This dual capacity . . . to make sense of things and to put them into language meaningful to large numbers of people gives the person who has it enormous leverage" [50, pp. 94–95].

2. *Using rituals or ceremonies.* Gameson and Scotch [221 noted the ritualistic function of firing managers and coaches of professional sports teams whose win-loss records were bad. The firings did not so much represent a substantive change as they did a symbolic one designed to give the impression that things would get better. Inaugurations, ceremonies, and commencements are symbolic functions used frequently to manage meanings and interpretations in order to influence organizational adaptation.

3. *Using time and measurement.* Time spent is one measure of the importance of organizational activities (47). Therefore, spending more time at one activity than another helps managers convey messages of priority to other organization members. Similarly, what is measured almost always receives more attention in organizations than what is not measured. Adaptation is facilitated by managers, therefore, through their use of time and quantitative measurement.

4. *Redesigning physical space.* Providing a new physical setting often conveys the message that something new is going on or that a different direction is being pursued. Similarly, attributes of physical settings often are interpreted as manifestations of power in offices and buildings (e.g., larger space, higher space, more central space, and so on). Pfeffer noted that "skilled managers understand well the importance of physical settings for their symbolic value. The size, location, and configuration of physical space provide the backdrop against which other managerial activity takes place, and thereby influence the interpretation and meaning of that other activity" [48, p. 41].

5. *Introducing doubt.* "The introduction of doubt into a loosely coupled system is a much more severe change intervention than most people realize. Core beliefs, such as the presumption of logic and the logic of confidence, are crucial underpinnings that hold loose events together. If these beliefs are questioned, action stops, uncertainty is substantial, and receptiveness to change is high" [66, p. 392].

Each of these strategies of adaptation under the symbolic action approach assumes substantial power on the part of managers to change the definition of the external environment and to change organizational behavior in response to those definitions. The environment is not assumed to be immutable (as with the population ecology approach); on the contrary, it is assumed to be almost entirely a product of social definition. Adaptation occurs by changing definitions.

Review

By way of review, approaches to organizational adaptation can be organized into at least four categories based on the importance of the roles played by the external environment and by management in influencing organizational survival. The population ecology approach assumes a prominent role for the environment and virtually no role for management action. The life cycles approach assumes a prominent role for the environment and evolutionary forces, but some discretion is assumed for management in altering those naturalistic forces. The strategic choice approach assumes a prominent role for both environment and management, but the balance is shifted toward management. The strategies implemented by managers can change the external environment as well as the organization. The symbolic action approach assumes a prominent role for management, through the ability to manipulate symbols and social definitions, and a less prominent role for the external environment.

Having reviewed the major approaches to adaptation, the question remains: What does this mean for institutions of higher education? Is one approach to adaptation better than another? What should managers and administrators in institutions do to make their organizations more adaptable?

To answer these questions, it is necessary to review the environmental conditions that are likely to face institutions of higher education in the future. That is, to understand how colleges should adapt, it is first necessary to understand what conditions will be characteristic of the external environment that perpetuate imbalances and require adaptation. The next section speculates on what future environments will be like for educational organizations.

Section 2. The Nature of Postindustrial Environments

It is generally acknowledged that factors in the external environment are increasing in their influence on organizations. Organizations are more frequently being required to be good at adaptation in order to survive. Roeber noted, for example:

> The characteristic mode of change in Western industrialized countries has been integrative, and the key characteristic is loss of slack. Partial equilibrium solutions are

becoming less satisfactory, particularly where interaction between organizations and their social environment is involved. Consequently, the environment is becoming more of a factor inside organizations and requires more explicit attention. [52, p. 154]

Roeber's point, that the environment is becoming more dominant at the same time that organizations are faced with less slack, suggests that adaptive strategies should constitute a critical concern of future managers.

Several authors have discussed the changes that are occurring in the external environment that make attention to it more crucial than ever before. These changes are leading to what some call postindustrial society [56, 6], the technetronic era [9], the information society [38], the telematic society [37], and the third wave [59]. These authors all point out that environments in the future will be radically different for institutions than are the current environments of industrialized society. In a recent provocative article, for example, Huber [28] pointed out several ways in which postindustrial environments will be different from present or past environments. He stated that "postindustrial society will be characterized by more and increasing knowledge, more and increasing complexity, and more and increasing turbulence. These, in combination, will pose an organizational environment qualitatively more demanding than those in our experience" [28, p. 4].

Taking "increasing knowledge" as an example, environments of the future will contain a great deal more knowledge than is currently available. Because knowledge feeds on itself, the current knowledge explosion is likely to continue at exponential rates. The availability of computers that are more "friendly" (i.e., little, if any, training needed), more "intelligent" (i.e., able to coach the user), and more up-to-date (i.e., have access to more cutting-edge data) will contribute to both the availability of existing knowledge to institutions and the generation of new knowledge. Because knowledge will be able to be distributed rapidly, managers and administrators in institutions will have more information upon which to base decisions and less need to interact in face-to-face meetings to obtain it. Knowledge will become more continuous in its availability, more wide-ranging in the subjects it covers, and more direct in its sources.

This increase in knowledge and its availability through computer technology is also likely to produce increased complexity in the environment. Complexity is generally defined by three dimensions: numerosity, specialization or diversity, and interdependence. Miller explained the relationship between these three factors: "As a system's components become more numerous, they become specialized, with resulting increased interdependence" [45, p. 5]. That is, managers and administrators in institutions in a postindustrial environment will be exposed to a greater number of environmental elements (i.e., time and distance buffers will be greatly reduced by communication and transportation technologies, and more elements in the environment will become directly relevant). This abundance of environmental elements will force a greater degree of specialization of managers and administrators since overload could quickly occur otherwise. Increased specialization will, in turn, lead to the requirement of even greater interdependence among managers and institutions. Although institutions will have to be more loosely coupled in structure to cope with this environmental complexity [31], they will also need to become more tightly coupled in their information exchange.

The knowledge explosion and the increased complexity of the environment also contribute to a greater degree of turbulence. That is, increased access to information will require more rapid decision making and action implementation. Events in this kind of an environment will, as a result, occur more rapidly, and the timeliness required of managers will produce a tendency toward short timeframe strategies. More decisions in less time, along with a tendency toward shorter and more numerous events, will lead to a major increase in the turbulence of organizational environments (see [28] for an elaboration).

Increases in knowledge, complexity, and turbulence in postindustrial environments will place enormous strains on managers of educational organizations. In particular, although the necessity of designing and implementing adaptive strategies will dramatically increase, the "bounded rationality" [36] of managers will act as a constraint on their ability to do so. That is, the cognitive capacity of managers can be exceeded easily by the necessity to consider all the information and events present in a postindustrial environment. It is simply impossible for managers to initiate adaptive strategies in the same ways in postindustrial environments as they do now. The institutions themselves will have to be designed so as to enhance their ability to adapt, aside from the manager's specific strategies. Simon explained this requirement in the following way:

> Organizational decision making in the organizations of the postindustrial world shows every sign of becoming a great deal more complex than the decision making of the past. As a consequence of this fact, the decision-making process, rather than the processes contributing immediately and directly to the production of the organization's final output, will bulk larger and larger as the central activity in which the organization is engaged in the postindustrial society, the central problem is not how lo organize to produce efficiently (although this will always remain an important consideration), but how to organize to make decisions—that is, to process information. [56, pp. 269–70]

In view of these turbulent conditions, it becomes clear that all four approaches to organizational adaptation will be required as managers and administrators encounter the postindustrial environment. Institutional forms will have to emerge that are compatible with a diversity of environmental elements (the population ecology approach). Transitions to new stages of development will have to be closely monitored and planned for since they will occur more rapidly and sporadically in a postindustrial environment (the life cycles approach). Strategic choices by managers will be required that enhance the adaptability of the institution by expanding information search capacities while constraining information-processing requirements in order to make the choices more reasonable (the strategic choice approach). interpreting the environment for the institution will become an even more critical task for managers due to its complexity and turbulence (the symbolic action approach).

Although none of these activities (i.e., designing diversity into institutions, managing rapid organizational transitions, implementing strategic choices, and interpreting the environment) are unknown to managers and administrators, the nature of the postindustrial environment and the phenomenon of bounded rationality will require that they be implemented in the kinds of institutions that have not been common in the past. That is, the nature of the institutions themselves will need to be different if they are to be adaptive to this new environment. The third section of this article proposes some characteristics that will be required by institutions of higher education and by managers in order to remain adaptable in future environments.

Section 3. Adaptability and the Janusian Institution

In discussing the challenges of managing organizations during turbulent times, Drucker observed some characteristics that managers must assure if organizations are to survive. "The one certainty about the times ahead, the times in which managers will have to work and to perform, is that they will be turbulent times. And in turbulent times, the first task of management is to make sure of the institution's capacity for survival, to make sure of its structural strength and soundness, of its capacity to survive a blow, to adapt to sudden change, and to avail itself of new opportunities" [19, p. 1]. For managers and administrators in higher education to assure capacity for survival, strength and soundness, adaptability to sudden change, and the ability to take advantage of new opportunities in a postindustrial environment with turbulence, information overload, rapid-fire events, and complexity all increasing at exponential rates, they will need to become Janusian thinkers and develop Janusian institutions.

Janusian Thinking

Rothenburg [53] introduced the concept of "Janusian thinking" while investigating the creative achievements of individuals such as Einstein, Mozart, Picasso, and O'Neill, as well as fifty-four highly creative artists and scientists in the United States and Great Britain. Janusian thinking is named after the Roman god Janus, who was pictured as having at least two faces looking in different directions at the same time. Janusian thinking occurs when two contradictory thoughts are held to be true simultaneously. The explanation or resolution of the apparent contradiction is what leads to major breakthroughs in insight.

> In Janusian thinking, two or more opposites or antitheses are conceived simultaneously, either as existing side by side, or as equally operative, valid, or true. In an apparent defiance of logic or of physical possibility, the creative person consciously formulates the simultaneous operation of antithetical elements and develops those into integrated entities and creations. It is a leap that transcends ordinary logic. What emerges is no mere combination or blending of elements: the conception does not only contain different entities, it contains opposing and antagonistic elements, which are understood as coexistent. As a self-contradictory structure, the Janusian formulation is surprising when seriously posited in naked form. [54, p. 55]

The surprising nature of Janusian formulations results from the pre-conception that two opposites cannot both be valid at the same time. However, holding such thoughts engenders the flexibility of thought that is a prerequisite for individual creativity. Such flexibility is also the key to effective problem solving. As pointed out by Interaction Associates:

> Flexibility in thinking is critical to good problem solving. A problem solver should be able to conceptually dance around the problem like a good boxer, jabbing and poking, without getting caught in one place or "fixated." At any given moment, a good problem solver should be able to apply a large number of strategies. Moreover, a good problem solver is a person who has developed, through his understanding of strategies and experiences in problem solving, a sense of appropriateness of what is likely to be the most useful strategy at any particular time. [30, p. 15]

Similarly, perpetuating Janusian characteristics in institutions also has the effect of producing flexibility and adaptability, and it enables organizations to cope better with unpredictable environmental events. A large variety of sometimes contradictory characteristics must be present in order to make adaptation effective on the institution level. For example, Weick pointed out some of these contradictory characteristics by asserting:

> The problem of organizational effectiveness has traditionally been punctuated into conclusions such as those that the effective organization is flexible and productive, satisfies its members, is profitable, acquires resources, minimizes strain, controls the environment, develops, is efficient, retains employees, grows, is integrated, communicates openly, and survives. I would like to propose a different set of punctuations. Specifically, I would suggest that the effective organization is (1) garrulous, (2) clumsy, (3) superstitious, (4) hypocritical, (5) monstrous, (6) octopoid, (7) wandering, and (8) grouchy. [64, p. 193]

Several Janusian characteristics are discussed below that are proposed as necessary in effective higher education institutions in postindustrial environments.

Janusian Institutions

In addition to being aware of and implementing all four of the approaches to adaptation discussed previously, managers and administrators will need to perpetuate the following characteristics in their postindustrial institutions. Both loose coupling and tight coupling will be required. A loosely coupled system is one where connections among elements are weak, indirect, occasional, negligible, or discontinuous (see [62, 66]). Diffusion from one part of the organization to another occurs unevenly, sporadically, and unpredictably, if it occurs at all. Loose coupling refers to process looseness, not necessarily structural looseness. Tightly coupled systems, on the other hand, are controlled and coordinated so as to achieve specified goals. Centralization and hierarchy are prevalent so that all organizational action is directed toward similar purposes. Structure and process are interdependent (see [55]).

Lutz [33, 34] recently pointed out that the main responsibility of managers in higher education is to reinforce and perpetuate the tightly coupled elements in their institutions. Weick's statement is used as support for this point of view: "The chief responsibility of the administrator in a loosely coupled system is to reaffirm and solidify those ties that do exist" [67, p. 276]. Lutz responded: "That is exactly the point I was trying to make in my article, hence its title. To reaffirm and strengthen organizational ties or couplings is the administrator's chief responsibility. As university administrators fail in that responsibility, higher education is going to be in trouble" [34, p. 297].

The point of view advocated in this article is contrary to that of Lutz. In order for institutions to be adaptive in postindustrial environments, both tight and loose couplings will need to be reinforced and reaffirmed by administrators. Neither can predominate permanently over the other. One reason for this is that initiating innovations requires loose coupling, but implementing innovation requires tight coupling. "During the initiation (discovery) stage, the organization needs to be as flexible and as open as possible to new sources of information and alternative courses of action. . . . During the implementation stage, however. . . . a singleness of purpose is required . . . in order to bring the innovation into practice" [20, p. 175].

Postindustrial institutions of higher education will be required to remain loose enough to develop multiple, innovative adaptations. At the same time, they must be tight enough to implement them quickly and to change major components of the organization as needed. The self-design characteristics called for by Hedberg, Nystrom, and Starbuck [26], Weick [63], and Galbraith [21]—where high levels of experimentation and temporariness exist—will need to be matched with the ability to communicate and act quickly and efficiently through tight coupling. To do this, new arrangements such as ad hoc structures, collateral or parallel processes, or matrix arrangements may have to become much more common.

Actions designed both to achieve stability and to achieve flexibility will be required. Adaptation, in a technical sense, is designed to re-establish equilibrium between the organization and its environment. As mentioned earlier, adaptation is motivated by an imbalance or discontinuity between the requirements of the environment and the organization. Adapting to meet these requirements, therefore, makes the organization more stable but also less flexible. Adaptation establishes a certain organizational history that provides continuity, but it makes less likely radical departures from current functioning.

Adaptability, on the other hand, generally refers to the ability to cope with novel changes in the environment by maintaining a repertoire of unique, unconnected responses. It is synonymous with flexibility. Maintaining adaptability requires that organizational histories be at least partially forgotten so that improvisations can occur as required. Too much flexibility inhibits a sense of continuity and identity, and too much stability inhibits the ability to respond to completely new environmental features [66].

In postindustrial environments, institutions will need to be both stable (i.e., maintain a strong identity and a common interpretation of the environment) and at the same time be flexible (i.e., have a high degree of experimentation, trial-and-error learning, detours, randomness, and improvisation) as they encounter environmental clements that they have never before experienced. Because pressures will be present to fragment institutions, a strong identity and sense of institutional history is needed, but that identity and history must be systematically ignored in some circumstances. Mechanisms designed to erase organizational memory and to kill previous frameworks will be as important as mechanisms designed to operationalize current frameworks and reinforce the institution's culture. Short-term stability and long-term adaptability will both be prerequisites of effectiveness.

A wider search for information as well as mechanisms to inhibit information overload will be required. Postindustrial environments will require that institutions increase their sensing and receptor capabilities because of the tremendous amount of knowledge that will be available. Not being aware of critical elements in the environment could lead to an institution's demise. With increasing turbulence and complexity coupled with an exponential growth in the amount of knowledge available, managers and administrators will have to increase markedly their abilities to acquire that knowledge (see [25]).

On the other hand, these same environmental characteristics can quickly lead to information overload. There will simply be too many fragmented elements to consider at one time. Because of the constraints of bounded rationality [36], mechanisms will have to be present to filter knowledge and reduce the amount that must be attended to [1].

To satisfy these two contradictory requirements, institutions may need to develop specialized scanning units, ad hoc probing and sensing groups, formalized interpretation systems, boundary spanning units, and so on [28]. The purpose of such units would be to both gather more information and to reduce, synthesize, or select out information required for adaptation decisions.

More consensus in decision making while also having more heterogeneity will be needed. In institutions where a high level of consensus exists, change and adaptation can occur both rapidly and efficiently. Time is not required to consider multiple, conflicting points of view or coalitional interests. The institution can be mobilized much more quickly when faced with disruptive environmental events than when the multiple stake holders do not agree on a common action.

Ashby's [4] "law of requisite variety" indicates, however, that complexity in one element must always be matched by equal complexity in another element. Contingency theorists (e.g., [10, 31]) have found that this principle applies to the relationship between organizations and their environments. Complexity in the environment must be met with complexity (i.e., heterogeneity) in the organization for equilibrium to occur. There will be a requirement in postindustrial environments, therefore, for intraorganizational heterogeneity (i.e., multiple view-points, specialization, diversity) to exist in order for institutions to maintain adaptability. Too much homogeneity, on the one hand, can lead to "groupthink" phenomena [29] and to narrowness of strategic alternatives. Too much heterogeneity can lead to revolution and anarchy in adaptation. Both consensus and homogeneity as well as diversity and heterogeneity, therefore, are needed simultaneously as prerequisites of adaptability.

To achieve these two contradictory states simultaneously, institutions will need to rely on new kinds of computer decision support systems that allow preferences and interests to be instantaneously aggregated and compared [28], new varieties of consensus-building group decision processes [60], formalized diffusion mechanisms that gather preferences and build commitment among institutional members when adaptation is required, redundant structures and process mechanisms that function independently, and so on.

Other characteristics of Janusian institutions also will be important to cope with postindustrial environments, such as high specialization as well as high generality of roles, proactivity and reactivity in strategic decisions, continuity of leadership and the infusion of new leaders with new ideas, deviation amplifying and deviation reducing processes, and so on. These characteristics are not elaborated here because of the constraint of space. However, the important point to be made is that the adaptability needed by institutions in postindustrial environments will require that Janusian characteristics be present. The deliberate redesign and restructuring of institutions will be a necessary prerequisite for these new environments.

The presence of Janusian thinking in individuals and Janusian characteristics in organizations often appears to be frightening (because of unpredictability) or even silly (because of inconsistency). However, it is precisely because of this attribute that both individuals and organizations operate successfully in turbulent and unknown environments. Initiating both continuity and change in leadership, specialization and generalization, proactivity and reactivity, and other seemingly contradictory characteristics will produce the adaptability necessary for effective institutions of higher education in the future.

Summary

The first section of this article reviewed different approaches to organizational adaptation. These approaches were categorized according to the amount of discretion they assumed for managers and the importance of the external environment. It was argued in the second section that each of these approaches will be required to operate simultaneously in institutions of higher education in a postindustrial environment. That environment was described as being characterized by more and increasing knowledge, complexity, and turbulence.

In addition to relying on these four common approaches to adaptation, however, it was proposed that managers and administrators will also be required to help design and perpetuate characteristics and processes in their institutions that have been somewhat uncommon in the past. That is, self-contradictory attributes will need to be developed and reinforced both in individual administrators and in their institutions in order to maintain adaptability in a postindustrial environment. Educational institutions with these characteristics and processes were labelled "Janusian" institutions because of the presence of contradictory phenomena that operate simultaneously within them.

The intent of this article, then, has been not only to review and provide a framework for the organizational adaptation literature but to propose how adaptation might be best facilitated in institutions of higher education. Liberal arts colleges, like other types of colleges and universities, will survive and prosper as they become adept at implementing adaptive strategies in the required ways and as they develop characteristics that match with the demands of the postindustrial environment.

Reprinted by permission from THE JOURNAL OF HIGHER EDUCATION, Vol. 55, April/May 1984, pp. 122-144. Copyright © 1984 by the Ohio State University Press. All rights reserved.

Kim S. Cameron is director, Organizational Studies Program, National Center for Higher Education Management Systems.

References

Ackoff. R. L. "Management Misinformation Systems." *Management Science,* 1967, 14 ; 147–56.

Aldrich, H. *Organizations and Environments.* Englewood Cliffs, N.J.: Prentice-Hall, 1979.

Aldrich, H., and J. Pfeffer. "Environments of Organizations." *Annual Review of Sociology,* 1976, 2; 79–105.

Ashby, W. R. "Principles of the Self-Organizing Dynamics System." *Journal of General Psychology,* 1947, 37; 13–25.

Barnard, C. I. *The Functions of the Executive.* Cambridge, Mass.: Harvard University Press. 1938.

Bell, D. *The Coming of Postindustrial Society.* New York: Basic Books, 1973.

Berger, P., and T. Luckmann. *The Social Construction of Reality.* New York: Doubleday, 1967.

Birnbaum, R. *Maintaining Diversity in American Higher Education.* San Francisco: Jossey-Bass, 1983.

Brezezinski, Z. *Between Two Ages: America's Role in the Technetronic Era*. New York: Viking Press, 1970.

Burns, T., and G. M. Stalker. *The Management of Innovation*. London: Tavistock. 1961.

Cameron, K. S. "Strategic Responses to Conditions of Decline: Higher Education and the Private Sector." *Journal of Higher Education*, July/August 1983, 54; 359–90.

Cameron, K. S., and R. E. Quinn. "The Field of Organizational Development." In *Classics in Organization Development*, edited by R. E. Quinn and K. S. Cameron. Oak Park, Ill.: Moore Publishing, 1983.

Cameron, K. S., and D. A. Whetten. "Perceptions of Organizational Effectiveness Over Organizational Life Cycles." *Administrative Science Quarterly*, 1981, 26; 525–44.

————. "Models of the Organization Life Cycle: Applications to Higher Education." *Review of Higher Education*, in press.

Chamberlain, N. W. *Enterprise and Environment: The Firm in Time and Place*. New York: McGraw-Hill, 1968.

Chandler, A. D. *Strategy and Structure: Chapters in the History of the American Enterprise*. Cambridge, Mass.: M.I.T. Press, 1962.

Child, J. "Organizational Structure, Environment, and Performance: The Role of Strategic Choice." *Sociology*, 1972, 6, 1–22.

Cohen, M. D., and J. G. March. *Leadership and Ambiguity: The American College President*. New York: McGraw-Hill, 1974.

Drucker, P. F. *Managing in Turbulent Times*. New York: Harper and Row, 1980.

Duncan, R. B. "The Ambidextrous Organization: Designing Dual Structures for Innovation." in *The Management of Organization Design: Strategies and Implementation*, edited by R. H. Kilmann, L. R. Pondy, and D. P. Slevin, New York: Elsevier North Holland, 1976; 167–88.

Galbraith, J. R. "Designing the Innovating Organization." *Organizational Dynamics*, 1982, 11; 5–25.

Gameson, W. A., and N. R. Scotch. "Scapegoating in Baseball." *American Journal of Sociology*, 1964, 70; 69–76.

Goodman, P. S. and L. B. Kurke. "Studies of Change in Organizations: A Status Report." in *Change in Organizations*, edited by P. S. Goodman, San Francisco: Jossey-Bass, 1982; 1–46.

Hannan, M. T., and J. Freeman. "The Population Ecology of Organizations." *American Journal of Sociology*, 1977, 82; 929–64.

Hedberg, B. L. T. "How Organizations Learn and Unlearn." In *Handbook of Organizational Design*. Vol. 1, edited by P. C. Nystrom and W. H. Starbuck. New York: Oxford University Press, 1981; 3–27.

Hedberg, B. L. T., P. C. Nystrom, and W. H. Starbuck. "Camping on Seesaws: Prescriptions for a Self-Designing Organization." Administrative Science Quarterly, 1976, 21; 41–65.

Huber, G. P. "Decision Support Systems: Their Present Nature and Future Applications." in *Decision Making: An Interdisciplinary Inquiry*. edited by G. R. Ungson and D. N. Braunstein. Boston: Kent, 1982.

————. "The Nature and Design of Postindustrial Organizations." *Management Science*, in press.

Janis, I. *Victims of Groupthink*. Boston: Houghton-Mifflin. 1972.

Interaction Associates. *Tools for Change*. San Francisco: Interaction Associates, 1971.

Lawrence, P., and J. W. Lorsch, *Organization and Environment*. Homewood, Ill.: Irwin, 1967.

Lindblom. C. E. "The Science of Muddling Through." *Public Administration Review*, 1959, 20; 79–88.

Lutz, F. W. "Tightening Up Loose Couplings in Organizations of Higher Education." *Administrative Science Quarterly*, 27 (1982), 653–69.

————. "Reply to More on Loose Coupling." *Administrative Science Quarterly*, 1983, 28; 296–98.

March, J. G. "Footnotes to Organizational Change." *Administrative Science Quarterly*, 1981, 26; 563–77.

March, J. G., and H. A. Simon. *Organizations*. New York: Wiley, 1958.

Martin, J. *Telematic Society: The Challenge for Tomorrow*. Englewood Cliffs, N.J.: Prentice-Hall, 1981.

Masuda. Y. *The Information Society*. Bethesda, Md.: World Future Society, 1980.

McKelvey, W. *Organizational Systematics: Taxonomy, Evolution, and Classification*. Berkeley: University of California Press, 1982.

Miles, R. E. and C. C. Snow. *Organizational Strategy, Structure, and Process*. New York: McGraw-Hill, 1978.

Miles. R. H. *Macro Organizational Behavior*. Glenview, Ill.: Scott Foresman, 1980.

Miles, R. H., and K. S. Cameron. *Coffin Nails and Corporate Strategies*. Englewood Cliffs, N.J.: Prentice-Hall, 1982.

Miller, D., and P. H. Friesen. "Archetypes of Organizational Transition." *Administrative Science Quarterly*, 1980, 25; 268–99.

————. "Momentum and Revolution in Organizational Adaptation." *Academy of Management Journal*, 1980, 23; 591–614.

Miller, J. G. "Living Systems: The Organization." *Behavioral Science*. 1972, 17; 1–182.

National Commission on Excellence in Education. *A Nation at Risk: The Imperative for Educational Reform*. Report to the Secretary of the U.S. Department of Education, Washington, D.C., 1983.

Peters, T. J. "Symbols, Patterns, and Settings: An Optimistic Case for Getting Things Done." *Organizational Dynamics*, 1978, 7; 3–23.

Pfeffer, J. "Management as Symbolic Action: The Creation and Maintenance of Organizational Paradigms." In *Research in Organizational Behavior*, Vol. 3, edited by I.. I.. Cummings and B. M. Staw, Greenwich, Conn." JAI Press, 1981; 1–52.

Pfeffer, J., and G. R. Salancik. *The External Control of Organizations*. New York: Harper and Row. 1978.

Pondy, L. R. "Leadership Is a Language Game." In *Leadership: Where Else Can We Go?*, edited by M. W. McCall and M. M. Lombardo. pp. 87–99. Durham, N.C.: Duke University Press, 1978.

Quinn, R. E.. and K. S. Cameron. "Organizational Life Cycles and Shifting Criteria of Effectiveness: Some Preliminary Evidence." *Management Science*, 1983, 29; 33–51.

Roeber, R. J. C. *The Organization in a Changing Environment*. Reading, Mass.: Addison-Wesley, 1973.

Rothenburg, A. *The Emerging Goddess*. Chicago: University of Chicago Press, 1979.

————. "Creative Contradictions." *Psychology Today*, June 1979; 55–62.

Scott, W. R. *Organizations: Rational, Natural, and Open Systems*. Englewood Cliffs, N.J.: Prentice-Hall, 1981.

Simon, H. A. "Applying Information Technology to Organization Design." *Public Administration Review*, 1973, 34; 268–78.

Snow, C. C., and L. G. Hrebiniak. "Strategy, Distinctive Competence, and Organizational Performance." *Administrative Science Quarterly*, 1980, 25; 317–35.

Toffler, A. *Future Shock*. New York: Random House, 1970.

————. *The Third Wave*. New York: Morrow, 1980.

Van Gundy, A. B. *Techniques of Structured Problem Solving*. New York: Van Nostrand Reinhold, 1981.

Wamsley, G., and M. N. Zald. *The Political Economy of Public Organizations*, Lexington, Mass.: D. C. Heath, 1973.

Weick, K. E. "Educational Organizations as Loosely Coupled Systems." *Administrative Science Quarterly*, 1976, 21; 1–19.

————. "Organizational Design: Organizations as Self-Designing Systems." *Organizational Dynamics*, 1977, 6; 30–46.

————. "Repunctuating the Problem" In *New Perspectives on Organizational Effectiveness*, edited by P. S. Goodman and J. M. Pennings, San Francisco: Jossey-Bass, 1977; 146–84.

————. *The Social Psychology of Organizing*. Reading, Mass.: Addison-Wesley. 1979.

————. "Managing Change Among Loosely Coupled Elements." In *Change in Organizations*, edited by P. S. Goodman, pp. 375–408. San Francisco: Jossey-Bass, 1982.

————. "Administering Education in Loosely Coupled Schools." *Phi Delta Kappan*, 1982, 63; 673–76.

Zammuto, R. F., and K. S. Cameron. "Environmental Decline and Organizational Response." Discussion paper. National Center for Higher Education Management Systems, Boulder, Colorado, 1983.

Measuring Organizational Effectiveness in Institutions of Higher Education

KIM S. CAMERON

This study examines the concept of organizational effectiveness in institutions of higher education. Some obstacles to the assessment of organizational effectiveness in higher education are discussed, namely criteria problems and the unique organizational attributes of colleges and universities, and criteria choices addressing these issues are outlined. Criteria were generated from dominant coalition members in six institutions, and nine dimensions of organizational effectiveness were derived. Reliability and validity of the dimensions were tested, and evidence was found for certain patterns of effectiveness across the nine dimensions.*

* * *

For the past 50 years, organizational researchers have been concerned with the "effectiveness" of organizations, yet confusion persists regarding what organizational effectiveness is. It has rarely been possible to compare studies of effectiveness, since few have used common criteria for indicating effectiveness (Campbell, 1973; Steers, 1975), and effectiveness has been a label pinned on a wide variety of organizational phenomena from a wide variety of perspectives. Difficulty in empirically assessing organizational effectiveness has arisen because no one ultimate criterion of effectiveness exists. Instead, organizations may pursue multiple and often contradictory goals (Warner, 1967; Perrow, 1970; Hall, 1972, 1978; Dubin, 1976), relevant effectiveness criteria may change over the life cycle of an organization (Yuchtman and Seashore, 1967; Kimberly, 1976; Miles and Cameron, 1977), different constituencies may have particular importance at one time or with regard to certain organizational aspects and not others (Friedlander and Pickle, 1968, Scott, 1977; Barney, 1978), criteria at one organizational level may not be the same as those at another organizational level (Price, 1972; Weick, 1977), and the relationships among various effectiveness dimensions may be difficult to discover (Seashore, Indik, and Georgopolous, 1960; Mahoney and Weitzel, 1969; Kirchhoff, 1975). In short, organizational effectiveness may be typified as being mutable (composed of different criteria at different life stages), comprehensive (including a multiplicity of dimensions), divergent (relating to different constituencies), transpositive (altering relevant criteria when different levels of analysis are used), and complex (having nonparsimonious relationships among dimensions).

A number of excellent papers have recently been published which outline many of the inadequacies and complexities of organizational effectiveness research, especially Goodman and Pennings (1977), and which also provide helpful suggestions for improving research methodology. Fewer empirical studies have been reported, however, which explicitly address

---

those issues. The purpose of this paper is to present the results of an empirical study that attempts to deal directly with several of the important problems currently plaguing organizational effectiveness research.

Problems in Assessing Organizational Effectiveness

Criteria problems are the major obstacles to the empirical assessment of organizational effectiveness, and they are of two general kinds. The first relates to the selection of the type of criteria indicating effectiveness, and the second relates to the sources or originators of the criteria. Problems of criteria type generally focus on (1) the aspect of the organization being considered, e.g., goal accomplishment, resource acquisition, internal processes, (2) the universality or specificity of criteria, (3) the normative or descriptive character of criteria, and (4) the static or dynamic quality of criteria.

Organizational Aspects

Outputs and goal accomplishment are probably the most widely used criteria of effectiveness (Georgopolous and Tannenbaum, 1957; Etzioni, 1964; Price, 1972; Hall, 1978). Not only were the earliest approaches to effectiveness guided by a rationalistic goal model, but recent writers (Price, 1968; Campbell, 1977; Scott, 1977) have continued to advocate accomplishment of goals as the defining characteristic of organizational effectiveness.

Others, however, have pointed out problems with specifying goal accomplishment as the criterion for effectiveness[1] (Merton, 1957; Blau and Scott, 1962; Rice, 1963; Scriven, 1967; Warner, 1967; Pfeffer, 1977). Consequently. alternatives to the goal approach have been proposed.

One alternative to the goal model—the system resource model or the natural systems approach—was introduced by Yuchtman and Seashore (1967). This approach focuses on the interaction of the organization with its environment, and defines organizational effectiveness as the ability of the organization to exploit its environment in the acquisition of scarce and valued resources. Organizational inputs and acquisition of resources replace goals as the primary criteria of effectiveness.[2]

Another approach relies on internal organizational processes as the defining characteristics of effectiveness. Steers (1977: 7), for example, stated, "One solution that at least minimizes many of the obstacles to addressing effectiveness is to view effectiveness in terms of a process instead of an end state." Similarly, Pfeffer (1977) suggested that to study organizational effectiveness, it was necessary to consider the process by which organizations articulate preferences, perceive demands, and make decisions. Organizational development approaches (Beckhard, 1969), organizational health models (Bennis, 1966) or Likert's (1967) "system 4" are variations on the process model in that each uses internal organizational activities or practices as the dominant criteria of effectiveness.[3]

Universality of Criteria

Georgopolous and Tannenbaum (1957), Caplow (1964), Friedlander and Pickle (1968), Mott (1972), and Duncan (1973) are among those who suggest that effective organizations are typified largely by the same criteria (e.g., adaptivity, flexibility, sense of identity, absence of strain, capacity for reality testing capacity) and that research on effectiveness should include the appropriate universal indicators. Others point out that organizations have different characteristics, goals, and constituencies, and that each organization (or each type of organization) requires a unique set of effectiveness criteria (Rice, 1961; Hall, 1972; Scott, 1977). The researcher, in other words, must choose a level of specificity for criteria.

Normative/Descriptive Criteria

A related problem refers to the extent to which the research selects derived or prescribed criteria (Price, 1972). McGregor (1960), Argyris (1962), Bennis (1966). Likert (1967), and others have all indicated what qualities effective organizations should possess, and they approach the problem of effectiveness deductively by stating that the organization must meet these standards to be effective. Other writers have used a descriptive approach in which organizational characteristics or criteria are.described (inductively derived) and a priori evaluative standards are avoided (Mahoney et al., 1967, 1969, 1974; Price, 1972 ; Webb, 1974; Steers, 1977). Thompson (1967) has suggested that the difference may be typified as goals for the organization versus goals of the organization.

Dynamic/Static Nature of Criteria

A fourth problem refers to static versus dynamic variables. Most studies of organizational effectiveness include static views of inputs, processes, or outcomes (Mahoney, 1967; Seashore and Yuchtman. 1967; Negandhi and Reimann, 1973; Hall, 1978) although a few use criteria indicating changes over time (Webb, 1974; Pennings, 1975, 1976). Even when change criteria are included, however, the approach is generally analogous to a blurred snapshot in which indications of movement can be detected than to a motion picture in which the criteria changes can be tracked as they occur. Research conducted by Kimberly (1976) and by Miles and Cameron (1977) are among the few examples of studies in which longitudinal data on effectiveness have been gathered and monitored over time.[4]

Sources of Criteria

Organizational effectiveness criteria are also likely to differ depending on whose viewpoint is taken, that is, on their sources. For example, the appropriate organizational constituency, the level of analysis specified by the criteria. and the use of organizational records versus perceptual reports are all choices facing the researcher.

Constituencies. Effectiveness criteria always represent someone's values and biases, but there are conflicting opinions about who should determine effectiveness criteria and who should provide data for their measurement. Some investigators advocate relying on major decision makers and directors, or the organization's dominant coalition, to generate the criteria and to supply effectiveness information (Yuchtman and Seashore, 1967; Gross 1968; Price, 1968; Pennings and Goodman, 1977). Others suggested that these top administrators or managers have narrow and biased perceptions, so that a broad range of constituencies should be tapped (Pfiffner and Sherwood, 1960; Steers, 1975; Katz and Kahn, 1978). Still another group (Bass, 1952; Friedlander and Pickle, 1968; Reinhardt, 1973, Scott, 1977) points out that constituencies outside the organization are relevant for generating criteria inasmuch as derived goals (Perrow, 1961), "macroquality" criteria (Reinhardt, 1973), or information concerning the organization's contribution to the supersystem (Katz and Kahn, 1978) are obtained from that group. Cameron (1978a) and Miles (1979) point out that various strategic constituencies exist for every organization, and that ratings from different constituencies may be more or less appropriate depending on the purpose of the evaluation and the domain of effectiveness.

Seashore (1976) and Scott (1977) both suggest that effectiveness criteria differ among separate constituencies because each constituency perpetuates criteria in its own self interest. Friedlander and Pickle (1968) and Molnar and Rogers (1976) found empirical evidence supporting this view.

LEVEL OF ANALYSIS

Bidwell and Kasarda (1975), Hirsch (1975), and Katz and Kahn (1978) are among those who advocate relying on the supersystem or the external organizational set to determine effectiveness criteria (they define effectiveness as the ability of the organization to adapt to, manipulate, or fulfill expectations of the external environment); whereas writers such as Webb (1974), Scott (1977), Steers (1977), and Weick (1977) suggest that criteria should relate to the organization as a unit (they see effectiveness related to the goals, processes, or characteristics of the organization itself). Pennings and Goodman (1977) propose an approach to effectiveness which focuses on organization subunits (organizational effectiveness is associated with the contributions of and the coordination among subunits), and Kaufman (1960), Argyris (1962), Lawler, Hall, and Old ham (1974) and others, focus on individual performance as criteria of organization effectiveness (organizational effectiveness is assumed to be indicated by individual behaviors and/or satisfaction).

ORGANIZATIONAL RECORDS VERSUS PERCEPTUAL CRITERIA

A third source of criteria concerns the use of organizational records instead of personal perceptions. Records are sources in which information concerning effectiveness criteria may be obtained with no direct involvement by organizational members (e.g., archival records such as organizational histories, changes in personnel, stock price changes) whereas personal perceptions are criteria collected directly from organizational members (generally through questionnaires, interviews, or direct observation). Campbell (1977) labeled criteria obtained from organizational records "objective criteria" and asserted that such measures are inappropriate and "preordained to fail in the end." Effectiveness criteria, according to him, should always be subjective. On the other hand, Seashore and Yuchtman (1967) relied totally on organizational records and argued that these were the most appropriate sources. Economists have generally relied on objective sources for criteria, whereas industrial and organizational psychologists have more often used perceptions. Studies such as those done by Pennings (1975, 1976) have included both objective and perceptual indicators.

Figure 1 compares the types and sources of effectiveness criteria which were selected in 20 recent empirical studies of organizational effectiveness. Empirical studies have been plotted in the figure based on the sources used to assess criteria and the types of criteria included in the investigation. The figure points out the variety of criteria choices made by researchers, since only 9 of 43 cells contain overlapping choices. Most empirical investigations, in other words, have used sources and types of effectiveness criteria which are not comparable with other empirical investigations. Furthermore, the large number of blank cells in the figure illustrates the difficulty of providing a complete picture of organizational effectiveness in any one study as well as the lack of information on a large number of possible criteria types. Organizational effectiveness criteria on one level of analysis, for example, may be different from criteria on other levels. Not only do the pragmatics of research constrain the types and sources of criteria that can be considered, but some choices of criteria may be more appropriate in one type of organization than in another (Molnar and Rogers, 1976).

In institutions of higher education, for example, unique organizational characteristics have presented special problems for researchers in selecting and assessing criteria for organizational effectiveness. Choices regarding the types and sources of criteria illustrated in Figure 1 have been particularly difficult to make in studying these organizations, so that the characteristics of the institutions as well as problems associated with the concept of organizational effectiveness have served as obstacles to empirical assessment of effectiveness in colleges and universities. In fact, almost no studies have been conducted to measure organizational effectiveness in institutions of higher education.

Although some instruments, such as the Educational Testing Service's *Institutional Functioning Inventory* (1970), Pace's *College and University Environment Scales* (1969), or WICHE's Management Information System materials have been widely distributed and used, none of these instruments purported to assess criteria of organizational effectiveness. Several researchers have conducted studies of quality of graduate programs (Cartter 1966, 1977; Blau and Margulis, 1973), while others have investigated objective correlates of those quality ratings (Beyer and Snipper, 1974). Still other researchers have focused on individual variables such as student achievement, teaching processes, and learning climates (Astin, 1968, 1971, 1977; Feldman and Newcomb, 1969; Bowen, 1977), but colleges and universities as organizations were not the primary focus in these studies. Clark (1970) and Blau (1973) reported two important empirical studies of colleges as organizations, but neither was interested in assessments of effectiveness per se.

Figure 1.

Selections of sources and types of criteria for 21 emperical studies of organizational effectiveness.

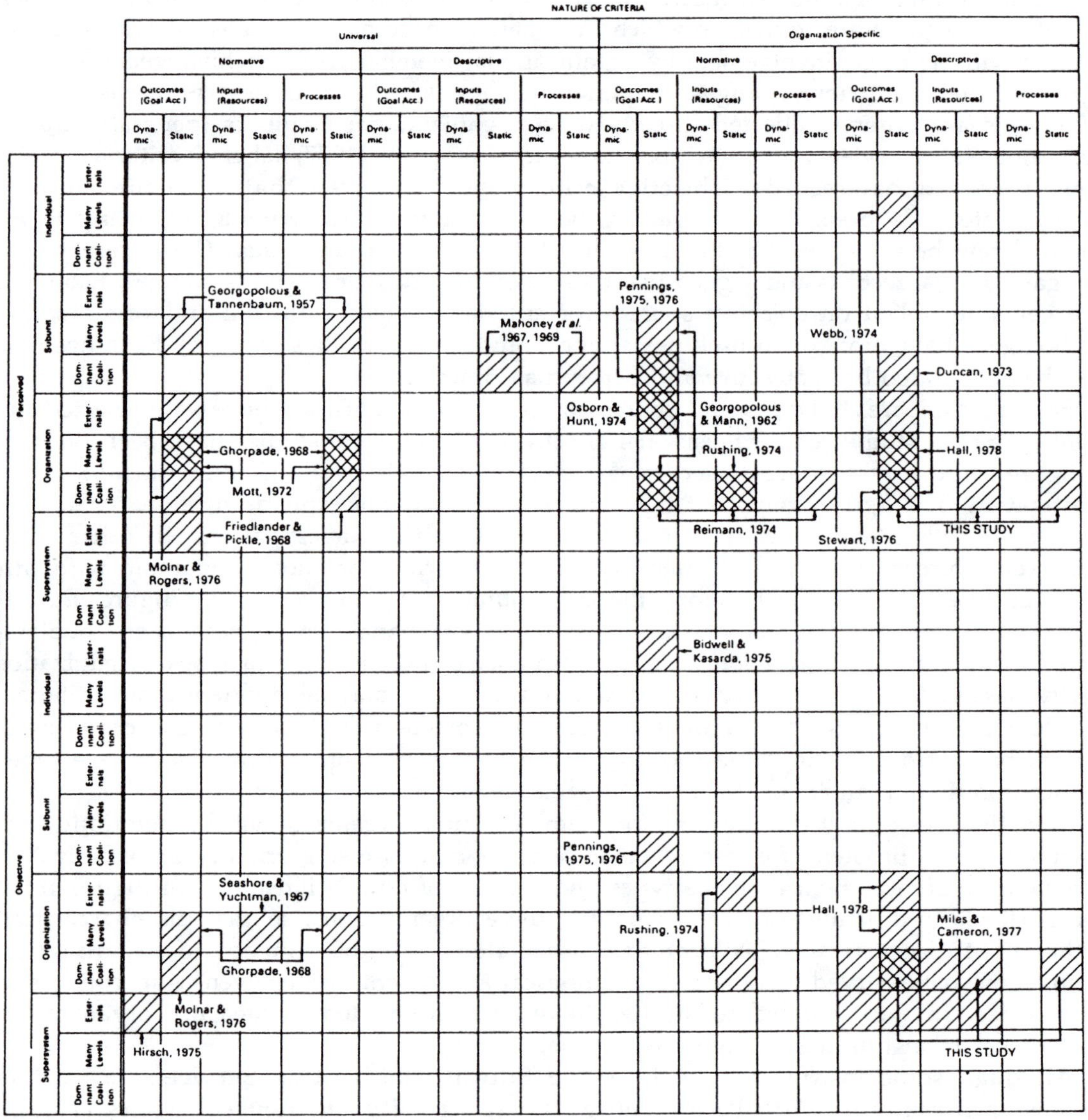

Studies referenced in the figure include: Georgopolous & Tannenbaum, 1957; Pennings, 1975, 1976; Mahoney et al. 1967, 1969; Webb, 1974; Duncan, 1973; Osborn & Hunt, 1974; Georgopolous & Mann, 1962; Ghorpade, 1968; Rushing, 1974; Hall, 1978; Mott, 1972; Friedlander & Pickle, 1968; Reimann, 1974; Stewart, 1976; THIS STUDY; Molnar & Rogers, 1976; Bidwell & Kasarda, 1975; Seashore & Yuchtman, 1967; Miles & Cameron, 1977; Hirsch, 1975.

Problems in Assessing Effectiveness in Higher Education

Some formidable problems stand as obstacles to the selection and assessment of criteria of effectiveness in institutions of higher education. First, it is difficult to specify concrete, measurable goals and outcomes. Some researchers have lamented the "complexity, diffuseness, ambiguity, and changeability" and typify educational goals and outcomes (National Institute of Education, 1975), and some have suggested that without meaningful and measurable objectives, it is impossible to assess the effectiveness of higher education (Warner and Havens, 1968; Chickering, 1971; Hayman and Stenner, 1971). Barro (1973), for example, stated that because information on effectiveness is not usually collected by colleges and universities, prospects for the evaluation of effectiveness "do not seem very good," and Hutchins (1977: 5) asserted:

> The only way you can criticize a university, the only way you can appraise it, the only way you can determine whether it's good or bad or medium or indifferent, is to know what it's about, what it's supposed to be, what it's supposed to be doing. It you don't know these things, you haven't any standards of criticism ... [Universities] haven't any very clear ideas of what they're doing or why. They don't even know what they are.

Second, the evaluation of institutional effectiveness engenders skepticism and defensiveness in the academic community. Several commentators (Dressel, 1972; Barro, 1973; Bowen, 1973) hypothesized that calls for evaluations of effectiveness or institutional accountability are seen as the public trying to scrutinize and control higher education, or as the existence of defects that need to be corrected. The implication of pressures to evaluate seems to be that freedom to experiment and innovate, to risk failure, or to establish unique quality standards is no longer the prerogative of the institution and that evaluations restrict academic freedom.

Individual institutions, furthermore, tend to view themselves as having unique characteristics and goals, and as not being comparable to other institutions. Dressel's (1971: 6. 7) report of an administrator's position on evaluation is illustrative of the approach taken by many administrators in higher education:

> This evaluation will be a waste of time, for either it will demonstrate that the program is excellent or that it is defective in some sense. In the first case it is a waste of time because we already know that it's a good program, and in the second, it's a waste of time because we would not believe any evidence of weakness.

Third, the financial concerns of colleges and universities have led to research on efficiency rather than on effectiveness. Meeth (1974) suggested that the central concern of higher education in the 1970s has been how to provide quality education for less money by focusing on efficiency. Efficiency has generally been defined as the ratio of costs to some output, or as the amount of energy lost in the production of organizational output (Katz and Kahn, 1978). In higher education, efficiency has most often been measured by indicators such as costs per student, student-faculty ratios, costs per faculty member, costs per square foot, etc. (Bowen and Douglas, 1971; O'Neill, 1971; Mood et al., 1972; Meeth, 1974; Hartmark, 1975). These criteria of efficiency, while being well used, are not sufficient for understanding institutional success inasmuch as educational institutions must not only demonstrate efficiency, i.e., using resources with little waste, but they must also be able to demonstrate the effective use of resources as well. Fincher (1972) pointed out that efficiency and effectiveness could not be assessed by the same criteria, and more emphasis was needed on criteria of effectiveness.

Finally, even the applicability of the concept of organizational effectiveness to colleges and universities has been questioned, as by writers who have applied the terms "organized anarchy" or "loosely coupled system" to colleges and universities (Cohen and March, 1974;

Weick, 1976). March and Olson (1976:176), for example, have suggested that organizations in higher education are "complex 'garbage cans' into which a striking variety of problems, solutions, and participants may be dumped." Any attempt to make statements about the effectiveness of such organizations, therefore, is seen as tenuous, since the rules, goals, and choices operating within these organizations are ambiguous, changing, and often not recognized.

It has been found (Cameron, 1978b), however, that institutions of higher education vary on a continuum from loose coupling, i.e., organized anarchies, to tight coupling i.e., structured bureaucracies. Some colleges for example, maintain a relatively homogeneous structure and operation with many effectiveness criteria being relevant for the subsystems within the institution. In others, common criteria are difficult to find since subsystems are mostly autonomous. The problem of studying organizational effectiveness in organizations which vary on the loosely coupled to tightly coupled continuum lies in identifying a core group of effectiveness criteria that are relevant to organizational members, applicable across subunits, and comparable across institutions. The criteria choices made in this study were oriented toward identifying such criteria.

Criteria Choices

Selections of Criteria

The problem of ambiguity and diffuseness of goals in colleges and universities was addressed by focusing on organizational characteristics rather than on goals, since it seemed unlikely that goals or outcomes were made operational in most institutions. Both objective and perceptual criteria were obtained from some institutions of higher education, and anonymity for both institutions and individuals was guaranteed in an attempt to reduce defensiveness and reporting bias. The study focused on the organizational level, since it has been the most neglected in research on higher education, and because it would allow for comparisons among institutions. Criteria specifically related to institutions of higher education were used instead of universal criteria applicable to all types of organizations. The generality of criteria often resulting from a universalistic approach and the unique organizational features of colleges and universities made this choice seem reasonable. Since there is no precedent for criteria of effectiveness in institutions of higher education, this study used an inductive approach in generating them rather than prescribing a priori standards. And, although indications of organizational change over time were sought as criteria, the study was not longitudinal, and the effectiveness indicators are best typified as static rather than dynamic. Figure 1 points out where this study falls in relation to other empirical investigations of effectiveness.

Many of the criteria used to assess organizational effectiveness were initially generated from a search of the literature.[5] Approximately 130 variables emerged from examining this literature, and they provided a framework from which interviews were later conducted with individuals at several colleges and universities.

Selections of Constituency

The strategic constituency chosen to be interviewed in deriving the effectiveness criteria for this study was the internal dominant coalition. The internal dominant coalition refers to representatives of the major subunits or interest groups within the college or university, who influence the direction and functioning of the organization (Thompson, 1967). In the institutions in this study, this included academic, financial, general, and student affairs administrators, deans, and heads of academic departments.[6] Only formal position holders or formal representatives were included in defining the dominant coalition. Whereas informal leaders or charismatic personalities may have an influence on organizational direction, resource allocation, or functioning, it is extremely difficult to identify who those individuals are; therefore, formal position holders were relied upon as being representative.

The dominant coalition was selected first because several writers (Yuchtman and Seashore, 1967; Price, 1972; Pennings and Goodman, 1977) argued that the organization's major decision makers or the dominant coalition should be the sources of criteria for organizational effectiveness and their measurement, since they comprised the resource allocators, the determiners of organizational policy, and the explicators of organizational goals. Thompson (1967) suggested that the dominant coalition was the most likely group to make specific both the cause and effect relationships within an organization and the hierarchy of outcomes to be preferred. Furthermore, as Pennings and Goodman (1977:152) noted, because members of the dominant coalition served as the representatives in the bargaining process within an organization, "consensus among members of the dominant coalition can be employed as a vehicle for obtaining effectiveness data." Van de Ven (1977) suggested, further, that solving the wrong problem with the right methods can be avoided only if users of information about organizational effectiveness are included as sources. Members of the dominant coalition are among the major users of information about organizational effectiveness.

Second, members of the dominant coalition were assumed to be a knowledgeable source about each of the organizational aspects under investigation at the institutional level. The mutability, comprehensiveness, divergence, transpositiveness, and complexity of organizational effectiveness require that a limited domain of effectiveness be specified in evaluations, or that a specific operationalization of the concept be determined. This domain of effectiveness is defined by the aspects of the organization being studied coupled with the level of analysis used (Cameron, 1978a). In this study, the focus was limited to institutional characteristics relating to acquisition of resources, the vitality and viablility of internal processes and practices, and organizational outcomes and emphases. The dominant coalition is likely to be a more reliable source of information for these organizational aspects than other constituencies—for example, most external constituencies.

Selections of Institutions

It was assumed that in large, diverse institutions, dominant coalition members had less college-wide information than in smaller institutions because of the size and autonomy of departments and programs. Thompson (1967) argued that dominant coalition members, as representatives in the internal organizational negotiations, became exposed to organization-wide information as they functioned in their roles, and he suggested that more information was available to them when the dominant coalition was smaller.

The size of the institutions included was therefore limited to those with under 10,000 undergraduate students, and the focus of the study was the undergraduate part of the institutions. These constraints eliminated from consideration large, loosely coupled universities having many semiautonomous professional schools from the study and helped increase the likelihood that respondents would have information related to the overall organizational level.

Method

Interviews were conducted with individuals associated with a variety of institutions of higher education to ensure that the effectiveness criteria had relevance for colleges and universities and that the criteria could be measured. Separate date were collected in two studies. The first study represented an initial attempt to assess the reliability and validity of the effectiveness criteria through questionnaires and interviews. The second study was designed primarily to effect refinements and improvements in the instruments and to improve their psychometric properties.

Institutional Sample

The first study included four colleges in New England with two more schools added in the second study. Two institutions were public and four were private, and their undergraduate enrollments ranged from approximately 1,000 to approximately 10,000. Two institutions were primarily computer schools, with the others being mostly residential; four had unionized faculties, while two did not; and one of the institutions was in a rural setting, while the other five were in or near cities with a population of over 100,000.

Interviews to Derive Dimensions

Four or five top administrators at six colleges in the northeastern United States along with about ten faculty members were interviewed. They were usually the provost or academic vice-president, the president, the financial or administrative vice-president, the dean of student affairs, an assistant to the president or a director of institutional research and one or two department heads on each campus. Individuals were asked to respond to questions, including the following:

1. What organizational characteristics do effective colleges possess?
2. What is it at this institution that makes a difference in terms of its effectiveness?
3. What would have to change in order to make this institution more effective?
4. Think of an institution of higher education that you judge to be effective. What is it that makes that institution effective?
5. Of the 130 or so items generated from the literature, which ones are not relevant to the effectiveness of this school?
6. Of the 130 items, which ones are not measurable or for which are data not available?

Interviews lasted from one and one half to four hours, and special emphasis was placed on criteria relating to the organizational level of analysis. For example, references to individuals or to specific departments or programs were avoided; instead, criteria were sought that characterized the entire institution. Therefore, the success of the president's personal leadership style or the characteristics of a unique program in one department were not generally included, whereas the institution's orientation toward participatory decision making involving the faculty, or the emphasis it placed on developing community-oriented programs were. Some of the effectiveness criteria resulting from the interviews did relate to aggregates of individuals, e.g., student educational satisfaction, but the focus in these criteria tended to be on the entire organization rather than on one institutional sub-unit.

Certain clusters of items became apparent as the criteria emerged from the interviews, and on an a priori, intuitive basis, nine separate groupings of criteria were formed. As a rationale for this strategy of combining criteria into dimensions on an intuitive basis, Campbell (1977: 23) stated, "Criterion combination quite properly is based on value judgments, and there is no algorithm or higher order truth to which we can appeal." Several alternative groupings were tried but the one used here represents the only grouping that encompassed all the effectiveness criteria generated from the interviews.

These nine dimensions represented conceptually different constructs, although they were not assumed to be independent. The nine effectiveness dimensions and the criteria they encompassed were:

1. Student educational satisfaction—criteria indicated the degree of satisfaction of students with their educational experiences at the institution.
2. Student academic development—criteria indicated the extent of academic attainment, growth, and progress of students at the institution.

3. Student career development—criteria indicated the extent of occupational development of students, and the emphasis on career development and the opportunities for career development provided by the institution.
4. Student personal development—criteria indicated student development in nonacademic. noncareer oriented areas. e.g. socially, emotionally, or culturally, and the emphasis on personal development and opportunities provided by the institution for, personal development.
5. Faculty and administrator employment satisfaction—criteria indicated satisfaction of faculty members and administrators with jobs and employment at the institution.
6. Professional development and quality of the faculty—criteria indicated the extent of professional attainment and development of the faculty, and the amount of stimulation toward professional development provided by the institution.
7. Systems openness and community interaction—criteria indicated the emphasis placed on interaction with, adaptation to, and service in the external environment.
8. Ability to acquire resources—criteria indicated the ability of the institution to acquire resources from the external environment, such as good students and faculty, financial support, etc.
9. Organizational health—criteria indicated benevolence, vitality, and viability in the internal processes and practices at the institution.

Instruments

Two types of instruments were developed to measure the criteria in the nine dimensions. The first was a questionnaire asking respondents to describe the extent to which their college possessed certain organizational characteristics (effectiveness criteria). Questionnaire items centered mostly on ratings of organizational traits (e.g., how much emphasis was given to college-community relations?) rather than on personal feelings or affect (e.g., how do you like this school?), in order to reduce the possibility of obtaining highly intercorrelated perceptions all related to the general satisfaction of respondents. Appendix A lists the questionnaire items assessing the effectiveness dimensions.

The second instrument included a set of questions designed to obtain objective data from the records of each institution. Appendix A also lists these items for the eight dimensions measured. These objective data were provided by the academic vice-president or provost, the financial vice-president, the dean of students, the director of institutional research, the director of development, or other appropriate administrators at each institution. The reason for developing both objective and perceived instruments was to provide data for testing the external validity of the dimensions, since there was no way to determine the amount of bias existing in the ratings of the dominant coalition members without such a test.

A modified form of Cattell's (1966) "marker item" procedure was used to guide the additions and refinements made to the questionnaire items for the second study. This procedure suggests that items be chosen which have meaning central to the concept being measured, i.e., face validity, and that overlap should occur with other criteria known to be indicators of the concept. Items were added to several of the scales, consequently, in order to make certain that the central concept indicated by the title of the effectiveness dimension was being measured. These new items were similar to Cattell's marker items. Mean within-dimension correlations ranged from .491 to .636 for the marker items, providing evidence that the central meanings of the dimensions, as specified by their titles, were being tapped.

Respondent Sample

The questionnaires were mailed, under a covering letter signed by the president or academic vice-president, to approximately 75 administrators and academic department heads at each of the six institutions. Anonymity for all respondents and institutions was guaranteed. Reports of the results of the study were promised to each participating institution, but respondents and institutional names were kept confidential. Respondents to the questionnaire were divided into five job categories: general, academic, financial, and student affairs administrators, and academic department heads. About half of the respondents were faculty members and about half were administrators. Usable questionnaires returned in the first study were 191 (70 percent); 134 (72 percent) were returned in the second study. The frequencies of returns for the five respondent categories are shown in Table 1.

Table 1

Response Rate for Five Categories of Respondents in Six Institutions				
	Responses*			
	Study 1		Study 2	
Job Category	N	%	N	%
Administrators				
General	23	82	20	77
Academic	37	70	15	68
Financial	16	70	7	54
Student affairs	34	85	32	70
Academic department head	81	62	60	77
Total	191	70	134	72

*Responses across institutions ranged from 54% to 84%.

Analysis

At least two different strategies were possible for analyzing the data obtained from these dominant coalition members. One was to emphasize the reliability or internal consistency of measures of the central concepts in the nine effectiveness dimensions, and the other was to ensure the inclusion of all variables generated by the interviews regardless of their relationships to the nine central concepts. The former strategy was adopted because, first, inasmuch as reliability is a prerequisite for validity (Nunnally, 1967; Kerlinger, 1973), it was important for the internal consistency (reliability) of the criteria to be demonstrated in order that the effectiveness dimensions could be validated. Since the questionnaire items were constructed to assess the criteria comprising the dimensions, if it was found that one of the items had low internal consistency in relation to other items thought to measure the same dimension, the item was dropped since there was no way to determine whether the variance in the item was attributable to another construct being assessed (trait variance) or to method or to random error. It was thought more important to demonstrate the reliability of the measures than to focus solely on the comprehensiveness of the criteria. This is similar to the strategies used by Mahoney (1967) and by Seashore and Yuchtman (1967) in the generation of their effectiveness criteria.

Second, it had been determined that institutional data were not available for every single criterion that emerged from the interviews. Therefore, unless a large number of questionnaire items turned out to be unrelated to the nine underlying dimensions, it was appropriate for reasons of meaningfulness and parsimony to concentrate on the nine central concepts indicated by the dimension titles.

Results

Internal Consistency and Discriminant Validity

Eight of the questionnaire items in the first study were found to have low correlations within their own effectiveness dimension as well as with items from the other eight effectiveness dimensions. These eight items, which had an average intrascale correlation below .20, included quality of written work of students, attrition of students because of too few extracurricular activities, faculty grievances, attrition of faculty because of dissatisfaction, proportion of the budget available for professional development, work efficiency, and pay satisfaction. Moreover, there were no high intercorrelations among the eight items themselves; consequently, they were not included in other statistical analyses of the dimensions. Coefficient alpha was applied to test the internal consistency reliability of the effectiveness dimensions and acceptable levels of reliability were found for each of them. Nunnally (1967) suggested that for exploratory research, a reliability of between .50 and .60 was acceptable, and in the first study the lowest reliability coefficient among the nine effectiveness dimensions was .601, while the highest was .928. In the second study, reliability coefficients ranged from .628 to .924. The relatively high correlations of the marker items in the second study with the appropriate effectiveness dimensions also provided some evidence for the face validity of the dimensions. The internal consistency reliability for each of the dimensions is shown in Table 2.

Factor analytic procedures also largely confirmed the existence of the dimensions. Oblique, varimax, and quartimax rotations were used in both studies, and the number of factors was limited to between six and twelve to try to uncover any underlying dimensions. Appendices B and C contain the factors produced by an orthogonal rotation pattern in which an eigenvalue of 1.0 specified the number of factors. In the first study, two of the effectiveness dimensions loaded on the same factor and two other dimensions split into two factors. After several questionnaire items were reworded to improve their meaningfulness and clarity for respondents, the second study produced a single factor for each of the dimensions except Student Educational Satisfaction, which did not load on any of the factors. Furthermore, a nine-factor rotation still did not produce a factor for this dimension.

Average within-dimensions correlations for each item were compared to the mean correlations of each item with all items outside its own effectiveness dimension as one test of the discriminant validity of the items. It was found that within-dimension mean correlations were higher than the mean outside correlations for every item except one in the first study and for all items in the second study. The single item in the first study (opportunities for personal development) was eliminated from further analysis. As Table 2 indicates, this finding confirmed that the dimensions were composed of items with high internal consistency and that they were distinguishable one from another. Also, after the median correlation coefficient for all items within a dimension was computed, correlations between the dimension and all outside items were inspected to determine overlapping among items. The purpose was to uncover the effectiveness items that correlated highly with more than one dimension and to determine which dimensions had overlapping items. Several items were slightly reworded prior to the second study as a result of this analysis in order to help clarify the conceptual differences among the effectiveness dimensions for future respondents.

The Student Educational Satisfaction dimension and the Organizational Health dimension in the second study were found to contain discriminating items, but the dimensions taken as a whole were weak in discriminant validity. Table 2 demonstrates, for example, that mean within-dimension correlations were not significantly higher than were correlations outside the dimension for either Student Educational Satisfaction or for Organizational Health. Whereas correlations within dimensions were higher in value for each of these two dimensions, an insignificant t-test indicated a relatively high intercorrelation between these two dimensions and others.

Table 2

Between-Dimension and Between-Item Correlations for the Nine Effectiveness Dimensions

	No. of items x	s.d.	Mean item Correlations Inside	Outside	1	2	3	4	5	6	7	8	9
†1.	4 3.78	.8	.37	.23*	(.70)‡								
	3 2.84	.7	.36	.29	(.63)								
2.	3 4.79	1.0	.38	.20*	.37	(.65)							
	5 3.79	1.0	.40	.26	.56	(.77)							
3.	4 3.65	.9	.27	.14	.33	.22	(.60)						
	5 4.27	1.0	.33	−.01***	.05	−.20	(.71)						
4.	3 4.24	.9	.63	.13***	.40	.54	.23	(.66)					
	4 3.23	1.2	.61	.29***	.56	.39	−.02	(.86)					
5.	6 3.94	1.1	.40	.21**	.49	.36	.31	.34	(.91)				
	6 4.74	1.5	.57	.30***	.60	.39	.05	.36	(.89)				
6.	4 4.62	.9	.31	.17*	.31	.32	.25	.32	.47	(.73)			
	5 4.48	1.1	.50	.24**	.42	.43	.02	.37	.37	(.83)			
7.	5 3.52	1.2	.47	.24**	.41	.33	.28	.34	.50	.46	(.90)		
	5 3.96	1.2	.51	.27**	.44	.46	.13	.55	.43	.45	(.84)		
8.	5 4.79	1.0	.46	.26**	.57	.56	.33	.46	.54	.42	.47	(.81)	
	6 4.49	1.1	.50	.33*	.68	.66	−.04	.59	.58	.55	.59	(.86)	
9.	15 3.79	1.0	.46	.23***	.48.	.28	.34	.39	.59	.41	.55	.50	(.92)
	17 3.91	1.2	.40	.30	.65	.57	−.10	.52	.69	.49	.56	.69	(.93)

* Significant differences between inside and outside correlations at the $p<.05$ level.

** Significant differences between inside and outside correlations at the $p<.01$ level.

*** Significant differences between inside and outside correlations at the $p<.001$ level.

† 1.Student Educational Satisfaction; 2. Student Academic Development; 3. Student Career Development; 4. Student Personal Development; 5. Faculty and Administrator Employment Satisfaction; 6. Professional Development and Quality of the Faculty; 7. System Openness and Community Interaction; 8. Ability to Acquire Resources; 9. Organizational Health.

‡ Numbers in parentheses are reliability coefficients.

Note: The top numbers for each dimension refer to the first study, and the bottom numbers refer to the second study.

Between-School and Between-Job Differences

Analyses of variance were performed to determine whether the effectiveness dimensions differentiated among the schools and among the respondent groups. For the scales to be employable in assessments of effectiveness, there needed to be some significant differences among the institutions. If all institutions scored the same on the nine effectiveness dimensions, the instruments would be of no use in assessing relative effectiveness in institutions of higher education. Furthermore, one method of testing construct validity is to demonstrate differences among groups expected to score differently on a measure (Cronbach and Meehl, 1955).

The five respondent job categories were also analyzed to determine if differences among them existed. Multivariate and univariate analysis of variance procedures were used to test for significant effects.

Table 3

Multivariate and Univariate Analysis of Variance for the Effectiveness Dimensions						
	Institution		Job		Interaction Institution X Job	
	F	Ø	F	Ø	F	Ø
MANOVA‡	4.76***	.281***	1.50*	.156	1.06	.174
	19.06***	.282***	1.08	.127	1.37	.228

Dimension	Multiple R^2	Institution		Job	Interaction Institution X Job	
		F	n^2	F	n^2	F
1. Student educational satisfaction	.124	6.08***	.09	1.71	.04	1.29
	.478	23.97***	.39	3.38**	.30	4.34
2. Student academic development	.185	9.73***	.13	3.39*	.06	1.51
	.517	44.55***	.50	.75	.12	2.50*
3. Student career development	.159	9.18***	.12	2.01	.03	.91
	.609	70.34***	.60	.32	.15	1.98
4. Student personal development	.087	2.61*	.03	2.91*	.05	2.05
	.366	12.56***	.60	1.24	.22	2.53*
5. Faculty and administrator employment satisfaction	.082	4.11**	.07	.62	.02	1.41
	4.080	18.34***	.37	1.24	.22	2.53*
6. Professional development and quality of faculty	.162	9.00***	.14	1.81	.03	.43
	.349	15.70***	.34	.20	.11	1.53
7. System openness and community interaction	.229	14.73***	.20	1.52	.05	1.57
	.282	3.54*	.15	2.04	.23	2.23
8. Ability to acquire resources	.207	11.53***	.17	2.19	.06	1.06
	.552	52.65***	.54	.51	.14	2.18
9. Organizational health	.223	13.38***	.18	2.31	.05	1.00
	.559	51.41***	.52	4.79***	.35	4.89***

* p <.05
** p <.01
*** p <.001
‡ Degrees of freedom were 27 and 476 for institution, 36 and 612 for job, and 108 and 1199 for the interaction in the first study, and 9 and 111 for institution, 36 and 417 for job, and 36 and 417 for the interaction in the second study.
Note: The top numbers for each dimension refer to the first study, and the bottom numbers refer to the second study.

The results, summarized in Table 3, suggest that institutional affiliations do have a significant effect on responses for combined organizational effectiveness (MANOVA p < .001), but that the job or position held is not as important. That is, in both studies, the differences are significant among the means of the institutions but not for the five job categories. In the first study, the MANOVA F-test based on Wilks' lambda for job resulted in a significance level of p

< .03 while the theta (Ø) value, normally a more conservative test, resulted in a significance level of greater than .05. No statistical significance for job resulted in the second study. Using univariate MANOVA procedures for each separate effectiveness dimension showed that the employing institution had a significant effect in determining the perceptions of the respondents for every dimension (p < .01). The amount of variance accounted for among the dimensions by this institutional factor (n2) ranged from 3 percent to 20 percent in the first study and 15 percent to 60 percent in the second effectiveness dimensions: Student Academic Development and Student Personal Development in the first study, and Student Education Satisfaction and Organizational Health in the second study. The interaction of the school and the job category was significant (p < .05) only for Student Personal Development in the first study and for four dimensions in the second study.

A profile analysis, shown in Figure 2, also confirmed the similarity of the different job categories. Mean scores for each respondent group included in the six institutions were plotted across the nine dimensions of effectiveness and tested for differences in levels (Nunnally, 1967). According to Van de Geer (1971), the MANOVA procedure had already tested for differences in parallelism. None of the respondent group pairs differed significantly (.50) in the levels of their ratings, so that it can be concluded that the dominant coalition members in these institutions had similar perceptions of effectiveness.

Figure 2

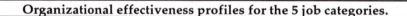

Organizational effectiveness profiles for the 5 job categories.

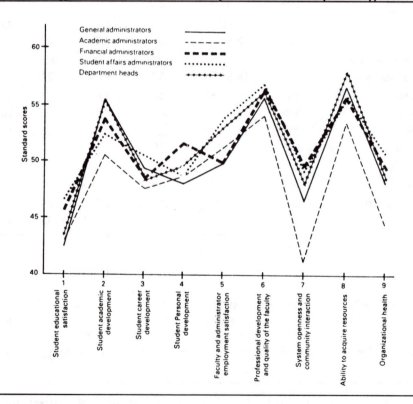

A second profile analysis plotting institutional means on the nine effectiveness dimensions revealed that the institutions not only varied significantly in their effectiveness profiles (significant differences exist among at least two of the institutions on every dimension), but that certain patterns of organizational effectiveness could be distinguished. Institution 5, for example, showed high effectiveness on all the dimensions except Student Career Development and System Openness and Community Interaction. This may indicate a tendency away from occupational and community involvement—an external emphasis—by this institution. Instituteness was achieved in the career and community oriented dimensions with low effectiveness scores on other dimensions. This occupational and community-oriented success may be somewhat surprising to the institution since the catalogues of each of all six institutions claimed a liberal arts undergraduate emphasis.

Institution 1 showed relatively high effectiveness on dimensions related to satisfaction and organizational morale, i.e., Student Educational Satisfaction, Faculty and Administrator Employment Satisfaction, and Organizational Health, while the academically oriented dimensions tended to be low, i.e., Student Academic Development and Professional Development and Quality of the Faculty. Institution 3, on the other hand, had relatively high effectiveness in Student Academic Development but was less effective in most other areas. Institution 2 had consistently high scores on the dimensions with the highest relative effectiveness being on the nonstudent-oriented dimensions. Institution 6 was almost exactly opposite to that pattern by being consistently low on the effectiveness dimensions but with the highest relative effectiveness being on the student oriented dimensions.

These results suggest that the institutions can be distinguished, on the basis of their effectiveness profiles, as those having very high or very low effectiveness on external dimensions (institutions 4 and 5), those with very high or low effectiveness on morale dimensions (institutions 1 and 3), and as those having high or low effectiveness on student oriented dimensions (institutions 2 and 6). Furthermore, whereas institutional effectiveness profiles differ significantly from one another and relative strengths and weaknesses are evident, some institutions do achieve higher overall effectiveness than others.

The analyses of these two studies indicated that the hypothesized dimensions had acceptable reliability and that they were useful in differentiating among colleges and universities for organizational effectiveness. Each institution was found to vary uniquely across the nine effectiveness dimensions, although certain patterns of effectiveness seemed to emerge. Furthermore, scores on the dimension were generally not significantly affected by different respondent categories.

Evidence for Validity

Supporting evidence for internal consistency and discriminant validity in these studies still left questions unanswered about the external validity and construct validity of the effectiveness dimensions. There was a dilemma, however, in attempting to deal with validity. On the one hand, no generally accepted criteria exist against which to compare these perceptual dimensions; therefore, testing for concurrent or criterion validity was impossible. On the other hand, construct validity—an approach to validity used when no valid external criteria are available (Cronbach and Meehl, 1955)—was similarly questionable since, as Nunnally (1967) indicated, proof of construct validity comes from determining the extent to which measures of a construct fit into a network of expected relations. Inasmuch as organizational effectiveness in institutions of higher education has never been measured, no theoretical or predictable network of relationships has been possible between effectiveness of colleges and universities—particularly these nine dimensions—and other constructs. Campbell (1973) pointed out that much of the explanatory research on organizational effectiveness had been done using individual behavior or performance. Very few studies have used organizational units as degrees of freedom. Consequently, there is no well-defined nomological network for organizational effectiveness in general, let alone college and university effectiveness. This study was designed to begin the development of a network.

Some indications of validity in this research project were needed, nevertheless, in order that followup research, in which explanatory data could be obtained and related to the effectiveness constructs, would prove meaningful and worthwhile. Two separate pieces of evidence were found which suggested that the effectiveness dimensions had some external and construct validity.

Objective indicators of the effectiveness dimensions had been obtained from each of the six institutions, and it was hypothesized that positive correlations between the two sets of data would provide some evidence for the external validity of the perceptual measures. Table 4 reports the nonparametric rank order correlations between the objective data and the perceptual ratings.

Moderate to high positive correlations for all but two of the effectiveness dimensions provided some support for external validity, although two of the dimensions had, unexpectedly, negative correlations indicating that either the objectives measures or the perceptual measures were faulty, that different and negatively correlated concepts were being assessed, that the concepts being measured were not unidimensional and had complex relationships with each other, or that the constructs being measured in the two effectiveness dimensions were confusing to respondents.

There was no sure way to determine the reason for the negative correlations in these two studies, particularly given the small sample, but a close examination of the objective and perceptual items for the eight dimensions did suggest that two separate concepts may have been assessed. In the case of Student Career Development, objective items focused on vocational counseling and work study, whereas the perceived items emphasized successful placement of students in desired post-college employment and the offering of a career oriented curriculum. The perceived items relating to Systems Openness and Community Interaction dealt mainly with community and professional activities of employees, whereas the objective items focused on continuing education and extension programs. Close examination of the items also revealed, however, that other dimensions had the same problem. That is, differences in objective and perceptual concepts could be hypothesized for almost all of the dimensions. For example, the objective measures for the Student Academic Development dimension seemed to emphasize continued academic attainment after leaving the institution whereas the perceptual measures emphasized academic development of students within the institution. Yet, the correlation coefficient for that dimension was high and positive.

Table 4

Rank-Order Correlations Between Objective and Perceptual Measures of the Effectiveness Dimensions		
Dimension	r	p<
1. Student educational satisfaction	.600	.10
2. Student academic development	.829	.02
3. Student career development	−.657	.08
4. Student personal development	.771	.04
5. Faculty and administrator employment satisfaction	.314	.27
6. Professional development and quality of the faculty	.943	.002
7. System openness and community interaction	−.600	.10
8. Ability to acquire resources	.714	.05
9. Organizational health	No objective data collected	

This is not an unusual difficulty when comparing objective and perceptual measures, and similar problems have been found in relation to other concepts, most notably environmental uncertainty (Tosi, Aldag, and Storey, 1973; Downey, Hellreigel, and Slocum, 1975). Researchers on environmental uncertainty have generally concluded that a choice should be made between the two types of measures and comparisons between them avoided. The dilemma in this study was that some evidence of external validity was needed to help determine the amount of bias existing in the perceptual ratings, yet comparisons with the objective data was tenuous. Limited support for external validity seemed to be justified for some of the dimensions since what appeared to be related concepts were being assessed by two types of measures, but no definitive conclusions can be drawn.

There is evidence that the objective measures of effectiveness in this research, furthermore, were not as reliable as would have been desirable. It was found, for example, that relatively little objective data were available on inputs, processes, and outcomes at the six institutions studied. Data were often in confidential files, in several offices, or unavailable altogether. Answers to many of the items, consequently, were guesses by the responding administrator, particularly when the data were not readily available or had not been centrally compiled. This objective data gathering made it understandable, in fact, why most studies of higher education avoid multivariate objective data on effectiveness and rely instead on cost ratios.

Figure 3

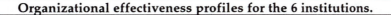

Organizational effectiveness profiles for the 6 institutions.

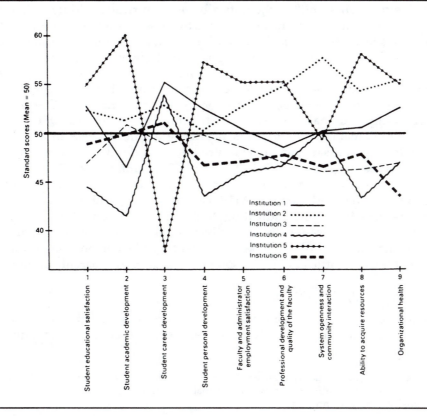

A second indication of validity was found by comparing scores on the nine effectiveness dimensions of institutions with unionized faculties and those without a union. Figure 3 shows that the institutions with a faculty union (institutions 1, 3, 4, and 6) scored lower than each institution without a unionized faculty (institutions 2 and 5) on four of the effectiveness dimensions: Faculty and Administrator Employment Satisfaction, Professional Development and Quality of the Faculty, Ability to Acquire Resources, and Organizational Health. These findings are consistent with research conducted by Duryea *et al.* (1973), Hedgepeth (1974), Garbarino (1975), Kemerer and Baldridge (1975), and others, which found lower faculty satisfaction, more emphasis on collective bargaining issues and less on faculty concerns, feelings of powerlessness or of being externally controlled, and less collegiality and organizational benevolence in unionized institutions. In terms of construct validity, these relationships between the effectiveness dimensions and other external concepts, i.e., faculty unionism, in predictable directions provides the beginnings of a nomological network that can be expanded with additional research.

Conclusion

Multidomain Character of Effectiveness.

Much of the lack of cumulativeness in past effectiveness research has resulted from confusion over what conceptual referent or effectiveness domain has been applied when referring to organizational effectiveness, and from the wide variety of types and sources of criteria used to indicate effectiveness. The emphasis on one best definition of organizational effectiveness that has been common in past literature has not advanced the development of studies of organizational effectiveness either theoretically or empirically. While acknowledging the multidimensional character of organizational effectiveness, researchers continue to write as if a unitary concept is being considered (Hall, 1972; Mott, 1972: Child, 1974; Hannan and Freeman. 1977; Weick, 1977). In this study it is proposed that since the concept of organizational effectiveness differs with different constituencies, different levels of analysis, different aspects of the organization, and different research or evaluation purposes, effectiveness not only possesses multiple dimensions, but it is not a unitary concept. Rather it is a construct composed of multiple domains which are therefore operationalized in different ways. Effectiveness in one domain may not necessarily relate to effectiveness in another domain. For example, maximizing the satisfaction and growth of individuals in an organization, the domain of effectiveness for Argyris (1962), Likert (1967), Cummings (1977), and others, may be negatively related to high levels of subunit output and coordination, the domain of effectiveness for Pennings and Goodman (1977). Specifically, publishing a large number of research reports may be a goal indicating high effectiveness to faculty members (on an individual level) while indicating low effectiveness at the subunit or organizational level (e.g., poor teaching quality, little time with students, little personal attention for students, graduate student teaching instead of professors) to legislators and parents of undergraduates.

Application of the Approach

This approach to the study of organizational effectiveness is probably most useful as a first step in approaching a fine-grained analysis of effectiveness in colleges and universities. Weick (1974: 366) pointed out that:

> We treat effects more crudely than we do causes. It we tried obsessively to discriminant subtle differences in effects, we would probably find more single-cause, single-effect relationships than we now see.

That is, one of the reasons for the lack of theoretical and methodological development in studies of organizational effectiveness is the tendency of researchers to do a fine-grained analysis of causes but a coarse-grained analysis of effects.

It has been discovered that no institution operates effectively on all effectiveness dimensions, but that certain effectiveness profiles are developed in which particular dimensions are emphasized. No single profile is necessarily better than any other, since strategic constituencies, environmental domain, contextual factors, etc., help determine what combination is most appropriate for the institution. Once a profile of effectiveness is identified for an institution, however, a fine-grained analysis of effectiveness can then really be made. That is, once a particular college or university is found to have high effectiveness in Organizational Health and the Ability to Acquire Resources, for example, and low effectiveness in Student Academic Development and in faculty satisfaction, detailed examinations of the causes, correlates, and components of its strengths and weaknesses are possible, whereas no such analyses can be made when general prestige rankings (Cartter, 1966) or internal efficiency ratios (Mood et al., 1972) are relied on.

The instrument used in assessing these nine dimensions of organizational effectiveness can be the first step in a fine-grained analysis of effectiveness on the institutional level in identifying relevant effectiveness dimensions. The instrument could now be developed into at least nine separate instruments in a fine-grained analysis of each of the nine dimensions in colleges and universities.

This approach to assessing organizational effectiveness also appears applicable to other types of loosely coupled organizations, particularly in the non-profit or public sectors. Rainey, Backoff, and Levine (1976), in reviewing differences between public and private organizations, suggested that one major difference lies in the availability of tangible, specifiable goals. In the private sector, goal accomplishment is more easily recognized, agreed upon, and quantifiable than in the public sector. It is suggested that by inductively deriving criteria, by focusing on organizational attributes rather than operationalized goals, and by carefully selecting sources and types of criteria to indicate effectiveness, important dimensions of effectiveness can be identified which can lead to more fine-grained analyses of public sector organizations.

Special thanks is given to Richard Hackman, Bob Miles, John Kimberly, and Larry Cummings as well as to the ASO reviewers for their helpful comments and suggestions on earlier versions of this paper. Financial support from the Richard D. Irwin Foundation is also gratefully knowledged.

Notes

[1] The following are some of the criticisms which have been advanced concerning the goal approach to effectiveness (1) There is a focus on official or management goals to the exclusion of the organizational member, organizational constituency, and societal goals (Blau and Scott. 1961: Scriven. 1967). (2) There is neglect of implicit, latent, or informal procedures and goals (Merton, 1957). (3) There is neglect of the multiple and contradictory nature of organizational goals (Rice. 1963) (4) Environmental influences on the organization and its goals are ignored (Lawrence and Lorsch. 1969) (5) Organizational goals are retrospective and serve to justify organizational action, not to direct it (Welch, 1969) (6) Organizational goals change as contextual factors and organizational behavior change (Warner, 1967: Pfiffner, 1977)

[2] Criticisms of the system-resource approach include the following: (1) Efficiency and effectiveness are not separated under this approach (Price, 1972) (2) Focusing only on inputs may have damaging effects on outputs (Scott, 1977). (3) This approach assumes that the only valuable aspects of organizations are those which aid further input acquisition (Scott, 1977). (4) Only the organizational directors' viewpoint is taken (Scott 1977). (5) It is really the same as the goal model since increasing inputs is an organizational operative goal (Kirchhoff, 1977). (6) This approach is inappropriate when considering nonprofit organizations (Molnar and Rogers. 1976)

[3] Criticisms of the process model include the difficulty of monitoring organizational processes (Dornbusch and Scott, 1975), the expense of gathering data on processes (Scott, 1977), the focus on means to the neglect of ends (Campbell, 1977), and the inaccuracy of most process data "Almost every individual instance of [process data] reporting has something wrong with it" (Haberstroh, 1965:182)

[4] Miles and Cameron (1977) in their study of the U S tobacco industry, for example, found that one firm, R J Reynolds, was most effective if static criteria were used, whereas another firm, Philip Morris, was most effective when dynamic criteria were considered.

[5] Several sources of organizational effectiveness criteria proved to be of particular value, among which were Price (1968), Pace (1969), the *Institutional Functioning Inventory* (1970), Mott (1972), Blau (1973), Campbell (1973, 1974), Balderston (1974), Micek and Wallhaus (1974), Hartmark (1975), the *Michigan Survey Research Center Assessment Package* (1975), National Institute of Education Reports (1975), and Steers (1975).

[6] Student representatives were not included in the study's dominant coalition because (1) students are not generally in a position to directly influence the direction and functioning of the institution; (2) they generally have more limited information about the overall institution than do other dominant coalition members; (3) they have been found in other studies not to differ significantly in their perceptions of the institution from faculty members or administrators (Educational Testing Service. 1970); and most importantly; (4) constraints on time and money prohibited a representative sample from being gathered from relevant student groups on various campuses.

References

Argyris, Chris. *Interpersonal Competence and Organizational Effectiveness.* Homewood, IL: Irwin, 1962.

Astin, Alexander W. *The College Environment.* Washington: American Council on Education, 1968.

―――. *Predicting Academic Performance in College.* Riverside, NJ: Free Press, 1971.

―――. *Four Critical Years.* San Francisco: Jossey-Bass, 1977.

Balderston, Frederick E. *Managing Today's Universities.* San Francisco: Jossey-Bass, 1974

Barney, Jay. "The electronic revolution in the watch industry: a decade of environmental changes and corporate strategies." In Robert H. Miles (ed.), *Organizational Adaptation to Environment: Working Paper No. 7*, Government and Business Relations Series. New Haven. CT: Yale University, 1978; 1–63

Barro, Stephen M. "Toward operational accountability systems for colleges and universities." In *Addresses and Proceedings.* Oakland, CA: Western College Association, 1973; 32–47.

Bass, Bernard M. "Ultimate criteria of organizational worth." *Personnel Psychology*, 1952, 5:157–173.

Beckhard, Richard. *Organizational Development.* Reading, MA: Addison-Wesley, 1969.

Bennis, Warren G. "The concept of organizational health." In Warren G. Bennis (ed.). *Changing Organizations.* New York: McGraw-Hill, 1966.

Beyer, Janice M., and Reuben Snipper. "Objective versus subjective indicators of quality in graduate education." *Sociology of Education*, 1974, 47; 541–557.

Bidwell, Charles E., and John D. Kasarda. "School district organization and student achievement." *American Sociological Review*, 1975, 40; 55–70.

Blau, Peter M. *The Organization of Academic Work.* New York: Wiley, 1973.

Blau, Peter M., and Rebecca Z. Margulis. "America's leading professional schools." *Change.* 1973, 5; 21–27.

Blau, Peter M., and W. Richard Scott. *Formal Organizations.* San Francisco: Chandler, 1962 .

Bowen, Howard R. "Holding colleges accountable." *The Chronicle of Higher Education*, March 1973, 12; 28.

―――. *Investment in Learning,* San Francisco: Jossey-Bass, 1977.

Bowen, Howard R., and Gordon K. Douglas. *Efficiency in Liberal Education: A Study of Comparative Instructional Costs for Different Ways of Organizing Teaching-Learning in a Liberal Arts College.* New York: McGraw-Hill, 1971.

Cameron, Kim. "On the domains of organizational effectiveness." Working paper, School of Business, University of Wisconsin, 1978a.

————. Organizational Effectiveness: Its Measurement and Prediction in Higher Education. Doctoral dissertation, Department of Administrative Science, Yale University, 1978b.

Campbell, John P. "Research into the nature of organizational effectiveness: an endangered species?" Working paper, Department of Psychology, University of Minnesota, 1973.

————. "Sources of organizational indicators" Proceedings from the Symposium on the Utilization of Indicator Data, Institute for Social Research, University of Michigan, 1974.

————. "On the nature of organizational effectiveness." In Paul S. Goodman and Johannes M. Pennings (eds), *New Perspectives on Organizational Effectiveness*, San Francisco: Jossey-Bass, 1977; 13–55.

Caplow, Theodore. *Principles of Organization.* New York: Harcourt Brace Jovanovich, 1964.

Cartter, Allan M. *An Assessment of Quality in Graduate Education.* Washington: American Council on Education, 1966.

————. "The Cartter report on the leading schools of education, law, and business." *Change*, 1977, 9; 44–48.

Cattell, Raymond B. "The meaning and strategic use of factor analysis." In Raymond Cattell (ed.), *Handbook of Multivariate Experimental Psychology.* Chicago: Rand McNally, 1966; 174–243.

Chickering, Arthur W.

"Research in action." in Paul Dressel (ed.), *The New Colleges*, Iowa City, IA: College Testing Program and the American Association of Higher Education, 1971; 25–52.

Child, John. "What determines organizational performance?" Organizational Dynamics (Summer), 1974; 2–18.

Clark, Burton R. *The Distinctive College*, Chicago: Aldine, 1970.

Cohen, Michael, and James G. March. *Leadership and Ambiguity: The American College President.* New York: McGraw-Hill, Carnegie Commission for the Future of Higher Education, 1974.

Cronbach, Lee J., and Paul E. Meehl. "Construct validity in psychological tests." *Psychological Bulletin*, 1955, 52; 281–302.

Cummings, Larry L. "Emergence of the instrumental organization." In Paul S. Goodman and Johannes M. Pennings (eds.), *New Perspectives on Organizational Effectiveness*, San Francisco: Jossey-Bass, 1977; 56–62.

Dornbusch, Sanford M., and William R. Scott. *Evaluation and the Exercise of Authority.* San Francisco: Jossey-Bass, 1975.

Downey, Kirk, Don Heilreigel, and John Slocum. "Environmental uncertainty: the concept and its operationalization." *Administrative Science Quarterly*,1975, 20; 613–629.

Dressel, Paul L. *The New Colleges: Toward an Appraisal.* Iowa City, IA: American College Testing Program and the American Association of Higher Education, 1971.

————. *Return to Responsibility: Constraints on Autonomy in Higher Education.* San Francisco: Jossey-Bass, 1972.

Dubin, Robert. "Organizational effectiveness: some dilemmas of perspective." *Organization and Administrative Sciences*, 1976, 7; 7–14.

Duncan, Robert B. "Multiple decision-making structures in adapting to environmental uncertainty: the impact on organizational effectiveness." *Human Relations*, 1973, 26; 273–291.

Duryea, E. D., R. S. Fisk, and Associates. *Faculty Unions and Collective Bargaining.* San Francisco: Jossey-Bass, 1973.

Educational Testing Service. *Institutional Functioning Inventory*, Princeton, NJ: Educational Testing Service, 1970.

Etzioni, Amitai. *Modern Organizations.* Englewood Cliffs. NJ: Prentice-Hall, 1964.

Feldman, Kenneth A., and Theodore M. Newcomb. *The Impact of College on Students.* San Francisco: Jossey-Bass, 1969.

Fincher, Cameron. "Planning models and paradigms in higher education." *Journal of Higher Education,* 1972, 43; 754–767.

Friedlander, Frank, and Hal Pickle. "Components of effectiveness in small organizations," *Administrative Science Quarterly,* 1968, 13; 289–304.

Garbarino, Joseph W. *Faculty Bargaining: Change and Conflict.* New York: McGraw-Hill, 1975.

Georgopolous, Basil S., and Floyd C. Mann. *The Community General Hospital.* New York: MacMillan, 1962.

Georgopolous. Basil S., and Arnold S. Tannenbaum. "The study of organizational effectiveness." *American Sociological Review,* 1957, 22; 534–540,

Ghorpade, Jaisingh V. *Study of Relative Effectiveness of Joint Stock and Cooperative Sugar Factories.* Doctoral dissertation, Graduate School, University of California, Los Angeles, 1968.

Goodman, Paul S., and Johannes M. Pennings, editors, *New Perspectives on Organizational Effectiveness.* San Francisco: Jossey-Bass, 1977.

Gross, Edward. "Universities as organizations: a research approach." American Sociological Review, 1968, 33; 518–544.

Haberstroh. Chadwick J. "Organizational design and systems analysis." In James G. March (ed.). *Handbook of Organizations,* Chicago: Rand McNally, 1965; 1171–1211.

Hall, Richard P. *Organizations: Structures and Process.* Englewood Cliffs, NJ: Prentice-Hall, 1972.

———. "Conceptual, methodological, and moral issues in the study of organizational effectiveness." Working Paper, Department of Sociology. SUNY-Albany, 1978.

Hannan, Michael T., and John Freeman. "Obstacles to comparative studies." in Paul S. Goodman and Johannes M. Pennings (eds.), *New Perspectives on Organizational Effectiveness,* San Francisco: Jossey-Bass, 1977; 106–131.

Hartmark, Leif. *Accountability, Efficiency, and Effectiveness in the State University of New York.* SUNY-Albany: Comparative Development Studies Center, 1975.

Hayman, John, and Jack Stenner. "Student performance." in Darrell Bushnell (ed.). *Planned Change in Education:* 47–62. New York: Harcourt Brace Jovanovich, 1971.

Hedgepeth, Royster C. "Consequences of collective bargaining in higher education." *Journal of Higher Education,* 1974, 45; 691–705.

Hirsch, Paul M. "Organizational effectiveness and the institutional environment." *Administrative Science Quarterly,* 1975, 20; 327–344.

Hutchins, Robert Maynard. "Interview with Robert Maynard Hutchins." *The Chronicle of Higher Education,* 1977, 14; 5.

Katz, Daniel, and Robert L. Kahn. *The Social Psychology of Organizations.* NY: Wiley, 1978.

Kaufman, Herbert. *The Forest Ranger.* Baltimore: Johns Hopkins Press, 1960.

Kemerer, Frank R., and J. Victor Baldridge. *Unions on Campus: A National Study of the Consequences of Faculty Bargaining.* San Francisco: Jossey-Bass, 1975.

Kerlinger, Fred N. *Foundations of Behavioral Research,* NY: Holt, Rinehart and Winston, 1973.

Kimberly, John R. "Contingencies in the creation of organizations: an example from medical education." New Haven: School of Organization and Management. Yale University, 1976.

Kirchhoff, Bruce A. "Examination of a factor analysis as a technique for determining organizational effectiveness." Proceedings: Midwest AIDS Conference, 1975, 6; 56–59.

———. "Organizational effectiveness measurement and policy research." *Academy of Management Review,* 1977, 1: 347–355

Lawler, Edward E., Douglas T. Hall, and Greg R. Oldham. "Organizational climate: relationship to organizational structure, process, and performance." *Organizational Behavior and Human Performance*, 1974, 11; 139–155.

Lawrence, Paul R., and Jay W. Lorsch. *Organization and Environment*, Homewood, IL: Irwin, 1969.

Likert, Rensis. *The Human Organization*. New York: McGraw-Hill, 1967.

Mahoney, Thomas A. "Managerial Perceptions of Organizational Effectiveness." *Administrative Science Quarterly*, 14: 357–365.

Mahoney, Thomas A., and William Weitzel. "Managerial Models of Oganizational Effectiveness." *Administrative Science Quarterly*, 1969, 14; 357–365.

Mahoney, Thomas A, and Peter J. Frost. "The Role of Technology in Models of Organizational Effectiveness." *Organizational Behavior and Human Performance*, 1974, 11; 122–138

March, James G., and Johan P. Olsen. *Ambiguity and Choice in Organizations*. Oslo: Univesiteisfortaget, 1976.

McGregor, Douglas. *The Human Side of Enterprise*, New York: McGraw-Hill, 1960.

Meeth, Richard L. *Quality Education for Less Money*. San Francisco: Jossey-Bass, 1974.

Merton, Robert K. *Social Theory and Social Structure*. New York: Free Press, 1957.

Micek, Sidney S., and Robert A. Wallhaus. *An Introduction to the Identification and Uses of Higher Education Outcome Information*. Boulder. CO: Western Interstate Commission on Higher Education, 1974.

Miles, Robert H. *Macro Organizational Behavior*. Santa Monica, CA: Goodyear (in press), 1979.

Miles, Robert H., and Kim Cameron. "Coffin Nails and Corporate Strategies: A Quarter Century View of Organizational Adaptation to Environment in the U.S. Tobacco Industry." *Working Paper No. 3*, Business-Government Relations Series. New Haven, CT: Yale University, 1977.

Molnar, Joseph J., and David C. Rogers. "Organizational Effectiveness: an Empirical Comparison of the Goal and System Resource Approaches." *Sociological Quarterly*, 1976, 17; 401–413.

Mood, Alexander M. Colin Bell, Lawrence Bogard, Helen Brownlee, and Joseph J. McCloskey, *Papers on Efficiency in the Management of Higher Education*. New York: McGraw-Hill, 1972.

Mott, Paul E. *The Characteristics of Effective Organizations*, New York: Harper & Row, 1972.

National Institute of Education. *Administration and Management in Educational Organizations: A Proposal for Research*. Watsonville. CA: National Institute of Education, 1975.

Negandhi, Anant, and Bernard Reimann. "Task Environment, Decentralization, and Organizational Effectiveness." *Human Relations*, 1973, 26; 203–214.

Nunnally, Jum C. Psychometric Theory. New York: McGraw-Hill, 1967.

O'Neill, June. *Resource Use in Higher Education: Trends in Outputs and Inputs*. New York: McGraw Hill, 1971.

Osborn, Richard N.. and James C. Hunt. "Environment and Organizational Effectiveness." *Administrative Science Quarterly*, 1974, 19; 231–246.

Pace, C. R. *College and University Environment Scales: Technical Manual*. Princeton, NJ: Educational Testing Service, 1969.

Pennings, Johannes M. "The Relevance of the Structure-Contingency Model for Organizational Effectiveness." *Administrative Science Quarterly*, 1975, 20; 393–410.

————. "Dimensions of Organizational Influence and Their Effectiveness Correlates." *Administrative Science Quarterly*, 1976, 21; 688–699.

Pennings, Johannes M., and Paul S. Goodman. "Toward a Workable Framework." In Paul S. Goodman and Johannes M. Pennings (eds.), *New Perspectives on Organizational Effectiveness*, San Francisco; Jossey-Bass, 1977; 146–184.

Perrow, Charles. "Goals in Complex Organizations." *American Sociological Review*, 1961, ; 854–865.

————. *Organizational Analysis: A Sociological View*, Belmont, CA: Brooks/Cole, 1970.

Pfeffer, Jeffrey. "Usefulness of the Concept." in Paul S Goodman and Johannes M. Pennings (eds.), *New Perspectives on Organizational Effectiveness*, San Francisco: Jossey-Bass, 1977; 132–143.

Pfiffner, John M., and Frank P. Sherwood. *Administrative Organization*. Englewood Cliffs. NJ: Prentice-Hall, 1960.

Price, James L. *Organizational Effectiveness: An Inventory of Propositions*. Homewood. IL: Irwin, 1968.

————. "The Study of Organizational Effectiveness." *Sociological Quarterly*, 1972, 13; 3–15.

Rainey, Hal, Robert Backoff, and Charles Levine

————. "Comparing public and private organizations." *Public Administration Review*, 1976, 36; 233–244.

Reimann, Bernard C. "Dimensions of structure in effective organizations." *Academy of Management Journal*, 1974, 17: 693–708.

Reinhardt, Uwe E. "Proposed changes in the organization of health care delivery: an overview and critique." *Milbank Memorial Fund Quarterly*, 1973, 51; 169–222.

Rice, A. K. *The Enterprise and its Environment*. London: Tavistock, 1963.

Rice, Charles E. "A Model for the Empirical Study of Large Social Organizations." *General Systems Yearbook*, 1961, 6: 101–106.

Rushing, William. "Differences in Profit and Non-Profit Organizations." *Administrative Science Quarterly*, 1974, 19; 474–484,

Scott, W. Richard. "Effectiveness of Organizational Effectiveness Studies." In Paul S. Goodman and Johannes Pennings (eds.) *New Perspectives on Organizational Effectiveness*, San Francisco: Jossey-Bass, 1977; 63–95.

Scriven, Michael. "The Methodology of Evaluation." In Ralph W. Tyler, Robert W. Gagne. and Michael Scriven (eds.), *Perspectives in Curriculum Evaluation*, Chicago: Rand McNally, 1967; 39–83.

Seashore, Stanley E. "Defining and Measuring the Quality of Working Life." In Louis E. Davis, Albert B. Cherns, and Associates (eds.), *The Quality of Working Life*, New York: Free Press, 1976; 105–118.

Seashore, Stanley E., B. P. Indik, and Basil S. Georgopolous. "Relationships Among Criteria of Job Performance." *Journal of Applied Psychology*, 1960, 44; 195–202.

Seashore, Stanley E., and Ephraim Yuchtman. "Factorial Analysis of Organizational performance." *Administrative Science Quarterly*, 1967, 12; 377–395.

Steers, Richard M. "Problems in Measurement of Organizational Effectiveness." *Administrative Science Quarterly*, 1975, 20; 546–558

————. *Organizational Effectiveness: A Behavioral View*. Santa Monica, CA: Goodyear, 1977.

Stewart, James H. "Factors Accounting for Goal Effectiveness." *Organization and Administrative Sciences*, 1976, 7; 109–121.

Survey Research Center. *Michigan Organizational Assessment Package*, Ann Arbor: University of Michigan, 1975.

Thompson, James D. *Organizations in Action*. New York: McGraw-Hill, 1967.

Tosi, Henry, Ramon Aldag, and Ronald Storey. "On the Measurement of the Environment: An Assessment of the Lawrence and Lorsch Environmental Uncertainty Scales." *Administrative Science Quarterly*, 1973, 18; 27–36.

Van de Geer, John P. *Introduction to Multivariate Analysis*. San Francisco: Freeman, 1971.

Van de Ven, Andrew. "A Process for Organizational Assessment." Working Paper, Wharton School, University of Pennsylvania, 1977.

Warner, W. Keith "Problems in Measuring the Goal Attainment of Voluntary Organizations." *Journal of Adult Education*, 1967, 19; 3–14.

Warner, W. Keith, and A. Eugene Havens. "Goal displacement and the intangibility of organizational goals." *Administrative Science Quarterly*, 1968, 12; 539–555.

Webb, Ronald J. "Organizational Effectiveness and the Voluntary Organization." *Academy of Management Journal*, 1974, 17; 663–677.

Weick, Karl E. *The Social Psychology of Organizing*. Reading, MA: Addison-Wesley, 1969.

———. "Middle Range Theories of Social Systems" *Behavioral Science*, 1974, 19; 357–367.

———. "Educational Organizations as Loosely Coupled Systems." *Administrative Science Quarterly*, 1976, 21; 1–19.

———. "Re-Punctuating the Problem." In Paul S. Goodman and Johannes M. Pennings (eds.), *New Perspectives on Organizational Effectiveness*; San Francisco: Jossey-Bass, 1977; 193–225.

Yuchtman, Ephraim, and Stanley E. Seashore "A System Resource Approach to Organizational Effectiveness." *American Sociological Review*. 1967, 32; 891–903

Assessment with Open Eyes

Patrick T. Terenzini

Pitfalls in Studying Student Outcomes

There can be little doubt that "assessment" is here to stay. At least seven national reports have appeared in the last five years, all critical of higher education in America and all giving a central role to "assessment"—the measurement of the educational impact of an institution on its students. At least eleven states have adopted formal assessment requirements [10], as many more are moving in that direction, and regional accrediting associations are writing student outcomes assessment activities into their reaccreditation requirements.

The fact that the origins of the push toward assessment are external to most campuses is significant. Surveys indicate that while "over 50 percent of college administrators support assessing general education, . . . only 15 percent report doing anything about it. In the more complex area of 'value-added' assessment, some 65 percent support the concept but less than 10 percent are fielding value-added programs" [10, p. 25]. The clear implication of these findings is that for many colleges and universities, assessment is a relatively new undertaking: they are either just beginning to explore and implement assessment programs, or they have not yet even begun.

In fact, through such activities as course examinations, senior comprehensive examinations, periodic program evaluations, or some types of student, alumni and employer surveys, many campuses have been engaged in "assessment," by one definition or another, for some time. These efforts, however, are typically undertaken by individuals or by individual offices or committees and are not coordinated in any way. Nor are they part of any comprehensive, institutional plan for ongoing, systematic self-study and improvement. Much of the discussion which follows will be useful to such discrete, individual assessment activities (for example, a department's evaluation of its courses or programs), but because the major thrust of state boards or agencies and regional accrediting bodies is for systematic, campus-wide assessment activities, this article focuses on potential problems in the development of institution-wide assessment programs.

Moreover, as Astin [1] has pointed out, we have for years tended to think of undergraduate program "quality" as synonymous with "resources invested." The "best" colleges and universities are frequently thought to be those with high-ability and high-achieving students, more books in their library, more faculty with terminal degrees, lower student-faculty ratios, larger endowments and so on. Although a reasonable argument can be made that undergraduate program quality and resources invested are not independent, the increased emphasis on assessment has radically altered the nature of discussions of undergraduate program quality. Increasingly, claims to quality must be based not on resources or processes, but on outcomes. The benefits to institutions and students of this reformulation of the issues are substantial. Because they are detailed elsewhere, however [for example, 9, 23], the major ones will be only suggested here.

Perhaps most importantly, assessment requires a redirection of institutional attention from resources to education. Now that the costs of a college education are identifiable and measurable, important people (for example, legislators, parents, students) now want to know what the return is on their investments. What *does* one get out of a college education? The question forces a fundamental introspection on the part of both individual faculty members and institutions. Assessment requires reconsideration of the essential purposes and expected academic and nonacademic outcomes of a college education. It also requires a clarity of institutional and programmatic purpose as well as a specificity of practice often absent on many campuses or hidden in the generalities of recruiting materials. What *should* students get out of attending college? What should they get out of attending *this* college? In addition, assessment requires that we try to understand whether the things we do and believe to be educational in fact produce the intended outcomes.

These are all substantial benefits. Many campuses, however, fail to recognize them, instead viewing assessment as merely one more external reporting obligation, as something to be done as quickly and as painlessly as possible. When assessment is seen in this light, significant opportunities to enhance educational programs are likely to be lost.

But though advice on how assessment programs should be designed and implemented is easy to come by, the pitfalls of assessment are more obscure, typically treated only cursorily (if at all) in the literature. This article calls attention to some of those pitfalls and suggests, however briefly, how at least some of them might be avoided. The article is not intended to discourage institutions from developing assessment programs. On the contrary. Its purpose is twofold: first, to identify some of the serious conceptual, measurement, organizational, and political problems likely to be encountered in the process of designing and implementing an assessment program; and second, by identifying some of the pitfalls, to help people who are involved in assessment to "do" it well. To accomplish these purposes, the article focuses on three major areas: (1) definitional issues, (2) organizational and implementational issues, and (3) methodologial issues.

Definitional Issues

One of the most significant and imposing obstacles to the advancement of the assessment agenda at the national level is the absence of any consensus on precisely what "assessment" means. Some have used the term to mean testing individual student achievement levels in various academic areas. To others it means a review of the general education program and an evaluation of whether students are receiving a "liberal education." To still others it means a series of surveys of current students, alumni, or even employers, undertaken for program evaluation and planning purposes. And to still others, it means nothing less than institution-wide self-study, applicable to teaching, research, service, and administrative and management functions. Lack of clarity about exactly what this term means on a campus constitutes a significant threat to the success of any assessment effort.

In thinking about what "assessment" can mean, it is useful to keep three questions in mind, for the answers will have a powerful influence on the kind of assessment in which a campus becomes involved, as well as on the issues and problems it will face. The first question is: "What is the *purpose* of the assessment?" *Why* is the assessment program being designed? Although something of an oversimplification, the answers to this question generally fall into one (or both) of two categories: assessment for the enhancement of teaching and learning or assessment for purposes of accountability to some organizationally higher authority, whether internal or external to an institution. The answers to this question parallel the purposes of formative and summative evaluation: the first is intended to guide program modification and improvement, while the second is undertaken to inform some final judgment about worth or value.

The second question is: "What is to be the *level* of assessment?" *Who* is to be assessed? Will the assessment focus on individual students, where the information gathered on each student is inherently interesting? Or will it focus on groups, where individual information is aggregated to summarize some characteristic of the group (for example, average performance on some measure)? In this instance, "group" refers to any of a wide variety of student aggregations, such as at the course, program, department, college/school, campus, or system level; or to students grouped by sex, race/ethnicity, class year, major, place of residence, or whatever.

The third question is: "*What* is to be assessed?" On which of a variety of possible educational outcomes will assessment efforts be focused? Several "outcomes" taxonomies are available [for example, 5, 6, 16, 17]. A simple yet useful general typology has been given by Ewell [9, 11], who suggests four basic dimensions of outcomes: (1) knowledge (both breadth and depth) outcomes; (2) skills outcomes (including basic, higher-order, and career-related skills); (3) attitudes and values outcomes (frequently overlooked); and (4) behavioral outcomes (what students do, both during and after college). If these three questions are juxtaposed in a three-dimensional matrix such as figure 1, one can begin to see how varying approaches to assessment can be categorized.

Figure 1

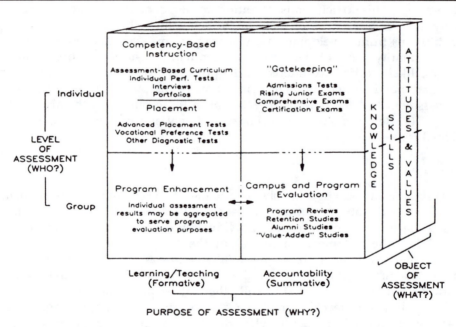

A Taxonomy of Approaches to Assessment.

Some would assert that assessment in its purest form has the improvement of learning and teaching as its primary purpose and that it focuses on individual students. In this approach, most notably practiced at Alverno College, but also at King's College in Pennsylvania and Clayton State College in Georgia, analysis of individual student performance is an integral part of the teaching and learning process. Students receive regular feedback on their knowledge and skill development, and teachers use the same information to shape their teaching strategies, activities and styles, as well as to guide individual student learning.

Some other standard assessment practices also fall in this category. For example, placement examinations and other diagnostic measures are clearly teaching- and learning-focused at the individual level. They are intended to determine a student's learning readiness and to permit assignment of the student to the most beneficial learning sequence (for example, developmental studies or honors programs).

Individual assessment results may, of course, be aggregated to evaluate program effectiveness where the evaluation is intended to be formative, facilitating program modifications and increased effectiveness. (The multiple, often overlapping uses of assessment data are indicated by the broken lines and arrows between the cells in figure 1.) For example, assessments of general education program outcomes might fall in this category, unless of course the major purpose of such an assessment is for accountability purposes (that is, summative).

Moving to the right-hand column of figure 1, one can note that assessment programs with a clear accountability orientation can be of two varieties. At the individual level, assessment serves a gatekeeping function, sifting and sorting the qualified from the unqualified. This category includes such practices as admissions testing (for example, ACT, SAT, and others) and "rising junior" examinations employed in Florida, Georgia, and elsewhere. Other varieties of the accountability-oriented conception of assessment include comprehensive examinations in the student's academic major field (a practice enjoying a revival) and certification examinations in professional fields (for example, nursing).

These latter sorts of examinations may, of course, also serve accountability assessment purposes at the group level. Assessment programs comprising this group-accountability cell focus on group mean scores rather than on individual scores. The principal interest is in program enhancement, in determining the level of effectiveness or quality at which a program, department, school or entire campus is functioning. Assessment activities in this cell include academic program reviews, analysis of student attrition rates and reasons, alumni follow-up studies, and various forms of "value-added" assessment. The focus or purpose is primarily evaluative and administrative, and the information so obtained may be used for accounting to external bodies, although it may also be highly useful for internal program improvement and planning and for enhancing teaching and learning.

Each institution must decide for itself, consistent with its mission, what the character of its assessment program is to be on each of these three dimensions (and for subsets within these major categories). The, point, here, is the importance of being clear on a more-or-less campus-wide basis about why assessment is being undertaken, who is to be assessed, and what educational outcomes are to be assessed. Time spent in committee work and in other forms of public discussion of these three questions will be time extremely well spent. An inadequate conceptual foundation for an assessment program will produce confusion, anxiety, and more heat than light.

Organizational and Implementational Issues

Assuming some reasonable level of agreement is reached on the purposes and objects of assessment, it is important to keep always in mind that institutional change is embedded in any conception of assessment. Depending upon where the changes occur and how they are managed, they can produce higher levels of individual and organizational performance and pride in accomplishment, or they can produce internal insurrection. Several significant organizational and implementational hazards must be addressed at the outset.

Mobilizing Support

A vital and difficult task involves enlisting the support of concerned parties. The active and visible support of senior executive officers (particularly the president and chief academic officer) is absolutely necessary but, unfortunately, not sufficient. Faculty support is also needed, and without it prospects for a successful assessment program are dim. According to Ewell, faculty objections are likely to come from either or both of two sources: first, the fear of being negatively evaluated, and second, a philosophical opposition based on the belief that the outcomes of college are inherently unmeasurable and that the evidence from such studies is "misleading, oversimplifying, or inaccurate" [9, p. 73].

If sufficient attention has been given to public discussion and review of the program's purposes and objects, much will already have been done to allay the fears of faculty members and others. Assessment—even when required by an external body—should be, and be seen by all, as a developmental, not punitive, undertaking. It should be a vehicle for individual and institutional improvement, not a search for documentation on which to evaluate individual faculty members, or to cut budgets, or retrench programs. Indeed, in some institutions (for example, in Tennessee and at Northeast Missouri State University), it is used not as a basis for withdrawing departmental support but for increasing it, whether to reward good work or to help a unit improve. Some basic level of trust must be established, and good faith participation in assessment activities should not be discouraged.

Ewell [12] recommends being publicly clear about what an assessment program is not intended to do. This would include a clear and public specification of what data are to be collected, by whom, for what purposes, the conditions under which the data will be made available, and to whom they will be available. Northeast Missouri State University [19], one of the assessment pioneers, recommends against using assessment data to support negative decisions, and Rossmann and El-Khawas [23] caution against mixing assessment procedures with faculty evaluation procedures. These latter authors also recommend sensitivity to the timing of the initiation of assessment efforts. If a financial crisis, retrenchment, or major reorganization is imminent (or underway), individual and unit anxiety levels may already be high enough without introducing a potentially threatening program [23].

Yanikoski [29] has suggested thinking and speaking in terms of *"progress assessment,"* rather than "outcomes assessment." The switch can be important symbolically as well as conceptually. "Assessing outcomes" implies a certain finality: that a summative evaluation and judgment are to be made, that the "bottom line" is about to be drawn. "Assessing progress," by contrast, implies an ongoing, formative process, which, in turn, suggests that time remains to make any necessary improvements. The whole tone of "progress assessment" is more positive, less threatening.

Faculty reservations about the measurability of outcomes must also be addressed, and several approaches are possible. One powerful way to allay faculty concerns about evaluation and the measurability of student progress is to include faculty in the design and implementation of the process and especially in the interpretation of results and development of recommendations. Respected faculty opinion leaders should be involved, and faculty members with technical specialties in research design, measurement, and other important areas should be recruited as consultants. Faculty members on most campuses constitute a significant, but untapped, source of technical and political support for an assessment effort.

Another way to ease concerns about the measurability of student progress is to ensure that multiple measures are incorporated into one's assessment program. The concept of triangulation in astronomy, surveying and map reading, and of successive approximations in probability theory, are familiar to most faculty members. Multitrait, multi-method matrices can be highly useful, arraying in the rows those content and skill areas to be assessed and across the columns the assessment techniques and approaches that might be used to assess each trait. One can then judge the extent to which each assessment area will be covered by multiple measures. Adoption of multiple measures is likely to have a face validity that will appeal to faculty members as well as increase the confidence that can be placed in interpretations of the data. The psychometric importance of using multiple measures is discussed further below.

Whatever approach is taken, however, everyone involved must recognize that judgments of program and institutional quality are made all the time by many different people. The issue is not really whether "assessments" should be made, but rather what is to be the nature, sources, and quality of the evidence on which those judgments are based.

Finally, assessment programs that start small, perhaps on a pilot basis, are more likely to draw support than elaborate plans. Most successful programs began small and grew incrementally [12]. The assessment efforts at Alverno College and Northeast Missouri State University have been underway for a decade and a half. It should be clear to all concerned, however, that any "pilot" project is not a test of whether the campus will proceed with assessment, but of how to do so in the most efficient and effective manner.

An inventory of current data collection activities (including the use of standardized measures, program review results, surveys, and standard institutional research studies) can be a politically and practically useful beginning. All academic and administrative offices should be surveyed to identify the information already on hand about students and about the effectiveness of their unit's activities, Such an inventory is likely to reveal far greater involvement in "assessment" than might at first have been believed.

In sum, one cannot overstate the importance of laying a strong political foundation. Without it, the assessment structure cannot stand. Faculty members, department heads, and deans are keen observers of their administrative superiors and readily discern which attitudes and behaviors are rewarded and which are not. For any assessment program to succeed, there simply must be some payoff for faculty members, whether in the form of additional funding to correct identified program deficiencies, rewards for a job well-done (say, some extra travel money), or other incentives to engage in asssessment and enhance the quality of teaching and learning in a department.

Coordination

Assessment requires the involvement of a wide variety of people and offices, crossing not only academic departmental lines, but vice-presidential areas as well. Alternative approaches to the campus-wide coordination problem include assignment of coordinating responsibility to a currently existing office already significantly engaged in assessment and controlling many of the necessary resources (for example, the office of institutional research), creation of a new office, or assignment to a committee with representatives from the major affected organizational areas [12]. Each of these approaches has its assets and liabilities, of course, and though space precludes a detailed discussion of each, the reporting line(s) for the office or group should be given careful attention. Whatever approach is adopted, what will be the likely effects on traditional areas of responsibility and lines of authority? On informal power networks? On traditional distinctions between academic and student affairs? Ways will have to be found to coordinate activities in such a way that lines of authority and responsibility are clear, existing functions and activities are not duplicated, and support is received from each area [12]. As noted earlier, experience indicates that the support of the institutions' top executives, particularly the president and chief academic officer, must be active and visible, especially in the early stages of the program's development.

Costs

How much should an institution invest in its assessment program? The answer, of course, will depend upon the purposes and the extensiveness of the assessment program and its activities. Ewell and Jones have argued that the real question is one of marginal costs: "How much *more* money beyond that already committed to outcomes-related information gathering do we have to spend to put in place an assessment program that is appropriate to our needs?" [13, p. 34]. These costs are incurred in four areas: (1) instruments, (2) administration, (3) analysis, and (4) coordination [13]. Rossmann and El-Khawas [23] also note start-up costs, which can include consultant services, conference attendance and visits to other campuses, on-campus workshops, and faculty and staff time for organizing and perhaps instrument development.

According to Rossmann and El-Khawas [23, p. 20], campuses with ongoing assessment programs spend $10-15 per enrolled student. Ewell and Jones [13], after making a series of assumptions about the nature of the assessment program likely to be mounted by institutions of varying types and sizes, estimate incremental costs ranging from $30,000 (for a small, private, liberal arts college) to $130,000 (for a major public research university). These latter estimates do not include personnel costs associated with faculty involvement in assessment.

Finally, opportunity costs must also be considered. Institutional resources (including time) invested in assessment are not available for investment elsewhere. Moreover, Governor Kean [15] of New Jersey has advised institutions not to ask for additional funds to cover assessment costs. According to Kean, legislators are unlikely to respond favorably to requests for money to determine whether past and current appropriations are being effectively utilized. If that is true, reallocation of currently appropriated funds will probably be necessary, although a variety of other sources are available, including grants from public agencies, private foundations, individuals, or even student fees to cover testing directly beneficial to students [23].

In considering the costs of assessment, however, the costs of not assessing educational outcomes must also be placed in the balance. Important opportunities may be missed, including, for example, the chance to clarify institutional goals, to review and revise (or reconfirm the value of) existing curricular purposes and structures, and to examine the successes and failures of current policies and practices. The costs of rejecting or deferring assessment may be substantial, if difficult to calculate.

Methodological Issues

The third major category of potential assessment pitfalls is methodological. Some of these problems are specific to particular approaches to assessment, whereas others are merely common and frequent violations of the canons of good research. Within this general area, potential problems fall into three subcategories: (1) design limitations, (2) measurement difficulties, and (3) statistical hazards.

Design Problems

From the outset it is important to keep in mind that research design is a series of compromises. Designs that increase the power of a study in one area come almost invariably at the expense of some other aspect of the study. Whenever something is gained, something else is given away. The key to useful and psychometrically sound inquiry is to know what is being gained and what ig being given away [see 25].

The dominant theme in the chorus of demands for "accountability" through assessment is the need to demonstrate that college and university attendance makes a difference, that students leave colleges and universities with knowledge, skills, attitudes, and values they did not have when they arrived. An impressive number of studies [for example, 6, 20] demonstrate the fact that students change in a variety of ways between their freshman and senior years. The problem lies in specifying the *origins* of those changes. Students may change during the college years in response to many influences, including their own precollege characteristics and their noncollege experiences, not to mention normal maturation. Thus, collegiate impact is only one of the possible sources of freshman-to-senior year change. Collegiate experiences may be a significant source of change, but knowing with any degree of certainty whether and to what extent college has an effect is a very complicated matter.

A common approach to the assessment of change in students is the use of a successive cross-sections design, typically involving cross-sectional samples of current freshmen and senior students. The freshmen (the control group) are compared with the seniors (the treatment group) on some measure of the variable(s) on which change is being studied. Observed differences are then taken as an indication of the effects of the college on students. Such designs have a number of limitations, however, including the need to assume that current seniors, at the time they matriculated, were similar in important respects to current freshmen—a questionable proposition. Such designs also leave selective dropout during the college years uncontrolled.

Not all students who begin college will finish it, and students who complete a college program, compared with those who do not, are likely to have higher aptitude and achievement records and greater commitment to college. Given such self-selection during the college years, freshman and senior group score means would probably be different even if the two classes had been identical at the time they entered college. Any changes over the period in admissions standards or recruiting strategies might also have produced initially nonequivalent groups in the two classes.

Pascarella [21] suggests several ways to reduce the nonequivalent-groups problem inherent in this design. One possibility is to control for age and entering academic aptitude through statistics, matching, or both. Use of samples of freshman and senior students of the same age is another option. Both are preferable, if imperfect, alternatives to the typical, unadjusted, successive cross-sections design.

Longitudinal designs are a frequently recommended alternative. One might measure the characteristics of an entering freshman class in a variety of areas and then, after a period of time (for example, two or four years) study the group again and compare students with themselves at the time they entered college, controlling for entering characteristics. At least some of the same people are being studied at the two different times, but the tendency of subjects to drop out of a study over time can be a significant problem with longitudinal research, particularly research that covers an extended period of time (for example, four years). As response rates drop, study generalizability is threatened.

Ideally, one would follow over the same period of time a control group of high-school graduates who do not attend college (but who are presumably personally and academically equivalent to one's freshmen) and who could be compared after some period of time with the freshman group who have presumably benefited from college attendance. Although the equivalency of groups might be questioned even under this sampling plan, the design has obvious advantages over a successive cross-sections design. Obtaining a sample of students who do not attend college may be difficult, however, it may be reasonable for institutions serving a largely local or regional population (for example, community and commuting colleges). Institutions that draw students from a national base will probably find this alternative impractical.

The price paid for adopting a longitudinal design comes in several forms. Because of the unavoidable subject mortality problem, longitudinal designs also require larger samples. Increased sample sizes mean higher direct and indirect costs for personnel and materials as well as more complex data management requirements. Finally, longitudinal studies take longer to complete, and all too often the need for information is (or is thought to be) immediate.

Another group assessment pitfall arises in developing a sampling plan. Have clearly in mind the kinds of subgroup analyses that are planned, for as the number of groups grows, or if one or more subgroups come from a small population (for example, minority students), simple random sampling may be inappropriate. Experience indicates, for example, that successful assessment programs provide unit-specific information. It is easy for deans or department heads to disregard assessment information when it comes from students or alumni of other schools or departments. The implication of this advice, however, often overlooked until it is too late, is that a census, not a sample, of students must be taken. Otherwise, group sizes may be too small to have face validity, political believability, or statistical stability. Costs and workload will, of course, go up accordingly.

Measurement Problems

However one defines "assessment," it will involve some form of measurement, and sooner or later one must deal with the problems and hazards of instrument selection. The common dilemma is whether to "buy, build, or borrow." Should one adopt a commercially available measure (for example, ACT's COMP or Collegiate Assessment of Academic Proficiency [CAAP], or ETS's Academic Profile)? Or should one devise an instrument locally, or perhaps use a measure developed for similar purposes on some other campus? As noted previously, research is a series of compromises. Nationally available measures have several advantages, the first of which is that they have been developed by experts. Second, they have been field-tested, and their psychometric properties are known. Third, national scores or norms are usually available so one can compare one's students with those of other campuses of similar size, type, and purpose. Finally, use of commercial instruments can save substantial amounts of time and expense that would be required for local instrument development.

Such advantages come at a cost, however. In order to be usable in a variety of settings and for a variety of purposes, commercial measures are necessarily general and lack the specificity needed to focus in any detail on local conditions. Standardized achievement measures also focus unavoidably on a limited number of learning objectives. Do the substantive knowledge and skills measured by those instruments coincide with those that faculty want students to learn? Centra calls attention to the "faulty assumption ...that commercial, standardized tests will adequately measure the student learning objectives of a typical general education program. But in fact it is unlikely that any of the tests measure more than half of what most faculty members believe should be part of general education" [7, p. 2].

Moreover, the format of any given measure constrains the range of what it can assess. For example, many standardized tests employ a multiple-choice structure that, no matter how clearly items may be written, limits the range of aspects of an educational outcome that can be examined [2]. One must remember that standardized, machine-scored tests were developed (and are popular) because they are comparatively easy to use, not because they are the best way to measure something. Centra [7] recommends, if commercial instruments are adopted, that they be supplemented with local measures.

On the other hand, though locally developed measures may be more carefully tailored to local purposes and educational objectives, they are also likely to be untested (at least in the short run) and, consequently, of unknown reliability and validity. Moreover, instrument construction is neither inexpensive nor an activity for novices. Many faculty members will have neither the time, commitment, nor competence to develop local measures.

As suggested earlier, the validity of assessments can be increased through the use of multiple measures. The allegory of the blind men seeking to describe the elephant has an important lesson to offer. Psychometricians know that each type of measurement has its characteristic sources of error [24], and reliance on one measure (or type of measure) is likely to produce data systematically biased by that measure's characteristic source(s) of error. In adopting multiple measures, one samples their strengths and their weaknesses, and as the number of different measures increases, so does the likelihood that any given measure's weakness(es) will be counterbalanced by the strength(s) of another.

One source of error characteristic of many of the assessment measures currently in use (commercially or locally developed) is their reactivity. Respondents to tests and surveys know they are being studied, and that knowledge may influence their responses in varying and unknown ways. Such intrusive methods influence and shape, as well as measure. Unobtrusive measures—ones that do not require a conscious response from the subject, can be highly useful as well as efficient. For example, if one wishes to know whether students are receiving a general education, one alternative to the intrusive testing of students is an analysis of their transcripts. How many credits does the typical undergraduate take in various disciplinary areas? When are those credits earned (for example lower-or upper-division years)? How do these course-taking patterns vary across major fields? Transcript analysis is a reasonable basis for inference about the breadth and depth of students' formal learning [27], and numerous other unobtrusive measures are available to creative researchers [26].

Even if one successfully avoids these measurement pitfalls, however, additional hazards lie ahead as one begins the analysis of the data those assessment devices produce. The certainty implied by statistical testing can mask problems that may lead to the serious misinterpretation of results.

Statistical Problems

As noted previously, assessment (particularly the accountability strain) has embedded in it the expectation that change will occur, that the institution's contribution to student learning can be made apparent and even measured with some precision. Unfortunately, we rely almost without exception on average changes (for example, a comparison of a group mean at Time 1 with the same group's mean at Time 2). Group change, however, often masks individual change. Any observed freshman-to-senior year group change is related to the number of students who change and to the amount of change each student experiences. It may be useful to give attention to the frequency, direction, and magnitude of individual changes [see 14, pp. 52-69].

Moreover, change is often construed as "value-added," a frequently-heard phrase that can be highly misleading and damaging if not understood. Warren [27] and Pascarella [21] offer thoughtful and detailed discussions of this concept, but certain aspects of it require attention here. "Value-added" is both a metaphor and a research design. As a metaphor, it is a vivid and useful term focusing our attention on institutional effects rather than resources. Unfortunately, it can sometimes be too vivid, leading people inside and outside the academy to expect more of our assessment programs than can possibly be delivered. The reason for this lies not only in the metaphor's implication that "change" occurs, but also that it is positive change or growth. Can "value" be "added" without positive change? Legislators and others are likely to say "No." And therein lies the perniciousness of the metaphor, for it is important to distinguish "change" from collegiate "impact." As Pascarella notes: "In some areas of development...the impact of college (or other educational experiences) may be to prevent or retard decline rather than to induce major positive changes. Consequently, approaches to value-added assessment which focus only on pre- to post-changes may be overlooking important college effects" [21, p. 78]. For example, Wolfle [28] found that mathematics performance among a national sample of high-school graduates declined over the seven years following graduation. The data suggest, however, that the effects of college attendance may be to maintain precollege mathematics performance levels, whereas math achievement declines among those who do not go to college.

Similarly, it will be well to remember that one variable (for example, some aspect of the college experience) can influence another variable (for example, some outcome measure) in both direct and indirect ways. For example, evidence indicates that whereas participation in a pre-matriculation orientation program has no direct influence on freshman persistence into the sophomore year, attendance at an orientation session does positively influence students' level of social integration, which, in turn, is positively related to sophomore year enrollment [22]. Thus, any "value-added" approach that fails to take into account the indirect, as well as the direct, effects of college is likely to underestimate the full range of the collegiate influence [20].

One must also remember that college effects may not manifest themselves right way. For example, it is probably unreasonable to expect significant student progress over a one- or two-year period in acquiring the intellectual and personal knowledge, skills, attitudes, and values presumed to characterize a liberal education. Faculty, administrators, students, parents, and legislators must not expect (nor be led to expect) more of assessment programs than can reasonably be delivered. The benefits college is supposed to impart are not acquired overnight, and the programs intended to assess these benefits take time to design, implement, and fine-tune.

The "value-added" metaphor also promotes an analytical design that is correspondingly simple but potentially more dangerous. Common sense suggests that if one wishes to know whether something changes over time, one should measure it at Time 1 and again at Time 2. The difference between the pre- and post-test scores, the "change" score, presumably reflects the effects of some process. To many, this change score reflects the institutional "value-added." In this instance, however, common sense may harm more than help. Indeed, change scores have some positively alarming characteristics.

For example, simple difference scores are highly unreliable, and they can be shown to be negatively correlated with pretest scores [4, 18]. Second, it can also be shown that the higher the correlation between pre- and post-test measures, the lower the reliability of the gain score [18]. Such unreliability makes detection of reliable associations with other variables (for example, aspects of the institutional experience thought to produce a portion of the change) more difficult.

Third, simple difference scores are also subject to ceiling effects: students with high pretest scores have little room for improvement and thus are likely to show smaller gains than students with lower initial scores. Similarly, gain scores are subject to regression effects, the tendency—due strictly to measurement error—for initially high (or low) scores to move ("regress") toward the group mean upon subsequent retesting.

One or more of these reasons probably lies behind the results reported by Banta, Lambert, Pike, Schmidhammer, and Schneider [3]. Many institutions are unable or unwilling to wait the usual two-to-four years needed for a longitudinal study following a cohort of entering freshmen through to the completion of a degree program. For that reason, and using the correlation between students' senior year "College Outcomes Measures Project" (COMP) scores and their freshman year ACT Assessment Composite scores, the American College Testing Program (ACT) has constructed concordance tables which permit institutions to estimate the COMP score gain, or value-added, that might have been recorded if the students had taken the COMP test in both freshman and senior years [3].

In a series of tests on these estimated gain scores, Banta et al. [3] made a number of striking (if not to say bizarre) findings. They found, for example, that the estimated gains for University of Tennessee-Knoxville students were underestimated by as much as 60 percent. Moreover, a large number of seniors had no ACT Assessment Composite score from which to estimate a gain score, and the students without assessment scores tended to be older, black, and from lower socioeconomic families, raising serious questions about the generalizability of any study based on estimated gain scores. Finally, the correlations between estimated gain scores and certain demographic and institutional variables were the opposite of what was expected. For example, the greatest gain scores tended to be those of students who had high school averages lower than 3.0, did not receive a scholarship, whose fathers did not graduate from college, who did not participate in honors mathematics sections, and who did not take more than two mathematics courses [3, p. 15]. In all likelihood, these startling findings are due to the unreliability of gain scores, as well as to ceiling and regression effects.

Such results raise serious questions about the reliability and validity of any estimated gain score, not just those produced using the ACT's COMP and assessment instruments. Indeed, Banta and her colleagues are quick to praise COMP as a "valuable tool for stimulating faculty discussion about the general education curriculum, and modes of instructions...What is called into question is the usefulness, the validity, of employing *estimated* student score gain on the COMP for the purpose of making precise judgments about program quality that can serve as the basis for decisions about the allocation of resources in higher education" [3, p. 19]. And though one might infer from this that the use of actual gain scores may be a way of circumventing the problems Banta and her colleagues identified, the same problems afflict actual gain scores as well.

Thus, in considering the use of the "value-added" metaphor in a specific measurement setting, one would be well advised to follow the suggestion of Cronbach and Furby, who advised "investigators who ask questions regarding gain scores...[to]...frame their questions in other ways" [8, p. 80]. Centra recommends "a criterion-referenced approach in which the level and content of student learning is compared to standards and objectives established by the faculty and staff of a college" [7, p. 8]. A variant on that approach is to examine the trend over time in the proportion of students who score above a faculty-determined threshold of "acceptable" performance on any given measure. Linn and Slinde [18] and Pascarella [21] suggest a number of other alternatives, although space precludes their review here. The point is that there are conceptually understandable and methodologically preferable alternatives to the use of simple difference scores.

Finally, whether one is dealing with design, measurement, or analytical issues, it will be well to remember that campus-based assessment programs are intended to gather information for instructional, programmatic and institutional improvement, not for journal publication. Methodological standards for research publishable in scholarly and professional journals can probably be relaxed in the interests of institutional utility and advancement. The most appropriate test of the suitability of a design, measure, or analytical procedure is probably that of reasonableness [21]: Was the study conducted with reasonable fidelity to the canons of sound research? Given the constraints on the research methods used and the data produced, is it reasonable to infer that college has had an effect on student change? Although the methodological issues reviewed here cannot and should not be ignored, neither should one's concern about them stifle action.

Conclusion

The assessment of student outcomes has much to offer colleges and universities. In linking stated institutional and programmatic goals to the measurement of progress toward their achievement, assessment represents a significant refocusing of institutional efforts on the purposes and effectiveness of undergraduate education. Assessment requires consideration of three questions: (1) What should a student get out of college?, (2) What should a student get out of attending this college?, and (3) What does a student get from attending this college? Addressing these questions in a systematic, periodic assessment program is likely to foster increased clarity about the purposes of an undergraduate program (one can also engage in assessment at the graduate level), increased consensus on those goals, and a better understanding of the consequences of educational policies and programs. In many respects, assessment is really only something higher education should have been doing all along.

The assessment of student outcomes, however, is not something that can be done quickly or casually. Several conceptual, administrative, political, and methodological issues may prove troublesome in developing a successful and beneficial assessment program. At the same time, and with a little preparation and care, those pitfalls can be rather easily avoided. This article has sought to help in those preparations by increasing the likelihood that when a campus starts down the path to assessment, it will do so with open eyes.

An earlier version of this article was presented at the Fifth Annual Conference on Research in Postsecondary Education at the University of Georgia, Institute of Higher Education, Athens, Georgia, December 1987.

Patrick T. Terenzini is professor of Higher Education at the Institute of Higher Education, University of Georgia.

References

Astin, A. W. *Achieving Educational Excellence*. San Francisco: Jossey-Bass, 1985.

Baird, L.L. "Diverse and Subtle Arts: Assessing the Generic Academic Outcomes of Higher Education." Paper presented to the Association for the Study of Higher Education, Baltimore, Md., 1987.

Banta, T. W., et al. "Estimated Student Score Gain on the ACT COMP Exam: Valid Tool for Institutional Assessment?" *Research in Higher Education*, 1987, 27; 195–217.

Bereiter, C. "Some Persisting Dilemmas in the Measurement of Change. "In *Problems in Measuring Change*, edited by C. W. Harris, pp. 3–20. Madison: University of Wisconsin Press, 1963.

Bloom, B. S., et al. *Taxonomy of Educational Objectives: Handbook I, Cognitive Domain*. New York: McKay, 1956.

Bowen, H. R. *Investment in Learning: The Individual and Social Value of American Higher Education*. San Francisco: Jossey-Bass, 1977.

Centra, J. A. "Assessing the Content Areas of General Education." Paper presented to the Association for the Study of Higher Education, Baltimore, Md., 1987.

Cronbach, L. J., and L. Furby. "How We Should Measure 'Change'—or Should We?" *Psychological Bulletin*, 1970, 74; 68–80.

Ewell, P. T. *The Self-Regarding Institution: Information for Excellence*. Boulder, Colo.: National Center for Higher Education Management Systems, 1984.

——————"Assessment: Where Are We?" *Change*, January/February 1987, 19; 23–28.

—————— "Establishing a Campus-based Assessment Program." In *Student Outcomes Assessment: What Institutions Stand to Gain*, edited by D. F. Halpern, *New Directions for Higher Education*, No. 59. San Francisco: Jossey-Bass, 1987; 9–24.

—————— "Implementing Assessment: Some Organizational Issues." In *Implementing Outcomes Assessment: Promise and Perils*, edited by T. W. Banta and H. S. Fisher. *New Directions for Institutional Research*, No. 59. San Francisco: Jossey-Bass, 1988.

Ewell, P. T., and D. Jones. "The Costs of Assessment." In *Assessment in American Higher Education: Issues and Contexts*, edited by C. Adelman, pp. 33–46. Washington, D.C.: U.S. Office of Education, Office of Educational Research and Improvement, 1986. (U.S. Government Printing Office, Document No. OR 86–301).

Feldman, K. A., and T. M. Newcomb. *The Impact of College on Students*. San Francisco: Jossey-Bass, 1969.

Kean, T. H. "Time to Deliver Before We Forget the Promises We Made." *Change*, 1987, 19; 10–11.

Krathwohl, D. R., B. S. Bloom, and B. B. Masia. *Taxonomy of Educational Objectives: The Classification of Educational Goals. Handbook II: Affective Domain*. New York: McKay, 1964.

Lenning, O. T. *The Outcomes Structure: An Overview and Procedure for Applying It in Postsecondary Education Institutions*. Boulder, Colo.: National Center for Higher Education Management Systems, 1979.

Linn, R. L., and J. A. Slinde. "The Determination of the Significance of Change Between Pre- and Posttesting Periods." *Review of Educational Research*, Winter 1977, 47; 121–50.

Northeast Missouri State University. *In Pursuit of Degrees with Integrity: A Value Added Approach to Undergraduate Assessment*. Washington,D.C.: American Association of State Colleges and Universities, 1984.

Pace, C. R. *Measuring the Outcomes of College: Fifty Years of Findings and Recommendations for the Future*. San Francisco: Jossey-Bass, 1979.

Pascarella, E. T. "Are Value-Added Analyses Valuable?" In *Assessing the Outcomes of Higher Education*, Proceedings of the 1986 ETS Invitational Conference. Princeton, N.J.: Educational Testing Service, 1987; 71–91.

Pascarella, E. T., P. T. Terenzini, and L. M. Wolfle. "Orientation to College and Freshman Year Persistence/Withdrawal Decisions." *Journal of Higher Education*, March/April 1986, 57; 155–175.

Rossmann, J. E., and E. El-Khawas. *Thinking About Assessment: Perspectives for Presidents and Chief Academic Officers*. Washington, D.C.: American Council on Education, 1987.

Sechrest, L., and M. Phillips. "Unobtrusive Measures: An Overview." In *Unobtrusive Measurement Today*, edited by L. Sechrest, *New Directions for Methodology of Behavioral Science*, No. 1. San Francisco: Jossey-Bass, 1969; 1–17.

Terenzini, P. T. "An Evaluation of Three Basic Designs for Studying Attrition." *Journal of College Student Personnel*, May 1980, 21; 257–63.

———. "The Case for Unobtrusive Measures." In *Assessing the Outcomes of Higher Education*, Proceedings of the 1986 ETS Invitational Conference. Princeton, N.J.: *Educational Testing Service*, 1987; 47–61.

Warren, J. "The Blind Alley of Value Added." *AAHE Bulletin*, September 1984, 37; 10–13.

Wolfle, L. M. "Effects of Higher Education on Ability for Blacks and Whites." *Research in Higher Education*, 1983, 19; 3–10.

Yanikoski, R. A. Comments made as part of a panel discussion on "Measuring the Value of College" at the annual meeting of the Illinois Association for Institutional Research, Champaign, Ill., November 1987.

References

PART II

AAUP/ACE/AGB. (Winter, 1966). "Statement on government of colleges and universities." *AAUP Bulletin* 52 (4): 375-379.

Berdahl, R. (1989). "Shared governance and external constraints." In J. Schuster, L. Miller, & Associates. *Governing tomorrow's campus: Perspectives and agendas*, pp. 167-179. New York:ACE/MacMillan.

Birnbaum, Robert. (1989). "The latent organizational functions of the academic senate: Why senates don't work but won't go away." *Journal of Higher Education*, 60(4):423-443.

Cameron, Kim S. (1978). "Measuring organizational effectiveness in institutions of higher education." *Administrative Science Quarterly*, 23 (4): 604-629.

Cameron, Kim S. (1984). "Organizational adaptation and higher education." *The Journal of Higher Education*, 55: 122-144.

Chaffee, Ellen E. (1983). "The role of rationality in university budgeting." *Research in Higher Education*, 19(4):387-406.

Chaffee, Ellen E. (1985). "Three models of strategy." *Academy of Management Review*, 10(1):89-98.

Cohen, Michael D., & March, James G. (1974). "The processes of choice." In M.D. Cohen and J.G. March, *Leadership and ambiguity: The American college president*, 2e. Boston: Harvard Business School Press.

Dill, David D. (1982). "The management of academic culture: Notes on the management of meaning and social integration." *Higher Education*, 11: 303-320.

Hackman, Judith D. (1985). "Power and centrality in the allocation of resources in colleges and universities." *Administrative Science Quarterly*, 30: 61-77.

Kotler, Philip, and Murphy, Patrick E. (1981). "Strategic planning for higher education." *The Journal of Higher Education*, 52: 470-489.

Mortimer, Kenneth P., & McConnell, T.R. (1978). "Process of academic governance." In K. Mortimer and T. McConnell, *Sharing authority effectively*, pp. 266-284. San Francisco: Jossey-Bass.

Rice, E., & Austin, A.E. (1988). "High faculty morale: What exemplary colleges do right." *Change*, 20:50-58. March-April, 1988.

Terenzini, Patrick. (1989). "Assessment with open eyes." *Journal of Higher Education*, 60(6):644-664.

Suggested Additional References

PART II

AAUP. (1983). "1982 Recommended Institutional Regulations on Academic Freedom and Tenure." *Academe*, January-February, 1983.

Cameron, Kim S. (1986). "Effectiveness as paradox: Consensus and conflict in conceptions of organizational effectiveness." *Management Science*, 32: 539-553.

Chaffee, Ellen E. (1984). "Successful strategic management in small private colleges." *Journal of Higher Education*, 55(2): 212-241.

Dill, D.D. and K.P. Helm. "Faculty Participation in Strategic Policy Making." In J. Smart (ed.), *Higher Education: Handbook of Theory and Research*, Vol. III. New York: Agathon Press, 1987.

Fenske, R.H. "Setting Institutional Goals and Objectives." In P. Jedamus, M. Peterson and Assoc. (eds.), *Improving Academic Management: A Handbook of Planning and Institutional Research*. San Francisco: Jossey-Bass, 1981, pp. 177-199.

Peterson, M.W. "Analyzing Alternative Approaches to Planning." In P. Jedamus, M. Peterson and Assoc. (eds.), *Improving Academic Management: A Handbook of Planning and Institutional Research*. San Francisco: Jossey-Bass, 1981, pp. 113-163.

Peterson, M.W. and L. Mets. "An Evolutionary Perspective on Governance, Management and Leadership." In M. Peterson and L. Mets (eds.), *Key Resources on Higher Education Governance, Management and Leadership*. San Francisco: Jossey-Bass, 1987.

Polishook, I. and R. Nielson. "Governance, Faculty Unions, and the Changing Workplace." In J. Schuster and L. Miller (eds.), *Governing Tomorrow's Campus: Perspectives and Agendas*. New York: ACE/Macmillan, 1989.

Volkswein, J.F. "State Regulation and Campus Autonomy." In J. Smart (ed.), *Higher Education: Handbook of Theory and Research*, Vol. III. New York: Agathon Press, 1987.

Zammuto, R.F. "Managing Decline in American Higher Education." In J. Smart (ed.), *Higher Education: Handbook of Theory and Research*, Vol. II. New York: Agathon Press, 1986.

PART III
LEADERSHIP
PERSPECTIVES

The Ambiguity of Leadership[1]

JEFFREY PFEFFER

Problems with the concept of leadership are addressed: (a) the ambiguity of its definition and measurement, (b) the issue of whether leadership affects organizational performance, and (c) the process of selecting leaders, which frequently emphasizes organizationally-irrelevant criteria. Leadership is a process of attributing causation to individual social actors. Study of leaders as symbols and of the process of attributing leadership might be productive.

* * *

Leadership has for some time been a major topic in social and organizational psychology. Underlying much of this research has been the assumption that leadership is causally related to organizational performance. Through an analysis of leadership styles, behaviors, or characteristics (depending on the theoretical perspective chosen), the argument has been made that more effective leaders can be selected or trained or, alternatively, the situation can be configured to provide for enhanced leader and organizational effectiveness.

Three problems with emphasis on leadership as a concept can be posed: (a) ambiguity in definition and measurement of the concept itself; (b) the question of whether leadership has discernible effects on organizational outcomes; and (c) the selection process in succession to leadership positions, which frequently uses organizationally irrelevant criteria and which has implications for normative theories of leadership. The argument here is that leadership is of interest primarily as a phenomenological construct. Leaders serve as symbols for representing personal causation of social events. How and why are such attributions of personal effects made? Instead of focusing on leadership and its effects, how do people make inferences about and react to phenomena labelled as leadership (5)?

The Ambiguity of the Concept

While there have been many studies of leadership, the dimensions and definition of the concept remain unclear. To treat leadership as a separate concept, it must be distinguished from other social influence phenomena. Hollander and Julian (24) and Bavelas (2) did not draw distinctions between leadership and other processes of social influence. A major point of the Hollander and Julian review was that leadership research might develop more rapidly if more general theories of social influence were incorporated. Calder (5) also argued that there is no unique content to the construct of leadership that is not subsumed under other, more general models of behavior.

Kochan, Schmidt, and DeCotiis (33) attempted to distinguish leadership from related concepts of authority and social power. In leadership, influence rights are voluntarily conferred. Power does not require goal compatability—merely dependence—but leadership implies some congruence between the objectives of the leader and the led. These distinctions depend on the ability to distinguish voluntary from involuntary compliance and to assess goal compatibility. Goal statements may be retrospective inferences from action (46, 53) and problems of distinguishing voluntary from involuntary compliance also exist (32). Apparently there are few meaningful distinctions between leadership and other concepts of social influence. Thus, an understanding of the phenomena subsumed under the rubric of leadership may not require the construct of leadership (5).

While there is some agreement that leadership is related to social influence, more disagreement concerns the basic dimensions of leader behavior. Some have argued that there are two tasks to be accomplished in groups—maintenance of the group and performance of some task or activity—and thus leader behavior might be described along these two dimensions (1, 6, 8, 25). The dimensions emerging from the Ohio State leadership studies—consideration and initiating structure—may be seen as similar to the two components of group maintenance and task accomplishment (18).

Other dimensions of leadership behavior have also been proposed (4). Day and Hamblin (10) analyzed leadership in terms of the closeness and punitiveness of the supervision. Several authors have conceptualized leadership behavior in terms of the authority and discretion subordinates are permitted (23, 36, 51). Fiedler (14) analyzed leadership in terms of the least-preferred-co-worker scale (LPC), but the meaning and behavioral attributes of this dimension of leadership behavior remain controversial.

The proliferation of dimensions is partly a function of research strategies frequently employed. Factor analysis on a large number of items describing behavior has frequently been used. This procedure tends to produce as many factors as the analyst decides to find, and permits the development of a large number of possible factor structures. The resultant factors must be named and further imprecision is introduced. Deciding on a summative concept to represent a factor is inevitably a partly subjective process.

Literature assessing the effects of leadership tends to be equivocal. Sales (45) summarized leadership literature employing the authoritarian-democratic typology and concluded that effects on performance were small and inconsistent. Reviewing the literature on consideration and initiating structure dimensions, Korman (34) reported relatively small and inconsistent results, and Kerr and Schriesheim (30) reported more consistent effects of the two dimensions. Better results apparently emerge when moderating factors are taken into account, including subordinate personalities (50), and situational characteristics (23, 51). Kerr, et al. (31) list many moderating effects grouped under the headings of subordinate considerations, supervisor considerations, and task considerations. Even if each set of considerations consisted of only one factor (which it does not), an attempt to account for the effects of leader behavior would necessitate considering four-way interactions. While social reality is complex and contingent, it seems desirable to attempt to find more parsimonious explanations for the phenomena under study.

The Effects of Leaders

Hall asked a basic question about leadership: is there any evidence on the magnitude of the effects of leadership (17, p. 248)? Surprisingly, he could find little evidence. Given the resources that have been spent studying, selecting, and training leaders, one might expect that the question of whether or not leaders matter would have been addressed earlier (12).

There are at least three reasons why it might be argued that the observed effects of leaders on organizational outcomes would be small. First, those obtaining leadership positions are selected, and perhaps only certain, limited styles of behavior may be chosen. Second, once in the leadership position, the discretion and behavior of the leader are constrained. And third, leaders can typically affect only a few of the variables that may impact organizational performance.

Homogeneity of Leaders

Persons are selected to leadership positions. As a consequence of this selection process, the range of behaviors or characteristics exhibited by leaders is reduced, making it more problematic to empirically discover an effect of leadership. There are many types of constraints on the selection process. The attraction literature suggests that there is a tendency for persons to like those they perceive as similar (3). In critical decisions such as the selections of persons for leadership positions, compatible styles of behavior probably will be chosen.

Selection of persons is also constrained by the internal system of influence in the organization. As Zald (56) noted, succession is a critical decision, affected by political influence and by environmental contingencies faced by the organization. As Thompson (49) noted, leaders may be selected for their capacity to deal with various organizational contingencies. In a study of characteristics of hospital administrators, Salancik (42) found a relationship between the hospital's context and the characteristics and tenure of the administrators. To the extent that the contingencies and power distribution within the organization remain stable, the abilities and behaviors of those selected into leadership positions will also remain stable.

Finally, the selection of persons to leadership positions is affected by a self-selection process. Organizations and roles have images, providing information about their character. Persons are likely to select themselves into organizations and roles based upon their preferences for the dimensions of the organizational and role characteristics as perceived through these images. The self-selection of persons would tend to work along with organizational selection to limit the range of abilities and behaviors in a given organizational role.

Such selection processes would tend to increase homogeneity more within a single organization than across organizations. Yet many studies of leadership effect at the work group level have compared groups within a single organization. If there comes to be a widely shared, socially constructed definition of leadership behaviors or characteristics which guides the selection process, then leadership activity may come to be defined similarly in various organizations, leading to the selection of only those who match the constructed image of a leader.

Constraints on Leader Behavior

Analyses of leadership have frequently presumed that leadership style or leader behavior was an independent variable that could be selected or trained at will to conform to what research would find to be optimal. Even theorists who took a more contingent view of appropriate leadership behavior generally assumed that with proper training, appropriate behavior could be produced (51). Fiedler (13), noting how hard it was to change behavior, suggested changing the situational characteristics rather than the person, but this was an unusual suggestion in the context of prevailing literature which suggested that leadership style was something to be strategically selected according to the variables of the particular leadership theory.

But the leader is embedded in a social system, which constrains behavior. The leader has a role set (27), in which members have expectations for appropriate behavior and persons make efforts to modify the leader's behavior. Pressures to conform to the expectations of peers, subordinates, and superiors are all relevant in determining actual behavior.

Leaders, even in high-level positions, have unilateral control over fewer resources and fewer policies than might be expected. Investment decisions may require approval of others, while hiring and promotion decisions may be accomplished by committees. Leader behavior is constrained by both the demands of others in the role set and by organizationally prescribed limitations on the sphere of activity and influence.

External Factors

Many factors that may affect organizational performance are outside a leader's control, even if he or she were to have complete discretion over major areas of organizational decisions. For example, consider the executive in a construction firm. Costs are largely determined by operation of commodities and labor markets; and demand is largely affected by interest rates, availability of mortgage money, and economic conditions which are affected by governmental policies over which the executive has little control. School superintendents have little control over birth rates and community economic development, both of which profoundly affect school system budgets. While the leader may react to contingencies as they arise, or may be a better or worse forecaster, in accounting for variation in organizational outcomes, he or she may account for relatively little compared to external factors.

Second, the leader's success or failure may be partly due to circumstances unique to the organization but still outside his or her control. Leader positions in organizations vary in terms of the strength and position of the organization. The choice of a new executive does not fundamentally alter a market and financial position that has developed over years and affects the leader's ability to make strategic changes and the likelihood that the organization will do well or poorly. Organizations have relatively enduring strengths and weaknesses. The choice of a particular leader for a particular position has limited impact on these capabilities.

Empirical Evidence

Two studies have assessed the effects of leadership changes in major positions in organizations. Lieberson and O'Connor (35) examined 167 business firms in 13 industries over a 20 year period, allocating variance in sales, profits, and profit margins to one of four sources: year (general economic conditions), industry, company effects, and effects of changes in the top executive position. They concluded that compared to other factors, administration had a limited effect on organizational outcomes.

Using a similar analytical procedure, Salancik and Pfeffer (44) examined the effects of mayors on city budgets for 30 U.S. cities. Data on expenditures by budget category were collected for 1951-1968. Variance in amount and proportion of expenditures was apportioned to the year, the city, or the mayor. The mayoral effect was relatively small, with the city accounting for most of the variance, although the mayor effect was larger for expenditure categories that were not as directly connected to important interest groups. Salancik and Pfeffer argued that the effects of the mayor were limited both by absence of power to control many of the expenditures and tax sources, and by construction of policies in response to demands from interests in the environment.

If leadership is defined as a strictly interpersonal phenomenon, the relevance of these two studies for the issue of leadership effects becomes problematic. But such a conceptualization seems unduly restrictive, and is certainly inconsistent with Selznick's (47) conceptualization of leadership as strategic management and decision making. If one cannot observe differences when leaders change, then what does it matter who occupies the positions or how they behave?

Pfeffer and Salancik (41) investigated the extent to which behaviors selected by first-line supervisors were constrained by expectations of others in their role set. Variance in task and social behaviors could be accounted for by role-set expectations, with adherence to various demands made by role-set participants a function of similarity and relative power. Lowin and Craig (37) experimentally demonstrated that leader behavior was determined by the subordinate's own behavior. Both studies illustrate that leader behaviors are responses to the demands of the social context.

The effect of leadership may vary depending upon level in the organizational hierarchy, while the appropriate activities and behaviors may also vary with organizational level (26,

40). For the most part, empirical studies of leadership have dealt with first line supervisors or leaders with relatively low organizational status (17). If leadership has any impact, it should be more evident at higher organizational levels or where there is more discretion in decisions and activities.

The Process of Selecting Leaders

Along with the suggestion that leadership may not account for much variance in organizational outcomes, it can be argued that merit or ability may not account for much variation in hiring and advancement of organizational personnel. These two ideas are related. If competence is hard to judge, or if leadership competence does not greatly affect organizational outcomes, then other, person-dependent criteria may be sufficient. Effective leadership styles may not predict career success when other variables such as social background are controlled.

Belief in the importance of leadership is frequently accompanied by belief that persons occupying leadership positions are selected and trained according to how well they can enhance the organization's performance. Belief in a leadership effect leads to development of a set of activities oriented toward enhancing leadership effectiveness. Simultaneously, persons managing their own careers are likely to place emphasis on activities and developing behaviors that will enhance their own leadership skills, assuming that such a strategy will facilitate advancement.

Research on the bases for hiring and promotion has been concentrated in examination of academic positions (e.g., 7, 19, 20). This is possibly the result of availability of relatively precise and unambiguous measures of performance, such as number of publications or citations. Evidence on criteria used in selecting and advancing personnel in industry is more indirect.

Studies have attempted to predict either the compensation or the attainment of general management positions of MBA students, using personality and other background information (21, 22, 54). There is some evidence that managerial success can be predicted by indicators of ability and motivation such as test scores and grades, but the amount of variance explained is typically quite small.

A second line of research has investigated characteristics and backgrounds of persons attaining leadership positions in major organizations in society. Domhoff (11), Mills (38), and Warner and Abbeglin (52) found a strong preponderance of persons with upper-class backgrounds occupying leadership positions. The implication of these findings is that studies of graduate success, including the success of MBA's, would explain more variance if the family background of the person were included.

A third line of inquiry uses a tracking model. The dynamic model developed is one in which access to elite universities is affected by social status (28) and, in turn, social status and attendance at elite universities affect later career outcomes (9, 43, 48, 55).

Unless one is willing to make the argument that attendance at elite universities or coming from an upper class background is perfectly correlated with merit, the evidence suggests that succession to leadership positions is not strictly based on meritocratic criteria. Such a conclusion is consistent with the inability of studies attempting to predict the success of MBA graduates to account for much variance, even when a variety of personality and ability factors are used.

Beliefs about the bases for social mobility are important for social stability. As long as persons believe that positions are allocated on meritocratic grounds, they are more likely to be satisfied with the social order and with their position in it. This satisfaction derives from the belief that occupational position results from application of fair and reasonable criteria, and that the opportunity exists for mobility if the person improves skills and performance.

If succession to leadership positions is determined by person-based criteria such as social origins or social connections (16), then efforts to enhance managerial effectiveness with the expectation that this will lead to career success divert attention from the processes of stratification actually operating within organizations. Leadership literature has been implicitly aimed at two audiences. Organizations were told how to become more effective, and persons were told what behaviors to acquire in order to become effective, and hence, advance in their careers. The possibility that neither organizational outcomes nor career success are related to leadership behaviors leaves leadership research facing issues of relevance and importance.

The Attribution of Leadership

Kelley conceptualized the layman as:

> an applied scientist, that is, as a person concerned about applying his knowledge of causal relationships in order to exercise control of his world (29, p. 2).

Reviewing a series of studies dealing with the attributional process, he concluded that persons were not only interested in understanding their would correctly, but also in controlling it.

> The view here proposed is that attribution processes are to be understood not only as a means of providing the individual with a veridical view of his world, but as a means of encouraging and maintaining his effective exercise of control in that world (29, p. 22).

Controllable factors will have high salience as candidates for causal explanation, while a bias toward the more important causes may shift the attributional emphasis toward causes that are not controllable (29, p. 23). The study of attribution is a study of naive psychology—an examination of how persons make sense out of the events taking place around them.

If Kelley is correct that individuals will tend to develop attributions that give them a feeling of control, then emphasis on leadership may derive partially from a desire to believe in the effectiveness and importance of individual action, since individual action is more controllable than contextual variables. Lieberson and O'Connor (35) made essentially the same point in introducing their paper on the effects of top management changes on organizational performance. Given the desire for control and a feeling of personal effectiveness, organizational outcomes are more likely to be attributed to individual actions, regardless of their actual causes.

Leadership is attributed by observers. Social action has meaning only through a phenomenological process (46). The identification of certain organizational roles as leadership positions guides the construction of meaning in the direction of attributing effects to the actions of those positions. While Bavelas (2) argued that the functions of leadership, such as task accomplishment and group maintenance, are shared throughout the group, this fact provides no simple and potentially controllable focus for attributing causality. Rather, the identification of leadership positions provides a simpler and more readily changeable model of reality. When causality is lodged in one or a few persons rather than being a function of a complex set of interactions among all group members, changes can be made by replacing or influencing the occupant of the leadership position. Causes of organizational actions are readily identified in this simple causal structure.

Even if, empirically, leadership has little effect, and even if succession to leadership positions is not predicated on ability or performance, the belief in leadership effects and meritocratic succession provides a simple causal framework and a justification for the structure of the social collectivity. More importantly, the beliefs interpret social actions in terms that indicate potential for effective individual intervention or control. The personification of social causality serves too many uses to be easily overcome. Whether or not leader behavior actually influences performance or effectiveness, it is important because people believe it does.

One consequence of the attribution of causality to leaders and leadership is that leaders come to be symbols. Mintzberg (39), in his discussion of the roles of managers, wrote of the symbolic role, but more in terms of attendance at formal events and formally representing the organization. The symbolic role of leadership is more important than implied in such a description. The leader as a symbol provides a target for action when difficulties occur, serving as a scapegoat when things go wrong. Gamson and Scotch (15) noted that in baseball, the firing of the manager served a scapegoating purpose. One cannot fire the whole team, yet when performance is poor, something must be done. The firing of the manager conveys to the world and to the actors involved that success is the result of personal actions, and that steps can and will be taken to enhance organizational performance.

The attribution of causality to leadership may be reinforced by organizational actions, such as the inauguration process, the choice process, and providing the leader with symbols and ceremony. If leaders are chosen by using a random number table, persons are less likely to believe in their effects than if there is an elaborate search or selection process followed by an elaborate ceremony signifying the changing of control, and if the leader then has a variety of perquisites and symbols that distinguish him or her from the rest of the organization. Construction of the importance of leadership in a given social context is the outcome of various social processes, which can be empirically examined.

Since belief in the leadership effect provides a feeling of personal control, one might argue that efforts to increase the attribution of causality to leaders would occur more when it is more necessary and more problematic to attribute causality to controllable factors. Such an argument would lead to the hypothesis that the more the *context* actually effects organizational outcomes, the more efforts will be made to ensure attribution to *leadership*. When leaders really do have effects, it is less necessary to engage in rituals indicating their effects. Such rituals are more likely when there is uncertainty and unpredictability associated with the organization's operations. This results both from the desire to feel control in uncertain situations and from the fact that in ambiguous contexts, it is easier to attribute consequences to leadership without facing possible disconfirmation.

The leader is, in part, an actor. Through statements and actions, the leader attempts to reinforce the operation of an attribution process which tends to vest causality in that position in the social structure. Successful leaders, as perceived by members of the social system, are those who can separate themselves from organizational failures and associate themselves with organizational successes. Since the meaning of action is socially constructed, this involves manipulation of symbols to reinforce the desired process of attribution. For instance, if a manager knows that business in his or her division is about to improve because of the economic cycle, the leader may, nevertheless, write recommendations and undertake actions and changes that are highly visible and that will tend to identify his or her behavior closely with the division. A manager who perceives impending failure will attempt to associate the division and its policies and decisions with others, particularly persons in higher organizational positions, and to disassociate himself or herself from the division's performance, occasionally even transferring or moving to another organization.

Conclusion

The theme of this article has been that analysis of leadership and leadership processes must be contingent on the intent of the researcher. If the interest is in understanding the causality of social phenomena as reliably and accurately as possible, then the concept of leadership may be a poor place to begin. The issue of the effects of leadership is open to question. But examination of situational variables that accompany more or less leadership effect is a worthwhile task.

The more phenomenological analysis of leadership directs attention to the process by which social causality is attributed, and focuses on the distinction between causality as perceived by group members and causality as assessed by an outside observer. Leadership is associated with a set of myths reinforcing a social construction of meaning which legitimates leadership role occupants, provides belief in potential mobility for those not in leadership roles, and attributes social causality to leadership roles, thereby providing a belief in the effectiveness of individual control. In analyzing leadership, this mythology and the process by which such mythology is created and supported should be separated from analysis of leadership as a social influence process, operating within constraints.

Jeffrey Pfeffer (Ph.D. - Stanford University) is Associate Professor in the School of Business Administration and Associate Research Sociologist in the Institute of Industrial Relations at the University of California, Berkeley.

Notes

[1] An earlier version of this paper was presented at the conference, Leadership: Where Else Can We Go?, Center for Creative Leadership, Greensboro, North Carolina, June 30 July 1, 1975.

References

Bales, R.F. *Interaction Process Analysis: A Method for the Study of Small Groups*, Reading, Mass.: Addison-Wesley, 1950.

Bavelas, Alex. "Leadership: Man and Function," *Administrative Science Quarterly*, 1960, 4; 491–498.

Berscheid, Ellen, and Elaine Walster. *Interpersonal Attraction*, Reading, Mass.: Addison-Wesley, 1969.

Bowers, David G., and Stanley E. Seashore. "Predicting Organizational Effectiveness with a Four-Factor Theory of Leadership," *Administrative Science Quarterly*, 1966, 11; 238–263.

Calder, Bobby J. "An Attribution Theory of Leadership," in B. Slaw and G. Salancik (Eds.), *New Directions in Organizational Behavior*, Chicago: St. Clair Press, 1976, in press.

Cartwright, Dorwin C., and Alvin Zander. *Group Dynamics: Research and Theory*, 3rd ed., Evanston, Ill.: Row, Peterson, 1960.

Cole, Jonathan R., and Stephen Cole. *Social Stratification in Science*, Chicago: University of Chicago Press, 1973.

Collins, Barry E., and Harold Guetzkow. *A Social Psychology of Group Processes for Decision-Making*, New York: Wiley, 1964.

Collins, Randall. "Functional and Conflict Theories of Stratification," *American Sociological Review*, 1971, 36; 1002–1019.

Day, R. C., and R. L. Hamblin. "Some Effects of Close and Punitive Styles of Supervision," *American Journal of Sociology*, 1964, 69; 499–510.

Domhoff, G. William. *Who Rules America?* Englewood Cliffs, N.J.: Prentice-Hall, 1967.

Dubin, Robert. "Supervision and Productivity: Empirical Findings and Theoretical Considerations," in R. Dubin, G. C. Homans, F. C. Mann, and D. C. Miller (Eds.), *Leadership and Productivity*, San Francisco: Chandler Publishing Co., 1965; 1–50.

Fiedler, Fred E. "Engineering the Job to Fit the Manager," *Harvard Business Review*, 1965, 43; 115–122.

Fiedler, Fred E. *A Theory of Leadership Effectiveness*, New York: McGraw-Hill, 1967.

Gamson, William A., and Norman A. Scotch. "Scapegoating in Baseball," *American Journal of Sociology*, 1964, 70; 69–72.

Granovetter, Mark. *Getting a Job*, Cambridge, Mass.: Harvard University Press, 1974.

Hall, Richard H. *Organizations: Structure and Process*, Englewood Cliffs, N.J.: Prentice-Hall, 1972.

Halpin, A. W., and J. Winer. "A Factorial Study of the Leader Behavior Description Questionnaire," in R. M. Stogdill and A. E. Coons (Eds.), *Leader Behavior: Its Description and Measurement*, Columbus, Ohio: Bureau of Business Research, Ohio State University, 1957; 39–51.

Hargens, L. L. "Patterns of Mobility of New Ph.D.'s Among American Academic Institutions," *Sociology of Education*, 1969, 42; 18–37.

Hargens, L. L., and W. O. Hagstrom. "Sponsored and Contest Mobility of American Academic Scientists," *Sociology of Education*, 1967, 40; 24–38.

Harrell, Thomas W. "High Earning MBA's," *Personnel Psychology*, 1972, 25; 523–530.

Harrell, Thomas W., and Margaret S. Harrell. "Predictors of Management Success." *Stanford University Graduate School of Business, Technical Report No. 3 to the Office of Naval Research*.

Heller, Frank, and Gary Yukl. "Participation, Managerial Decision-Making, and Situational Variables," *Organizational Behavior and Human Performance*, 1969, 4; 227–241.

Hollander, Edwin P., and James W. Julian. "Contemporary Trends in the Analysis of Leadership Processes," *Psychological Bulletin*, 1969, 71; 387–397.

House, Robert J. "A Path Goal Theory of Leader Effectiveness," *Administrative Science Quarterly*, 1971, 16; 321–338.

Hunt, J. G. "Leadership-Style Effects at Two Managerial Levels in a Simulated Organization," *Administrative Science Quarterly*, 1971, 16; 476–485.

Kahn, R. L., D. M. Wolfe, R. P. Quinn, and J. D. Snoek. *Organizational Stress: Studies in Role Conflict and Ambiguity*, New York: Wiley, 1964.

Karabel, J., and A. W. Astin. "Social Class, Academic Ability, and College 'Quality'," *Social Forces*, 1975, 53; 381–398.

Kelley, Harold H. *Attribution in Social Interaction*, Morristown, N.J.: General Learning Press, 1971.

Kerr, Steven, and Chester Schriesheim. "Consideration, Initiating Structure and Organizational Criteria-An Update of Korman's 1966 Review," *Personnel Psychology*, 1974, 27; 555–568.

Kerr, S., C. Schriesheim, C. J. Murphy, and R. M. Stogdill, "Toward A Contingency Theory of Leadership Based Upon the Consideration and Initiating Structure Literature," *Organizational Behavior and Human Performance*, 1974, 12; 62–82.

Kiesler, C., and S. Kiesler. *Conformity* Reading, Mass.: Addison-Wesley, 1969.

Kochan, T. A., S. M. Schmidt, and T. A. DeCotiis. "Superior-Subordinate Relations: Leadership and Headship," *Human Relations*, 1975, 28; 279–294,

Korman, A. K. "Consideration, Initiating Structure, and Organizational Criteria—A Review," *Personnel Psychology*, 1966, 19; 349–362.

Lieberson, Stanley, and James F. O'Connor. "Leadership and Organizational Performance: A Study of Large Corporations," *American Sociological Review*, 1972, 37; 117–130.

Lippitt, Ronald. "An Experimental Study of the Effect of Democratic and Authoritarian Group Atmospheres," *University of Iowa Studies in Child Welfare*, 1940, 16; 43–195.

Lowin, A., and J. R. Craig. "The Influence of Level of Performance on Managerial Style: An Experimental Object-Lesson in the Ambiguity of Correlational Data," *Organizational Behavior and Human Performance*, 1968, 3; 440–458.

Mills, C. Wright. "The American Business Elite: A Collective Portrait," in C. W. Mills, *Power, Politics, and People*, New York: Oxford University Press, 1963; 110–139.

Mintzberg, Henry. *The Nature of Managerial Work* New York: Harper and Row, 1973.

Nealey, Stanley M., and Milton R. Blood. "Leadership Performance of Nursing Supervisors at Two Organizational Levels," *Journal of Applied Psychology*, 1968, 52; 414–442.

Pfeffer, Jeffrey, and Gerald R. Salancik. "Determinants of Supervisory Behavior: A Role Set Analysis," *Human Relations*, 1975, 28; 139–154.

Pfeffer, Jeffrey, and Gerald R. Salancik. "Organizational Context and the Characteristics and Tenure of Hospital Administrators," *Academy of Management Journal*, 1977, 20, in press.

Reed, R. H., and H. P. Miller. "Some Determinants of the Variation in Earnings for College Men," *Journal of Human Resources*, 1970, 5; 117–190.

Salancik, Gerald R., and Jeffrey Pfeffer. "Constraints on Administrator Discretion: The Limited Influence of Mayors on City Budgets," *Urban Affairs Quarterly*, in press.

Sales, Stephen M. "Supervisory Style and Productivity: Review and Theory," *Personnel Psychology*, 1966, 19; 275–286.

Schutz Alfred. *The Phenomenology of the Social World* Evanston, Ill.: Northwestern University Press, 1967.

Selznick, P. *Leadership in Administration*, Evanston, Ill.: Row, Peterson, 1957.

Spaeth, J. L., and A. M. Greeley. *Recent Alumni and Higher Education*, New York: McGraw-Hill, 1970.

Thompson, James D. *Organizations in Action*, New York: McGraw-Hill, 1967.

Vroom, Victor H. "Some Personality Determinants of the Effects of Participation," *Journal of Abnormal and Social Psychology*, 1959, 59; 322–327.

Vroom, Victor H., and Phillip W. Yetton. *Leadership and Decision-Making* Pittsburgh: University of Pittsburgh Press, 1973.

Warner, W. L., and J. C. Abbeglin. *Big Business Leaders in America* New York: Harper and Brothers, 1955.

Weick, Karl E. *The Social Psychology of Organizing* Reading, Mass.: Addison-Wesley, 1969.

Weinstein, Alan G., and V. Srinivasan. "Predicting Managerial Success of Master of Business Administration (MBA) Graduates," *Journal of Applied Psychology*, 1974, 59; 207–212.

Wolfle, Dael. *The Uses of Talent*, Princeton: Princeton University Press, 1971.

Zald, Mayer N. "Who Shall Rule? A Political Analysis of Succession in a Large Welfare Organization," *Pacific Sociological Review*, 1965, 8; 52–60.

Comparative Reflections on Leadership in Higher Education

MARTIN A. TROW

I

In this chapter I want, first, to explore in somewhat general terms what we mean by "leadership" in universities, what its major dimensions may be; second, to contrast the American university presidency with its counterparts in other European countries; and third, to sketch the historical sources of the unique role of the university president that we have developed in America.

Finally, I will try to identify some of the structures and institutional mechanisms through which the American university president does in fact take initiatives, deploy resources, and exercise leadership. (The male pronoun will here be used conventionally to refer to both sexes.) One caveat: many of these observations about the presidency of American universities also apply to four-year colleges, and particularly to the best of them. But this chapter will focus on the role of the presidency as it can be seen in the great American research universities, perhaps thirty or so in all. Moreover, when I refer to university "presidents," I will be speaking mainly about chief campus officers, though in some multi-campus universities—for example, those in Illinois and California—the chief campus officer is called "Chancellor." The special problems of the heads of multi-campus systems deserve a lecture, or a library, of their own.[1]

Leadership in higher education in large part is the taking of effective action to shape the character and direction of a college or university, presumably for the better. That leadership shows itself chiefly along symbolic, political, managerial, and academic dimensions. *Symbolic* leadership is the ability to express, to project, indeed to seem to embody, the character of the institution, its central goals and values, in a powerful way. Internally, leadership of that kind serves to explain and justify the institution and its decisions to participants by linking its organization and processes to the larger purposes of teaching and learning in ways that strengthen their motivation and morale. Externally, a leader's ability to articulate the nature and purposes of the institution effectively helps to shape its image, affecting its capacity to gain support from its environment and to recruit able staff and students.[2] *Political* leadership refers to an ability to resolve the conflicting demands and pressures of many constituencies, internal and external, and in gaining their support for the institution's goals and purposes, as they are defined. *Managerial* leadership is the familiar capacity to direct and coordinate the various support activities of the institution; this includes good judgment in the selection of staff, the ability to develop and manage a budget, to plan for the future, and to build and maintain a plant. *Academic* leadership shows itself, among other ways, as the ability to recognize excellence in teaching, learning, and research; in knowing where and how to intervene to strengthen academic structures; in the choice of able academic administrators; and in support for the latter in their efforts to recruit and advance talented teachers and scholars.

Any particular university president need not excel personally in all these dimensions of his office; leaders vary in how their talents and energies are distributed among these facets of academic life. Some are largely "external presidents," presenting the image of the institution to its external constituencies and seeking their support, while giving to a provost or dean the main responsibility for academic affairs and to a vice-president for administration the chief responsibility for internal management. Other presidents spend more of their time and attention on internal matters.

But however a leader fills the several dimensions of the role—in the definition of its character and purpose, in its quest for resources, in the management of its organization, or in the pursuit of ever higher levels of academic excellence—effective action in all areas requires that the president have the legal authority and resources to act, to choose among alternatives, even to create alternatives, in short, to exercise discretion. Without that discretion and the authority and resources behind it, a president or chancellor cannot exercise leadership, whatever his personal qualities.

So a discussion of leadership in American higher education must involve, first, a comparison of the potential for leadership—the power and opportunities for discretionary decisions and action—of American college and university presidents as compared with their counterparts abroad; second, some suggestions as to why those differences exist—an historical reference that allows us to see more clearly how and why our institutions and their presidents are as they are; and third, a somewhat closer examination of how American college and university presidents exercise power, and a look at some of the institutional characteristics and mechanisms that allow them to take initiatives.

II

The American university presidency in recent years has received bad press. Some of the most influential theorists about the organization and governance of higher education argue that colleges and universities are really ungovernable, and that leadership in them is impossible. James March in his various writings, alone and with collaborators, has stressed the sheer chaos and unmanageability of organizations within higher education, institutions characterized by "garbage-can decision processes," in which problems are more often evaded than solved. Colleges and universities, in his view, are prototypical "organized anarchies," characterized by ambiguous goals, unclear technology, and fluid participation.[3] Since their goals are ambiguous, nobody is sure where the organization is going or how it will get there. Decisions are often by-products of activity that is unintended and unplanned. They are not so much "made" as they "happen"—they are events in which problems, choices and decision-makers happen to coalesce to form temporary solutions. From this point of view, "an organization is a collection of choices looking for problems, issues and feelings looking for decision situations in which they might be aired, solutions looking for issues to which they might be the answer, and decision-makers looking for work."[4] Such inept, leaderless organizations must be unable to initiate anything or to innovate. As Cohen and March put it somewhat epigrammatically, "anything that requires the coordinated effort of the organization to start is unlikely to be started. Anything that requires a coordinated effort of the organization in order to be stopped is unlikely to be stopped."[5] And if the university cannot be led or moved, then consistently enough in their view,

> the presidency is an illusion. Important aspects of the role seem to disappear on close examination. In particular, decision making in the university seems to result extensively from a process that decouples problems and choices and makes the president's role more commonly sporadic and symbolic than significant.[6]

Similarly, George Keller cites Cohen, et al., approvingly when he says that "Universities love to explore process and methodology but hate to make decisions. . . . Decisions in a university often get made randomly—by deans, legislators, a financial officer, the president."[7]

But oddly enough, all of Keller's illustrative cases show just the contrary, whether he is talking about planning for cuts at the University of California; the survival of a private college in Maryland; responses to cuts at the University of Minnesota; Carnegie-Mellon; or Teachers College, Columbia. These institutions are not exceptions. While each of course is unique, with its own configuration of problems and leaders, the capacity of American colleges and universities to adapt to new circumstances, whether a demographic crisis, budget cuts, cultural and religious change, or technological explosions, is on the whole astonishing; and most of the gloomiest prophecies in recent decades have not been fulfilled. To take only one example: for at least a decade we have been told that starting in 1979 enrollments in American colleges and universities would begin to decline, impelled inexorably by a decline in the size of the college-age cohorts, a decline nationally of some 23 percent between 1979 and 1992 when these cohorts would be at their lowest levels. And according to these forecasts, the population of college-age youth would not start to grow again until perhaps 1995. It is true that the number of high school graduates peaked in 1979 as predicted; by 1984 the size of the graduating class had already fallen some 13 percent below the 1979 peak. But to almost everyone's surprise, enrollments in colleges and universities nationally did not fall; on the contrary, they actually grew by 6 percent between 1979 and 1984 overall during this time of shrinking college-age cohorts.[8]

Of course there are variations by region and by type of institution. But nevertheless, American colleges and universities have shown a remarkable capacity to respond both to recession and to declining age cohorts, and have continued to attract growing numbers. I would suggest that much of this capacity to respond creatively and successfully to difficult, and in some cases to life-threatening, circumstances must be attributed to the ability of institutional leaders to innovate, to motivate, and above all to lead. Our task is to learn more about the nature of that effective and creative leadership and how it works, rather than to assert in the face of much contrary evidence that it is impossible.

The thoughtful 1984 report of the Commission on Strengthening Presidential Leadership,[9] is also rather gloomy about the state of the college and university presidency. In the course of giving sound advice to institutions, presidents, and governing boards, the report identifies and discusses some recent and current developments that the commission believes have made the college and university presidency less attractive now to able people than it was formerly. Its authors are especially concerned with the growing constraints on the presidency ("more barbed wire around smaller corrals," as one of their informants put it). Oddly enough, though they reach the somber conclusion that "the American college and university presidency is in trouble," they note that "about one-fourth of all presidents [whom they interviewed] are quite satisfied with their situations (some are even euphoric); about one-half are clearly more satisfied than dissatisfied most of the time; and about one-fourth are dissatisfied—some even in despair."[10] But upon reading this report one is struck by the fact that many of the problems that university presidents face, including some of those that have grown in difficulty recently, arise out of the very strength and centrality of the role, a role that has no real counterpart outside the United States.

III

However constrained American college and university presidents may seem to observers, however weak and ineffective they may appear to students of university organization, they look very strong by contrast with the power and influence of their "counterparts" abroad. The question may be raised as to whether they *have* any true counterparts abroad. Certainly in any genuine sense they do not. The weakness of the "chief campus officer" (the rectors, vice-chancellors, or presidents) of European institutions of higher education, arises out of the history and development of those universities. They arose, as we know, initially as guilds of masters, in some places with important initiatives from students. European universities retained their character as corporate bodies of academics that in modern times came to be regulated, funded, and in varying degrees governed by agencies of the state. The basic power relationship in European higher education has been between the guild of academics and its chairman (the rector) on one side and the relevant church authorities or governmental ministries on the other. Their discussions have centered on the issues of autonomy and support. The leading university academic officer, whether he is called rector, vice-chancellor or president, was and still is largely a chairman of the corporate body, and on the continent and in the British ancient universities was until recently elected by the guild from among its own members. On the continent, he is still elected, though now from a wider and more politicized electorate.

Since the Second World War there has been much talk in European academic circles about the desirability of strengthening the hand of the chief officer, making him more like his American counterparts, and indeed sometimes an effort has been made to do so merely by changing his name from "rector" to "president." But I do not think that European countries or institutions have actually gone very far in that direction, beyond the change of name. The broad reforms of higher education introduced since 1968 in almost all European countries have had the effect less of strengthening the president or rector than of weakening the professoriate, "democratizing" governance internally by giving more power and influence to the nonprofessorial staff and to students; and externally, by increasing the influence of politicians, civil servants, and organized economic interest groups on institutional and regional governing boards. The literature on these reforms and reorganizations is not about more powerful institutional leadership, but about more and more complex internal group politics, with central government trying to retain and extend its influence on the nature and direction of the institutions in the face of their claims to traditional autonomies and their newly expanded participatory democracy.[11]

The comparative perspective on American higher education and its leadership is one of American exceptionalism, of a sharp contrast between the role of institutional leadership here as compared with that in almost every other modern society, as well as one of quite astonishing success. We can understand better the highly particularized character of the American college and university presidency if we look at it in historical perspective. The strength of the university presidency in this country, as compared with its overseas counterparts, arose out of the weakness of the academic profession in America throughout most of our history in conjunction with the tradition of noninvolvement by the federal government in education generally, and in higher education particularly.

These two factors—the weak academic guild and weak central government—are also related to the strength of lay boards as the chief governing bodies of colleges and universities. The lay board originated at Harvard, the first American university. The founders of Harvard, community leaders most of whom had studied at the University of Cambridge, had intended to carry on the English tradition of resident faculty control. The senior academic members of the Oxford and Cambridge colleges, the "dons," comprised then, as now, a corporate body that governed each of the constituent colleges comprising those ancient universities. But in the colonial United States there simply were no scholars already in residence. Harvard had to be founded and not just developed. Without a body of scholars to be brought together who could govern themselves, the laymen who created the institution had to find someone to take responsibility for the operation of the infant university, and that person was the president. He was in fact the only professor to begin with, and he both governed and carried a major part of instruction himself, with some younger men to help him. And this pattern lasted for quite a long time in each new institution—long enough to set governing patterns throughout our history. Harvard was established for more than eighty-five years, Yale for some fifty, before either had another professor to stand alongside its president. For a very long time, both before and after the American Revolution, many colleges and universities relied wholly on the college president and a few tutors who would serve for a few years and then go on to another career.[12]

To this set of historical facts we may attribute the singular role of the college and university president in American higher education. He combined in himself the academic role with the administration of the institution. The members of the lay governing boards from the very beginning have had other things to do, and have delegated very large powers to the president whom they appointed, a president who did not until this century have to deal with a large or powerful body of academic peers. The American college and university president still holds his office wholly at the pleasure of the external board that appoints him. Most of the rest of the academic staff have tenure in their jobs. But the president of a college or university never has tenure, at least not as president (though he may return to a professorship if he has such an appointment in the institution). That lack of tenure in office partly accounts for the broad power the board delegates to him; they can always take it back, and often do.

For a long time in American history there were very few who made academic life a career; as long as that was true there was no real challenge to the authority of the president so long as he had the support of the lay board that governed the institution. This of course is quite unlike arrangements in most other countries. European universities, as we know, arose out of guilds, the corporations of doctors and masters and other learned men in Paris, Bologna, and elsewhere. And where they arose differently, as in the modem universities, the academics in their faculties claimed the same powers as their counterparts in the ancient universities. In America, by contrast, colleges and universities were created by a lay board and a president. This has had an enormous impact on the development of our institutions.

The near absolute authority of the American college president has been lost in most of our universities over time, especially with the rise of the research university and the emergence of a genuine academic profession in the last decade of the nineteenth century. In this century, and especially in the stronger universities, a great deal of autonomy over academic affairs has been delegated to the faculty and its senates. But the American college or university president remains far more powerful than his counterparts in European institutions, whose formal authority is shared with the professoriate, the junior staff, government ministries, advisory boards, student organizations, and trade unions. The European rector or vice-chancellor really is a political man, a power broker, a negotiator, a seeker for compromise without much power or authority of his own.

IV

The role of the faculty in the governance of the leading colleges and universities in the United States is substantial and important, but it is as much a source of presidential power as a limitation on it. The two generations of presidential giants—White at Cornell, Eliot at Harvard, Angell at Michigan, Gilman at Hopkins, Harper at Chicago, Van Hise at Wisconsin, Jordan at Stanford, Wheeler at California, among others—the men who governed the great American universities between the Civil War and the First World War, essentially created the American academic profession, a development that coincided with the emergence and growth of the great research universities. Those creative presidents flourished, however, before their universities had large numbers of specialized scholars and scientists with high prestige in American society as well as national and international reputations in their disciplines. Those presidents recruited distinguished scholars and scientists, paid them decent salaries, rewarded their scholarship and research, and thus created the faculty of the modern research university, a body of men and women who could meet them, collectively at least, as equals. The American academic profession and its instruments—the senates on campus and the American Association of University Professors (AAUP) and various disciplinary associations nationally—were the institutionalized expression or reflection of those scholars and scientists brought together in the new research universities by this generation of great university presidents. It was the growth of that body of academics, increasingly aware of their collective importance to the university and to its supporters and constituents outside the university, that gave rise to the modern university faculty, determined to be treated as members and not merely as employees of the university. They thus came to be included in the governance of the universities, in a role that stressed their right to be consulted on matters of importance to them.

In the leading universities, both public and private—though matters are quite different in the second- and third-tier universities—what has evolved is a system of shared governance, marked by a degree of cooperation and mutual trust that has survived the political stresses of the 1960s, the demands for greater accountability from state governments of the 1970s, the growth of federal law and regulation, the consequent elabortion and formalization of procedures, record-keeping and reporting, and the explosion of litigation against the university over the past two decades. Despite all of these forces and the internal stresses they have engendered, academic senates and committees in the leading universities still gain the willing and largely unrewarded participation of active and leading scholars and scientists in the process of governance by consultation. The nature of this shared governance by consultation is extremely complicated and subtle, never adequately captured in the description of the formal arrangements that differ on every campus. Moreover, the power of the faculty varies sharply depending on the status of the university and of its faculty.

It is sometimes suggested that a strong academic senate reduces the power of the president or chancellor. I believe, on the contrary, that a strong senate enhances that power. An academic senate is, above all, an instrument for the defense of academic and scholarly standards in the face of all the other pressures and demands on the university and on its president. Senates function on the whole through committees; committees are, or can be, excellent bodies for articulating and applying academic values to a variety of conditions and issues that arise. Though committees are splendid at saying no, they are poor instruments for taking initiatives or implementing them. By being consulted routinely on a wide variety of initiatives emanating from the office of the president, the senate may in fact give wise and useful advice. But above all, it makes itself and faculty sentiments felt by giving or withholding its approval and legitimacy to presidential initiatives. Without that consultation and support, the relation of president and faculty would be largely adverserial—which is what we often see where the senate has been replaced by a faculty union, or where the faculty and president are deeply at odds. And there the power of the president is certainly diminished.

Of course, there are frictions between senate and president; the relationship at its best is marked, in Jacques Barzun's words, by "the good steady friction that shows the wheels are gripping." In such a happy relationship, faculty members recognize that just as the effectiveness of the president depends in large part on a strong senate, so also does the strength of the senate depend on a strong president. It is *not* a zero sum game. For much of the senate's power is exercised through its advice to and influence on the president: where *h e* has little power, *they* have little power. Effective power then lies outside the institution altogether, in the hands of politicians or ministries, as in European nations or some American states.

V

I have suggested that on historical and comparative grounds that the president of a leading American college or university can exercise leadership: symbolic, political, intellectual, and administrative. But what are his resources for the exercise of leadership, especially when looked at in a comparative perspective? What I will say here is familiar to all, and yet is often dismissed or discounted by commentators except when they are actually describing specific leaders and policies.

First, a president has substantial control over the budget of his institution and its allocation, even though his discretion is constrained by the very large fraction of the budget that is committed to tenured faculty salaries and to support services that must he funded if the institution is to continue functioning. In a public university, he usually works with a block grant; thus he can view the budget as a whole and make internal adjustments subject to the above constraints. By contrast, most European institutions are funded by central state authorities on what is closer to a line item budget—sums are earmarked for particular chairpersons and the support staff around them, and to particular services, such as a library. The rector or president ordinarily has little power over these internal allocations of funds. Moreover, in the United States it is now widespread practice, if not quite universal, that faculty vacancies resulting from death or retirement revert to the president's office and are not the property of the departments where the vacancy occurred. This reversion of resources permits the president and his associates over time to modify the internal distribution of faculty places in response to changing student demand or market demand, to developments in the disciplines themselves, or to his own ideas about the right mix of fields and subjects.

Academic autonomy is related, if not perfectly, to the multiplicity of funding sources.[13] Here again, by contrast with their European counterparts, American universities are funded in a variety of ways, which in itself gives presidents a certain power to bargain from strength in the face of demands from one or another funding source. Even such public universities as the University of California are not state-supported so much as "state-aided." The University of California gets about 40 percent of its current operating budget from state sources; about 15 percent from federal grants and contracts; about 13 percent from fees, tuition, gifts and endowment; and about 30 percent from various enterprises such as teaching hospitals, educational extension, and sales of educational serviced.[14]

But in addition to the sheer multiplicity of sources, some of them are more discretionary than others. The use of unearmarked private contributions, research overhead funds, some of the return on the endowment, is largely at the discretion of the president or chancellor, though over time, of course, those discretionary funds become encumbered by expectations if not by formal programmatic commitments. Programs and people supported by such discretionary funds come to expect that they will continue to be supported. But presidents and their staffs can vary the levels of those commitments, especially if they do so incrementally, and thus maintain a genuine degree of discretionary power over their allocations.

Even where discretion is not total, it may be large within a category. For example, "student services" is a very broad rubric indeed, and gives a president equally broad discretion for shaping the mix of such services as between a learning center, medical services, counseling services, intramural athletics, recruitment and admissions, and various forms of remedial education and outreach to the secondary school system, among others. The very size of student support services in American universities, as compared with those overseas, increases the power of presidents; where academic staff is largely tenured, and their programs and departments difficult to modify except slowly and incrementally, the president has far greater (though never total) freedom to restructure support services whose staff members are not tenured (though increasingly unionized). These large support staffs report to someone directly in the president's office, and they constitute a substantial body of resources and people whom the president can draw on in support of his own priorities, again within certain political, legal, and normative constraints. A large staff provides the resources to put behind the president's own ideas about a stronger development office, or larger affirmative action programs, or whatever it is he may think important.

But the discretionary resources built into student services are only part of the staff resources available to American university presidents. In the United States, the great authority of lay governing boards, much of it delegated to the president, together with the relatively smaller role of central government, ensured that as the public universities grew and needed larger administrative staffs, those staffs would be extensions of the president's office rather than civil servants responsible to a faculty body or to state authorities. As a result, the strong president, supported by his own large administrative staff, has been able to preserve much autonomy and power inside the university. Having his own internal staff allows the college or university president to deal with state authorities with equal skill and expertise, rather than as a scholarly amateur against a body of professional planners and managers. Several points need to be made about this large internal staff:

Many staff people (and most of those at the upper levels) owe their appointments to the president they serve, and hold those appointments at his discretion. In some institutions there are "untouchables" on the staff, who have independent ties to the board or powerful alumni; these sometimes constitute a problem for new presidents.[15] But on the whole, few members of the administrative staff have any formal or informal security of employment, and even they owe their advancement, and sometimes their jobs in periods of contraction, to the sitting president. They are for the most part his employees, in a part of the university that much more closely resembles the hierarchical structures of bureaucracies than the collegial structures of departments and research centers. Presidential leadership is often found in programs that rest largely on this administrative staff rather than on the reshaping of the academic programs directly; and that, I think, is because that is where so many of his discretionary resources lie.

These support staffs under the president's direction and leadership can also develop programs that further increase his discretion. For example, strengthening a development office, increasing the effectiveness of market research and student recruitment, writing better proposals for government or foundation grants, all increase the discretion of top administrators. These activities and funds can provide the staff support for new academic programs, new links to secondary schools, remedial courses, creative connections with local industry, and other colleges and universities. They give the president the needed resources to create priorities, to be an entrepreneur and to take advantage of opportunities as they arise.

In the United States the president of a college or university is the link between "the administration" and its support services on the one hand, and the faculty and its programs of teaching, learning, and research on the other. And here again the American college and university differs fundamentally from its overseas counterparts. Almost everywhere else, alongside the rector or president stands a registrar, a "curator," an administrative officer who is not appointed by the president, and who is not really responsible to him but is appointed by the lay governing council or by a government ministry. In the United Kingdom, a vice-chancellor plays a large part in the appointment of the registrar, but the appointment is rather like a senior civil service post, and ordinarily continues beyond the term of any sitting vice-chancellor. And that sharp separation of the academic (and symbolic) leadership from the day-to-day management and administration of the institution enormously reduces the authority and discretion of the chief campus officer of European universities, as compared with his American counterparts.

In addition to the support staff I have spoken of, the American college or university president also appoints the chief academic officers; the vice-president for academic affairs, the provost, the deans, and through them the department chairmen, who are both heads of their departments and administrative officers. The president appoints them, and he can replace them. Of course he cannot do so frivolously or too often without loss of respect and credibility. Nevertheless, the fact that the president appoints the senior academic administrators, unlike his counterparts overseas (and the British case is intermediate in this regard), gives him a degree of leverage over changes in the academic program: for example, the opportunity to influence the balance of subjects, the sub-disciplines represented, and above all the quality and character of new appointments.

Another consequence of the fact that the president appoints his senior administrative colleagues, his cabinet so to speak, is that he largely defines their areas of authority and responsibility; they are not inherent in the job or office, or in fixed regulations of the institution or ministry. University presidents in the United States (unlike their European counterparts) can and indeed often do change the administrative structures under them in the service of their own purposes and conceptions of the interests of the institution. And that restructuring—ordinarily at the beginning or early in the tenure of a president—may be one of his most creative acts. Moreover, presidents can modify the charge and scope of responsibility of any given academic administrator in response to the interests, talents, and capacities of the individual whom they appoint to a post, as well as to new problems and opportunities that develop around it. In addition, leaders can create decision-making structures *ad hoc*, in response to different issues that arise.

If we ask what is the decision-making process at a college or university, we have to answer, "it depends on the issue." Different people and interests are brought together to solve or address different problems. But who is brought together to address what problems is determined chiefly by the president, and that indeed is an important area for the exercise of his discretion and the demonstration of his capacity for leadership. Should a senior academic officer be brought into a discussion of changes in admission procedures, which often conceal changes in academic standards? Should faculty members or academic senate committees be involved in decisions about the athletic program? Should a university financial officer be involved in discussions about a change in the requirements for graduation? What interests, what expertise, what individuals and perspectives should be brought together to deal with a particular problem; at what point will a greater diversity of perspectives not improve and inform a decision, but paralyze it? Those are among the most consequential judgments and decisions that a college or university president makes.

There is another mechanism of presidential power and initiative, one that lies directly at the heart of the academic enterprise, but which I think has not been adequately studied or discussed by students of American college and university life, and that is the power of a president to take a department or program "into receivership." Various observers have emphasized that colleges and universities are organizationally "bottom-heavy," in that expertise, both with respect to teaching and research, is located among the faculty members and in the departments. This is certainly true, and under ordinary conditions college and university presidents are wise not to interfere in the private life of departments, in what and how they teach, what they study, who they appoint, and who they promote. The autonomy of departments, rooted in their expertise, is an important constraint on the power of administrators, including presidents.

But in American colleges and universities, that autonomy can be overridden and set aside when something goes wrong: when, for example, factional fights within a department make it ungovernable, or prevent new appointments from being made, or block all promotions; or other tendencies and events lead to a decline in the unit's standing in the periodic national ranking of departments, or a fall-off in its external research support, or a degree of politicization that affects the quality of instruction, or a loss in the department's ability to attract able students or junior staff. These are among the reasons that lead presidents to take departments into receivership. When they do, they take the government and management of the unit out of the hands of the department members themselves, and of their chairman, and put it in the hands of others, with a clear understanding on how to proceed and what to do. The caretaker may be a person from another related department, or from the same discipline in another university, or even a committee of leading scientists and scholars from within the same institution. In my own university, this has happened to five or six departments over the past decade, including most recently to all of the biological sciences in some twenty-five departments and schools.[16]

The surprising thing is that when a department is "put into receivership," there is remarkably little resistance or opposition within the faculty—probably because it happens rarely enough and in extreme cases, so that there is a general consensus that something really has gone wrong. That is to say, it can be treated as an exceptional case, and the treatment of that case is not going to be an attack on the ordinary processes of academic governance in which the faculty plays a major role. Something has gone wrong, and the president or his senior advisers intervene to help put it right, so that the action is in the service of the fundamental values of the faculty anyway. It does not happen very often, but it is extremely important that it can, and there are times when departments know "we can't let things go on like this or they will come and take us over." Like all drastic sanctions, the power to put departments into receivership is a powerful threat as well as an act, and affects behavior even when it is not employed.

Control over the budget and especially over the discretionary resources in "student services"; the relatively large staff appointed by and responsible to the president; his power to set the institution's priorities, define problems, and specify who is to solve them; his power to take departments into receivership—these are some of the organizational resources and mechanisms for intervention and change by which presidential leadership can be exercised in American research universities.

VI

To sum up, this chapter is an effort to get beyond the descriptions of universities as "organized anarchies" engaged in "garbage-can processes of decision making." I believe those conceptions of the university stand in the way of a clearer description and understanding of what leadership in higher education consists of and how it functions. But if they are not true, if indeed the presidency of great research universities is as strong and effective as I claim, why has it had such bad press in recent years; why is it seen as weak, ineffective, and unattractive? Some speculations, if not explanations, may be helpful here.

First, much of the gloomiest writing about university leadership addresses the situation of weaker second- and third-rank institutions. In the American system, marked by a very high level of competitiveness among institutions for students, for faculty, for resources, for prestige and rank, the power of the leading universities as models, both as organizations and as nonnative communities, is very great. All universities judge themselves by the standards and criteria of the leading universities, and share their high expectations regarding research, graduate work, and institutional autonomy. But those second- and third-ranking institutions do not command the resources of the leading ones: their financial support, both public and private, their libraries and laboratories, their eminent faculties, all the traditions of autonomy that the leading institutions have gained over the years. It may be that the difficulties of university presidents in most institutions commonly arise out of the tension between their high aspirations and inadequate resources, and their resulting sense of relative failure when they compare themselves to Harvard, Stanford, Berkeley, Michigan, or Illinois.

In addition to the costs of this kind of "relative deprivation" are the often frustrating experiences of university presidents even in the leading institutions. The corral does sometimes seem smaller, the barbed wire higher than it was, or at least as it is remembered.[17] It may be that the presidency of a research university is a more effective than attractive position. In one of the most poignant commentaries on the role, the report of the Commission on Presidential Leadership quotes one president as follows:

> On any issue I will enjoy an incredibly high 90 to 95 percent of faculty support. Even so, five percent are dissatisfied with my decision, and they remember. On the next issue, I'll again enjoy the same 90 to 95 percent support, but the five to ten percent of dissenters will be a different group, and they, too, will remember. Eventually one manages to make at least one decision against the convictions of virtually every member of the faculty. By recognizing and providing an outlet for such accumulated discontent, the formal evaluation process merely increases the speed by which courageous decision makers are turned over. This does nothing for attracting the best people into the jobs.[18]

This "accumulation of discontent" threatens to make the aggregate of many small successes into one big failure. And the inexorable erosion of support that this process describes casts its pall over both the role and the office.

Moreover, university presidents are most likely to underplay their power and effectiveness, and exaggerate the importance of the process of "shared governance" of which they are a part, than they are to claim undue credit for their achievements. In this democratic, indeed populist, age, the towering figures of the heroic age of the university presidency would surely find themselves under attack as authoritarian, power-driven, and without a sensitive concern for the interests of their varied constituencies in the university.

One example: Clark Kerr was, as we all know, a very strong chancellor of the University of California, Berkeley, from 1952 to 1958 and an equally strong chancellor of the University of California system from 1958 to 1967. In both roles he had an enormous impact on the institutions that he led—for example, he shaped the quite distinct characteristics of the new campuses of the university that were established during his tenure as president. And yet, in his seminal book, *The Uses of the University*, perhaps the most illuminating essay on the modern research university (and after some nostalgic references to the giants of the past), Kerr observes that in his own time a university president is likely to be "the Captain of the Bureaucracy who is sometimes a galley slave on his own ship."[19] And he quotes Allan Nevins's observations that the type of president required by the new university, the "multiversity" as Kerr called it, "will be a coordinator rather than a creative leader...an expert executive, a tactful moderator...." In Kerr's own words, "he is mostly a mediator."[20]

This, I suggest, is at odds with the realities of university leadership both as Clark Kerr employed it and as it now exists. Of course, leadership may be more visible and dramatic during periods of growth and expansion, and not all presidents carry to the role the talents that Kerr did. Of course, coordination and mediation were important parts of the job, both then and now. But boldness, the undertaking of initiatives, the acting by a president on and through the institution in the service of his own conception of its nature and future—in my view, all of that does not have the weight and emphasis in Kerr's analysis of university leadership that it did in his own exercise of leadership. Kerr's analysis reflects his concern (reflected again in the report of the Commission on Strengthening Presidential Leadership that he chaired) regarding the decline of institutional leadership as a result of the growth of countervailing forces and complex power centers within and around the university. I believe his analysis also reflects his sense that modern university leaders, if they are to be effective, must keep a low profile, must appear to be finding "a sense of the meeting," rather than imposing themselves on the institution and taking important initiatives within it. If we compare the modern university president to those of the heroic age, we find today more problems, more restraints, even more resources, more of everything except authority. The exercise of authority is today often "authoritarian," and successful presidents have learned the trick of exercising authority without appearing to do so: to lead while appearing to follow, facilitate, mediate, or coordinate.

Of course the interplay among the characteristics of the person who occupies the office, the role, and the university's institutional environment is tremendously complex, and successful leadership today requires high skills and careful attention to the process of governance. And finally, even when the presidency is successful, expectations rise, troubles multiply and opposition accumulates: it is perhaps inevitably a case of "doing better and feeling worse."

This may be why presidents tend to underplay their own effectiveness. But why do observers and analysts do likewise? I have already set forth some of the reasons, but there is one other, and that is the apparent anarchy of intertwined purposeful policies in universities. I suspect that observers have been looking at the university president's role as if it were a cross-section of a thick cable, made up of many-colored strands or wires, each strand representing another program or activity, and all together in cross-section representing a heterogeneous collection of issues, solutions, and problems, showing little coherence or purpose. But in the research university this model is misleading. For if this rope is cut along the dimension of time, we see that each strand extends backwards and forwards, moving along in its own coherent, purposeful, even rational way, each marked by its own set of purposes that are largely insulated from other strands even as they intertwine.[21] So what appears as a random or haphazard collection of events, problems, evasions, and solutions when viewed in cross section at a given moment, looks more like a set of purposeful programs each being pursued in relative isolation within the boundaries of the same institution when viewed along the dimension of time. And the variety of these programs in their purposes and participants will be greater the more comprehensive and varied the role of the university in society at large.

It is this multiplicity of activities, governed by different norms and purposes in different ways, that defines the comprehensive university. And it is of some interest to consider how these activities, apparently governed by different and even incompatible values, can be pursued on the same campus, under the general authority of the same president. The key lies in the institutional insulations of activities governed by different values, and the ways in which these activities are brought together in the office of the president. One common situation finds presidents serving what appear to be the mutually incompatible values of academic excellence and social equity, the latter taking the form of increased access to the institution of underrepresented groups. In Berkeley currently, the commitment to excellence is represented by a major reform of the biological sciences very much keyed to strengthening modern currents in biology, both in research and teaching. This involved a major intervention by the chancellor with the advice and support of leading biologists on campus, an intervention that required the creation of new institutional forms and the temporary but substantial reduction of the power and autonomy of the existing biological departments to control their own faculty recruitment, graduate training, and the like. At the same time, other units of the chancellor's office were engaged in major efforts to upgrade the secondary education of minority groups in the cities surrounding Berkeley, from which many of its undergraduates are drawn. These activities come together in the office of the chancellor, and only there, although they are carried on quite separately and in many ways are highly insulated from one another. It is doubtful if any of the distinguished biologists involved in the renewal of their discipline at Berkeley know very much about the outreach programs into the Oakland secondary schools, or the outreach staff know anything about developments in the biological sciences on campus. In the particular circumstances of Berkeley at the moment—and I suspect this is true much more widely—it is necessary for the university to serve the values of both excellence and equity, and to be seen doing so. How that is done depends very much on the sensitivity of a university leader both to his external political environment and to the internal groups and values with whom he must work, most notably the faculty.

There is of course an apparent contradiction in the values that govern these two kinds of programs. But these two strands of policy, differently colored and serving different ends and values, are not competitive but supportive, closely intertwined as they move along the dimension of time. It is, I suggest, the task of university leadership to tend both of these strands of university policy, and to weave them together. And if that is done effectively, it may not be visible to observers of the office of the president or chancellor, observers who may be more impressed by the illogic or inconsistency of the values served than by the skills and initiative that enter into their accommodation within the same institution. Of course, incoherence and the loss of institutional integrity always threaten the American research university, which says yes to almost all claims on its energies, resources, and attention. But it is precisely the nature of leadership in American universities, the broad conceptions of power and the resources at its disposal, that enable the president or chancellor to give coherence, character, and direction to an institution so large in size and aspiration, so various in its functions and constituencies, so deeply implicated in the life of learning and of action, with links to so many parts of the surrounding society. These great research universities are among the most successful institutions in the world. They could not be if their presidents were unable to give them direction as well as the capacity for responding to what is almost always an unanticipated future. It is in the office of the president that the necessary resources and opportunities lie.

VII

Problems with which we have the resources to cope can also be seen as opportunities. The great research universities currently face a series of such problems (or opportunities) that are uniquely the responsibility of their presidents, however useful their aides and staff members may be. Each of us will have his or her own short list of grave problems that face university presidents, and these lists will change over time, but my own list would include at least the following, though not necessarily in this order of importance:

(i) There is the problem each president faces of accommodating to or reconciling demands for broadened access by students from historically underrepresented groups with the maintenance of the highest standards in teaching and research. This is the familiar tension in education between equity and excellence, both served in different ways within the same institution, and to differing degrees by different institutions.

(ii) There is the problem of the evolving relations between research universities and industry. The question presents itself as how to serve industry while using its funds, research facilities, and know-how for the university's own purposes, at the same time maintaining the unique qualities—the very integrity—of the university as a place committed to the pursuit of truth in an atmosphere of open inquiry and free communication.

(iii) There are the problems created for the university by the very rapid growth of scientific knowledge, and the impact of that growth on the organization of the schools and departments of science and technology, and on the physical facilities in which science is done within the university.

(iv) Closely linked to the third is the problem of maintaining a flow of new scientists and scholars into departments and research labs, without institutional growth and with a largely tenured and aging faculty that is not retiring in large numbers until the 1990s or later.

(v) On the other side of the campus, there is the problem of sustaining the humanities and the performing arts—that is, of maintaining the crucial balance of subjects within the university—in the face of the expansion of scientific and technological knowledge, and the growing attractiveness of professional training, especially at the undergraduate level.

(vi) Finally, there is the problem upon which perhaps all others depend: the defense of freedom of speech and of academic freedom on campus in the face of intense pressure from vocal minorities of students and faculty who, unlike the rest of us, do not have to pursue the truth since they already possess it, and who are loathe to permit others with whom they disagree to express and propagate what they view to be error and pernicious doctrines. (The theological language here is intentional.)

What a list! Yet we expect presidents to cope with large problems, as no other national university system does, because in fact our society gives them the authority and the resources to cope. There are never enough resources, in their view, yet by and large they do cope. It is still in part a mystery how they cope so successfully when so much of the theory of organizational leadership tells us they cannot and should not be able to do so.

But I think that the office of the university president has not been properly appreciated; it has been the object more of compassion and criticism than of understanding. The university presidency deserves understanding, though I suspect that incumbents will continue to speak of it deprecatingly and, with good reason, as fraught with difficulties and constraints. And meanwhile, under their leadership in that extraordinary office, our research universities go on from strength to strength.

Notes

[1] On multi-campus systems, see Eugene Lee and Frank Bowen, *The Multi-campus University: A Study of Academic Governance*, New York: McGraw-Hill, 1971.

[2] On the distinction between organizations and institutions, and the role of leadership in defining purpose and mission, see Philip Selznick, *Leadership in Administration*, Evanston, Ill., Row, Peterson, 1957, esp. 5–28.

[3] M. Cohen and J. G. March, *Leadership and Ambiguity*, New York: McGraw-Hill, 1974; 3.

[4] Ibid., 81.

[5] Ibid., 206.

[6] Ibid., 2.

[7] George Keller, *Academic Strategy*, Baltimore: Johns Hopkins, 1983; 86.

[8] Martin Trow, "American Higher Education: Past, Present and Future," in G. W. Lapidus and G. E. Swanson, eds., *Social Welfare and the Social Service*: USA/USSR, Berkeley, 1986.

[9] The Commission on Strengthening Presidential Leadership, *Presidents Make a Difference* Washington, D.C.: The Association of Governing Boards, 1984.

[10] Ibid., xix and xviii.

[11] See Guy Neave, "Strategic Planning, Reform and Governance in French Higher Education," *Studies in Higher Education*, 1985, 10, no. 1; and Alain Bienayme, "The New Reforms in French Higher Education, *European Journal of Education*, 1984, 19, no. 2; See for example, Maurice Kogan, "Implementing Expenditure Cuts in British Higher Education, in Rune Premfors, ed., *Higher Education Organization*, Stockholm: Almqvist and Wiksell, 1984.

[12] See Frederick Rudolph, *The American College and University*, New York: Alfred A. Knopf, 1962; 161–166.

[13] See Martin Trow, "Defining the Issues in University-Government Relations," *Studies in Higher Education*, 8, no, 2, 1983.

[14] Private communication, University of California Budget Office.

[15] Clark Kerr and Marian L. Gade, *The Many Lives of Academic Presidents: Time, Place & Character*, Washington, D.C.: Association of Governing Universities and Colleges, 1986, 27.

[16] See Martin Trow, "Leadership and Organization: The Case of Biology at Berkeley," in Rune Premfors, ed., *Higher Education Organization*, Stockholm: Almqvist and Wiksell, 1984.

[17] The phrase is drawn from the Commission on Strengthening Presidential Leadership, op. cit.

[18] Ibid., 54.

[19] Clark Kerr, *The Uses of the University*, Cambridge, Mass. Harvard University Press, 1963, 33.

[20] Ibid., 36.

[21] This image, and the next few paragraphs, are drawn from my essay "Leadership and Organization: The Case of Biology at Berkeley," op. cit., 166–167.

The Nature of Administrative Behavior in Higher Education[1]

DAVID D. DILL

The rapid growth of American higher education after World War II produced several outputs in large measure. In addition to the largest number of faculty members and students in the world, a significant volume of research and a vast and growing literature on the enterprise itself resulted. A sizable portion of the literature on higher education has addressed a still amorphous area usually referred to as higher education administration. The intent of this review is to focus on a particular slice of that literature: the research on administrative behavior.

The focus of the review was prompted by three important publications that appeared over a two-year period. In 1974, Peterson published the only extant review of the research literature on the organization and administration of higher education.[2] As his review made clear, the large volume of research as of 1974 addressed colleges and universities as organizations—their goals and purposes, organizational climate, institutional decision making, governance structures, patterns of influence, and processes of conflict, innovation, participation, and change. Peterson also identified and reviewed a growing literature on planning and management techniques in higher education. In contrast, empirical studies on administrative behavior or on what administrators in these settings actually did were rare, and Peterson identified this as a particular weakness of the literature at the time.

In the same year, March presented a classic but generally unknown address on educational administration.[3] In it, March argued that the training of higher education administrators should be based on knowledge of the context of education. This knowledge should ideally include the nature of educational organizations as well as what educational managers actually do. As March pointed out, a persistent difficulty with attempts to improve administrative effectiveness has been that efforts in that direction are often unrelated to the ordinary organization and conduct of administrative life. Unless one begins with some appreciation of what administrators do and why they organize their lives the way they do, such efforts are unlikely to improve administrative performance.

In the prior year, Mintzberg's landmark book, *The Nature of Managerial Work*, was published.[4] Mintzberg's original investigations as well as his codification of existing research revealed consistent patterns in managerial work. These patterns were at variance with existing models of administrative behavior that tended to emphasize the rational processes of planning, organizing, and controlling. Subsequent research by Kurke and Aldrich,[5] Kotter,[6] and Lau and his associates[7] has generally supported Mintzberg's findings. Taken as a whole, this research raised the question of whether or not the successful implementation of technologies and processes advocated for contemporary managers was seriously compromised by a failure to understand the nature of managerial work itself.

Following the lead of these three publications, this review will focus on the state of knowledge on administrative behavior in institutions of higher education.

Method

A review of research represents a fundamental activity in the behavioral sciences, but the methods, techniques, and procedures for conducting such reviews are sometimes ambiguous or unstated.[8] As a result, it is quite likely that two people conducting a similar review may arrive at substantially different conclusions. This variation may be due to the questions asked, the methods of selecting material, the form the analysis takes, and/or to unstated biases that shape each of the above. In sum, reviews of research are subject to the same sources of error as traditional research studies.

The review that follows is an integrative review, that is, a review "inferring generalizations about substantive issues from a set of studies directly bearing on those issues."[9] To increase the potential value of the review, several strategies were employed. First, the basic organization of the review was derived from a framework that is reliably grounded in the nature of managerial work. Second, some care was taken in selecting the material for the review. A computerized search was conducted of both the *Social Sciences Citation Index* and *ERIC*. The key words utilized were: "administrative behavior," "management," "leadership," "higher education," "college," and "university." Citations were collected for the period of 1974 (i.e., the date of the last such review by Peterson) through September 1983. This yielded 345 references. In addition, a separate review was made of the best known research journals in the field. These journals were: the *Educational Administration Quarterly*, *Higher Education*, *Journal of Higher Education*, *Research in Higher Education*, and *The Review of Higher Education*. This resulted in an additional 50 references. Each of these was reviewed to determine those articles that presented the results of empirical research, and 30 more references were identified. To these were added a number of articles and book chapters reporting research that was known to be relevant by the author but that had not been uncovered in the keyword search.

It is at this point that substantial bias can enter into a review. Therefore, one important control is for the author to state his or her own bias(es). The writer's own views of management and academic organizations have been heavily influenced by the writings of Clark,[10] March,[11] and Mintzberg.[12] As a result, personal knowledge of references in the field was likely to over-represent literature on subjects such as "ambiguity," "culture," "influence," and "political models," as well as research pertinent to the categories of Mintzberg's framework. In contrast, literature addressing "rational" analyses and techniques were apt to be underrepresented. Furthermore, although the techniques of decision analysis, cost-benefit analysis, and MBO may, if implemented, lead to improvements in academic management, the empirical research supporting the utility of such models for managerial work is scant in the writer's judgment. Finally, the author's knowledge of material relating to research universities is greater than for other types of institutions. Having stated these biases, it is incumbent on the writer to attend to contradictory research evidence in the articles reviewed.

An additional control employed in this review was the means of presenting and analyzing the results of the primary materials.[13] Because the variety of research methodologies and approaches employed in the field of higher education administration and management compromise the additive results of different studies, the present review will attend principally to general trends in research results as well as to issues related to methodology.

Finally, this discussion of method must conclude with an important *caveat*. The plan for selecting material for the review has limitations which may affect the results. In addition to the title keyword search, subject key words or key words reflecting the organizing or analytical framework employed in the review could have been pursued. Furthermore, dissertations and books could have been included along with journal articles. The decision to restrict the search and material considered was mandated by limitations of time and funds. One implication of the procedure used is that the review over-represents research published in traditional research journals. As such, the research results may under-represent new directions in inquiry not yet evident in published sources. However, it can be assumed that the review in representative of the accrued knowledge in the field to date.

Analytical Framework

The concept of "administrative behavior" refers to the behavior of those within the boundaries of organizations who occupy administrative positions.[14] Traditionally the research in this area has focused on leadership traits and patterns of individual or group decision making. The literature has also included normative prescriptions for the managerial activities of planning, coordinating, and controlling that have been based on little if any research. Because classical perspectives on administrative behavior have been supplanted by more recent observational approaches, the general managerial skill framework of Katz[15] will be linked with the empirically derived categories of Mintzberg[16] as a means of organizing and presenting the research analyzed in this review. Katz has argued that successful managers exhibit three categories of skills: human relations skills, conceptual skills, and technical skills. Anderson[17] has suggested that linking these categories with the behavior exhibited by the executives observed by Mintzberg provides greater insight to the understanding of managerial behavior (see Figure 1).

Figure 1

Framework for Administrative Behavior Based Upon Katz and Mintzberg (1973, 1974)

Katz	Mintzberg
Human Relations Skills	Peer-related Behavior
	Leadership Behavior
	Conflict-resolution Behavior
	Information-related Behavior
	Decision-making Behavior
Conceptual Skills	Resource Allocation Behavior
	Entrepreneurial Behavior
	Introspective Behavior
Technical Skills	Profession-related Behavior

SOURCE: Adapted from K. Anderson, *Management: Skills, Functions, and Organizational Performance (Dubuque, IA: W.C. Brown, 1984).*

By human relations skills, Katz means those interpersonal skills that are applied when a manager relates to superiors, peers, and subordinates. They are thereby relevant to every managerial level. In terms of Mintzberg's research, human relations skills include: (1) peer-related behavior such as developing contacts in the organization, maintaining information networks, and negotiating and communicating with peers; (2) leadership behavior that relates to dealing effectively with subordinates; and (3) conflict resolution behavior.

Conceptual skills relate to the manager's ability to think through the coordination and integration of the organization's diverse activities, what in contemporary terms is thought of as "strategic thinking." Mintzberg discovered five types of behavior that may be categorized as conceptual skills: (1) information processing behavior or the monitoring of one's networks for obtaining information, extracting and assimilating information, and communicating the "pictures" the manager develops; (2) decision making in unstructured and ambiguous situations;

(3) resource allocation behavior or the allocation of the organization's critical assets (i.e., time, money, and skill) among competing demands; (4) entrepreneurial behavior that relates to discovering problems and opportunities for which "improvement projects" will be initiated; and (5) introspective behavior that relates to the manager's understanding of the job, sensitivity to his or her personal impact, and learning from these insights.

By technical skill Katz means two things: first, the technique or expertise of "management" (e.g., knowledge of budgeting and accounting), and second, the professional expertise or skill that the individual practiced prior to becoming a manager. In the case of the academic manager, professional expertise is equivalent to academic expertise, that is, knowledge of a disciplinary field as well as acknowledged capabilities in teaching and research. Because several of Mintzberg's categories of observed management behavior (e.g., conflict resolution behavior, decision-making behavior, and resource allocation behavior) are relevant to Katz's first meaning of technical skill, technical skill in this review will be limited to a discussion of the relevance of the aspect of this skill area referred to as professional expertise. Both Katz and Mintzberg argue that professional expertise becomes less relevant as one moves up the managerial hierarchy and assumes responsibility for a broader range of activities. However, a distinctive aspect of academic management is the attempts of faculty members to sustain their professional expertise by teaching and conducting research while occupying administrative positions. Thus, the relationship of technical academic skills to managerial behavior is of special interest in higher education administration.

There is no assumption here that the research on administrative behavior in higher education will be evenly distributed among these various categories or that the results within each category will be unequivocal. Some categories will probably contain no research at all, and further, some material may well logically be placed in more than one of the classification categories. Nevertheless, by organizing the review in this fashion, the state of knowledge regarding what administrators in higher education do can be codified and implications for practice and research can be more effectively drawn.

Knowledge concerning the allocation of administrative time and patterns of communication is an important contribution of the research of Mintzberg and others who study managerial work. This review will begin with the related research on academic administrators as an introduction. In the sections of the review that follow, the published research will be reviewed in terms of the above categorization of administrative behavior. Put another way, what little is known about how administrators in higher education distribute their time will be discussed first. Then the skills and behavior associated with the categories of human relations skills, conceptual skills, and professional technical skills will be explored in turn.

Managerial Time in Academia

Mintzberg's study of five managers of large organizations concluded that the managers performed a great deal of work at an unrelenting pace; that managerial work was characterized by variety, fragmentation, and brevity; and that managerial work was conducted essentially in a verbal medium. Related analyses of the time allocations of college presidents and deans or department heads have reached similar conclusions about academic managerial work.

Cohen and March in a national survey of college presidents discovered that these executives worked an average of 60 hours a week.[18] This compared with 55 hours of weekly work for the average dean or department head in Lewis and Dahl's small sample study done at the University of Minnesota.[19] As Cohen and March have pointed out, such an average work week is consistent with reported work schedules of academics generally, and it is at the high end of the scales in terms of studies of managers in other fields.

Cohen and March's data on university presidents were comparable in other ways to those on general managers. For example, the presidents spent proportionately similar amounts of time around their office (approximately 30%), in the vicinity of the university (approximately 60%), and out of town (approximately 22%) as did the executives in Mintzberg's study. University presidents were also similar to the executives in terms of their distribution of contact time with other parties. Approximately one-third of their contact time was with those outside the organization, less than 10% was with trustees, and over 50% was with subordinates (i.e., students, faculty, and administrators). Although the university presidents came in contact with a wide variety of people, more time was spent by them with fellow administrators than with any other single group.

University presidents, department heads or deans, and managers from other fields are also alike in that they spend approximately 25% of their time alone, but over 40% of their time in meetings, usually with two or more people. Similarly, management in all settings is a reactive job. Further, the majority of meetings that all these managers attend is initiated by others.

The studies of academic managers reveal some interesting variations and similarities in role both by institution and administrative level. For example, presidents of large universities are more likely to be alone, in town, and spending time with "academic" administrators and dealing with people in groups. In contrast, deans and department heads reported only 45% of their time in administrative work. (The sample in the Lewis and Dahl study contained more department heads than deans.) Approximately 9% of their time was reported in the area of research, 16% in teaching, and over 20% in university service. Lewis and Dahl also reported that the administrators indicated greatest stress came from their administrative duties and that the greatest stress reducer would be increasing the number of hours each week voluntarily devoted to management. This is consistent with the survey results of Weisbord, Lawrence, and Charns of academics in a large medical complex who perceived the functions of research, teaching, patient care, and departmental administration as essentially conflicting functions.[20]

In summary, academic administrators lead a busy, reactive life in which they heavily utilize their verbal skills, particularly in meetings. Observed variations exist as a result of differences in role between full-time administrators (e.g., presidents) and part-time administrators (e.g., department heads). How academic managers apportion their time and contacts is of interest, but what do they actually do? That is, what are their characteristic administrative behaviors? In the following sections, the available research will be discussed according to the framework established for this review.

Human Relations Skill

There is high level of agreement in the literature on administrative behavior that human relations or interpersonal skills are critical to the role of manager, particularly as one moves up the hierarchy of an organization. Mintzberg clarified those skills by focusing on peer-related behavior that deals with the manager's behavior in entering into and effectively maintaining peer or horizontal relationships. Leadership behavior, on the other hand, was conceived by Mintzberg (and many others as well) as the vertical relationships between managers and their subordinates. In this sense, leadership addresses the interpersonal processes of motivation, training, helping, and dealing with issues of authority and dependence. Conflict resolution behavior was described as attempting to mediate between conflicting individuals and decisions or handling disturbances.

Peer-Related Behavior

Cohen and March reported that the amount of time spent by university presidents on peer-related behavior was substantial. Over a third of their time was spent with outsiders and nearly 30% was spent with constituents (trustees, students, and faculty members) who were not direct subordinates. (Cohen and March also quoted very comparable data from a study conducted in New York State that included community college presidents.)

The large amount of external contact suggests that high level administrators become more distinct and isolated. Lunsford has argued: "The growth in size and importance of universities, together with increasing specialization, has sharpened the separation of administrators from the rest of university life. Their authority is consequently mixed and precarious."[21] In his ethnographic study at the University of California at Berkeley, Lunsford observed that certain core values or beliefs reinforced this isolation and made it a more significant problem for academic managers than for their industrial counterparts. These core values were beliefs in the esoteric quality of specialized research, in academic freedom, in "collegial" decision making, and in the separation of powers between academic and non-academic decisions. Whitson and Hubert in a national study of department chairmen in large public universities confirmed that decision-making authority was perceived to reflect a separation of powers.[22] Department heads reported primary influence or greater influence than all other groups or individuals in personnel decisions, faculty selection and evaluation, salary decisions, dismissal and nonreappointment of faculty, and administration of the budget. Faculty were reported as having had primary influence in student admissions' policy, departmental academic standards, and the selection and recruitment of graduate students. Department heads and faculty had equal influence in tenure and promotion issues. Lunsford further suggested that academic beliefs in conjunction with the impacts of institutional growth and increased administrative accountability have led to the isolation of high-level administrators. The specialization of administrative tasks, the nature of associations (less with faculty and students, and more with trustees, alumni, and legislators), the visibility and prestige of executive status, and the unwelcome burden of conveying bad news have led in Lunsford's analysis to a separate administrative culture, one distinct and alien.

As a consequence of this separation, Lunsford observes that managers must spend time building channels of communication and support. This involves seeking opportunities for frequent, informal communication with internal constituents such as faculty and students (for example, through teaching a class as a means of staying in touch or using task forces composed of faculty members to address administratively defined problems). Another such possible means is through the use of special assistants drawn from the faculty at large, Stringer, in a study within a large public university, found these "colleague" special assistants to be the most influential of all "assistant-to" types.[23] The relationships of these assistants to executives was what Stringer termed, "collegial": that is, they participated in all major policy discussions and had frequent informal contacts with the executives. As Stringer pointed out, this type of staff role is unique to higher education.

The earlier analysis of administrator time devoted to peer contacts and this modest research suggests that peer-related behavior is both a significant part of an academic manager's job and, given the potential for isolation, a potentially critical component of behavior. However, little work has been done on the means managers use to develop and maintain their networks of contacts. Also lacking is knowledge about how academic managers negotiate with peers for needed resources or how they consult effectively with the many colleagues and experts that they must utilize.

Leadership Behavior

Cohen and March reported that contact with direct subordinates, such as members of the president's staff as well as academic and non-academic administrators, occupied the largest single block of the university president's time. There is also some evidence that this time is perceived as important to administrative success and satisfaction. Peterson asked four-year college presidents in public midwestern colleges to identify incidents critical to their success.[24] Staffing problems and subordinate ineffectiveness (i.e., subordinate incompetence in decision making or handling a problem that still necessitated presidential intervention) were mentioned by both new and experienced presidents as the major constraint on their productivity. Solmon and Tierney in a national study of administrative job satisfaction in higher education discovered that a great emphasis on authority relationships between leaders and subordinates was negatively correlated with satisfaction.[25] In contrast, when interpersonal behaviors were emphasized, satisfaction increased. Given the apparent importance of leadership behavior, how do higher education managers act in these kinds of situations?

A number of studies have been conducted with department chairpersons. Hoyt and Spangler, using a sample drawn from four diverse universities, studied the relationship between department chairperson management emphases and rated performance of the chair by the faculty.[26] Personnel management—faculty recruitment; allocating faculty responsibilities; stimulating research scholarship and teaching; maintaining faculty morale; and fostering faculty development—represented six of the nine positive relationships in this regard. Coltrin and Glueck,[27] and Glueck and Thorp[28] reported analyses of data collected from research-oriented departments at the University of Missouri. These studies revealed that a leadership style emphasizing ethical behavior, helpfulness in research projects, accurate and complete communication, frequency of communication, and a willingness to represent the interests of the staff was positively associated with faculty satisfaction with the department head in all departments. There was also some evidence that keeping track of research activities in progress through discussion rather than formal report was also positively related to faculty satisfaction. In contrast, attempts to restrict the selection of projects by researchers was negatively associated with faculty satisfaction. When given a choice of leader roles, faculty members consistently preferred the leader as a "resource person/coordinator." That is, they ideally saw the administrator as a "facilitator" or one who smoothed out problems and sought to provide the resources necessary for the research activities of faculty members. Researchers' perceptions of department heads' attempts to reward them were also positively associated with both satisfaction and effort (i.e., reported hours worked). However, there was no observed direct relationship between leader style and faculty publications, although a later reanalysis led Coltrin and Glueck to question whether an "ideal style" was or was not department independent.

This issue has also been raised in a number of related studies. Neumann and Boris found support that highly ranked paradigmatic departments (e.g., physics and chemistry) were characterized by task-oriented leaders, while lesser ranked paradigmatic departments and highly ranked preparadigmatic departments (e.g., sociology and political science) were both characterized by task and people-oriented department heads.[29] Similarly, Groner used the Group Atmosphere Scale of Fiedler to measure the quality of leader-member relations.[30] He found that the quality of department head-faculty member relations was positively associated with feelings of control over the destiny of the department. But, in both the community college and the university settings, leader-member relations also correlated positively with the amount of task clarity in the department (i.e., extent to which the department was paradigmatic). More specifically, in the university setting there was a strong negative relationship between the heterogeneity of faculty research interests and department head-faculty member relationships.

One traditional argument about the role of department chair is that it is a marginal position in which the chairperson is presented with conflicting demands from above to be a manager and from below to be an academic colleague. Carroll[31] applied the Kahn et al. model for studying role conflict with a sample of department heads from Florida universities.[32] He reported that intersender conflict, a situation in which the focal person perceives incompatible expectations from individuals having influence on his or her position, was most commonly reported and was negatively associated with chairperson satisfaction. As Carroll noted, intersender conflict appears to stem primarily from hierarchical relationships of superiors and subordinates.

Two studies, one within a single university and the other a survey of physical education departments, utilized the Leadership Behavior Description Questionnaire to study department heads. Madron, Craig, and Mendel found that high consideration by the department head was related to departmental morale.[33] They also found a negative relationship between morale and department size suggesting that departmental size may serve as a constraint on leadership style. Milner, King, and Pizzini discovered no significant difference between male and female department heads in their perceptions of ideal leadership qualities or in their rating of their actual qualities.[34] In contrast, faculty members in the departments reacted differently to the department head depending on their sex. Faculty members of both sexes tended to perceive heads of the same sex as more considerate.

When viewed from the perspective of research on leadership generally, the studies reported above offer at best modest insights. However, within this review, leadership behavior has been defined consistent with Mintzberg's emphasis as relational behavior between leaders and subordinates. Viewed from this perspective, the studies indicate the potential contribution that the quality of leader-subordinate relationships has for the morale and satisfaction of *both* parties. As well, the research gives some indication that the nature of leader-subordinate relations may vary by department size, type of department, and the sex match of leaders and followers. Nonetheless, it is unclear whether the findings about the leadership behavior of department chairpersons is generalizable to other levels of the academic hierarchy. What is clear from such studies, given their limitations, is that there is a need to investigate leadership behavior in the higher education context and to study the leadership of administrators at all levels of the organizational hierarchy. Uniquenesses and potentially substantial complexities argue for the need for carefully conducted studies that account for a variety of variables and control for known sources of variation. Conversely, the tendency to continue to rely on correlational research methods in leadership studies can be questioned in terms of the insights they will yield into the practice of leadership.

Conflict Resolution Behavior

Only two studies were found that directly addressed managerial mediation and disturbance-handling behavior. Hobbs focused on the management of academic disputes utilizing a critical incident methodology.[35] The disputes studied included those involving academic administrators, faculty, nonfaculty professionals, and ancillary personnel as well as community versus institutional personnel. In all categories, disputes were held sub rosa; they were avoided or muted whenever possible. The nature of disputes varied, however, among the constituencies. Non-professional personnel tended to have conflicts of interest, and faculty and administrators more often engaged in value conflicts. Administrative disputes were generally settled through compromise or resignation after due consideration of the tactical or sometimes strategic value of compromise. Compromising behavior was less characteristic of conflict resolution involving the other groups. Hobbs inferred that compromise was more endemic to the role of administrators—it was seen as more familiar and legitimate. Administrators also often assumed the third party role in disturbances involving other parties. They seldom served in the role of the mediator but, rather, as the intervenor—intruding into events after crises, adjudicating issues in question, and establishing parameters for future interactions. Intervention was most typical in disputes among ancillary personnel. In these cases, administrators imposed new arrangements in order to terminate controversy. With non-faculty professionals, administrators attempted to optimize the needs of both parties while observing institutional priorities. From the sides of the disputants, however, such interventions were usually perceived as one more aspect of the conflict. The specific tactics of administrative intervention employed depended on astute timing and the use of the substance of the administrator's own participation. "I learned from watching (another third party administrator) when to act and when not to. At times he'd listen, at times he'd cajole and at times he'd question. But sometimes he'd say, 'stop; that's it; go no further.' And things would stop."[36] In contrast to this prevalent use of a personal style of intervention, Hobbs found little evidence of the use of quasi-legal practices such as grievance committees.

Some support for Hobbs' research comes from Weisbord, Lawrence, and Charns' study of conflict management practices in academic medical centers.[37] They found that bargaining or splitting differences in an attempt to maximize one's own interest was the preferred mode for resolving conflicts between departments as well as between faculty and administrators. Smoothing or letting people discuss issues in which differences existed without dealing with substantive issues was the second most preferred method of resolving conflict. Weisbord, Lawrence, and Charns suggested that these results contrasted dramatically with the industrial setting where confronting and forcing or where using power plays were identified as the major means of conflict management.

The research on conflict-resolution behavior is quite modest. Available research on peer-related behavior, leadership behavior, and conflict-resolution behavior in higher education partially confirms Mintzberg's research. Such behaviors are part of the managerial repertoire, and they are important components of overall managerial skill. The nature of behavior in this skill area is partially obscured by the researchers' tendencies to ignore it and by the tendency of some to fragment it through methodological reductionism. This problem was graphically revealed in the contrast of the rich insights on disturbance-handling behavior in Hobbs' research with the more limited observations on administrative behavior provided in other reported studies.

Conceptual Skills

Conceptual skills include the manager's capacity to collect and use different types of information for decision making in ambiguous situations. These decisions often entail allocating resources (e.g., money, space, and the manager's time). Mintzberg has provided additional insight into this area by his discovery that conceptual skills also involve the manager's capacity for identifying opportunities for change and gaining insight into the managerial role itself. Essentially these are the cognitive and creative behaviors of managers.

Information-Related Behavior

Fenker developed a questionnaire for evaluating administrators that he distributed among the faculty and staff of a single university.[38] A factor analysis of the responses yielded four factors, one of which was an information/communication factor. Components of this factor included the accumulation of pertinent information before acting and communicating important information. Although information is important, Lunsford observed that it often comes from unconventional sources.[39] The hierarchical separation of academic administrators means they have restricted associations. Therefore, they place a premium on "political" information and informal knowledge of constituent attitudes as well as their academic knowledge based on past faculty experience. In contrast, the everyday knowledge of operating information for administrators is variable. Astin and Christian studied the variance between administrators' everyday knowledge of basic institutional information and the "actual" data.[40] The study, which was conducted in liberal arts colleges, resulted in the finding that there was an average error of between 6 and 8% among all administrators on data about student enrollment, faculty size, and finances or budgets. Directors of development had the greatest error and academic administrators the least. Presidents were most accurate on student-related data, least accurate on faculty data, and consistently overestimated revenues—what Astin and Christian characterized as "wishful thinking." Administrators use their political information and experience, Lunsford has argued, to explain and define the institution with "socially integrating myths."[41] These broad abstractions help to hold a loosely coordinated institution together and provide members a sense of mission. Patrick and Caruthers in a national survey of college and university presidents provided some support for Lunsford's ethnographic insights.[42] The presidents perceived communicating institutional strengths to internal constituencies, trustees, and the public as a major current focus. There was almost universal agreement among the presidents, however, that data and analytical reports were of low priority. Adams, Kellogg, and Schroeder discovered that when administrators provided information to guide operational decision making, it was often limited.[43] That is, at most it included a due date, guidelines for a report format, and individual or group responsibilities. Rarely were administrators precise about the types of final output needed or about assumptions, constraints, or implementation issues. In sum, while information is deemed critical to administrators, the sources and uses of information appear somewhat unconventional when viewed in the light of the recommendations of traditional management texts.

Administrative behavior in relationship to management, especially computer-based, information systems, has received particular attention in the research literature. Wyatt and Zeckhauser conducted in-depth interviews at six different sized institutions including both public and private universities.[44] The attitudes of administrators toward quantitative data and management reports appeared to be a function of individual background, discipline, and prior experience. Size of institution[45] also seemed positively related to the use of such data. Some individuals with a non-quantitative background tended to hold a "technological mystique" and were unrealistic about the kind of improvements that were possible with improved management information. Management information systems that were in use were often manual, idiosyncratic, and ad hoc—the information was in an individual's head and the procedures were unwritten. Centralized information systems were criticized for being too late, being too hard to decipher, or lacking critical data. Baldridge in a comparable study of liberal arts colleges observed that reports contained too much "junk" (or unfocused data).[46] If administrators had to stop and translate raw data, it was perceived as slowing down the decision-making process. Baldridge also discovered that, to the extent data were used, their major value was in facilitating "hot spot" analyses—the data highlighted or made more obvious those issues previously neglected. Wyatt and Zeckhauser concluded that the difficulties with using existing information systems led to three typical administrative responses.[47] The first was to use data that were available on the spur of the moment, the second was to use interpreters who understood and could translate existing information, and the third was to create parochial or local level information systems.

Research on particular types of quantitative information has resulted in similar conclusions.[48] Large amounts of data are often available, but they are used principally for operating purposes and for outside reporting. The management applications of the information (e.g., for establishing recruitment costs per student admitted) are minimal, and relevant management analytical techniques (e.g., long-term cash budgeting) are rarely utilized. In concluding, Adams, Kellogg, and Schroeder argued that these results were due overwhelmingly to utilization rather than to availability factors.[49]

Feldman and March have provided insight into the information-related behavior of academic managers.[50] Consistent with the research just reviewed they observed that academic administrators appear to value information that has no great decision relevance—they gather information and do not use it, they ask for reports and do not read them, and they act first and ask for information later. Feldman and March suggested that this behavior can be understood as a function of belief, that is, a general academic commitment to reason and rational discourse as well as to a decision theory perspective on the nature of life. As a result, displaying the use of information symbolizes a commitment to rational choice and signals personal and organizational competence. This dichotomy between the symbolic and the real may be attributed to the background and training of academic managers as well as to the organizational characteristics of academic institutions. It can also be attributed, as Mintzberg discovered in business organizations, to a general ignorance about the true nature of managerial work among those who design and develop information systems.

Decision-Making Behavior

Research on decision making behavior falls into three general arenas: the locus or location of decision making, the sources of influence on decision making, and actual decision-making behavior.

In a survey of Canadian community colleges, Heron and Friesen discovered a parallel between structuring and decentralization of decision making.[51] That is, as institutions grew and aged, the size of the administrative component and the use of formal documents in administration increased. But decentralization of decision making also increased in these institutions. This was particularly true when institutional growth was accompanied (as it usually was) by increasing academic specialization. Similarly, Ross, using a national data set found that organizational complexity and certain aspects of administrative apparatus, such as administrative use of the computer and presence of an institutional research office, were positively associated with decentralized decision making.[52] Ross concluded that culture—local traditions, beliefs, and values as influenced by an institution's history—may be a better predictor of the locus of decision making than are structural variables. Studies such as these are helpful in indicating the pitfalls of simplistic or dichotomous thinking about the location of decision making. Put another way, a large administrative structure or a high degree of structuring activity is not necessarily incompatible with decentralization of authority.

In studies of influences on managerial decision making, the type of decision influenced appears to vary with administrative position.[53] Faculties, department heads, deans, and central level administrators in public universities were perceived as having primary influence on different clusters of decisions although they partially influence one another on many decisions. Demographic factors such as the region of the country, type of field, size, and existence of collective bargaining also affected the pattern of influence within an institution. McLaughlin, Montgomery, and Sullins suggested that the pattern of influence was associated with the decisions made by the chairmen.[54] When faculty were most influential, the chairman's goals were faculty oriented. In contrast, chair-dominated departments were characterized by goals less orientated to faculty development. There has also been limited research on the influence of individual differences on decision making. In a survey of public university administrators in California, Walker and Lawler discovered an association between political orientation, expectations regarding the impact of collective bargaining, and support for implementation of collective bargaining.[55] Strong opposition to collective bargaining was, therefore, partially explained by unfavorable perceptions and political attitudes. Two studies that investigated sex differences, however, suggested that the decision-making behavior of male and female academic administrators was more similar than dissimilar.[56] In sum, level in the hierarchy, distribution of influence, and personal perceptions and attitudes have all been found to relate to decision-making behavior.

In a study of administrators in community colleges, four-year colleges, and one university, Taylor provided one of the few direct studies of decision-making behavior.[57] Utilizing the well known Vroom-Yetton model of decision styles, in the study administrators chose a style of encouraging faculty participation over two-thirds of the time. They also preferred decision styles which protected the "quality" of a decision rather than those that ensured decision acceptance or implementation. Nonetheless, a closer analysis by Taylor revealed little relationship between the nature of the problem and the preferred style of decision making. For example, in those situations where more information was required, where commitment to the decision was critical to success, where non-acceptance could generate high conflict, or where fairness was at issue, the administrators often selected autocratic styles. Taylor's evidence also indicated support for faculty participation was an ideological response among department heads as opposed to an explicitly considered decision-making style. As Lunsford argued, administrators seemed to assume that universities are united by strongly shared and well understood values that provide guidelines for tough decisions.[58] The administrator, therefore, can make decisions as a benevolent representative of the institution. The interests of the institution, like the public interest, are assumed to be equivalent to the interests of all participants and thereby become a basis for choice. As a consequence, academic administrators rely strongly on the myth of consultation as a legitimizing force for their decisions. Taylor's research, when combined with Lunsford's analysis, suggests a potential dichotomy between what is espoused and what is practiced in academic decision making. The gap is likely to vary by institution depending both on institutional history and on the prior socialization of faculty.

Several studies examined decision-making behavior related to substantive areas such as budgeting and program evaluation. Moyer and Kretlow in a national study of vice-presidents of finance in colleges and universities found little use of commonly employed business techniques in program evaluation decisions or in capital investment decisions.[59] Instead of capital evaluation techniques, current demand—usually expressed as demonstrated academic need—was not only the primary, but usually also the exclusive criterion. Adams, Kellogg, and Schroeder in an in-depth study of decision making and information systems at small colleges came to similar conclusions.[60] In faculty position allocations, institutional goal setting, and budgeting, decision making was responsive rather than anticipatory and was characterized by reacting to requests for expansion and setting goals only when demand was great. Again, the technical apparatus which might have been appropriate or supportive of these decision processes was not in evidence. At least well through the 1970s, therefore, decision making continued to be present oriented and subject to both influence and negotiation.

The research on decision-making behavior is not inconsistent with, and to some extent supports, the well known "garbage can" model of decision making developed by Cohen, March, and Olsen.[61] In this model, university decision making frequently does not resolve problems. Choices are more likely to be made in these settings by flight or oversight, and the decisions made are apt to be among those of intermediate importance rather than of most or least importance. The matching of problems, choices, and decision makers is partly determined by problem content, problem relevance, and the competence of the decision maker. However, decision choices are sensitive to timing, the current catalog of problems, and the overall load on the system. For example, Cohen and March suggested that decision-making style was apt to vary by institutional size and wealth as well as by changes in organizational slack or the relative availability of financial resources.[62] The research on decision making just reviewed, provides detailed insight into the dynamics of the garbage can model. The possible effects of demographic factors, influence, personality, beliefs, and technology are suggested, and the tendency toward decision making by flight and oversight is quite apparent.

Resource-Allocation Behavior

Mintzberg characterized resource allocation behavior as involving the allocation of all resources—the manager's time, the delegation of responsibility, and the allocation of financial resources. As discussed previously in the section on time-related behavior, academic administrators are similar to managers generally in the amount of their time that they allocate to different constituencies, activities, and media. That is, academic administrators allocate their largest block of work time to other administrators (peers and subordinates), to meetings and committee work, and to the verbal medium, particularly telephone conversations and informal discussions. Contact with faculty and students, and solitary work (and, by inference, reading and analytical activity) receive less time. Of particular importance is the fact that academic managers are largely responsive to the demands of others in allocating their time. The most distinctive characteristic of time allocation, particularly at the departmental level, is the high allocation of time to academic work (averaging between 45-50%) as contrasted to managerial or administrative work. Although this behavior undoubtedly diminishes as one moves up the administrative hierarchy, the continued allocation of time to academic work helps to explain much of the dissatisfaction and stress in academic administration as well as the frequent observation that academic institutions are undermanaged.[63] It also seems to influence the behavior of subordinates. Glueck and Thorp reported a negative relationship between perceived amount of time department heads spend on their own research and faculty satisfaction with the administrator.[64]

There was no direct research evidence on delegation behavior, although the previously discussed research on the decentralization of decision making and the use or non-use of participative decision making by department heads could be viewed from this perspective. There has, however, been substantial research on the allocation of financial resources. In a national sample of college presidents, Patrick and Caruthers discovered that fiscal resource allocation and reallocation were among the two highest current priorities for change.[65] Moyer and Kretlow reported that facilities allocations were usually based on presidential "wish lists." Although institutional standards for space needs had been developed, no institution in their study had assigned facilities costs to programs or used discounting methods of cost/revenue matching techniques.[66] Similarly, Adams, Kellogg, and Schroeder found little use of class size and teaching load standards or unit costs in the allocation of faculty positions and discretionary budgets.[67]

A series of related studies have suggested that administrators base their resource allocations on perceptions of influence and power. The results of the studies, all conducted in major research universities, reveal that universalistic criteria such as workload or numbers of students are less powerful predictors of the allocation of faculty slots and discretionary funds than are various measures of subunit power.[68] In the most recent test of this model, it was discovered that the state of paradigm development of a unit increases its power since high paradigm units are more likely to receive outside funds.[69] High paradigm departments also possess greater consensus and, therefore, act as a stronger coalition in fights for internal resources.[70] Power, operationalized as the ability to attract grants and contracts as well as student enrollments, was thus inferred to be a de facto administrative criterion for the allocation of scarce resources. Finally, power was a more important criterion during periods of resource scarcity, suggesting that attempts to develop more universalistic criteria for allocation decisions during retrenchment may run counter to normal managerial behavior.[71]

Of particular interest in the research on resource allocation behavior is the tendency toward present-oriented responsiveness to other's demands, the relative lack of independent criteria or values on which to base resource allocation decisions, and the avoidance by administrators of management technology or expertise as inputs to resource allocation decision processes.

Entrepreneurial Behavior

Mintzberg's concept of entrepreneurial behavior is metaphorically similar to the process of project management. Managers search their organizations for problems or opportunities for change and then initiate improvement projects to address them. Some of these projects are supervised personally, such as a study of the age distribution of faculty, and others are delegated by the manager to staff members while retaining responsibility for review and quality control. Implicit in Mintzberg's analysis are two critical assumptions: (1) that the manager is constantly involved in developing and implementing improvement projects and is juggling a number of such projects at any one time; and (2) that, like R and D projects, many improvement projects fail or lead to no implementable result. These insights derived from the observation of managers at work have a face validity for those who have been involved in academic management. Patrick and Caruthers in their national survey reported that college presidents identified with certain managerial change priorities and placed greater importance on developing procedures for managerial change than on reports and data analysis of results.[72] However, the research analyzed for this review does not directly address entrepreneurial behavior. In part, this may be due to a methodological or conceptual bias in which organizational change has been interpreted as a response to changes in the external environment.[73] For example, Manns and March discovered a measurable relationship between changes in resource availability and departmental curricula change at Stanford University, but because of the methods and variables selected, no insight was provided about how this process was managed at the departmental level.[74] Similarly, Salancik, Staw, and Pondy studied the relationship between external change and department chair turnover, and they concluded that the largest amount of turnover was explained by factors associated with organization and context, and was not directly affected by the individual capacities or characteristics of administrators (although these characteristics and capacities were not measured and, therefore, could not be controlled in the study).[75] Mintzberg's interpretation of the manager as a change agent also conflicts with the prevailing model of organizational development which advocates an external change agent.[76] A possible result of such methodological and theoretical biases, therefore, is a relative lack of knowledge about the means by which academic managers act in an entrepreneurial manner to bring about change in their organizations. The implications of this will be explored below.

Introspective Behavior

Mintzberg suggested that managers need the capacity to thoroughly understand their jobs, that they should be sensitive to their own impact on their organizations, and that they should have the ability to learn by introspection. Argyris developed a model of organizational learning, based in part on research with academic administrators, that takes a similar position to that taken by Mintzberg.[77] Argyris advocates that academic professionals need the capacity to take technical actions and, simultaneously, to reflect on their practice. This in effect double-loop learning will become even more critical in the future, Argyris believes, because the management dilemmas that will be encountered will require examination of both current values and underlying policies. Argyris therefore advocates double loop learning as a theoretical basis for professional and executive education.

Academic managers, of course, are not by and large professionally trained in management. Further, research continually suggests that professionals learn little from seminars and continuing professional education opportunities; instead, they are most influenced by learning that takes place in conjunction with the job itself. What would be of most value for the higher education setting would be research on effective patterns of learning and introspective behavior of academic managers in the context of their work. Regrettably, such research does not appear to have been conducted. Lewis and Dahl's research suggested that academic administrators at the department head and dean levels either deny, resist, or do not fully comprehend the obligations of their administrative duties.[78] The greatest amount of stress was induced for these administrators because they appeared to resist allocating sufficient time to administrative demands. This suggests that accurate knowledge of the job, of the current demands of the job, and of their own preferences was inadequate. McLaughlin, Montgomery, and Sullins discovered a relationship between a chairperson's perception of who has influence and his or her own professional goals.[79] If these administrators perceived themselves in control or as making the major decisions, they characteristically spent more time in guiding the growth and development of the department as well as its personnel and programs, and had a greater desire to continue in administration. In contrast, if they perceived control to be above them, they typically spent more time in working with students, in doing liaison work, and in activities with expected return to the faculty. Similarly, Solmon and Tierney found that institutional reward systems that were perceived to foster acceptance of authority created less job satisfaction for administrators because they created a sense that the job was not challenging, that the administrator had little autonomy in decision making, and that the job had little variety.[80] Although this research can be related to the issue of introspective behavior, it is insufficiently illuminating because it does not provide any insight into the nature of the behavior itself.

Technical Skills: Profession-Related Behavior

Mintzberg suggested that managerial behavior can be separated from profession-related behavior in that the manager makes the transition from technical activity such as teaching and research to managerial activity. However, in the academic environment, this transition is rarely completed. Most academic administrators, in fact, continue to engage in academic responsibilities. The allocation of time between profession-related and administrative activities and its relationship to administrative stress and satisfaction has already been addressed. A more fundamental question involves the relationship between academic skill or background and interpersonal behavior, conceptual behavior, and overall management success. For example, research in a related setting—R and D organizations—suggests that scientific expertise is an important predictor of managerial effectiveness.[81] The results from anecdotal evidence in recent publications on computer modelling provide an indication that the disciplinary background of senior academic administrators can be of primary importance in influencing the successful implementation of contemporary planning and management techniques.[82] It is worth noting that, although a number of the research studies reported here identify discipline or field as a variable with implications for faculty behavior, departmental leadership style, and centralized allocation behavior, no study directly examined the relationship between the technical and professional skills of administrators and administrative behavior.[83] This seems odd, because there is well validated research on substantive differences in behavior among faculty members from different disciplines.[84] Such studies suggest that the relationship between technical skill or background and administrative behavior could be a fruitful and particularly important component of research in higher education administration and would have practical implications for management selection, training, and development.

Discussion

In the sections above, the available research over the last ten years on administrative behavior in higher education has been analyzed utilizing the combined conceptual frameworks of Katz and Mintzberg. In this section some broader issues will be explored including the author's possible bias, methodological issues of research in this area, and implications for future research.

The available research on higher education suggests that the use and allocation of time among academic administrators is not untypical of managers generally. Academic managers: (1) perform a great quantity of work at a continual pace; (2) carry out activities characterized by variety, fragmentation, and brevity; (3) prefer issues that are current, specific, and ad hoc; (4) demonstrate a preference for verbal media (telephone calls, meetings, and brief discussions); and (5) develop informal information systems. Unlike their management counterparts in other organizations, academic managers are apt to sustain substantial academic technical activity while in their managerial roles. They are also, particularly department heads and deans, less likely to be comfortable with full-time administrative responsibilities. Both interpersonal skill and what Katz terms conceptual skill play an important part in academic managerial work. Research on interpersonal skills has been addressed somewhat in terms of leadership skills. Given the organizational structure and belief systems of academic organizations, the development of horizontal peer networks for information and influence could, however, be more important to academic administrators than to other managers. Unfortunately, there has been little definitive research on this topic. Similarly, conflict negotiation and dispute settlement deserve more attention, and Hobbs has suggested some fruitful leads in this regard.[85] In the category of conceptual behavior, substantial attention has been given to information-processing, decision-making, and resource allocation behavior, but relatively little is known about the entrepreneurial and introspective behavior of academic managers. Since the management of change is routinely advocated as the role of the administrator, the apparent paucity of research on how academic administrators *actually manage* change is somewhat surprising.

The writer began this review effort with a certain bias—that is, that academic management is an ambiguous process highly dependent on flows of influence and power, and subject to the beliefs and values of the academic culture. If anything, this bias has been strengthened by the analysis of available research. First, it is apparent that informal influence, negotiations, and networks of contacts are important aspects of academic administration as it is currently practiced. Second, the results of research on information-related behavior, decision making, and resource allocation provide some indication that academic management is still highly intuitive, tends to avoid the use of quantitative data or available management technology, and is subject to the political influence of various powerful groups and interests. Third, the traditions, beliefs, and values of individuals, disciplines, and institutions appear to play a more substantial role than is generally acknowledged in the extant prescriptive literature on management. In short, the garbage can model of decision making and the institutional context of organized anarchy as articulated by March and his colleagues receives much support from the available research on administrative behavior.

Nevertheless, it is wise to be cautious about these generalizations. Although the models of ambiguity and influence may better fit the available data than do the highly rational models, current understandings are based on historical evidence. Furthermore, the contextual environment which obviously influences the development of current patterns of administrative behavior is currently changing, perhaps dramatically. Those studies that have sampled administrative behavior over time provide evidence of differing patterns of managerial behavior under various environmental circumstances. For example, Cohen, March, and Olsen's simulation of the garbage can model predicted modification of administrative decision-making behavior (i.e., organizational learning) over time and as organizational slack was reduced.[86] In other words, it is important to maintain a constant willingness to test models and biases against current empirical data.

In sum, available research, not surprisingly, prompts the notion that a better understanding of administrative behavior is critical to improved management: (1) for example, sophisticated information systems that are planned without sufficient attention to the needs and working habits of academic administrators appear to make little (immediate) impact; (2) further, since human beings need and seek meaning, an important part of academic administration involves the creation and maintenance of academic beliefs;[87] and finally, (3) interpersonal relationships and skills are an important part of management in organizations that depend for their effectiveness on the talent of autonomous, creative, and often "spikey" individuals. It is reasonable to assume that managerial behavior in academic organizations may change in response to new conditions. However, the understanding of that process is most apt to occur through research on the relationships between administrative behavior, technology, and structure.

The methodologies of studies reviewed deserve special attention. In the first place, sampling strategies vary substantially. Some studies are focused on single institutions and the elite, research institutions are over-represented in this respect. Other studies have surveyed particular clusters of institutions such as private liberal arts colleges, public universities, or community colleges. Overall, research seems to be heavily focused on larger research universities and published studies of administrative behavior in small or community colleges are far less common. While available information on the focus and source of data for each study was included in the analysis above, specificity in this regard was often difficult to ascertain. One of the consistently reliable findings of research in this area is that institutions of higher education vary in organization and management by type and level of institution.[88] The research reviewed here confirms that institutional type, level, region, size, and culture can all contribute to variance in administrative behavior. It is reasonable, of course, to argue that the study of a single case can provide a model suitable for testing in later studies. March and Pfeffer, and their colleagues, have demonstrated the value of this approach. However, among the research studies reviewed for this article, more than half seem to be unaware of the obvious weaknesses in terms of their focus and sampling procedures, or of the relevant research on institutional types. Future research on administrative behavior in higher education needs to give significantly greater attention to measuring and controlling for variance between types of institutions.

A second major issue relates to the conceptual frameworks employed in some of the studies. Studies tend to employ a psychological model that reduces behavior to the study of relationships between variables relevant to the psychological models used, or they employ a sociological unit of analysis which tends to bypass individual behavior altogether. There are, of course, fundamentally important reasons for such selectivity. The psychological approach places emphasis on precision of measurement and the potential for prediction, often with some penalty in overall understanding. The sociological logic has been well expressed by March.[89] Throughout his work, March has evolved a Tolstoyan perspective on academic administrators that argues that great leadership is unlikely, particularly in organizations of this type. Academic administration, in this view, is an art of small adjustments in which larger and, by inference, slow-moving forces determine the evolution of events. But each of these two perspectives, the psychological and the sociological, limits the understanding of administrative behavior. The framework and precision of the psychological view causes overlook key interpersonal processes. For example, the means researchers to by which administrators build and maintain networks for information and influence were ignored by traditional management researchers until they were emphasized in the observational work of Mintzberg and his followers. Even today, there has been little informative research that suggests the relationships of importance in this domain. Although the sociological point of view provides an appropriate sense of humility toward administrative accomplishment, its results are similarly impoverished in terms of advancing knowledge. If the contribution of management is at the margin through small adjustments and improvements, then *how is this accomplished*? As the results of research on managers continually indicate, it is a profession of action. Therefore, illuminating the nature of administrative action and its consequences in different settings is apt to be of substantial value to theory and to practice. With the exception of a few of the studies reviewed, there is little insight into administrative behavior in action. This criticism is *not* a plea for a particular type of methodology but, rather, for a more creative application and interchange between the disciplines and methodologies available to inquirers.

Conclusion

The research on administrative behavior in higher education over the last ten years has helped to fill an important gap that Peterson observed in his 1974 review of the field. While the research is modest in amount and limited in approach, it provides some insight into the nature of managerial work in higher education as well as suggestions for promising directions in both research and practice.

The nature of academic organizations and of administration in these settings highlights the centrality of human behavior, beliefs, and values. Although organizational structure and management technology are very important, studies of those mechanisms and processes in the absence of an understanding of administrative behavior at best make a limited contribution to theory or to practice. Ironically, while the best known research on academic organizations provides a rich understanding of the role of human behavior, culture, and meaning in the development of these institutions (see, for example, the many writings of Burton Clark, James

March, David Riesman, and Lawrence Veysey), it is currently the students of business organizations who argue most strongly for an emphasis on entrepreneurship, organizational culture, the development of human assets, and the importance of interpersonal skills.[90]

The intent of this review was to provide an integrative understanding of the current knowledge concerning administrative behavior in higher education. Taking stock at certain periods is a necessary and important part of the ongoing attempts to advance both practice and research. To paraphrase A. N. Whitehead, the scientist does not inquire in order to know, the scientist knows in order to inquire.

David D. Dill is Associate Professor of Education and Assistant to the Chancellor at the University of North Carolina at Chapel Hill.

Notes

[1] The writer would like to acknowledge the help of Peter Cistone, Ralph Kimbrough, James Lemons, Sandra Reed, Jay Smout, John Walker, and two anonymous reviewers in the preparation of this article.

[2] M. W. Peterson, "Organization and Administration in Higher Education: Sociological and Socio-Psychological Perspectives," in *Review of Research in Education*, Volume 2, F. N. Kerlinger and J. B. Carroll, eds. (Itasca, Ill.: F. E. Peacock, 1974).

[3] J. G. March, "Analytical Skills and University Training of Educational Administrators, *Education and Urban Society* (6, 4 (August 1974): 382–427.

[4] H. Mintzberg, *The Nature of Managerial Work* (New York: Harper and Row, 1973).

[5] L. B. Kurke and H. E. Aldrich, "Mintzberg Was Right!: A Replication and Extension of *The Nature of Managerial Work*" (Paper presented at the Annual Meeting of The Academy of Management, Atlanta, Ga., 1979).

[6] J. P. Kotter, *The General Managers* (Glenco, Ill.: The Free Press, 1982).

[7] C. M. Pavett and A. W. Lau, "Managerial Roles, Skills, And Effective Performance," *Proceedings of the Forty-Second Annual Meeting of The Academy of Management* (New York: The Academy, 1982).

[8] G. B. Jackson, "Methods for Integrative Reviews," *Review of Educational Research* 50, 3 (Fall 1980): 438–460.

[9] Ibid., p. 438.

[10] 10. Burton Clark's collective work on academic organizations has had a substantial impact on the field. For a useful synthesis of his findings, see B. R. Clark, *The Higher Education System* (Berkeley, Calif.: University of California Press, 1983).

[11] M. D. Cohen and J. G. March, *Leadership and Ambiguity: The American College President* (New York: McGraw-Hill, 1973); M. D. Cohen, J. G. March, and J. P. Olsen, "A Garbage Can Model of Organizational Choice," *Administrative Science Quarterly* 17 (March 1972): 1–25; M. S. Feldman and J. G. March, "Information in Organizations as Signal and Symbol," *Administrative Science Quarterly* 26 (1981): 171–186; C. L. Manns and J. G. March, "Financial Adversity, Internal Competition and Curriculum Change in a University," *Administrative Science Quarterly* 23, 4 (1978): 541–552; and J. G. March, "How We Talk and How We Act: Administrative Theory and Administrative Life" (Seventh David D. Henry Lecture in Higher Education, University of Illinois, September, 1980).

[12] Mintzberg, *Nature of Managerial Work*.

[13] Jackson, "Methods for Integrative Reviews."

[14] H. R. Bobbitt and O. C. Behling, "Organizational Behavior: A Review of the Literature," *Journal of Higher Education* 52, 1 (January/February 1981): 29–44,

[15] R. L. Katz, "Skills of an Effective Administrator," *Harvard Business Review* (September/October 1974): 90–102.

[16] Mintzberg, *Nature of Managerial Work*.

[17] K. Anderson, *Management: Skills, Functions, and Organizational Performance* (Dubuque, Iowa: W. C. Brown Company, 1984).

[18] Cohen and March, *Leadership and Ambiguity*.

[19] D. R. Lewis and T. Dahl, "Time Management in Higher Education Administration: A Case Study," *Higher Education* 5 (1976): 49–66.

[20] M. R. Weisbord, P. R. Lawrence, and M. P. Charns, "Three Dilemmas of Academic Medical Centers," *Journal of Applied Behavioral Sciences* 14, 3 (1978): 284–304.

[21] T. F. Lunsford, "Authority and Ideology in the Administered University," in *The State of the University: Authority and Change*, C. E. Kruytbosch and S. L. Messinger, eds. (Beverly Hills, Calif.: Sage Publications, 1970).

[22] L. J. Whitson and F. W. R. Hubert, "Interest Groups and The Department Chairperson: The Exertion of Influence in the Large Public University," *Journal of higher Education* 53, 2 (1982): 163–176.

[23] J. Stringer, "The Role of the 'Assistant To' in Higher Education," *Journal of Higher Education* 48, 2 (March/April): 193–201.

[24] W. D. Peterson, "Critical Incidents for New and Experienced College and University Presidents," *Research in Higher Education* 3 (1975): 45–50.

[25] L. C. Solmon and M. L. Tierney, "Determinants of Job Satisfaction among College Administrators," *Journal of Higher Education* 48, 4 (July/August 1977): 412–431.

[26] D. P. Hoyt and R. K. Spangler, "The Measurement of Administrative Effectiveness of the Academic Department Head," *Research in Higher Education* 10, 4 (1979): 291–303.

[27] S. Coltrin and W. Glueck, "Effect of Leadership Roles on Satisfaction and Productivity of University-Research Professors," *Academy of Management Journal* 20, 1 (1977): 101–116.

[28] W. F. Glueck and C. D. Thorp, "The Role of the Academic Administrator in Research Professors' Satisfaction and Productivity," *Educational Administration Quarterly* 10, 1 (Winter 1974): 72–90.

[29] Y. Neumann and S. B. Boris, "Paradigm Development and Leadership Style of University Department Chairmen," *Research in Higher Education* 9 (1978): 291–302.

[30] N. E. Groner, "Leadership Situations in Academic Departments: Relations among Measures of Situational Favorableness and Control," *Research in Higher Education* 8 (1978): 125–143.

[31] A. B. Carroll, "Role Conflict in Academic Organizations: An Exploratory Examination of the Department Chairman's Experience," *Educational Administration Quarterly* 10, 2 (Spring 1974): 51–64.

[32] R. L. Kahn, D. M. Wolfe, R. P. Quinn, J. D. Snoek, and R. A. Rosenthal, *Organizational Stress: Studies in Role Conflict and Ambiguity* (New York: John Wiley, 1964).

[33] T. M. Madron, J. R. Craig, and R. M. Mendel, "Departmental Morale as a Function of the Perceived Performance of Department Heads," *Research in Higher Education* 5 (1976): 83–94.

[34] E. K. Miner, H. A. King, and E. L. Pizzini, "Relationship Between Sex and Leadership Behavior of Department Heads in Physical Education," *Research in Higher Education* 10, 2 (1979): 113–121.

[35] W. C. Hobbs, "The 'Defective Pressure-Cooker' Syndrome," *Journal of Higher Education* 45, 8 (1974): 569–581.

[36] Ibid, p. 578.

[37] Weisbord, Lawrence and Charns, "Three Dilemmas."

[38] R. M. Fenker, "The Evaluation of University Faculty and Administrators: A Case Study," *Journal of Higher Education* 56, 6 (November/December 1975): 665–686.

[39] Lunsford, "Authority and Ideology."

[40] A. W. Astin and C. E. Christian, "What do Administrators Know about Their Institutions?" *Journal of Higher Education* 49, 4 (July/August 1977): 389–400.

[41] Lunsford, "Authority and Ideology."

[42] C, Patrick and J. K. Caruthers, "Management Priorities of College Presidents," *Research in Higher Education* 12, 3 (1980): 195–214.

[43] C. R. Adams, T. E. Kellogg, and R. G. Schroeder, "Decision-Making and Information Systems in Colleges," *Journal of Higher Education* 47, 1 (January/February 1976): 33–49.

[44] J. B. Wyatt and S. Zeckhauser, "University Executives and Management Information: A Tenuous Relationship," *Educational Record* 56, 3 (Summer 1975): 175–189.

[45] R. C. Moyer and W. J. Kretlow, "The Resource Allocation Decision in U. S. Colleges and Universities: Practice, Problems and Recommendations," *Higher Education* 7 (1978): 35–46.

[46] J. V. Baldridge, "Impact on College Administration: Management Information Systems and Management by Objectives Systems," *Research in Higher Education* 10, 3 (1979): 263–282.

[47] Wyatt and Zeckhauser, "University Executives and Management Information."

[48] Adams, Kellogg, and Schroeder, "Decision-Making and Information Systems"; and Moyer and Kretlow, "The Resource Allocation Decision."

[49] Adams, Kellogg, and Schroeder, "Decision-Making and Information Systems."

[50] Feldman and March, "Information Organizations."

[51] R. P. Heron and D. Friesen, "Growth and Development of College Administrative Structures," *Research in Higher Education*, Vol. 1 (1973): 333–346.

[52] R. D. Ross, "Decentralization of Authority in Colleges and Universities," *Research in Higher Education* 6, 2 (1977): 97–123.

[53] G. W. McLaughlin, J. R. Montgomery, and W. R. Sullins, "Roles and Characteristics of Department Chairmen in State Universities as Related to Level of Decision Making," *Research in Higher Education* 6 (1977): 327–341; Whitson and Hubert, "Interest Groups and the Department Chairperson."

[54] McLaughlin, Montgomery, and Sullins, "Roles and Characteristics."

[55] J. M. Walker and J. D. Lawler, "University Administrators and Faculty Bargaining," *Research in Higher Education* 16, 4 (1982): 353–372.

[56] O. Andruskin and N. J. Howes, "Dispelling a Myth: That Stereotypic Attitudes Influence Evaluations of Women as Administrators in Higher Education," *Journal of Higher Education* 51, 5 (1980): 475–496; and Milner, King, and Pizzini, "Relationship between Sex and Leadership Behavior."

[57] A. L. Taylor, "Decision-Process Behaviors of Academic managers," *Research in Higher Education* 16, 2 (1982): 155–173.

[58] Lunsford, "Authority and Ideology."

[59] Moyer and Kretlow, "The Resource Allocation Decision."

[60] Adams, Kellogg, and Schroeder, "Decision-Making and Information Systems."

[61] Cohen, March, and Olsen, "A Garbage Can Model."

[62] Cohen and March, *Leadership and Ambiguity.*

[63] Adams, Kellogg, and Schroeder, "Decision-Making and Information Systems"; Lewis and Dahl, "Time Management"; and G. W. McLaughlin, J. R. Montgomery, and L. F. Malpass, "Selected Characteristics, Roles, Goals, and Satisfactions of Department Chairmen in State and Land-Grant Institutions," *Research in Higher Education* 3 (1975): 243–259.

[64] Glueck and Thorp, "The Role of the Academic Administrator."

[65] Patrick and Caruthers, "Management Priorities."

[66] Moyer and Kretlow, "The Resource Allocation Decision."

[67] Adams, Kellogg, and Schroeder, "Decision-Making and Information Systems."

[68] F. S. Hills and T. A Mahoney, "University Budgets and Organizational Decision Making," *Administrative Science Quarterly* 23, 3 (1978): 454–465; J. Pfeffer and G. R. Salancik, "Organizational Decision Making as a Political Process: The Case of a University Budget," *Administrative Science Quarterly* 19, 2 (1974): 135–151; G. R. Salancik and Jeffrey Pfeffer, "The Bases and Use of Power in Organizational Decision Making: The Case of a University," *Administrative Science Quarterly* 19, 4 (1974): 453–473; and Manns and March, "Financial Adversity."

[69] J. Pfeffer and W. L. Moore, Power in University Budgeting: A Replication and Extension," *Administrative Science Quarterly* 25, 4 (1994): 637–653.

[70] Groner, "Leadership Situations"; and Pfeffer and Moore, "Power in University Budgeting."

[71] Hills and Mahoney, "University Budgets"; and Pfeffer and Moore, "Power in University Budgeting."

[72] Patrick and Caruthers, "Management Priorities."

[73] D. Katz and R. L. Kahn, *Social Psychology of Organizations,* 2nd Edition (New York: John Wiley, 1978).

[74] Manns and March, "Financial Adversity."

[75] G. Salancik, B. Staw, and L. Pondy, "Administrative Turnover as a Response to Unmanaged Organizational Interdependence." *Academy of Management Journal* 23, 3 (1980): 422–437.

[76] Bobbitt and Behling, "Organizational Behavior."

[77] C. Argyris, "Educating Administrators and Professionals," in *Leadership in the '80s,* C. Argyris and R. M. Cyert (Cambridge, Mass.: Institute for Educational Management/Harvard University, 1980).

[78] Lewis and Dahl, "Time Management."

[79] McLaughlin, Montgomery, and Sullins, "Roles and Characteristics."

[80] Solmon and Tierney, "Determinants of Job Satisfaction."

[81] N. Rosen, R. Billings, J. Turney, "The Emergence and Allocation of Leadership Resources Over Time in a Technical Organization," *Academy of Management Journal* 20 (1976): 165–183.

[82] D. S. P. Hopkins and W. F. Massey, *Planning Models for Colleges and Universities* (Stanford, Calif.: Stanford University Press, 1981).

[83] Coltrin and Glueck, "Effect of Leadership Roles"; Groner, "Leadership Situations"; Neumann and Boris, "Paradigm Development"; Pfeffer and Moore, "Power in University Budgeting"; Salancik, Straw, and Pondy, "Administrative Turnover."

[84] J. M. Beyer and T. M. Lodahl, "A Comparative Study of Patterns of Influence," *Administrative Science Quarterly* 21 (1976): 104–129; and A. Biglan, "Relationships Between Subject Matter Characteristics and the Structure and Output of University Departments," *Journal of Applied Psychology* 57, 3 (1973): 204–213.

[85] Hobbs, "The Syndrome."

[86] Cohen, March, and Olsen, "A Garbage Can Model."

[87] D. Dill, "The Management of Academic Culture," *Higher Education* 11, 3 (1982): 303–320.

[88] J. V. Baldridge, D. V. Curtis, G. Ecker, and G. L. Riley, *Policy Making and Effective Leadership* (San Francisco: Jossey-Bass, 1978).

[89] March, "How We Talk."

[90] See, for example, T. E. Deal and A. A. Kennedy, *Corporate Cultures* (Reading, Mass.: Addison-Wesley, 1982); W. G. Ouchi, *Theory Z* (Reading, Mass.: Addison-Wesley, 1981); and T. J. Peters and R. H. Waterman, Jr., *In Search of Excellence* (New York: Harper and Row, 1982).

Higher Education and Leadership Theory

ESTELLA M. BENSIMON, ANNA NEUMANN,
AND ROBERT BIRNBAUM

This section examines works on leadership in the literature of higher education from the perspective of theories discussed in the previous section, suggesting implications of these studies for effective leadership in higher education.

Although studies of leadership in higher education have for traditionally been atheoretical, a resurgence of theoretical research has occurred in recent years, and several works have attempted to integrate findings in the higher education literature with more general theories of leadership. A review of the strengths and weaknesses of several conceptual approaches to studying leadership in the context of academic organizations, for example, provides a clear and concise summary of the major theories of leadership along with a comprehensive annotated bibliography of works on leadership, corporate management, and higher education administration keyed to each theory (Dill and Fullagar 1987). Another essay emphasizes the role of leaders in organizational improvement and gives considerable attention to characteristics and behaviors of leaders as developed through the Ohio State leadership studies (Fincher 1987), not only recognizing the contingent nature of leadership but also including a critical analysis of several works on the presidency.

Trait Theories

Trait theory continues to be influential in images of effective leadership in higher education, even though it is no longer a major approach to research among organizational theorists. Works concerned primarily with describing successful presidents, with identifying the characteristics to look for in selecting individuals for positions of leadership, or with comparing the characteristics of effective and ineffective leaders are the most likely to reflect a trait approach. Even though trait theory may not necessarily be the authors' primary orientation, the tendency to associate leaders with specific traits is so common that many works on leadership refer to traits or individual qualities (see, e.g., Kerr 1984; Kerr and Gade 1986; Vaughan 1986; Walker 1979).

Successful academic leaders have been described in terms of personal attributes, interpersonal abilities, and technical management skills (Kaplowitz 1986). Personal attributes include humor, courage, judgment, integrity, intelligence, persistence, hard work, vision, and being opportunity conscious; interpersonal abilities include being open, building teams, and being compassionate. Technical management skills include producing results, resolving conflicts, analyzing and evaluating problems, being able to shape the work environment, and being goal oriented (Gilley, Fulmer, and Reithlingshoefer 1986; Vaughan 1986).

A portrait of the effective president suggests the following personal traits:

> . . . a strong drive for responsibility, vigor, persistence, willingness to take chances, originality, ability to delegate, humor, initiative in social situations, fairness, self-confidence, decisiveness, sense of identity, personal style, capacity to organize, willingness to act or boldness... (Fisher 1984, p. 24).

A belief persists that in selecting candidates for positions of leadership, one should look for individuals who appear to have such characteristics. Most often cited are confidence, courage, fairness, respect for the opinions of others, and sensitivity. Undesirable characteristics include being soft-spoken, insecure, vain, concerned with administrative pomp, and graveness (Eble 1978). The trouble, of course, is that judgments on the presence or absence of these characteristics are highly subjective. No research has shown, for example, that a college president who speaks in an assertive and strong voice will be more effective than a soft-spoken president. One study of presidential effectiveness compares the traits and behaviors of 412 presidents identified as highly effective by their peers with a group of 412 "representative" presidents (Fisher, Tack, and Wheeler 1988). The prototypical effective president was self-described as a "strong risk-taking loner with a dream" who was less likely to form close collegial relationships than typical presidents, worked longer hours, made decisions easily, and confided less frequently in other presidents. Closer examination of the data reveals, however, that effective and representative presidents were probably more alike than different. In four of five leadership factors derived from a factor analysis of survey items (managing style, human relations, image, and social reference), no significant differences were found between the two groups of presidents. Significant differences were found only for the confidence factor, which consisted of items that assessed the extent to which presidents believed they can make a difference in their institutions.

While this study suggests that effective leaders are "loners" who maintain social distance, the findings of another study suggest that successful colleges are headed by presidents who are "people-oriented—caring, supportive, and nurturing" (Gilley, Fulmer, and Reithlingshoefer 1986, p. 115). Similarly, while the former study maintains that effective leaders are risk takers, the other says that successful presidents "work feverishly to minimize risk at every step of the way" (p. 65). These studies' conflicting findings suggest the problems of analyzing the effectiveness of leadership from a trait perspective. Few people exhibit consistent traits under all circumstances, so that both "distance" and "nurturing" may accurately represent effective leadership as manifested in different situations. If this in fact is the case, these studies provide a strong argument for the need to define the effectiveness of leadership in dynamic rather than static terms.

Power and Influence Theories

Power and influence theories fall into two types, those that consider leadership in terms of the influence or effects that leaders may have on their followers (social power theory and transformational leadership theory) and those that consider leadership in terms of mutual influence and reciprocal relationships between leaders and followers (social exchange theory and transactional leadership theory).

Social Power Theory

From this perspective, effective leaders are those who can use their power to influence the activities of others. Concepts of social power appeared to be an important influence in shaping presidents' implicit theories of leadership in one study (Birnbaum 1989a). When asked to explain what leadership meant to them, most of the presidents participating in an extensive study of institutional leadership provided definitions describing leadership as a one-way process, with the leader's function depicted as getting others to follow or accept their directives. For a small minority, the role of the leader was not to direct the group but to facilitate the emergence of leadership latent within it. Definitions that included elements of other conceptual orientations (trait theories, contingency theories, and symbolic theories) were mentioned infrequently.

The most likely sources of power for academic leaders are expert and referent power rather than legitimate, coercive, or reward powers (see the discussion of power and influence theories in the previous section): it has been proposed that college presidents can exert influence over their campuses through charismatic power, which has been questionably identified as analogous to referent power (Fisher 1984). This particular perspective maintains that academic leaders can cultivate charismatic power by remaining distant or remote from constituents, by attending to their personal appearance and style, and by exhibiting self-confidence. To establish distance and remoteness, presidents are counseled not to establish close relationships with faculty, not to be overly visible, and to emphasize the importance of the trappings of the office as symbols of its elevated state. Style consists of presidential comportment, attitude, speech, dress, mannerisms, appearance, and personal habits. Self-confidence relates to cultivating a style of speaking and walking that conveys a sense of self-assuredness. The concept of charismatic power that has been proposed here appears to be much different from referent power, which traditionally has been defined as the willingness of followers to accept influence by a leader they like and with whom they identify.

Practitioners and scholars tend to question the importance given to charismatic traits as well as whether leaders stand to gain by creating distance between themselves and their constituents. it has been suggested (Keohane 1985) that a leader who is concerned with creating an image of mystery and separateness cannot be effective at building coalitions, a critical part of leadership. High levels of campus discontent have been attributed to leaders who were considered to be too distant from their internal and external constituencies and who tended to take constituents' support for granted or to feel it was not needed (Whetten 1984). Reacting to the current preoccupation with charismatic leadership, a recent commentary published in *The Wall Street Journal* says "leadership is more doing than dash."

> It has little to do with "leadership qualities" and even less to do with "charisma...Charisma becomes the undoing of leaders. It makes them inflexible, convinced of their own infallibility, unable to change. This is what happened to Stalin, Hitler, and Mao, and it is a commonplace in the study of ancient history that only Alexander the Great's early death saved him from becoming an ineffectual failure" (Drucker 1988).

Social Exchange Theory/Transactional Theory

College and university presidents can accumulate and exert power by controlling access to information, controlling the budgetary process, allocating resources to preferred projects, and assessing major faculty and administrative appointments (Corson 1960). On college campuses, however, the presence of other sources of power—the trustees' power to make policy and the faculty's professional authority—seriously limits the president's discretionary control of organizational activities. For this reason, social exchange theory is particularly useful for examining the principles of shared governance and consultation and the image of the president as first among equals, which undergirds much of the normative values of academic organizations.

Transactional theory can be particularly useful for understanding the interactions between leaders and followers. The idiosyncrasy credit (IC) model (Hollander 1987), a major transactional approach to leadership, is of particular relevance to the understanding of leaders' influence in academic organizations. This model suggests that followers will accept change and tolerate a leader's behavior that deviates from their expectations more readily if leaders first engage in actions that will demonstrate their expertise and conformity to the group's norms. The IC model, for example, explains why new presidents initially may find it beneficial to concentrate on getting to know their institutions' history, culture, and key players before proclaiming changes they plan to introduce. A study of new presidents suggests that first-time presidents, not wanting to appear indecisive, may overlook the potential benefits of "getting to know" and "becoming known" by the institution. In contrast, experienced presidents, in assuming office at a new institution, recognized the importance of spending time learning about the expectations of followers (Bensimon 1987, 1989a).

Two works relate presidential failure and success in accomplishing change to presidents' initial actions. These studies show the relevance of concepts underlying the IC model. For example, a member of a new university administration attributed the failure to implement radical changes and reforms to the inability of the new president and his academic administrators to build loyalty—and to gain credits—among respected members of the faculty.

> We succeeded in infusing new blood...but we failed to recirculate the old blood. We lost an opportunity to build loyalty among respected members of the veteran faculty. If veteran faculty members had been made to feel that they, too had a future in the transformed university, they might have embraced the academic reorganization plan with some enthusiasm. Instead the veteran faculty members were hurt, indignant, and—finally—angry (Bennis 1972, p. 116).

In contrast, another study illustrates that time spent accumulating credits (e.g., fulfilling the expectations of constituents) can lead to positive outcomes (Gilley, Fulmer, and Reithlingshoefer 1986). The authors observed that presidential success was related to gaining acceptance and respect from key constituents through low-key, pleasant, and noncontroversial actions early in the presidential term. In their judgment, change and departure from established patterns were tolerated because "of the safety zone of good will they ha[d] created" (p. 66).

The influence of social exchange theory can also be detected in works that downplay the charismatic and directive role of leaders. These studies portray leaders as coordinators of ongoing activities rather than as architects of bold initiatives. This view of leadership is related to the anarchical (Cohen and March 1974), democratic-political (Walker 1979), atomistic (Kerr and Gade 1986), and cybernetic (Birnbaum 1988) models of university leadership that will be discussed in the next section.

Transformational Theory

This perspective suggests that effective leaders create and promote desirable "visions" or images of the institution. Unlike goals, tasks, and agendas, which refer to concrete and instrumental ends to be achieved, vision refers to altered perceptions, attitudes, and commitments. The transforming leader must encourage the college community to accept a vision created by his or her symbolic actions (Green 1988b; Hesburgh 1979).

Transformation implies a "metamorphosis or a substitution of one state or system for another, so that a qualitatively different condition is present" (Cameron and Ulrich 1986, p. 1). Fear that higher education is suffering a crisis in leadership has made calls for transformational leadership a recurrent theme in recent studies. Some suggest it is an "illusion, an omnipotent fantasy" (Bennis 1972, p. 115) for a change-oriented administrator to expect that academic organizations would be receptive to this kind of leadership. In higher education, transformational leadership more appropriately may refer to the inspirational role of the leader. For example, the description of leadership as the "poetic part of the presidency" that "sweeps listeners and participants up into the nobility of intellectual and artistic adventures and the urgency of thinking well and feeling deeply about the critical issues of our time" (Keller 1983, p. 25) is unmistakably transformational in tone, as is the following eloquent and inspiring call:

> ...in the years ahead, higher education will be sorely tested. If we believe that our institutions have value, we must articulate that value and achieve adequate understanding and support. We must find leaders who are dedicated enough to the purpose of higher education that they will expend themselves, if necessary, for that

purpose.... The qualities of transforming leadership are those that restore in organizations or society a sense of meaning and purpose and release the powerful capacity humankind has for renewal (Kauffman 1980, pp. 114-15).

A modern example of the transformational leader may be found in Theodore Hesburgh, who has been described as "brilliant, forceful, and charismatic...a legend on campus, where stories of students scampering up the fire escape outside his office for a glimpse of the great man are a part of the Notre Dame lore, like winning one for the Gipper" (Ward 1988, pp. 32-33). Images like this one, along with the popular belief that transformational leaders are concerned with "doing the right things" while managers are concerned with "doing things right" (Bennis and Nanus 1985; Cameron and Ulrich 1986), make transformational leadership irresistible to leaders and nonleaders alike.

A five-step agenda derived from an analysis of the qualities possessed by great leaders like Ghandi, Martin Luther King, Jr., and Winston Churchill attempts to put transformational leadership into practical terms (Cameron and Ulrich 1986). The list includes the following steps: (1) create readiness for change by focusing attention on the unsatisfactory aspects of the organization; (2) overcome resistance by using non-threatening approaches to introduce change; (3) articulate a vision by combining rational reasoning and symbolic imagery; (4) generate commitment; and (5) institutionalize commitment. Suggested approaches on how to implement each step came mostly from examples drawn from industry and tested in case studies of two colleges in crisis whose presidents took actions that corresponded to the agenda prescribed for transformational leadership. Of course, while following these steps might result in changes that make the campus more adaptable to the demands of the environment, it might not result in changes in the perceptions, beliefs, and values of campus constituents that are at the core of transformational leadership as initially proposed (Burns 1978).

The nature of colleges and universities appears to make the exercise of transformational leadership extremely difficult except under certain conditions. Three such conditions have been suggested—institutional crisis, institutional size, and institutional quality (Birnbaum 1988). Institutional crisis is likely to encourage transformational leadership because campus members and the external community expect leaders to take strong action. Portrayals of presidents exercising transformational leadership can be found in case-study reports of institutions suffering adversity (see, e.g., Cameron and Ulrich 1986; Chaffee 1984; Clark 1970; Riesman and Fuller 1985). Transformational leadership is also more likely to emerge in small institutions where leaders can exert a great deal of personal influence through their daily interactions with the campus. Leaders in 10 small private liberal arts colleges identified as having high faculty morale displayed characteristics of the transformational orientation (Rice and Austin 1988). These leaders were seen by others as powerful influences in the life of their colleges and were credited with singlehandedly turning their institutions around. Institutions that need to be upgraded to achieve comparability with their peers also provide an opportunity for transformational leadership. Such presidents have been described as "pathbreaking leaders" (Kerr and Gade 1986).

Although with few exceptions (see Bass 1985) leaders tend to be considered as being either transactional or transformational, a recent study comparing the initial activities of new presidents in institutions in crisis suggests that leaders who use transactional means (e.g., conforming to organizational culture) may be more successful in attaining transformational effects (e.g., improving the organizational culture) than leaders whose behavior reflects the pure form (one-way approach) of transformational leadership (Bensimon 1989c). Even in institutions in distress, a leadership approach that conforms to the group's norms while also seeking to improve them may be of greater benefit than heroic attempts at redesigning an institution.

Behavioral Theories

Behavior of the Leader

These theories examine whether the leader is task (initiating structure) or people (consideration) oriented or both. Blake and Mouton (1964) adapted their managerial grid into an academic grid and applied it to higher education. Their model suggests five styles of academic administration (Blake, Mouton, and Williams 1981): caretaker, authority-obedience, comfortable-pleasant, constituency-centered, and team. The optimum style is identified as team administration, which is characteristic of leaders who scored high on both concern for institutional performance and concern for people on their grid.

Some limited empirical tests of this theory have been performed. A study of department chairs found that those judged as effective by the faculty scored high both in initiating structure (task) and consideration of people (Knight and Holen 1985). On the other hand, a case study of a single institution reports that departments with high faculty morale had chairs who scored high on measures of consideration of people and participative leadership style but not in initiating structure (Madron, Craig, and Mendel 1976). The academic grid appears to have found its greatest use as a tool for self assessment. For example, the grid was adapted into a questionnaire to assist department chairs in determining their personal styles of leadership (Tucker 1981).

Presidents' perceptions of the similarity of their role to other leadership roles were used to describe two types of presidents—mediative and authoritative, which are roughly comparable to emphasizing consideration of people and initiating structure (task), respectively (Cohen and March 1974). Mediative presidents tended to define their roles in terms of constituencies, while authoritative presidents appeared to be more directive. Additionally, mediative presidents were more likely to measure their success on the basis of faculty respect, while authoritative presidents were more likely to base it on the quality of educational programs.

Administrative styles based on the self-reported behaviors of presidents were found to be related to faculty and student outcomes in 49 small private liberal arts colleges (Astin and Scherrei 1980). These findings, however, may be influenced by the size of the institutions.

Managerial Roles

A comprehensive essay (Dill 1984) reviews the literature on administrative behavior in higher education, employing the behavioral framework developed by Mintzberg (1973). The findings (p. 91) suggest that like managers in other settings, senior administrators in higher education:

- Perform a great variety of work at a continuous pace;
- Carry out activities characterized by variety, fragmentation, and brevity;
- Prefer issues that are current, specific, and ad hoc;
- Demonstrate preference for verbal media (telephone calls, meetings, brief discussions); and
- Develop informal information systems.

Although academic leaders are likely to learn from their actions, almost no attention has been given to what leaders learn on the job. A qualitative study based on interviews with 32 presidents reports that what presidents learn from their actions varies, depending on whether they feel the action they took was wrong (substantive error) or whether they feel the action was justified but the process used (process error) was inappropriate (Neumann 1988). New presidents who made substantive errors learned how to sense situational differences that called for diverse (and new) responses, they began to identify new behaviors that were more appropriate to their new settings, and they gave up the behaviors that worked in their old settings but appeared to be dysfunctional in their new ones. From process errors, presidents tended to learn the degree of influence organizational members have on what presidents can accomplish. Some presidents also made action errors, which consisted of taking action when none should have been taken. From these errors, presidents gained respect for personal and organizational limitations.

Contingency Theories

From this perspective, effective leadership requires adapting one's style of leadership to situational factors. Applying four contingency theories to higher education, Vroom (1983) found that if used to determine the kind of leader best suited to chair academic departments, each would prescribe a different type of leader. Situational variables in Fiedler's contingency model and in House's path-goal theory prescribe a task-oriented leader who would do whatever is necessary to drive the group to complete a job. In contrast, Hersey and Blanchard's life-cycle theory and the Vroom-Yetton decision process theory identify individuals with a delegating and participative style of leadership. The contradictory prescriptions may be the result of their development in organizational settings with clearly delineated superior and subordinate roles. Thus, they may have limited applicability to the study of leadership in higher education. The Vroom-Yetton model appears to be better suited to higher education organizations, because it uses multiple criteria to determine participative or autocratic decision making (Floyd 1985).

Although the observation that "a president may be egalitarian one day and authoritarian the next" (Gilley, Fulmer, and Reithlingshoefer 1986, p. 66) is commonplace, little systematic application of contingency theory has occurred to determine under what conditions alternative forms of leadership should be displayed. Generally, contingency theories have found their greatest applicability in the study of leadership in academic departments, probably because decision making at this level is less equivocal than at higher levels of the academic organization. An application of the Vroom-Yetton model to the study of decision making among department chairs concludes that they frequently chose autocratic styles of decision making in situations where a consultative style would have increased the likelihood of the faculty's acceptance of the decision (Taylor 1982). Hersey and Blanchard's theory was used to develop a questionnaire that would help department chairs determine departmental level of maturity and select a corresponding style of leadership (Tucker 1981). An analysis of studies on the behavior of leaders (Dill 1984) suggests that "when given a choice of leader roles, faculty members consistently preferred the leader as a...'facilitator' or one who smoothed out problems and sought to provide the resources necessary for the research activities of faculty members" (p. 79).

Kerr and Jermier's theory of substitutes for hierarchical leadership may be highly relevant for academic organizations. Despite being one of the few contingency theories in which leadership is not seen as residing solely with the official leader, it has received little attention in the study of academic leadership. If leadership in higher education were to be viewed from this perspective, one could conclude that directive leadership may not be effective because characteristics of academic organizations (such as faculty autonomy and a reward structure that is academic discipline and peer-based) substitute for or neutralize the influence of leaders (Birnbaum 1989a). Similarly, a consideration of the influence of administrators on the faculty's motivation asks, "What are university administrators to do in the face of so many 'substitutes' for their leadership?" (Staw 1983, p. 312). Because alternatives such as stressing local (e.g., primary identification is with the institution) rather than professional orientation (e.g., primary identification is with the academic discipline) or reducing self-governance and self-motivation are not in the best interests of the university, it may be more fruitful for administrators to assume the role of facilitator than controller.

Cultural and Symbolic Theories

Occasionally effective leaders give symbolic meaning to events that others may see as perplexing, senseless, or chaotic. They do so by focusing attention on aspects of college life that are both familiar and meaningful to the college community. Cultural and symbolic approaches to studying leadership appear in works on organizations as cultural systems (Chaffee and Tierney 1988; Kuh and Whitt 1988). Understanding colleges and universities as cultures was originally introduced in a now-classic case study of Reed, Swarthmore, and Antioch (Clark 1970, 1972). This study suggests that leaders may play an important role in creating and maintaining institutional sagas. The role of academic leaders in the preservation of academic culture may be even more critical today than in the past, because increased specialization, professionalization, and complexity have weakened the values and beliefs that provided institutions with a common sense of purpose, commitment, and order (Dill 1982). Although leaders may not be able to change culture through management, their attention to social integration and symbolic events may enable them to sustain and strengthen the culture that already exists (Dill 1982).

Cultural and symbolic perspectives on leadership have figured prominently in a small handful of recent works that examine the actions of leaders and their effects on campus during times of financial decline. A recent study suggests that college presidents who are sensitive to the faculty's interpretation of financial stress are more likely to elicit the faculty's support for their own leadership (Neumann 1989a). One of the most important contributions to the understanding of leadership from a cultural perspective is the work on the role of substantive and symbolic actions in successful turn-around situations (Chaffee 1984, 1985a, 1985b). The examination of managerial techniques of presidents in institutions suffering financial decline discloses three alternative strategic approaches—linear, adaptive, and interpretive. Linear strategists were concerned with achieving goals. Adaptive strategists were concerned with aligning the organization with the environment, for example, by changing the organizational orientation to meet current demands and thus to ensure the continued flow of resources. Interpretive strategists reflected the cultural/symbolic perspective in that they were concerned with how people saw, understood, and felt about their lives. Interpretive leaders believed that effective action involves shaping the values, symbols, and emotions that influence the behaviors of individuals. The use of interpretive strategy in combination with adaptive strategy was considerably more effective in turning institutions around than the use of adaptive strategy alone (Chaffee 1984). Presidents who employed interpretive strategies were careful to protect the essential character of their institutions and to refrain from actions and commitments that compromise or disrupt the institution's self-identity and sense of integrity by only introducing new programs that were outgrowths of the old ones. For example, they reaffirmed the existing institutional mission and did not attempt to pursue programmatic thrusts that were outside the expertise of the faculty.

Strategies of change that make sense to institutional members and that therefore are likely to elicit acceptance and support may depend upon leaders' understanding an organization from cultural perspectives. To do so, leaders may be required to act as anthropologists uncovering the organizational culture by seeking to identify metaphors embedded in the language of the college community (Corbally 1984; Deshler 1985; Peck 1983; Tierney 1988). Frameworks for organizational cultures suggest that leaders can begin to understand their institutional cultures by identifying internal contradictions or incongruities between values and structure, by developing a comparative awareness, by clarifying the identity of the institution, by communicating so as "to say the right things and to say things right," and by acting on multiple and changing fronts (Chaffee and Tierney 1988, pp. 185-91).

Leaders should pose organizational questions to help them identify characteristics of the organizational environment, the influence of institutional mission on decision making, processes of socialization, the uses of information, the approaches used to make decisions, and constituents' expectations of leaders (Tierney 1988). Researchers also can gain insights into leadership by examining the symbols embedded in the language of leaders. A study of 32 presidents reveals that they used six categories of symbols—metaphorical, physical, communicative, structural, personification, and ideational—when they talked about their leadership role. Understanding the use of symbolism can help academic leaders to become more consistent by sensitizing them to contradictions between the symbols they use and the behaviors they exhibit on their campuses. Leaders may become more effective by using symbols that are consistent with the institution's culture (Tierney 1989).

The "techniques of managing meaning and social integration are the undiscussed skills of academic management" (Dill 1982, p. 304). For example, it has been suggested that leaders in community colleges have consistently failed to interpret and articulate their missions and to create positive images among their publics (Vaughan 1986). While it is clear that cultural and symbolic leadership skills are becoming increasingly important to presidents, scholars still have much to learn about the characteristics of these skills and effective ways of teaching them to present and aspiring leaders (Green 1988b). A recent examination of colleges and universities from a cultural perspective provides administrators with the following insights: Senior faculty or other core groups of institutional leaders provide continuity and maintain a cohesive institutional culture; institutional policies and practices are driven and bound by culture; culture-driven policies and practices may denigrate the integrity and worth of certain groups; institutional culture is difficult to modify intentionally; and organizational size and complexity work against distinctive patterns of values and assumptions (Kuh and Whitt 1988, p. vi).

Cognitive Theories

Cognitive theories have important implications for perceptions of leaders' effectiveness. In many situations, presidential leadership may not have measurable outcomes other than social attribution —or the tendency of campus constituents to assign to a president the credit or blame for unusual institutional outcomes. From this perspective, leaders are individuals believed by followers to have caused events (Birnbaum 1989b). Leaders themselves, in the absence of clear indicators, are subject to cognitive bias that can lead them to make predictable errors of judgment (Birnbaum 1987) and to over-estimate their effectiveness in campus improvements (Birnbaum 1986).

Summary

Trait theories and power and influence theories appear to be particularly influential in works on leadership in higher education. Several of the works reviewed tend to relate effectiveness of leaders to individual characteristics, although not necessarily the same ones. For example, while some consider "being distant" as a desirable characteristic, others propose that "being nurturing" is more important.

Even though exchange theories are more relevant to the understanding of leadership in academic organizations, works that consider leadership from the perspective of power and influence theories tend to emphasize one-way, leader-initiated and leader-directed approaches. Transformational theory, in particular, has received considerable attention, while transactional theory hits for the most part been ignored.

Behavioral and contingency theories may have limited application in higher education because these theories focus their attention on the relationship between superior and subordinate roles. Within the category of behavioral theories, the most promising approach may be in the study of administrative behavior, particularly as a way of understanding how leaders learn from their actions and mistakes. Examining how leaders learn from a behavioral perspective may provide new directions and ideas for the design of training programs for academic leaders.

Within the category of contingency theories, Kerr and Jermier's theory of substitutes for hierarchical leadership may be of greatest use, even though it has been almost totally overlooked by scholars of academic leadership.

Although cultural and symbolic perspectives on leadership were first suggested in the early 1970s in Burton Clark's case study of Reed, Swarthmore, and Antioch, only recently has this view of leadership attracted serious attention. Cultural and symbolic perspectives have been shown to be especially useful for understanding the internal dynamics of institutions in financial crisis, particularly in differentiating the strategies leaders use to cope with financial stress and to communicate with constituents. Cognitive theories offer a promising new way of studying leadership, but their use in higher education to date has been limited.

Leadership in an Organized Anarchy

Michael D. Cohen and James G. March

The Ambiguities of Anarchy

The college president faces four fundamental ambiguities. The first is the ambiguity of *purpose*. In what terms can action be justified? What are the goals of the organization? The second is the ambiguity of *power*. How powerful is the president? What can he accomplish? The third is the ambiguity of *experience*. What is to be learned from the events of the presidency? How does the president make inferences about his experience? The fourth is the ambiguity of *success*. When is a president successful? How does he assess his pleasures?

These ambiguities are fundamental to college presidents because they strike at the heart of the usual interpretations of leadership. When purpose is ambiguous, ordinary theories of decision making and intelligence become problematic. When power is ambiguous, ordinary theories of social order and control become problematic. When experience is ambiguous, ordinary theories of learning and adaptation become problematic. When success is ambiguous, ordinary theories of motivation and personal pleasure become problematic.

The Ambiguity of Purpose

Almost any educated person can deliver a lecture entitled "The Goals of the University." Almost no one will listen to the lecture voluntarily. For the most part, such lectures and their companion essays are well-intentioned exercises in social rhetoric, with little operational content.

Efforts to generate normative statements of the goals of a university tend to produce goals that are either meaningless or dubious. They fail one or more of the following reasonable tests. First, is the goal clear? Can one define some specific procedure for measuring the degree of goal achievement? Second, is it problematic? Is there some possibility that the organization will accomplish the goal? Is there some chance that it will fail? Third, is it accepted? Do most significant groups in the university agree on the goal statement? For the most part, the level of generality that facilitates acceptance destroys the problematic nature or clarity of the goal. The level of specificity that permits measurement destroys acceptance.

Recent discussions of educational audits, of cost-benefit analysis in education, and of accountability and evaluation in higher education have not been spectacularly successful in resolving this normative ambiguity, even in those cases where such techniques have been accepted as relatively fruitful. In our judgment, the major contributions (and they are important ones) of operational analysis in higher education to date have been to expose the inconsistencies of current policies and to make marginal improvements in those domains in which clear objectives are widely shared.

Similarly, efforts to infer the "real" objectives of a university by observing university behavior tend to be unsuccessful. They fail one or more of the following reasonable tests. First, is the goal uniquely consistent with behavior? Does the imputed goal produce the observed behavior and is it the only goal that does? Second, is it stable? Does the goal imputed from past behavior reliably predict future behavior? Although it is often possible to devise a statement of the goals of a university by some form of revealed preference test of past actions, such goal statements have poor predictive power.

The difficulties in imputing goals from behavior are not unique to universities. Experience with the complications is shared by revealed preference theorists in economics and psychology, radical critics of society, and functionalist students of social institutions. The search for a consistent explanation of human social behavior through a model of rational intent and an imputation of intent from action has had some successes. But there is no sign that the university is one of the successes, or very likely to become one.

Efforts to specify a set of consciously shared, consistent objectives within a university or to infer such a set of objectives from the activities or actions of the university have regularly revealed signs of inconsistency. To expose inconsistencies is not to resolve them, however. There are only modest signs that universities or other organized anarchies respond to a revelation of ambiguity of purpose by reducing the ambiguity. These are organizational systems without clear objectives, and the processes by which their objectives are established and legitimized are not extraordinarily sensitive to inconsistency. In fact, for many purposes the ambiguity of purpose is produced by our insistence on treating purpose as a necessary property of a good university. The strains arise from trying to impose a model of action as flowing from intent on organizations that act in another way.

College presidents live within a normative context that presumes purpose and within an organizational context that denies it. They serve on commissions to define and redefine the objectives of higher education. They organize convocations to examine the goals of the college. They write introductory statements to the college catalog. They accept the presumption that intelligent leadership presupposes the rational pursuit of goals. Simultaneously, they are aware that the process of choice in the college depends little on statements of shared direction. They recognize the flow of actions as an ecology of games (Long, 1958), each with its own rules. They accept the observation that the world is not like the model.

The Ambiguity of Power

Power is a simple idea, pervasive in its appeal to observers of social events. Like *intelligence* or *motivation* or *utility*, however, it tends to be misleadingly simple and prone to tautology. A person has power if he gets things done, if he has power, he can get things done.

As students of social power have long observed, such a view of power has limited usefulness.[1] Two of the things the simple view produces are an endless and largely fruitless search for the person who has "the real power" in the university, and an equally futile pursuit of the organizational locale "where the decision is *really* made." So profound is the acceptance of the power model that students of organizations who suggest the model is wrong are sometimes viewed as part of the plot to conceal "the real power" and "the true locus of decision." In that particular logic the reality of the simple power model is demonstrated by its inadequacy.

As a shorthand casual expression for variations in the potential of different positions in the organization, *power* has some utility. The college president has more potential for moving the college than most people, probably more potential than any one other person. Nevertheless, presidents discover that they have less power than is believed, that their power to accomplish things depends heavily on what they want to accomplish, that the use of formal authority is limited by other formal authority, that the acceptance of authority is not automatic, that the necessary details of organizational life confuse power (which is somewhat different from diffusing it), and that their colleagues seem to delight in complaining simultaneously about presidential weakness and presidential willfulness.

The ambiguity of power, like the ambiguity of purpose, is focused on the president. Presidents share in and contribute to the confusion. They enjoy the perquisites and prestige of the office. They enjoy its excitement, at least when things go well. They announce important events. They appear at important symbolic functions. They report to the people. They accept and thrive on their own importance. It would be remarkable if they did not. Presidents even occasionally recite that "the buck stops here" with a finality that suggests the cliché is an observation about power and authority rather than a proclamation of administrative style and ideology.

At the same time, presidents solicit an understanding of the limits to their control. They regret the tendency of students, legislators, and community leaders to assume that a president has the power to do whatever he chooses simply because he is president. They plead the countervailing power of other groups in the college or the notable complexities of causality in large organizations.

The combination is likely to lead to popular impressions of strong presidents during good times and weak presidents during bad times. Persons who are primarily exposed to the symbolic presidency (e.g., outsiders) will tend to exaggerate the power of the president. Those people who have tried to accomplish something in the institution with presidential support (e.g., educational reformers) will tend to underestimate presidential power or presidential will.

The confusion disturbs the president, but it also serves him. Ambiguity of power leads to a parallel ambiguity of responsibility. The allocation of credit and blame for the events of organizational life becomes—as it often does in political and social systems—a matter for argument. The "facts" of responsibility are badly confounded by the confusions of anarchy; and the conventional myth of hierarchical executive responsibility is undermined by the countermyth of the nonhierarchical nature of colleges and universities. Presidents negotiate with their audiences on the interpretations of their power. As a result, during the recent years of campus troubles, many college presidents sought to emphasize the limitations of presidential control. During the more glorious days of conspicuous success, they solicited a recognition of their responsibility for events.

The process does not involve presidents alone, of course. The social validation of responsibility involves all the participants: faculty, trustees, students, parents, community leaders, government. Presidents seek to write their histories in the use of power as part of a chorus of history writers, each with his own reasons for preferring a somewhat different interpretation of "Who has the Power?"

The Ambiguity of Experience

College presidents attempt to learn from their experience. They observe the consequences of actions and infer the structure of the world from those observations. They use the resulting inferences in attempts to improve their future actions.

Consider the following very simple learning paradigm:

1 At a certain point in time a president is presented with a set of well-defined, discrete action alternatives.
2 At any point in time he has a certain probability of choosing any particular alternative (and a certainty of choosing one of them).
3 The president observes the outcome that apparently follows his choice and assesses the outcome in terms of his goals.
4 If the outcome is consistent with his goals, the president increases his probability of choosing that alternative in the future; if not, he decreases the probability.

Although actual presidential learning certainly involves more complicated inferences, such a paradigm captures much of the ordinary adaptation of an intelligent man to the information gained from experience.

The process produces considerable learning. The subjective experience in one of adapting from experience and improving behavior on the basis of feedback. If the world with which the president is dealing is relatively simple and relatively stable, and if his experience is relatively frequent, he can expect to improve over time (assuming he has some appropriate criterion for testing the consistency of outcomes with goals). As we have suggested earlier, however, the world in which the president lives has two conspicuous properties that make experience ambiguous even where goals are clear. First, the world is relatively complex. Outcomes depend heavily on factors other than the president's action. These factors are uncontrolled and, in large part, unobserved. Second, relative to the rate at which the president gathers experimental data, the world changes rapidly. These properties produce considerable potential for false learning.

We can illustrate the phenomenon by taking a familiar instance of learning in the realm of personnel policies. Suppose that a manager reviews his subordinates annually and considers what to do with those who are doing poorly. He has two choices: he can replace an employee whose performance is low, or he can keep him in the job and try to work with him to obtain improvement. He chooses which employees to replace and which to keep in the job on the basis of his judgment about their capacities to respond to different treatments. Now suppose that, in fact, there are no differences among the employees. Observed variations in performance are due entirely to random fluctuations. What would the manager "learn" in such a situation?

He would learn how smart he was. He would discover that his judgments about whom to keep and whom to replace were quite good. Replacements will generally perform better than the men they replaced; those men who are kept in the job will generally improve in their performance. If for some reason he starts out being relatively "humane" and refuses to replace anyone, he will discover that the best managerial strategy is to work to improve existing employees. If he starts out with a heavy hand and replaces everyone, he will learn that being tough is a good idea. If he replaces some and works with others, he will learn that the essence of personnel management is judgment about the worker.

Although we know that in this hypothetical situation it makes no difference what a manager does, he will experience some subjective learning that is direct and compelling. He will come to believe that he understands the situation and has mastered it. If we were to suggest to the manager that he might be a victim of superstitious learning. he would find it difficult to believe. Everything in his environment tells him that he understands the world, even though his understanding is spurious.

It is not necessary to assume that the world is strictly random to produce substantially the same effect. Whenever the rate of experience is modest relative to the complexity of the phenomena and the rate of change in the phenomena, the interpretation made of experience will tend to be more persuasive subjectively than it should be. In such a world, experience is not a good teacher. Although the outcomes stemming from the various learned strategies in the personnel management example will be no worse because of a belief in the reality of the learning, the degree of confidence a manager comes to have in his theory of the world is erroneously high.

College presidents probably have greater confidence in their interpretations of college life, college administration, and their general environment than is warranted. The inferences they have made from experience are likely to be wrong. Their confidence in their learning is likely to have been reinforced by the social support they receive from the people around them and by social expectations about the presidential role. As a result, they tend to be unaware of the extent to which the ambiguities they feel with respect to purpose and power are matched by similar ambiguities with respect to the meaning of the ordinary events of presidential life.

The Ambiguity of Success

Administrative success is generally recognized in one of two ways. First, by promotion: An administrator knows that he has been successful by virtue of a promotion to a better job. He assesses his success on the current job by the opportunities he has or expects to have to leave it. Second, by widely accepted, operational measures of organizational output: a business executive values his own performance in terms of a profit-and-loss statement of his operations.

Problems with these indicators of success are generic to high-level administrative positions. Offers of promotion become less likely as the job improves and the administrator's age advances. The criteria by which success is judged become less precise in measurement, less stable over time, and less widely shared. The administrator discovers that a wide assortment of factors outside his control are capable of overwhelming the impact of any actions he may take.

In the case of the college president all three problems are accentuated. As we have seen earlier, few college presidents are promoted out of the presidency. There are job offers, and most presidents ultimately accept one; but the best opportunity the typical president can expect is an invitation to accept a decent version of administrative semiretirement. The criteria of success in academic administration are sometimes moderately clear (e.g., growth, quiet on campus, improvement in the quality of students and faculty), but the relatively precise measures of college health tend neither to be stable over time nor to be critically sensitive to presidential action. For example, during the post-World War II years in American colleges, it was conventional to value growth and to attribute growth to the creative activities of administrative leaders. In the retrospective skepticism about the uncritical acceptance of a growth ethic, we have begun to reinterpret a simple history that attributed college growth to the conscious prior decision of a wise (or stupid) president or board. The rapid expansion of higher education, the postwar complex of student and faculty relations and attitudes, and the massive extension of governmental subsidies to the research activities of colleges and universities were not the simple consequences of decisions by Clark Kerr or John Hanna. Nor, retrospectively, does it seem plausible to attribute major control over those events to college administrators.

An argument can be made, of course, that the college president should be accustomed to the ambiguity of success. His new position is not, in this respect, so strikingly, different from the positions he has held previously. His probable perspective is different, however. Success has not previously been subjectively ambiguous to him. He has been a success. He has been promoted relatively rapidly. He and his associates are inclined to attribute his past successes to a combination of administrative savoir-faire, interpersonal style, and political sagacity. He has experienced those successes as the lawful consequence of his actions. Honest modesty on the part of a president does not conceal a certain awareness of his own ability. A president comes to his office having learned that he is successful and that he enjoys success.

The momentum of promotion will not sustain him in the presidency. Although, as we have seen, a fair number of presidents anticipate moving from their present job to another, better presidency, the prospects are not nearly as good as the hopes. The ambiguities of purpose, power, and experience conspire to render success and failure equally obscure. The validation of success is unreliable. Not only can a president not assure himself that he will be able to lead the college in the directions in which others might believe, he also has no assurance that the same criteria will be applied tomorrow. What happens today will tend to be rationalized tomorrow as what was desired. What happens today will have some relation to what was desired yesterday. Outcomes do flow in part from goals. But goals flow from outcomes as well, and both goals and outcomes also move independently.

The result is that the president is a bit like the driver of a skidding automobile. The marginal judgments he makes, his skill, and his luck may possibly make some difference to the survival prospects for his riders. As a result, his responsibilities are heavy. But whether he is convicted of manslaughter or receives a medal for heroism is largely outside his control.

One basic response to the ambiguities of success is to find pleasure in the process of presidential life. A reasonable man will seek reminders of his relevance and success. Where those reminders are hard to find in terms of socially validated outcomes unambiguously due to one's actions, they may be sought in the interactions of organizational life. George Reedy (1970) made a similar observation about a different presidency: "Those who seek to lighten the burdens of the presidency by easing the workload do no occupant of that office a favor. The workload—especially the ceremonial work load—are the only events of a president's day which make life endurable."

Leader Response To Anarchy

The ambiguities that college presidents face describe the life of any formal leader of any organized anarchy. The metaphors of leadership and our traditions of personalizing history (even the minor histories of collegiate institutions) confuse the issues of leadership by ignoring the basic ambiguity of leadership life. We require a plausible basic perspective for the leader of a loosely, coupled, ambiguous organization.

Such a perspective begins with humility. It is probably a mistake for a college president to imagine that what he does in office affects significantly either the long-run position of the institution or his reputation as a president. So long as he does not violate some rather obvious restrictions on his behavior, his reputation and his term of office are more likely to be affected by broad social events or by the unpredictable vicissitudes of official responsibility than by his actions. Although the college library or administration building will doubtless record his presidency by appropriate portraiture or plaque, few presidents achieve even a modest claim to attention 20 years after their departure from the presidency; and those who are remembered best are probably most distinguished by their good fortune in coming to office during a period of collegiate good times and growth, or their bad fortune in being there when the floods came.

In this respect the president's life does not differ markedly from that of most of us. A leadership role, however, is distinguished by the numerous temptations to self-importance that it provides. Presidents easily come to believe that they can continue in office forever if they are only clever or perceptive or responsive enough. They easily come to exaggerate the significance of their daily actions for the college as well as for themselves. They easily come to see each day as an opportunity to build support in their constituencies for the next "election."

It is an old story. Human action is frequently corrupted by an exaggeration of its consequences. Parents are intimidated by an exaggerated belief in their importance to the process of child-rearing. Teachers are intimidated by an exaggerated belief in their importance to the process of learning. Lovers are intimidated by an exaggerated belief in their importance to the process of loving. Counselors are intimidated by an exaggerated belief in their importance to the process of self-discovery.

The major consequence of a heroic conception of the consequences of action is a distrust of judgment. When college presidents imagine that their actions have great consequences for the world, they are inclined to fear an error. When they fear an error, they are inclined to seek social support for their judgment, to confuse voting with virtue and bureaucratic rules with equity. Such a conception of the importance of their every choice makes presidents vulnerable to the same deficiencies of performance that afflict the parents of first children and inexperienced teachers, lovers, or counselors.

A lesser, but important, result of a heroic conception of the consequences of action is the abandonment of pleasure. By acceding to his own importance, the college president is driven to sobriety of manner. For reasons we have detailed earlier, he has difficulty in establishing the correctness of his actions by exhibiting their consequences. He is left with the necessity of communicating moral intent through facial intensity. At the same time, he experiences the substantial gap between his aspirations and his possibilities. Both by the requirements of their public face and by their own intolerant expectations, college presidents often find the public enjoyment of their job denied to them.

The ambiguities of leadership in an organized anarchy require a leadership posture that is somewhat different from that implicit in most discussions of the college presidency. In particular, we believe that a college president is, on the whole, better advised to think of himself as trying to do good than as trying to satisfy a political or bureaucratic audience; better advised to define his role in terms of the modest part he can play in making the college slightly better in the long run than in terms of satisfying current residents or solving current problems. He requires an enthusiasm for a Tolstoyan view of history and for the freedom of individual action that such a view entails. Since the world is absurd, the president's primary responsibility is to virtue.

Presidents occupy a minor part in the lives of a small number of people. They have some power, but little magic. They can act with a fair degree of confidence that if they make a mistake, it will not matter much. They can be allowed the heresy of believing that pleasure is consistent with virtue.

The Elementary Tactics of Administrative Action

The tactics of administrative action in an organized anarchy are somewhat different from the tactics of action in a situation characterized by clearer goals, better specified technology, and more persistent participation. Nevertheless, we can examine how a leader with a purpose can operate within an organization that is without one.

Necessarily, any presentation of practical strategies suggests a minor Machiavellianism with attendant complications and concerns. There is an argument that strategies based upon knowledge contribute to administrative manipulation. There is a fear that practical strategies may be misused for evil ends. There is a feeling that the effectiveness of the strategies may be undermined by their public recitation.

We are aware of these concerns, but not persuaded by them. First, we do not believe that any major new cleverness that would conspicuously alter the prevailing limits on our ability to change the course of history will be discovered. The idea that there are some spectacularly effective strategies waiting to be discovered by some modern Machiavelli seems implausible. Second, we believe that the problem of evil is little eased by know-nothingness. The concern about malevolent manipulation is a real one (as well as a cliché), but it often becomes a simple defense of the status quo. We hope that good people interested in accomplishing things will find a list of tactics marginally helpful. Third, we can see nothing in the recitation of strategic recommendations that changes systematically the relative positions of members of the organization. If the strategies are effective, it is because the analysis of organization is correct. The features of the organization that are involved are not likely to change quickly. As a result, we would not anticipate that public discussion of the strategies would change their effectiveness much or distinctly change the relative positions of those (e.g., students, presidents) who presumably stand to profit from the advice if it is useful.

As we will indicate later in this chapter, a conception of leadership that merely assumes that the college president should act to accomplish what he wants to accomplish is too narrow. A major part of his responsibility is to lead the organization to a changing and more complex view of itself by treating goals as only partly knowable. Nevertheless, the problems of inducing a college to do what one wants it to do are clearly worthy of attention. If presidents and others are to function effectively within the college, they need to recognize the ways in which the character of the college as a system for exercising problems, making decisions, and certifying status conditions their attempts to influence the outcome of any decision.

We can identify five major properties of decision making in organized anarchies that are of substantial importance to the tactics of accomplishing things in colleges and universities:

1. Most issues most of the time have *low salience* for most people. The decisions to be made within the organization secure only partial and erratic attention from participants in the organization. A major share of the attention devoted to a particular issue is tied less to the content of the issue than to its symbolic significance for individual and group esteem.

2. The total system has *high inertia*. Anything that requires a coordinated effort of the organization in order to start is unlikely to be started. Anything that requires a coordinated effort of the organization in order to be stopped is unlikely to be stopped.

3. Any decision can become a *garbage can* for almost any problem. The issues discussed in the context of any particular decision depend less on the decision or problems involved than on the timing of their joint arrivals and the existence of alternative arenas for exercising problems.

4. The processes of choice are easily subject to *overload*. When the load on the system builds up relative to its capabilities for exercising and resolving problems, the decision outcomes in the organization tend to become increasingly separated from the formal process of decision.

5. The organization has a *weak information base*. Information about past events or past decisions is often not retained. When retained, it is often difficult to retrieve. Information about current activities is scant.

These properties are conspicuous and ubiquitous. They represent some important ways in which all organizations sometimes, and an organization like a university often, present opportunities for tactical action that in a modest way strengthen the hand of the participant who attends to them. We suggest eight basic tactical rules for use by those who seek to influence the course of decisions in universities or colleges.

RULE 1: SPEND TIME

The kinds of decision-making situations and organizations we have described suffer from a shortage of decision-making energy. Energy is a scarce resource. If one is in a position to devote time to the decision-making activities within the organization, he has a considerable claim on the system. Most organizations develop ways of absorbing the decision-making energy provided by sharply deviant participants; but within moderate boundaries, a person who is willing to spend time finds himself in a strong position for at least three significant reasons:

- By providing a scarce resource (energy), he lays the basis for a claim. If he is willing to spend time, he can expect more tolerant consideration of the problems he considers important. One of the most common organizational responses to a proposal from a participant is the request that he head a committee to do something about it. This behavior is an acknowledgment both of the energy-poor situation and of the price the organization pays for participation. That price is often that the organization must allow the participant some significant control over the definition of problems to be considered relevant.[2]

- By spending time on the homework for a decision, he becomes a major information source in an information-poor world. At the limit, the information provided need have no particular evidential validity. Consider, for example, the common assertions in college decision-making processes about what some constituency (e.g., board of trustees, legislature, student body, ethnic group) is "thinking." The assertions are rarely based on defensible evidence, but they tend to become organizational facts by virtue of the shortage of serious information. More generally, reality for a decision is specified by those willing to spend the time required to collect the small amounts of information available, to review the factual assertions of others, and to disseminate their findings.

- By investing more of his time in organizational concerns, he increases his chance of being present when something important to him is considered. A participant who wishes to pursue other matters (e.g., study, research, family, the problems of the outside world) reduces the number of occasions for decision making to which he can afford to attend. A participant who can spend time can be involved in more arenas. Since it is often difficult to anticipate when and where a particular issue will be involved (and thus to limit one's attention to key times and domains), the simple frequency of availability is relatively important.

RULE 2: PERSIST

It is a mistake to assume that if a particular proposal has been rejected by an organization today, it will be rejected tomorrow. Different sets of people and concerns will be reflected each time a problem is considered or a proposal discussed. We noted earlier the ways in which the flow of participants leads to a flow of organizational concerns.[3] The specific combination of sentiments and people that is associated with a specific choice opportunity is partly fortuitous, and Fortune may be more considerate another day.

For the same reason, it is a mistake to assume that today's victory will be implemented automatically tomorrow. The distinction between decision making and decision implementation is usually a false one. Decisions are not "made" once and for all. Rather they happen as a result of a series of episodes involving different people in different settings, and they may be unmade or modified by subsequent episodes. The participant who spends much time celebrating his victory ordinarily can expect to find the victory short-lived. The loser who spends his time weeping rather than reintroducing his ideas will persistently have something to weep about. The loser who persists in a variety of contexts is frequently rewarded.

RULE 3: EXCHANGE STATUS FOR SUBSTANCE

As we have indicated, the specific substantive issues in a college, or similar organization, typically have low salience for participants. A quite typical situation is one in which significant numbers of participants and groups of participants care less about the specific substantive outcome than they do about the implications of that outcome for their own sense of self-esteem and the social recognition of their importance. Such an ordering of things is neither surprising nor normatively unattractive. It would be a strange world indeed if the mostly minor issues of university governance, for example, became more important to most people than personal and group esteem.

A college president, too, is likely to become substantially concerned with the formal acknowledgment of office. Since it is awkward for him to establish definitively that he is substantively important, the president tends to join other participants in seeking symbolic confirmation of his significance.

The esteem trap is understandable but unfortunate. College presidents who can forgo at least some of the pleasures of self-importance in order to trade status for substance are in a strong position. Since leaders receive credit for many things over which they have little control and to which they contribute little, they should find it possible to accomplish some of the things they want by allowing others to savor the victories, enjoy the pleasures of involvement, and receive the profits of public importance.

RULE 4: FACILITATE OPPOSITION PARTICIPATION

The high inertia of organizations and the heavy dependence of organizational events on processes outside of the control of the organization make organizational power ambiguous.

Presidents sense their lack of control despite their position of authority, status, and concern. Most people who participate in university decision making sense a disappointment with the limited control their position provides.

Persons outside the formal ranks of authority tend to see authority as providing more control. Their aspirations for change tend to be substantially greater than the aspirations for change held by persons with formal authority. One obvious solution is to facilitate participation in decision making. Genuine authoritative participation will reduce the aspirations of oppositional leaders. In an organization characterized by high inertia and low salience it is unwise to allow beliefs about the feasibility of planned action to outrun reality. From this point of view, public accountability, participant observation, and other techniques for extending the range of legitimate participation in the decision-making processes of the organization are essential means of keeping the aspirations of occasional actors within bounds. Since most people most of the time do not participate much, their aspirations for what can be done have a tendency to drift away from reality. On the whole, the direct involvement of dissident groups in the decision-making process is a more effective depressant of exaggerated aspirations than is a lecture by the president.

RULE 5: OVERLOAD THE SYSTEM

As we have suggested, the style of decision making changes when the load exceeds the capabilities of the system. Since we are talking about energy-poor organizations, accomplishing overload is not hard. In practical terms, this means having a large repertoire of projects for organizational action; it means making substantial claims on resources for the analysis of problems, discussion of issues, and political negotiation.

Within an organized anarchy it is a mistake to become absolutely committed to any one project. There are innumerable ways in which the processes we have described will confound the cleverest behavior with respect to any single proposal, however imaginative or subjectively important. What such processes cannot do is cope with large numbers of projects. Someone with the habit of producing many proposals, without absolute commitment to any one, may lose any one of them (and it is hard to predict a priori which one), but cannot be stopped on everything.

The tactic is not unlike the recommendation in some treatments of bargaining that one should introduce new dimensions of bargains in order to facilitate more favorable trades.[4] It is grounded in the observation that the press of proposals so loads the organization that (as we noted in Chapter 5) a large number of actions are taken without attending to problems. Where decisions are made through oversight or flight, considerable control over the course of decision making lies in the hands of two groups: the initiators of the proposals, who get their way in oversight, and the full-time administrator, who is left to make the decision in cases of flight. The college president with a program is in the enviable position of being both a proposal initiator and a full-time administrator. Overload is almost certainly helpful to his program. Other groups within a college or university are probably also advantaged by overload if they have a positive program for action, but their advantage is less certain. In particular, groups in opposition to the administration that are unable to participate full time (either directly or through representatives) may wish to be selective in the use of overload as a tactic.

RULE 6: PROVIDE GARBAGE CANS

One of the complications in accomplishing something in a garbage can decision-making process is the tendency for any particular project to become intertwined with a variety of other issues simply because those issues exist at the time the project is before the organization. A proposal for curricular reform becomes an arena for a concern for social justice. A proposal for construction of a building becomes an arena for concerns about environmental quality. A proposal for bicycle paths becomes an arena for discussion of sexual inequality.

It is pointless to try to react to such problems by attempting to enforce rules of relevance. Such rules are, in any event, highly arbitrary. Even if they were not, it would still be difficult to persuade a person that his problem (however important) could not be discussed because it is not relevant to the current agenda. The appropriate tactical response is to provide garbage cans into which wide varieties of problems can be dumped. The more conspicuous the can, the more garbage it will attract away from other projects.

The prime procedure for making a garbage can attractive is to give it precedence and conspicuousness. On a grand scale, discussions of overall organizational objectives or overall organizational long-term plans are classic first-quality cans. They are general enough to accommodate anything. They are socially defined as being important. They attract enough different kinds of issues to reinforce their importance. An activist will push for discussions of grand plans (in part) in order to draw the garbage away from the concrete day-to-day arenas of his concrete objectives.

On a smaller scale, the first item on a meeting agenda is an obvious garbage can. It receives much of the status allocation concerns that are a part of meetings. It is possible that any item on an agenda will attract an assortment of things currently concerning individuals in the group, but the first item is more vulnerable than others. As a result, projects of serious substantive concern should normally be placed somewhat later, after the important matters of individual and group esteem have been settled, most of the individual performances have been completed, and most of the enthusiasm for abstract argument has waned.

The garbage can tactic has long-term effects that may be important. Although in the short run the major consequence is to remove problems from the arena of short-term concrete proposals, the separation of problem discussion from decision making means that general organizational attitudes develop outside the context of immediate decisions. The exercise of problems and the discussion of plans contribute to a building of the climate within which the organization will operate in the future. A president who uses the garbage can tactic should be aware of the ways in which currently irrelevant conversations produce future ideological constraints. The same tactic also provides a (partly misleading) device for the training and selection of future leaders of the organization. Those who perform well in garbage can debates are not necessarily good leaders, though they may frequently be identified as potential leaders. Finally, the tactic offers a practical buffer for the organization from the instabilities introduced by the entry and exit of problems that drift from one organization to another. In recent years universities have become an arena for an assortment of problems that might have found expression in other social institutions. Universities and colleges were available and accessible to people with the concerns. Although the resulting strain on university processes was considerable, the full impact was cushioned by the tendency of such problems to move to decision-irrelevant garbage cans, to be held there until they could move on to another arena in another institution.

RULE 7: MANAGE UNOBTRUSIVELY

If you put a man in a boat and tell him to plot a course, he can take one of three views of his task. He can float with the currents and winds, letting them take him wherever they wish; he can select a destination and try to use full power to go directly to it regardless of the current or winds; or he can select a destination and use his rudder and sails to let the currents and wind eventually take him where he wants to go. On the whole, we think conscious university leadership is properly seen in third light.

A central tactic in high-inertia systems is to use high-leverage minor actions to produce major effects—to let the system go where it wants to go with only the minor interventions that make it go where it should. From a tactical point of view, the main objection to central direction and control is that it requires an impossible amount of attention and energy. The kinds of organizations with which we have been concerned are unable to be driven where we want them to go without making considerable use of the "natural" organizational processes. The appropriate tactics of management are unobstrusive and indirect.

Unobtrusive management uses interventions of greater impact than visibility. Such actions generally have two key attributes: (1) They affect many parts of the system slightly rather than a few parts in a major way. The effect on any one part of the system is small enough so that either no one really notices or no one finds it sensible to organize significantly against the intervention. (2) Once activated, they stay activated without further organizational attention. Their deactivation requires positive organizational action.

Given all the enthusiasm for elaborating a variety of models of organizations that bemoan bureaucracy and the conventional managerial tools associated with bureaucratic life, it is somewhat surprising to realize that the major instruments of unobstrusive management are bureaucratic. Consider the simple act of committing the organization by signing a piece of paper. By the formal statutes of many organizations, some people within the organization are conceded authority to sign pieces of paper. College presidents tend, in our judgment, to be timid about exercising such authority. By signing a piece of paper the president is able to reverse the burden of organizing the decision-making processes in the system. Many people have commented on the difficulty of organizing the various groups and offices in a college or university in order to do something. What has been less frequently noted is that the same problems of organization face anyone who wants to overturn an action. For example, the official charter of an institution usually has some kind of regulation that permits a desired action, as well as some kind of regulation that might be interpreted as prohibiting it. The president who solicits general organizational approval for action is more likely to obtain it if the burdens of overcoming organizational inertia are on his opposition. He reverses the burden of organization by taking the action.

Major bureaucratic interventions lie in the ordinary systems of accounting and managerial controls. Such devices are often condemned in academic circles as both dreary and inhibiting. Their beauty lies in the way in which they extend throughout the system and in the high degree of arbitrariness they exhibit. For example, students of business have observed that many important aspects of business life are driven by accounting rules. What are costs? What are profits? How are costs and profits allocated among activities and subunits? Answers to such questions are far from arbitrary. But they have enough elements of arbitrariness that no reasonable business manager would ignore the potential contribution of accounting rules to profitability. The flow of investments, the utilization of labor, and the structure of organization all respond to the organization of accounts.

The same thing is true in a college or university, although the process works in a somewhat different way because the convenient single index of business accounting, profit, is denied the university executive. Universities and colleges have official facts (accounting facts) with respect to student activities, faculty activities, and space utilization. In recent years such accounting facts have increased in importance as colleges and universities struggled first with the baby boom and now with fiscal adversity. These official facts enter into reports and filter into decisions made throughout the system. As a typical simple example, consider the impact of changing the accounting for faculty teaching load from number of courses to student credit hours taught. Or, consider the impact of separating in accounting reports the teaching of language (number of students, cost of faculty) from the teaching of literature in that language at a typical American university. Or, consider the impact of making each major subunit in a university purchase services (e.g., duplication services, computer services, library services) at prices somewhat different from the current largely arbitrary prices. Or, consider the consequences of allowing transfer of funds from one major budget line to another within a subunit at various possible discount rates depending on the lines and the point in the budget year. Or, consider the effect of having students pay as part of their fees an amount determined by the department offering the instruction, with the amount thus paid returning to the department.

RULE 8: INTERPRET HISTORY

In an organization in which most issues have low salience, and information about events in the system is poorly maintained, definitions of what is happening and what has happened become important tactical instruments. If people in the organization cared more about what happened (or is happening), the constraints on the tactic would be great. Histories would be challenged and carefully monitored. If people in the organization accepted more openly the idea that much of the decision-making process is a status-certifying rather than a choice-making system, there would be less dependence on historical interpretation. The actual situation, however, provides a tactically optimal situation. On the one hand, the genuine interest in keeping a good record of what happened (in substantive rather than status terms) is minimal. On the other hand, the belief in the relevance of history, or the legitimacy of history as a basis for current action, is fairly strong.

Minutes should be written long enough after the event as to legitimize the reality of forgetfulness. They should be written in such a way as to lay the basis for subsequent independent action—in the name of the collective action. In general, participants in the organization should be assisted in their desire to have unambiguous actions taken today derived from the ambiguous decisions of yesterday with a minimum of pain to their images of organizational rationality and a minimum of claims on their time. The model of consistency is maintained by a creative resolution of uncertainty about the past.

Presidents and Tactics

As we observed at the outset, practical tactics, if they are genuine, will inevitably be viewed as somewhat cynical. We will, however, record our own sentiments that the cynicism lies in the eye of the beholder. Our sympathies and enthusiasm are mostly for the invisible members of an organized anarchy who make such tactics possible. We refer, of course, to the majority of participants in colleges and universities who have the good sense to see that what can be achieved through tactical manipulation of the university is only occasionally worth their time and effort. The validity of the tactics is a tribute to their reluctance to clutter the important elements of life with organizational matters. The tactics are available for anyone who wants to use them. Most of us most of the time have more interesting things to do.

But presidents, as full-time actors generally occupying the best job of their byes, are less likely to have more interesting things to do. In addition, these tactics, with their low visibility and their emphasis on the trading of credit and recognition for accomplishment, will not serve the interests of a president out to glorify himself or increase his chances to be one of the very few who move up to a second and "better" presidency. Instead, they provide an opportunity chiefly for those who have some conception of what might make their institution better, more interesting, more complex, or more educational, and are satisfied to end their tenures believing that they helped to steer their institutions slightly closer to those remote destinations.

The Technology of Foolishness

The tactics for moving an organization when objectives are clear represent important parts of the repertoire of an organizational leader.[5] Standard prescriptions properly honor intention, choice, and action; and college presidents often have things they want to accomplish. Nevertheless, a college president may sometimes want to confront the realities of ambiguity more directly and reconsider the standard dicta of leadership. He may want to examine particularly the place of purpose in intelligent behavior and the role of foolishness in leadership.

Choice and Rationality

The concept of choice as a focus for interpreting and guiding human behavior has rarely had an easy time in the realm of ideas. It is beset by theological disputations over free will, by the dilemmas of absurdism, by the doubts of psychological behaviorism, and by the claims of historical, economic, social, and demographic determinism. Nevertheless, the idea that humans make choices has proved robust enough to become a matter of faith in important segments of contemporary Western civilization. It is a faith that is professed by virtually all theories of social policy making.

The major tenents of this faith run something like this:

> Human beings make choices. Choices are properly made by evaluating alternatives in terms of goals and on the basis of information currently available. The alternative that is most attractive in terms of the goals is chosen. By using the technology of choice, we can improve the quality of the search for alternatives, the quality of information, and the quality of the analysis used to evaluate alternatives. Although actual choice may fall short of this ideal in various ways, it is an attractive model of how choices should be made by individuals, organizations, and social systems.

These articles of faith have been built upon and have stimulated some scripture. It is the scripture of the theories of decision making. The scripture is partly a codification of received doctrine and partly a source for that doctrine. As a result, our cultural ideas of intelligence and our theories of choice display a substantial resemblance. In particular, they share three conspicuous interrelated ideas:

The first idea is the *preexistence of purpose*. We find it natural to base an interpretation of human-choice behavior on a presumption of human purpose. We have, in fact, invented one of the most elaborate terminologies in the professional literature: "values," "needs," "wants," "goods," "tastes," "preferences," "utility," "objectives," "goals," "aspirations," "drives." All of these reflect a strong tendency to believe that a useful interpretation of human behavior involves defining a set of objectives that (1) are prior attributes of the system. and (2) make the observed behavior in some sense intelligent vis-à-vis those objectives.

Whether we are talking about individuals or about organizations, purpose is an obvious presumption of the discussion. An organization is often defined in terms of its purpose. It is seen by some as the largest collectivity directed by a purpose. Action within an organization is justified or criticized in terms of purpose. Individuals explain their own behavior, as well as the behavior of others, in terms of a set of value premises that are presumed to be antecedent to the behavior. Normative theories of choice begin with an assumption of a preexistent preference ordering defined over the possible outcomes of a choice.

The second idea is the *necessity of consistency*. We have come to recognize consistency both as an important property of human behavior and as a prerequisite for normative models of choice. Dissonance theory, balance theory, theories of congruency in attitudes, statuses, and performances have all served to remind us of the possibilities for interpreting human behavior in terms of the consistency requirements of a limited-capacity, information-processing system.

At the same time, consistency is a cultural and theoretical virtue. Action should be consistent with belief. Actions taken by different parts of an organization should be consistent with each other, Individual and organizational activities are seen as connected with each other in terms of their consequences for some consistent set of purposes. In an organization, the structural manifestation of consistency is the hierarchy with its obligations of coordination and control. In the individual, the structural manifestation is a set of values that generates a consistent preference ordering.

The third idea is the *primacy of rationality*. By rationality we mean a procedure for deciding what is correct behavior by relating consequences systematically to objectives. By placing primary emphasis on rational techniques, we have implicitly rejected—or seriously impaired—two other procedures for choice: (1) the processes of intuition, through which people do things without fully understanding why; and (2) the processes of tradition and faith, through which people do things because that is the way they are done.

Both within the theory and within the culture we insist on the ethic of rationality. We justify individual and organizational action in terms of an analysis of means and ends. Impulse, intuition, faith, and tradition are outside that system and viewed as antithetical to it. Faith may be seen as a possible source of values. Intuition may be seen as a possible source of ideas about alternatives. But the analysis and justification of action lie within the context of reason.

These ideas are obviously deeply embedded in the culture. Their roots extend into ideas that have conditioned much of modern Western history and interpretations of that history. Their general acceptance is probably highly correlated with the permeation of rationalism and individualism into the style of thinking within the culture. The ideas are even more obviously embedded in modem theories of choice. It is fundamental to those theories that thinking should precede action: that action should serve a purpose: that purpose should be defined in terms of a consistent set of preexistent goals; and that choice should be based on a consistent theory of the relation between action and its consequences.

Every tool of management decision making that is currently a part of management science, operations research, or decision-making theory, assumes the prior existence of a set of consistent goals. Almost the entire structure of microeconomic theory builds on the assumption that there exists a well-defined, stable, and consistent preference ordering. Most theories of individual or organizational choice accept the idea that goals exist and that (in some sense) an individual or organization acts on those goals, choosing from among some alternatives on the basis of available information. Discussions of educational policy with their emphasis on goal setting, evaluation, and accountability, are in this tradition.

From the perspective of all of man's history, the ideas of purpose, consistency, and rationality are relatively new. Much of the technology currently available to implement them is extremely new. Over the past few centuries, and conspicuously over the past few decades, we have substantially improved man's capability for acting purposively. consistently, and rationally. We have substantially increased his propensity to think of himself as doing so. It is an impressive victory, won—where it has been won—by a happy combination of timing, performance, ideology, and persistence. It is a battle yet to be concluded, or even engaged, in many cultures of the world; but within most of the Western world individuals and organizations see themselves as making choices.

The Problem of Goals

The tools of intelligence as they are fashioned in modern theories of choice are necessary to any reasonable behavior in contemporary society. It is inconceivable that we would fail to continue their development, refinement, and extension. As might be expected, however, a theory and ideology of choice built on the ideas outlined above is deficient in some obvious, elementary ways, most conspicuously in the treatment of human goals.

Goals are thrust upon the intelligent man. We ask that he act in the name of goals. We ask that he keep his goals consistent. We ask that his actions be oriented to his goals. We ask that a social system amalgamate individual goals into a collective goal. But we do not concern ourselves with the origin of goals. Theories of individual, organizational, and social choice assume actors with preexistent values.

Since it is obvious that goals change over time and that the character of those changes affects both the richness of personal and social development and the outcome of choice behavior, a theory of choice must somehow justify ignoring the phenomena. Although it is unreasonable to ask a theory of choice to solve all the problems of man and his development, it is reasonable to ask how such conspicuous elements as the fluidity and ambiguity of objectives can plausibly be ignored in a theory that is offered as a guide to human choice behavior.

There are three classic justifications. The first is that goal development and choice are independent processes, conceptually and behaviorally. The second is that the model of choice is never satisfied in fact and that deviations from the model accommodate the problems of introducing change. The third is that the idea of changing goals is so intractable in a normative theory of choice that nothing can be said about it. Since we are unpersuaded of the first and second justifications, our optimism with respect to the third is somewhat greater than that of most of our fellows.

The argument that goal development and choice are independent behaviorally seems clearly false. It seems to us obvious that a description that assumes that goals come first and action comes later is frequently radically wrong. Human choice behavior is at least as much a process for discovering goals as for acting on them. Although it is true enough that goals and decisions are "conceptually" distinct, that is simply a statement of the theory, not a defense of it. They are conceptually distinct if we choose to make them so.

The argument that the model is incomplete is more persuasive. There do appear to be some critical "holes" in the system of intelligence as described by standard theories of choice. Incomplete information, incomplete goal consistency, and a variety of external processes facilitate goal development. What is somewhat disconcerting about the argument, however, is that it makes the efficacy of the concepts of intelligent choice dependent on their inadequacy. As we become more competent in the techniques of the model and more committed to it, the "holes" become smaller. As the model becomes more accepted, our obligation to modify it increases.

The final argument seems to us sensible as a general principle, but misleading here. Why are we more reluctant to ask how human beings might find "good" goals than we are to ask how they might make "good" decisions? The second question appears to be a more technical problem. The first seems more pretentious. It claims to say something about alternative virtues. The appearance of pretense, however, stems directly from the prevailing theory of choice and the ideology associated with it.

In fact, the conscious introduction of goal discovery for consideration in theories of human choice is not unknown to modern man. For example, we have two kinds of theories of choice behavior in human beings. One is a theory of children. The other is a theory of adults. In the theory of children, we emphasize choices as leading to experiences that develop the child's scope, his complexity, his awareness of the world. As parents, teachers, or psychologists, we try to lead the child to do things that are inconsistent with his present goals because we know (or believe) that he can develop into an interesting person only by coming to appreciate aspects of experience that he initially rejects.

In the theory of adults, we emphasize choices as a consequence of our intentions. As adults, educational decision makers, or economists, we try to take actions that (within the limits of scarce resources) come as close as possible to achieving our goals. We try to find improved ways of making decisions consistent with our perceptions of what is valuable in the world.

The asymmetry in these models is conspicuous. Adults have constructed a model world in which adults know what is good for themselves, but children do not. It is hard to react positively to the conceit. The asymmetry has, in fact, stimulated a large number of ideologies and reforms designed to allow children the same moral prerogative granted to adults—the right to imagine that they know what they want. The efforts have cut deeply into traditional childrearing, traditional educational policies, traditional politics, and traditional consumer economics.

In our judgment, the asymmetry between models of choice for adults and for children is awkward; but the solution we have adopted is precisely wrong-headed. Instead of trying to adapt the model of adults to children, we might better adapt the model of children to adults.

For many purposes, our model of children is better. Of course, children know what they want. Everyone does. The critical question is whether they are encouraged to develop more interesting "wants." Values change. People become more interesting as those values and the interconnections made among them change.

One of the most obvious things in the world turns out to be hard for us to accommodate in our theory of choice: A child of two will almost always have a less interesting set of values (indeed, a worse set of values) than a child of 12. The same is true of adults. Values develop through experience. Although one of the main natural arenas for the modification of human values is the arena of choice. our theories of adult and organizational decision making ignore the phenomenon entirely.

Introducing ambiguity and fluidity to the interpretation of individual, organizational, and societal goals obviously has implications for behavioral theories of decision making. We have tried to identify and respond to some of those difficulties in the preceding chapters. The main point here, however, is not to consider how we might describe the behavior of systems that are discovering goals as they act. Rather it is to examine how we might improve the quality of that behavior, how we might aid the development of interesting goals.

We know how to advise a society, an organization, or an individual if we are first given a consistent set of preferences. Under some conditions, we can suggest how to make decisions if the preferences are consistent only up to the point of specifying a series of independent constraints on the choice. But what about a normative theory of goal-finding behavior? What do we say when our client tells us that he is not sure his present set of values is the set of values in terms of which he wants to act?

It is a question familiar to many aspects of ordinary life. It is a question that friends, associates, students, college presidents, business managers, voters, and children ask at least as frequently as they ask how they should act within a set of consistent and stable values.

Within the context of normative theory of choice as it exists, the answer we gave is: First determine the values, then act. The advice is frequently useful. Moreover, we have developed ways in which we can use conventional techniques for decision analysis to help discover value premises and to expose value inconsistencies. These techniques involve testing the decision implications of some successive approximations to a set of preferences. The object is to find a consistent set of preferences with implications that are acceptable to the person or organization making the decisions. Variations on such techniques are used routinely in operations research, as well as in personal counseling and analysis.

The utility of such techniques, however, apparently depends on the assumption that a primary problem is the amalgamation or excavation of preexistent values. The metaphors— "finding oneself," "goal clarification," "self-discovery," "social welfare function," "revealed preference"—are metaphors of search. If our value premises are to be "constructed" rather than "discovered," our standard procedures may be useful: but we have no a priori reason for assuming they will.

Perhaps we should explore a somewhat different approach to the normative question of how we ought to behave when our value premises are not yet (and never will be) fully determined. Suppose we treat action as a way of creating interesting goals at the same time as we treat goals as a way of justifying action. It is an intuitively plausible and simple idea, but one that is not immediately within the domain of standard normative theories of intelligent choice.

Interesting people and interesting organizations construct complicated theories of themselves. To do this, they need to supplement the technology of reason with a technology of foolishness. Individuals and organizations sometimes need ways of doing things for which they have no good reason. They need to act before they think.

Sensible Foolishness

To use intelligent choice as a planned occasion for discovering new goals, we require some idea of sensible foolishness. Which of the many foolish things that we might do now will lead to attractive value consequences? The question is almost inconceivable. Not only does it ask us to predict the value consequences of action, it asks us to evaluate them. In what terms can we talk about "good" changes in goals?

In effect, we are asked either to specify a set of supergoals in terms of which alternative goals are evaluated, or to choose among alternatives *now* in terms of the unknown set of values we will have at some future time (or the distribution over time of that unknown set of future values). The former alternative moves us back to the original situation of a fixed set of values—now called "supergoals"—and hardly seems an important step in the direction of inventing procedures for discovering new goals. The latter alternative seems fundamental enough, but it violates severely our sense of temporal order. To say that we make decisions now in terms of goals that will be knowable only later is nonsensical—as long as we accept the basic framework of the theory of choice and its presumptions of preexistent goals.

As we challenge the dogma of preexistent goals, we will be forced to reexamine some of our most precious prejudices: the strictures against imitation, coercion, and rationalization. Each of those honorable prohibitions depends on the view of man and human choice imposed on us by conventional theories of choice.

Imitation is not necessarily a sign of moral weakness. It is a prediction. It is a prediction that if we duplicate the behavior or attitudes of someone else, not only will we fare well in terms of current goals but the chances of our discovering attractive new goals for ourselves are relatively high. If imitation is to be normatively attractive, we need a better theory of who should be imitated. Such a theory seems to be eminently feasible. For example, what are the conditions for effectiveness of a rule that one should imitate another person whose values are close to one's own? How do the chances of discovering interesting goals through imitation change as the number of people exhibiting the behavior to be imitated increases? In the case of the college president we might ask what the goal discovery consequences are of imitating the choices of those at institutions more prestigious than one's own, and whether there are other more desirable patterns of imitation.

Coercion is not necessarily an assault on individual autonomy. It can be a device for stimulating individuality. We recognize this when we talk about education or about parents and children. What has been difficult with coercion is the possibility for perversion, not its obvious capability for stimulating change. We need a theory of the circumstances under which entry into a coercive relationship produces behavior that leads to the discovery of interesting goals. We are all familiar with the tactic. College presidents use it in imposing deadlines, entering contracts, making commitments. What are the conditions for its effective use? In particular, what are the conditions for goal-fostering coercion in social systems?

Rationalization is not necessarily a way of evading morality. It can be a test for the feasibility of a goal change. When deciding among alternative actions for which we have no good reason, it may be sensible to develop some definition of how "near" to intelligence alternative "unintelligent" actions lie. Effective rationalization permits this kind of incremental approach to changes in values. To use it effectively, however, we require a better idea of the metrics that might be possible in measuring value distances. At the same time, rationalization is the major procedure for integrating newly discovered goals into an existing structure of values. It provides the organization of complexity without which complexity itself becomes indistinguishable from randomness.

The dangers in imitation, coercion, and rationalization are too familiar to elaborate. We should, indeed, be able to develop better techniques. Whatever those techniques may be, however, they will almost certainly undermine the superstructure of biases erected on purpose, consistency, and rationality. They will involve some way of thinking about action now as occurring in terms of a set of future values different from those that the actor currently holds.

Play and Reason

A second requirement for a technology of foolishness is some strategy for suspending rational imperatives toward consistency. Even if we know which of several foolish things we want to do, we still need a mechanism for allowing us to do it. How do we escape the logic of our reason?

Here we are closer to understanding what we need. It is playfulness. Playfulness is the deliberate, temporary relaxation of rules in order to explore the possibilities of alternative rules. When we are playful, we challenge the necessity of consistency. In effect, we announce—in advance—our rejection of the usual objections to behavior that does not fit the standard model of intelligence.

Playfulness allows experimentation at the same time that it acknowledges reason. It accepts an obligation that at some point either the playful behavior will be stopped or it will be integrated into the structure of intelligence in some way that makes sense. The suspension of the rules is temporary.

The idea of play may suggest three things that are, in our minds, quite erroneous in the present context. First, play may be seen as a kind of "holiday" for reason, a release of the emotional tensions of virtue. Although it is possible that play performs some such function, that is not the function with which we are concerned. Second, play may be seen as part of some mystical balance of spiritual principles: fire and water, hot and cold, weak and strong. The intention here is much narrower than a general mystique of balance. Third, play may be seen as an antithesis of intelligence, so that the emphasis on the importance of play becomes a support for simple self-indulgence. Our present intent is to propose play as an instrument of intelligence, not a substitute.

Playfulness is a natural outgrowth of our standard view of reason. A strict insistence on purpose, consistency, and rationality limits our ability to find new purposes. Play relaxes that insistence to allow us to act "unintelligently" or "irrationally" or "foolishly" to explore alternative ideas of purposes and alternative concepts of behavioral consistency. And it does this while maintaining our basic commitment to intelligence.

Although play and reason are in this way functional complements, they are often behavioral competitors. They are alternative styles and alternative orientations to the same situation. There is no guarantee that the styles will be equally well developed, that all individuals, organizations, or societies will be equally adept in both styles; or that all cultures will be sufficiently encouraging to both.

Our design problem is either to specify the best mix of styles or, failing that, to assure that most people and most organizations most of the time use an alternation of strategies rather than persevering in either one. It is a difficult problem. The optimization problem looks extremely complex on the face of it, and the learning situations that will produce alternation in behavior appear to be somewhat less common than those that produce perseverance.

Consider, for example, the difficulty of sustaining playfulness as a style within contemporary American society. Individuals who are good at consistent rationality are rewarded early and heavily. We define consistent rationality as intelligence, and the educational rewards of society are associated strongly with it. Social norms press in the same direction, particularly for men. "Changing one's mind" is viewed as feminine and undesirable. Politicians and other leaders will go to enormous lengths to avoid admitting an inconsistency. Many demands of modern organizational life reinforce the same rational abilities and preferences for a style of unchanging purposes.

The result is that many of the most influential and best-educated citizens have experienced a powerful overlearning with respect to rationality. They are exceptionally good at maintaining consistent pictures of themselves, of relating action to purposes. They are exceptionally poor at a playful attitude toward their own beliefs, toward the logic of consistency, or toward the way they see things as being connected in the world. The dictates of manliness, forcefulness, independence, and intelligence are intolerant of playful urges if they arise. The playful urges that arise are weak ones, scarcely discernible in the behavior of most businessmen, mayors, or college presidents.

The picture is probably overdrawn, but we believe that the implications are not. Reason and intelligence have had the unnecessary consequence of inhibiting the development of purpose into more complicated forms of consistency. To move away from that position. we need to find some ways of helping individuals and organizations to experiment with doing things for which they have no good reason, to be playful with their conceptions of themselves. We suggest five things as a small beginning:

First, we can treat *goals as hypotheses*. Conventional theories of decision making allow us to entertain doubts about almost everything except the thing about which we frequently have the greatest doubt—our objectives. Suppose we define the decision-making process as a time for the sequential testing of hypotheses about goals. If we can experiment with alternative goals, we stand some chance of discovering complicated and interesting combinations of good values that none of us previously imagined.

Second, we can treat *intuition as real*. We do not know what intuition is or even if it is any one thing. Perhaps it is simply an excuse for doing something we cannot justify in terms of present values or for refusing to follow the logic of our own beliefs. Perhaps it is an inexplicable way of consulting that part of our intelligence and knowledge of the world that is not organized in a way anticipated by standard theories of choice. In either case, intuition permits us to see some possible actions that are outside our present scheme for justifying behavior.

Third, we can treat *hypocrisy as a transition*. Hypocrisy is an inconsistency between expressed values and behavior. Negative attitudes about hypocrisy stem mainly from a general onus against inconsistency and from a sentiment against combining the pleasures of vice with the appearance of virtue. It seems to us that a bad man with good intentions may be a man experimenting with the possibility of becoming good. Somehow it seems more sensible to encourage the experimentation than to insult it.

Fourth, we can treat *memory as an enemy*. The rules of consistency and rationality require a technology of memory. For most purposes, good memories make good choices. But the ability to forget or overlook is also useful. If you do not know what you did yesterday or what other people in the organization are doing today, you can act within the system of reason and still do things that are foolish.

Fifth, we can treat *experience as a theory*. Learning can be viewed as a series of conclusions based on concepts of action and consequences that we have invented. Experience can be changed retrospectively. By changing our interpretive concepts now, we modify what we learned earlier. Thus we expose the possibility of experimenting with alternative histories. The usual strictures against "self-deception" in experience need occasionally to be tempered with an awareness of the extent to which all experience is an interpretation subject to conscious revision. Personal histories and national histories need to be rewritten continuously as a base for the retrospective learning of new self-conceptions.

If we knew more about the normative theory of acting before thinking, we could say more intelligent things about the functions of management and leadership when organizations or societies do not know what they are doing. Consider, for example, the following general implications.

First, we need to reexamine the functions of management decision making. One of the primary ways in which the goals of an organization are developed is by interpreting the decisions it makes, and one feature of good managerial decisions is that they lead to the development of more interesting value premises for the organization. As a result, decisions should not be seen as flowing directly or strictly from a preexistent set of objectives. College presidents who make decisions might well view that function somewhat less as a process of deduction or a process of political negotiation, and somewhat more as a process of gently upsetting preconceptions of what the organization is doing.

Second, we need a modified view of planning. Planning can often be more effective as an interpretation of past decisions than as a program for future ones. It can be used as a part of the efforts of the organization to develop a new consistent theory of itself that incorporates the mix of recent actions into a moderately comprehensive structure of goals. Procedures for interpreting the meaning of most past events are familiar to the memoirs of retired generals, prime ministers, business leaders, and movie stars. They suffer from the company they keep. In an organization that wants to continue to develop new objectives, a manager needs to be tolerant of the idea that he will discover the meaning of yesterday's action in the experiences and interpretations of today.

Third, we need to reconsider evaluation. As nearly as we can determine, there is nothing in a formal theory of evaluation that requires that criteria be specified in advance. In particular, the evaluation of social experiments need not be in terms of the degree to which they have fulfilled our prior expectations. Rather we can examine what they did in terms of what we now believe to be important. The prior specification of criteria and the prior specification of evaluational procedures that depend on such criteria are common presumptions in contemporary social policy making. They are presumptions that inhibit the serendipitous discovery of new criteria. Experience should be used explicitly as an occasion for evaluating our values as well as our actions.

Fourth, we need a reconsideration of social accountability. Individual preferences and social action need to be consistent in some way. But the process of pursuing consistency is one in which both the preferences and the actions change over time. Imagination in social policy formation involves systematically adapting to and influencing preference. It would be unfortunate if our theories of social action encouraged leaders to ignore their responsibilities for anticipating public preferences through action and for providing social experiences that modify individual expectations.

Fifth, we need to accept playfulness in social organizations. The design of organizations should attend to the problems of maintaining both playfulness and reason as aspects of intelligent choice. Since much of the literature on social design is concerned with strengthening the rationality of decision making managers are likely to overlook the importance of play. This is partly a matter of making the individuals within an organization more playful by encouraging the attitudes and skills of inconsistency. It is also a matter of making organizational structure and organizational procedures more playful. Organizations can be playful even when the participants in them are not. The managerial devices for maintaining consistency can be varied. We encourage organizational play by insisting on some temporary relief from control, coordination. and communication.

Presidents and Foolishness

Contemporary theories of decision making and the technology of reason have considerably strengthened our capabilities for effective social action. The conversion of the simple ideas of choice into an extensive technology is a major achievement. It is, however, an achievement that has reinforced some biases in the underlying models of choice in individuals and groups. In particular, it has reinforced the uncritical acceptance of a static interpretation of human goals.

There is little magic in the world, and foolishness in people and organizations is one of the many things that fail to produce miracles. Under certain conditions, it is one of several ways in which some of the problems of our current theories of intelligence can be overcome. It may be a good way, for it preserves the virtues of consistency while stimulating change. If we had a good technology of foolishness, it might (in combination with the technology of reason) help in a small way to develop the unusual combinations of attitudes and behaviors that describe the interesting people, interesting organizations. and interesting societies of the world. The contribution of a college president may often be measured by his capability for sustaining that creative interaction of foolishness and rationality.

Notes

[1]For anyone who wishes to enter the literature, see by way of introduction Raymond Wolfinger (1971a, 1971b), and Frederick W. Frey (1971).

[2] For a discussion of this point in the context of public school decision making, see Stephen Weiner (1972).

[3] For a discussion of the same phenomenon in a business setting. see R. M. Cyert and J. G. March (1963).

[4] See, for example. Iklé (1964) and Walton and McKersie (1965).

[5] These ideas have been the basis for extended conversation with a number of friends. We want to acknowledge particularly the help of Lance Bennett, Patricia Nelson Bennett, Michael Butler, Soren Christensen, Michel Crozier, Claude Faucheux, James R. Glenn, Jr., Gudmund Hernes, Heiga Hernes, Jean Carter Lave, Harold J. Leavitt, Henry M. Levin. Leslie Lincoln, André Massart, John Miller, Johan Olsen, Richard C., Snyder, Alexander Szalai, Eugene J. Webb, and Gail Whitacre.

The Meaning of "Good Presidential Leadership": A Frame Analysis

Estella M. Bensimon

The idea that managers should be able to examine problems from different perspectives and along more than one value dimension (Lombard 1971) is not new. Contingency theorists, for example, have maintained that differences in the subsystems of an organization demand different administrative approaches (Kast and Rosenzweig 1973) such as the ability to use both closed and open system logic (Thompson 1967). However, models of administrative practice to help managers understand situations, problems, and the general day-to-day life of their organizations from multiple vantage points are relatively new.

Recently, Lee Bolman and Terrence Deal (1984) proposed four different organizational lenses through which managers can understand their organizations: structural, human resources, political, and symbolic. They suggest that organizations have multiple realities and that a manager who can use multiple lenses will likely be more effective than one who deals with problems from a single perspective. Similarly, Robert Birnbaum (1988) suggests that administrators must recognize the interactions between the bureaucratic, collegial, political, and symbolic processes in colleges and universities if they are to be effective. Though this concept is gaining acceptance, it is unclear how many business or educational leaders do, in fact, incorporate multiple "vantage points."

This study explores empirically the extent to which college and university presidents incorporate single or multiple vantage points in their descriptions of good leadership. Presidential vantage points are classified according to Birnbaum's adaptation of Bolman and Deal's framework for understanding academic organizations and governance patterns. Specifically, they suggest that leaders implicitly use different cognitive "frames" to define their roles and understand organizational behavior. A frame represents a distinctive cognitive lens that helps the manager of an organization or the president of a college determine what is important and what can be safely ignored. Cognitive frames determine what questions might get asked, what information is collected, how problems are defined, and what courses of action should be taken (Bolman and Deal 1984; Goleman 1985). Frames influence what leaders see and do.

Cognitive Frames

Bolman and Deal and Birnbaum find four frames that provide important conceptual maps for understanding organizations and effective leadership behavior. Birnbaum proposes that each frame reflects "institutional functioning in some ways, at some times, in some parts of all colleges and universities" (1988, 175).

The Bureaucratic Frame

This frame views organizations as mechanistic hierarchies with clearly established lines of authority. According to this model: (1) the organization's goals are clear, (2) the organization is a closed system insulated from environmental penetration, and (3) administrative leaders have the power to analyze a problem, determine alternate solutions, choose the best, and execute it.

The classic schools of thought associated with the bureaucratic frame include scientific management (Taylor 1947), administrative principles (Fayol 1949), and bureaucracy (Weber 1947). More contemporary applications of the structural frame are found in such decision-making systems as management by objectives and planning, programming, and budgeting systems.

The bureaucratic frame is more useful for understanding stable organizations or parts of organizations in which preferences of superiors direct the preferences of subordinates (Birnbaum 1998). Presidents with a bureaucratic frame are likely to emphasize their role in making decisions, getting results, and establishing systems of management.

The Collegial Frame

Within this frame, organizations are viewed as collectivities with organizational members as their primary resource. The emphasis is on human needs and how organizations can be tailored to meet them. Schools of thought associated with this frame include human relations (Mayo 1949; Likert 1961) and Theory X and Theory Y (McGregor 1960).

This frame pictures colleges and universities as communities of scholars (Millett 1962) who, by virtue of their professional expertise and a shared value system, control organizational goals. The collegial frame is useful for understanding stable organizations, or organizational subunits, in which preferences are developed by consensus through interaction (Birnbaum 1988). Presidents who use a collegial frame seek participative, democratic decision making and strive to meet people's needs and help them realize their aspirations. Emphasis here is on interpersonal skills, motivating others, and putting the interests of the institution first.

The Political Frame

This frame sees organizations as formal and informal groups vying for power to control institutional processes and outcomes. Decisions result from bargaining, influencing and coalition building. This frame assumes that colleges and universities are pluralistic entities made up of groups with different interests and values and that conflict will erupt when resources are scarce (Baldridge 1971). Conflict, not salient in the two previous frames, is here a central feature of organizational life.

In the political frame, the president is a mediator or negotiator between shifting power blocs. The president must "assemble a winning or dominant coalition that will support proposed actions—as one would in a parliamentary form of government" (Whetten 1984, 40). Presidents should administer through persuasion and diplomacy, be open and communicative, and stay flexible on means but rigid on ends (Walker 1979). Presidents with a political frame are also sensitive to external interest groups and their strong influence over the policy-making process.

The Symbolic Frame

Within this frame, organizations are cultural systems of shared meanings and beliefs in which organizational structures and processes are invented. Leaders construct and maintain "systems of shared meanings, paradigms, and shared languages and cultures" (Pfeffer 1981, 9) by sustaining rituals, symbols, and myths that create a unifying system of belief for the institution (Dill 1982). Works such as Thomas Peters and Robert Waterman's *In Search of Excellence* (1982), Terrence Deal and Allan Kennedy's *Corporate Cultures* (1982), and Edgar Schein's *Organizational Culture and Leadership* (1985) exemplify symbolic approaches to the understanding of organizations and leadership.

In higher education Michael Cohen and James March's *Leadership and Ambiguity* (1974) gives the best analysis of the presidency with a symbolic orientation. Cohen and March dub universities "organized anarchies" because of their problematic goals, unclear technology, and fluid participation. Presidents who adhere to this symbolic frame are primarily catalysts or facilitators of an ongoing process. They do not so much lead the institution as channel its activities in subtle ways. They do not plan comprehensively but try to apply preexisting solutions to current problems (Baldridge et al. 1978). They emphasize expressive rather than instrumental actions (Pfeffer 1981).

How Frames Work

Each of these frames focuses on different aspects of organizational behavior; they also function as cognitive blinders in that whatever is "out of frame" is likely to be ignored or overlooked. For example, the president who analyzes problems through the cognitive lens of the bureaucratic frame will probably propose solutions that stress efficiency but overlook impacts on institutional members, political ramifications, or symbolic interpretations others in the organization may attach to the solution.

The difference between seeing through one frame or many frames may be related to cognitive style, specifically to the theory of integrative complexity (Tetlock 1983). Those who use several frames and switch from one to another may demonstrate a higher level of cognitive differentiation (e.g., recognizing a variety of aspects) and integration (e.g., developing complex connections among different aspects). Leaders who incorporate elements of several frames are likely to have more flexible responses to different administrative tasks because they have different images of the organization and can interpret events in a variety of ways.

This more complicated type of understanding may be particularly important as college and university environments become more complex. On a more practical level, college and university presidents are expected to play many roles (Kerr 1963). The president who can think and act using more than one frame may be able to fulfill the many, and often conflicting, expectations of the presidential office more skillfully than the president who cannot differentiate among situational requirements.

Espoused Theories of Leadership

Presidents use these frames in a variety of ways: to solve problems, interpret events, describe proper leadership roles, or act as presidents. This study identifies the preferred cognitive frames implicit in presidents' interpretations of good leadership. These interpretations are called "espoused theories" (Argyris and Schon 1974) because they represent what presidents say good leadership should be, the way they see themselves or the way they would like others to see them. Even though espoused theories may not accurately represent what presidents actually do, they are likely to influence the expectations presidents have of themselves as leaders as well as their behavior.

Methodology and Data

I used data collected through on-site, semi-structured interviews with the presidents of thirty-two colleges and universities participating in the Institutional Leadership Project (ILP), a five-year longitudinal study conducted by the National Center for Postsecondary Governance and Finance. For the purposes of the ILP and its stratified sampling procedure, see Birnbaum, Bensimon, and Neumann 1989. I examined interview data reflecting espoused leadership theories to identify the thirty-two presidents' cognitive frames and constructed the espoused theories of leadership by abstracting data from the total interview transcript and the presidents' responses to the following question: "How does President X [the respondent] define good presidential leadership?" To identify presidents' frames, I analyzed espoused theories of leadership as if they were made up of two distinct components: leadership as the process of providing direction to a group or an institution and the ways in which presidents prefer to provide direction.

I used content analysis to code references to elements of the four frames in a sustained interview passage. I considered that presidents used a frame if their responses contained at least two references to it. Presidents could thus espouse as many as four frames and as few as one. For example, when President #1 said that a good leader "understands and respects the institution and reads the written histories," he described a characteristic stance found in the symbolic frame and was recorded as espousing that frame. In the interviews, President #1 never espoused the bureaucratic frame, gave three separate depictions of the collegial frame, five of the political, and two of the symbolic frame. The dominant espoused theory was thus classified as including three frames, all except the bureaucratic.

I then created a three-part classification: presidents who espoused a single-frame theory, those who combined two frames, and those with multi-frame orientations.

Results

Of the thirty-two presidents interviewed, thirteen espoused a single frame, eleven espoused two frames, seven espoused three frames, and one espoused four frames.

In the first part of this section, I describe the three frame categories using excerpts from the interviews with the presidents. Next, I analyze the findings by institutional type and length of president's tenure.

Single-frame Theories

Single-frame theories of good presidential leadership have one clearly identifiable theme with a specific organizational model. The language describing the process of providing leadership and the tactics of leadership is consistent with a single-focus orientation. Of course, the content of single-frame theories varies according to the frame in use.

Presidents espousing single-frame theories sometimes mentioned other viewpoints, but more to reinforce the single-frame perspective than to introduce a second dimension. For example, one president with a bureaucratic frame explained that "coming across with your main priorities is important so that you can show you are in control, that you are the president." Even though establishing priorities seems to have symbolic rather than instrumental value, the intent is to show control, to solidify a bureaucratic image of good presidential leadership. As Table 1 shows, presidents expressed single-frame orientations of all four kinds; however, I will use only two interview excerpts as examples.

Table 1

Espoused Theories with a Single-Frame Orientation	
Frames	Number
Bureaucratic	5
Collegial	4
Political	1
Symbolic	3
Total	13

One president with a bureaucratic frame looked at leadership as "the person who sets the pace and commands the respect of those that follow him and who accomplishes what he sets out to do.... The president's principal responsibility is to make decisions." In true bureaucratic form, this president described the leader as being at the top of the hierarchy. Implicit within this definition is the image of the president as decisive and as action- and results-oriented.

Another president spoke about leadership almost exclusively through the collegial frame: "I define a leader as a person who provides a vision or direction for a group which takes the capability of the group and potential benefits into account.... A [president] has to understand what the faculty is feeling and needing and address oneself to meeting the needs and getting people to feel good about the institution." Unlike the president in the first sample, this one emphasizes being responsive to group needs rather than being a decision-maker. For her, strong leaders attend to the needs of people to build commitment and loyalty to the institution. Although the realities these two presidents construct and the ways in which they enact their roles are different, both presidents have a single-frame orientation to leadership.

Thirteen presidents (41 percent) had single-frame theories. Table 1 shows that though presidents expressed single-frame orientations of all four kinds, they were more likely to espouse the bureaucratic and collegial frames than the political and symbolic.

Paired-frame Theories

Paired-frame theories are two frames coupled in a complementary way. There may be a functional division between the two frames, one frame providing a global definition of what it means to be a good presidential leader, while more concrete explanations, elaborations, or clarifications are provided through the second frame. Even though one frame gives the initial meaning of good presidential leadership and another translates or enhances it, each frame by definition contributes a different dimension and completes the full viewpoint.

Complementary use of two frames may be illustrated by a president who articulated his theory of good leadership through the collegial and symbolic frames. Starting with the collegial frame, this president explained that good presidential leadership means "accomplishing commonly determined goals in such a way that all involved are satisfied with the path taken to get there." He continued, shifting to a symbolic frame: "Presidential leadership also means the development and interpretation of the vision, and granting permission to pursue the vision, and free up...the obstacles that prevent the institution from doing it effectively." By introducing the second frame, a fairly conventional response became a significantly more important and interesting statement about the meaning of good presidential leadership.

Another president who combined the collegial and symbolic frames said, in the symbolic frame, that good leadership requires a president to: "do a lot of listening and solicit the dreams and hopes from the people; tell the people about the good things you are finding and in three to six months take these things and report them as the things you would like to see happen." A good leader, in this president's eyes, searches among the activities of the institution and selects those that should be retained as institutional goals. For this president, the presidential role is sense-making, and leadership is the management of meaning (Smircich and Morgan 1982). Reality is constructed not by imposing the president's image of what the institution should be doing, but by transforming people's desires and ambitions for the institution ("the good things you are finding") into its plans and goals. Even though this president uses primarily the symbolic frame to describe good presidential leadership, he is influenced by the collegial frame. This is particularly evident when he adds, "Leaders are good listeners, they are able to paraphrase back to people what they have said accurately. You need to work with what they have said and how they feel. You have to be able to read people's emotions."

Another president provided a different complementary pairing. First he used the symbolic frame perspective to explain the importance of having different repertoires: "The trick is to know what guise to put on and to be able to do it. Some people can only use one guise and as a result they are good leaders only in certain situations." Then, he listed important tasks: "[You should] do your homework, get to know your immediate staff—their backgrounds, make them relax with you. Get a master key and drop in around campus. Accept all speaking engagements.

Go to the faculty leaders' offices and talk to them so they will know that you are willing to listen to them. Have a beer with them. But don't make any promises."

Here we see a noticeable shift to the political frame in the emphasis of understanding key individuals who could be potential friends or, opponents. Had this president continued to speak through the symbolic lens, he might have stressed a simpler theme of establishing an image of accessibility.

Summarizing the approach used, this president also speaks from the symbolic frame: "There is a need for a president to coast over a total problem and know when to swoop down and give total attention to one issue. At such points, I call the people with information and suck up everybody's files. I can do that in one night. It is total immersion. I decide what needs to be done. I give it to my staff to do. And then I soar again. This is an important thing for a president to do." The scanning and selecting" technique allows this president to limit the number of problems on which to concentrate and singles out important problems by taking symbolic and dramatic action. He then delegates to the staff responsibility for implementing the solutions he has worked out. (But this president is also involved in dramatically solving problems and making decisions.)

Of the thirty-two presidents, eleven (34 percent) used two frames to express the meaning of good presidential leadership. Table 2 shows that paired-frame theories are distributed among four possible combinations. No one combined bureaucratic-collegial and bureaucratic-symbolic. Almost half of the paired-frame theories were collegial-symbolic. Interestingly, the symbolic frame, with either the collegial or the political frames, was present in seven of the paired-frame theories.

Table 2

Theories Espousing a Paired-Frame Orientation	
Frame Combinations	Number
Bureaucratic/collegial	0
Bureaucratic/political	1
Bureaucratic/symbolic	0
Collegial/political	3
Collegial/symbolic	5
Political/symbolic	2
Total	11

Multi-frame Theories

Multi-frame theories display at least three of the four possible frames and represent, therefore, the greatest frame complexity. Espousing a multi-frame theory implies the ability to shift frames in response to situational circumstances. The one president who espoused all four frames was "new" and the only first-time president in the sample with a multi-frame orientation. This president combined the collegial and bureaucratic frames to explain that good presidential leadership "means to help a group of people achieve a set of agreed upon goals. There are things that make that happen—having clear goal-setting, good communication, good management."

This president then listed additional characteristics, spanning all four frames, all needed "to make it all move forward." The bureaucratic frame was obvious in the stated necessity to "have a clear sense of what the important goals are and a real desire to take leadership responsibility." The collegial frame underlay a sense that "to get the group to the goals," a president needs "a real affirming attitude toward all the players in the group." "Affirming people," this president explained, "means people getting credit for what they are doing and being told that it is important, and being encouraged to be creative. But this is not a pretense; you must be honest with them. It requires honesty; it is not pablum. You must give authentic recognition and encouragement. You must respect the individual's special contributions."

In giving examples of good leadership tactics, she shifted to the political frame: "I would say invest time out with the troops—with faculty, students, the administration. Be very close to the ground. Being liked is not trivial." And the president concluded by combining the symbolic and political models: "I am really good at being casual and talking to people, but I remain clear on what path we will go down. You need a leadership game plan. You can't get the long view if you constantly have your ear to the ground. But it is important for a leader to be a cheerleader, an affirmer."

This president showed a keen awareness of the four approaches and was able to switch from one to the other. From the outset, she framed the explanation in a bureaucratic perspective, for example, by stressing the importance of goal-setting and good management. But at the same time, we see a sensitivity to the importance of communication as a way of projecting an image of respect for others and flexibility in using their talents. So it is instructive to note that this president used collegial tactics symbolically, to temper the bureaucratic orientation.

Table 3 shows the frame combinations among the eight presidents espousing multi-frame theories. With three frames five different combinations were possible; however, all eight clustered in three combinations.

Table 3

Espoused Theories with a Multi-Frame Orientation	
Frames	Number
Bureaucratic/collegial/political/symbolic	1
Bureaucratic/collegial/political	2
Bureaucratic/political/symbolic	0
Bureaucratic/collegial/symbolic	0
Collegial/political/symbolic	5
Total	8

More than one-half of the multi-frame theories were a combination of collegial, political, and symbolic frames. Looking back at the paired-frame theories, we can see that these, like the multi-frame theories, had a similar distribution pattern, tending to cluster in collegial and symbolic frames and, less frequently, collegial and political pairings.

The excerpts included in this section illustrate ways in which the frames singly and in combination result in vastly different interpretations of good presidential leadership, and the data tables show the kinds of frame combinations most and least likely to occur within the pair- and multi-frame category. The data analysis presented thus far has focused on the distribution of the espoused theories in relation to frame content. The following section presents the results in terms of frame complexity (i.e., single versus multi-frame orientations) relating to two variables—institutional type and president's length of tenure.

Frame Analysis by Institutional Type

Table 4 shows the distribution of single, paired, and multi-frame theories by institutional type. The most striking aspect of the distribution is that universities, public comprehensive colleges, and independent colleges appear in all the three frames; community colleges, on the other hand, converge in single-frame theories.

Table 4

	Frame Analysis by Institutional Type		
	Single-Frame	Paired-Frame	Multi-Frame
Universities	2	3	3
Public colleges	3	3	2
Independent colleges	3	3	2
Community colleges	5	2	1
Total	13 (41%)	11 (34%)	8 (25%)

The five single-frame theories provided by community college presidents were spread out across three of the four frames. The bureaucratic and collegial frames were found in two each, and the symbolic frame in one. Nine of the eleven paired-frame theories were espoused in equal numbers by presidents of universities, public four-year colleges, and independent colleges. Both paired-frame theories espoused by community college presidents fell into the collegial and symbolic frames.

I found multi-frame orientations in only one-fourth of the espoused theories: one from a community college president; two each from presidents of public four-year colleges and independent colleges, and three from university presidents.

Frame Analysis and Presidents' Length of Tenure

The results of frame analysis by presidents' length of tenure, shown in Table 5, reveal different cluster patterns for old and new presidents. All but five of the old presidents espoused theories classified as paired or multi-frame. In contrast, one-half of the new presidents clustered, in the single-frame category. New presidents espousing single-frame theories came from three institutional types: three were presidents of community colleges, three of public four-year colleges, and two of independent colleges. Old presidents espousing single-frame theories included two from universities, two from community colleges, and one from an independent college.

Table 5

	Frame Categories and Presidents' Length of Tenure	
	Old*	New**
Single-frame	5	8
Paired-frame	6	5
Multi-frame	5	3
Total	16	16

*In office five or more years.

**In office one to three years.

There were three recently appointed presidents in the sample who had previously been presidents of at least one other institution. Notably, two of these espoused a multi-frame theory; the third one had a paired-frame theory. Only one of the three new presidents with a multi-frame theory was a first-time president.

Discussion

The findings show that the theories of leadership presidents espouse were more likely to have a single or paired-frame orientation than a multi-frame orientation. Multi-frame orientations may be unusual in presidents. Furthermore, multi-frame theories are more likely to be formed by integrating three rather than four frames. A four-frame orientation is probably exceptional, and few individuals may have the cognitive complexity and flexibility implied by this orientation.

The most distinct pattern emerging from the analysis by institutional type involves the distribution of community colleges and universities. Community colleges cluster in the single-frame category and universities in the paired- and multi-frame categories. Public and independent colleges are more uniformly distributed across the three frame categories.

Two factors might influence theories espoused by community college presidents to concentrate in the single-frame category. Structurally and administratively, community colleges are more closely aligned with the bureaucratic model of governance because of a high level of administrative dominance (Baldridge et al. 1978; Bensimon 1984; Reyes and Twombly 1987). But the results of this study do not support this commonly accepted view. Only two of the five community college presidents with a single frame had a bureaucratic orientation. The other three had either collegial or symbolic frames.

The finding that four out of the five single-frame theories espoused by community college presidents have either a bureaucratic or collegial orientation may reveal tendencies to view the organization as a closed system. Presidents of community colleges are perhaps prone to closed system views because decision-making is centralized; and they, rather than the faculty, control transactions with the external environment.

Furthermore, three of the five community college presidents with a single-frame orientation were recent appointees; and none of them had a bureaucratic orientation. The two who did had served in their positions for some time. Possibly, as George Vaughan (1986) had suggested, the newer generation of community college presidents favors leadership approaches encouraging greater participation and shared decision-making.

Results from this study showed that new presidents were likely to hold leadership theories with a single-frame orientation, while multi-frame views were found almost exclusively in old presidents and new appointees who had been presidents of at least one other college. Quite possibly the more experienced presidents have assimilated the potential complexities of their role and so can more easily shift among frames. Research studies of cognitive complexity and managerial experience show, as common sense would suggest, that the move toward greater complexity is developmental (Bartunek, Gordon, and Weathersby 1983).

Similarly, new managers take charge in a series of stages by performing progressively complex tasks (Gabarro 1987). These studies imply that cognitive complexity relates to experiential learning and the absence of multi-frame theories among new presidents relates to newness. A study of the pre- and postselection rhetoric of national presidential candidates has shown, for example, that their policy statements became more complex after their election (Tetlock 1983).

New college and university presidents may also initially appear to have a single-frame orientation because their espoused leadership theories reflect normative perceptions of the presidential role rather than their own experience. On the other hand, we could argue that few new presidents evolve into multi-frame leaders. For most, the presidency culminates their academic careers (Cohen and March 1974); their espoused theories of leadership (and their behavior) represent what has worked for them in the past. Thus, if presidents' past experiences and successes have had a single-frame orientation they may resist change, unless confronted with alternatives (Brookfield 1987).

Implications

The four-frame scheme used in this study is not in itself a novel approach to understanding leaders and leadership. But previous treatments have, for the most part, been highly abstract; consequently, only two kinds of manifestations, either the simplest single-frame level or the most complicated four-frame one, have generally been considered. This study makes it possible to look for all possible combinations and to uncover combinations not readily seen in more abstract treatments.

The three frame categories emerging from this study, and the finding that most espoused theories were concentrated in the single and paired-frames, aid us in understanding presidential leadership in higher education. Leading proponents of the four-frame/model concept suggest that qualitative differences exist among leaders with a single rather than a multi-frame perspective. Bolman and Deal assert that modern organizations are so complex that they cannot be understood from a single-frame perspective and that a single-frame perspective "is likely to produce error and self-imprisonment" (1984, 4) for the manager. They suggest that "managers who understand and use only one or two of the frames are like a highly specialized species: They may be well adapted to a very narrow environment but extremely vulnerable to changes in climate or competition" (1984, 278).

If multi-frame leadership is better suited to a turbulent environment, then quite a few presidents are not effective. Perhaps rather than looking for leaders who have successfully integrated the four frames into their leadership style, we should form executive teams whose members have complementary frame orientations to attain multi-frame leadership (Sayles 1979).

Questions raised as a result of exploring the cognitive lenses implicit in the theories of good leadership may help develop new understandings of presidential frames and their consequences for effective leadership.

Estella M. Bensimon is assistant director and research associate, Institutional Leadership Project, National Center for Postsecondary Governance and Finance at Teachers College, Columbia University.

References

Argyris, Chris, and Donald A. Schon. *Theory in Practice: Increasing Professional Effectiveness*. San Francisco: Jossey-Bass Publishers, 1975.

Baldridge, J. Victor. *Power and Conflict in the University*, New York: John Wiley and Sons, 1971.

Baldridge, J. Victor, David V. Curtis, George Ecker, and Gary L. Riley. *Policy Making and Effective Leadership: A National Study of Academic Management*. San Francisco: Jossey-Bass Publishers, 1978.

Bartunek, Jean M., Judith R. Gordon, and Rita Preszler Weathersby. "Developing 'Complicated' Understanding in Administrators." *Academy of Management Review* 8 (April 1983): 273–84.

Bensimon, Estela M. "Selected Aspects of Governance: An ERIC Review." *Community College Review* 12 (Fall 1984): 54–61.

Birnbaum, Robert. How Colleges Work: *The Cybernetics of Academic Organization and Leadership*. San Francisco: Jossey-Bass Publishers, 1988.

Birnbaum, Robert, Estela M. Bensimon, and Anna Neumann. "Leadership in Higher Education: A Multidimensional Approach to Research." *Review of Higher Education* 12, no. 2 (Winter 1989): 101–105.

Bolman, Lee G., and Terrence E. Deal. *Modern Approaches to Understanding and Managing Organizations*. San Francisco: Jossey-Bass Publishers, 1984.

Brookfield, Stephen. *Developing Critical Thinking*. San Francisco: Jossey-Bass Publishers, 1987.

Cohen, Michael D., and James G. March. *Leadership and Ambiguity: The American College President*. New York: McGraw-Hill Book Company, 1974.

Deal, Terrence E., and Allan A. Kennedy. *Corporate Cultures: The Rites and Rituals of Corporate Life*. Reading, Mass.: Addison-Wesley, 1982.

Dill, David D. "The Management of Academic Culture: Notes on the Management of Meaning and Social Integration." *Higher Education* 11 (May 1982): 303–20.

Fayol, H. "General Principles of Management." 1949. Reprint. In Pugh 1984, 135–56.

Gabarro, John J. *The Dynamics of Taking Charge*. Boston: Harvard Business School Press, 1987.

Goleman, Daniel. *Vital Lies, Simple Truths: The Psychology of Self-Deception*. New York: Simon and Schuster, Inc., 1985.

Kast, Fremont E., and James E. Rosenzweig. *Contingency Views of Organization and Management*. Chicago: Science Research Associates, 1973.

Kerr, Clark. *The Uses of The University*. Cambridge: Harvard University Press, 1963.

Likert, R. "The Principle of Supportive Relationships." 1961. Reprint. In Pugh 1984, 293–316.

Lombard, George F. F. Relativism in Organizations. *Harvard Business Review* 49 (March-April 1971): 55-65.

Mayo, E. "Hawthorne and the Western Electric Company." 1949. Reprint. In Pugh 1984, 279–92.

McGregor, D. "Theory X and Theory Y." 1960 Reprint. In Pugh 1984, 317–33.

Millett, John D. *The Academic Community: An Essay on Organization*. New York: McGraw-Hill, 1962.

Peters, Thomas J., and Robert Waterman, Jr. *In Search of Excellence: Lessons from America's Best-Run Companies*. New York: Harper and Row, 1982.

Pfeffer, Jeffrey. "Management as Symbolic Action: The Creation and Maintenance of Organizational Paradigms." In *Research in Organizational Behavior* 3, edited by L. L. Cummings and Barry M. Staw, 1–52. Greenwich, Conn.: Arjai Press, Inc., 1979.

Pugh, D. S., ed. *Organization Theory*. Middlesex, England: Penguin Books, Ltd., 1984.

Reyes, Pedro, and Susan B. Twombly. "Perceptions of Contemporary Governance in Community Colleges: An Empirical Study." *Community College Review* 14 (Winter 1986–87): 4–12.

Sayles, Leonard R. Leadership: *What Effective Managers Really Do ...And How They Do It*. New York: McGraw-Hill Book Company, 1979.

Schein, Edgar H. *Organizational Culture and Leadership*. San Francisco: Jossey-Bass, 1985.

Smircich, Linda, and Gareth Morgan. "Leadership: The Management of Meaning." *The Journal of Applied Behavioral Science* 18, no. 3 (1982): 257–73.

Taylor, F. W. "Scientific Management." 1947. Reprint. In Pugh 1984, 157–76.

Tetlock, Philip E. "Cognitive Style and Political Ideology." *Journal of Personality and Social Psychology* 45 (July 1983): 118–26.

Thompson, James D. *Organizations in Action*. New York: McGraw-Hill, Inc., 1967.

Vaughan, George B. *The Community College Presidency*. New York: ACE/MacMillan, 1986.

Walker, Donald E. *The Effective Administrator*. San Francisco: Jossey-Bass Publishers, 1979.

Weber, M. "Legitimate Authority and Bureaucracy." 1947. Reprint. In Pugh, 1984, 15–27.

Whetten, David A. "Effective Administrators: Good Management on the College Campus." *Change* 16 (November/December 1984): 38–43.

Symbolism and Presidential Perceptions of Leadership

WILLIAM G. TIERNEY

In the last decade, organizational researchers have shown considerable interest in the interpretive aspects of organizational life. Rather than viewing an organization as rational and objective, theorists have used the perspective that organizations are socially constructed and subjective entities. Symbolism has emerged as a critical theme. For example, Birnbaum (in press) has investigated the symbolic aspects of the academic senate, Pfeffer (1981) has considered management as symbolic action; and Tierney has undertaken a semiotic analysis of a private, liberal arts college (1987).

Researchers have also noted the significance of a leader's use of symbols. "The only thing of real importance that leaders do is to create and manage culture," asserts Edgar Schein. "The unique talent of leaders is their ability to work with culture" (1985, 2). Birnbaum has commented, "To emphasize the importance of leadership as myth and symbol is not to denigrate the role of leaders, but rather to identify a particularly critical function that they play" (1988, 208). If a central task of leadership is managing the symbolic aspects of the organization, then obviously it is helpful to investigate what leaders perceive leadership to be and what activities leaders perceive they have used to realize those perceptions.

This paper seeks to shed light on the discussion of leadership in higher education from the perspective of its symbolic dimensions. By investigating presidential perceptions of leadership using the National Center of Postsecondary Governance and Finance's Institutional Leadership Project, I developed a schema of symbolic categories leaders use to accomplish their goals. First, I consider leadership and symbolism from an interpretive perspective. Second, I discuss the methodology and how I developed the symbolic categories; I then incorporate the data used from the Institutional Leadership Project to examine the symbolic aspects of presidential perceptions of leadership. I conclude by discussing the implications for administrators of understanding the symbolism of their leadership.

Leadership and Symbolism

First, how does one think about a symbol? Second, how does symbolism enhance and help define leadership? Third, what constraints does the organization impose on a leader's use of symbols?

The Nature of Symbols

Organizational theorists (Dandridge, Mitroff, and Joyce 1980; Peters and Waterman 1982; Pettigrew 1979; Trice and Beyer 1984) have tended to view symbols either as objects or as reified objects that serve as vehicles for conveying meaning. I assume, however, that symbols connote more than objectivized meaning, and they are not simply vehicles in which meaning resides—tabernacles which hold institutional beliefs.

Symbols exist within an organization whether or not the organization's participants are aware of these symbols. To speak of organizations is to speak of interpretation and symbols. An organization void of symbolism is an organization bereft of human activity. Given that symbols exist wherever human activity occurs, a central question for researchers is how to define and uncover symbols in organizations. Particularly germane for this paper is how to interpret symbols of leadership.

Symbols reside in a wide variety of discursive and nondiscursive message units: an act, event, language, dress, structural roles, ceremonies, or even spatial positions in an organization. Hence, we must understand the context in which symbols function and how leaders communicate symbols to create and interpret their organizational reality.

Symbols and Leadership

As with any act of communication, the audience that receives a message must necessarily interpret what the message means. A manager who walks around a building, casually talking with subordinates, for example, may be considered a symbol of management's respect for everyone in the organization. Conversely, organizational participants may feel that the leader is "checking up" on everyone and that such symbolic behavior is intrusive.

Similarly, leaders who remain in their offices and, never converse informally with subordinates may symbolize in their business-oriented approach the message that formalized tasks, rules, and procedures are what the organization values. The point is not that a leader must use this or that trait to be an effective leader. Rather, I suggest that "management by walking around," as well as any other management strategy, is a symbolic act, open to interpretation. Indeed, a manager's informal style can symbolize any number of messages to different constituencies—friendship, accessibility, intrusiveness, or harassment, to name but a few possible interpretations.

As conscious or unconscious forms for participant understanding of the organization, symbols change and evolve due to historical ruptures, responses to the exterior environment, and individual influence. Individuals attach significance to any number of phenomena, and it is in the context of the organization itself that symbols acquire shared meaning. Thus, the key to understanding organizational symbols lies in delineating the symbolic forms whereby the participants communicate, perpetuate, and develop their knowledge about and attitudes toward life (Geertz 1973).

Conversely, symbolism enhances and helps define leadership. Clifford Geertz observes that leaders

> . . . justify their existence and order their actions in terms of a collection of stories, cere-
> monies, insignia, formalities, and appurtenances that they have either inherited . . . or
> invented. It is these—crowns and coronations, limousines and conferences—that mark the
> center as center and give what goes on there its aura of being not merely important but in
> some odd fashion connected with the way the world is built (1983, 124).

Symbolism is intertwined with participants' expectation and understanding of leadership. The symbolic role of a college or university president allows an individual to try to communicate a vision of the institution that other individuals are incapable of communicating. We understand leadership through such symbols as the president's yearly speech at convocation or, as will be shown, by a host of activities that "mark the center as center."

Organizational Constraints

Yet leaders are not entirely free to define what is or is not symbolic. Organizations channel activity and interpretation, constraining a leader's use of symbols. Merely because a college president intends for an open door to signify open communication does not assure that the faculty will so interpret it. Almost all leaders in higher education inherit organizations with a history; thus, the parameters of the organization's culture and ideology help fix not only what is or is not symbolic but also what that symbol signifies.

Organizational participants need to feel that they comprehend what is going on in the organization. To do so, they interpret abstractions, often following suggestions made by their leaders. Bailey notes, "We focus on some things and ignore others; we impose a pattern on the flow of events, and thus 'falsify' them if only by simplifying the diversity and the complexity . . . and so make the real world comprehensible" (1983, 18).

College presidents highlight some activities and ignore others; they employ a wide variety of symbolic forms to communicate their messages to different constituencies. To adequately understand how leaders make sense of the organizational universe for their followers, it is important to deconstruct the underlying conceptual orientations that presidents bring to their leadership roles and contexts. It is these concepts and ideologies that shape presidents' perceptions of their organizations and presidential actions within those organizations. Symbolism both defines leadership and is defined by the organization in which the leader resides.

Methodology and Data

Research teams collected data through on-site, semi-structured interviews with the presidents of thirty-two colleges and universities participating in the Institutional Leadership Project (ILP), a five-year longitudinal study conducted by the National Center for Postsecondary Governance and Finance. (For the purposes of the ILP and its purposive stratified sampling procedure, see Birnbaum, Bensimon, and Neumann 1989.)

Data for this paper comes from the presidents' responses to three analytical questions.

1. What is the meaning of "good" presidential leadership?
2. What have you done as a presidential leader?
3. What are you like as a presidential leader?

I reviewed the transcripts of presidential responses, looking especially for comments that were symbolic in nature. Building on previous discussions of what defines a symbol (Deal and Kennedy 1982; Eco 1979; Trice and Beyer 1984), I then disaggregated the data into six categories: metaphorical, physical, communicative, structural, personification, and ideational. These categories are not always mutually exclusive; a symbol may fail within more than one category or reinforce another symbolic category. Nor do these six categories necessarily cover all organizational symbols. This is an "essay" in the root sense of the word—a trial of some ideas.

It is also important to point out that I built the categories from previous work on symbolism. The presidents did not devise them. Needless to say, when presidents act they do not generally think, "I am now using a structural symbol." Indeed, one intent of this paper is to provide a provisional framework which presidents might use in reflecting on their leadership acts and thinking about the use of symbols.

In reviewing the data I neither found differences due to institutional type in how presidents symbolically perceived leadership nor did I find substantial differences between presidents appointed within the last three years and "old" presidents. Instead, I found similarities across type and between new and old presidents, as well as differences within type and among the same presidential generation. However, as we will see, what is particularly important when we analyze symbols in an organization is the manner and intention with which presidents use symbols. That is, two presidents may use the same symbolic form with the same frequency, but their purposes will be quite different.

The limitations of this study have already been referred to in the Introduction to these articles. We have analyzed presidents' responses but not the context surrounding those responses. That is, the data of this paper comes from the mouths of presidents. Analyzing the data of faculty and other constituents about their perceptions of presidential symbols is yet to come. It also was not my purpose to count or gradate the frequency of symbolic categories. Prior to such a task we will first need a clearer understanding of symbolic categories. What follows is a discussion of each category that highlights how presidents act symbolically.

Metaphorical Symbols

Metaphors are figures of speech. Presidents provide figures of speech for themselves, their organization, environment, and activities as if something were that particular other. The metaphors an individual uses provide participants with a portrait of how the organization functions. One president noted:

> My philosophy of leadership is to have a team approach to managing the university. The executive committee is a group that shares certain values and expectations, and we push each other hard for the good of the college. What is essential is that we have an effective team, and that we portray that to the board and the community.

Another individual consistently mentioned how it was important "to provide the glue" so that the organization "sticks together." And still another president spoke of organizational participants as "troops" that needed to be rallied.

Presidents also use different metaphors to describe themselves. "I am militaristic...like a football coach," observed one. "I am their counselor," commented another. And a third individual was a maestro: "Being president is like an orchestra conductor."

Metaphors give participants a way of seeing and, hence, of acting in the organizational universe. The organization where the participants see themselves as a team presumably interacts differently than the organization led by a general who commands troops. Similarly, an organization that needs glue is different from an organization where it is unimportant to stick together but where a prime metaphorical value concerns "everyone pulling his or her own weight."

Presidents perceive themselves as leaders in a multitude of ways. By focusing on particular metaphors, a president simplifies the organizational universe by providing an image of leadership and the organization. However, the success or failure of a metaphor as a strategy may depend on how the metaphor fits with the organization's culture. That is, a faculty that sees itself as an academy of scholars may rebel at the idea that they are troops being led by a general.

Physical Symbols

Physical symbols refer to objects that are meant to mean something other than what they really are and are perhaps the most common symbols. Artifacts are tangible examples of a particular message. However, as with all symbols, physical symbols may not signify what the leader intends. For example, one president said that getting personal computers for each faculty members made "a statement about the distinctiveness of the learning experience here. The purpose of this action was not to give PC's to the faculty but to set forth a philosophy, to make a statement that we are changing teaching here."

As the president notes, the intention was to make a statement with physical symbols. Clearly, on some campuses, alternative interpretations may exist. A humanities faculty might interpret the uninvited appearance of computers in their offices as the sciences' encroachment on their turf. A science faculty who already owned personal computers but worked in a building that needed renovation could interpret computers as a sign that the president was pandering to the liberal arts. The point is not that one interpretation is right and the other wrong, but rather that physical objects need to be seen within the context of the organization and its constituencies.

New libraries, attention to the grounds, a faculty club, school ties and scarves, and a host of other physical artifacts are designed as symbolic representations to various constituencies by presidents. Another president observed that the university had remained open when students took over the administration building. The president noted how the campus "carried on." By the president's symbolic use of space the president intended for the community to understand that the college was more than buildings and that, even under duress, the institution would continue.

Communicative Symbols

Communication entails not only symbolic acts of oral discourse but also written communicative acts and nonverbal activities that convey particular meanings from a president to a constituency. "I try to rub elbows with students and faculty on a regular basis," related one president. "I spend evenings in the student center. I try to make faculty council meetings, and I talk to faculty on campus." Another individual reported, "I call each of the faculty by their first name. During the year, all of them will be entertained in my home. I send birthday cards to all full-time faculty," noted a third leader. And a fourth commented:

> During a normal workday I will walk over to some other person's office maybe seven or eight times. It is really time consuming to be doing that, and I could save time by just picking up the phone. But I get mileage out of doing that, however, that is immeasur able . . . . I am visible.

Given the popularity of such texts as *In Search of Excellence* and *Corporate Cultures*, it is commonplace to hear leaders refer to their style as "management by walking around." And, indeed, many leaders do "walk around." As American organizations struggle to emulate what they perceive to be Japanese models of effectiveness and efficiency, communicative symbols serve as functional vehicles for organizational success.

Talking with students "on their turf," entertaining faculty, strolling around campus, or walking into offices are all presidential perceptions of symbolic communication. Most often, the symbol is meant to communicate presidential concern; presidents think of themselves as caring individuals when they talk with students about student concerns. To use yet another symbolic metaphor, presidents perceive themselves as understanding their constituencies when they know everyone's first name or send someone a birthday card.

Structural Symbols

Symbolic structures refer to institutional structures and processes that signify more than who reports to whom. Of the six symbolic forms mentioned in this paper, the structural form most often differentiates new presidents from old. New presidents, those in office three years or less, often feel the need to alter the organizational structure to signify change. Birnbaum has noted, "New presidents...may talk off the record to colleagues...and complain (but with a certain degree of pride), 'You wouldn't believe the mess I found when I got here, but I've finally begun to get it turned around'" (1986, 392). Although I have not uncovered any aggregated differences between new and old presidents' symbolic perceptions—including the structural form—within the structural form, I have found Birnbaum's comment correct. That is, the intent of new presidents differs from that of old presidents when they use the structural form.

New presidents tend to embrace decision-making structures as symbols of change more than individuals who have served in their positions longer. Although older presidents use structures as symbols, structures do not necessarily connote change. Instead they may imply any number of significations. Commented one new president: "I did not create the faculty council. It was here when I arrived. But under my predecessor, people on that council were selected by the president and it was an at-large position. I have changed that so that there is one faculty representative per division and they are elected by the faculty."

Another new president set up a task force primarily composed of senior faculty who helped the president create fundamental changes in the university. An older president said, "When I came in, I developed the traditional vice presidential offices. The first thing I did was to create a traditional administrative structure, an administrative team."

One new college president spoke indirectly about the symbolic implications of structural changes:

> I created two vice president positions—one for academic affairs and the other for public relations; I upgraded the dean of research to vice president. More reorganization took place at the deans' level too. I had to change the football coach and the athletic director. This situation enabled me to establish the fact that the president would be running the university, not the athletic director.

None of these examples, indeed, no examples of symbols in general, serve a singular purpose. When a president takes office, it is certainly conceivable that an administrative structure may be unsuitable to the president's style or needs. Changing such a structure may achieve particular goals. At the same time, by changing a structure the president also signals to the college community that life as it previously existed will change. From this perspective, the president's action accounts not only for structural change but also for the perception of change.

Borrowing from Merton (1957), Birnbaum (in press) has termed symbols such as those noted here as functionally "latent." Although structural change may produce needed outcomes, Birnbaum contends that some latent functions "are meeting less obvious, but still important, organizational needs." The findings from the data tend to suggest that new presidents use structural change in large part because of its latent function; they draw heavily on structural symbols to place their imprimatur on the institution.

Task forces may provide someone with good ideas and a different electoral system may be an improvement upon a previous system; but in essence, the president uses these devices to symbolize change. An older president commented, "During my rime, we have elaborated the administrative style of the university. [My predecessor] was more of a one-person operator." Again, the administrative structure had come into play as a presidential perception of structural change or evolution.

Personification Symbols

Symbolic personification refers to a leader's intent to represent a message with an individual or group. For example, on a national level, we often find political appointees who symbolize an elected leader's commitment to a particular constituency. President Reagan's appointing a woman to the Supreme Court was intended to symbolize his concern for women.

College presidents also perceive that particular groups or individuals symbolize particular messages to different communities. One president noted, "When we changed the governance structure, we put the president of the student government on [it]; and he or she is involved in everything we discuss. The individual is a full member of the administrative structure." Thus, the president perceived not only that the administrative structure symbolized a message but also that who sat on the governing body symbolized, in this case, concern for student ideas.

Another president commented about the rising quality of the student body and noted, "We have finally started getting the recognition we deserve to have." This recognition was that the Big Eight accounting firms had been recruiting on campus. The presence of major marketing companies symbolized a rise in the institution's quality.

One college president felt the need to emphasize "excellent teaching." A potent symbol was appointing "three campus deans and a VP who have all had teaching experience and have had department chair experience. And I told the deans that they were required to teach also." Thus, this president's perception of leadership was to use personal symbols as a means of reorienting the culture of the organization.

Presidents also see themselves as symbols of the institution. One president spoke for many: "I had to get out in the community because no one had been out there before. I wanted people to think of the college as entering a new era." The presidents' willingness to meet the public was perhaps the most tangible example of symbolic personification. Presidents are the university; or, at least, they perceive themselves to be.

Ideational Symbols

Ideas as symbols refer to images leaders convey about the mission and purpose of the institution. Presidents generate ideas that serve as symbolic ideologies about their institutions. Clark's (1980) concept of an institutional saga is a cogent example of an ideational symbol by which leaders attempt to seize a unique role for their institution. A president perceives that leadership is often inextricably bound up with the symbolic generation of an institutional mission or ideology.

Ideational symbols are often the most difficult symbols for constituents to interpret if the symbol is divorced from tangible contexts. That is, particular ideas that presidents perceive as important may appear to be no more than presidential rhetoric to a constituency if the symbol cannot be palpably interpreted to them.

"I wanted a new image, a comprehensive quality," commented one leader. A second downgraded the importance of football at the institution:

> The first statement I would make as president would be about athletics, and I knew that it would be heard throughout all the towns and cities. I wanted it to be a statement not about athletics but about what the institution would be and do in the future. I want us to be known for great education and not great athletics. I wanted it to be a statement about the kind of students we want.

The images that presidents struggle to convey to their constituencies are symbolic representations of institutional values. What a president perceives to be the value of the institution is oftentimes what the institution will struggle to achieve. By definition, an institution with a unique identity cannot be all things to all people. The symbolic idea serves as the unifying principle for the organization. Many colleges and universities are committed to distinctive ideas. College presidents who emphasize one idea over another impart to constituents what they believe to be the primary goal of the institution.

Discussion

I offer organizational leaders three suggestions about the symbolic aspects of leadership. Rather than formulaic prescriptions of how to function in the organizational universe, I tender three proposals for understanding one's own perceptions and the culture in which one operates. The suggestions are components of a diagnostic frame of reference, a way of interpreting one's organization. I propose ways for leaders to identify what they must do to comprehend the symbolic dimensions of their leadership.

1. SYMBOLS DEMAND CORROBORATION

As noted, the research team queried the presidents about how they defined good leadership and what they had done as leaders. The interviews revealed several contradictions between what the individuals used as a symbol and how they acted. That is, on occasion discrepancies existed between what leaders perceive as good leadership and how they actually act.

One president who believes in visibility, for example, meets formally with the faculty only once a year. Another president's ideational symbol was "excellence" and to be known as a top-rate institution yet later in the interview spoke of institutional survival as the top priority. A third president cited the faculty council as a structural-personal symbol to communicate the critical importance of the faculty, yet no formal vehicles existed whereby the president actually met with them. Still another president tried to communicate symbolically that open, frank discussion was extremely important yet simultaneously demanded "extraordinary loyalty" to the president.

The point is not that individuals seek to deceive their constituencies. Instead, leaders should be aware of how symbolic forms may contradict one another. Walking around a campus or stressing "teamwork" does not necessarily confirm that collegiality exists. Leaders need to contextualize their perceptions and search for contradictions. We all have discrepancies between what we say and what we do. For an organizational leader, greater consistency between words and deeds allows followers a clearer understanding of a leader's intention.

2. USE SYMBOLS CONSISTENT WITH THE ORGANIZATION'S CULTURE

The culture of an organization is a social construction, dependent not only on the perceptions of a leader but also on the unique history of the organization, the individual orientations and perceptions of followers, and larger environmental influences. The cultural paradigm assumes that an organization does not consist of rational, "real" entities (Tierney 1988).

Everyday existence is a constant matter of interpretation among organizational participants. Rather than assume a functional view of symbols and a passive view of individuals, we need to reconceptualize culture as an interpretive dynamic whereby a leader's symbols may or may not be interpreted the way he or she intended. Thus, dissonance will occur even when a president's symbols corroborate each other if he or she has used symbols that are inconsistent with the organization's culture.

A new president, for example, may want to symbolize care and concern for the faculty and structurally reorganize the decision-making process, adding councils and committees to make it more participative. The president's perception and symbolic intent is to highlight a structural symbol. The strategy may fail, however, if the culture has relied for a generation on presidential informality and one-on-one conversations with faculty.

The challenge for the president is not only to search for contradictions in symbolic forms but also to understand how those symbolic forms exist within the organization's culture. If symbols are neither reified nor functional, then we must necessarily investigate their contextual surroundings to understand them.

3. USE ALL SYMBOLIC FORMS

Leaders, not unlike most individuals, are intuitively aware that particular objects or activities are highly imbued with symbolism. This essay has reported on the use of new buildings or new computers to convey a message. Similarly, the well-read manager today believes that management tips about communication hold symbolic value.

Yet as we have seen, leaders may employ a wide array of symbolic forms. Within each category exist a potential multitude of symbols. Further, an abundance of activities, acts, and the like also exist within a symbolic form. Rather than rely on the symbolic content of a single convocation speech every year, a president might benefit from employing a wide array of consistent symbolic forms. We tend to compartmentalize activities to simplify them, yet that is not how organizational participants experience reality.

All acts within an organization are open to interpretation. Virtually everything a leader does or says (or does not do or say) is capable of symbolic intent or interpretation. To acknowledge the pervasiveness of symbols in an organization does not imply that a leader is in charge of an anarchic organization that interprets messages any way it wants. Instead, a central challenge for the leader is to interpret the culture of the organization and to draw upon all of the symbolic forms effectively so that organizational participants can make sense of organizational activities.

Conclusion

A symbolic view of leadership and organizations needs to move beyond functionalist definitions of organizational symbolism. We need to pay attention to the processes whereby organizational members interpret the symbolic activities of leaders, rather than assume that all individuals march to the same organizational beat. We need to investigate why a particular symbol may be potent in one organization at one particular time and relatively useless in another organization.

The assumption at work in this paper has been that, although both the structure and expressions of colleges and universities change, the inner necessities that drive them do not. "Thrones may be out of fashion," states Geertz, "and pageantry too; but authority still requires a cultural frame in which to define itself and advance its claims" (1983, 143). If symbolism helps define authority, then we should continue the quest to understand the symbolic manifestations of organizational life and leadership.

William G. Tierney is assistant professor and research associate, Center for the Study of Higher Education, Pennsylvania State University.

This document was prepared with financial support from the Office of Educational Research and Improvement/Department of Education (OERI/ED). However, the opinions expressed herein do not necessarily reflect the position, policy, or official endorsement of the OERI/ED.

References

Bailey, Frederick George. *The Tactical Uses of Passion.* Ithaca, NY: Cornell University Press, 1983.

Birnbaum, Robert. *How Colleges Work: The Cybernetics of Academic Organization and Leadership.* San Francisco: Jossey-Bass Publishers, 1988.

————. "Leadership and Learning." *Review of Higher Education* 9, no. 4 (1986): 381–95.

————. "The Latent Organizational Functions of the Academic Senate." *Journal of Higher Education* in press.

Birnbaum, Robert, Estela M. Bensimon, and Anna Neumann. "Leadership in Higher Education: A Multidimensional Approach to Research." *Review of Higher Education* 12, no. 2 (Winter 1989): 101–105.

Clark, Burton R. "The Making of an Organizational Saga." In *Readings in Managerial Psychology,* edited by Harold J. Leavitt and Louis R. Pondy. Chicago: University of Chicago Press, 1980.

Dandridge, Thomas C., Ian Mitroff, and William F. Joyce. "Organizational Symbolism: A Topic to Expand Organizational Analysis." *Academy of Management Review* 5, no. 1 (1980): 77–82.

Deal, Terrence, and Allan A. Kennedy. *Corporate Cultures: The Rites and Rituals of Corporate Life.* Reading, Mass.: Addison-Wesley, 1982.

Eco, Umberto. *A Theory of Semiotics.* Bloomington: Indiana University Press, 1979.

Geertz, Clifford. *The Interpretation of Cultures.* New York City: Basic Books, 1973.

————. "Reflections on the Symbolics of Power." In *Local Knowledge,* edited by Clifford Geertz. New York City: Basic Books, 1983.

Merton, Robert K. *Social Theory of Social Structure.* Glencoe, Ill.: Free Press, 1957.

Peters, Thomas J., and Robert H. Waterman, Jr. *In Search of Excellence.* New York: Harper and Row, 1982.

Pettigrew, Andrew M. "On Studying Organizational Cultures." *Administrative Science Quarterly* 24 (1979): 570–81.

Pfeffer, Jeffrey. "Management as Symbolic Action." In *Research in Organizational Behavior,* edited by Larry L. Cummings & Barry Staw. Greenwich, Conn.: JAI Press, 1981.

Schein, Edgar H. *Organizational Culture and Leadership.* San Francisco: Jossey-Bass Publishers, 1985.

Tierney, William G. "The Semiotic Aspects of Leadership: An Ethnographic Perspective." *The American Journal of Semiotics* 5, no. 1 (1987): 223–50. In press-a.

————. "Organizational Culture in Higher Education: Defining the Essentials." *Journal of Higher Education* 59, no. 1 (1988): 2–21. In press-b.

Trice, Harrison M., and Janice M. Beyer. "Studying Organizational Cultures through Rites and Ceremonials." *Academy of Management Review* 9 (1984): 653–69.

Administrative and Professional Authority

Amitai Etzioni

The ultimate source of the organizational dilemmas reviewed up to this point is the incomplete matching of the personalities of the participants with their organizational roles. If personalities could be shaped to fit specific organizational roles, or organizational roles to fit specific personalities, many of the pressures to displace goals, much of the need to control performance, and a good part of the alienation would disappear. Such matching is, of course, as likely as an economy without scarcity and hence without prices. But even if all the dilemmas which result from the incomplete articulation of personality and organization were resolved, there still would remain those which are consequences of conflicting tendencies built into the organizational structure.

Probably the most important structural dilemma is the inevitable strain imposed on the organization by the use of knowledge. All social units use knowledge, but organizations use more knowledge more systematically than do other social units. Moreover, most knowledge is created in organizations and passed from generation to generation — i.e., preserved — by organizations. It is here that Weber overlooked one necessary distinction: He viewed bureaucratic or administrative authority as based on technical knowledge or training; the subordinates, he thought, accept rules and orders as legitimate because they consider being rational being right, and regard their superiors as more rational.[1] One is not "stretching" Weber much to suggest that he thought that the higher the rank of an official the better equipped he tends to be either in terms of formal education e.g., academic degrees or in terms of merit and experience. Examinations and promotion according to merit, Weber pointed out, help to establish such association between rank and knowledge. To a degree, this conception is valid. There is considerable evidence that persons who have only a high-school education will be more frequently found in lower ranks, and college-educated persons in the higher ones. There is probably some correlation between IQ and rank, in the sense that on the average the IQ of the top third of an organization is likely to be higher than that of the lowest third. One could argue that when the superiority-of-knowledge requirement is not fulfilled, when the higher in rank knows less or has a lower IQ than the lower in rank, his orders might still be followed because of his power to enforce them; but Weber would counter that such orders would not be considered legitimate and hence the official would have power but not authority.

Still the reader is correct in his intuition that there is something fundamentally wrong with the notion of viewing the bureaucracy as a hierarchy in which the more rational rule the less rational. There are two reasons. First, by far most of the trained members of the organization are found not in the highest but in the middle ranks, and not in the regular line or command positions but around them. Depending on the type of organization, they are referred to as experts, staff, professionals, specialists, or by the names of their respective professions. Second, the most basic principle of administrative authority and the most basic principle of authority based on knowledge — or professional authority — not only are not identical but are quite incompatible.

Administrative vs. Professional Authority

Administration assumes a power hierarchy. Without a clear ordering of higher and lower in rank, in which the higher in rank have more power than the lower ones and hence can control and coordinate the latter's activities, the basic principle of administration is violated; the organization ceases to be a coordinated tool. However, knowledge is largely an individual property; unlike other organization means, it cannot be transferred from one person to another by decree. Creativity is basically individual and can only to a very limited degree be ordered and coordinated by the superior in rank. Even the application of knowledge is basically an individual act, at least in the sense that the individual professional has the ultimate responsibility for his professional decision. The surgeon has to decide whether or not to operate. Students of the professions have pointed out that the autonomy granted to professionals who are basically responsible to their consciences (though they may be censured by their peers' and in extreme cases by the courts) is necessary for effective professional work. Only if immune from ordinary social pressures and free to innovate, to experiment, to take risks without the usual social repercussions of failure, can a professional carry out his work effectively. It is this highly individualized principle which is diametrically opposed to the very essence of the organizational principle of control and coordination by superiors — i.e., the principle of administrative authority. In other words, the ultimate justification for a professional act is that it is, to the best of the professional's knowledge, the right act. He might consult his colleagues before he acts, but the decision is his. If he errs, he still will be defended by his peers. The ultimate justification of an administrative act, however, is that it is in line with the organization's rules and regulations, and that it has been approved — directly or by implication — by a superior rank.

The Organization of Knowledge

The question is how to create and use knowledge without undermining the organization. Some knowledge is formulated and applied in strictly private situations. In the traditional professions, medicine and law, much work is carried out in non-organizational contexts — in face-to-face interaction with clients. But as the need for costly resources and auxiliary staff has grown, even the traditional professions face mounting pressures to transfer their work to organizational structures such as the hospital and the law firm. Similarly, while most artistic work is still conducted in private contexts, often in specially segregated sectors of society in which an individual's autonomy is particularly high, much of the cognitive creativity, particularly in scientific research, has become embedded in organizational structures for reasons similar to those in medicine and law.

In addition there are several professions in which the amount of knowledge (as measured in years of training) and the degree of personal responsibility (as measured in the degree to which privileged communications — which the recipient is bound not to divulge — or questions of life and death are involved) are lower than in the older or highly creative, cognitive professions. Engineering and nursing are cases in point. These professions can be more easily integrated into organizational structures than can medicine or law, for example. Most professional work at this level is carried out within organizations rather than in private practice, and it is more given to supervision by persons higher in rank (who have more administrative authority but no more, or even less, professional competence) than the work of the professions discussed above.

To some degree, organizations circumvent the problem of knowledge by "buying" it from the outside, as when a corporation contracts for a market study from a research organization; i.e., it specifies the type of knowledge it needs and it agrees with the research group on price, but then it largely withdraws from control over the professional work. There are, however, sharp limitations on the extent to which knowledge can be recruited in this way, particularly since organizations consume such large amounts of knowledge and they tend to need more reliable control on its nature and flow. There are three basic ways in which knowledge is handled within organizations:

1. Knowledge is produced, applied, preserved, or communicated in organizations especially established for these purposes. These are *professional organizations*, which are characterized not only by the goals they pursue but also by the high proportion of professionals on their staff (at least 50 per cent) and by the authority relations between professionals and non-professionals which are so structured that professionals have superior authority over the major goal activities of the organization, a point which is explored below. Professional organizations include universities, colleges, most schools, research organizations, therapeutic mental hospitals, the larger general hospitals, and social-work agencies. For certain purposes it is useful to distinguish between those organizations employing professionals whose professional training is long (5 years or more), and those employing professionals whose training is shorter (less than 5 years). The former we call *full-fledged professional* organizations; the latter, *semi-professional* organizations. Generally associated with differences in training of the professionals in these two types of organizations are differences in goals, in privileges, and in concern with matters of life and death. "Pure" professional organizations are primarily devoted to the creation and application of knowledge; their professionals are usually protected in their work by the guarantee of privileged communication, and they are often concerned with matters of life and death. Semi-professional organizations are more concerned with the communication and, to a lesser extent, the application of knowledge, their professionals are less likely to be guaranteed the right of privileged communications, and they are rarely directly concerned with matters of life and death.
2. There are *service organizations* in which professionals are provided with the instruments, facilities, and auxiliary staff required for their work. The professionals however are not employed by the organization nor subordinated to its administrators.
3. Professionals may be employed by organizations whose goals are *non-professional*, such as industrial and military establishments. Here professionals are often assigned to special divisions or positions, which to one degree or another take into account their special needs.

We shall first discuss the relation between the two authority principles — that of knowledge and that of administration — in non-professional organizations, then in "full-fledged" professional organizations, in semiprofessional organizations, and finally in service organizations.

Professional Authority in Non-professional Organizations

Superiority of Administrative Authority

By far the largest and most common non-professional organizations are the production organizations which are privately owned and managed. The organizational goal of private business is to make profits. The major means are production and exchange. While professionals deal with various aspects of the production and exchange process — that is, with means such as engineering, quality control, and marketing — the manager (the corporation's equivalent of the administrator) is expected to coordinate the various activities in such a way that the major organizational goal — profit-making — will be maximized. This seems to be one of the reasons why modern corporations prefer to have as top executives people with administrative experience rather than professionals. (In a study of the occupational backgrounds of the chief executives of American industry in 1950, administration was found to have been the principal occupation of 43.1 per cent; 11.8 per cent were defined as entrepreneurs; finance had been the field of 12.4 per cent; and only 12.6 per cent had been engineers.[2] People with scientific backgrounds such as research workers are even less likely to become heads of private business. Only about 4 per cent of the presidents of American corporations had such a background.[3])

In general, the goals of private business are consistent with administrative orientations. The economic orientation of the organization and the bureaucratic orientation of the administrative role share an orientation toward rational combination of means and development of rational procedures to maximize goals which are considered as given. The social and cultural conditions that support modern economic activities also support modern administration (see below, Ch. 10). Professional and economic orientations are less compatible.

When people with strong professional orientations take over managerial roles, a conflict between the organizational goals and the professional orientation usually occurs. Homans reports an interesting case in which the influence of professionally oriented participants was greater than in most corporations.[4] He discusses an electrical equipment company which was owned, managed, and staffed by engineers. Management, which was in the hands of administration-oriented engineers, suffered from pressure to pursue uneconomic goals by the professionally oriented design engineers. The design engineers were charged with being indifferent to the "general welfare of the company" — that is, to profit-making — as "shown by their lack of concern with finance, sales, and the practical needs of the consumer and by their habit of spending months on an aspect of design that had only theoretical importance." This caused considerable tension between the managerial and professionally oriented groups, tension to which this company was especially sensitive because of its high dependence on professional work and the special structure of ownership. A power struggle resulted which ended with a clearer subordination of the design engineers (staff) to the managerial engineers (line). This was mandatory "if the company was to survive and increase its sales," as Homans put it. The treasurer (a non-professional in this context) became the most influential member of the new management. In short, in a corporation where the professionals exerted a strong influence, the existence of the organization was threatened, considerable internal tension was generated, and finally the organizational power structure was changed toward a more usual structure, with the professionally minded more clearly subordinated. In other words, the organizational authority structure was made more compatible with the goals of the organization. The orientations of the managers and the goals of private business seem to match. When a professional orientation dominates, this tends to "displace" the profit goal of privately owned economic organizations.

Staff and Line

The way the two kinds of authority are combined in corporations and other non-professional organizations is often referred to as "staff and line." The managers, whose authority is administrative, direct the major goal activities; the professionals deal with knowledge as a means, and with the knowledge aspect of other means. They are in a subordinate position to the managers. Thus, in cases of conflict between the two criteria for decision-making, the organizational power structure is slanted in favor of the administrative authority. However, professional subordinates are treated differently from regular subordinates; they are not treated as are lower ranks in a line structure, but as "staff," a term which designates positions outside the regular chain of command or "line" and implies a certain amount of autonomy.

There are two interpretations of the relationship between staff and line. According to one approach, the staff has no administrative authority whatsoever. It advises the administrators (line authority) on what action to take. The staff does not issue orders to those lower in rank; if it desires any action or correction, this must be achieved through those in the line rank. According to the second approach, the staff, while advising the line on various issues, also takes responsibility for limited areas of activity.[5] That is, on some matters the staff directly issues orders to the lower participants.

Both combinations of the two authority principles generate considerable strain. In the first, where the line alone issues orders, the line tends to be overloaded by demands for decisions, and tends to repel at least some of the professional advice and requests for action of the staff. Line personnel have a large number of other functional requirements they must look after. They rarely comprehend fully the bases of actions requested by the staff, and they tend to neglect or at least to under-represent the staff demands. In the second approach the lower line is subordinated to two authorities at a time. There is a functional division of control between the two authorities, in the sense that professional matters are assigned to staff control and all the others to line control. In practice, while there are some matters that fall clearly into one category or the other, many issues can be viewed as either professional or administrative matters or both. This leads to the issuance of conflicting orders and gives the lower in rank the opportunity to play one authority against the other.

Dalton called attention to the tendencies of the higher- and lower-ranking line personnel to form a coalition against the staff personnel. He found the reason in the sociological differences that unite the line against the staff. The staff is generally younger and much more likely to be college-educated than the line, although the latter have greater organizational experience and hence resent advice and suggestions from the relatively inexperienced staff. Furthermore, the two groups are divided by differences in patterns of speech and dress, recreational preferences, etc.[6] In these areas, the higher-ranking line is often closer to the lower-ranking line than to the staff. Thus the tensions between staff and line derive not only from the organizational conflicts resulting from overloading or lack of clear division of authority, but also from differences in sociological background. (These differences might decline as more and more higher line officials gain college education, or a new division might emerge between the A.B. and B.S. on the one hand, and the Ph.D.'s on the other.)

In spite of important differences between the two approaches, staff authority in both is subordinate to line authority and the line is identified with administrative authority and the staff with professional authority. While it is obvious that there are some staff functions which are not carried out by professionals, and that there are some professionals among the line personnel, there is a high correlation between staff and professionals, and between line and non-professionals.

In organizations whose goal is non-professional (e.g., profit-making), it is considered desirable for administrators to have the major (line) authority because they direct the major goal activity. Professionals deal only with means, with secondary activities. Therefore it is functional for the organization that they have no, or only limited (staff), authority, and they be ultimately subordinated to administrators. This generally is the case in corporations and armies.

Professionals in Professional Organizations

In full-fledged professional organizations the staff-professional line-administrator correlation, insofar as such distinctions apply at all, is reversed. Although administrative authority is suitable for the major goal activities in private business, in professional organizations administrators are in charge of secondary activities; they administer *means* to the major activity carried out by professionals. In other words, to the extent that there is a staff-line relationship at all, professionals should hold the major authority and administrators the secondary staff authority. Administrators offer advice about the economic and organizational implications of various activities planned by the professionals. The final decision is, functionally speaking, in the hands of the various professionals and their decision-making bodies, such as committees and boards. The professor decides what research he is going to undertake and to a large degree what he is going to teach; the physician determines the treatment to be given to the patient.

Administrators may raise objections. They may point out that a certain drug is too expensive or that a certain teaching policy will decrease the number of students in a way that endangers the financing of a university. But functionally the professional is the one to decide on his discretion to what degree these administrative considerations should be taken into account. It is interesting to note that some of the complaints usually made against professionals in non-professional organizations are made against administrators in professional organizations: They are said to lose sight of the major goal of the organization in pursuit of their specific limited responsibilities. Professionals in private business are sometimes criticized as being too committed to science, craftsmanship, and abstract ideas; administrators in professional organizations are deprecated because they are too committed to their specialties —"efficiency" and economy.

Many of the sociological differences between professionals and managers in private business are reversed in professional organizations. Professionals enter professional organizations younger and at lower positions (i.e., as students, research assistants, or interns) than managers do. The range of mobility of administrators is usually relatively limited, and a professional is more likely to reach the top position of institutional head.

In private business, overinfluence by professionals threatens the realization of organizational goals and sometimes even the organization's existence. In professional organizations overinfluence by the administration, which takes the form of ritualization of means, undermines the goals for which the organization has been established and endangers the conditions under which knowledge can be created and institutionalized (as, for instance, academic freedom).

Who Is Superior?

Heading a professional organization constitutes a special dilemma. It is a typical case of institutionalized role conflict.[7] On the one hand, the role should be in the hands of a professional in order to ensure that the commitments of the head will match organizational goals. A professional at the head of the authority structure will mean that professional activity is recognized as the major goal activity, and that the needs of professionals will be more likely to receive understanding attention. On the other hand, organizations have needs that are unrelated to their specific goal activity. Organizations have to obtain funds to finance their activities, recruit personnel to staff the various functions, and allocate the funds and personnel which have been recruited. Organizational heads must know how to keep the system integrated by giving the right amount of attention and funds to the various organizational needs, including secondary needs. A professional may endanger the integration of the professional organization by over-emphasizing the major goal activity and neglecting secondary functions. He may lack skill in human relations. In short, the role of head of professional organizations requires two incompatible sets of orientations, personal characteristics, and aptitudes. If the role is performed by either a lay administrator or a typical professional, one set of considerations is likely to be emphasized to the neglect of the other.

The severity of the dilemma is increased because of the motivational pattern of typical professionals. Most successful professionals are not motivated to become administrators. Some would refuse any administrative role, including the top one of university president or hospital chief, because of their commitment to professional values and ties to professional groups, and because they feel that they would not be capable of performing the administrative role successfully. Even those professionals who would not reject the distinguished and powerful role of organizational head avoid the administrative roles that are training grounds for and channels of mobility to these top positions. Thus many academicians refuse to become deans, not to mention associate or assistant deans, and try to avoid if possible the role of department chairman. Those who are willing to accept administrative roles are often less committed to professional values than their colleagues,[8] or view it as a transitional status, not a career. The same can be said about administrative appointments in hospitals. For instance, in the mental hospital studied by Stanton and Schwartz, the role of administrative psychiatrist is fulfilled at the beginning of the training period.[9] It is considered an undesirable chore that must be endured before turning to the real job. Psychiatrists who complete their training tend to withdraw to private practice. From other studies, especially those of state mental hospitals, it appears that those who stay are often less competent and less committed to professional values than those who leave.

The Professionally Oriented Administrator

There are various solutions to this dilemma. By far the most widespread one is the rule of the professionally oriented administrator. Such an administrator is one who combines a professional education with a managerial personality and practice. Goal as well as means activities seem to be handled best when such a person is the institutional head. Because of his training, he is more likely to understand the special needs of a professional organization and its staff than a lay administrator, and, because of his personal characteristics, he is more likely to be skilled in handling the needs and requests of his professional colleagues as well as those of the administrative staff.

There are two major sources of professionally oriented administrators. One is the professionals themselves. Some feel that they have little chance of becoming outstanding professionals in their field. Often the same people find that they are relatively more skilled in administrative activities. Thus they gravitate toward administrative jobs by serving on committees and by assuming minor administrative roles; some eventually become top administrators. Contrary to the popular belief, most university presidents are former professors. Wilson found that out of the 30 universities he studied, 28 had presidents who bad been professors, albeit none a very eminent scholar.[10] It seems that academicians who are inclined to take administrative jobs, or who are organization-oriented, not only publish less in quantity and quality after they have entered administrative positions but also tended to publish less before they accepted such jobs.

Of the heads of mental hospitals studied, 74.2 per cent are physicians.[11] Although there is no study on their professional eminence as compared to that of private practitioners, it seems that the heads of mental hospitals do not include the most successful psychiatrists. Only about 22 per cent of the heads of general hospitals are physicians. Where these are full-time jobs, the statement made about the heads of mental hospitals seems to apply here also.

The second source of professionally-oriented administrators is special training. In recent years there has been a movement toward developing training programs for specialized administration, such as hospital administration and research administration. A considerable number of teachers, for example, return to universities to take courses in administrative education before they become school principals.

The advantages of specialized administrators over lay administrators are obvious. They are trained for their particular role and have considerable understanding of the organization in which they are about to function before they enter it. They are sensitized to the special tensions of working with professionals, and they share some of their professional values. On the other hand, they are less prepared for their role than the professionally oriented administrators from the first source who have a deeper commitment to professional values, command more professional respect, and have a greater number of social ties with professionals.

Although most professional organizations are controlled by professional or professionally oriented administrators, some are controlled by lay administrators. By lay administrators we mean administrators who have no training in serving the major goal activities of the organization. This holds for 2 out of the 30 universities studied by Wilson, for fewer than 10 per cent of the schools, for 20.5 per cent of the mental hospitals, and for about 38 per cent of the general hospitals. (Wilson's study is small, the other data is based on large populations).

The strain created by lay administrators in professional organizations leads to goal displacement. When the hierarchy of authority is in inverse relation to the hierarchy of goals and means, there is considerable danger that the goals will be subverted. Of course there are many other factors which may have such a distorting influence; but lay administrators are more likely to cause displacement than are other administrators.

Notes

[1]Max Weber (Talcott Parsons, ed.; A. M. Henderson and Talcott Parsons, trans.), *The Theory of Social and Economic Organization* (New York: Oxford University Press, 1947), p. 339

[2]M. Newcomer, *The Big Business Executive* (New York: Columbia University Press, 1955), p. 92.

[3] See G. H. Copeman, *Leaders of British Industry* (London: Gee and Co., 1955).

[4]George C. Homans, *The Human Group* (New York: Harcourt, Brace, 1950), pp. 369-414.

[5] On the two approaches, see H. A. Simon, D. W. Smithburg, and V. A. Thompson, *Public Administration* (New York: Knopf, 1956), pp. 280-295; and A. W. Gouldner, *Patterns of Industrial Bureaucracy* (Glencoe, Ill.: The Free Press, 1954), pp. 224-228.

[6] Melville Dalton, "Conflicts Between Staff and Line Managerial Officers," *American Sociological Review* (1950), 15:342-351.

[7] By role we mean the behavior expected from a person in the particular position. Seeman, "Role Conflict and Ambivalent Leadership," *American Sociological Review* (1953), 18:373-380.

[8] A. W. Gouldner, "Cosmopolitans and Locals: Toward an Analysis of Latent Social Roles," *Administrative Science Quarterly* (1957), 2:281-306. For a more recent study, see Barney C. Glaser, "Attraction, Autonomy, and Reciprocity in the Scientist-Supervisor Relations," *Administrative Science Quarterly* (1963), 8-379-398.

[9] A. H. Stanton and M. S. Schwartz, *The Mental Hospital* (New York: Basic Books, 1954).

[10] L. Wilson, *The Academic Man* (New York: Oxford University Press, 1942), p. 85.

[11] L. Block, "Ready Reference Of Hospital Facts," *Hospital Topics* (1956), 34:23.

Faculty Organization and Authority

BURTON R. CLARK

As we participate in or study various faculties in American higher education, we observe decisions being made through informal interaction among a group of peers and through collective action of the faculty as a whole. Formal hierarchy plays little part, and we have reason to characterize the faculty as a collegium.[1] At the same time we sense that what we now observe is not a counterpart of the collegiality of the days of old. The modern faculty in the United States is not a body to be likened to the guilds of the medieval European university,[2] or to the self-government of a dozen dons in a residential college at Oxford or Cambridge,[3] or to the meagre self-rule that was allowed the faculty in the small liberal art's college that dominated American higher education until the end of the last century.[4] The old-time collegium has modern reflections, as in the Fellowships of the colleges at Yale, but for the most part it is no longer winningly with us, and the kind of collegiality we now find needs different conceptualization. We also observe on the modern campus that information is communicated through formal channels, responsibility is fixed in formally-designated positions, interaction is arranged in relations between superiors and subordinates, and decisions are based on written rules. Thus we have reason to characterize the campus as a bureaucracy. But, at the same time, we sense that this characterization overlooks so much that it becomes misleading. Though the elements of bureaucracy are strong, they do not dominate the campus; and though they grow, their growth does not mean future dominance if other forms of organization and authority are expanding more rapidly.

The major form of organization and authority found in the faculties of the larger American colleges and universities, and toward which many small campuses are now moving, is now neither predominantly collegial nor bureaucratic. Difficult to characterize, it may be seen as largely "professional," but professional in a way that is critically different from the authority of professional men in other organizations such as the business corporation, the government agency, and the hospital. To approach this unusual pattern, we will first discuss trends in the organization and culture of the campus as a whole and then turn to the related trends in the organization and authority of the faculty.

We begin with broad changes in the nature of the campus because they condition the structure of authority. Authority is conditioned, for example, by the nature of work, the technology of an organization. The mass assembly of automobiles does not allow much personal discretion on the part of the worker; surgery in the hospital operating room requires on-the-spot judgment and autonomous decision by the surgeon and one or two colleagues. To understand faculty authority, we need some comprehension of what academic work has in common with work in other settings and how it differs from work elsewhere. Authority is also conditioned by patterns of status. Status comes in part from formal assignment, hence men called deans usually have much of it, but status is also derived in academia from one's standing in a discipline, and this important source of status is independent of the official scheme.[5] Authority is also conditioned by traditional sentiments. Legends and ideologies have a force of their own. Conceptions of what should be are formed by what has been or by ideals handed down through the generations. The stirring ideologies of community of scholars and academic freedom are forces to be reckoned with when one is dealing with faculties and in understanding their organization. Thus, the work itself, the status system, the traditional sentiments, all affect authority.

Trends in the Social Organization of the Campus

Four trends in the campus, closely related, are as follows: unitary to composite or federal structure; single to multiple value systems; non-professional to professional work; consensus to bureaucratic coordination.

Unitary to Federal Structure

The history of American higher education is a history of movement from unitary liberal arts colleges to multi-structured colleges and universities. The American college of 1840 contained a half dozen professors and fifty to a hundred students;[6] in 1870, average size was still less than 10 faculty and 100 students (Table 1). All students in a college took the same curriculum, a "program of classical-mathematical studies inherited from Renaissance education."[7] There was no need for sub-units such as division and department; this truly was a unitary structure. In comparison, the modern university and college is multi-structured. The University of California at Berkeley in 1962-63, with over 23, 000 students and 1,600 "officers of instruction," was divided into some 15 colleges or schools (e.g., College of Engineering, School of Public Health); over 50 institutes, centers and laboratories; and some 75 departments (including Poultry Husbandry, Romance Philology, Food Technology and Naval Architecture). In three departments and three schools, the sub-unit itself contained over 50 faculty members. Such complexity is not only characteristic of the university: a large California state college contains 40 or so disciplines, grouped in a number of divisions; and even a small liberal arts college today may have 20 departments and three or four divisions.

Table 1

Size of Colleges, 1870-1956					
Year	Colleges	Faculty		Students	
		Total Number	Average Size	Total Number	Average Size
1870	563	5,553	10	52,000	92
1880	811	11,552	14	116,000	143
1890	998	15,809	16	157,000	157
1900	977	23,868	24	238,000	244
1910	951	36,480	38	355,000	373
1920	1,041	48,615	47	598,000	574
1930	1,409	82,386	58	1,101,000	781
1940	1,708	146,929	86	1,494,000	875
1950	1,851	246,722	134	2,659,000	1,436
1956	1,850	298,910	162	2,637,000	1,425

Source: U. S. Bureau of the Census, *Historical Statistics of the United States, Colonial Times to 1957*, Washington, D.C.: Government Printing Office, 1960, pp. 210-211.

The multiplication of sub-units stems in part from increasing size. The large college cannot remain as unitary as the small one, since authority must be extensively delegated and subsidiary units formed around the many centers of authority. The sub-units also stem from plurality of purpose; we have moved from single- to multi-purpose colleges. Goals are not only more numerous but also broadly defined and ambiguous. Those who would define the goals of the modern university speak in such terms as "preserving truth, creating new knowledge, and serving the needs of man through truth and knowledge."[8] The service goal has a serviceable ambiguity that covers anything from home economics for marriage to research and development for space. A tightly integrated structure could not be established around these goals. Organizational structure accommodates to the multiplicity of goals by dividing into segments with different primary functions, such as liberal arts and professional training, scientific research and humanistic education. The structure accommodates to ambiguity of goals with its own ambiguity, overlap, and discontinuity. We find some liberal arts disciplines scattered all over the campus (e.g., statistics, psychology) , residing as components of professional schools and of "other" departments as well as in the appropriately-named department. No neat consistent structure is possible; the multiple units form and reform around functions in a catch-as-catch-can fashion. Needless to say, with a multiplicity of ambiguous goals and a variety of sub-units, authority is extensively decentralized. The structure is federal rather than unitary, and even takes on some likeness to a loosely-joined federation.

Single to Multiple Value Systems

Most colleges before the turn of the century and perhaps as late as the 1920s possessed a unified culture that extended across the campus,[9] and this condition still obtains in some small colleges of today. But the number of colleges so characterized continues to decline and the long-run trend is clear: the campus-wide culture splits into subcultures located in a variety of social groups and organizational units. As we opened the doors of American higher education, we admitted more orientations to college—college as fun, college as marriage, college as preparation for graduate school, college as certificate to go to work tomorrow, college as place to rebel against the Establishment, and even college as a place to think. These orientations have diverse social locations on campus, from fraternity house to *cafe espresso* shop to Mrs. Murphy's desegregated rooming house. The value systems of the students are numerous.

The faculty is equally if not more prone to diversity in orientation, as men cleave to their specialized lines of work and their different perspectives and vocabularies. Faculty orientations differ between those who commit themselves primarily to the local campus and those who commit themselves primarily to their farflung discipline or profession; between those who are scientists and those who are humanists; between those who think of themselves as pure researchers or pure scholars and those who engage in a professional practice and train recruits. The value systems of the faculty particularly cluster around the individual disciplines and hence at one level of analysis there are as many value systems as there are departments.

Non-Professional to Professional Work

Intense specialization characterizes the modern campus; academic man has moved from general to specific knowledge. The old-time teacher—Mr. Chips—was a generalist. He covered a wide range of subject-matter, with less intensity in any one area than would be true today, and he was engaged in pure transmission of knowledge. In the American college of a century ago, the college teacher had only a bachelor's degree (in the fixed classical curriculum) plus "a modest amount of more advanced training, perhaps in theology ..."[10] There was no system of graduate education, no reward for distinction in scholarship, and the professor settled down into the groove of classroom recitation and the monitoring of student conduct. We have moved from this kind of professor, the teacher generalist, to the teacher of physics, of engineering, of microbiology, of abnormal psychology, and to the professor as researcher, as consultant, as professional-school demonstrator. We have moved from transmission of knowledge to innovation in knowledge, which has meant specialization in research. Taking the long view, perhaps *the* great change in the role of academic man is the ascendance of research and scholarship—the rise of the commitment to create knowledge. This change in the academic role interacts with rapid social change: research causes change, as in the case of change in technology and industrial processes; and such changes, in turn, encourage the research attitude, as in the case of competition between industrial firms, competition between nations, competition between universities. In short, the research component of the academic role is intimately related to major modern social trends.

In his specialism, modern academic man is a case of professional man. We define "profession" to mean a specialized competence with a high degree of intellectual content, a specialty heavily based on or involved with knowledge. Specialized competence based on involvement in knowledge is the hallmark of the modern professor. He is preeminently an expert. Having special knowledge at his command, the professional worker needs and seeks a large degree of autonomy from lay control and normal organizational control. Who is the best judge of surgical procedure—laymen, hospital administrators, or surgeons? Who is the best judge of theories in chemistry—laymen, university administrators, or professors of chemistry? As work becomes professionalized—specialized around esoteric knowledge and technique—the organization of work must create room for expert judgment, and autonomy of decision-making and practice becomes a hallmark of the advanced profession.

Not all professional groups need the same degree of autonomy, however. Professionals who largely give advice or follow the guidelines of a received body of knowledge require extensive but not great autonomy for the individual and the group. They need sufficient leeway to give an honest expert opinion or to apply the canons of judgment of their field. Those requiring great autonomy are those who wish to crawl along the frontiers of knowledge, with flashlight or floodlight in hand, searching for the new—the new scientific finding, the new reinterpretation of history, the new criticism in literature or art. Academic man is a special kind of professional man, a type characterized by a particularly high need for autonomy. To be innovative, to be critical of established ways, these are the commitments of the academy and the impulses of scientific and scholarly roles that press for unusual autonomy.

Consensual to Bureaucratic Coordination

As the campus has moved from unitary to composite structure, from single to multiple systems of values, from general to specialized work, it has moved away from the characteristics of community, away from "community of scholars. " A faculty member does not interact with most other members of the faculty. In the larger places, he may know less than a fifth, less than a tenth. Paths do not cross. The faculty lounge is no more, but is replaced by coffee pots in dozens of locations. The professor retains a few interests in common with all others, such as higher salaries, but he has an increasing number of interests that diverge. Even salary is a matter on which interests may diverge, as men bargain for themselves, as departments compete for funds, as scientists are paid more, through various devices, than the men of the humanities.

In short, looking at the total faculty, interaction is down, commonality of interest is down, commonality of sentiments is down. With this, coordination of work and policy within the faculty is not so much now as in the past achieved by easy interaction of community members, by the informal give-and-take that characterizes the true community—the community of the small town where everyone knows nearly every one else, or the community of the old small college where the professors saw much of everyone else in the group. The modern campus can no longer be coordinated across its length and breadth by informal interaction and by the coming together of the whole. Informal consulting back and forth is still important; the administration and the faculty still use the lunch table for important business. But campus-wide coordination increasingly moves toward the means normal to the large-scale organization, to bureaucratic means. We appoint specialists to various areas of administration, give them authority, and they write rules to apply across the system. They communicate by correspondence, they attempt to make decisions fairly and impartially by judging the case before them against the criteria of the rulebook. Thus we move toward bureaucratic coordination, as the admissions officer decides on admissions, the registrar decides on the recording of grades, the business officer decides proper purchasing procedures, and various faculty committees decide on a wide range of matters, from tenure to travel funds to the rules of order for meetings of an academic senate.

In sum: the campus tends toward composite structure, toward a multiplicity of subcultures, toward intense professionalism, and toward some bureaucratic coordination.

Change in Faculty Organization and Authority

The organization and authority of the faculty accommodate to these trends in at least three ways: by segmentation, by a federated professionalism, and by the growth of individual power centers.

Segmentation

As campuses increase in size, complexity, and internal specialization, there is less chance that the faculty will be able to operate effectively as a total faculty in college affairs, less as the governmental body we have in mind when we speak of a community of scholars. The decision-making power and influence of the faculty is now more segmented—segmented by sub-college, by division, and particularly by department. Since the interests of the faculty cluster around the departments, faculty participation in government tends to move out to these centers of commitment. Who selects personnel, decides on courses, and judges students? The faculty as a whole cannot, any more than the administration. Indeed, as departments and professional schools grow in size and complexity, even they often do not; it is a wing of the department or a part of the professional school that has most influence. A liberal arts department that numbers 40 to 80 faculty members may contain six or eight or a dozen specialties. The day has arrived when a department chairman may not even know the name, let alone the face and the person, of the new instructors in "his" department.

What happens to the governmental organs designed for the faculty as a whole ? They move in form from Town Hall to representative government, with men elected from the various "states" coming together in a federal center to legislate general rules, which are then executed by the administration or the faculty committees that constitute an administrative component of the faculty. With the move to representative government, there is greater differentiation in participation: a few Actives participate a great deal; a considerably larger group constitutes an alert and informed public and participates a modest amount; the largest group consists of those who are not very interested or informed and who participate very little. The structure of participation parallels that found in the larger democratic society, and apparently is normal to a representative mass democracy. The situation is, of course, vexing to those who care about faculty government.

Professionalization

The authority of the faculty which flows out toward the departments and other units of the campus becomes located in the hands of highly specialized experts; and, as suggested earlier, takes on some characteristics of professional authority. Almost everywhere in modern large-scale organizations, we find a tug-of-war going on between administrative and professional orientations. In the hospital, the basic conflict in authority lies between the control of the non-medical hospital administrator and the authority of the doctors. In industry, a fascinating clash is occurring between management and the scientist in the research and development laboratory.[11] The fantastic expansion of research and development has brought over 400, 000 scientists and engineers into industry, there to be committed to innovation and to the development of new inventions to the point of practical utility. Many of these technologists have a high degree of expertise, a strong interest in research—often "pure" research—and they press for a large degree of freedom. Their fondest wish is to be left alone; they make the point that in scientific work it seems rational to do just that, that basic discoveries stem not from managerial direction but from the scientist following up his own initial hunches and the leads he develops as he proceeds. Management has found such men difficult to deal with; their morale suffers easily from traditional forms of management, and they present unusual demands on management to change and accommodate. In this situation, professional authority and bureaucratic authority are both necessary, for each performs an essential function: professional authority protects the exercise of the special expertise of the technologist, allowing his judgment to be preeminent in many matters. Bureaucratic authority functions to provide coordination of the work of the technologists with the other major elements of the firm. Bureaucratic direction is not capable of providing certain expert judgments; professional direction is not capable of providing the overall coordination. The problem presented by the scientist in industry is how to serve simultaneously the requirements of autonomy and the requirements of coordination, and how to accommodate the authority of the professional man and his group of peers to the authority of management and vice versa.[12]

The professional-in-the-organization presents everywhere this special kind of problem. He gains authority, compared to most employees, by virtue of his special knowledge and skills; he loses authority, compared to a man working on his own, by virtue of the fact that organizations locate much authority in administrative positions. The problem of allocation of authority between professionals and bureaucrats does, however, vary in intensity and form in different kinds of organizations. As mentioned earlier, advisers and practitioners need a modest degree of authority, while scientists and academics have perhaps the highest requirements for autonomy to engage in research, in unfettered teaching, and in scholarship that follows the rules of consistency and proof that develop within a discipline.

The segmentation of the faculty into clusters of experts gives professional authority a special form in academic organizations. In other situations, there usually are one or two major professional groups within the organization who, if they are influential, substitute professional control for administrative control. This occurs in the case of medical personnel in the hospital who often dominate decision-making. The internal controls of the medical profession are strong and are substituted for those of the organization. But in the college or university this situation does not obtain; there are 12, 25, or 50 clusters of experts. The experts are prone to identify with their own disciplines, and the "academic profession" overall comes off a poor second. We have wheels within wheels, many professions within a profession. No one of the disciplines on a campus is likely to dominate the others; at a minimum, it usually takes an alliance of disciplines, such as "the natural sciences" or "the humanities," to put together a bloc that might dominate others. The point is that with a variety of experts—chemists, educationists, linguists, professors of marketing—the collective control of the professionals over one another will not be strong. The campus is not a closely-knit group of professionals who see the world from one perspective. As a collection of professionals; it is decentralized, loose and flabby.

The principle is this: where professional influence is high and there is one dominant professional group, the organization will be integrated by the imposition of professional standards. Where professional influence is high and there are a number of professional groups, the organization will be split by professionalism. The university and the large college are fractured by expertness, not unified by it. The sheer variety of the experts supports the tendency for authority to diffuse toward quasi-autonomous clusters. Thus, faculty authority has in common with professional authority in other places the protection of individual and group autonomy. It is different from professional authority in other places in the extremity of the need for autonomy and in the fragmentation of authority around the interests of a large variety of groups of roughly equal status and power. The campus is a holding company for professional groups rather than a single association of professionals.

Individualization

When we speak of professional authority we often lump together the authority that resides with the individual expert and the authority that resides with a collegial group of experts. Both the individual and the group gain influence at the expense of laymen and the general administrator. But what is the division of authority between the individual and the group? Sometimes group controls can be very tight and quite hierarchical, informally if not formally, as young doctors learn in many hospitals, and as assistant professors learn in many departments. The personal authority of the expert varies widely with the kind of establishment, and often with rank and seniority. The campus is a place where strong forces cause the growth of some individuals into centers of power. We will review several of these sources of personal authority.

First, we have noted the expertise of the modern academy. The intense specialization alone makes many a man into king of a sector in which few others are able to exercise much judgment. Thus, *within* a department, men increasingly feel unable to judge the merits of men in specialties they know nothing about. The technical nature of the specialized lines of work of most academic men, then, is a source of personal authority. If we want to provide a course on Thomas Hardy, we are likely to defer on its content to the judgment of the man in the English Department who has been knee-deep in Hardy for a decade. The idea of such a course would really have been his in the first place; Hardy falls within his domain within the English Department, and his judgment on the need for the course will weigh more than the judgment of others.

Second, some professorial experts now have their personal authority greatly enhanced by money. Despite his location within an organization, the professor in our time is becoming an entrepreneur. It used to be that the college president was the only one on campus, other than an enterprising and dedicated member of the board of trustees, who was capable of being an entrepreneur. Many of the great presidents were great because they were great at coming home with the loot—adventurers who conquered the hearts and pocketbooks of captains of industry and then with money in hand raided wholesale the faculties of other institutions. Presidents who can raise money and steal faculty are still with us, but they have been joined by professors. Kerr has suggested that the power of the individual faculty member is going up while the power of the collective faculty is going down because the individual as researcher, as scholar, and as consultant relates increasingly to the grant-giving agencies of the Federal government and to the foundations.[13] He has direct ties to these major sources of funds and influence; indeed, he participates in their awarding of grants and even has problems of conflict of interest. A professor-entrepreneur, by correspondence and telephone and airplane trips, lines up money for projects. He sometimes arranges for the financing of an entire laboratory; occasionally he even brings back a new building. Even when the professor does little of the arranging, it is *his* presence that attracts these resources. He represents competence, and the grant-givers pursue competence.

The entrepreneurial activity and resources-gaining influence of professors, which extends down to assistant professors in the social as well as the natural sciences, has had remarkable growth since World War II, and the personal autonomy and power thus achieved in relation to others in the university is considerable. A professor does not have to beg postage stamps from a departmental secretary nor a two hundred dollar raise from the department chairman nor travel money to go to a meeting from a dean or a committee if he has monies assigned to him to the tune of $37,000, or $175,000, or $400,000. His funds from outside sources may be called "soft" funds, in the jargon of finance, but they are hard enough to hire additional faculty members and assistants, to cover summer salaries, and to provide for travel to distant, delightful places.

The following principle obtains: a *direct* relation of faculty members to external sources of support affects the distribution of influence within the campus, redistributing influence from those who do not have such contacts to those who do, and moving power from the faculty as a whole and as smaller collectivities to individual professors. In the university of old, members of the faculty achieved a high degree of influence by occupying the few professorial positions available in a structure that narrowed at the top. Their source of influence was structural and internal. The source of great influence in the modern American university is less internal and less tied to particular positions; it is more external and more tied to national and international prestige in a discipline, and to contact with the sources of support for research and scholarship that are multiplying and growing so rapidly.

This individualization in faculty organization and authority excites impulses in the faculty and the administration to establish some collective control, for much is at stake in the balance of the curriculum, the equality of rewards in the faculty, and even the character of the institution. But the efforts at control do not have easy going. Collective bodies of the faculty and the administration are hardly in a position, or inclined, to tell the faculty member he can have this contract but not that one, since the faculty member will define the projects as part of his pursuit of his own scholarly interests. When the faculty member feels that this sensitive right is infringed, he will run up the banners of academic freedom and inquiry, or he will fret and become a festering sore in the body politic of the campus, or he will retreat to apathy and his country house, or he will make it known in other and greener pastures that he will listen to the siren call of a good offer.

Third, personal authority of the professorial expert is increased in our time by the competitiveness of the job market. The expansion of higher education means a high demand for professors, and the job market runs very much in the professor's favor in bargaining with the administration. His favorable position *in* the market enhances his position *on* campus. He can demand more and get it, he can even become courageous. In the world of work, having another job to go to is perhaps the most important source of courage.

To recapitulate: faculty organization and authority tends in modern times to become more segmented, more professional in character, and somewhat more individualized. We are witnessing a strong trend toward a federated structure in colleges and especially in universities with the campus more like an United Nations and less like a small town and this trend affects faculty authority by weakening the faculty as a whole and strengthening the faculty in its many parts. Faculty authority becomes less of a case of self-government by a total collegium, and more of a case of authority exercised department by department, sub-college by sub-college. The *role* of faculty authority is shifting from protecting the rights of the entire guild, the rights of the collective faculty, to protecting the autonomy of the separate disciplines and the autonomy of the individual faculty member.

Faculty authority in our time tends to become professional authority in a federated form. We have a loose alliance of professional men. The combination of professional authority and loosely-joined structure has the imposing function of protecting the autonomy of the work of experts amidst extensive divergence of interests and commitments. The qualities of federation are important here. The federation is a structure that gives reign to the quasi-autonomous, simultaneous development of the interests of a variety of groups. Within an academic federation, a number of departments, divisions, colleges, professional schools, institutes, and the like can co-exist, each pushing its own interests and going its own way to a rather considerable extent. Professional authority structured as a federation is a form of authority particularly adaptive to a need for a high degree of autonomous judgment by individuals and sub-groups.

This trend toward a federation of professionals is only part of the story. To hold the separate components of the campus together, we have a superimposed coordination by the administration, and, as Kerr has suggested, this coordination increasingly takes on the attributes of mediation.[14] The administration attempts to keep the peace and to inch the entire enterprise another foot ahead. The faculty, too, in its own organization, also counters this divisive tread with a machinery of coordination. The very fact of a diffusion of authority makes the faculty politician more necessary than ever, for the skills of politics and diplomacy are needed. There must be faculty mediators; men who serve on central committees, men with cast iron stomachs for lunch table discussions and cocktail parties, men who know how to get things done that must be done for the faculty as a whole or for part of the faculty. There must be machinery for setting rules and carrying them out impartially across the faculty. The modern campus is, or is becoming, too large and complicated for collegial or professional arrangements to provide the over-all coordination, and coordination is performed largely by bureaucratic arrangements—e.g., the rulebook, and definite administrative domains.

Federated professionalism within an organization, like many other trends, thus promotes counter-trends. Specialization and individualization seriously weaken the integration of the whole. The weakness of collegiality or professionalism in the large organization, as suggested earlier in the case of industry, is that it cannot handle the problem of order, it cannot provide sufficient integration. Thus the above trends in faculty organization and authority open the door to bureaucracy—more bureaucracy in the administration, more within the faculty itself. The modern large faculty, therefore, combines professionalism, federated structure, and bureaucracy perhaps in a mixture never before evidenced in human history.

This combination of what seem contradictory forms of organization perplexes observers of academia. Is the faculty collegial? Yes, somewhat. Is it split into fragments? Yes, somewhat. It is professional? Yes, somewhat. Is it unitary? Yes, somewhat. Is it bureaucratic? Yes, somewhat. Different features of the faculty strike us according to the occurrences of the week or the events we chance to observe. The ever-mounting paperwork firmly convinces us that the campus is doomed to bureaucratic stagnation. The fact that the president often gets what the president wants convinces us that he really has all the authority. The inability of a campus to change a department that is twenty years behind in its field convinces us that departmental autonomy has run amok and the campus is lacking in leadership and in capacity to keep up with the times. One observer will see the campus as a tight ship, the next will speak of the same campus as a lawless place where power lies around loose. No wonder we are confused and no wonder that outsiders are so often even more confused or more irrelevant in giving advice.

But in the combination of forms of organization and forms of authority that we find today within the campus and within the faculty itself, there are certain trends that are stronger than others and certain features that tend toward dominance. The society at large is tending to become a society of experts, and the campus has already arrived at this state. Expertise is a dominant characteristic of the campus, and organization and authority cluster around it. Because of its expertness, together with its ever-growing size, the faculty moves away from community, moves away from collegiality of the whole. The faculty moves toward decentralized or federated structure, and authority moves toward clusters of experts and the individual expert. Thus professional authority tends to become the dominant form of authority, and collegial and bureaucratic features fall into a subsidiary place. In short, when we say college, we say expert. When we say expert, we say professional authority.

Burton R. Clark, Associate Research Sociologist, Center for the Study of Higher Education, University of California, Berkeley

Notes

[1] A major type of collegiality is that involving collegial decision: "In such cases an administrative act is only legitimate when it has been produced by the cooperation of a plurality of people according to the principle of unanimity or of majority." Max Weber, *The Theory of Social and Economic Organization*, translated by A. M. Henderson and Talcott Parsons, New York: Oxford University Press, 1947, p. 400.

[2] Hastings Rashdall, *The Universities in Europe in the Middle Ages*, edited by T. M. Powicke and A. B. Emden, Oxford: At the Clarendon Press, 1936, three volumes.

[3] C. P. Snow, *The Masters*, New York: The Macmillan Co., 1951.

[4] Richard Hofstadter and Walter P. Metzger, *The Development of Academic Freedom in the United States*, New York: Columbia University Press, 1955; George P. Schmidt, *The Liberal Arts College*, New Brunswick, New Jersey: Rutgers University Press, 1957.

[5] Logan Wilson, *The Academic Man*, New York: Oxford University Press, 1942; Theodore Caplow and Reece J. McGee, *The Academic Marketplace.*, New York: Basic Books, Inc., 1958.

[6] Hofstadter and Metzger, op. cit., pp. 222–223.

[7] *Ibid.*, p. 226.

[8] Clark Kerr, *The Uses of the University*, The Godkin Lectures, Harvard University, 1963.

[9] Hofstadter and Metzger, *op. cit.,*: Schmidt, op. cit.

[10] Hofstadter and Metzger, *op. cit.*, p. 230.

[11] See William Kornhauser, *Scientists in Industry: Conflict and Accommodation*, Berkeley: University of California Press, 1962; and Simon Marcson, *The Scientist in American Industry*, New York: Harpers and Brothers, 1960.

[12] Kornhauser, *op. cit.*

[13] Kerr, *op. cit.*

[14] *Ibid.*

Administrative Effectiveness in Higher Education

David A. Whetten and Kim S. Cameron

For at least two decades after World War II, higher education administrators had a relatively easy job. By traditional standards, administrative effectiveness was almost universal. Enrollments were increasing, revenues were growing, innovations in the form of new and experimental programs were common, and almost unprecedented prestige was associated with college professors and administrators in the minds of the public. The environment in which higher education existed was largely protected from outside competition (e.g., almost no corporations offered degree granting programs, and accreditation was restricted, for the most part, to college and university campuses), and costs of college were offset by the availability of large amounts of federal dollars.

All that changed in the 1970s and was magnified in the 1980s: the availability of federal funds was severely curtailed; the legitimacy and usefulness of college degrees was called into question; private corporations began entering the higher education business at a rapid pace and now spend more on education than do colleges and universities; shifting demographics resulted in declining enrollments; and, the public prestige associated with faculty and administrator status plummeted along with their relative earnings. Colleges currently have more than twice the mortality rate that businesses have and are five times more likely to fail than government organizations (see Cameron & Ulrich, in press, for an elaboration of these conditions). By traditional standards, administrative effectiveness has eroded markedly.

Of course, the problem with traditional standards of administrator effectiveness is that criteria such as those listed above are largely a product of environmental forces and beyond administrative control. They, therefore, are of limited value as legitimate indicators of administrator performance. The effectiveness of administrators in higher education must be evaluated on other bases in order to be valid and useful. In this article, we discuss indicators of administrator effectiveness that we have uncovered in our investigations of college and university performance. We make the assumption that the effectiveness of colleges and universities is highly dependent on the effectiveness of administrators. Evidence for this assumption comes from Cameron's (in press) studies of higher education effectiveness which discovered that the most powerful predictor of organizational effectiveness in colleges and universities is administrative behavior. Results from that research show that administrators are more important than environment, structure, age, institution type, and control in accounting for performance.

Characteristics of Effective Administrators

While no author has yet proposed a universal, unified model of effectiveness for institutions as a whole, research on this topic has shed considerable light on the characteristics of effective administrators in higher education. Close examination of the many "centers of excellence" in higher education has produced a collage of principles that seem to characterize unusually successful administrators. Most of the principles we identify below have emerged from empirical research conducted in past investigations at the Organizational Studies Division at NCHEMS (Cameron & Whetten, 1983; Chaffee, 1983). This research serves as the primary source of these characteristics inasmuch as it is one of the only projects ever conducted to investigate the effectiveness of higher education institutions and administrators.

In the past, many have characterized the field of educational administration primarily as a translation process. That is, the major activity was searching for leading edge management theories and ideas in business administration and then translating them into an educational context. There is some indication that this trend is waning, however, with the emergence of new research on higher education. Increasingly, administrators are able to look to educational researchers as sources of new approaches and models of organizational excellence, rather than to remain merely as consumers of knowledge adapted from other sectors.

This research on organizational effectiveness in higher education has generated a list of eight characteristics of effective administrators. Although we seldom found that any single administrator implemented all eight principles, we were able to build a composite picture of administrative effectiveness based on the assessments of faculty, staff, and peers at a large number of institutions. These characteristics are of sufficient generality that they apply across institutional types in higher education. The informed reader will undoubtedly note that there is considerable overlap between our list of characteristics and those described recently by other investigators (e.g., Peters & Waterman, 1982; Keller, 1983). We take heart in this convergence, rather than despair at the overlap. Recalling Will Rogers' sage observation that "common sense ain't necessarily common practice," we believe that reinforcement of basic administrative principles is important, since university administrators, like their athletic teams, are most successful when they emphasize proper execution of sound fundamentals. Furthermore, our research indicates it is especially important that administrative fundamentals be explicated during this period of decline and retrenchment in higher education when many administrators are searching for new potions to cure what they perceive as novel organizational problems. What follows, then, are the eight fundamental principles of administration:

1. Place Equal Emphasis on Process and Outcomes

Effective administrators recognize that the how of their work is just as important as the what and the why. They treat administration as a verb as much as a noun. They are as concerned about the process of implementing a decision as with the content of the decision itself.

Studies of effective administrators have consistently highlighted their preference for action (Peters & Waterman, 1982; Mintzberg, 1975). They are doers who take the initiative to make things happen. Our observation is related, but different in an important way. Many action oriented administrators focus primarily on putting programs together, reaching objectives, improving the bottom line, etc., and are insensitive to the manner in which they accomplish these outcomes. In other words, they tend to be mainly interested in results. This orientation is consistent with the "management by objectives" approach to administration advocated during the early 1970s by many writers on administration. They argued that effective managers were oriented primarily to outcomes, and that they should avoid the pettiness of holding subordinates accountable for doing things "by the book." What was important was whether the job got done, not how it was done. This orientation has some value, particularly as a check against stultifying supervision that discourages experimenting with new approaches to solving problems and reaching objectives. However, our research on university administrators' responses to declining resources convinced us that in many situations organizational members are more sensitive to how decisions are made than the final outcome of the decision making process. Under conditions of austerity where considerable uncertainty exists regarding job security, funding allocations, programmatic cuts, and so forth, we found effective administrators described very differently than ineffective administrators by faculty members and peers. These individuals described effective administrators as fair, open to different viewpoints, equalitarian, and trustworthy, regardless of whether specific decisions benefited or harmed their own particular interests.

This description is important because we found that members of the university community tend to evaluate the quality of a retrenchment decision to a large extent on the basis of whether it conforms with their expectations of how critical academic decisions ought to be made. Frequently members who benefited from, or were only minimally harmed by, a retrenchment decision are openly critical of the process used by administrators to collect information, solicit alternative proposals, and listen to contrasting points of view. The ability of administrators to manage this dynamic is critical to effectiveness.

2. LOW FEAR OF FAILURE—WILLINGNESS TO TAKE RISKS

In the systems management literature a distinction is made between fail-safe and safe-fail systems (DeGreene, 1982). In the fail-safe system great precautions are taken to protect against the chance of failure, which is viewed as catastrophic. The objective of the fail-safe approach is to literally make a system failure proof. In contrast, a safe-fail system provides a supportive environment in which experimentation is encouraged and failure is not abhorrent. Indeed, the system views periodic failure as evidence that its members are experimenting with highly innovative and, therefore, risky ideas.

In our studies of administrative effectiveness in higher education we have found that leaders who are more likely to institutionalize the norms of a safe-fail system do not personally over identify with the success of their organization. Leaders whose self-esteem is tightly linked with receiving credit for organizational successes become risk-aversive. They recognize that taking credit for an accomplishment that represents the aggregate efforts of many members (and generally a good measure of luck) encourages others to be quick to blame them for faulty leadership when organizational failures occur. Therefore, as they learn through experience that a single failure can wipe out the personal credits accumulated from several successes, they gradually place more and more emphasis on avoiding making mistakes. In the process, they adopt a conservative leadership style that significantly affects the strategic posture of their organization. They become reactors instead of initiators, and defenders instead of prospectors (Miles, Snow, Meyer, & Coleman, 1978). They treat emerging crises as threats to the security of their reputation, rather than as an opportunity to capitalize on a mandate for change and to make important improvements in the organization.

The proposition that some failures or set backs are healthy for an organization is borne out in the management of decline literature (Whetten, 1980a,b; Hedberg, Nystrom, & Starbuck, 1977; Argenti, 1978). One of the best predictors of organizations declaring bankruptcy (rather than recuperating) as a consequence of decline is the organization's previous experience with decline. Organizations that have enjoyed spectacular, continuous success are often so ill-prepared to deal with the consequences of a period of retrenchment that they never recover. In contrast, the organization that has continually experienced set backs and has had to struggle during every stage of its development is in the long run much more robust and resilient. So pronounced is this linkage between early success and response to subsequent failure that it has been labeled the "success breeds failure" syndrome.

At the individual administrator's level, leaders who have had little opportunity to develop personal coping mechanisms for dealing with either personal or organizational failure often find the prospects of being labeled a failure so devastating that they become immobilized when decisive action is required. In contrast, risk neutral administrators benefit from what might be described as an innoculation theory of failure. While they avoid taking excessive risks that might be viewed as irresponsible, they have a healthy respect for what can be learned from failure. They are highly introspective and oftentimes keep a record of the lessons learned from various experiences, including failures. Over time they learn how to cope with the stress associated with uncertainty, scarcity, or criticism, and how to support others undergoing similar experiences. In this manner, they, in effect, develop a measure of resistance to failure and are less threatened by its prospects.

3. NURTURE THE SUPPORT OF STRATEGIC CONSTITUENCIES

Given the fact that universities have been described as "loosely coupled systems" (Weick, 1976) and "organized anarchies" (Cameron, 1980) it should not be surprising that our research has indicated that an important characteristic of effective educational administrators is successful coalition management. Effective presidents spend a great deal of time nurturing the support of internal and external interest groups vital to the success of the organization's goals. They delegate to others as much as possible the administrative detail required to operate the institution and devote large chunks of their personal time to cultivating political and financial support. Many of these leaders even describe their organization in coalitional terms (e.g., as a fragile amalgam of interests). Administrators most effective at this pursuit generally share at least three distinguishing characteristics: they are politically astute, pragmatic, and skillful bargainers. That is, they are sensitive to shifts in political currents pervading the organization; and they are seldom inflexibly wedded to an ideological orientation; and, they are not put off by the notion that interest groups want something in return for their support.

The need to continually nurture the support of vital constituencies is most commonly overlooked during periods of organizational success. During a period of rapid growth and generous financial support, for example, it is easy to take members of the coalition for granted. Deterioration in student services may go unchecked; aggressive annual giving campaigns may lose momentum; and local support groups that have made significant sacrifices in the past for a struggling school may be overlooked. This scenario is illustrated by several small, private, religiously affiliated colleges during the early 1970s. As the college aged population increased rapidly, many state education systems were unprepared to meet the demand. This was particularly the case in several eastern states where the community college concept was slow to develop and large state universities or elite private colleges were not accessible to a large number of high school graduates. Therefore, many of them applied to relatively unknown colleges in the Midwest and the South. The result was that the enrollments of these institutions grew dramatically, massive physical plant expansion projects were initiated, and administrators and faculty fancied that they had joined the elite group of colleges capable of consistently attracting a national student body. In the process, many of these colleges ignored their traditional support groups. They hired professional recruiters in the East but failed to send representatives to maintain contacts with high school counselors in neighboring communities, many of whom openly disparaged the college's rush to national prominence. Campus leaders also became increasingly reluctant to allow local church groups to use campus facilities for religious retreats, youth camps, etc. Unfortunately, many of these colleges had their aspirations dashed within a few years as the community college network expanded nation wide and as a period of economic prosperity encouraged many marginal students to pursue full time employment instead of college. As a result, as enrollments plummeted, campus administrators were forced to take retrenchment actions such as closing new dormitories, and laying off recently hired faculty, They were forced once again to approach their old constituencies seeking desperately needed support. Many of these groups were reluctant to bail the school out of trouble, and were instead inclined to make the college suffer for its fickle allegiance. Administrators of these schools learned a painful lesson, that it is easier to sustain support than to rekindle it.

4. DON'T SUCCUMB TO THE TYRANNY OF "LEGITIMATE DEMANDS"

Effective university administrators recognize that, while it is important to nurture the support of key interest groups, there is a fine line between taking responsive action and acting responsibly. If interest groups perceive that the administration of a school does not have a clear sense of purpose and the courage to advocate unpopular actions when necessary, sensing that policy is being formed in response to pressure, they will push harder and harder for self-interests. Effective administrators are able to distinguish between legitimate needs strongly advocated and strong advocation for effect.

For example, a newly appointed dean may make a particularly forceful argument to the president for a budget increase in his college, primarily to solidify his political position with the faculty. Research on bargaining has shown that negotiators who are representing constituencies tend to make stronger demands than negotiators who represent only themselves because they perceive that their constituency expects forceful advocacy (Shaw, 1976). The effective administrator avoids the tendency of weak leaders to be whipsawed by strong interest groups. To accomplish this they rely on several specific tactics. For example, they pit competing interest groups against each other. Avoiding a cross fire between conflicting parties, they place the responsibility on the competing groups to resolve their differences and to present a single, unified proposal. Or they might capitalize on competing internal demands for resources and build their case to external funding bodies on the necessity of satisfying the needs of both parties. Above all, the effective administrator manages the conflicting demands by combining a strong commitment to core organizational policies or objectives with flexibility in implementing personal mission or agenda in order to take into account the legitimate needs and concerns of critical interest groups.

5. LEAVE A DISTINCTIVE IMPRINT

Whether they are described as strong independent personalities or masters at building on the ideas of others, the most effective educational administrators leave distinctive imprints on the history of their institution. In our interviews with individuals, especially in small colleges, we have been impressed with the tendency of faculty and administrators to demarcate their institution's history into presidential eras. Frequently, when we would ask a question about campus activities during a specific period of time, before the respondents could formulate an answer, they would have to first identify who the president was at that time. Their memories were clearly indexed by presidential tenure, and their recollections of what transpired on campus during each term was strongly colored by their overall evaluation of the effectiveness of each president. Events that transpired during the term of an uninspiring, ineffective president were described in a bland, colorless manner. In contrast, descriptions of activities during the tenure of spirited, effective presidents were conveyed using very emotional language and with a sense of institutional pride.

This experience made us aware of the need for administrators to periodically examine their actions from the point of view of a future historian. The importance of being sensitive to the global, composite impression others are forming was made very clear in an interview with the president of a major research university. In response to several probing questions covering a range of topics, including strategic plans, responses to crises, personal satisfaction, and the use of time, he paused and made the following observation:

> "Seldom does a day go by that I don't go home at night and see myself being interviewed on television, or read the description of something I have done during the day in the local newspaper. When I think back on the collage of activities reported in the media, I might as well be the president of General Foods, or 3M. The image I am portraying is that of an efficient administrator who is concerned about budgets, lobbying to obtain more favorable government treatment, and so forth. What is missing is a clear identification with educational issues. We lament the fact that our institution is underrated by our academic colleagues and now I can see the need to take a more active personal role in identifying our university with key educational problems and challenges in our society."

In general, we have found that administrators who are most effective in leaving a distinctive imprint on their institution began their tenure with a thorough analysis of the organization's strengths and weaknesses, strategic competencies, morale of the faculty, and concerns of the students. These leaders then had the capacity to generate excitement and commitment to a plan of action emerging from this analysis. They also demonstrated remarkable flexibility in assuming a variety of leadership roles in order to facilitate the accomplishment of communal objectives. Ineffective administrators, in contrast, generally approached their responsibilities with preconceived and somewhat rigid notions of what the university's pressing needs were and what the role of the president should be. These conceptions generally were linked to previous personal successes at other universities, an inflexible definition of personal capacities or leadership style, or an unvalidated supposition regarding others' expectation of the administrative role often based on conversations with an unrepresentative sample of the university community during the interviewing process, or second and third hand reports about the performance of the previous president.

In our discussions regarding the importance of flexible leadership behaviors adapted to situational needs, we have found the leadership model developed by Quinn and Rohrbaugh (1981) very useful (see Faerman & Quinn in this issue). Based on previous research on the determinants of organizational effectiveness, Quinn described leadership roles using the conjunction of two dimensions. These roles vary in terms of their emphasis on adaptiveness and tolerance versus organization and precision and an emphasis on peacefulness and serenity versus aggressiveness and assertiveness. The four quadrants shown in Figure 1 give rise to eight leadership roles that vary in terms of their emphasis on these two dimensions. For example, the mentor role in the top left hand quadrant is a combination of an adaptive, tolerant orientation and a peaceful, serene orientation. Research using this model has shown that the most effective administrators are those who can assume a wide variety of these roles. Like an amoeba, effective administrators shift the focus of their activities to capitalize on available opportunities, and to satisfy pressing needs and expectations. Our own work confirms this view of effective leadership. Specifically, we have found that the administrators most likely to leave a distinctive mark on their institution demonstrate this capacity for accurate assessment of situational demands combined with the ability to alter their administrative role accordingly.

Figure 1

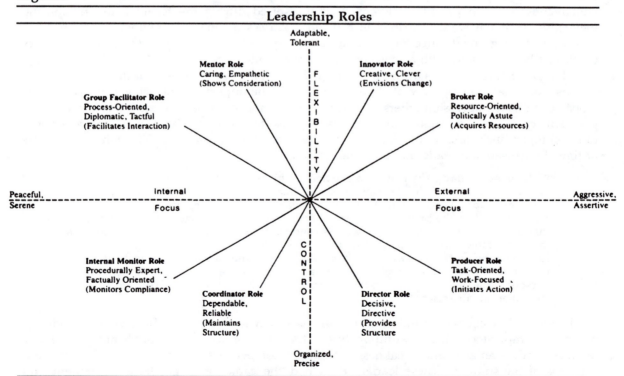

6. ERROR IN FAVOR OF OVERCOMMUNICATION, ESPECIALLY SURING TIMES OF FLUX

A basic axiom of communication theory is that information reduces uncertainty (Galbraith, 1977). The more information individuals have, the less apprehensive they are about what might happen in the future. Therefore, the more uncertainty members are experiencing because of declining enrollments, smaller state appropriations, or proposed curricular changes, the greater the need for the administration to communicate information regarding priorities, time schedules, constraints, etc. Research has shown that individuals have a significant need to make sense out of uncomfortable situations. They want to know why this experience is occurring, how long it is likely to last, and what the likely outcomes are. In the absence of adequate "official" information about these things, members generate their own based on rumors, personal suppositions, and inferences from guarded official pronouncements. Furthermore, these self-generated explanations and predictions are typically more negative (i.e., have greater personally threatening implications and contain less favorable evaluations of the ability of organizational leaders to cope with the situation), than is actually warranted. Consequently, the common practice of not sharing information regarding the details of a change because administrators fear it might damage morale oftentimes produces the opposite result.

Our research has shown that effective administrators are able to work around an apparent contradiction in faculty attitudes about governance. On the one hand, most faculty members abhor committee meetings. When asked to serve on a policy task force or a planning committee, they are quick to point out how this activity will adversely affect their performance in the really important professional activities of research and teaching. Furthermore, many such declinations contain overtones that administrators are abrogating their duties and responsibilities under the guise of getting, faculty input. On the other hand, during periods of high stress on campus (due to declining enrollments or under-funding from external sources, for example), the same faculty members will often criticize the campus administration for being secretive and imperialistic in its decision making activities. While these sentiments appear contradictory on the surface, they are actually a reasonable statement of a consistent set of preferences. By and large most faculty members want to be kept informed and feel that they can have input on important decisions, but they view most committee assignments as an inefficient use of their time because only a small percentage of most issues discussed are germane to their interests. Therefore, it is important that effective administrators not confuse lack of faculty enthusiasm for being involved in the detailed minutia of making decisions—even critical ones, and their desires to be kept informed to and feel influential. As one member of a prestigious faculty stated:

> "We don't like being surprised by administrative decisions, or presented with a fait acompli. What is really needed is more interactive communication between the faculty and the administration before, during, and after major decisions. This is especially critical during periods of change when there is a natural tendency for misunderstandings and rumors to break down that vital element of trust and mutual respect between the faculty and the administration."

7. RESPECT THE POWER OF ORGANIZATIONAL CULTURES

Effective administrators understand and respect the indigenous campus culture. Over time, norms, values, and expectations governing the administrative process crystalize at each university. These pertain to how aggressive the administration should be in pursuing new opportunities; how much initiative they should take on their own without input from the faculty; whether critical budgetary and personnel decisions are handled at the campus, college, or department levels of administration; and so forth. Effective administrators recognize that these norms have evolved in response to local particularistic conditions and are not easily modified. Research on emergent leadership has shown that groups with strong cultures are most readily influenced by new leaders who are perceived as personifications of, rather than threats to, their shared cultural values (Hollander, 1958). This will most likely be the case when promotions come from within the ranks of organizational members. If an outsider is brought into an organization with a strong culture, that leader must win the trust and loyalty of the community by embracing their norms and values.

On the surface this principle of effective administration appears to contradict our early point regarding the need to leave a distinctive imprint on the university. The basis for reconciling these prescriptions is timing. The research on emergent leadership we referred to earlier does not report that members of an organization will resist all efforts to change their culture, only that they will resist threats from individuals viewed as outsiders. If new administrators demonstrate a full awareness of and sensitivity to the sacred local values, they can gradually win the trust and confidence of long time members. When this occurs recommendations for changing the traditional power structure or the strategic posture of the university will not be dismissed outright. This process follows the oriental adage: "only Chinese can change Chinese."

In summary, effective administrators are sensitive to members' strong allegiance to core cultural values and norms. However, they also do not treat these as immutable elements of the university. When they perceive that a traditional view of governance is hindering the aggressive pursuit of important new objectives they are willing to work to change the anachronistic beliefs. However, they do this after they have obtained the confidence of organizational members, and confidence is engendered by suggesting new approaches rather than directly assaulting accepted practice as bad, inferior, or unenlightened. They justify their proposed changes in terms of staying in touch with a changing environment, and keeping up with competition, rather than belittling past practice, per se.

This is an important distinction because effective administrators recognize that an organization's culture is not simply a potential source of resistance to change. Seldom has a truly excellent college or university emerged that was not driven by a unique and pervasive culture. Clark (1970) pointed out the importance of a distinctive organizational ideology in the development of elite private colleges (e.g., the Swathmore saga), and Keller (1983) has reaffirmed this linkage in his analysis of the rise to prominence of institutions like Michigan State and the University of Chicago. The importance of a distinctive culture also pervades Peters and Waterman's (1982) discussion of excellent business firms (e.g., IBM blue, The Hewlett Packard way). Indeed, the effective manipulation of cultural symbols is at the heart of the distinction many make between managers and leaders. While managers make sure the books balance, leaders instill institutional pride and the relentless pursuit of excellence. They seize opportunities to make dramatic statements regarding important organizational priorities through the use of cultural symbols (Chafee, 1983). For example, when the administration of a major state university was having difficulty convincing the state legislature that the quality of their institution was eroding with each year's niggardly budget, one enterprising faculty member, noting the number of prominent state leaders attending home football games, suggested that during half time the marching band should form the outline of the graduate library; then, to the accompaniment of the school song the library would begin crumbling floor by floor.

Our research has identified similarly dramatic, although somewhat more conventional uses of symbols to staunch the gradual erosion of a school. For example, the president of a small, private, liberal arts college during a period of significant decline in student body purchased a neighboring campus in an effort to diversify the college geographically and in curricular offerings. This move stunned many members of the college who questioned the practicality of encumbering large debts when revenues were failing. What they underestimated was the symbolic impact of the decision. It served as the focal point for launching a drive to significantly upgrade the college. Faculty, students, and alumni became intrigued by the emerging opportunities resulting from this decision. It also instilled a sense of institutional pride that became self-reinforcing. Instead of grumbling about how bad the college was, people began to think, "We can't be all that bad if we are expanding to two campuses." Campus recruiters finally had something to get animated about; faculty members worked hard to bring their performance up to the new status of the school; and, alumni gave willingly to support such an enterprising initiative. Overall, a decision that seemed irrational and impractical from a management perspective became the badly needed symbol of effective leadership for transforming an institution.

8. Preserve and Highlight Sources of Opportunity at an Institution—At Any Cost

As we began our research on the management of organizational decline, we believed that bright, aggressive, capable individuals were attracted to growing organizations for financial reasons. To some extent, this explanation was based on research that reports the best predictor of the chief executive officer of a company is the size of the organization (rather than its profitability) (Haire, 1959). However, our experience in the field has altered that view. Our current belief is that very capable individuals are attracted to what they perceive as "centers of opportunity," and these just happen to be more commonly associated with conditions of organizational growth, rather than retrenchment. However, our research has convinced us that one of the critical ingredients of the effective management of retrenchment is preserving the belief that opportunities will continue to abound in an organization regardless of its financial condition (Whetten, 1981). Retrenching organizations that have been successful in this regard have been able to retain, and even attract, the best students and faculty. They do this by finding ways to decouple the presumed causal link between abundant resources and opportunity. While it is obviously easier to provide opportunities for members during periods of abundance, ineffective administrators are too quick to assume that scarcity necessarily must drive out opportunity. Indeed, the term retrenchment implies that the most effective responses to scarcity are to cut back recent additions to preserve the oldest and most traditional part of the institution. The obvious fallacy of this logic is that so-called peripheral activities may be most relevant for current environmental conditions, and what is treated as core or central may be anachronistic, having lost its functional utility.

During periods of scarcity ineffective administrators become preoccupied with crises and constraints. They assume that crises are necessarily detrimental because they disturb the current equilibrium. Therefore, they focus on downplaying the magnitude of serious problems, as a mistaken balm for sagging faculty and student morale. They also worry a great deal about not violating emerging constraints. When members suggest new ideas to them, they are quick to point out why each is no longer feasible. In contrast, effective administrators convert crises into mandates for improvement. They deflect the faculty's attention away from highly visible signs of financial erosion, such as low salaries or large class sizes, by generating enthusiasm for new opportunities. Specifically, they do everything possible to generate moral and financial support for new ideas. They preserve some organizational slack by, for example, withholding one percent of each unit's budget to form a new program's fund, and they aggressively pursue nontraditional sources of support, such as multi-university, or university/business consortia. Even when they do not have as much money as before to fund new programs they go to great lengths to reinforce initiative by expressing appreciation for the time spent to develop a proposal and admiration for the quality of the ideas.

Our discussions with faculty members indicate that their decision to stay or leave a retrenching university is influenced as much by their perceptions of the administration's reaction to the situation as the objective impact retrenchment has on their personal work activities or financial well being. Of course, quality faculty are not going to wait around to serve as pall bearers at the funeral of a great university, but neither are they anxious to move on at the first sneeze. There is a "wait and see" period during which faculty attitudes are heavily influenced by administrative action, or lack thereof. During this time, effective administrators maintain an offensive posture. They recognize that, while football teams may win by emphasizing good defense, administrators do not. Hence, they use crises to illuminate organizational problems and to galvanize resolve to sustain excellence through improvement, rather than engaging in debilitating, self-defeating debates over causes of, and blame for, serious problems. They view constraints as challenges to be outwitted and they place a high premium on creative suggestions even when they run counter to conventional wisdom. Staying on the offensive does not imply that administrators should act like naive optimists, which quickly erodes their credibility. Instead they must become astute opportunists, aggressively pursuing all leads. Kenneth Boulding (1975) has argued that this is one of the greatest challenges facing academic administrators as we shift from an era of abundance to a period of scarcity. In the past, administrators have been reinforced for exhibiting characteristics of primitive gatherers, rather than hunters. With resources in abundance (literally there for the picking), administrators were able to pursue a fairly passive and short term approach to procurement (spending a few minutes to gather only what is necessary for the next meal). As the environment shifts, university administrators must take on more of the characteristics of hunters, who must organize collective hunting parties, move their families in pursuit of migrating herds, store food for use during the winter, etc.

Summary and Conclusion

This article has focused on determinants of organizational and administrative effectiveness in higher education. We began by noting that traditional views of administrative and institutional effectiveness have little legitimacy because they are based on indicators more typical of the environment than of administrative behavior. We have summarized characteristics associated with maintaining and enhancing institutional effectiveness via administrative action. These characteristics are generalizable across most institutional types. The relevance of the eight characteristics lies in the guidance they can provide, especially in the increasingly complex, turbulent environment typical of higher education.

In a 1974 study conducted at the Stanford Research Institute, the eight most significant threats to our society were identified (DeGreene, 1982). Among the typical concerns about the quality of the environment, maintaining a skilled labor force, and so forth, this study identified "the increasingly difficult tasks of effectively managing large complex systems." We see this list of effective administrative characteristics being helpful in addressing such a challenge in higher education. On the other hand, we are encouraged that, despite the enormity of the challenge, many colleges and universities are being administered in a very effective manner. This arena clearly represents a bona fide source of principles governing administrative excellence.

For researchers, the relevance of these eight characteristics lies in their hypothetical character. No one of these characteristics has been a rigorously tested variable in any empirical research in higher education to date. Contingencies and refinements still need to be made. Whereas each is derived from our investigations of institutional and administrative performance, none has been subjected to serious scrutiny in a single study. Questions such as the following are still unanswered: What administrative characteristics are associated with what domains of institutional effectiveness? Under what conditions should these administrative characteristics be modified? What is the relationship of personal style and individual demographics to these principles? To which levels of administrators in the institutional hierarchy are these characteristics most applicable? What are the appropriate methods for assessing these characteristics, especially when little objective data exists?

David A. Whetten is at the University of Illinois and Kim S. Cameron is at the University of Michigan.

References

Argenti, J. *Corporate Collapse.* New York: Halstead. (1978).

Boulding, K. E. "The Management of Decline." *Change,* (1975), 7(5); 8–9.

Cameron, K. S. "Critical Questions in Assessing Organizational Effectiveness." *Organizational Dynamics,* (1980), 9; 66–80.

Cameron, K. S. "A Study of Organizational Effectiveness and its Predictors." *Management Science.* (in press).

Cameron, K. S., & Ulrich, D. O. "Transformational Leadership in Higher Education." In J. R. Smart (Ed.), *Higher Education: Handbook of Theory and Research* (Vol. 2). New York: Agathon Press. (in press).

Cameron, K. S., & Whetten, D. A. *Organizational Effectiveness: A Comparison of Multiple Models.* New York: Academic Press. (1983).

Chaffee, E. E. *Cases in college Strategy.* Boulder, CO: NCHEMS. (1983).

Clark, B. R. *The Distinctive Colleges.* Chicago: Aldine. (1970).

DeGreene, K. G. *The Adaptive Organization.* New York: Wiley. (1982).

Galbraith, J. R. *Organization Design.* Reading, MA: Addison-Wesley. (1977).

Haire, M. "Biological Models and Empirical Histories of the Growth of Organizations." In M. Haire (Ed.), *Modern Organization Theory.* New York: Wiley. (1959).

Hedberg, B. L. T., Nystrom, P. C., & Starbuck, W. H. "Designing Organizations to Match Tomorrow." In P. C. Nystrom & W. H. Starbuck (Eds.), *Prescriptive Models of Organizations* (North-Holland/TIMS *Studies in the Management Sciences,* Vol. 5). Amsterdam: North-Holland Publishing. (1977).

Holland, E. "Conformity Status and Idiosyncrasy Credit." *Psychological Review,* (1958), 65; 117–127.

Keller, G. *Academic Strategy: The Management Revolution in American Higher Education.* Baltimore: Johns Hopkins University Press. (1983).

Miles, R. E., Snow, C. C., Meyer, A. D., & Coleman, H. J. "Organizational Strategy, Structure, and Process." *Academy of Management Review,* (1978), 3; 546–562.

Mintzberg, H. "The Manager's Job: Folklore and Fact." *Harvard Business Review,* (1975), 53; 49–71.

Peters, T., & Waterman, R. *In search of Excellence.* Chicago: Harper-Row. (1982).

Quinn, R. E., & Rohrbaugh, J. "A Competing Values Approach to Organizational Effectiveness." *Public Productivity Review,* (1981), 5; 122–140.

Shaw, M. E. *Group Dynamics: The Psychology of Small Group Behavior* (2nd ed.). New York: McGraw-Hill. (1976).

Weick, K. E. "Educational Organizations as Loosely Coupled Systems." *Administrative Science Quarterly,* (1976), 21; 172–181.

Whetten, D. A. "Organizational Decline: Causes, Responses, and Effects." In J. Kimberly & R. Miles (Eds.), *The Organization Life Cycle: Creation, Transformations, and Decline.* San Francisco: Jossey-Bass. (1980a).

Whetten, D. A. "Organizational Decline: A Neglected Topic in Organizational Science." *Academy of Management Review,* (1980b), 5; 577–588.

Whetten, D. A. "Organizational Response to Scarcity: Exploring the Obstacles to Innovative Approaches to Retrenchment in Education." *Educational Administrative Quarterly,* (1981), 17; 80–97.

References

PART III

Bensimon, Estella M. (1989). "The meaning of 'good presidential leadership': A frame analysis." *The Review of Higher Education*, 12(2):107-123.

Bensimon, Estella M., Neumann, Anna, & Birnbaum, Robert. (1989). "Higher education and leadership theory." In Bensimon, et al., *Making sense of administrative leadership: The "L" word in higher education.* ASHE-ERIC #1. Washington, D.C.: School of Education and Human Development, George Washington University.

Clark, Burton R. (1963). "Faculty organization and authority." In T. Lunsford (ed.), *The study of academic administration*, pp. 37-51. The Western Interstate Commission for Higher Education.

Cohen, Michael D., and March, James G. (1986). "Leadership in an organized anarchy." In M. Cohen and J. March, *Leadership and ambiguity: The American college president, 2e.* Boston: Harvard Business School Press.

Dill, David D. (1984). "The nature of administrative behavior in higher education." *Educational Administration Quarterly*, 20: 69-99.

Etzioni, Amatai. (1964). "Administrative and professional authority." In A. Etzioni, *Modern organizations*, pp.75-84. Englewood Cliffs, NJ: Prentice-Hall, Inc.

Pfeffer, J. (1977). "The ambiguity of leadership." *Academy of Management Review*, 2: 104-119.

Tierney, William G. (1989). "Symbolism and presidential perceptions of leadership." *Review of Higher Education*, 12(2):153-166.

Trow, Martin. (1987). "Comparative reflections on leadership in higher education," In, P. Altbach and R. Berdahl (eds.), *Higher education in American society*, Revised ed. Buffalo: Prometheus Books.

Whetten, David A., & Cameron, Kim S. (1985). "Administrative effectiveness in higher education." *Review of Higher Education*, 9(1):35-49.

Suggested Additional References

PART III

Bensimon, E.M., A. Neumann, and R. Birnbaum. "Making Sense of Administrative Leadership." *ASHE-ERIC Research Report*, Vol. 1, 1989.

Birnbaum, R. "Presidential Searches and the Discovery of Organizational Goals." *Journal of Higher Education*, Vol. 59, 1988, pp. 489-509.

Birnbaum, R. "Responsibility Without Authority: The Impossible Job of the College President." In J. Smart (ed.), *Higher Education: Handbook of Theory and Research*, Vol. V. New York: Agathon Press, 1989.

Cameron, K.S. and D.D. Ulrich. "Transformational Leadership in Colleges and Universities." In J. Smart (ed.), *Higher Education: Handbook of Theory and Research*, Vol. II. New York: Agathon Press, 1986.

Dill, D.D. and P.K. Fullagar. "Leadership and Administrative Style." In M. Peterson and L. Mets (eds.), *Key Resources on Higher Education Governance, Management and Leadership*. San Francisco: Jossey-Bass, 1987.

Ingram, R.T. and L.E. Henderson. "Institutional Governing Boards and Trustees." In M. Peterson and L. Mets (eds.), *Key Resources on Higher Education Governance, Management and Leadership*. San Francisco: Jossey-Bass, 1987.

PART IV.
OTHER
RESOURCES

Supplementary Texts, Edited Volumes, and Monograph Series

Single Authored Texts: Each of these volumes focuses on Organization, Governance, or Leadership in higher education. They are readily available for reference or as supporting texts. Chapters from them are not included in this Reader.

Birnbaum, R. *How Colleges Work: The Cybernetics of Academic Organization*. San Francisco: Jossey-Bass, 1988.

Chaffee, E.E. and W.G. Tierney. *Collegiate Culture and Leadership Strategy*. New York: ACE/Macmillan, 1988.

Clark, B.R. *The Higher Education System: Academic Organization in Cross-National Perspective*. Berkeley, CA: University of California Press, 1983.

Cohen, M.D. and J.G. March. *Leadership and Ambiguity, 2e*. Boston: Harvard Business School Press, 1986.

McGuiness, A.C. *State Postsecondary Structures Handbook: 1988*. Denver, CO: Education Commission of the States.

Mortimer, K.P. and T.R. McConnell. *Sharing Authority Effectively: Participation, Interaction, and Discretion*. San Francisco: Jossey-Bass, 1978.

Edited Volumes: Each of these volumes includes several chapters especially relevant to Organization and Governance which are not included in this Reader.

Bess, J. (ed.) *College and University Organization from the Behavioral Sciences*. New York: New York University Press, 1984.

Jedamus, P. and M.W. Peterson (eds.) *Improving Academic Management: A Handbook of Planning and Institutional Research*. San Francisco: Jossey-Bass, 1981.

Peterson, M.W. and L. Mets (eds.) *Key Resources on Higher Education Governance, Management, and Leadership*. San Francisco: Jossey-Bass, 1987.

Smart, J.C. (ed.) *Higher Education: Handbook of Theory and Research*. New York: Agathon Press. Volumes I-VI, 1985-1990.

Monograph Series: These series regularly include individual volumes which may be relevant to Organization and Governance. Chapters from volumes in these series are not included in this Reader.

The Jossey-Bass *New Directions Series* in:
    Community Colleges
    Higher Education
    Institutional Research

The *ASHE/ERIC Research Report Series*